Pro Oracle Application Express 4

Second Edition

Tim Fox
John Edward Scott
Scott Spendolini

Apress®

Pro Oracle Application Express 4, Second Edition

Copyright © 2011 by Tim Fox, John Edward Scott, and Scott Spendolini

ISBN-13 (pbk): 978-1-4302-3494-4

ISBN-13 (electronic): 978-1-4302-3495-1

President and Publisher: Paul Manning
Lead Editor: Jonathan Gennick
Technical Reviewer: Alex Fatkulin
Editorial Board: Steve Anglin, Mark Beckner, Ewan Buckingham, Gary Cornell, Jonathan Gennick, Jonathan Hassell, Michelle Lowman, James Markham, Matthew Moodie, Jeff Olson, Jeffrey Pepper, Frank Pohlmann, Douglas Pundick, Ben Renow-Clarke, Dominic Shakeshaft, Matt Wade, Tom Welsh
Coordinating Editor: Jessica Belanger
Copy Editor: Kim Burton-Weisman
Compositor: Bytheway Publishing Services
Indexer: BIM Indexing & Proofreading Services
Cover Designer: Anna Ishchenko

Distributed to the book trade worldwide by Springer Science+Business Media, LLC., 233 Spring Street, 6th Floor, New York, NY 10013. Phone 1-800-SPRINGER, fax (201) 348-4505, e-mail orders-ny@springer-sbm.com, or visit www.springeronline.com.

For information on translations, please e-mail rights@apress.com, or visit www.apress.com.

Apress and friends of ED books may be purchased in bulk for academic, corporate, or promotional use. eBook versions and licenses are also available for most titles. For more information, reference our Special Bulk Sales–eBook Licensing web page at www.apress.com/bulk-sales.

I would like to dedicate this effort to my father, Louis Fox,
for introducing me to software development by bringing home a TRS-80 when I was 14.
— Tim Fox

Contents at a Glance

Contents

About the Authors

 **Tim Fox** has been using Oracle since version 5 in 1989. At that time, the Oracle Forms version was 1.x and procedural code had not yet arrived. Since that time, Tim has been constantly involved in projects where some version of an Oracle database or development tool was being used. Tim has worked in corporate IT for the State of Indiana and The Associates, spent ten years as a manager at Andersen Consulting / Accenture, and is currently the Director of Development at Enkitec, a Dallas-based Oracle services provider.

While at Enkitec, Tim has been an instrumental figure in development projects across dozens of companies and has greatly assisted in the uptake of Oracle Application Express. As a result, Tim is a frequent contributor to the Dallas Oracle User Group (DOUG), Oracle-sponsored Tech Days, and other regional user groups and conferences. In 2010, Tim became heavily involved in implementation and training related to Oracle's Exadata database machine. Given his background in APEX development and his access to Enkitec's Exadata machine, he has APEX 4 running directly on Exadata.

John Edward Scott has been using Oracle since version 7 (around 1993), and has used pretty much every release since then. He has had the good fortune to work on a wide range of projects for a varied group of clients. He was lucky enough to start working with Oracle Application Express when it was first publicly released, and has worked with it nearly every day since (and loves it). John is an Oracle ACE Director and was named Application Express Developer of the Year 2006 by Oracle Magazine. He is also the cofounder of ApexEvangelists (http://www.apex-evangelists.com), a company that specializes in providing training, development, and consulting specifically for the Oracle Application Express product. You can contact John at john.scott@apex-evangelists.com.

Scott Spendolini is president & co-founder of Sumneva™, a world-class Oracle® Application Express (APEX) consulting, training, and solutions firm founded in 2010. He has assisted a number of clients from various verticals with their Oracle APEX development and training needs. Spendolini has presented at a number of Oracle-related conferences, including Oracle OpenWorld, ODTUG, and IOUG, and is a regular contributor to the Oracle APEX Forums on OTN. Spendolini is also the host & conference chair of APEXposed, an APEX-specific annual conference. He is a recent recipient of the Oracle Ace Director designation and is also a co-author of the book Pro Oracle Application Express. In 2009, Spendolini along with ODTUG was presented with the Oracle Innovation Award for his work on ODTUG's public web site, odtug.com. Spendolini is also an Oracle Certified Oracle Application Express developer.

Previous to co-founding Sumneva, Spendolini founded and ran Sumner Technologies from 2005 through 2009, which also focused on Oracle APEX consulting, training, and solutions. Before that, he was employed by Oracle Corporation for almost 10 years, the last three of which he was a Senior Product Manager for Oracle APEX. He holds a dual bachelors degree from Syracuse University in Management Information Systems and Telecommunications Management and currently resides in Ashburn, Virginia with his wife and two children.

About the Technical Reviewer

Alex Fatkulin is master of the full range of Oracle technologies. This mastery has been essential in addressing some of the greatest challenges his customers have met. Alex draws on years of experience working with some of the world's largest telco companies, where he was involved with almost everything related to Oracle databases, from data modeling to architecting high availability solutions and resolving performance issues of extremely large production sites.

With companies that rely on technologies such as RAC, Oracle Streams, and Data Guard, Alex's intimate knowledge of client, data, and software gives them robust and dependable production systems that allow them to run their businesses smoothly and stay ahead of their competitors.

Alex holds a Bachelor of Computer Sciences degree from Far Eastern National University in Vladivostok, Russia.

Acknowledgments

Working on a project like this is not a singular effort. In my case, my family had to give me time to work on a daily basis, which wasn't easy for Reese and Ryan, my four- and seven-year-old daughters. They didn't really understand what I was doing (they're not APEX developers … yet), but they knew that I was "working on the book" almost every night. My wife, Thanh, probably paid the highest price as I tried only to work after the kids were tucked in for the night. She was very supportive of this project and fell asleep next to me on the couch more times than I can count. For all of that, I thank my family more than they know.

During the course of writing this book, I learned a great deal more than I had anticipated, but I did not do it alone. The team that is Enkitec (my day job) is a group of people I like to call "home run hitters," many of whom are currently working on critical APEX projects. You'll see a few of their first names in this book, but I'd like to thank our core APEX team formally now: Brian Hill, David Little, and Toby Marks. I feel very lucky to be associated with a group of really smart people who genuinely enjoy what they do.

I ultimately have Kerry Osborne to thank for getting me into this project in the first place. He and another Enkitec colleague, Randy Johnson, were embarking on writing the *Pro Oracle Exadata* book and he encouraged me to join in the fun of technical writing. I actually thought at the beginning that I would be able to work on this project during business hours, but that didn't happen. It didn't happen for Kerry and Randy either so now we share stories of marathon writing sessions and comparing amusing comments from the editors.

Speaking of the editors, without their experience and guidance, this would be a very different book. Jonathan Gennick and Jessica Belanger of Apress worked diligently with me to ensure that I had all the resources I needed and that I stayed on schedule. Alex Fatkulin was also instrumental as a technical reviewer.

Since this book is a revision of the original *Pro Oracle Application Express*, I have to give the original authors their due. John Edward Scott and Scott Spendolini are obviously APEX experts in the truest sense of the word. The body of APEX knowledge that they created in the first edition is still relevant today and is a must for any serious APEX developer. Many of the concepts they describe apply to any Oracle-based development whether APEX, Java, or otherwise.

As for APEX in general, I continue to be amazed by the completeness and the professional feel of the development interface and applications created with it. APEX 4.0 takes application look and feel to a higher level than ever before and I find it truly amazing how easy APEX makes it is to create fully functional, professional applications. In my day job, I always offer APEX as the development language of choice for web-based applications. I explain it to my customers like this: in the time it takes to describe how a form should work, I can have it built in APEX. Development productivity can't be matched by any other environment (in my opinion). Maybe the best thing about APEX is that it's still 100% free.

—Tim Fox

Foreword

I consider myself a pragmatic person—one who uses the right tools for a job and employs the most straightforward and easy way to accomplish a task. To that end, I've been a great supporter and fan of Oracle's Application Express (APEX) from before the day it was introduced. I say "before the day" because I've had the honor and pleasure of using APEX long before it was released to the public at large. My web site, http://asktom.oracle.com, is one of the first ever built with the software that was to become known as APEX.

APEX is one of the most pragmatic database development tools I know of. It does one thing and one thing well: it rapidly implements fully functional *database* applications—applications that are used to predominantly access, display, and modify information stored in the database (you know, the *important* applications out there). It facilitates using the database and its feature set to the fullest, allowing you to implement some rather complex applications with as little work (code) as possible. It is possible to build extremely scalable applications with a huge user base (http://shop.oracle.com, for example, is built with APEX). It is possible to build extremely functional applications, with seriously powerful user interfaces (APEX itself is written in APEX, as proof of this). It is easy to build applications rapidly; for example, the current version of http://asktom.oracle.com was developed in a matter of days by two developers—in their spare time; it was not a full-time job.

While it all sounds wonderful and easy so far, APEX is a rather sophisticated tool with many bits of functionality and a large degree of control over how the generated application will look and feel. To fully utilize the power of APEX, you need to have a guide and a mentor to show you how to do so, very much akin to what I do with people regarding the Oracle database.

This book, *Pro Oracle Application Express 4*, is that guide. The authors, Tim Fox, John Scott, and Scott Spendolini are those mentors. The book walks you through the steps you need to understand after you've installed and started using APEX, to go beyond the sample applications. Covering diverse topics such as using the database features to full advantage (one of my favorite topics), to SQL injection attacks (what they are and how to avoid them in APEX), to printing, you'll find many real-world issues you will be faced with explained, demystified, and solved in this book.

This second edition of the book has been enhanced to cover some of the very latest additions to APEX. One of the most powerful new features is the ability to create your own components using a new plug-in architecture. You can create new components, and you can share those components in standardized ways. Chapter 12 goes into more detail on this exciting aspect of APEX development.

Other new features covered in this edition include Websheets and Dynamic Actions. Websheets provide a friendly and accessible way for end users to create their own applications. Dynamic Actions represents APEX 4.0's new support for Ajax, helping you to create highly interactive applications that run in the browser without constantly needing to refresh and load new pages.

Chapter 4, "Data Security," covers a wide breadth of topics about securing your database application, which is an even greater concern now than when the first edition was published. There is a section on URL injection issues that discusses what they are, how they are exploited, why you should care about them, and how to protect yourself from them. There is a section on session state protection that follows the same format: what it is, how it is exploited, why you should care, and how to protect yourself. The same mentoring occurs with data-level access, where the authors introduce how to use Virtual Private Database, a core database feature (not really an APEX feature) to protect your data from unauthorized access. Lastly, a critical application feature, auditing, is discussed in depth using the same "what it is, why it is, why you should care, and then how to do it" approach. While some of the content in this chapter is not specific to APEX, it is needed to give you a holistic view to building database applications, which is what this book is about.

This book covers not just the nitty-gritty details of building a secure application, but it also covers all you need to know to build database applications with APEX. When they are finished with security, the authors move on to other necessary topics, such as how to perform screen layout and application screen navigation, how to integrate reports and charts, how to integrate web services—enabling you to perform application integration—in an APEX environment, and much more.

If you are an APEX developer just starting out, or an APEX developer with experience under your belt and want to learn more about the environment you are using, this book is for you. It describes from start to finish how to build secure, functional, scalable applications using the APEX application development environment.

—Thomas Kyte
http://asktom.oracle.com

Introduction

If you're new to APEX development, prepare yourself for one of the most productive tools available for Oracle application development. The speed with which you can create fully functional, secure, web-based applications is truly astounding, especially when compared to using a tool like Java. If you are used to writing procedural or object-oriented code, you may find APEX's declarative development methodology a little challenging at first, but the learning curve is not significant. When you consider that you only need an Oracle database to get started, the barriers to beginning APEX development are minimal.

The first edition of this book, *Pro Oracle Application Express*, was written in 2008 using APEX 3.2. In 2010, Oracle released APEX 4.0, which included a significant number of new features along with a major upgrade of the development environment's user interface. Along with the much improved look and feel, Oracle included several Web 2.0 features like Dynamic Actions, Plug-ins, and RESTFul web service support. Prior to APEX 4.0, you could implement the newest web features, but it usually required custom coding. With APEX 4.0, you can use the familiar declarative development techniques to add an Ajax feature, for example. The inclusion of these significant new features obviated the need for a revision of the original book.

In general, APEX 4.0 lets you create professional looking, feature-laden applications with less effort than ever before.

Development Best Practices

Oracle Application Express (APEX) makes it extremely easy to quickly prototype and develop a web application. However, as a software developer, you're probably aware that speed of development is only one of a number of criteria that will contribute to the perceived success (or failure) of your project.

Of course, perceptions about a project's success can vary. For example, the people who encounter a typical project might include developers, testers, managers, production support, and end users. The developers may feel that the project was a success because development went quickly, Production support might feel like the project was a failure because no one has a clear strategy for performing application upgrades. The end users may dread using the application because it runs incredibly slowly. Clearly, for the project to be considered a success, you need to satisfy the expectations of all these people (or as many as you reasonably can). Ideally, you should strive for an application that has the following characteristics:

- Easy to develop

- Easy to deploy and upgrade

- Easy to maintain and debug

- Enjoyable for end users to use

- Fast enough for the users' requirements

- Stable from the end users' perspective

- Secure enough to protect your data from unauthorized access

You should never end up feeling like developing, deploying, maintaining, or (even worse) using the application is seen as a chore. Each of these areas can often benefit from the adoption of some best practices to ensure that everyone involved sees your application as a success.

Chapter 1 is the best place to introduce best-practice techniques, since they should form the foundation of every significant development project you undertake. You can certainly create applications without using any of the techniques we'll discuss, but adopting techniques like these will make your job as a developer easier, and your applications will be considerably more successful.

APEX Installation Decisions

This book will not cover the details of installing APEX version 4.0, since that information is already bundled with the product, as well as discussed in detail in several online resources. It is worth mentioning, however, that APEX 4.0 supports another connection type via the Oracle Application Express Listener. The APEX Listener is a Java-based web server that is certified to run under Web Logic, Tomcat, OC4J with Oracle WebLogic Server, OC4J, and Oracle Glassfish.

Indeed, many people enjoy using APEX without bothering with installation, either because someone else has installed it for them or they are using a hosted environment (such as the public Oracle apex.oracle.com site or one of the commercial providers such as Shellprompt). Others use Oracle Database Express Edition (XE), a free edition of the database that includes a preinstalled version of APEX.

However, if you are installing APEX, one important decision is which tablespace to use for the product. The installer usually defaults to installing APEX into the SYSAUX tablespace, and if you're using the 11g version of the database, the SYSAUX tablespace will be selected by default. I highly recommend that instead of using SYSAUX you create a dedicated tablespace that you'll use specifically for the APEX database objects and metadata. By using a dedicated tablespace, you can gain a far greater degree of control and flexibility over the administration of the APEX environment. For example, should it become necessary to recover the tablespace using point-in-time recovery from an Oracle Recovery Manager (RMAN) backup, you'll be confident that you haven't affected any other database components, like AWR (which may not be the case if you install into SYSAUX).

Installing into a separate, dedicated tablespace also allows the database administrator (DBA) to make decisions about where that dedicated tablespace should be stored on disk (to reduce contention), control the storage growth of the tablespace, and perhaps also take advantage of advanced Oracle features, such as transportable tablespaces to quickly move the tablespace to another database instance.

Application Development Considerations

The decisions related to how to create and organize your application within the APEX and database environment will greatly affect how easily you'll be able to deploy and migrate your application later on. By structuring your development environment in a logical and organized way, you'll encounter far fewer problems when your application needs to be deployed or updated to your live environment.

Users and Administrators

When APEX is installed, an Application Express instance administrator is created. You can connect to APEX as this instance administrator in two ways:

- Connect to one of the following URL's:

- PL/SQL Plugin: http://server:port/pls/apex/apex_admin

- APEX Listener or EPG: http://server:port/apex/apex_admin

Use the username ADMIN and the password you used when you installed the product.

- Connect to the same URL you'd use to log into any workspace, such as

    `http://server:port/pls/apex/apex_login`, and use `INTERNAL` as the workspace and `ADMIN` as the username with the password you used when you installed the product.

Including the instance administrator, four different types of users exist for APEX:

Application Express instance administrator. This is the user you'll use to administer the APEX installation. The instance administrator can connect only to the `INTERNAL` workspace to perform administration tasks, such as creating workspaces and users, monitoring activity, and managing the APEX service. Instance administrators can't create any applications themselves; they must create workspaces and other users for applications to be created. The instance administrator can create workspace administrators, developers, and built-in users for any of the workspaces.

Workspace administrator. A workspace administrator is responsible for the administration of a particular workspace. As a workspace administrator, you are able to create developers and users for that workspace, and create applications. Workspace administrators can also log into any application within the same workspace that uses APEX account credentials.

Application developer. Application developers are created within a particular workspace by workspace administrators. They can create and maintain an application within that workspace. They can't log in to other workspaces, but they are able to log in to any application within the same workspace that uses APEX account credentials.

Application user. Application users can take two forms. They can be created and managed within the APEX environment and are then known as *built-in users* (or *cookie users*). Alternatively, they can be created and managed outside the APEX environment; for example, they could be stored within a database table or as part of a Lightweight Directory Access Protocol (LDAP) directory. Built-in users are able to log in to any application within the same workspace that uses APEX account credentials.

For small projects with a single developer, it is quite possible to perform all application development as the workspace administrator. However, for any development that uses two or more developers, it's best to create a specific developer account for each physical developer, since this lets you use features such as page-locking, as well as track changes to the application at the developer level.

Although the workspace administrator could be one of the physical developers, a better idea is to create a developer account to use for development. Use the workspace administrator account only when necessary to perform administration duties.

Workspaces and Schemas

When you create an application in APEX, you must select a schema as the default parsing schema. In other words, if you built a report that issued a query like this:

```
select empno, ename from emp;
```

the query would use the emp table in the schema you selected as the parsing schema when you created your application. If you wanted to access an object in a different schema, you could prefix the object name with the schema name, like this:

```
select empno, ename from payroll.emp;
```

Because the application will be executed using the parsing schema (and its privileges), accessing objects in other schemas requires that the appropriate privileges are granted to the parsing schema. Objects in other schemas can also be accessed via synonyms or a view, which effectively hides the schema and enables you to reference the object without needing to specify the schema name yourself.

Choosing a Parsing Schema

The schemas assigned to the workspace you are currently logged into define the choice of schemas that can be used as the parsing schema. When you create a workspace (as an APEX administrator), you must specify whether to use an existing schema or create a new one, as shown in Figure 1-1. If no other schemas are assigned to the workspace, you will be able to select only this schema as the parsing schema when you create your application.

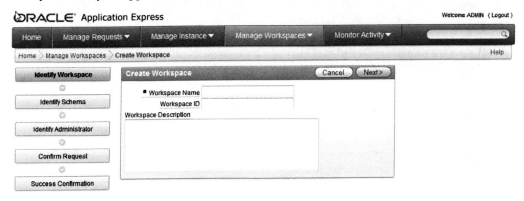

Figure 1-1. Creating a new workspace

This means that if you already have an existing schema with a lot of objects you'd like to access, you can select that schema. Then, any applications that are created within the schema will be able to access those schema objects directly. This way, you can create an application in APEX that provides a front end to existing data very quickly.

Although you can select only a single schema during the provisioning of the workspace, extra schemas can be assigned to the schema later on. After these additional schemas have been assigned to the workspace, they are available to workspace developers to use as the default parsing schema when they create an application within that workspace.

If you choose to create a new schema during the provisioning of the workspace, a new tablespace and corresponding datafile will be created for that schema automatically. The disadvantage is that the tablespace and datafile will have nondescriptive names, such as APEX_1400423609989676 and APEX_1400423609989676.dbf. Moreover, if you later decide to remove the workspace, that tablespace and datafile will not be deleted. If you regularly provision and delete a lot of workspaces, you can end up with many tablespaces and datafiles cluttering up your disk (and perhaps being unnecessarily included in your backups).

For small developments or evaluation, it may be fine to create a new schema through the APEX wizard. However, from a maintenance point of view, this approach often increases the difficulty in correlating schemas, tablespaces, datafiles, and workspaces because of the nondescriptive names. While this may not be a primary concern to you as a developer, it can be critical to how quickly the DBA is able to restore your schema from a backup if necessary.

Generally, for larger developments, if you are not using an existing schema, you may find it beneficial to manually create the tablespace and schema yourself, using a tool such as Enterprise Manager. For example, you can create a tablespace called APEXDEMO, which has a single datafile named APEXDEMO01.dbf that's allowed to grow to 2GB. You can then create a user APEXDEMO that has the APEXDEMO tablespace as its default tablespace. Figure 1-2 shows how the schema would look after being created in Enterprise Manager.

Select	UserName	Account Status	Expiration Date	Default Tablespace	Temporary Tablespace	Profile	Created	User Type
●	APEXDEMO	OPEN	Apr 30, 2011 6:17:37 PM CDT	APEXDEMO	TEMP	DEFAULT	Nov 1, 2010 6:17:37 PM CDT	LOCAL

Figure 1-2. Creating a schema in Enterprise Manager

You could now create a workspace named APEXDEMO and select the APEXDEMO schema you just created in Enterprise Manager, as shown in Figure 1-3. This naming scheme ties together your workspace with the underlying schema and related tablespace and datafiles. If you should accidentally drop some tables (forgetting for the moment about the recycle bin in Oracle Database 10*g*/11*g*), you can use RMAN to recover them easily, since their schema and tablespace will be obvious.

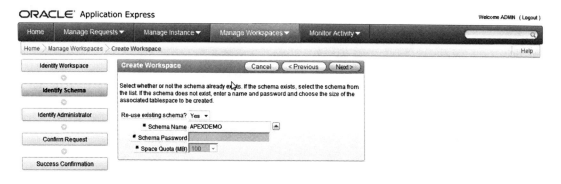

Figure 1-3. Creating a workspace using an existing schema

Although the APEX administrator can view reports that show which schemas and tablespaces particular workspaces are using, adopting a sensible naming convention makes it easier to get this information. For example, the DBA could look at a tablespace called APEXDEMO and be able to understand the purpose of that tablespace, which would not be clear from a generic tablespace name like APEX_1400423609989676.

> ■ **Note** Naming and coding standards can be extremely subjective. For example, some people may prefer to name the tablespace as APEXDEMO_TS while others prefer TS_APEXDEMO. If you already have an existing policy that details how you should name database objects, it makes sense to adopt that same policy for your development with APEX. If you do not currently have a policy in place, you should consider adopting one. The standards policy you use should be detailed enough to aid you in your work, but not so draconian that it actually hinders you.

Once the workspace is provisioned, additional schemas can be assigned to it. For example, you can create an APEXDEMO_TEST schema in Enterprise Manager, log in as the Application Express instance administrator, choose Manage Workspaces↗Manage Workspace to Schema Assignments, and select that schema, as shown in Figure 1-4.

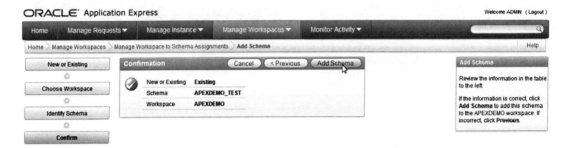

Figure 1-4. Adding a schema to a workspace

Controlling Access to New Schemas

Now the workspace administrator can specify which application developers can use the new schema (or, indeed, any of the assigned schemas). Figure 1-5 shows an example of a new developer account being created. By default, the developer will be able to access both schemas (APEXDEMO and APEXDEMO_TEST), since both schemas have been assigned to this workspace.

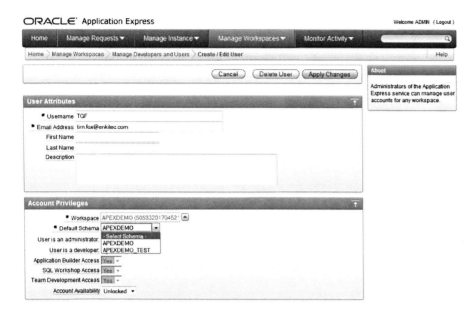

Figure 1-5. Creating a new developer with access to all assigned schemas

When this developer logs into the workspace, he or she can see the list of schemas that are available by clicking on the Administration⬈Manage Instance menus, as shown in Figure 1-6. Any application this developer creates can use any of the available schemas as its default parsing schema, as shown in Figure 1-7.

Figure 1-6. Schemas available to the developer

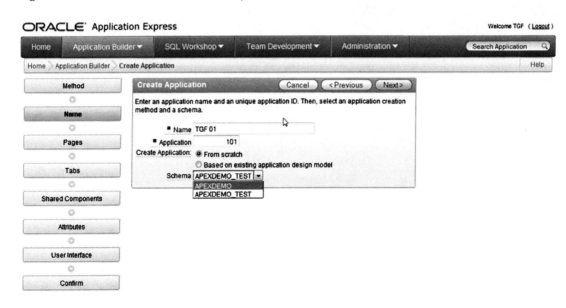

Figure 1-7. Selecting a default parsing schema for an application

Creating Workspaces

Generally, workspaces should be used to group together applications that are related. In other words, if you have a number of developers collaborating on applications that are related to each other and operate on the same data and schemas, ideally you'd create a workspace specifically for those applications.

It is possible, using multiple schemas assigned to a workspace, to establish a development/testing/live environment all within the same workspace. For example, you could create a single workspace that has a schema for development, a schema for testing, and a schema for live objects and data. You could then have three copies of your application: one pointing to the development schema, one to the testing schema, and one to the live schema. However, with this approach, it is all too easy to become confused about which schema you are operating in, with potentially disastrous effects.

It's best to create separate workspaces for development, testing, and live environments. This forces you to specifically log in to an environment, and helps to minimize the risk of making application or schema changes in the wrong environment. The APEX environment helpfully displays which workspace you are logged in to (and which user you are logged in as), so it definitely pays to double-check this information before you perform any drastic operations.

You also need to consider how the development, testing, and production environments will be staged. You may have each environment running on a different database instance (for example, a development instance, a testing instance, and a production instance). If you have only one database instance, it is possible to have the three (or two if you choose to forgo the testing environment!) environments all installed on the same database instance.

Application Deployment

An APEX application consists of three main components:

- The APEX application itself

- Any external images and files (such as CSS files), stored in the web server file system

- Database objects and data contained in the schema

The definition of the application itself—that is, the metadata that represents the pages, branches, processing logic, and so on—is stored in the schema that was created when the product was installed. This is quite distinct from the database objects on which your application performs operations, which are the database objects that reside in the parsing schema of your application and any other schemas that your application accesses.

In order to deploy your application from one database to another (where APEX has already been installed), you need to deploy the application definition as well as any database objects on which it is depends. You also need to deploy any static files (CSS files, images, and so on).

Deploying Workspaces

When moving an application from one APEX instance to another (*instance* here refers to a database with the APEX software installed), you need to have created the workspace on the destination instance. The instance administrator can choose to either create the workspace manually or export the existing workspace from the source instance. Exporting the workspace creates a file containing the SQL needed to re-create that workspace, and the instance administrator can then import that SQL file to the destination instance. Figure 1-8 shows the APEXDEMO workspace being exported. Note that you can specify a file format to use (either UNIX or DOS), which will determine the newline sequence used in the file.

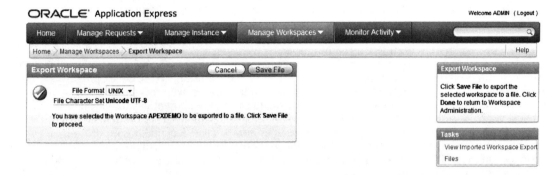

Figure 1-8. Exporting a workspace

The advantage of using a workspace export file is that this also re-creates all the users and developers created within that workspace, so it's a quick way of migrating all the existing users (and their permissions) to a new server. It also demonstrates an advantage of using the built-in users. If you use another method to authenticate your users, you'll need to handle their migration manually. Listing 1-1 shows the contents of the file that is created by exporting the APEXDEMO workspace.

Listing 1-1. Contents of a Workspace Export File

```
set serveroutput on size 1000000

set feedback off
-- Company, user group and user export
-- Generated 2006.07.17 12:58:25 by ADMIN
-- This script can be run in sqlplus as the owner of the Oracle flows engine.
begin
    wwv_flow_security.g_security_group_id := 1635127392255802;
end;
/
----------------
-- W O R K S P A C E
-- Creating a workspace will not create database schemas or objects.
-- This API will cause only meta data inserts.
prompt  Creating workspace APEXDEMO...
begin
wwv_flow_fnd_user_api.create_company (
  p_id                    => 1635220613255830,
  p_provisioning_company_id => 1635127392255802,
  p_short_name            => 'APEXDEMO',
  p_first_schema_provisioned=> 'APEXDEMO',
  p_company_schemas       => 'APEXDEMO:APEXDEMO_TEST');
end;
```

```
/
----------------
----------------
-- G R O U P S
--
prompt  Creating Groups...
----------------
-- U S E R S
-- User repository for use with apex cookie based authenticaion.
--
prompt  Creating Users...
begin
wwv_flow_fnd_user_api.create_fnd_user (
  p_user_id       => '1428202658421752',
  p_user_name     => 'ADMIN',
  p_first_name    => '',
  p_last_name     => '',
  p_description   => '',
  p_email_address=> 'admin@enkitec.com',
  p_web_password  => '1E6287A65491647783288E3C9E1A87D1',
  p_web_password_format => 'HEX_ENCODED_DIGEST_V2',
  p_group_ids     => '',
  p_developer_privs=> 'ADMIN:CREATE:DATA_LOADER:EDIT:HELP:MONITOR:SQL',
  p_default_schema=> 'APEXDEMO',
  p_account_locked=> 'N',
  p_account_expiry=> to_date('201011011826','YYYYMMDDHH24MI'),
  p_failed_access_attempts=> 0,
  p_change_password_on_first_use=> 'Y',
  p_first_password_use_occurred=> 'N',
  p_allow_app_building_yn=> 'Y',
  p_allow_sql_workshop_yn=> 'Y',
  p_allow_websheet_dev_yn=> 'Y',
  p_allow_team_development_yn=> 'Y',
  p_allow_access_to_schemas => '');
end;
/
begin
wwv_flow_fnd_user_api.create_fnd_user (
  p_user_id       => '1437223003555234',
  p_user_name     => 'TGF',
  p_first_name    => '',
  p_last_name     => '',
  p_description   => '',
  p_email_address=> 'tim.fox@enkitec.com',
  p_web_password  => 'D72DA6B4C47475A502A29CA604ACCCBC',
  p_web_password_format => 'HEX_ENCODED_DIGEST_V2',
  p_group_ids     => '',
  p_developer_privs=> 'CREATE:EDIT:HELP:MONITOR:SQL:MONITOR:DATA_LOADER',
  p_default_schema=> 'APEXDEMO',
  p_account_locked=> 'N',
  p_account_expiry=> to_date('201011011848','YYYYMMDDHH24MI'),
  p_failed_access_attempts=> 0,
```

11

```
      p_change_password_on_first_use=> 'N',
      p_first_password_use_occurred=> 'N',
      p_allow_app_building_yn=> 'Y',
      p_allow_sql_workshop_yn=> 'Y',
      p_allow_websheet_dev_yn=> 'N',
      p_allow_team_development_yn=> 'Y',
      p_allow_access_to_schemas => '');
end;
```

When possible, you should use workspace exports. They enable you to rapidly create a copy of an existing workspace and reduce the chance that you'll forget to create a particular user or developer.

■ **Note** Since the export file is a series of Data Definition Language (DDL) statements, it can be edited, such as to change the name of the workspace. However, you really shouldn't do this unless you have been specifically advised to do so by Oracle.

Deploying Applications

An application developer (or workspace administrator) can export an application from the Application Builder interface. This creates a file similar to the workspace export file, in that the file will contain all the statements necessary to create the metadata required for the application. However, the application export file does not contain the DDL to create any of the database objects your application uses, nor does the application export file contain any data from the database objects that your application uses. Such data would normally be handled with specialized data-loading tools, such as the import and export utilities, or copied over a database link.

You can use the APEX export options, shown in Figure 1-9, to affect the file that is created. For the most part, you won't need to change application export settings. However, you should understand what each of these options do. Here are descriptions of some of the more useful options:

File Format: This allows you to specify whether you want to use a DOS or UNIX format. Your choice will affect which newline sequences will be used in the resulting export file.

Owner Override: This lets the owner of an application specify that a different schema should be used rather than the one that is currently specified. It allows you to import the schema into a workspace that's completely different from the workspace from which the application was exported.

Build Status Override: This lets you specify whether the resulting export file will contain an application that developers can access (Run and Build Application) or one that only end users can access (Run Application Only).

As of __ minutes ago: This allows you to export an application as it existed some time ago. For example, you could export an application the way it was before you deleted a page.

Export Preferences: This set of options is new in APEX 4.0 and allows for some additional control during the export process.

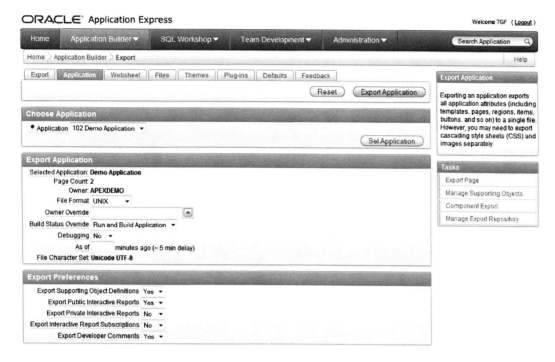

Figure 1-9. *Exporting an application*

An important consideration is whether you want developers to be able to access your application when it is imported to the target server. There is a trade-off between the added security you gain by exporting the application as Run Application Only versus not allowing your developers to access and debug the application via the Application Builder.

When you set an application to Run Application Only, you lose the ability to debug (by changing the `NO` in the URL to `YES`) and trace that application (by adding `p_trace=YES` to the URL). Generally, you want to set your production applications to Run Application Only, so that end users can't gain direct access to debug information that they shouldn't be able to see.

Deploying Static Files

APEX applications can include references to many different types of static files, including Cascading Style Sheets (CSS), images (JPG, GIF, and so on), JavaScript libraries, and Flash movies. You can reference these static files in two ways:

- They can be stored on a file system that's accessible by the Oracle HTTP Server (OHS).

- They can be uploaded to the database via the Application Builder interface.

Both methods have advantages and disadvantages, and you should be aware of how each method will affect your application. Whether you choose to store files in the file system or in the database

13

ultimately comes down to how you intend to manage those files and whether they need to be used by other external systems.

Uploading Static Files to the Database

You can upload static files to the database simply by using a browser. This means that you can upload a new image to the database and use it in your application immediately, without needing to involve the person in charge of administering the web server. When you reference these static files in your application, they are actually downloaded to the end user's browser via a database procedure. For example, if you uploaded a static file called `logo.jpg`, you could reference that file in an HTML region in your application with the following line of code:

```
<img src="#WORKSPACE_IMAGES#logo.jpg"></img>
```

When that HTML region is processed, the `#WORKSPACE_IMAGES#` directive will be translated into something like this:

```
<img src="wwv_flow_file_mgr.get_file?p_security_group_id=16&p_fname=logo.jpg"></img>
```

■ **Note** In the example, the value used for `p_security_group_id` is modified so that it fits onto a single line on this book page. In reality, you would have a number such as `1635127392255802`.

Any static files you reference in this way will be downloaded to the end user's browser as a result of making a call to the `get_file` routine. This approach has two downsides:

- Each file you reference in this way requires a separate call to the `get_file` routine.

- Quite often, browsers fail to store the image in their cache. In these cases, the static file will be rerequested every time the page is displayed, resulting in slower-loading pages and images that appear to flicker as they reload.

You can write your own `get_file` replacement procedure to enable the browser to cache the static files, as you'll learn in Chapter 9.

Storing Static Files on the Server File System

Storing files directly in the web server file system usually makes caching the static files happen transparently, since the OHS can add some default expiry headers to the file as it is requested by the user's browser. When the user views the same page again, his browser determines whether the image can be reloaded from the browser cache or if it needs to be requested again from the web server. By taking advantage of caching for static files, your application will appear far more responsive to your end users, as well as put less load on your database.

The downside of storing static files directly in the file system is that they aren't as integrated with your application. For example, you'll need to ensure that they are backed up as a separate process, since they won't be backed up as part of the database. You also need to ensure that the file names on the file system correspond to the names you used to reference the files in your application.

Application Portability and Code Reuse

APEX offers several features to make your application more portable between environments. We'll look at a few of these features, as well as how to separate data and application logic from style and presentation.

Using Substitution Strings to Avoid Hard-Coding References

Every application in APEX has a unique identifier—an application ID—assigned to it. This ID is used to identify the application and the associated metadata within the APEX repository.

When you move applications between different APEX environments, such as between your development and test environments, you might encounter problems if you've hard-coded any references to values that may be different in these environments. Unless you can be absolutely certain that the application ID and any other references are exactly the same in the different environments, you shouldn't hard-code any of these references.

You can avoid hard-coding the application ID by using the `APP_ID` substitution string. Here's an example of a typical URL where the application ID (112) has been hard-coded:

```
f?p=112:1:&APP_SESSION.:
```

If you import your application into an APEX environment that already has an application that uses the same application ID, forcing you to use a different ID, you may forget to update your hard-coded references. In that case, your links will point to the wrong application.

To avoid this, you should use the `APP_ID` substitution string, which will be replaced with the actual ID of your application at runtime. Using this substitution string, the URL now looks like this:

```
f?p=&APP_ID.:1:&APP_SESSION.:
```

This makes your application more portable between APEX environments.

Although it is not common for pages to be renumbered, you can also avoid having to hard-code a page ID by using the `APP_PAGE_ID` substitution string. This can be useful where you have a branch on a page that branches back to the same page.

A page within an application can also have an alias defined for it. For example, you may give page 1 the alias of `HOME`, as shown in Figure 1-10. Now, rather than using a URL such as this:

```
f?p=&APP_ID.:1:&APP_SESSION.:
```

you can use this URL:

```
f?p=&APP_ID.:HOME:&APP_SESSION.:
```

Figure 1-10. Defining an alias for the page

By using the alias in the reference, you'll be able to renumber the pages and the URL will still be pointing to the correct page.

You should use substitution strings to avoid hard-coding any references to resources (such as style sheets) in templates and HTML regions. This will give you great flexibility to change the location of those resources, whether they are uploaded into the database or are stored in the file system. For example, if you stored all your images in the database by uploading them through the Application Builder interface, you might refer to a particular image file like this:

```
<img src="#APP_IMAGES#logo.gif" type="image/jpeg" />
```

At runtime, this will be expanded to reference the download procedure that is used for accessing static files that have been uploaded into the database. The text that is substituted at runtime will be something like this:

```
wwv_flow_file_mgr.get_file?p_security_group_id=986113558690831&p_flow_id=112&p_fname
=logo.gif
```

In this section, I described #WORKSPACE_IMAGES# and #APP_IMAGES#. The simple difference between the two is that workspace images are available to any application in a workspace while application images are available only in the application to which they're assigned. If you want to assign an image to an application, you specify the application name during the upload process. If you don't specify an app name, the image will be available to all applications in the workspace.

However, if you now wanted to store the images in the file system rather than in the database, you'd need to change every reference like this one to use a different path to the file.

To simplify and minimize the number of changes you'll need to make, you can define a substitution string that will be used in place of the #APP_IMAGES# substitution string. You can find the Substitution Strings section on the Application Definition page in the Shared Components part of the Application Builder, as shown in Figure 1-11. When you define the substitution string IMAGE_PATH for the value #APP_IMAGES#, the URL then looks like this:

```
<link rel="stylesheet" href="&IMAGE_PATH.logo.gif" type="text/css" />
```

Figure 1-11. Defining the alias to reference the #APP_IMAGES# substitution string

Effectively, this creates a substitution string that references a substitution string. At runtime, this will be expanded to reference the same download procedure that was used before. The advantage of using this technique is that if you later decide to store the static files in the file system, rather than storing them within the database, you can simply change the value of your substitution string to reflect the new location, Figure 1-12 shows the substitution string modified to use a reference to the file system instead.

Figure 1-12. Changing the substitution string value to use the file system

This greatly reduces the number of references you'll need to change when moving your application between different APEX environments where the static files are stored in different locations, Figure 1-13 shows how the substitution string would be set in the development environment.

Figure 1-13. Substitution string set in the development environment

Using the Publish/Subscribe Feature

The publish/subscribe feature allows you to reuse certain common components among applications. You can define your component in an application, and then other applications can reference that common component by subscribing to it. Any changes that are made to the master component can then easily be incorporated into the applications that subscribe to the component.

Changes can be propagated from the master component to the subscribing component in two ways:

From the master component: The master component publishes the changes to all subscribing applications. If you want the changes to the master component to be reflected in all subscribing components, you publish the changes from the master component.

From within applications: The subscribing applications refresh the components that subscribe to a master component. If you want only certain applications to have their subscribing components updated, you refresh the components from within those applications.

The following components can make use of the publish/subscribe feature:

- Authentication schemes
- Authorization schemes
- Lists of values
- Navigation bar entries
- Shortcuts
- Templates

When you create any of these component types, you have the option of subscribing to an already existing component of the same type. For example, suppose you create a master application that has a named List of Values (LOV) component that uses the following query:

```
select ename d, empno r

from    emp

order by 1
```

Figure 1-14 shows the results of using this LOV in a select list.

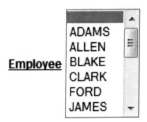

Figure 1-14. *Using the master LOV in a select list*

In another application within the same workspace, you can create a new LOV and choose to create it based on an existing LOV, as shown in Figure 1-15. The LOV creation wizard will then allow you to select which application (in the same workspace) should be used to list the available LOVs to subscribe to, as shown in Figure 1-16.

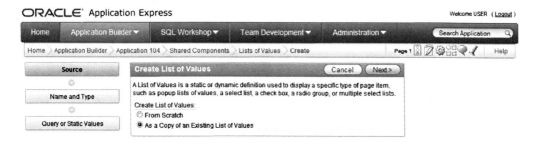

Figure 1-15. *Creating an LOV that will subscribe to the master LOV*

Figure 1-16. *Copying the LOV from the master application*

Once you've selected an application, the LOVs available in that application will be displayed, as shown in Figure 1-17, allowing you to copy and subscribe to them.

Figure 1-17. *Subscribing to the master LOV*

If you now create a select list in the application that uses the LOV you've subscribed to, you will see the same list of employees displayed in the master application, as shown in Figure 1-18.

Employee
ADAMS
ALLEN
BLAKE
CLARK
FORD
JAMES

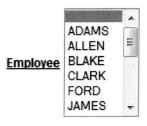

Figure 1-18. *A select list based on the subscribing LOV*

If you decide you want to change the definition of the LOV so that the employees are listed in descending alphabetical order, you can go back to the master application and change the query as follows:

```
select ename d, empno r
from   emp
order by 1 desc
```

At this point, the master application would display the employees in descending alphabetical order, while the application that subscribes to the LOV would still display the employees in ascending order. To update the subscribing LOV, you need to either publish the changes from the LOV in the master application, as shown in Figure 1-19, or refresh the LOV in the subscribing application, as shown in Figure 1-20.

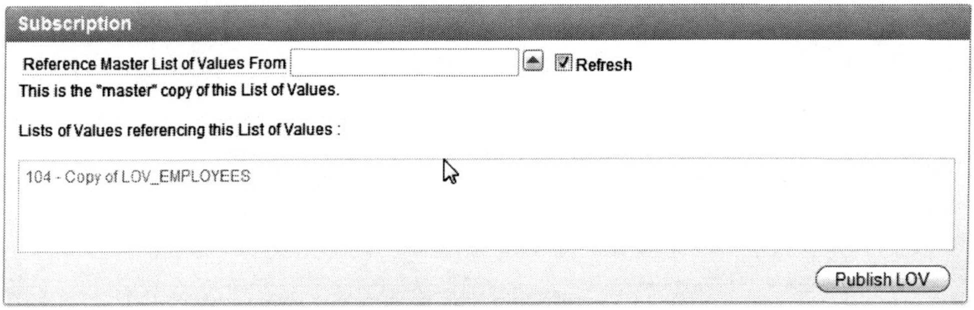

Subscription
Reference Master List of Values From
Refresh
This is the "master" copy of this List of Values.
Lists of Values referencing this List of Values :
104 - Copy of LOV_EMPLOYEES
Publish LOV

Figure 1-19. *Publishing the changes from the master LOV*

Subscription

Reference Master List of Values From 105: LOV_EMPLOYEES
Copied from Application : **105, LOV_EMPLOYEES**

No Lists of Values subscribe to this List of Values.

Refresh LOV

Figure 1-20. Refreshing the subscribing LOV

After you either publish the changes from the master application or refresh the subscribing LOV, the select list in the application will use exactly the same query that was defined in the master application. Figure 1-21 shows the select list now displaying the employees in descending alphabetical order.

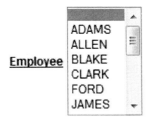

Employee

ADAMS
ALLEN
BLAKE
CLARK
FORD
JAMES

Figure 1-21. Subscribing LOV refreshed with the master LOV

The publish/subscribe functionality makes it far easier to maintain consistent appearance and behavior across common applications. You could create a single application that's used as the master for all of your common applications, and then make changes to the common components in the master application and synchronize the changes to the other applications by publishing from the master application or refreshing from individual applications.

Separating Data and Application Logic from Style and Presentation

To ensure that your applications and code are as portable and reusable as possible, you should strive to keep the data itself distinct from its presentation. This means that in general you shouldn't embed HTML markup into the data-retrieval process. For example, suppose you want to display employee names in bold in a report. You could use a query like this:

```
select '<b>' || ename || '</b>' as ename, deptno, sal from emp
```

However, it's better to keep the HTML markup out of the query. You could use a custom report template or use the column formatting section within the report attributes to apply some CSS formatting to the individual column. Then the query to bold the names would look like this:

```
select ename, deptno, sal from emp
```

Even in this simple example, it's far easier to see at a glance exactly what this query is doing. You can also change the way the data is presented without needing to modify the query definition.

By keeping the HTML markup out of the query, you may find that your application performs better if you use the query in multiple places. Because the query is already stored in the shared pool, Oracle can take advantage of this by soft-parsing the query. If you embed the HTML markup in the query, Oracle will treat two queries as being different, even if only the embedded markup is different. For example, this query:

```
select '<b>' || ename || '</b>' as ename, deptno, sal from emp
```

would not be considered the same query as this one:

```
select '<i>' || ename || '</i>' as ename, deptno, sal from emp
```

If you run the first query and then the second query (for the first time), Oracle won't find the second query in the shared pool. It would need to hard-parse the query, which would be more CPU-intensive than if it had found the query in the shared pool (and therefore could skip the hard-parse).

Whenever you find yourself including HTML in a query, rethink your approach. Consider how you can use SQL features (such as DECODE, NVL, and so on) to add conditional logic to a report template to distinguish how different columns or rows should be displayed.

Using Page Zero

If you want to display the same page element on all or multiple pages of your application, consider making use of page zero. When you place a page element on page zero, that element can be seen on all other pages of your application. By including some conditional display logic, you can restrict the element to appear only on certain pages.

A common use for page zero is to include a navigational menu in an application. You can create a region on page zero that contains the menu, which then appears on every page. You can also include a region that contains a navigational menu for administrators. You would include a conditional display that shows this menu only if the application user is an administrator.

By using page zero, you can centralize common components and functionality within your application. This also leads to a more consistent look and feel, since you can control the layout ofthe elements in a single place.

Performance Considerations

You need to consider performance during the design and implementation of a system, rather than investigate it only after you've rolled out your application to the live environment (at which point it might be too late to correct any fundamental flaws in the design).

Since the APEX environment runs entirely within the database, many of the recommendations for writing code and good schema design that perform and scale well are the same as for any PL/SQL programs or SQL queries. A sound understanding of SQL and PL/SQL is a definite benefit when developing with APEX. Take the time to learn about the latest features available in the database that might enable you to achieve your aims in a different way. For example learning how to use analytics might simplify many of your existing queries and make them perform better.

Bind Variables

The importance of using bind variables in your code can't be overstated. Bind variables not only help your code perform better, they also help protect you from SQL-injection attacks.

For example, say we use the following piece of code to return the SQL that should be used in a report. The code checks whether the user has entered a value for the page item P1_SEARCH. If the page item is not null, the value is appended to the text that is returned.

```
declare
  v_sql VARCHAR2(2000);
begin
  v_sql := 'select name, salary from payroll where deptno = 10 ';
  if p_search is not null then
    v_sql := v_sql || 'and name=''' || p_search || '''';
  end if;
  return v_sql;

end;
```

So, if the user entered SMITH into the search box, the following SQL would be returned:

```
select deptno, name, salary from payroll
  where deptno = 10 and name = 'SMITH';
```

However, suppose a malicious user knows you have a function called delete_user with the following signature:

```
function delete_user(p_id IN INTEGER) return integer
```

That user could enter this into the search box:

```
 or delete_user(id) = 1
```

The query now looks like this:

```
select id, deptno, name, salary from payroll
  where deptno = 10 and name = ' or delete_user(id) = 1'
```

The seemingly innocent search becomes a mass employee-deletion routine. The proper way to handle this would be to not concatenate the user input directly to the SQL text:

```
declare
  v_sql VARCHAR2(2000);
begin
  if :P1_SEARCH is not null then
    v_sql := 'select name, salary from payroll where deptno = 10';
  else
    v_sql := 'select name, salary from payroll '
             || ' where deptno = 10 and name = :P1_SEARCH';
```

```
    end if;

    return v_sql;
end;
```

Another potential danger in writing code that allows SQL injection is that a malicious user can add code like this:

```
    'or'1'='1
```

As you can see, this code snippet can cause injected SQL to evaluate to true, potentially allowing users to access data they were not intended to see.

Report Pagination Style

Different report pagination styles affect performance when displaying a report. For example, some pagination styles will display something like "Row Ranges X to Y of Z," If you don't need to display how many total rows are returned from the query, choose a pagination style that displaysonly "Row Ranges X to Y." It is worth noting that if you decide to display the total number records the report will return, the database will fetch all the rows, even though you may not display them all. If you don't need to display the total number of rows, the report will be rendered after the rows for the first page are fetched.

Error and Exception Handling

Your APEX application can use many different anonymous PL/SQL blocks, functions, procedures, and packages as it executes. If an error or exception occurs during the execution of some code, you need to be able to handle that error or exception gracefully, in such a fashion that flow of execution by the APEX engine is not broken. For example, the following code catches an exception and sets the value of an application item:

```
declare
  v_salary INTEGER;
begin
  select
    salary
  into
    v_salary
  from
    emp
  where
    empno = :P1_EMPNO;
  return v_salary;
  :APP_ERROR_MSG := null;
exception
  when no_data_found then
```

```
    :APP_ERROR_MSG := 'Could not find the employee record.';
end;
```

You can then display the application item on the page in an HTML region using this syntax:

```
&APP_ERROR_MSG.
```

You would then create a branch on the page to branch back to itself if the value of the application item is not null, thereby enabling the user to see the error and correct it.

Packaged Code

APEX allows you to write SQL and PL/SQL codedirectly in a number of places via the Application Builder interface. For example, suppose you create the following after-submit process in your login page to audit that a user logged in to the application.

```
begin
  insert into tbl_audit
    (id, user_name, action)
  values
    (seq_audit.nextval, :APP_USER, 'Logged On');
end;
```

Now, while this would work, it means that if you ever want to modify the logic of the auditing, you need to change the application. For example, notice that you aren't currently storing a timestamp of when the audit action was performed. To add that functionality, you'd need to modify the `tbl_audit` table and add an extra column to store the timestamp information (if that column didn't already exist), and then edit the application to change the PL/SQL page process to include the timestamp information, like this:

```
begin
  insert into tbl_audit
    (id, ts, user_name, action)
  values
    (seq_audit.nextval, sysdate, :APP_USER, 'Logged On');
end;
```

So, for a very simple change, you might need to modify the application in development, export a new version of the application, import that version into a test environment, and so on through to production.

A much more efficient approach is to try to isolate the number of places you directly code logic into your application by placing that code into a package and then calling the packaged procedure or function from your application. For example, you could change the PL/SQL page process to simply do this:

```
begin

  pkg_audit.audit_action('Logged On');

end;
```

This allows you to encapsulate all of the logic in the packaged code. Assuming you aren't making fundamental changes to the package signature, you can modify the internal logic without needing to change the application. This design allows you to change the table that the audit information is stored in or to add new columns and reference session state items without needing to change anything in the application itself. All you'd need to do is recompile the new package body in the development, test, or production environment. This would result in much less downtime for the application, since you no longer need to remove the old version of the application and import the new version. This method really does allow downtimes of just a few seconds (the time it takes to recompile the package body), as opposed to minutes, or potentially hours, while new versions of the applications are migrated. If you're using the 11gR2 database, you can take advantage of edition-based redefinition, which allows for the creation of multiple versions of PL/SQL objects. Obviously, you won't always be able to completely encapsulate your logic in packages. And sometimes, even if you do encapsulate the logic, you may need to change something in the application (for example, to pass a new parameter to the packaged code). However, it is good practice to use packaged logic where you can. Using packaged code can save you a lot of time later on, as well as encourage you to reuse code rather than potentially duplicating code throughout your application.

Another benefit of using packaged code is security. The parsing schema can be granted execution privileges on the packaged code only, without having direct grants on the underlying objects. This obviates the need for at least two schemas, one to own the objects and another to act as the parsing schema. If the parsing schema is compromised, the underlying objects are still protected as only the packaged code is accessible via this schema.

Team Development

The Team Development toolset is new in APEX 4.0. These tools enable management of the development process and tracking of new feature requests, bugs, and milestones. Before I delve into how these tools are used, it should be noted that Team Development does not perform source code control. That activity, sadly, is still handled as it was in previous versions of APEX and HTMLDB. What Team Development does provide is a centralized mechanism for recording requests and tracking the progress of development activities. The interface is straightforward but highly configurable, so some planning is required before putting these tools to full use. For businesses that use tools like Microsoft Project or Mercury Quality Center to track projects, Team Development may not be necessary. But for those without enterprise tools, these new features can be very beneficial—especially because they're free.

Using Team Development

To access the Team Development tools, simply log in to APEX as a developer. On the home page, you'll see the Team Development icon as shown in as shown in Figure 1-22.

Figure 1-22. Team Development icon

Once inside the Team Development system, you will see the types of project information that can be tracked. Figure 1-23 shows the Team Development dashboard. Before attempting to use these tools, a little planning is recommended.

Figure 1-23. Team Development dashboard

Preparing for Team Development

To get the maximum benefit from the Team Development tools, it is important to understand the interrelationships among its five components. Features and milestones are the anchor components in a development project. Milestones are just what you'd think—a date that has some significance to the project. Once a milestone is defined, it can stand alone or be assigned to features, to dos, and bugs. Features are a little more complex since milestones, bugs, and to dos can be associated with a feature. In addition, one feature can be the parent of another. This allows for an endless hierarchy of features, which is why planning is important. You don't want project management to be more complicated than the development process.

Figure 1-24 shows how you could build a hierarchy of features, bugs, to dos, and milestones with several parent-child relationships. Figure 1-25 shows a simplified method of managing a project. If you equate features to forms or reports, you can see that it's easier to track features, bugs, to dos, and milestones using the simplified method.

In any case, the Team Development tool offers managers and developers a centralized, web-based repository for storing bug reports, user requests, requirement changes, and so forth. This is a significant improvement over the traditional methods for recording this type of information: verbal conversations, handwritten notes, e-mail, etc. Since the Team Development interface is web-based, it can be used by anyone, whether APEX is being used for development or not.

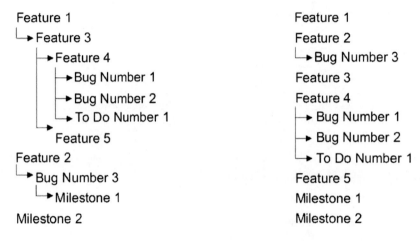

Figure 1-24. Possible feature hierarchy   *Figure 1-25. Recommended feature hierarchy*

To enable Team Development for a project, the team lead should prepare by identifying the main functions of the application and recording them as features. Specific forms and reports are good candidates to record as features since users routinely report problems and request changes at these levels. In addition, if any milestones are known, they too can be recorded. From that point on, to dos and bugs should be recorded and associated to a feature or a milestone. As new features are added, they should be recorded as well.

A simple workflow for setting up Team Development would include the following:

1. Create features for all known forms, reports, etc.

2. Assign any known to dos to their related features

3. Assign dates to any known milestones

As the project progresses, new bugs and to dos can be assigned and the status of completed tasks can be updated.

Creating Features

To create a feature, click on the Features icon on the Team Development dashboard and then click the Create button. Figure 1-26 shows the Feature entry screen. It is important to note that this form allows you to not only create a feature, but also to populate LOVs, which are used throughout the Team Development system. Fields used to build LOVs are:

- New Owner

- New Contributor

- New Focus Area

- New Release

Because the data entered into these fields is accepted without validation, it can easily become polluted. Please note that the "Release" LOV is populated using this form. If Team Development is to be used effectively, data like Release numbers must be tightly controlled. For this reason, it is recommended that access to the Create Feature page be restricted to team leads.

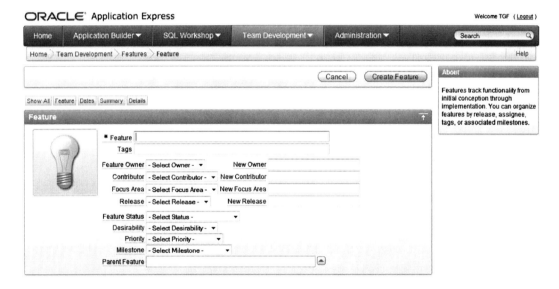

Figure 1-26. Create Feature form

The following LOVs are prepopulated at installation and can't be changed via the Team Development interface:

- Feature Status

- Desirability

- Priority

While many of the fields on this form accept free-form text, Feature Status does not. It is used, as you will see later, to aid in project status reporting. The remaining attributes of this form are self-explanatory and are common to most project management methodologies.

Recording Bugs and To Dos

Once the testing process begins, your users will inevitably begin reporting bugs. The Bug form in the Team Development interface is used to record and manage this information. The Create Bug form, shown in Figure 1-27, is similar in functionality to the Create Feature form. As noted, bugs should be associated with features that equate to a form, report, etc.

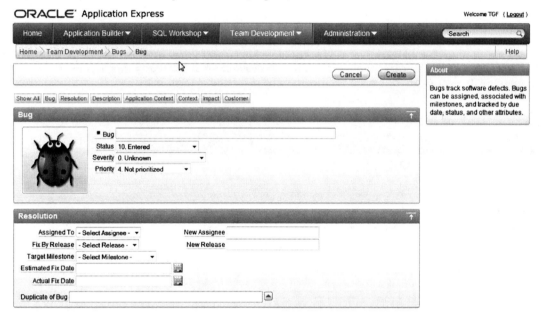

Figure 1-27. Create Bug page

To dos are similar to bugs in that they are a record of some activity that needs to be done by some date. You could consider a to do as anything except a bug. Figure 1-28 shows the Create To Do page. Determining whether to use the Bug page or the To Do page is up to the team lead. As all developers know, testers often report bugs that may actually be requests for new or changed functionality. In such cases, the team lead may want to create a To Do so that the development team can address the issues appropriately. The main difference between these two objects is that the Bug page can record much more detailed information about the context of the issue.

Like the Create Feature page, the Create Bug and To Do pages contain free-form text fields, LOVs, and fields used to populate LOVs. Using the recommended project management process, a bug or to do would be created and minimally assigned to a feature and to a developer.

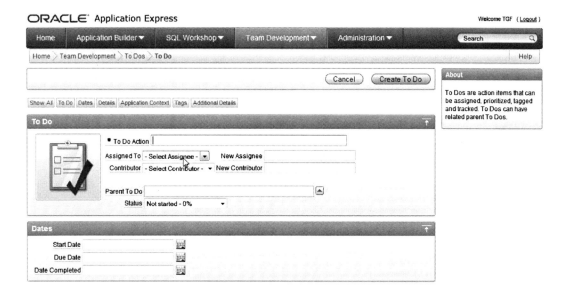

Figure 1-28. Create To Do page

It is worth noting that to dos, like features, can be created in a hierarchical fashion. Although this is a powerful feature, it does allow complex hierarchies, which are difficult to track and manage. At least in the beginning, it is recommended that the depth of to do (or feature) hierarchies be kept to one or two levels.

Recording a Milestone

A milestone is a significant date within a project plan. It can signify the required completion date of some unit of work, a business critical date like the end of a fiscal year, or something unrelated to the project like a public holiday. The Create Milestone page, shown in Figure 1-29, allows you to create a milestone, which can then be associated to a Feature, Bug, or To Do.

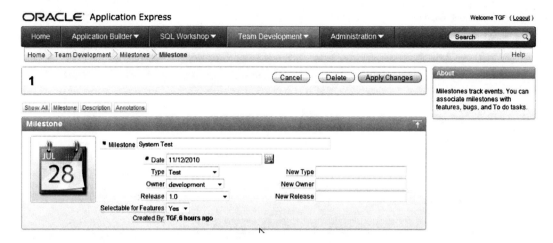

Figure 1-29. *Create Milestone page*

Once a milestone is set, it will show up on its assigned date on the project Calendar as shown in Figure 1-30. The annotation of the milestone (November 12 on the Calendar) is actually a hyperlink that, when clicked, causes the Edit Milestone page to be displayed.

Figure 1-30. *Project Calendar*

Milestones can stand alone or can be assigned to any or all of the project's features, bugs, or milestones. While this can be beneficial in managing a project, it does require the team lead to be diligent in determining how to associate milestones with other objects. It is important to note that any feature, bug, or to do can be assigned only one milestone at a time.

Gathering User Feedback

New in APEX 4.0 is the ability to quickly create a page that lets users report system issues to the development team lead. While this may sound like a handy feature, I may recommend you avoid it for the following reasons:

- Nontechnical users sometimes have trouble describing system problems in a way that makes sense to developers

- If you make it very easy to provide feedback, you'll get lots of it. You will then have to spend time filtering out the "noise" in an effort to determine what is relevant and what is not.

I've been writing code and working with users for more than 20 years, and during that time I've followed one simple approach regarding user feedback: without meaning any disrespect, I don't believe what anyone says about an application bug until I see it myself. When you are intimately familiar with a piece of code, no one can describe a bug in that code better than you. If at all possible, I recommend having a lead developer meet with the user community (or their reasonable facsimile) on a regular basis. The developer can then translate users' concerns into actionable items for the development team.

If you decide you want to include a Feedback page in your system, here's is a brief description of how to do it:

1. Add a page to an application, selecting "Feedback" as the type.

2. Select "Yes" to add a Navigation Bar entry.

3. Set the label for the Navigation Bar entry.

4. Select "Yes" to Enable Feedback for this application.

Once you complete this process, your users can access the Feedback page from the Navigation Bar (next to the Login / Logout link). An example is shown in Figure 1-31.

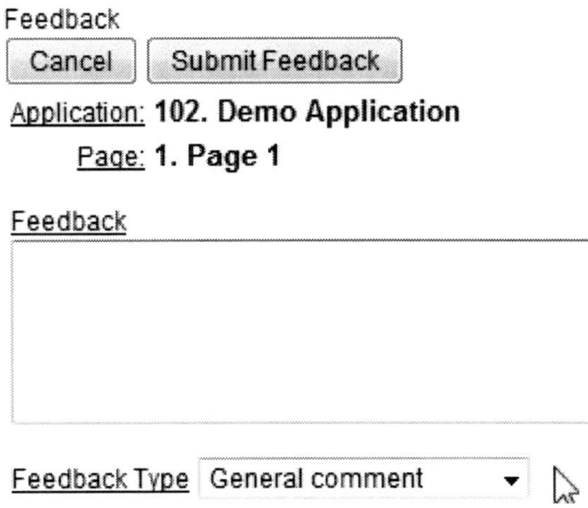

Figure 1-31. Feedback page

One more time, though, beware of asking for unfiltered end-user feedback. You'll get it.

Tracking Development Progress

Without progress reporting, all the time and effort spent recording features, bugs, and to dos would be a waste of time. APEX 4.0 addresses this reality by providing mainly dashboards to track project activities. The dashboard for each type of work shows progress and status at a glance, but to get more detailed information, additional reports are available. The APEX 4.0 Team Development system does not contain a consolidated report that shows the status of objects across Features, Bugs, and To Dos, but does have a the Team Development home page that contains dashboards for all types of work.

The main drawbacks to the Team Development system's reporting capabilities are:

- Inconsistent status labels across Features, Bugs, and To Dos

- No built-in report that consolidates Features, Bugs, and To Dos

Despite these drawbacks, it is still possible to effectively manage a project using the Team Development tools.

Feature Dashboard

When accessing the Features dashboard from the Team Development home page, you'll see a graphic that shows the percentage of Features that are complete and additional information on the total number of recorded features. This dashboard is unique in that a feature is considered complete when its status is set to "Functionally Complete – 80%" as opposed to 100% complete for a bug or a to do. The difference in status labels is a little annoying, especially since there is no way to set your own status labels via the Team Development interface. A feature (or a "page" in this example) that is marked "80% Functionally Complete " is shown in Figure 1-32.

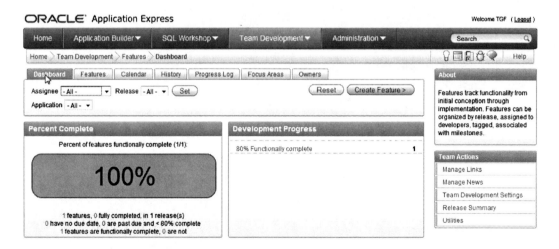

Figure 1-32. Feature dashboard

Bug Dashboard

When you access the Bug dashboard from the Team Development home page, you'll see a percentage graphic showing the number of "closed" bugs. A closed bug is one that has a status of "100.Complete." If you have recorded 2 bugs and closed one, the Bug dashboard will show that 50 percent of the bugs are closed. Several additional links on the dashboard, as shown in Figure 1-33, can be used to navigate to the Bug details page.

Figure 1-33. Bug dashboard

To Dos Dashboard

The To Dos dashboard is decidedly different from the Features and Bugs dashboards. While this page does show the completion status of all recorded To Dos as a percentage, it also contains a doughnut-shaped graphic that shows the percentage of to dos assigned to each developer. If you have two developers and each is assigned one to do, the doughnut will be divided in half to show that each developer is responsible for 50% of the to dos. The graphic also acts as a hyperlink for navigating to a report of to dos by developer. Like bugs, to dos must be 100% complete before the dashboard will show a completion percentage. Figure 1-34 shows the To Do dashboard.

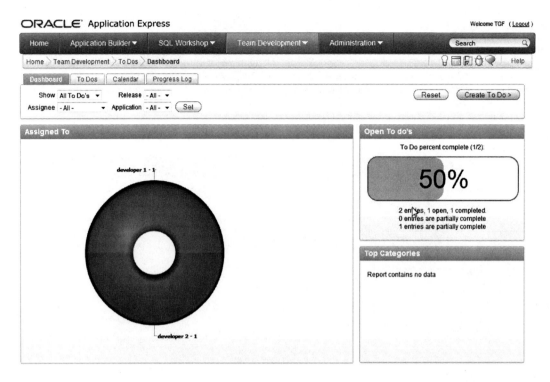

Figure 1-34. *To Do dashboard*

Although it may be difficult to see in gray-scale, the doughnut-shaped graphic is divided in half and is shown in two distinct colors. Clicking either half of the graphic or any of the other hyperlinks on this page results in navigation to the associated to do detail page.

New Development Features in APEX 4.0

APEX 4.0 includes some interesting new features to assist in development and debugging. The APEX Advisor, for instance, is a utility that will scan your application (either completely or by specific page) and report on deviations from "APEX best practices." You may or may not agree with what the Advisor says, but it makes finding certain type of errors much easier than digging through the code. For example, if you intend to include help on every field on all pages, the Advisor can quickly tell you whether you achieved your goal.

APEX Development Advisor

You access the APEX Development Advisor from the Utilities menu of an application home page, as shown in Figure 1-35. You should review each of the Checks to Perform to ensure that you get only the information you need. In the Check Pages section, you can include a comma-separated list of page numbers to scan, or leave this area blank to scan all pages.

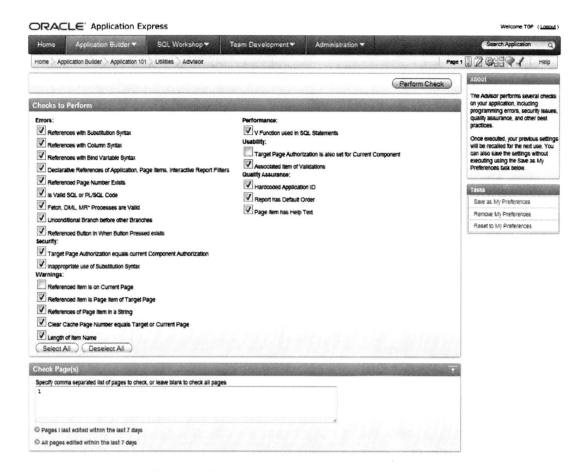

Figure 1-35. APEX Development Advisor

The resulting "report" shows all of the areas that don't meet the requirements of the Advisor. Using the example stated above (make sure all fields have help text defined), the Advisor was run on Page 1 of the Buglist application. The resulting APEX Development Advisor report shown in Figure 1-36 identifies a field as having no help text and includes a "View" link to take you directly to the item in question.

Figure 1-36. *APEX Development Advisor report*

APEX Code Debugger

The integrated Code Debugger has a clean, graphical user interface to view detailed application execution details. Debugging can be enabled or disabled for an application using the Edit Application Properties button on the Application Home Page. Once debugging has been enabled, it can be activated at any time during execution (when running in development mode) by pressing the "Debug" button at the bottom of the application page. Clicking the "View Debug" button at the bottom of any page brings up the Debug Message page, as shown in Figure 1-37. This page displays a history of the debug sessions that have been run for this application and their relative time of execution.

Help

| Items | Pages | Queries | Tables | PL/SQL | Images | Debug | Session | Errors |

Reset

Go   Actions ▼

View Identifier	Session	User	Application	Page	Entries	Timestamp	Seconds
341	3446010111957025	BRIAN	101	1	62	29 seconds ago	0.2415
322	3446010111957025	BRIAN	101	1	47	9 minutes ago	0.1137
321	3446010111957025	BRIAN	101	1	63	9 minutes ago	0.2185

1 - 3

Figure 1-37. *APEX debug history*

Clicking on the most recent debug session identifier opens another window showing the details of that session, as shown in Figure 1-38. The bar graph in the details window shows the execution times of each recorded activity. Hovering your mouse over the bars pops up some help text that describes the activity. Clicking on the bar will navigate to that activity in the debug details.

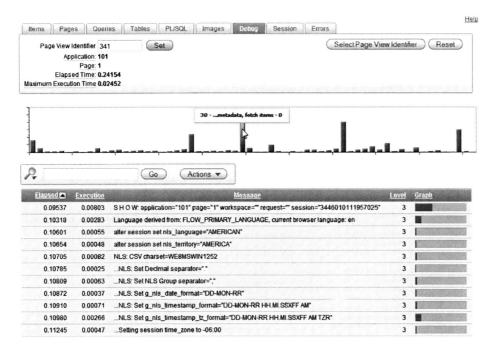

Figure 1-38. *APEX Debugger*

Summary

This chapter covered some best practices for using APEX. You don't need to follow our advice. Many people just charge in and begin coding without thinking to lay a solid foundation for their work. Some of what we advocate in this chapter may actually slow you down at first, but it will save you time in the long run. Helping you to work more efficiently, and taking a long-term view of doing that, is one of the reasons we've written this book.

As for project management, we are discussing art as opposed to science. Each project manager has his own way of doing things so no single methodology works in every case. In instances where formal project management tools are not available, APEX 4.0's Team Development tools can be a vast improvement over traditional methods that include e-mail, Excel, pencil and paper, and so forth. Hopefully, this chapter has exposed you to enough of the functionality that you can benefit from at least a portion of it.

CHAPTER 2

Authentication and User Management

Controlling who can and who can't access your application is an extremely important consideration when designing your applications. The authentication method you choose for your application will define how the identity of users is determined and verified. A comprehensive security model will also address authorization—the process of specifying what a user can do once he is logged into an application.

As you'll learn in this chapter, APEX allows you to define many different authentication schemes in your application. However, only one of the schemes can be set as the current one. You can use one of the preconfigured authentication schemes or create your own from scratch, enabling you to build any logic you like into your authentication scheme.

With APEX, you can specify, on a page-by-page basis, whether that particular page requires authentication or is public. If the page is public, anyone can directly access that page by typing its URL into a browser.

Once users have successfully authenticated to your application, they will be able to access any pages in the application that require authentication without having to reauthenticate (assuming the user passes any authorization checks, which we will cover in the next chapter). In other words, authentication is a one-time process—once you have authenticated, you remain authenticated for the duration of your session. Given increasing focus on application security, it is a common practice to time a session out after a period of inactivity. In earlier versions of APEX, you may have used custom functions to implement a session timeout, but this is no longer necessary in APEX 4.0. Both the session timeout (defaulted to 3600 seconds) and the maximum session length (defaulted to 28,800 seconds) can be set via the Security Settings section of the Manage Instance page.

Preconfigured Authentication Schemes

APEX offers a number of built-in authentication schemes, including the following:

Open door credentials: This scheme allows users to successfully authenticate using any username, without having to provide a password. The username is not checked against any sort of repository, so this scheme is really useful only for testing purposes or where you don't need to enforce any form of account uniqueness. This scheme also allows you to simulate (in your development environment) what happens when you authenticate as a particular user in another environment (for example the production environment).

No authentication: This scheme allows anyone to access the pages in your application, as long as the Oracle username and password specified in the database access descriptor (DAD) are correct. You will not be able to uniquely identify users in your application, since they will all be using the username specified in the DAD (for example, `APEX_PUBLIC_USER` or `HTMLDB_PUBLIC_USER`).

Application Express account credentials: This scheme uses the built-in users and groups created by a workspace administrator within the workspace where the application is installed. This method is often referred to as *cookie user accounts*. It offers a quick way to manage and maintain a simple user repository without having to create your own user-management routines.

Database account authentication: This scheme allows you to use Oracle accounts to authenticate your users against. Users need to specify a valid database username and password in order to successfully authenticate to your application. This scheme is ideal if you have already created a database user for each of your end users. Note that using database account authentication will not affect the parsing schema for your application. In other words, the authentication scheme uses only the username and password to authenticate with; it is not establishing a session to the database as that user, nor is it running any code as that particular user.

LDAP directory: Using this scheme, you can authenticate users against any LDAP directory, which includes Oracle Internet Directory (OID), Microsoft Active Directory, and Sun iPlanet, among many others.

Application server single sign-on: If you use Oracle Application Server, you can take advantage of single sign-on (SSO) against an OID LDAP server. Using SSO enables users to authenticate once against the SSO server, and then be able to access many different applications without needing to reauthenticate.

To use a preconfigured authentication scheme, within your application in Application Builder, choose to create a new authentication scheme and select "Based on a preconfigured scheme from the gallery." You will see the page shown in Figure 2-1.

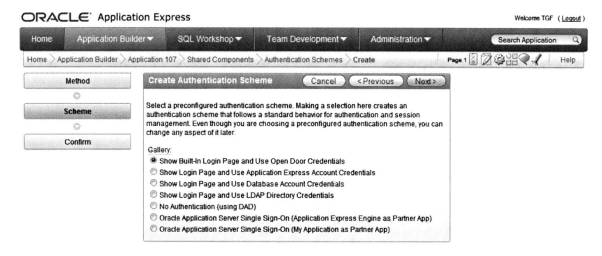

Figure 2-1. APEX preconfigured authentication schemes

You can view the existing authentication methods for your application by navigating to Shared Components➚Authentication Schemes. This takes you to a page that displays all of the authentication schemes defined for your application. The scheme that is currently being used is indicated with a check mark. Figure 2-2 shows an example of an application with the Application Express credentials and database account authentication methods defined, with Application Express credentials as the active method.

Figure 2-2. Authentication schemes defined for the application

Rather than apply a preconfigured scheme, you can instead use a custom authentication scheme, which gives you complete control over how your authentication scheme works. Typically, you might write a routine that authenticates a username and password against details that have been stored in a table.

This chapter covers all the preconfigured authentication methods, except the LDAP directory and SSO authentication schemes, as well as creating custom authentication schemes.

Open Door Credentials

With open door credentials, you are essentially declaring, "I want to allow anyone to authenticate to my application, just as long as they type in a username." To use open door credentials, choose to create a new authentication scheme and select "Based on a preconfigured scheme from the gallery." Then choose Show Built-In Login Page and Use Open Door Credentials (see Figure 2-1).

When users run your application and try to connect to a page requiring authentication, they will be presented with a login screen similar to the one shown in Figure 2-3, where they will need to enter a username.

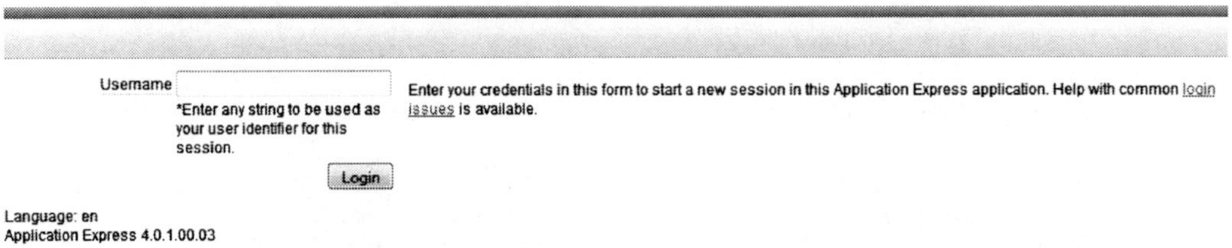

Username [   ]   Enter your credentials in this form to start a new session in this Application Express application. Help with common login
*Enter any string to be used as   issues is available.
your user identifier for this
session.

[Login]

Language: en
Application Express 4.0.1.00.03

Figure 2-3. Open door credentials login screen

Whatever the user enters as the username will be used as the `APP_USER` substitution variable. Since no password is requested and no validation is performed, users are free to use any username they like; for example, they could choose `ADMIN` or something else completely undesirable.

Using the open door credentials authentication method is a good way to quickly test your application using different users without needing to maintain a user repository. This lets you track down problems that are perhaps related to the username (for example, authorization issues) without having that user in your user repository.

Open door credentials authentication is rarely used outside development and testing environments. You will usually want to either make an application completely public (no authentication) or be able to differentiate among your individual users. Since the open door credentials method does not require a password, you won't be able prevent different users from using the same username.

No Authentication

It may seem strange in a chapter devoted to authentication to discuss no authentication. However, it is completely valid to have all of your pages accessible without requiring users to log in.

To set up an application with no authentication, choose to create a new authentication method based on one from the gallery, and then select No Authentication (using DAD), as shown in Figure 2-1. Once you've chosen this scheme, users will be able to access the application without needing to authenticate.

When you use the no-authentication method, the `APP_USER` substitution string that is used to identify the currently logged-in user will be set to the database user specified in the DAD configuration file. Typically, the user in the DAD will be specified as `HTMLDB_PUBLIC_USER` or `APEX_PUBLIC_USER`, but it depends on your particular configuration. Since the DAD configuration file usually specifies both the username and password to connect to the database, the user will not need to authenticate.

This authentication method is useful if you don't need to protect your application in any way. If you want to allow anyone to view all the pages in your application, and you're not concerned about the data they might be able to view and modify, this method is ideal. You may find it suitable when your application is essentially read-only—the end users just view the data (and that data is not deemed sensitive).

You should also take into account that with the no-authentication method, any form of auditing you might be performing (for example, keeping track of records being deleted) will be of limited use. Every user will be identified as `APEX_PUBLIC_USER` or `HTMLDB_PUBLIC_USER` (as specified in your DAD), so you won't be able to correlate the audit entries to a particular user.

Application Express Account Credentials

Application Express account credentials, commonly referred to as *cookie users* or *built-in users*, is an authentication scheme that relies on a user repository within the APEX environment. Any user that is defined within the workspace in which the application is installed can be used to authenticate to the application.

Using Application Express account credentials allows you to quickly and easily create and maintain users. The ease with which you can set up users makes this authentication scheme attractive for quick prototyping.

One drawback to using Application Express account credentials is that users will be able to successfully authenticate to any application in the workspace that uses Application Express account credentials. However, you can use group membership and a custom authentication method to limit which users can successfully authenticate to your application. The following sections describe how to create users and groups, including how to use a custom authentication method to take group membership into account.

Creating New Application Users

To create a new user who can authenticate to your application, log in to the workspace as a workspace administrator and navigate to Administration ↗ Manage Application Express Users. From here, you can create a new end user for your application, as shown in Figure 2-4.

Figure 2-4. *Creating a new end user*

Bear in mind that any end users you create will be able to authenticate to any application in that workspace that uses the Application Express account credentials authentication scheme. If you want to use this authentication method but would like to restrict the applications that users can log in to, you can use different workspaces to effectively partition your applications.

Once users have been authenticated, some applications may display the logged-in username, depending on the theme used. For example, the Light Blue theme (theme 15) shows the current username in the top-right corner of the page, as shown in Figure 2-5. Other themes may display the username in a different position, and some themes may not display the username at all.

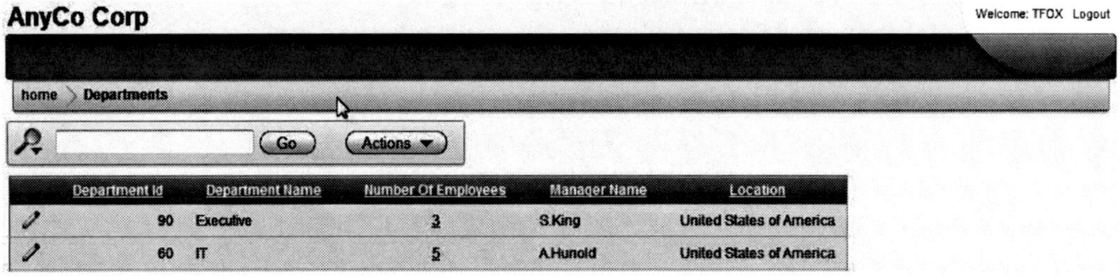

AnyCo Corp   Welcome: TFOX Logout

home Departments

	Department Id	Department Name	Number Of Employees	Manager Name	Location
✎	90	Executive	3	S.King	United States of America
✎	60	IT	5	A.Hunold	United States of America

Figure 2-5. *Username displayed in an application after a user has authenticated*

■ **Tip** If your application requires users to authenticate, displaying the username somewhere on the screen can be helpful. Being able to see the username at a glance can help to narrow down any problems you might have that affect one user but not another. Also, it's a quick and simple visual cue for users, allowing them to see exactly which account they have logged in as.

Creating Groups

As well as being able to create individual users with the Application Express account credentials authentication scheme, you can also create groups and then add individual users to particular groups. A group can contain more than one user, and a user can belong to multiple groups.

To create a group, use the Manage Application Express Users link in the Application Builder. Figure 2-6 shows an example of a new group called End Users being created. After you create the group, you can make users members of that group. To do this, edit the individual user and select each group you want the user to be a member of, as shown in Figure 2-7.

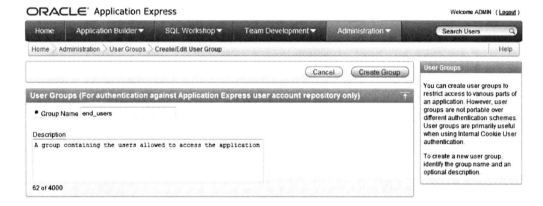

Figure 2-6. Creating a new group

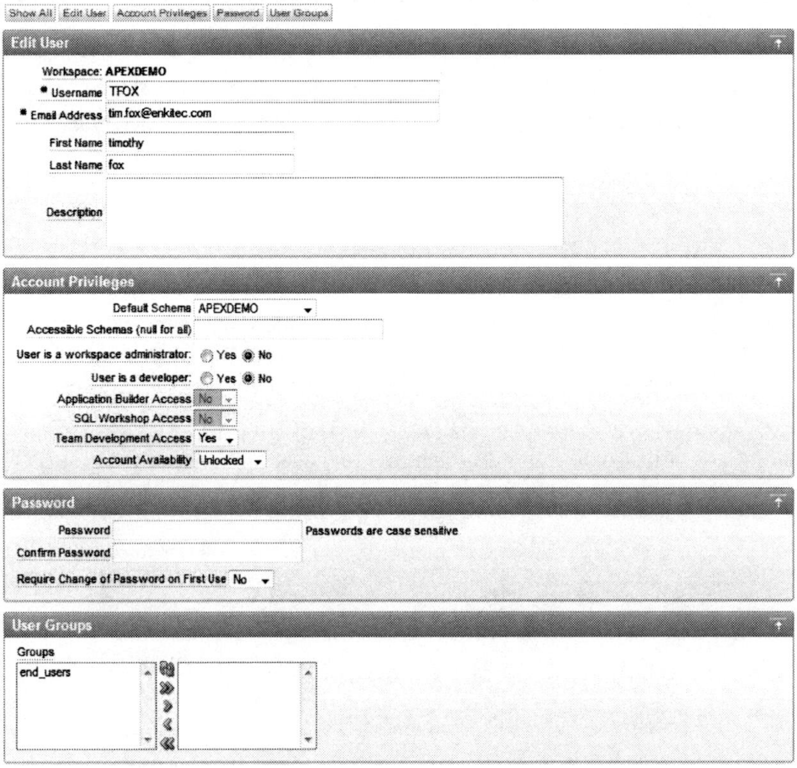

Figure 2-7. Adding a user to a group

Controlling Authentication with Groups

As noted earlier, with groups, you can use a custom authentication method to limit which users can authenticate to your application. As shown in Figure 2-8, the default authentication function used for the Application Express account credentials method is the `-BUILTIN-` function. This method will automatically check the username and password being used against the cookie (or built-in) users for the workspace.

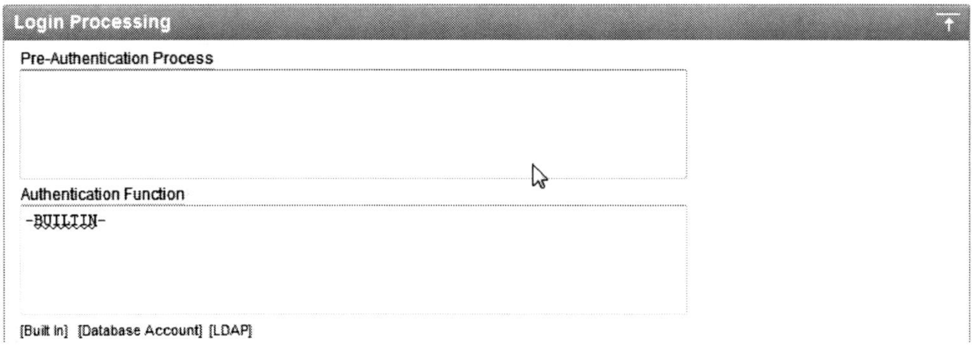

Figure 2-8. Using the -BUILTIN- authentication function

In order to take group membership into account, you'll need to replace the -BUILTIN- function with your own function, which should not only verify that the username and password are correct but also check that the user is in a particular group. To replace the existing -BUILTIN- authentication function with your own, you need to provide a function with the following signature:

```
(p_username in varchar2, p_password in varchar2) return Boolean
```

The function should take two parameters: one for the username and one for the password. It needs to return a Boolean value that indicates whether the authentication succeeded or failed. For example, Listing 2-1 shows a custom authentication function that allows any user to authenticate (we'll get to a more useful function in a moment).

Listing 2-1. A Simple Authentication Function That Always Succeeds

```
create or replace function authenticate(p_username in varchar2,
  p_password in varchar2) return boolean is
begin
  return true;
end authenticate;
```

You can then use your custom authentication function by replacing -BUILTIN- in the Authentication Function section of the Login Processing page with the following:

```
return authenticate;
```

This tells the APEX engine that it should call your **authenticate** function, passing in the username and password as parameters. The return result of your function is used to determine whether the user should be allowed to log in.

It is extremely important that your function have the exact signature that is expected; otherwise, you may receive an error similar to this:

```
ORA-06550: line 2, column 8: PLS-00306: wrong number or types of arguments in call
 to 'AUTHENTICATE' ORA-06550: line 2, column 1: PL/SQL: Statement ignored
```

The first step to making the authentication function useful is to modify it to verify the username and password in the same way that the -BUILTIN- method does. Fortunately, you don't need to know the internals of where the usernames and passwords are stored, since APEX provides many helper packages, functions, and procedures to make your job easier.

The apex_util package is one of these helper packages. It contains a number of functions and procedures directly related to working with cookie users. One such function is is_login_password_valid, which can be used to validate a username and password against the cookie users defined in the workspace in which the application resides. This function has the following signature:

```
function is_login_password_valid(p_username in varchar2,
  p_password in varchar2) returns boolean
```

■ **Note** The apex_util package was introduced in APEX version 2.2. If you have an earlier version, use htmldb_util or wwv_flow_user_api instead; for example, htmldb_util.is_login_password_valid.

As discussed in Chapter 1, it's generally a good idea to put code such as a custom authentication method in a package, rather than using it as a stand-alone function. Using a package allows you to specify different authentication routines, perhaps one for development and another for a live environment. Then you can specify which authentication should be used in the package itself, rather than needing to modify the application when it is installed into the live environment.

Listing 2-2 shows the new packaged function, which can be used as a direct replacement for the -BUILTIN- method.

Listing 2-2. Authentication Packaged Function

```
create or replace package pkg_auth as

  function authenticate(p_username in varchar2,
    p_password in varchar2) return boolean;
end;

create or replace package body pkg_auth as
  function authenticate(p_username in varchar2,
                        p_password in varchar2) return boolean is
  begin
    return apex_util.is_login_password_valid(p_username,
                                             p_password);
  end authenticate;

end;
```

You will also need to change the Authentication Function section of the Login Processing page so that it references the packaged function:

```
return pkg_auth.authenticate;
```

Using this authentication function, any of the cookie users will be able to log in to the application, just as they could with the -BUILTIN- method. You now need to modify the function to take group membership into account.

The apex_util package also contains a function called get_groups_user_belongs_to, which returns a string containing each group the user belongs to, delimited by commas. If the user doesn't belong to any groups, the function actually returns NULL, rather than an empty string (which you might expect). The function also returns NULL if you query the groups for a user that does not exist.

Listing 2-3 shows the updated packaged function that takes group membership into account.

Listing 2-3. Authentication Package Function That Takes Group Membership into Account

```
create or replace package pkg_auth as

  -- define a constant to represent the group name
  c_end_user constant varchar2(9) := 'end_users';

  function authenticate(p_username in varchar2,
                        p_password in varchar2) return boolean;
end;

create or replace package body pkg_auth as
  function authenticate(p_username in varchar2,
                        p_password in varchar2) return boolean is
    v_groups varchar2(32767);
    v_arrgroups apex_application_global.vc_arr2;
    b_group_member boolean := false;
    b_login_correct boolean;
  begin
    -- check the username and password are correct
    b_login_correct :=
      apex_util.is_login_password_valid(p_username,
                                        p_password);

    -- retrieve comma delimited string containing each group
    v_groups := apex_util.get_groups_user_belongs_to(p_username);

    -- convert the comma delimited string into an array
    v_arrgroups := apex_util.string_to_table(
                              p_string => v_groups,
                              p_separator => ',');

    -- loop round the array and compare each entry to the constant
    -- representing the group
    for i in 1 .. v_arrgroups.count
    loop
      if(v_arrgroups(i) = c_end_user) then
        b_group_member := true;
      end if;
    end loop;
```

```
        return(b_login_correct and b_group_member);

    end authenticate;

end;
```

The package checks whether the username and password are valid, and whether the user is a member of the End Users group. In reality, you'd probably check one of these first, and then check the other only if the first condition evaluated to true. I wrote the example in this way so that it's easier to see how the return result depends on both the b_login_correct value and the b_group_member value.

You might think the package is more complicated than it needs to be, due to the use of the call to apex_util.string_to_table. You might be tempted to simply use INSTR or SUBSTR to determine whether the comma-delimited string contains the group name of interest. However, you'd need to be extremely careful about the group names you were searching for. For example, Listing 2-4 shows how a false match can be made, since the group being searched for (Admin) appears as a substring of another group that the user is a member of (Payroll Admin).

Listing 2-4. Incorrectly Matching the Group Name Using an INSTR Match

```
jes@10gR2> var mygroups varchar2(200);

jes@10gR2> var check_group varchar2(200);
jes@10gR2> exec :mygroups := 'Payroll Admin,End User';
jes@10gR2> exec :check_group := 'Admin';
jes@10gR2> col is_member format a10
jes@10gR2> select decode(instr(:mygroups, :check_group), 0, 'N', 'Y') is_member ⏎
from dual

IS_MEMBER
----------

Y
```

Although this example shows how the INSTR function was used incorrectly, you don't have to completely avoid it; APEX itself uses INSTR to parse the input string. To ensure that the :mygroups string is parsed correctly, your decode must look for not only the group name, but also the delimiters. The code in Listing 2-5 shows the corrected decode statement.

Listing 2-5. Correctly Matching the Group Name Using an INSTR Match

```
jes@10gR2> select decode(instr(','||:mygroups||',', ','||:check_group||','), 0, 'N', 'Y')
is_member from dual
```

■ **Note** The example in Listing 2-4 is not actually that contrived. In a very similar way, users of a production system (not an APEX system) were suddenly able to access parts of the system they should not have been able to reach. It was an absolute nightmare to track down the cause, mainly because developers swore that no code had been changed. Yet the application was behaving "incorrectly."

Using the `string_to_table` routine to convert the comma-delimited string into an array makes searching through the entries much less error-prone when looking for an exact match. Whenever you write routines that deal with authentication and authorization, it's important to consider how they could be abused. You need to check whether an end user could make the routine behave in a way you wouldn't expect and possibly circumvent the security of your application, even unintentionally. It's also a good idea to hand your routine to a colleague and ask her to "break this if you can." It's far better to have one of your colleagues find a security risk than have it discovered by an end user (or even worse, someone who shouldn't even be an end user).

The `string_to_table` routine is incredibly useful. The `apex_util` package also contains a `table_to_string` routine, which converts an array into a delimited string. These routines can save you a lot of time and effort when you need to pass multiple values around in your application.

So, with the new packaged authentication function in place, you should find that you'll be able to successfully authenticate to the application only if you enter a valid username and password, and the username you enter is a member of the End Users group. For example, the `jes` user will be able to log in, but the `peterw` user will receive the "Invalid Login Credentials" message. If you add the `peterw` user to the End Users group, then you'll be able to successfully authenticate as `peterw`.

You can now completely control which cookie users are able to successfully authenticate to your application. You can also deploy multiple applications within the same workspace and easily partition them from each other so that cookie users can't access your application unless they are in a particular group. You can easily use this method to allow different users to authenticate depending on whether the application is running in the development, test, or live environment.

Maintaining Cookie Users Within Your Application

Using the Application Express account credentials method is a very quick and easy way to establish a user repository for your application. However, many people don't like having to connect to the workspace as a workspace administrator in order to create and maintain the users and groups.

Once again, the `apex_util` package comes to the rescue—with routines that enable you to programmatically perform many of the tasks that you'd otherwise need to perform as a workspace administrator. For example, if you want to be able to create new users from within the application itself, you could use the `apex_util.create_user` function:

```
procedure create_user
```

and get the following results:

```
argument name                  type          in/out default?

------------------------------ ------------- ------ --------
p_user_id                      number        in     default
p_user_name                    varchar2      in
p_first_name                   varchar2      in     default
p_last_name                    varchar2      in     default
p_description                  varchar2      in     default
p_email_address                varchar2      in     default
p_web_password                 varchar2      in
p_web_password_format          varchar2      in     default
p_group_ids                    varchar2      in     default
p_developer_privs              varchar2      in     default
p_default_schema               varchar2      in     default
p_allow_access_to_schemas      varchar2      in     default
```

p_attribute_01	varchar2	in	default
p_attribute_02	varchar2	in	default
p_attribute_03	varchar2	in	default
p_attribute_04	varchar2	in	default
p_attribute_05	varchar2	in	default
p_attribute_06	varchar2	in	default
p_attribute_07	varchar2	in	default
p_attribute_08	varchar2	in	default
p_attribute_09	varchar2	in	default
p_attribute_10	varchar2	in	default

This function might look a bit overwhelming, but the majority of the parameters have default values. At the minimum, you could pass in just the **p_user_name** and the **p_web_password** parameters. For example, you could create a page process that contains the PL/SQL anonymous block code shown in Listing 2-5, passing in some of the page items as parameters.

Listing 2-5. Calling the apex_util.create_user *Function from a PL/SQL Page Process*

```
apex_util.create_user(p_user_name => :P1_USERNAME,

                    p_email_address => :P1_EMAIL,
                    p_first_name => :P1_FIRST_NAME,
                    p_last_name => :P1_SURNAME,

                    p_web_password => :P1_PASSWORD);
```

Note that you can successfully call the **apex_util.create_user** function (and many of the other routines in the **apex_util package**) only if you are logged in to the application as a cookie user with workspace administrator privileges. If you attempt to execute the call while logged in to the application as a developer or end user, you will get an error similar to this:

```
ORA-20001: User requires ADMIN privilege to perform this operation.
```

Anytime you see this error on your page, it's a sure sign you're trying to call one of the **apex_util** routines while logged in to the application as a user who does not have **ADMIN** privileges.

The **apex_util** package contains other useful routines for managing users, such as **delete_user, create_user_group**, and **edit_user**, as well as routines to get and set particular attributes, such as **set_email_address**. Using these routines, you can fully manage the cookie user repository from within your application. You could also use a separate administration application, which would enable you to present a more uniform appearance and seamless integration with your applications than you can with the workspace administration tools.

▪ **Caution** Many of the packages, functions, procedures, and views available in APEX work correctly only when they are used from within the APEX environment. For example, if you try to use them while connected to a SQL*Plus session, you may find that views return no rows and the functions and procedures don't work, or they appear to work but don't give the correct results.

The `create_user` function has attribute parameters, such as `p_attribute_01, p_attribute_02`, and so on, which you can use to store up to ten additional bits of information related to a particular user. For example, to store the telephone extension number for the user, modify the `create_user` call as shown in Listing 2-6.

Listing 2-6. Using Custom Attributes in the `apex_util.create_user` Function

```
apex_util.create_user(p_user_name => :P1_USERNAME,

                      p_email_address => :P1_EMAIL
                      p_first_name => :P1_FIRST_NAME,
                      p_last_name => :P1_SURNAME,
                      p_web_password => :P1_PASSWORD,

                      p_attribute_01 => :P1_EXT_NUMBER);
```

This example uses page items from page 1 in the application as the parameters to the procedure. For example, `P1_FIRST_NAME` is a page item where the user can enter a first name.

You can then use the `get_attribute` function to retrieve the value for a particular attribute. For example, putting the following piece of code in a PL/SQL anonymous block region would display the value of the first attribute for the logged-in user:

```
htp.p(apex_util.get_attribute(p_username => :APP_USER,
                              p_attribute_number => 1));
```

Note that you refer to the attribute by number, not by name, so you need to be sure you're consistent when you use the attributes. It's easy to forget to change all references if you move the attributes around—for example, if you decide to store the extension number in `p_attribute_02` rather than `p_attribute_01`.

You can also store attributes with a user who has already been created by using the `set_attribute` function, as shown in Listing 2-7. One quirk of using `set_attribute` is that, rather than passing in the username as a string, you need to pass in the numeric ID of the username. (Not including an overridden `set_attribute` procedure that allows you to pass in the username as a string seems like an oversight, since many of the other administration routines in the `apex_util` package let you pass in either a string or numeric identifier.) Fortunately, you can easily retrieve this numeric ID for a particular username by using the `get_user_id` function, as shown in Listing 2-7.

Listing 2-7. Using `set_attribute` to Store a User-Defined Attribute

```
apex_util.set_attribute(p_userid =>

                        apex_util.get_user_id(:APP_USER),
                        p_attribute_number => 1,

                        p_attribute_value => :P1_EXT_NUMBER);
```

■ **Note** The `apex_util` package contains many other useful procedures and functions. We encourage you to spend some time looking at its features. You can use it to build an extremely powerful and flexible user repository, which can be easily exported from one environment and imported into another.

Database Account Authentication

Database account authentication was added in APEX version 2.2 (and is also available in the 2.1 release bundled with Oracle XE). This method allows you authenticate your users against real Oracle database accounts.

To set up an application with database account credential authentication, choose to create a new authentication method based on one from the gallery, and then select Show Login Page and Use Database Account Credentials, as shown in Figure 2-9.

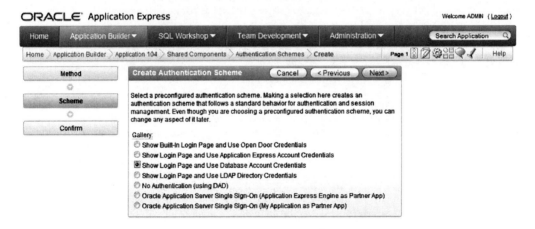

Figure 2-9. Creating an authentication scheme using database account credentials

When you create the authentication scheme, you need to specify which login page you wish you use. You can usually select page 101 (assuming that's specified as your existing login page), or you can use a built-in login page. You can change this option later by editing the authentication scheme, so it doesn't really matter which you choose at this point. The disadvantage of using the built-in login page is that you can't customize it as easily. When you use your own login page, you can modify it to make it more integrated with your application.

Users will be able to successfully authenticate to your application only if they use a valid database username and password. This is an ideal solution if you are already using database accounts as a user repository for other applications.

To allow a new user to authenticate to your application, you'll need to create a new database user in the database. For example, you might create a `demouser` user while connected to the database with SQL*Plus:

```
system@10gR2> create user demouser identified by demopassword;
```

```
User created.
```

You can now use this username and password to authenticate to the application, as shown in Figure 2-10.

Figure 2-10. Authenticated as the demouser database account

The database authentication method obeys the rules regarding whether the account is locked. For example, the **demouser** account can be locked from a SQL*Plus session:

```
system@10gR2> alter user demouser account lock;
```

```
User altered.
```

If you then tried to authenticate as **demouser** user, you'd receive the message shown in Figure 2-11. The user will not be able to successfully authenticate to your application until the account is unlocked, as follows:

```
system@10gR2> alter user demouser account unlock;
```

```
User altered.
```

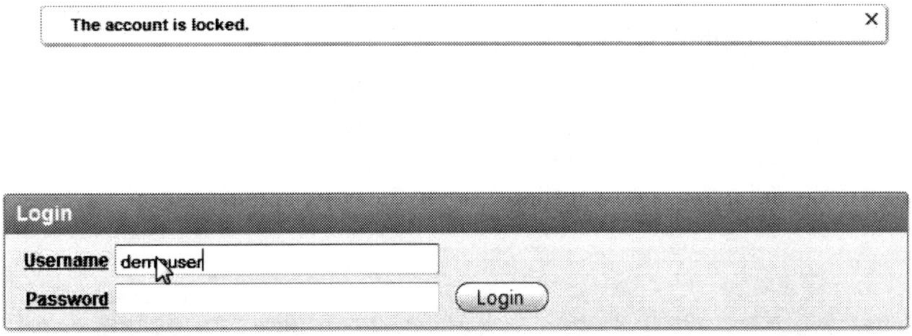

> The account is locked.   ×

Login

Username demouser

Password _____   (Login)

Figure 2-11. Attempting to authenticate with a locked account

At this point, you might start thinking of all the possibilities that have suddenly become open. For example, you might try to prevent an account from being shared by multiple people by restricting the number of times the user can be logged in simultaneously. This sort of functionality is relatively simple to achieve using Oracle accounts and profiles, as in this example:

```
system@10gR2> grant create session to demouser;

Grant succeeded.

system@10gR2> create profile demo_profile
  limit sessions_per_user 1;
Profile created.

system@10gR2> alter user demouser profile demo_profile;

User altered.
```

Now if you were to use two different SQL*Plus sessions to connect to the database as demouser, the first connection would succeed, but the second SQL*Plus session would result in an error:

```
Enter user-name: demouser

Enter password:
ERROR:

ORA-02391: eceeded simultaneous SESSIONS_PER_USER limit
```

The second SQL*Plus session will not be able to succeed until the first SQL*Plus session is ended. However, you'll find that if you launch two separate browser sessions and try to log in to your application as the demouser in each session, both sessions will be allowed to successfully authenticate! The profile restriction you witnessed with a SQL*Plus session does not apply in your application. This demonstrates a very important point to remember when you use database authentication:

- *Database account credentials are only used to authenticate against.* You are not actually connecting to the database as that user. The connection to the database is made using the credentials specified in the DAD.

If you look closely at the example of setting up the restriction, you'll see that it uses `grant create session to demouser`. This is necessary to log in to the account using SQL*Plus; otherwise, you would receive this error:

```
ORA-01045: user DEMOUSER lacks CREATE SESSION privilege; logon denied
```

However, you are able to authenticate to the application before that grant is performed. This clearly shows that database account authentication is not creating a session to the database as the username you logged in with.

Custom Authentication

By creating your own custom authentication scheme, you are in complete control over how and where your user repository is stored and how you authenticate users against that repository. Your custom authentication scheme can be as simple or as complex as you need. You can create a custom authentication scheme that extends or adapts one of the preconfigured schemes in the gallery, or you can build an entirely new authentication scheme.

One common custom authentication scheme can be referred to as "table-driven authentication." With this type of scheme, you store your user repository in a table or across a number of tables. When a user tries to authenticate to your application, your authentication scheme checks to see if the supplied username and password match an entry stored in the table. The scheme can also include any other logic you'd like, such as checking to see if the account is active or inactive (similar to the locked/unlocked status for database account credentials).

To demonstrate creating a custom authentication scheme, this section describes how to build a simple application using an Excel spreadsheet as the source. This application will be the basis for most of the examples in this and following chapters. Once the application is built, you'll set up table-driven authentication. I'll also cover some typical business requirements you might come across, including locking accounts and automating user registration.

Creating an Application from a Spreadsheet

The previous version of this text went into greater detail on how to create applications using desktop tools as the source. While the ability to use desktop tools is a powerful feature, we will discuss it only as a method for creating a basic application, which we will then modify.

Figure 2-12 shows the spreadsheet we'll use to create the Buglist application. It is a basic spreadsheet with headings in row 1 and data in the subsequent rows. Apex will consume this file and create a report and a corresponding form for data entry and modification.

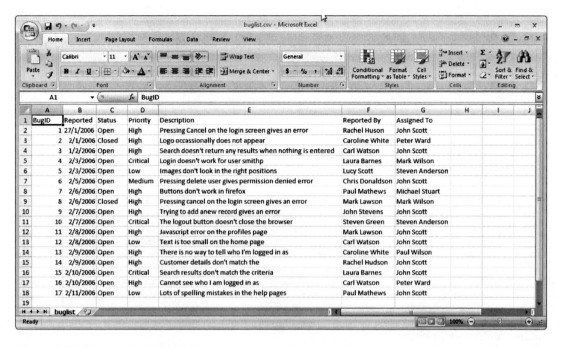

Figure 2-12. Bug Report spreadsheet

To create an application from this spreadsheet, navigate to the Application Builder and click the Create button. Choose the option to create a Database Application and click next. The screen shown in Figure 2-13 allows you to specify that the new application will be based on a spreadsheet.

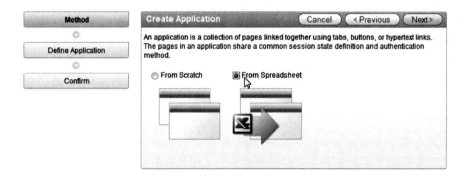

Figure 2-13. Create Application wizard

The spreadsheet wizard is very easy to use and creates a usable Apex application very quickly. In the next step of the process, you can either upload or cut and paste your spreadsheet into Apex as shown in Figure 2-14. If your spreadsheet is built such that you can use all of the contents, we recommend that you upload the file. If you only want to use a portion of an existing spreadsheet, cutting and pasting is the way to go.

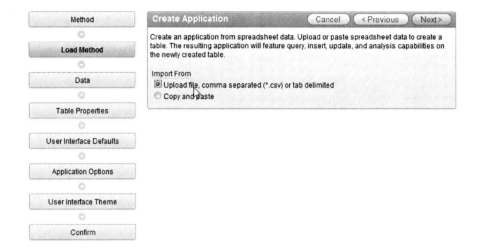

Figure 2-14. Preparing to upload a csv file or spreadsheet

To ensure that you get the data and only the data from the spreadsheet, the wizard asks for the field separator and for any delimiter that may be used to enclose strings of text. In most cases that use csv files, the field delimiter is the comma and the optional enclosing delimiter is the double quote mark. For the buglist file, the data is delimited by commas and there's no optional enclosure, as shown in Figure 2-15.

■ **Caution** Excel does not export CSV or tab-delimited data in UTF-8 by default. The data may become corrupted if you export from Excel using either of those formats and subsequently load that data into a UTF-8 database. If your database uses UTF-8, make sure to export from Excel in UTF-8.

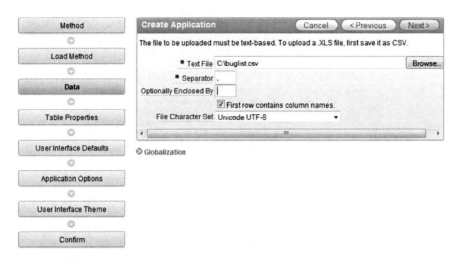

Figure 2-15. *Uploading a csv file or spreadsheet*

Once the file has been uploaded, you can define the properties of the table that will contain the data from the spreadsheet. In this case, we called the table "BUGLIST" as shown in Figure 2-16. Since the column names from the spreadsheet are nice and neat, they don't need to be changed. As you can see, you have complete control over the properties of each column in the source data.

Figure 2-16. *Table Properties*

Following the table definition, the Create Application wizard allows you to define the labels for each column on the data entry form as shown in Figure 2-17. The default values for column labels are the column names themselves. Since the column names are descriptive enough for a sample application, they can be left alone with the possible exception of "Bugid," which could be changed to "Bug Id." The singular and plural names are used on forms that we'll develop later. You can use "Bug" and "Bugs" for now, but either can be changed later.

Figure 2-17. *Setting user interface defaults*

During the final steps of the creation process, you can assign the name, type, and visual attributes of the application. The available creation types are:

- Read Only
- Read and Write; use this setting for the Buglist application
- Report Implementation Type

Apex 4.0 provides two choices for Report Implementation:

- Interactive
- Classic; use this report type

The "Classic" report contains standard text items and search buttons that can be easily manipulated using the standard features. The "Interactive" report type includes a Search field and a Go button, but they are not as accessible as the same values in a classic report. We will get into interactive reporting in later chapters.

You also set the theme, or look and feel, of the application at this point. For the Buglist application, I selected the light blue theme (theme 15).

Running the Application

If you run the application you just created, you'll be presented with a page asking for your username and password. This is because the application was created using APEX authentication, which means you'll need to log in using the credentials of an APEX user created by a workspace administrator. Figure 2-18 shows the page that's displayed once you have logged into the application.

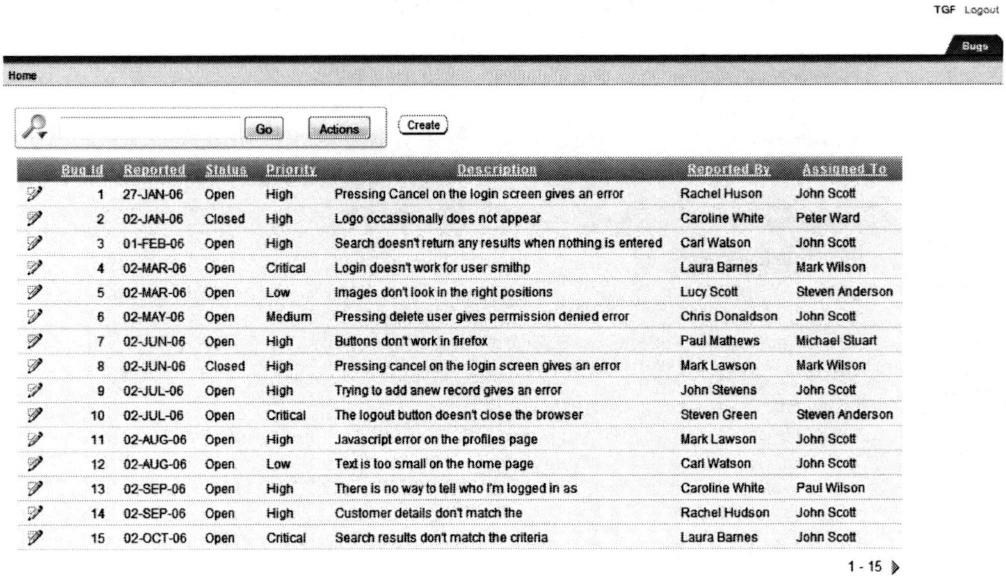

	Bug Id	Reported	Status	Priority	Description	Reported By	Assigned To
	1	27-JAN-06	Open	High	Pressing Cancel on the login screen gives an error	Rachel Huson	John Scott
	2	02-JAN-06	Closed	High	Logo occassionally does not appear	Caroline White	Peter Ward
	3	01-FEB-06	Open	High	Search doesn't return any results when nothing is entered	Carl Watson	John Scott
	4	02-MAR-06	Open	Critical	Login doesn't work for user smithp	Laura Barnes	Mark Wilson
	5	02-MAR-06	Open	Low	Images don't look in the right positions	Lucy Scott	Steven Anderson
	6	02-MAY-06	Open	Medium	Pressing delete user gives permission denied error	Chris Donaldson	John Scott
	7	02-JUN-06	Open	High	Buttons don't work in firefox	Paul Mathews	Michael Stuart
	8	02-JUN-06	Closed	High	Pressing cancel on the login screen gives an error	Mark Lawson	Mark Wilson
	9	02-JUL-06	Open	High	Trying to add anew record gives an error	John Stevens	John Scott
	10	02-JUL-06	Open	Critical	The logout button doesn't close the browser	Steven Green	Steven Anderson
	11	02-AUG-06	Open	High	Javascript error on the profiles page	Mark Lawson	John Scott
	12	02-AUG-06	Open	Low	Text is too small on the home page	Carl Watson	John Scott
	13	02-SEP-06	Open	High	There is no way to tell who I'm logged in as	Caroline White	Paul Wilson
	14	02-SEP-06	Open	High	Customer details don't match the	Rachel Hudson	John Scott
	15	02-OCT-06	Open	Critical	Search results don't match the criteria	Laura Barnes	John Scott

Figure 2-18. *Home page of Buglist application based on the spreadsheet.*

Creating the User Repository

For the custom authentication example, we will modify the Buglist application so that all of the user account information is stored in a table. At the very least, we want to be able to store the following pieces of information about a user:

- Username
- Password
- First name
- Surname
- E-mail address

Listing 2-8 shows the script for creating this user repository.

Listing 2-8. Script for Creating the User Repository

```
apexdemo@10gR2> create table user_repository(

username varchar2(8),
password varchar2(8),
forename varchar2(30),
surname  varchar2(30),
email    varchar2(50),
primary key (username)
);

Table created.

apexdemo@10gR2> insert into user_repository values
('john', '1234', 'john', 'scott', 'jes@apex-evangelists.com');

1 row created.

apexdemo@10gR2> insert into user_repository values
('peterw', '9876', 'peter', 'ward', 'peterw@apex-evangelists.com');
1 row created.


apexdemo@10gR2> commit;
```

Listing 2-8 shows two records inserted into the table, representing two different user accounts. This table definition is relatively simple. We will extend this definition later to make it more realistic and useful. For example, Listing 2-8 uses plain-text passwords, which is obviously extremely bad practice. Later in the chapter, you'll see how we can avoid using plain text and make the application much more secure.

Notice that the username is specified as the primary key. This works because it's unlikely you'd store two usernames with the same value. However, some people like to allow users to be able to change their usernames, and this approach would cause problems if the username were being used as a foreign key. For example, you might want to let a user who just got married change her username from anne_smith to anne_jones, but also want to maintain all of the user's history. In that case, you might prefer to use a sequence as a surrogate primary key, rather than the username.

▨ **Note** Some people (such as the author) believe that entities such as usernames should be immutable. If the user wants to use a different username, you should create a new account with that new username, rather than letting the user change her username. The user can then stop using the old account and begin using the new one. Allowing identifiers such as usernames to be modified can create all sorts of headaches, particularly if you are trying to correlate audit log entries with a particular user. However, this is a personal preference. You may believe you have a valid business reason for allowing users to change their existing usernames.

Creating a New Authentication Scheme

You can now create a new authentication scheme. When you create an authentication scheme from scratch, you can use the creation wizard to step through each setting, or you can create the scheme and then edit it later to make your configuration changes. Figure 2-19 shows a new authentication scheme being created.

Figure 2-19. *Creating a custom authentication scheme from scratch*

You can define many attributes for a custom authentication scheme, so it's worth taking the time to understand precisely what each attribute means:

> *Page Sentry Function*: You can specify a function that will be executed before a page in your application is requested or submitted. The function will return a Boolean value to indicate whether the page should be displayed or the user should be redirected to a login page, or some other page of your choice. If you don't specify anything here, the built-in logic will be used.

Session Verify Function: The page sentry function will call this function to determine if a valid session exists for the current page request or submission. If you specified your own page sentry function, you don't need to specify anything here, since your page sentry function should also perform the session verification. If you are using the built-in page sentry functionality, you can either specify your own session verification function here or leave it blank—in which case, the built-in functionality will be used.

Invalid Session Target: You can specify the target that will be used if the page sentry function returns false, which indicates that the session is considered invalid. You can redirect the user to the built-in login page, a page in your application, a URL, or an Oracle SSO application server.

Pre-Authentication Process: You can specify code that will be executed immediately before the user's account credentials are verified.

Authentication Function: This is where you can specify the function that will perform the credentials verification. The function you specify must accept two parameters: `p_username` and `p_password,` which are both of type `VARCHAR2`, and it must return a Boolean result, which is used to indicate whether the user has been successfully authenticated.

Post-Authentication Process: This is similar to the preauthentication process, except it allows you to specify code that will be executed after the credentials have been verified.

Cookie Attributes: This allows you to specify the cookie attributes for your application, such as the cookie name, path, and domain.

Logout URL: This allows you to specify the value that will be used for the application attribute `LOGOUT_URL`, which is commonly displayed on the page for the user to click to log out of an application. You can include many substitution variables here, such as `&APP_ID.` (note the terminating period).

For now, create the scheme by clicking Create Scheme. You can go back and change the individual items after you've created the function to perform the actual authentication.

Your authentication function must have this signature:

```
(p_username in varchar2, p_password in varchar2) return Boolean
```

The function will need to compare the username and password with the rows stored in the `user_repository` table, returning true if the username and password match a row in the table, or returning false if no matching row can be found. Listing 2-9 shows the `pkg_auth.authenticate` function originally used in the Application Express Account Credentials section modified to verify users against the `user_repository` table.

Listing 2-9. The pkg_auth.authenticate Function Modified to Verify Users Against a Table

```
create or replace package pkg_auth as

   function authenticate(p_username in varchar2,
                         p_password in varchar2) return boolean;
end;

create or replace package body pkg_auth as
   function authenticate(p_username in varchar2,
                         p_password in varchar2) return boolean is
     -- default the result to 0
     v_result integer := 0;
   begin
     -- store 1 in v_result if a matching row
     -- can be found
     select 1
     into v_result
     from user_repository
     where username = lower(p_username)
     and password = p_password;

     -- return true if a matching record was found
     return(v_result = 1);
   exception
   -- if no record was found then return false
   when no_data_found then
     return false;
   end authenticate;

end;
```

This authenticate function is straightforward. It simply tries to find a row in the user_repository table where the username and password match the parameters that were passed to the function. Notice that the p_username variable is being forced to lowercase. This is done for two reasons:

1. The usernames inserted into the user_repository table are in lowercase

2. The p_username variable will be passed in as uppercase from the application. Using lower() on the variable ensures that the cases in this comparison match. We avoid using a function on the username column as it may make an index on this column unusable.

Another way to handle this situation would be to populate the user_repository table with uppercased values. Since the application passes in uppercase values, the comparison would not require case conversion.

You can verify that the packaged function works correctly by calling the function from some anonymous PL/SQL code in SQL*Plus, as shown in Listing 2-10.

Listing 2-10. Confirming the **authenticate** *Function Works*

```
apexdemo@10gR2> set serveroutput on;

apexdemo@10gR2> declare
  bres boolean := false;
begin

  -- use the correct username and password

  bres := pkg_auth.authenticate('john', '1234');
  if (bres = true) then
    dbms_output.put_line('Authentication was successful');
  else
    dbms_output.put_line('Authentication failed');
  end if;
end;


Authentication was successful


PL/SQL procedure successfully completed.

apexdemo@10gR2> declare
  bres boolean := false;
begin

  -- use an incorrect password

  bres := pkg_auth.authenticate('john', '12345');
  if (bres = true) then
    dbms_output.put_line('Authentication was successful');
  else
    dbms_output.put_line('Authentication failed');
  end if;
end;


Authentication failed


PL/SQL procedure successfully completed.
```

You can now modify the authentication scheme to use the packaged function, as shown in Figure 2-20.

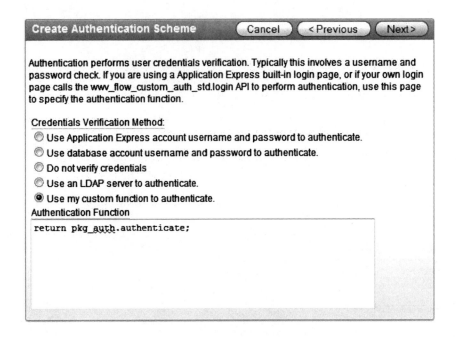

Figure 2-20. *Using the packaged authentication function*

▪ **Note** You could, if you prefer, remove the case-sensitivity match altogether to make it even more difficult for someone to guess usernames and passwords (in other words, not only does he need to guess the username, he also needs to know the exact case of the username). This means that JScott would be treated differently from jscott, for example. In general, though, you should not make usernames case-sensitive unless you have specific reason to do so. However, passwords should most definitely be case-sensitive.

Actually, you can use another method to completely remove the issue of the username being automatically uppercased. If you are using a login page that was generated for you automatically by the application creation wizard (as in the case of the Buglist application), there will be an after-submit page process on the login page called Login. If you examine this page process, you'll find that it runs an anonymous PL/SQL block like this:

```
wwv_flow_custom_auth_std.login(
    P_UNAME      => :P101_USERNAME,
    P_PASSWORD   => :P101_PASSWORD,
    P_SESSION_ID => v('APP_SESSION'),
    P_FLOW_PAGE  => :APP_ID||':1'

    );
```

This piece of code will set the :APP_USER item and redirect to the value specified by the P_FLOW_PAGE parameter after a successful login.

To prevent the username from being uppercased before it is passed to your authentication function, you can use the P_PRESERVE_CASE parameter to the wwv_flow_custom_auth_std.login function, as in this example:

```
wwv_flow_custom_auth_std.login(

    P_UNAME         => :P101_USERNAME,
    P_PASSWORD      => :P101_PASSWORD,
    P_SESSION_ID    => v('APP_SESSION'),
    P_FLOW_PAGE     => :APP_ID||':1',

    P_PRESERVE_CASE => TRUE

    );
```

Regarding Index Usage

Although we're not going to go into depthabout optimizing your queries, since that's a topic that could easily span several books, it's worth looking at the impact of modifying the query into one that performs a case-insensitive search against the username if you have a relatively large number of entries in the table.

Suppose you insert an extra 9,999 rows into the user_repository table from a SQL*Plus session:

```
apexdemo@10gR2> insert into user_repository (username, password)

(select 'user' || rownum, 'pass' || rownum from all_objects ⤶
where rownum < 10000);

9999 rows created.

apexdemo@10gR2> commit;
```

The user repository now has more than 10,000 entries (including the 2 original ones). A user repository of this size is certainly not unusual for an Internet application or an intranet application of a large corporation.

Make sure the statistics on the table are up-to-date:

```
apexdemo@10gR2> exec dbms_stats.gather_table_stats('APEXDEMO',

    'USER_REPOSITORY');


PL/SQL procedure successfully completed.
```

Now if you view the explain plan for the original query, where the username is not uppercased:

```
apexdemo@10gR2> select 1 as x from user_repository
  where username = 'john' and password = '1234'
```

you'll see something similar to this

```
          X
---------
          1
```

Execution Plan

```
    0       SELECT STATEMENT Optimizer=ALL_ROWS (Cost=2 Card=1 Bytes=18)
    1    0    TABLE ACCESS (BY INDEX ROWID) OF 'USER_REPOSITORY' (TABLE)
                (Cost=2 Card=1 Bytes=18)

    2    1      INDEX (UNIQUE SCAN) OF 'SYS_C008389' (INDEX (UNIQUE))
(Cost=1 Card=1)
```

Statistics

```
          1  recursive calls
          0  db block gets
          3  consistent gets
          0  physical reads
          0  redo size
        386  bytes sent via SQL*Net to client
        512  bytes received via SQL*Net from client
          2  SQL*Net roundtrips to/from client
          0  sorts (memory)
          0  sorts (disk)

          1  rows processed
```

Notice this line:

```
INDEX (UNIQUE SCAN) OF 'SYS_C008389'
```

This shows that the query used the system-generated index that was created due to the primary key on the **username** column. Also, you can see that the query resulted in three consistent gets. Compare this with the explain plan you'd get for the query where you uppercase the username column:

```
apexdemo@10gR2> select 1 as x from user_repository

  where upper(username) = 'JOHN' and password = '1234'

          X
---------
          1
```

```
Execution Plan
-----------------------------------------------------------
   0      SELECT STATEMENT Optimizer=ALL_ROWS (Cost=9 Card=1 Bytes=18)
   1   0    TABLE ACCESS (FULL) OF 'USER_REPOSITORY' (TABLE) (Cost=9 Card=1
             Bytes=18)


Statistics
-----------------------------------------------------------
       0   recursive calls
       0   db block gets
      39   consistent gets
       0   physical reads
       0   redo size
     386   bytes sent via SQL*Net to client
     512   bytes received via SQL*Net from client
       2   SQL*Net roundtrips to/from client
       0   sorts (memory)
       0   sorts (disk)

       1   rows processed
```

This time, the query results in a full scan of the user_repository table, because the upper function meant that the system-generated index could not be used. And as a result of the full scan, the consistent gets increase to 39.

To avoid having to full-scan the table, you can create a function-based index, which will be used by the query that contains the function call on the column:

```
apexdemo@10gR2> create index user_repository_upper_idx

  on user_repository(upper(username));


Index created.
```

Note that the function uses the same function call that is used in the query. In other words, the function has been applied to the data for that column, and the result of the function call is then contained in the index, rather than the original data.

If you now rerun the query containing the upper function call and look at the explain plan, you'd see something similar to this:

```
apexdemo@10gR2> select 1 as x from user_repository

2 where upper(username) = 'JOHN' and password = '1234';

        X
----------
        1
```

```
Execution Plan
---------------------------------------------------------------
   0      SELECT STATEMENT Optimizer=ALL_ROWS (Cost=2 Card=1 Bytes=18)
   1    0    TABLE ACCESS (BY INDEX ROWID) OF 'USER_REPOSITORY' (TABLE)
             (Cost=2 Card=1 Bytes=18)

   2    1       INDEX (RANGE SCAN) OF 'USER_REPOSITORY_UPPER_IDX' (INDEX
             ) (Cost=1 Card=40)
```

```
Statistics
---------------------------------------------------------------
        0   recursive calls
        0   db block gets
        4   consistent gets
        0   physical reads
        0   redo size
      386   bytes sent via SQL*Net to client
      512   bytes received via SQL*Net from client
        2   SQL*Net roundtrips to/from client
        0   sorts (memory)
        0   sorts (disk)

        1   rows processed
```

You can see that the function-based index `user_repository_upper_idx` is now being used, and the number of consistent gets has dropped to 4.

If you are not storing your usernames in uppercase in your table and you are making a call to the `upper` function in your query, investigate using a function-based index. You may feel that it's not worthwhile if you don't expect to have many users stored in your table repository. However, many huge systems have evolved from small ones, and quite often you don't get the chance to check things until performance problems start to occur.

Hash Rather Than Crypt

It's a very bad idea to store a password in a table as plain text, since anyone who can access that table will be able to view the list of valid usernames and their corresponding passwords.

As an alternative, you might decide to store the username in an encrypted format. While this is obviously more secure, it still poses a security risk. Encrypting the password implies that there is a decryption method. If your encryption method uses an encryption key, you'll need to ensure that the key does not fall into the wrong hands; otherwise, the security can be easily compromised by running the encrypted value through the decryption routine using the key.

A far better solution is to use a cryptographic hashing function such as MD5. A hash function will, for a given input, produce an output called the *hash value*. You can use this function to store the hash value, rather than the actual plain text password, in the table. The authentication function will then use the same hash function against the supplied password and produce a hash value that can be compared against the hash value stored in the user repository. Hash functions are one-way functions—you can't obtain the original input value from the hash value.

Depending on the actual hash function, the chance of two inputs producing the same hash value can vary substantially. A hash value that can be produced by two different input values is known as a *collision*. If a function produces many collisions, malicious users would have an easier time gaining access, because they would only need to guess a password that produced the same hash value, rather than the precise password. The MD5 function produces very few collisions. In other words, it is mathematically unlikely that two input values will produce the same hash value.

The `dbms_obfuscation_toolkit` package contains many procedures and functions related to encryption and hashing, including some for calculating MD5 hashes. Listing 2-11 shows how you can use the MD5 function call to convert a plain-text string into an MD5 hash value.

Listing 2-11. Using the `dbms_obfuscation_toolkit` Package

```
apexdemo@10gR2> var plaintext varchar2(30)

apexdemo@10gR2> var hashvalue varchar2(32)
apexdemo@10gR2> exec :plaintext := 'password';

PL/SQL procedure successfully completed.

apexdemo@10gR2> exec :hashvalue := UTL_I18N.STRING_TO_RAW(
  dbms_obfuscation_toolkit.md5(input_string => :plaintext));

PL/SQL procedure successfully completed.

apexdemo@10gR2> print hashvalue

HASHVALUE
------------------

5F4DCC3B5AA765D61D8327DEB882CF99
```

The `dbms_obfuscation_toolkit` package contains two overloaded MD5 functions. One accepts a RAW parameter and returns the result as a RAW. The other accepts a VARCHAR2 parameter and returns the result as a VARCHAR2. However, since the RAW data type is a subtype of the VARCHAR2 data type, this can lead to all sorts of problems when you try to call the MD5 function. Fortunately, the two functions have differently named parameters:

```
FUNCTION MD5(INPUT IN RAW) RETURNS RAW(16)


FUNCTION MD5(INPUT_STRING IN VARCHAR2) RETURNS VARCHAR2(16)
```

Listing 2-11 specifies the named parameter `input_string` so that the correct overloaded function will be used. Also, it uses the UTL_I18N package so that the `string_to_raw` function can be employed to cast the string returned from the MD5 function into the RAW format. This is a much friendlier hexadecimal format to read and store than the string, which would likely contain unprintable characters.

You can now modify the `user_repository` table to add a column for storing the hashed password:

```
apexdemo@10gR2> alter table user_repository add (password_hash raw(16));
Table altered.
```

Ideally, you'd update the table so that the `password_hash` column contains the MD5 hash of the password stored in the `password` column. However, if you try that, you'll run into the overloaded function issue mentioned earlier:

```
apexdemo@10gR2> update user_repository set password_hash = UTL_I18N.STRING_TO_RAW(

   dbms_obfuscation_toolkit.md5(password));
update user_repository set password_hash = UTL_I18N.STRING_TO_RAW(
   dbms_obfuscation_toolkit.md5(password))
                                                                   *
ERROR at line 1:

ORA-06553: PLS-307: too many declarations of 'MD5' match this call
```

You can't use named parameters in SQL either, so it would be no good trying to specify `input_string` in the query:

```
apexdemo@10gR2> update user_repository set password_hash = UTL_I18N.STRING_TO_RAW(

   dbms_obfuscation_toolkit.md5(input_string => password))
apexdemo@DBTEST> /
update user_repository set password_hash = UTL_I18N.STRING_TO_RAW(
   dbms_obfuscation_toolkit.md5(input_string => password))
                                                            *
ERROR at line 1:
```

ORA-00907: missing right parenthesis

Starting in 11g, you can use the `utl_raw.cast_to_raw` function instead of `utl_i18n.string_to_raw` and the following `update` statement will work:

```
update user_repository set password_hash =
UTL_raw.cast_TO_RAW(dbms_obfuscation_toolkit.md5(input_string => password ))
```

To work around this problem in 10g versions of the database, you can create a function that will act as a wrapper around the MD5 call:

```
apexdemo@10gR2> create or replace function md5hash

   (p_input in varchar2)
return varchar2 is
begin
  return upper(dbms_obfuscation_toolkit.md5
    (input => utl_i18n.string_to_raw(p_input)));
end md5hash;

Function created.
```

In 11g, the function would look like this:

```
apexdemo@10gR2> create or replace function md5hash
(p_input in varchar2)
return varchar2 is

begin
  return utl_raw.cast_to_raw(dbms_obfuscation_toolkit.MD5(input_string=>p_input));
end md5hash;
```

Although the dbms_obfuscation_toolkit package is still available in 11*g* (11.2.0.1), it is set to be deprecated. Its replacement is the dbms_crypto package, which you should start using instead of the dbms_obfuscation_toolkit. You can modify the md5hash function to use the new encryption package as follows:

```
function  md5hash (p_input in varchar2) return varchar2 is
begin
  return dbms_crypto.hash(utl_raw.cast_to_raw(p_input),2);
end md5hash;
```

The dbms_crypto.hash function expects an input value of type raw and an encryption algorithm designator. The hash encryption types are as follows:

1 = MD4
2 = MD5
3 = SH1

To ensure that you get the same results from both the dbms_obfuscation_toolkit and the dbms_crypto packages, use the MD5 designator (2) in the call to dbms_crypto.

```
apexdemo@10gR2> select md5hash('password') from dual;

MD5HASH('PASSWORD')
----------------------------------------------------------

5F4DCC3B5AA765D61D8327DEB882CF99
```

You can now use this wrapper function to update the user_repository table:

```
apexdemo@10gR2> update user_repository

2  set password_hash = md5hash(password);

2 rows updated.

apexdemo@10gR2> commit;

Commit complete.

apexdemo@10gR2> select * from user_repository;
```

```
apexdemo@10gR2> select username, password, password_hash
2  from user_repository;

USERNAME PASSWORD PASSWORD_HASH
-------- -------- --------------------------------
john     1234     81DC9BDB52D04DC20036DBD8313ED055

peterw   9876     912E79CD13C64069D91DA65D62FBB78C
```

You can make another improvement to this routine. The MD5 checksum is based only on the password, so two users who have the same password would have the same value in the password_hash column, as shown in Listing 2-12.

Listing 2-12. Two Users with the Same Password Have the Same Password Hash

```
apexdemo@10gR2> insert into user_repository ↵

(username, password, forename, surname, email) ↵
values ('jimb', '1234', 'James', 'Brookfield', 'jimb@apex-evangelists.com')
1 row created.

apexdemo@10gR2> update user_repository ↵
set password_hash = md5hash(password);

3 rows updated.

apexdemo@10gR2> select username, password, password_hash ↵
from user_repository;

USERNAME PASSWORD PASSWORD_HASH
-------- -------- --------------------------------
john     1234     81DC9BDB52D04DC20036DBD8313ED055
peterw   9876     912E79CD13C64069D91DA65D62FBB78C

jimb     1234     81DC9BDB52D04DC20036DBD8313ED055
```

This sort of information could potentially be used as an attack vector if a malicious user discovered that he and another user had the same password hash value. Since the malicious user already knows his own password, he would be able to deduce the other user's password from the fact that their hashes are the same. You can avoid this issue by passing in a string containing the concatenated username and password to the MD5 wrapper function, as shown in Listing 2-13.

Listing 2-13. Combining the Username and Password in the Hash Function

```
apexdemo@10gR2> update user_repository

set password_hash = md5hash(upper(username) || password);

3 rows updated.

apexdemo@10gR2> commit;
```

```
Commit complete.

apexdemo@10gR2> select username, password, password_hash from user_repository;

USERNAME PASSWORD PASSWORD_HASH
-------- -------- --------------------------------
john     1234     9B57B72DA06D24A934DEC92457B44974
peterw   9876     F635746DF6E7E69D1B6698B79D65CD7F

jimb     1234     DF2270203A47F5A0A51D484D77C2FFC5
```

With this approach, even if two users have the same password, their hash values will be completely different. Note that you also uppercase the username before passing it to the MD5 hash function, since the username will uppercased before being passed to the custom authentication function, as described earlier.

The authentication function can now be modified so that it performs the same hash function on the username and password the user is trying to authenticate with, and then compares that hash value with the hash value that is stored in the **user_repository** table, as shown in Listing 2-14.

Listing 2-14. Modified pkg_auth Package to Work with Password Hashes Using dbms_crypto

```
create or replace package pkg_auth as

  function authenticate(p_username in varchar2, p_password in varchar2) ↵
return boolean;
end;

create or replace package body pkg_auth as
  -- wrapper function to compute the MD5 hash
  function  md5hash (p_input in varchar2) return varchar2 is
begin
  return dbms_crypto.hash(utl_raw.cast_to_raw(p_input),2);
end md5hash;

  function authenticate(p_username in varchar2, p_password in varchar2)
      return boolean is
    v_result integer := 0;
    v_hash varchar2(32);
  begin

    v_hash := md5hash(p_username || p_password);

    select 1
    into v_result
    from user_repository
    where upper(username) = upper(p_username)
     and password_hash = v_hash;
    return(v_result = 1);

  exception
  when no_data_found then
    return false;
```

```
      end authenticate;

end;
```

Now you just need to remember to drop the plain-text password column from the **user_repository** table so that it can't be viewed:

```
apexdemo@10gR2> alter table user_repository drop(password);
```

```
Table altered.
```

With a few relatively simple changes to the **user_repository** table and your authentication scheme, you have made your whole application much more secure. Also, by keeping the authentication code within a package, you are forming the basis of a security module that can be easily reused in different applications.

Implementing Locked User Accounts

The ability to lock and unlock user accounts is very useful. For example, when employees leave a company, you probably don't want them to be able to access your applications and systems. However, you may have problems deleting their accounts if their usernames (or other surrogate keys) are being used as foreign keys from other tables, such as an audit trail. An easier solution is to introduce an attribute into the account record that indicates whether it is locked. If an account is locked, the user can't authenticate using that account.

You can add an extra column to the **user_repository** table—a flag indicating the locked status. A value of Y indicates locked, and a value of N indicates that the account is not locked (and therefore the user is allowed to authenticate with it). Listing 2-15 shows the modifications.

Listing 2-15. Adding the locked_flag and Constraint to the user_repository Table

```
-- add the new columnn to the table
apexdemo@10gR2> alter table user_repository
2   add(locked_flag char(1));

Table altered.

-- set one record to be a locked status
apexdemo@10gR2> update user_repository set locked_flag = 'Y'
2   where username = 'john';
```

```
1 row updated.

-- set all the other records to unlocked
apexdemo@10gR2> update user_repository set locked_flag = 'N'
2  where locked_flag is null;

2 rows updated.

apexdemo@10gR2> commit;

-- add a not null constraint to the column
apexdemo@10gR2> alter table user_repository
2  modify locked_flag not null;

Table altered.

-- add a check constraint to ensure that the locked_flag is either 'Y' or 'N'
apexdemo@10gR2> alter table user_repository add constraint
2  locked_flag_yn check (locked_flag in ('Y','N'));

Table altered.

apexdemo@10gR2> select username, locked_flag from user_repository;

USERNAME LOCKED_FLAG
-------- ---------------
david    Y
tim      N

brian    N
```

You can now modify the authentication function to take the value in the locked_flag column into account when deciding whether to allow the user to authenticate. The simplest case would be to just include an additional where clause restriction in the query to search for a record where the username and password hash match and the account is not locked, like this:

```
select 1
   into v_result
   from user_repository
   where upper(username) = upper( p_username)
    and upper(password_hash) = v_hash

.......................................
```

You will now find that if you attempt to authenticate to the application with a username that has the locked_flag set to 'Y' (or more correctly it isn't set to 'N'), you won't be able to log in.

When you attempt to log in with a locked account, you'll be presented with the "Invalid Login Credentials" message, as shown in Figure 2-21. Depending on your particular requirements, this may not be the most logical message to display.

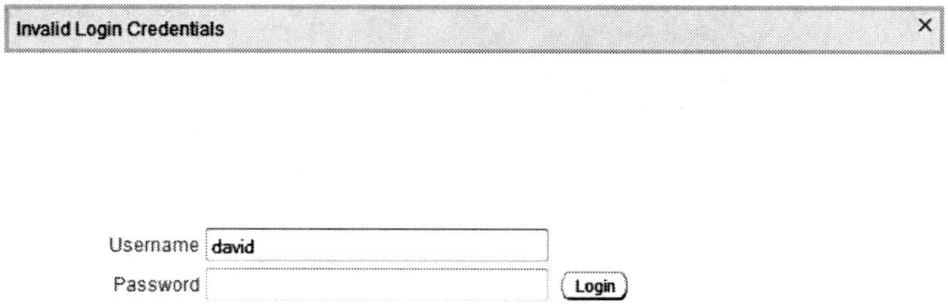

Figure 2-21. Attempting to authenticate with a locked account

This message appears because the page template for the login page includes the substitution item #NOTIFICATION_MESSAGE#. You might think it would be straightforward to change the message to something like "The Account Is Locked," but that's not the case. To understand why changing this message is not straightforward, you need to know what happens when a user tries to log in to the application.

Understanding the Login Process

When a login page is created automatically by a wizard, it contains a page process with code similar to the following:

```
wwv_flow_custom_auth_std.login(

    P_UNAME       => :P101_USERNAME,
    P_PASSWORD    => :P101_PASSWORD,
    P_SESSION_ID  => v('APP_SESSION'),
    P_FLOW_PAGE   => :APP_ID||':1'

);
```

The `wwv_flow_custom_auth_std.login` procedure is also known as the Login API. The Login API is responsible for performing the authentication and session registration for a user. It determines your current authentication scheme and interfaces with all of the authentication scheme items described earlier in this chapter (such as the authentication function). You can think of the Login API as a wrapper around the authentication scheme.

The Login API produces the "Invalid Account Credentials" message if the authentication function returns false. There is no way to pass in an alternative message. The only way to change the message is by removing the call to `wwv_flow_custom_auth_std.login` and using your own logic to determine what should happen if the authentication fails. To help with this, you can use some of the built-in session-handling features. For example, you can replace the code in the login page process with the code in Listing 2-16.

Listing 2-16. Invoking a Custom Post-Login Procedure

```
declare
  bresult boolean := FALSE;
begin
  -- use the existing authenticate function
  bresult := pkg_auth.authenticate(upper(:P101_USERNAME),
                                    :P101_PASSWORD);

  -- call the post_login procedure if the
  -- authentication was successful
  if (bresult = true) then

    wwv_flow_custom_auth_std.post_login(

    P_UNAME       => :P101_USERNAME,
    P_PASSWORD    => :P101_PASSWORD,
    P_SESSION_ID  => v('APP_SESSION'),
    P_FLOW_PAGE   => :APP_ID||':1'
    );
  end if;

end;
```

Here, you need to call the packaged `authenticate` function yourself. Since you are no longer using the Login API, the authentication scheme settings you've configured won't automatically be used. Therefore, you need to replicate the implementation details of the authentication scheme.

You call the `post_login` procedure if the `authenticate` function returns true (the authentication was successful). The `post_login` procedure's signature is very similar to that of the `login` procedure; however, the `post_login` procedure is responsible for the session registration part of authentication. So unless you want to manually handle the session information yourself, it's better to use the built-in methods.

You should now find that you can still log in if you use a valid username and password (and the account is unlocked). However, if you use an invalid username or password or the account is locked, you are presented with a blank page. This is because you haven't included any logic to specify what should happen if the `authenticate` function returns false.

You can use two different ways to return users to the login page if their login was unsuccessful:

- Add a conditional branch to the page that fires when the Login button is clicked and branches back to login page. If the login is successful, this branch will not be executed. If the login is unsuccessful, this branch will fire and the user will be taken back to the login page.

- Perform a redirect (using the `owa_util.redirect_url` procedure) back to the login page as part of the login page process logic.

Listing 2-17 shows the modified login page process, which now performs a redirect if the authentication was unsuccessful.

Listing 2-17. Performing a Redirect Back to the Login Page

```
declare
   -- use the existing authenticate function
   bresult boolean := FALSE;
begin
   bresult := pkg_auth.authenticate(upper(:P101_USERNAME),
                                    :P101_PASSWORD);

   -- call the post_login procedure if the
   -- authentication was successful
   if (bresult = true) then
    wwv_flow_custom_auth_std.post_login(
     P_UNAME       => :P101_USERNAME,
     P_PASSWORD    => :P101_PASSWORD,
     P_SESSION_ID  => v('APP_SESSION'),
     P_FLOW_PAGE   => :APP_ID||':1'
     );
   else
     -- perform a redirect back to the login page

     owa_util.redirect_url('f?p=&APP_ID.:101:&SESSION.');

   end if;

end;
```

Here, the login page ID is hard-coded (a bad practice!), to clearly illustrate which page is the target of the redirection. However, you could quite easily use a substitution item to avoid hard-coding the page ID.

■ **Note** You could actually use the ID of any page that requires authentication, since the default behavior of trying to navigate to a protected page when you are not currently authenticated is to redirect you to the login page. However, for clarity, you should use the login page as the target for the redirection.

However, you don't want to use page redirection for the redisplayed login page, because it could be treated as a completely new session (although sometimes the APEX engine is smart enough to detect that situation and issue the same session again). The correct way is to remove the redirection from the login page process and to use a page branch instead, as you'll see in the next section.

Modifying the Notification Message

Now that you've replaced the Login API with your own logic, you've gained full control over how the login process is handled. With this control, you can give users a meaningful error message if the account they try to authenticate with is locked.

First, you create a new application item to use to store the message. You can then reference this application item in an HTML region on the page to display the message. Figure 2-22 shows the new LOGIN_MESSAGE application item. Notice that we set the session state protection to Restricted; we will cover this setting in more detail in Chapter 5.

Figure 2-22. Creating the LOGIN_MESSAGE application item

The LOGIN_MESSAGE application item is then referenced in a new HTML region, as shown in Figure 2-23. This HTML region is positioned above the region containing the login page items, such as the username text field, so that the message will appear in a similar position to the notification message produced by the Login API. The region source simply uses the value of the application item, which is specified as &LOGIN_MESSAGE. (Note the trailing period.) Also, specify that no template should be used for the region.

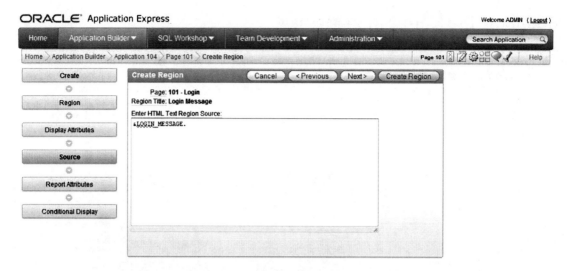

Figure 2-23. HTML region referencing the `LOGIN_MESSAGE` *application item*

Using the condition shown in Figure 2-24, this region will display only if the `LOGIN_MESSAGE` application item is not null; in other words, if a message has been set.

Figure 2-24. Conditional logic to show the region only if a message has been set

Listing 2-18 shows the modified `pkg_auth` package body that will set the `LOGIN_MESSAGE` application item to a meaningful message. (Important changes are in bold.)

Listing 2-18. Setting the Application Item from the `pkg_auth.authenticate` *Function*

```
create or replace package body pkg_auth as

  function  md5hash (p_input in varchar2) return varchar2 is
  begin
    return upper(dbms_obfuscation_toolkit.md5 (input =>
                  utl_i18n.string_to_raw(p_input)));
  end md5hash;

  function authenticate(p_username in varchar2,
                        p_password in varchar2) return boolean is
```

```
   v_locked_flag char(1);
   v_hash varchar2(32);
begin
   v_hash := md5hash(p_username || p_password);

   select locked_flag
   into v_locked_flag
   from user_repository
   where upper(username) = upper( p_username)
    and upper(password_hash) = v_hash;


   if v_locked_flag = 'N' then
     return true;
   else
     apex_util.set_session_state('LOGIN_MESSAGE',
                     'Your account is currently locked');

     return false;
   end if;

 exception
   when no_data_found then

     apex_util.set_session_state('LOGIN_MESSAGE',
       'Invalid username or password');

   return false;
 end authenticate;

end;
```

As you can see, the query is modified so that if a record is found for that particular username and password, the value of the locked_flag is stored in the v_locked_flag variable. If the value of the locked flag is set to 'N' (meaning that the account is unlocked), the function returns true, allowing the user to successfully authenticate. If the value of the locked flag is not set to 'N', you use the apex_util.set_session_state procedure to set the value of the LOGIN_MESSAGE application item to 'Your account is currently locked'.

If no matching account is found, the query will generate a no_data_found exception (due to the select...into... clause), and the no_data_found exception handler uses the apex_util.set_session_state procedure to set the application item to a meaningful message. The authenticate function then returns false (meaning the authentication was not successful) as before. Figure 2-25 shows the new logic for the login page process.

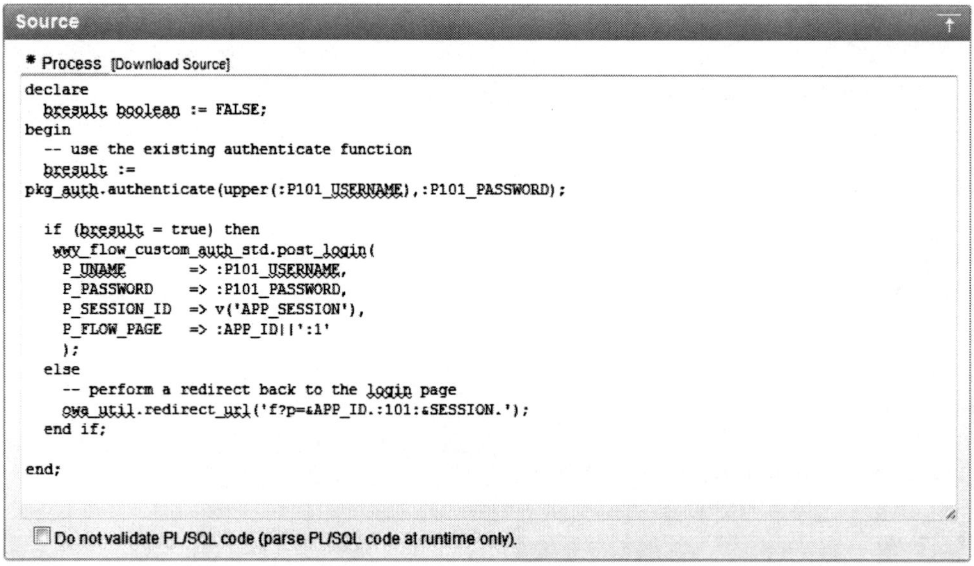

```
Source                                                                          ↑

 * Process  [Download Source]

declare
  bresult boolean := FALSE;
begin
  -- use the existing authenticate function
  bresult :=
pkg_auth.authenticate(upper(:P101_USERNAME),:P101_PASSWORD);

  if (bresult = true) then
    wwv_flow_custom_auth_std.post_login(
    P_UNAME        => :P101_USERNAME,
    P_PASSWORD     => :P101_PASSWORD,
    P_SESSION_ID   => v('APP_SESSION'),
    P_FLOW_PAGE    => :APP_ID||':1'
    );
  else
    -- perform a redirect back to the login page
    owa_util.redirect_url('f?p=&APP_ID.:101:&SESSION.');
  end if;

end;
```

☐ Do not validate PL/SQL code (parse PL/SQL code at runtime only).

Figure 2-25. *New login process logic*

You should also create a page branch that will branch back to the login page whenever the Login button is clicked, and an after-footer page process that clears the value for the LOGIN_MESSAGE application item. You need to clear the value so that the message is effectively reset each time the page is displayed; otherwise, the message would be displayed unnecessarily.

After you've made these changes, you should find that users receive a meaningful error message if they use the incorrect credentials or if the account is locked, as shown in Figures 2-26 and 2-27.

Invalid username or password

| Username | david |
| Password | | Login |

Figure 2-26. *Message the user receives after using incorrect credentials*

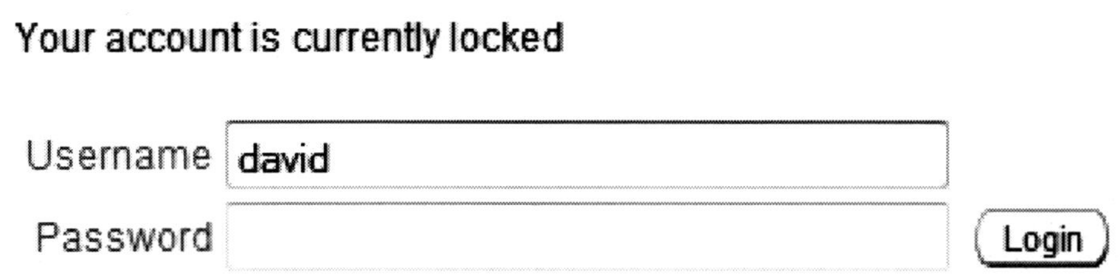

Your account is currently locked
Username
david
Password
Login

Figure 2-27. Message the user receives if the account is locked

Just to complete the example, you can replicate the way the original message looked when the login page process used the Login API. You can search through the HTML source for the page where the Login API is used to find where the "Invalid Login Credentials" message is displayed. You will find something like this:

```
<div class="t15Notification">Invalid Login Credentials</div>
```

Depending on which theme you chose for your application, you may find that a different class is used. Change the region source for the HTML region used to display the message to the following:

```
<div class="t15Notification">&LOGIN_MESSAGE.</div>
```

The message will now be formatted in the same way as if you used the Login API, as shown in Figure 2-28.

Your account is currently locked
Username
david
Password
Login

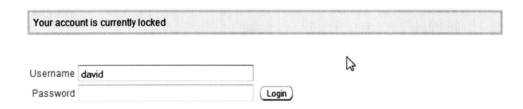

Figure 2-28. Using the original formatting of the notification message

A Note About Session Management

In our example that modified the login page process, we used the standard `wwv_flow_custom_auth_std.post_login` procedure to complete the session registration once the user authenticated. By using the existing built-in session registration and session management functionality, we let the APEX engine take care of handling all of the details surrounding whether the user has a valid session, whether a new session needs to be established, and so on, which drastically reduced the amount of code we needed to provide in the authentication process logic.

In the vast majority of cases, you should take advantage of the built-in session registration and session management functionality by using the `post_login` procedure in your custom authentication processing. The Oracle developers behind APEX have put a lot of time and effort into making sure the built-in session-handling functionality works, and works well. It is tried-and-tested logic that is being used by many applications around the world.

If you do feel you want to perform your own session-handling functionality, you should be prepared to do the following:

- Replicate the majority of the existing functionality and include your own custom handling.

- Test your custom session handling ruthlessly to destruction and back again. Session-handling code is one area of your application that you really do not want to have bugs, since trying to recover from the aftermath of buggy session-handling code in a live environment is not for the faint-hearted.

■ **Note** Applications that require their own custom session management routines are the exception rather than the norm. If you believe that your application requires custom session management, reconsider your business case to see if your requirements can be achieved in a different (and simpler) way.

Automating User Registration

Many applications allow new users to register without manual intervention from an administrator. Typically, the registration process follows this series of steps:

1. User enters details into a form, including e-mail address.

2. An e-mail message is sent to the e-mail address provided. This message gives either a verification code that the user needs to enter on a web page, or contains a link the user should click to verify the account.

3. Upon successful verification, the user will be able to authenticate to the application.

You can implement automatic user registration in the following ways:

- Create the user record directly in the `user_repository` table and use a flag to determine whether the account has been verified.

- Create the user record in a holding table, and then insert it into the `user_repository` table once the user has responded to the verification e-mail.

Which method to use depends on your requirements. If you think a lot of people might indicate they want to register but then not respond to the verification e-mail, you may want to use a holding table. This avoids ending up with a lot of unverified records in the `user_repository` table, which could incur a performance penalty due to the need to search through more records when users try to authenticate. Or you may prefer to create the records directly in the `user_repository` table, so that you don't need to go through the process of copying the record from the holding table into the user_repository table and then deleting the original record from the holding table.

Creating the records directly in the user_repository table has some other benefits. You can use a flag to indicate whether the account is verified. If you also record the timestamp of when the record was created, you can use a scheduled job to remove records that have not been verified within a certain period (for example, within 48 hours), so that you don't end up with unverified accounts in your user repository. You could also take advantage of features such as table partitioning so that records that are verified are stored in one partition, while unverified accounts are stored in a different partition. This way, the query used in your authentication function will benefit from needing to look at only the records in the partition containing the verified records (unless you wanted to provide a meaningful "Your account is not verified" type of message).

To demonstrate, let's walk through the process of allowing user registration for the Buglist application. Although this functionality might not really be practical for this application, the same techniques apply to other applications.

Modifying the User Repository

The first step is to modify the user_repository table to include a verified_flag column. Listing 2-19 shows the table being modified, as well as the current records being updated so that they are all in a verified status.

Listing 2-19. Adding a Verified Flag to the user_repository Table

```
-- add the new column
apexdemo@10gR2> alter table user_repository
  2  add(verified char(1));

Table altered.

-- set one account to an unverified state
apexdemo@10gR2> update user_repository set verified = 'N' where username = 'brian';

1 row updated.

apexdemo@10gR2> update user_repository set verified = 'Y' where username <> 'brian';

2 rows updated.

apexdemo@10gR2> commit;

Commit complete.

-- add a not null constraint to the new column
apexdemo@10gR2> alter table user_repository
  2  modify verified not null;

Table altered.

-- add a check constraint to the column
```

```
apexdemo@10gR2> alter table user_repository
  2  add constraint verified_yn check (verified in ('Y','N'));


Table altered.
```

Modifying the Authentication Method

Now you need to modify the pkg_auth.authenticate routine slightly to take the verified flag into
account, as shown in Listing 2-20.

Listing 2-20. Modified pkg_auth to Handle Account Verification Status

```
create or replace package body "pkg_auth" as

  function  md5hash (p_input in varchar2) return varchar2 is
begin
  return upper(dbms_obfuscation_toolkit.md5 (input =>
          utl_i18n.string_to_raw(p_input)));
end md5hash;

  function authenticate(p_username in varchar2,
                        p_password in varchar2) return boolean is
    v_locked_flag char(1);
    v_verified char(1);
    v_hash varchar2(32);
  begin
    v_hash := md5hash(p_username || p_password);

    select locked_flag, verified
    into v_locked_flag, v_verified
    from user_repository
    where upper(username) =upper( p_username)
     and upper(password_hash) = v_hash;

  -- if the account is not verified then set the login message
  -- and fail authentication
  if v_verified = 'N' then
    apex_util.set_session_state('login_message',
      'your account has not been verified yet');
     return false;
  else
    if v_locked_flag = 'N' then
      return true;
```

```
  else
     apex_util.set_session_state('login_message',
        'your account is locked');
     return false;
  end if;
end if;

exception
when no_data_found then
  apex_util.set_session_state('login_message',
     'invalid username or password');
  return false;
end authenticate;

end;
```

Now if you try to log in with an account that has not been verified (the verified column contains `'N'`), you will receive the message shown in Figure 2-29.

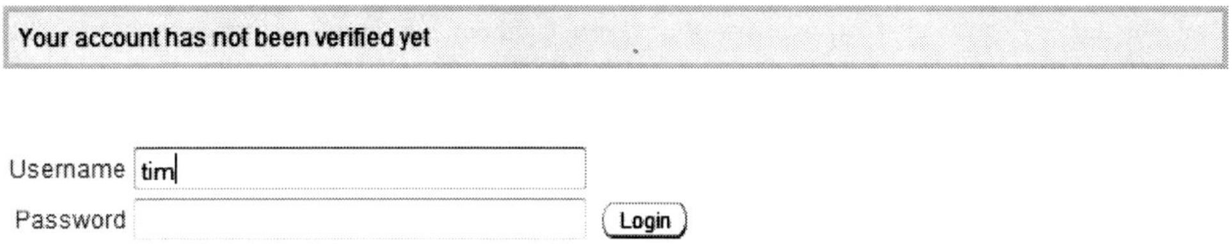

Figure 2-29. Authentication message with an unverified account

Creating a Registration Form

Next you need to create a simple registration form where users can enter their details. Figure 2-30 shows the form to capture the basic details to store in the `user_repository` table.

Figure 2-30. A simple user registration page

Adding a Verification Link Table

Create an additional table to store the verification link that will be sent to the user, as shown in Listing 2-21. In theory, you could store the verification link in the user_repository table; however, since the verification link should be used only during the registration process, it seems unnecessary to clutter up the user_repository table with this data.

Listing 2-21. Creating the verification_link Table

```
apexdemo@10gR2> create table verification_link(

  2  username varchar2(8) not null,
  3  registered timestamp,
  4  verification_code raw(16),
  5  primary key (username));


Table created.
```

You're storing the timestamp of when the user registered the account in the registered column. This column can be used within a cleanup routine that removes accounts over a certain age that haven't been registered yet.

Adding a User Registration Procedure

Add a register_user procedure to the pkg_auth package, as shown in Listing 2-22. This procedure inserts the user details into the user_repository table, and generates a verification link for that user and sends it via e-mail.

Listing 2-22. User Registration Procedure

```
procedure register_user(p_username in varchar2,

                        p_password in varchar2,
                        p_forename in varchar2,
                        p_surname in varchar2,
                        p_email in varchar2) is
    v_hash varchar2(32);
    v_code raw(32);
  begin
    -- generate the password hash for the user
    v_hash := md5hash(upper(p_username) || p_password);

    -- generate the verification link that will be used

    v_code := md5hash(p_username || dbms_random.string('A',   8));


    insert into verification_link
        (username,
        registered,
```

```
        verification_code)
      values
        (p_username,
         sysdate,
         v_code);

    -- store the new account in the user_repository table
    -- the account is stored unlocked and unverified
    insert into user_repository
      (username,
       forename,
       surname,
       email,
       password_hash,
       locked_flag,
       verified)
    values
      (p_username,
       p_forename,
       p_surname,
       p_email,
       v_hash,
       'N',
       'N');

    -- send the verification email

    send_verification_email(p_username, p_email, v_code);
  end register_user;
```

This procedure uses the following code in generating the verification link:

```
v_code := md5hash(p_username || dbms_random.string('A',    8));
```

The code uses the same md5hash helper function we used to generate an MD5 hash of the user's password. However, in this case, you are using it to generate a verification link that is based on the username and a random string of characters (generated by using the dbms_random.string function). It's perhaps easiest to visualize what the dbms_random.string function returns with an example:

```
apexdemo@10gR2> select dbms_random.string('A', 8) as X from dual;


X
--------------------
ZStZMclU

apexdemo@10gR2> /

X
--------------------
KBwWsrmj
```

```
apexdemo@10gR2> /

X
--------------------

FQzCCTPI
```

You concatenate the random string onto the end of the username before passing it to the md5hash function, just so the generated verification link is harder to deduce. This can be very important in an automated registration procedure where you want to prevent account generation from being abused by an automated tool written by a malicious user.

Here we are going to modify the user registration page and add a PL/SQL page process, which calls the pkg_auth.register_user procedure, using the page items as the parameters when the user clicks the Register button. Note that you can modify the c_base_url variable to reflect the fully qualified URL the user should use.

Although you could send a simple, single-line e-mail message from within the body of the register_user procedure, we'll put the actual e-mailing of the verification link into a separate procedure so we can send a nicely formatted text e-mail message. You could even extend the example to send an HTML e-mail instead of a plain-text message, by using the P_BODY_HTML parameter to the APEX_MAIL procedure.

Adding the Procedure to Send the Verification

Listing 2-23 shows the procedure for sending the verification e-mail message. Note that you'll need to use the correct values for the address and port number of your own e-mail server in order to have the e-mail sent.

Listing 2-23. Procedure to Send Verification E-mail

```
procedure send_verification_email(p_username in varchar2,

                                  p_email in varchar2,
                                  p_code in raw) is
    l_body clob;
    l_link clob;
    c_smtp_server varchar2(10) := 'localhost';
    c_smtp_port integer := 25;
    c_base_url varchar2(200) :=
      'http://apexdemo/pls/apex/apexdemo.pkg_auth.verify_user?p_user=';
    c_from varchar2(30) := 'register@apex-evangelists.com';
    begin
l_body := '=============================================' ||
 utl_tcp.crlf;
      l_body := l_body ||
'= This Is an Automated Message, Do Not Reply =' || utl_tcp.crlf;
      l_body := l_body ||
  '=============================================' || utl_tcp.crlf;
      l_body := l_body || utl_tcp.crlf;
      l_body := l_body || utl_tcp.crlf;
      l_body := l_body || 'Hello ' || p_username || ',' ||
              utl_tcp.crlf;
```

```
    l_body := l_body || utl_tcp.crlf;
    l_body := l_body || 'Thanks for taking the time to register.'
             || utl_tcp.crlf;
    l_body := l_body || utl_tcp.crlf;
    l_body := l_body ||
'in order to complete your registration you will need to verify
your email address.' || utl_tcp.crlf;
    l_body := l_body || utl_tcp.crlf;
    l_body := l_body || 'to verify your email address, simply
 click the link below, or copy it and paste it into the address
field of your web browser.' || utl_tcp.crlf;
    l_body := l_body || utl_tcp.crlf;
    l_link := c_base_url || p_username || '&p_code=' || p_code;
    l_body := l_body || l_link || utl_tcp.crlf;
    l_body := l_body || utl_tcp.crlf;
    l_body := l_body || 'You only need to click this link once,
and your account will be updated.' || utl_tcp.crlf;
    l_body := l_body || utl_tcp.crlf;
    l_body := l_body || 'You need to verify your email address
within 5 days of receiving this mail.' || utl_tcp.crlf;

    apex_mail.send(p_to => p_email,
                   p_from => c_from,
                   p_body => l_body,
                   p_subj => 'Your verification email');
    apex_mail.push_queue(c_smtp_server,
                         c_smtp_port);

  end send_verification_email;
```

Notice that we call the `apex_mail.push_queue` procedure immediately after calling the `apex_mail.send` procedure. The send procedure just puts the mail into the APEX mail queue. Usually, a scheduled job will run every 10 or so minutes and push out all e-mail messages in the queue. Calling `push_queue` yourself sends the messages immediately, rather than waiting for the scheduled job. You can actually omit the hostname and port parameters from the `apex_mail.push_queue` procedure, since it picks up the server settings for those values (so you don't need to know them yourself). You may wish to work with your e-mail server administrator to determine the best option for your system.

Here's an example of an e-mail message sent to a registering user.

```
==================================================
= This Is an Automated Message, Do Not Reply =
==================================================


Hello markw,

Thanks for taking the time to register.

In order to complete your registration you will need to verify your email address.
```

To verify your email address, simply click the link below, or copy it and paste it into the address field of your web browser (note this should be a single line, but is broken for clarity here).

```
http://apexdemo/pls/apex/apexdemo.pkg_auth.verify_user
   ?p_user=markw&p_code=F6C61F52B08B5F9E5A684EFDD63D5709
```

You only need to click this link once, and your account will be updated.

You need to verify your email address within 5 days of receiving this mail.

Tying all these pieces together, you now have a process that does the following:

- Allows a user to submit their details into a page

- Creates a new user in the user_repository table, with a status of unverified (verified is set to 'N')

- Stores a record in the verification_link table that contains the username, when the account was registered, and the verification code

Handling the Verification Link

The last ,step is to write the procedure that handles the verification link in the e-mail that the user will click. Listing 2-24 shows the definition of the pkg_auth.verify_user procedure.

Listing 2-24. Procedure for Verifying Users

```
procedure verify_user(p_user in varchar2, p_code in varchar2) is

  begin
    update user_repository ur
      set ur.verified = 'y'
      where upper(ur.username) = upper(p_user)
      and exists (select 1 from verification_link  vl
                            where
                                  vl.username = ur.username and
                                  vl.verification_code = p_code);
    if sql%rowcount > 0 then
      htp.p('Thank you, your account has now been verified.');
    else
      htp.p('Sorry the link you have used is invalid.');
    end if;

  end verify_user;
```

Before this procedure can be called via a URL, you need to grant execute rights on it to the user specified in the DAD:

```
apexdemo@DBTEST> grant execute on pkg_auth to apex_public_user;
```

Grant succeeded.

The user should now be able to click the link, and the `verify_user` procedure will try to match the username and the code used with the entry in the `verification_link` table. If a match is found, the corresponding user account in the `user_repository` table will have the verified flag set to `'Y'`.

Note the use of `SQL%ROWCOUNT`, so you can send a simple message back to the user's browser to let the user know whether the verification succeeded.

This simple example should give you some ideas about how you can set up an automated registration system. You could quite easily use this type of automated sign-up with some of the other authentication schemes. For example, with cookie user accounts, you could store the verified flag and the verification code using the custom attributes such as `p_attribute_01`, `p_attribute_02`, and so on. You could also make many improvements to this automated registration procedure, such as checking to see if the username is already registered.

Managing Session Timeouts

In APEX 4.0, session timeout management is a built-in feature. You can set both a session-timeout value, which invalidates a session after some period of inactivity, and a maximum session-length value, which terminates an active session after a specified time period. To set these parameters, you must log in as an APEX administrator (using the `http://…/apex/apex_admin` URL).

Both parameters are set in seconds via the Security screen under the Manage Instance menu as shown in Figure 2-31.

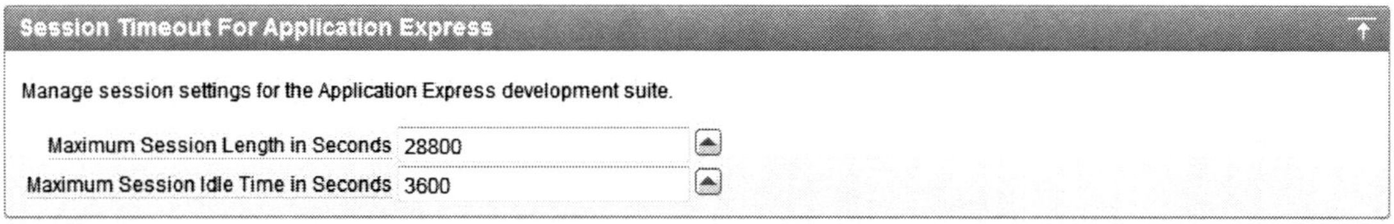

Session Timeout For Application Express	
Manage session settings for the Application Express development suite.	
Maximum Session Length in Seconds	28800
Maximum Session Idle Time in Seconds	3600

Figure 2-31. Entering session settings

The values you set for the session timeouts should be based on either your corporate security guidelines (if they exist) or the usage patterns of your user base. If normal user operations include significant "think time" between transactions, you should set the Maximum Idle Time accordingly. You don't want your users to have to re-login during a normal transaction.

It is important to note that you can't set an "unlimited" value for either parameter. The pop-up lists of values restrict entries to one of the following values:

> 1 Minute
>
> 5 Minutes
>
> 10 Minutes

30 Minutes

1 hour

2 Hours

5 Hours

10 Hours

Summary

Authentication is important to any application because it's the mechanism by which you ensure that users really are who they say they are. Authentication is a necessary precursor to authorization. You must first know who a user is before you can set appropriate limits on what that user can do.

You can take advantage of several built-in authentication schemes that APEX provides, or build your own mechanism for authenticating users who log in to your applications. You can manage users individually, or you can place them into groups. Placing users into groups makes it more efficient to manage large numbers of users, because you define policies for a group at a time rather than one at a time.

Chapter 3 builds on what you've just learned to demonstrate how to set limits on what users can do. Combining robust authentication with well-thought-out authorization ensures that application users can do only what they are supposed to be able to do—no more and no less.

Conditions and Authorization Schemes

This chapter covers two APEX features: conditions and authorization schemes. These two features can often be used to achieve the same thing: controlling the areas of your application the user can access and use.

You can use conditions to control the rendering of page elements (such as regions, reports, and page items), as well as to control the execution of certain pieces of logic (such as processes and computations). Many application elements allow a condition to be applied to them. Authorization schemes similarly allow you to control the display and processing of elements within your application, but in a more secure manner.

The key difference between conditions and authorization schemes is that a condition is used to control the *rendering and processing* of a specific element of your application (a page, a region, an item, and so on), whereas an authorization scheme is used to control *access* to a specific element in your application. The difference can be quite subtle, but as you'll learn in this chapter, it's also quite important.

Specifying Condition Types

APEX offers many different condition types, and the number seems to increase with each new release. Figure 3-1 shows just a few of the condition types available.

Each of these condition types is well-documented and -defined in the Oracle documentation. Here, you'll see how to use some of the more common condition types in your applications, as well as some of the places you can use conditions to affect the elements that are displayed and processed on your page. We suggest that you refer to the Oracle documentation to review all of the condition types and experiment with them yourself. We also encourage you to check the list of available condition types whenever you upgrade to a new release of APEX to see if any new types have been introduced.

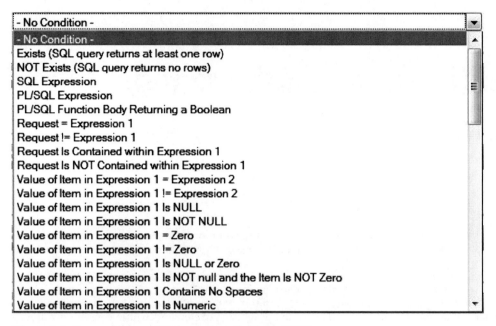

Figure 3-1. Some of the condition types available in APEX

As you will see, quite often, you can achieve the same result using different condition types. Your choice will depend on your particular situation and personal preferences. For example, although one condition type may perform better than another that achieves the same goal, if the condition isn't evaluated that often, the performance aspect may not be as important as using a condition type that is easy to read. The key is to be aware of all of the different condition types available to you and how you can use them in your application.

No Condition

The wording of the No Condition type varies depending on the actual element type you're using. For example, it may read "Button NOT Conditional" if you are using a button, or simply "No Condition" for a report region. However, the result is the same: the page element will always be displayed. This is the default condition for newly created elements (unless you change it during the creation). It's sometimes helpful to use the No Condition type during debugging to ensure that elements you wouldn't normally see are working as intended.

Exists (SQL Query Returns at Least One Row)

The Exists (SQL query returns at least one row) condition is perhaps among the first and most common condition types you'll use. It allows you to easily tie the conditional display of an item to the existence of a record (or records) in the database. If you're familiar with SQL, you've probably used this type of conditional SQL.

For example, the Buglist application currently allows everyone to create new records, as shown in Figure 3-2. You can modify this behavior so that only certain users will be able to see the Create button.

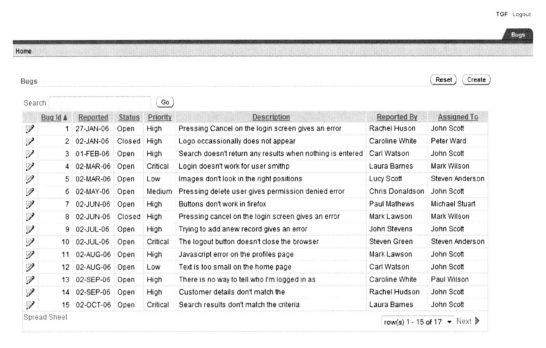

Figure 3-2. Everyone is allowed to see the Create button in the Buglist application.

Let's say you want to show the Create button only to users who are designated as administrators. First, in the user_repository table, you need to identify which users are administrators. You can do that by adding a new column to hold an admin flag, as shown in Listing 3-1.

Listing 3-1. Adding an admin Flag to the user_repository Table

```
apexdemo@10gR2> desc user_repository;

Name                   Null?     Type
---------------------  --------  ----------------
USERNAME               NOT NULL  VARCHAR2(8)
FORENAME                         VARCHAR2(30)
SURNAME                          VARCHAR2(30)
EMAIL                            VARCHAR2(50)
PASSWORD_HASH                    RAW(16)
LOCKED_FLAG            NOT NULL  CHAR(1)
VERIFIED              NOT NULL  CHAR(1)

-- add the new column
apexdemo@10gR2> alter table user_repository
2  add(admin char(1) default 'N');

Table altered.
```

```
-- modify the existing records so that 'toby' is an administrator
apexdemo@10gR2> update user_repository
2  set admin = 'Y' where username = 'toby';

1 row updated.

apexdemo@10gR2> update user_repository
2  set admin = 'N' where username <> 'toby';

3 rows updated.

apexdemo@10gR2> commit;

Commit complete.

-- add a not null constraint to the new column
apexdemo@10gR2> alter table user_repository
  2  modify admin not null;

Table altered.

-- add a check constraint to the column
apexdemo@10gR2> alter table user_repository
  2  add constraint admin_yn check (admin in ('Y','N'));

Table altered.
```

Next, you need to check whether the user currently logged in to the application is an administrator, which will determine whether that user sees the Create button. In essence, you want to check whether a row exists in the user_repository table where the username is the same as the logged-in user and the admin flag is set to 'Y', as shown by the query in Listing 3-2.

Listing 3-2. Query to Determine if the Current User Is an Administrator

```
select 1 from user_repository
  where upper(username) = :APP_USER
  and admin = 'Y'
```

You might wonder about the select 1 used in this query. You need to select something to return to the outer query, because the query is actually being used as an exists subquery. You could select the username or any other column or constant you preferred; however, doing a select 1 is a very common convention that you should follow, unless you have specific reasons not to use this convention. Also notice the uppercasing of the username, since the :APP_USER substitution variable will be in uppercase (as discussed in Chapter 2).

You can now modify the condition type of the Create button to the Exists (SQL query returns at least one row) condition type and add the query, as shown in Figure 3-3.

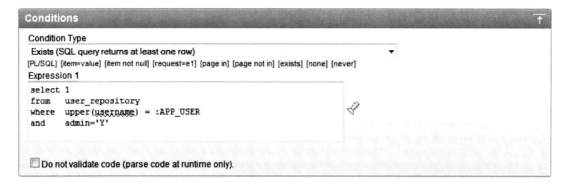

Figure 3-3. *Adding the Exists (SQL query returns at least one row) condition type to the Create button*

Now if you run the application while logged in as a nonadministrator, such as the brian user, you won't see the Create button, as shown in Figure 3-4. If you log in as peterw, who is an administrator, you will see the Create button (as in Figure 3-2).

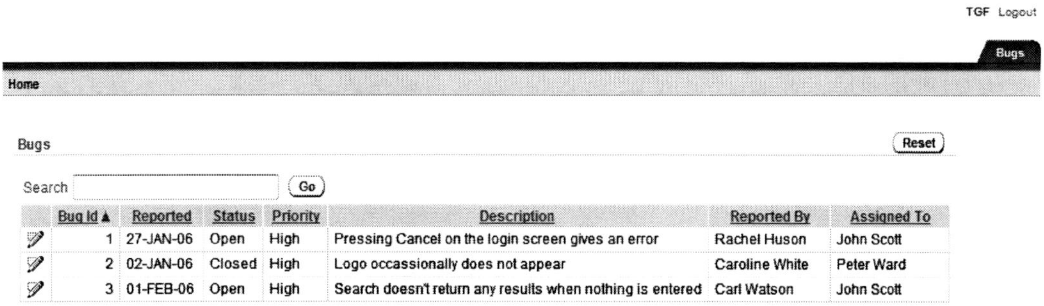

TGF Logout

Bug Id ▲	Reported	Status	Priority	Description	Reported By	Assigned To
1	27-JAN-06	Open	High	Pressing Cancel on the login screen gives an error	Rachel Huson	John Scott
2	02-JAN-06	Closed	High	Logo occassionally does not appear	Caroline White	Peter Ward
3	01-FEB-06	Open	High	Search doesn't return any results when nothing is entered	Carl Watson	John Scott

Figure 3-4. *Nonadministrators no longer see the Create button.*

■ **Caution** At this point, you might be thinking that conditions are a great way of preventing people from doing things you don't want them to do. Using conditions *will* stop page elements from being displayed or processed. However, knowledgeable users may still be able to get to a particular feature (such as the page to add a bug), even though you've used a condition to hide a button from them. In the "Authorization Schemes" section later in the chapter, you'll see how users can circumvent conditional processing to reach areas of the application they shouldn't be allowed to access. You should use authorization schemes (together with other techniques) to protect restricted areas of your application.

NOT Exists (SQL Query Returns No Rows)

The NOT Exists (SQL query returns no rows) condition type, as you can guess from the name, is the inverse of the Exists (SQL query returns at least one row) condition type. In this case, if the query returns a single row (or more), the overall result of the condition is deemed to be false and the element will not be displayed or processed.

In the previous example, we modified the application so that the Create button would appear only if the logged-in user was an administrator. This means that you can't add any bugs until an administrator is defined. You could modify the logic so that if there are no administrators defined, everyone gets to see the Create button. In other words, you check the user_repository table to see if there are any records where the admin flag is set to 'Y' and the username is not the same as the current user. In a nutshell, what you're asking is, "Is there another user who is an administrator?" To keep the example simple, we'll assume that only one administrator is ever defined in the application. Listing 3-3 shows the new query logic.

Listing 3-3. Query to Determine If Any Other User Is an Administrator

```
select 1 from user_repository
  where upper(username) <> :APP_USER
  and admin = 'Y'
```

You would modify the existing condition type to a NOT Exists type (you actually want to know if no other users are administrators) and put in the new query, as shown in Figure 3-5. If you now run the application and log in as the brian user, who is a not an administrator, the Create button will not be displayed, since the query will return a record for the peterw user, who is an administrator. And if you log in as the peterw user, you will see the Create button (since the query does not return any rows because there are no other administrators).

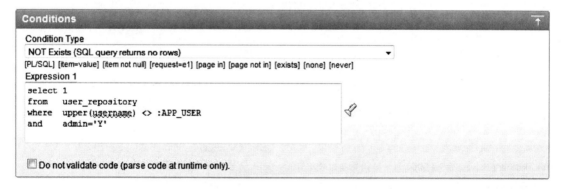

Figure 3-5. Adding the NOT Exists (SQL query returns no rows) condition type to the Create button

To see the NOT Exists condition in action, update the user_repository so that no administrator is defined:

```
apexdemo@10gR2> update user_repository set admin = 'N';
```

4 rows updated.

```
apexdemo@10gR2> commit;
```

Commit complete.

Then when you log in as any user, you will see the Create button.

Although the logic for this condition is probably not something you'd use in production, it does show that sometimes a NOT Exists condition may be a more logical choice than an Exists condition.

SQL Expression

A SQL expression is essentially any Boolean expression that you might place into a where clause. In fact, the logic in SQL expressions is effectively evaluated as a where clause restriction in a SQL statement. In other words, the APEX engine will perform a query such as the following:

```
select 1 from dual
  where <your expression here>
```

where the condition evaluates to true if a row is returned from the query, and evaluates to false if no rows are returned.

The earlier example of using an Exists condition type used the following piece of SQL (Listing 3-2):

```
select 1 from user_repository
  where upper(username) = :APP_USER
  and admin = 'Y'
```

The equivalent SQL expression logic would be something like this:

```
:APP_USER in
  (select username from user_repository where admin ='Y')
```

This would effectively become the following SQL statement:

```
select 1 from dual
where :APP_USER in
  (select upper(username) from user_repository where admin = 'Y')
```

SQL Expression condition types can be useful when you simply want to write the logic of your condition in a shorter, more concise form than the full select statement (as you would with an Exists condition). For example, you could compare the current date in *dd/mm/yyyy* format against a page item P1_DATE with the following SQL expression:

```
to_char(sysdate, 'dd/mm/yyyy') = :P1_DATE
```

This is more readable than the slightly longer equivalent Exists condition:

```
select 1 from dual where to_char(sysdate, 'dd/mm/yyyy') = :P1_DATE
```

Whether to use a SQL Expression condition type or an Exists condition type is often a matter of personal preference—whether you prefer to write out the entire query yourself or use the shortened form of a SQL expression.

PL/SQL Expression

A PL/SQL Expression condition can consist of any valid PL/SQL syntax that evaluates to a true or false value. For example, you could use logic such as the following:

```
length(:P1_USERNAME) < 8
```

This returns true if the value contained in the P1_USERNAME page item is less than eight characters long.

Suppose that Buglist users must meet certain performance targets for the number of bugs they've successfully fixed and cleared each month. You can modify the application to display some text that reminds the users that they need to clear as many bugs as they can before the month ends. You want to display this message during the last week of every month. To do this, simply add a new HTML Text region to the page, as shown in Figure 3-6.

Figure 3-6. Creating the new Month End Reminder region

■ **Note** This example uses the Sidebar Region template and positions the region in column 2. This means that it will display on the right side of the report on the page. Positioning and layout are covered in Chapter 5.

Since this is an HTML Text region, you can also include some HTML markup in the actual region source, as shown in Figure 3-7. Now if you run the application, you should see something like the screen shown in Figure 3-8. The reminder appears because it displays by default (remember that No Condition is the default).

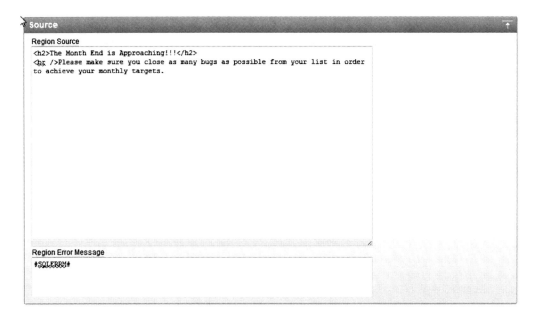

Figure 3-7. HTML region source for the Month End Reminder region

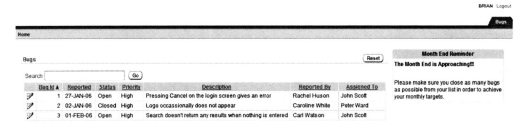

Figure 3-8. Displaying the Month End Reminder region

To determine the last week of the month, you can use some date and time functions available in Oracle, as shown in Listing 3-4.

Listing 3-4. Determining the Last Week of the Month

```
-- get today's date
apexdemo@10gR2> select to_char(sysdate, 'dd/mm/yyyy')
2  as value from dual;
```

```
VALUE
----------
11/18/2010

-- get the last day of the month
apexdemo@10gR2> select to_char(last_day(sysdate), 'dd/mm/yyyy')
2  as value from dual;

VALUE
----------
11/30/2010

-- determine the current week number
apexdemo@10gR2> select to_char(sysdate, 'w')
2  as value from dual;

VALUE
----------
3

-- determine the week number for the last day of the month
apexdemo@10gR2> select to_char(last_day(sysdate), 'w')
2  as value from dual;

VALUE
----------
5
```

The method used in Listing 3-4 actually counts weeks in terms of days from the start of the month; that is, the first seven days in the start of the month are considered the first week, and then the next seven days are the second week, as opposed to running from Monday to Sunday.

You can modify the Month End Reminder region to use a PL/SQL Expression condition that compares the current week number to the week number of the last day of the month, as shown in Figure 3-9. The region will now be shown only in the last seven days of the month.

***Figure 3-9.** Comparing the week numbers with a PL/SQL Expression condition*

PL/SQL Function Body Returning a Boolean

The PL/SQL Function Body Returning a Boolean condition type, as you'd guess, allows you to use a PL/SQL function that returns true or false to determine whether the condition succeeds or fails. For example, you could use something like the following code:

```
begin
  if :APP_USER = 'BOB' then
    return true;
  else
    return false;
  end if;
end;
```

However, as discussed in Chapter 1, you should aim to put as much of your code as you can into packages, and to reference those packaged functions and procedures from your application. Therefore, rather than including the previous code in your application, you could put that code into a packaged function, then call that function in the condition:

```
pkg_auth.check_for_bob;
```

The advantage of using a package is threefold:

- It's easy to reuse the code in another condition without having to copy and paste a lot of code.

- If you want to change the actual logic of the condition, you can change it in only one place (the package), regardless of how many places you're using it in your application.

- You can change the logic in the package without needing to modify your application. You can modify and recompile the underlying package without having to recode anything in your application (since it is just calling the function).

Remember, it will be far easier to send a new package body to customers and tell them to recompile it than to give them an entire application—which they will need to upgrade—just because you want to change something in a single routine.

Request = Expression 1

Whenever a page is submitted, the value of the REQUEST application attribute is set to the name of the object that caused the page to be submitted. This happens, for example, when a user clicks a button or a particular tab. Using the REQUEST application attribute means you can perform different actions depending on what the user actually did.

Now, let's say you want to keep track of the search phrases people are using in the Buglist application. For example, you want to record that the user searched for the phrase "logo" as shown in Figure 3-10.

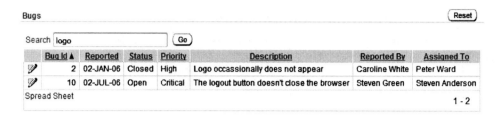

Figure 3-10. *Searching for a particular phrase*

To accomplish this, first you need to create a table to store the search text, as shown in Listing 3-5.

Listing 3-5. *Creating the user_searches Table*

```
apexdemo@10gR2> create table user_searches(id number,
  2  logged date not null,
  3  username varchar2(8),
  4  search_phrase varchar2(50),
  5 primary key (id));

Table created.

-- create a sequence to use as the PK of the table
apexdemo@10gR2> create sequence search_seq cache 100;

Sequence created.
```

Next, you need to create a new PL/SQL page process that will fire after a page submission, as shown in Figure 3-11. The PL/SQL for the process will simply insert a record into the user_searches table:

```
insert into user_searches
  (id, logged, username, search_phrase)
values
  (search_seq.nextval, sysdate, :APP_USER, :P23_SUBJECT)
```

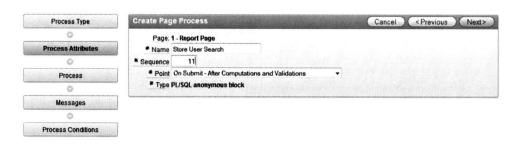

Figure 3-11. *Creating a PL/SQL page process to store the user search*

You also need to make sure that this process fires only if the user has clicked the Go button; otherwise, it will end up inserting rows into the user_searches table when the user performs other actions, such as navigating to the page using the Bugs tab. The key to doing this is to use the value of the REQUEST setting for the Go button, as shown in Figure 3-12.

Figure 3-12. Setting the REQUEST value associated with the Go button

Often, with an automatically generated element, the REQUEST value will already be defaulted to something sensible. If not, you can set or change the value. It's also very important to notice that you're using the REQUEST value, not the name or label of the button. Many people get caught out by trying to use the label of the element rather than the REQUEST value, and then can't figure out why their condition isn't working the way they thought it should.

With the REQUEST value of the Go button set to Go, you can use that value in the PL/SQL page process condition, as shown in Figure 3-13.

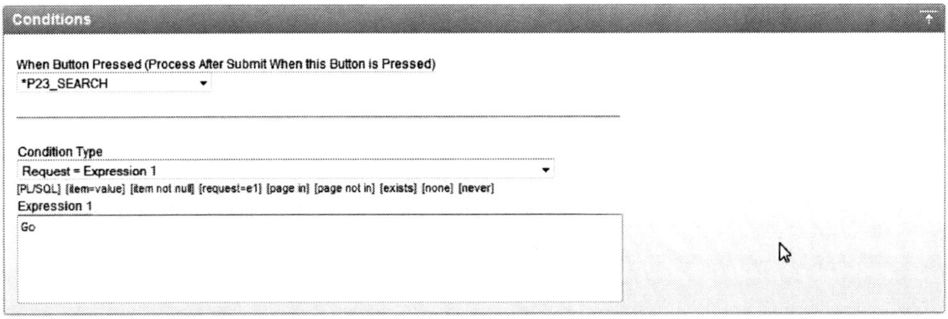

Figure 3-13. Using the Request = Expression 1 condition type to control the page process

Now run the application and search for a particular phrase, such as "browser," as shown in Figure 3-14.

113

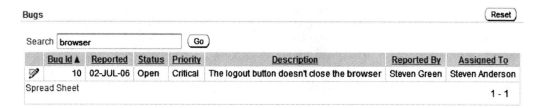

Figure 3-14. Searching for the phrase "browser"

Listing 3-6 shows that the search phrase, the username, and the timestamp of the search were all stored in the user_searches table.

Listing 3-6. Querying the Entries in the user_searches Table

```
apexdemo@10gR2> select * from user_searches;

     ID LOGGED     USERNAME SEARCH_PHRASE
------- --------- -------- -------------------
      1 20-NOV-10 TIM      browser
```

Great, it all works. But you may have also spotted a problem with this way of recording searches. Currently, the PL/SQL page process will execute only if the user clicks the Go button. Many people simply press the Enter/Return key after they've entered something in the Search field. The existing logic won't log those searches into the user_searches table. A simple way to address this problem is to make the REQUEST value of the Go button and the REQUEST value of the P1_REPORT_SEARCH text field the same. Then you'd need to check for only a single REQUEST value in the PL/SQL page process condition, regardless of whether the page was submitted as a result of the user clicking the Go button or hitting Enter/Return.

However, if you examine the attributes of the P1_REPORT_SEARCH text field, you'll see that, unlike for the button, you can't specify your own REQUEST value for the text field. In the case of a text field (and other element types), the REQUEST value is defined to be the actual element name; that is, the REQUEST value for the P1_REPORT_SEARCH text item is P1_REPORT_SEARCH. Since you can't change the REQUEST value of the text field to be the same as the button, you will need to change the REQUEST value of the button to be the same as the text field, as shown in Figure 3-15. You also need to modify the PL/SQL process condition so that it compares the REQUEST value against P1_REPORT_SEARCH rather than Go, as shown in Figure 3-16.

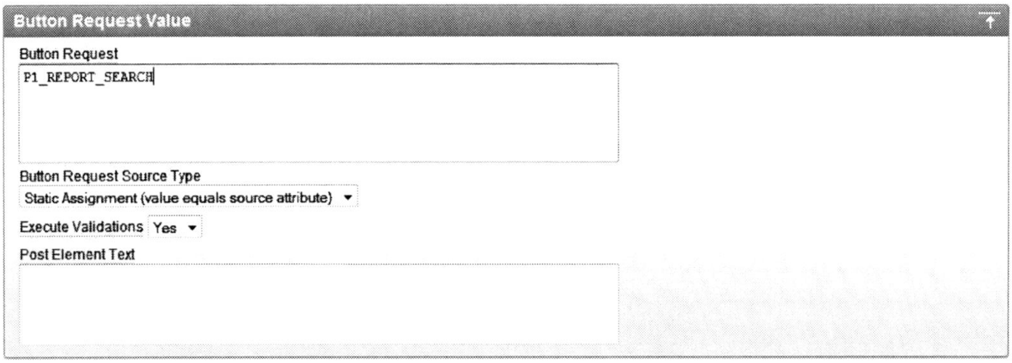

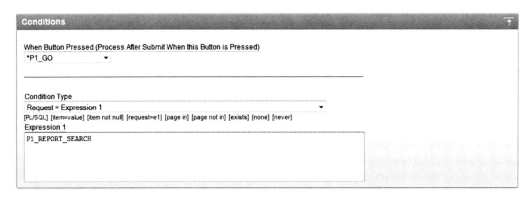

Figure 3-15. Setting the button REQUEST value to be the same as the text field

Figure 3-16. Using the shared REQUEST value in the PL/SQL page process

All search queries will now be logged, regardless of whether the user clicks the Go button or presses the Enter/Return key.

Request != Expression 1

The Request != Expression 1 condition type is the reverse of the Request = Expression 1 type. This condition evaluates to true if the value of the REQUEST item does not match the value in Expression 1. The way to use this condition type should be fairly obvious from the example in the previous section.

Request Is Contained Within Expression 1

The Request Is Contained within Expression 1 condition type allows you to compare the REQUEST value against the multiple values specified in Expression 1.

In the previous example that used the Request = Expression 1 condition, we modified the REQUEST value of the Go button to match the REQUEST value of the P23_SUBJECT text field so we could compare a single REQUEST value. Using the Request Is Contained within Expression 1 condition type instead, you can simply use the two different REQUEST values, rather than needing to make the REQUEST values the same.

If you change the REQUEST value of the Go button back to its original value of Go, you can modify the PL/SQL page process to use a condition like the one shown in Figure 3-17.

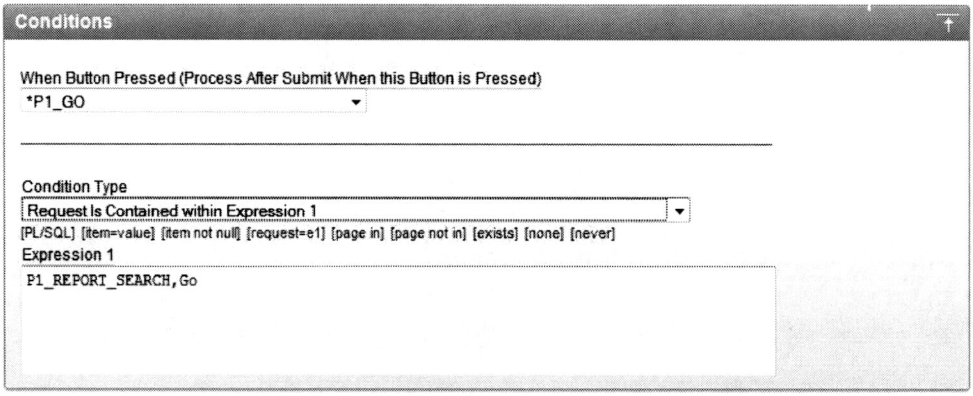

Figure 3-17. Using the Request Is Contained within Expression 1 condition type

Notice that this example uses a comma-separated list of values in Expression 1. However, the text in Expression 1 is actually evaluated using an INSTR test, so the REQUEST value is tested like this:

```
INSTR(text in expression 1, value of REQUEST item) > 0
```

and the condition is effectively evaluated as this:

```
INSTR('P23_SUBJECT,Go', :REQUEST) > 0
```

So it does not really matter which delimiter you use. You could use a colon, an exclamation point, or any other symbol, since the values contained in Expression 1 are not being parsed into their individual values. Instead, the entire text in Expression 1 is searched to see if the string containing the REQUEST value appears anywhere within it.

You need to be very careful when using Contained within Expression conditions, because of the opportunities for false-positive matches to be made. If you make poor choices for your REQUEST values, you may end up matching against a REQUEST value you didn't intend to match against.

As an example, imagine you have two buttons on your page: one used to submit the page, with a REQUEST value of Go, and another used to log the user out of the application, with a REQUEST value of Goodbye. Suppose you want to run a PL/SQL process when the user clicks the logout button, and therefore use the condition shown in Figure 3-18. The problem is that when the user clicks the submit button, which has a REQUEST value of Go, the APEX engine will perform this evaluation:

```
if instr('Goodbye', 'Go') > 0 then

  return true;
else
  return false;
end if;
```

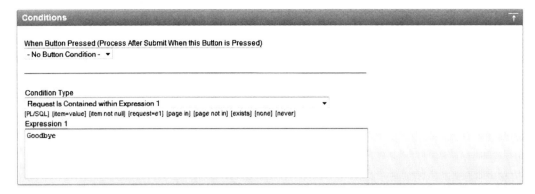

Figure 3-18. *Using a bad choice of REQUEST value*

Because the letters *Go* appear in the text "Goodbye," the condition will return true and the process will run, even though the user clicked the submit button rather than the logout button.

■ **Caution** Check your REQUEST values to make sure that they will match only when you want them to, and try to avoid using a REQUEST value that is a substring of another REQUEST value. Note that you don't need to worry about this issue when you use one of the condition types that deal with properly delimited values, such as those that are colon-delimited.

Value of Item in Expression 1 = Expression 2

The Value of Item in Expression 1 = Expression 2 condition type allows you to perform a case-sensitive comparison of the value of an item specified in Expression 1 with a string contained in Expression 2. For example, say you wanted to modify your application so that rather than logging every search phrase, it logs only the use of the search phrase "secure." You can achieve this by modifying the conditional logic for the PL/SQL page process, as shown in Figure 3-19.

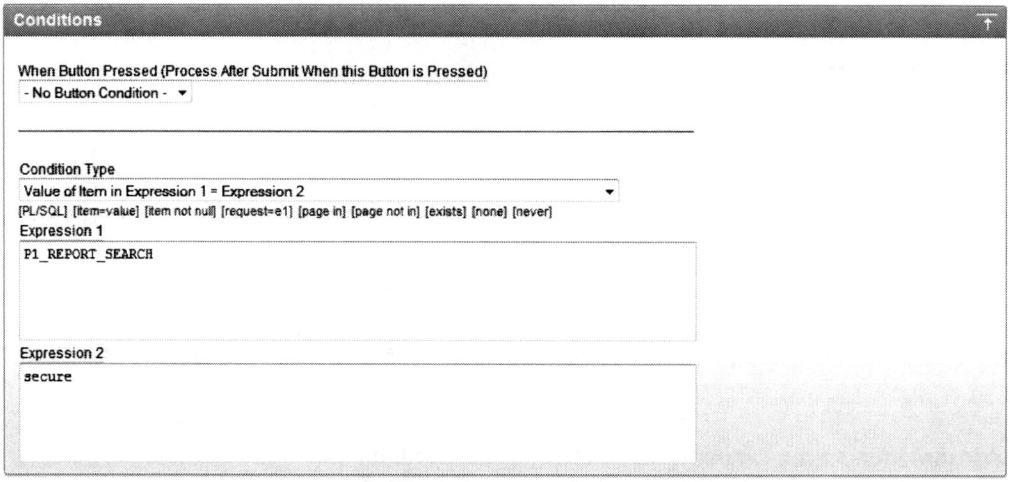

Conditions

When Button Pressed (Process After Submit When this Button is Pressed)
- No Button Condition - ▾

Condition Type
Value of Item in Expression 1 = Expression 2   ▾
[PL/SQL] [item=value] [item not null] [request=e1] [page in] [page not in] [exists] [none] [never]
Expression 1
P1_REPORT_SEARCH

Expression 2
secure

Figure 3-19. Comparing the value of the P1_REPORT_SEARCH item with a string

Here you enter the name of the item P23_SUBJECT as Expression 1 and the text you wish to compare it with as Expression 2. Now an entry will be added to the user_searches table only if the user enters the word "secure" into the Search text field. Note that this performs an exact, case-sensitive match against the text in Expression 2. If the user enters "is it secure" or "Secure" in the Search text field, the condition will not evaluate to true and the search phrase will not be logged into the user_searches table.

Value of Item in Expression 1 Is NULL

The purpose of the Value of Item in Expression 1 Is NULL condition type should be fairly obvious. This condition can be very useful. For example, you can easily modify your application so that users are given a warning if they click the Go button without entering a search phrase into the Search text field. Usually, the best way to achieve this is to use a validation, but you can implement similar functionality by creating a new field with warning text that will appear only if the Search text field is empty and the user clicked Go. Figure 3-20 shows the new text field.

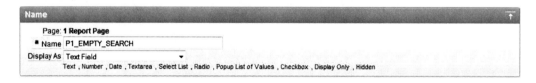

Page: **1 Report Page**
* Name P1_EMPTY_SEARCH
Display As Text Field   ▾
   Text , Number , Date , Textarea , Select List , Radio , Popup List of Values , Checkbox , Display Only , Hidden

Figure 3-20 Creating a new text field

Set this text to display just to the right of the Go button by setting the Begin On New Line property to false as shown in Figure 3-21. Also change the template to Required, which will make the text appear in red. You can now check the value of the P23_SUBJECT item for a null value, as shown in Figure 3-22. Users will see the text warning if they click the Go button or hit the Return/Enter key without entering a search phrase, as shown in Figure 3-23.

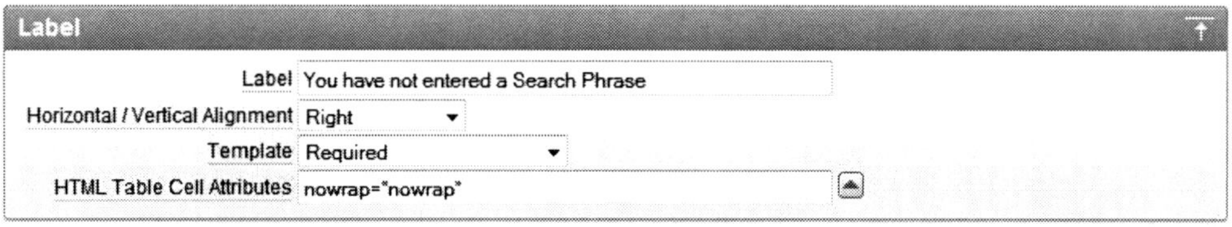

Figure 3-21. *Setting the display text to appear like a warning*

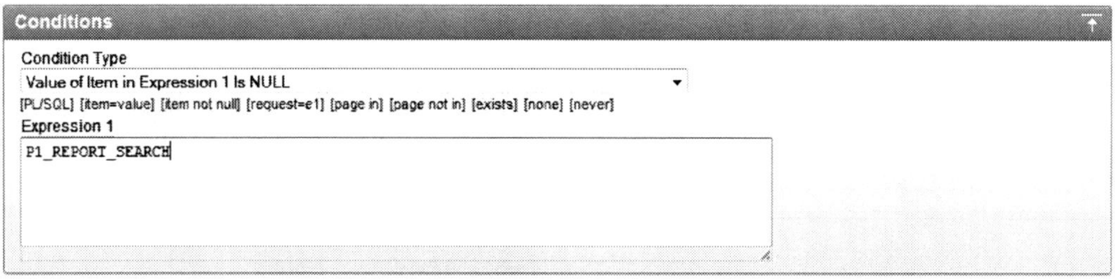

Figure 3-22. *Checking for a null search phrase*

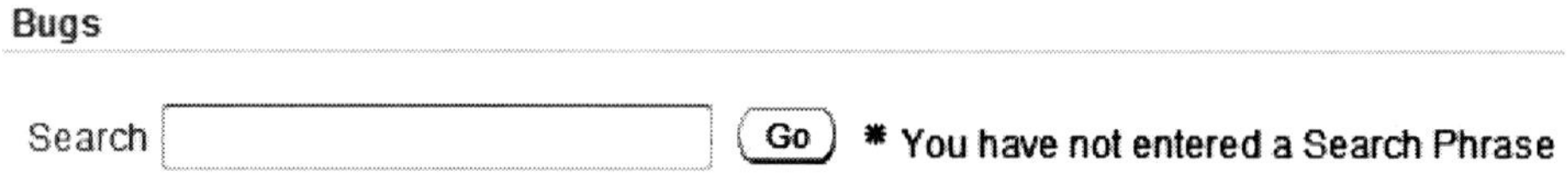

Figure 3-23. *A warning message is displayed if no search phrase is entered.*

As mentioned, using a validation would be a far more sensible way of performing this check. However, sometimes methods like the one shown here can prove useful.

Current Page = Expression 1

The Current Page = Expression 1 condition is ideal when you use shared components or make use of page zero (covered in Chapter 1) and want to conditionally display or process a page element based on which page the user is currently viewing.

For example, the Logout link is currently displayed in the top-right corner of the Buglist application screen. Suppose you want to make it visible only when the user is on the page containing the Bug report (page 1 in the application). To accomplish this, you can edit the navigation bar entry and use the condition shown in Figure 3-24. Now when the user clicks the Analyze tab, which will take him to page 5, the Logout link will no longer be visible, as shown in Figure 3-25.

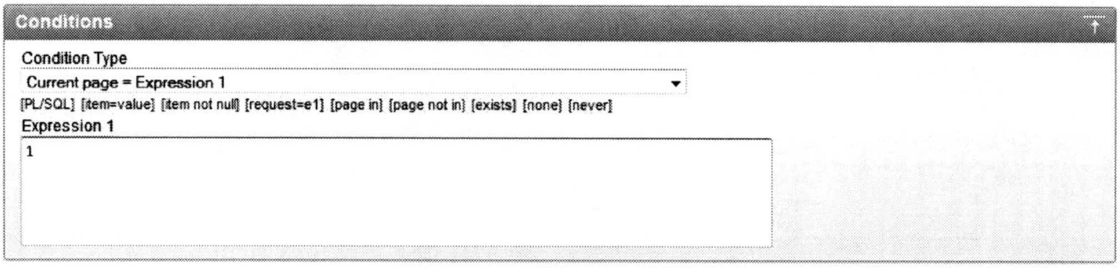

Figure 3-24. Comparing the current page with an expression

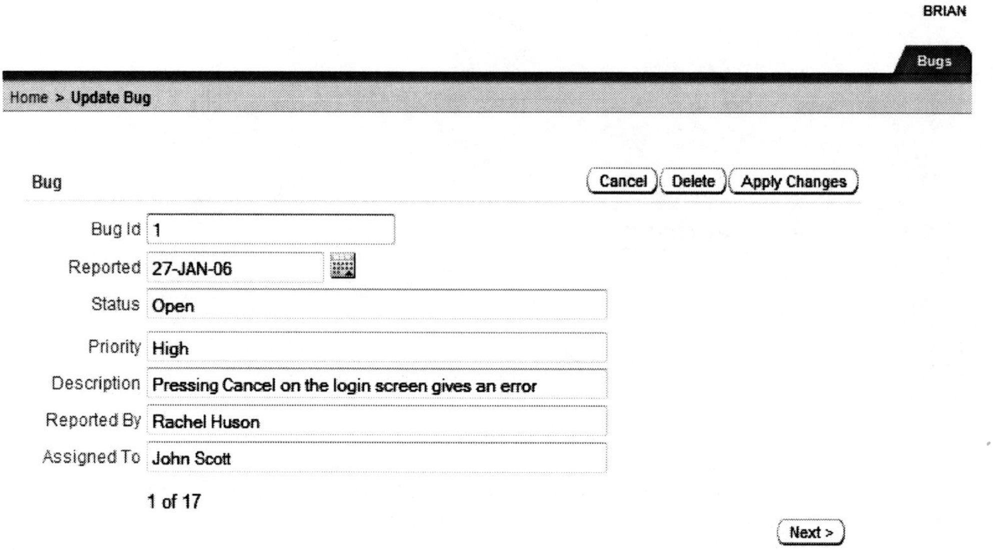

Figure 3-25. The Logout link is no longer visible on any page other than page 1

Current Page Is Contained Within Expression 1 (Comma Delimited List of Pages)

The Current Page Is Contained within Expression 1 (comma delimited list of pages) condition is similar to the Current Page = Expression 1 condition, but it allows you to supply a comma-delimited list of pages rather than just limiting you to a single page. For example, you could modify the previous example to display the Logout link for both pages 1 and 5, as shown in Figure 3-26.

Using conditions like these, combined with features such as page zero, can lead to some incredibly sophisticated applications. They allow you to display page elements selectively on many different pages, without needing to add that page element to each individual page. Take advantage of this power to minimize the amount of manual work you need to do wherever you can.

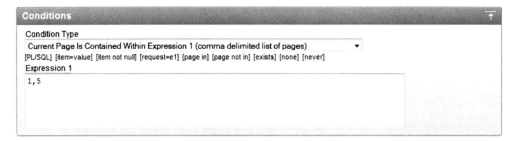

Figure 3-26. The Logout link is no longer visible on pages 1 and 5

User Is Authenticated (Not Public)

The User is Authenticated (not public) condition evaluates to true if the user has successfully authenticated to the application using the current authentication scheme, which can be either one of the built-in schemes or a custom authentication scheme.

A typical use of this condition is to display different information to users depending on whether or not they are logged in to your application. For example, you might have a navigation menu that gives extra options to people after they have logged in.

The previous example showed how to display the Logout link only if users are currently on page 1 or 5. A far more sensible usage would display the Logout link only if the user has actually logged in (is authenticated), as shown in Figure 3-27.

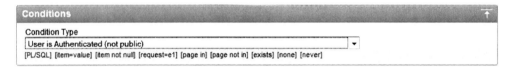

Figure 3-27. The Logout link is displayed only if the user is authenticated.

User Is the Public User (User Has Not Authenticated)

The User is the Public User (user has not authenticated) condition is the reverse of the User is Authenticated (not public) type. It will evaluate to true if the user is not authenticated to the application. Here, *Public User* refers to whether the username is the same as the username that is specified in the DAD in your Apache configuration file, which is used to connect to the database. This username will typically be something like HTMLDB_PUBLIC_USER (if you have upgraded from an older version of APEX) or APEX_PUBLIC_USER; if you are using Oracle XE, it will typically be defined as ANONYMOUS.

At the application level, you can set which value to use for Public User, as shown in Figure 3-28. Whenever the APP_USER variable equals the same value as you have specified at the application level, the user is deemed to be a public user.

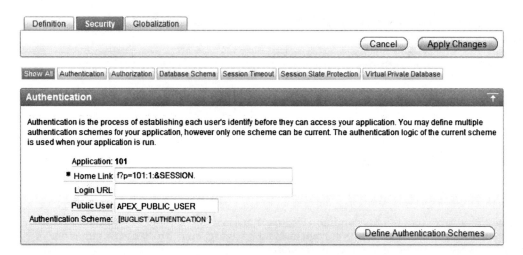

Figure 3-28. Defining the Public User variable at the application level

Figure 3-28 shows APEX_PUBLIC_USER specified as the Public User application attribute, which is the username specified in the DAD in this example. Until you log in to the application as another user, the APP_USER variable will be set to APEX_PUBLIC_USER (since that's the username specified in the DAD). And until you successfully authenticate to the application, your current session will be classified as a Public User session. If you alter the Public User value to be something else (such as nobody), it will no longer match the username specified in the DAD, and so your unauthenticated session will not be classified as a Public User session.

Current Language Is Contained Within Expression 1

The Current Language is Contained within Expression 1 condition is extremely useful for enabling your application to take advantage of multiple-language support. Using this condition type, you can perform different processing depending on the language setting of the web browser that the user is using. For example, to detect whether the user's browser is set to either French or German, you could use a condition such as the one shown in Figure 3-29.

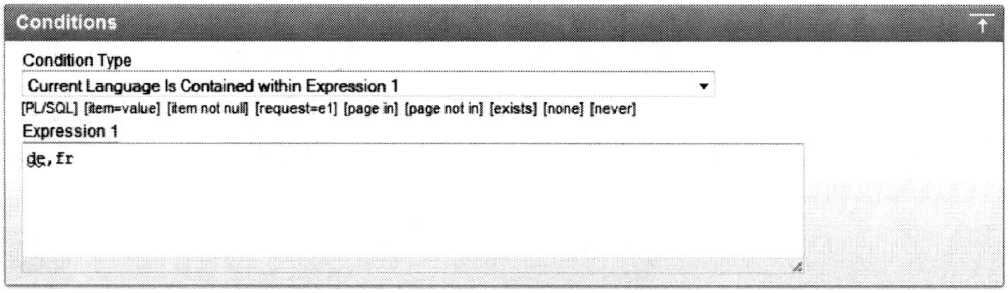

Figure 3-29. Checking the browser language setting for French and German

In Chapter 11, you will learn how you can use this type of condition to build an application that uses the browser settings to determine the correct language translations and character set when displaying the pages. This lets you make your application accessible to a far wider audience.

Never

As the name suggests, the Never condition will never be active—the page element will never be displayed or processed. You would typically use this condition type if you wished to temporarily disable a page element for debugging purposes. You might also use it to disable an element but not remove it completely from your application (in case you wanted to revert back to using it again in the future). However, leaving a lot of unused code lying around is generally not a good long-term strategy.

Using Conditions Appropriately

Conditions can make it incredibly easy to dynamically modify the way your application behaves at runtime. However, sometimes it's easy to misuse conditions to make your application behave in a particular way when another way of achieving the same result would be more appropriate.

For example, suppose you want to modify your application so that only administrators are able to see the Submitted By and Assigned To columns in the report. You can define conditional display logic against individual columns in the report by selecting the column from the Report Attributes tab, as shown in Figure 3-30.

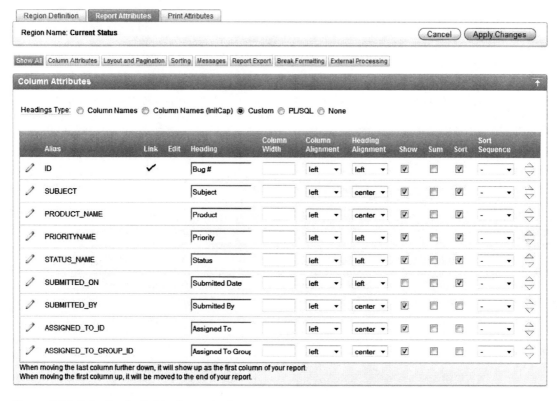

Figure 3-30. Selecting individual report columns

You can use the same query we saw in the earlier example for determining whether the current user has the admin flag set to 'Y' (Listing 3-2). Figure 3-31 shows the conditional logic applied to the Submitted By column. After also applying the same condition to the Assigned To column, anyone who is not an administrator will no longer be able to view these columns, as shown in Figure 3-32.

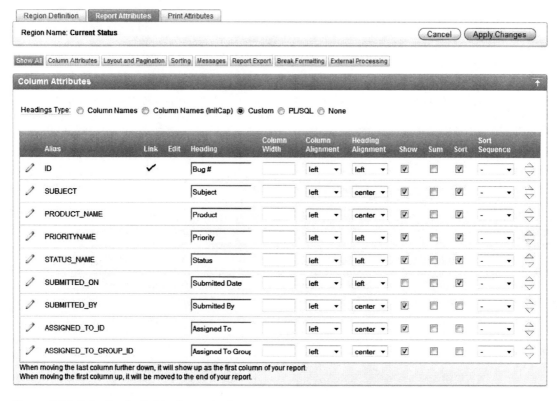

Figure 3-31. Using an Exists (SQL query returns at least one row) condition to display an individual report column

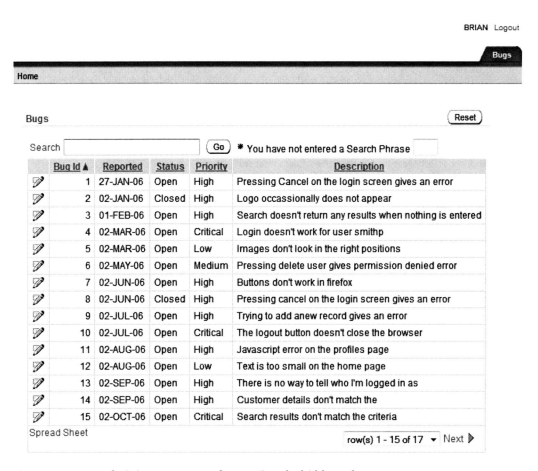

Figure 3-32. Nonadministrators can no longer view the hidden columns.

Using conditional display in this way is perfectly acceptable. In fact, it's an extremely elegant way to dynamically change the way that the data is presented to different users (or different classes of user).

Now suppose you also want to hide the Status and Priority fields from nonadministrators. You could easily do that by adding the same conditions you placed on the Submitted By and Assigned To columns to those two columns. In this case, you are now hiding four columns of data from the nonadministrators. However, the query is still selecting the data from those columns, regardless of whether or not the user is an administrator. This is where you need to use your judgment to determine whether applying conditions in this way is the best choice for your particular case. For example, if your application has 1 administrator and 99 nonadministrators, then (on average) you will be displaying all the fields that are being selected in the query only every 1 in a 100 times. In other words, the vast majority of the time you are having the query select columns you are not actually going to use—making the database perform extra, unnecessary work.

It's very important to realize that when you place conditions on report columns, you are not modifying the actual query that is being performed. You are affecting only which columns will be displayed after the query has been performed.

125

To achieve the same end result, you could have two different report regions: one with the query to select the columns that administrators should be able to see, and the other whose query selects the columns that nonadministrators should be able to see. You would then use mutually exclusive conditions so that only one report region was shown at a time—if the user is an administrator, the report region relevant to administrators is processed and vice versa. However, duplicating the report region in this way adds extra overhead in terms of maintenance for your application, meaning that if you wanted to change something, you might need to change it in two places rather than just one place.

Perhaps a better alternative would be to change the report region type from SQL Query to SQL Query (PL/SQL function body returning SQL query). This would allow you to use a PL/SQL function to return a different SQL query for the report to use depending on whether the user was an administrator.

Don't be afraid to reevaluate your options when the requirements change. You may find that the method that used to suit your needs perfectly has now become less attractive.

Authorization Schemes

Like conditions, authorization schemes allow you to control the display and processing of elements within your application. However, unlike a condition, an authorization scheme is a far more secure choice when it comes to restricting the areas of your application that a user should be able to access.

An authorization scheme is similar to an authentication scheme and condition type in that it is a piece of logic that returns a true or false value. If it returns true, the authorization is deemed to have been successful; otherwise, the authorization fails.

You can create new authorization schemes for your application from the Shared Components section of the application builder, as shown in Figure 3-33. Any existing authorization schemes can also be accessed from here.

Figure 3-33. The Authorization Schemes page

Creating an Authorization Scheme

The difference between a condition and an authorization scheme starts with the way in which you define the two. Whereas the logic for a condition is defined for a particular element (for example, a page item or a region), an authorization scheme is defined in one place and is then available to be used by one or more of your application elements.

As an example, we will create an authorization scheme that determines whether the current user is an administrator. First, you need to create the scheme itself. The wizard gives you the choice of whether you wish to create a scheme from scratch or to base the scheme on an existing schema, as shown in Figure 3-34.

Figure 3-34. *Creating a new authorization scheme*

As when you define the logic for a condition, you can select from different authorization scheme types, such as Exists SQL Query and PL/SQL Function Returning a Boolean. The list of types is nowhere near as comprehensive as the list of condition types, but it is usually sufficient to cover the vast majority of authorization schemes you might want to create.

As shown in Figure 3-35, name the new scheme USER_IS_ADMIN and choose the Exists SQL Query scheme type. For Expression 1, use the same query as the one you used earlier (Listing 3-2) for the Exists (SQL query returns at least one row) condition. You must also specify an error message that will be displayed to a user when the authorization scheme fails. Supplying an error message is mandatory for an authorization scheme, unlike with a condition.

Figure 3-35. Defining the authorization scheme logic

An important configuration setting you can define for an authorization scheme is called the *evaluation point*, as shown in Figure 3-36. You can use the evaluation point setting to define whether the authorization scheme logic should be evaluated every time you view a page that uses it or evaluated only once per session. For this example, choose once per session.

Evaluation Point

Validate authorization scheme
- ○ Once per page view
- ◉ Once per session

Figure 3-36. Defining an evaluation point

When you choose once per session for the evaluation point, the result of the authorization scheme is cached, and the cached value is used whenever an element references the authorization scheme. If the logic in your scheme is particularly time-consuming and the results probably won't change that often, taking advantage of the caching facility will lead to a much more responsive application for the user. For example, if the logic takes one second to perform and you use that authorization scheme on a lot of different pages, the user won't need to wait that extra second per page (and shaving a second off your page-delivery times can make a big difference to the users' perception of your application). We'll discuss the evaluation point choice in more detail in the "To Cache or Not to Cache" section later in this chapter.

Next, return to the Home page in your application and ensure that the condition type for the Create Bug link is set to No Condition Specified, as shown in Figure 3-37. As mentioned earlier, this is a quick way of disabling the condition without needing to remove the code. Then use the Authorization Scheme drop-down list, shown in Figure 3-38, to select the USER_IS_ADMIN scheme you created.

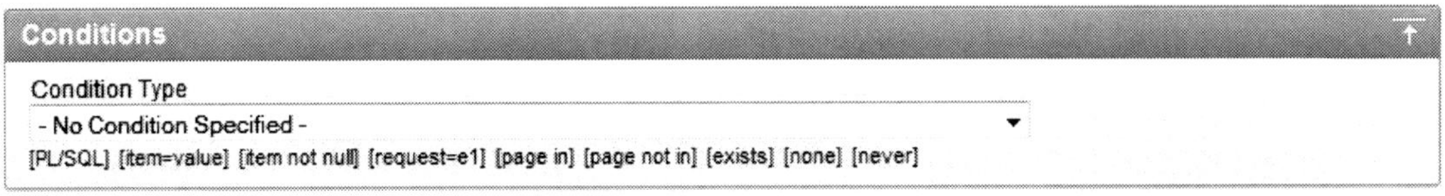

Figure 3-37. Defining the authorization scheme logic

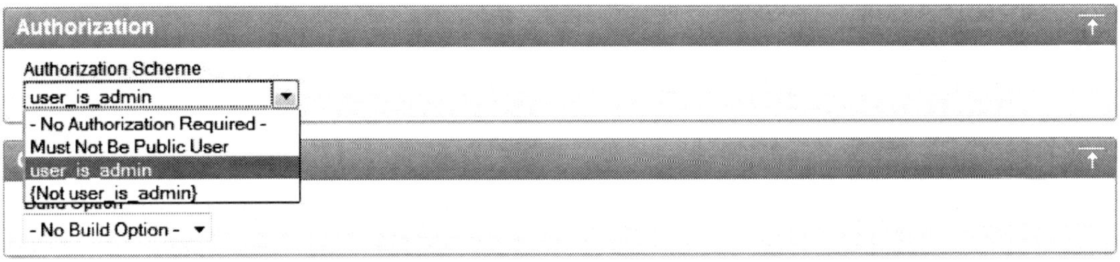

Figure 3-38. Selecting one of the available authorization schemes

As you can see, three schemes are available, even though you created only one:

> *Must Not Be Public User.* This scheme is added automatically. As the name suggests, it is a good way to determine if the user is authenticated to the application. This scheme uses the value of the Public User application attribute that was discussed earlier in the section about the User is the Public User (user has not authenticated) condition type.

> *USER_IS_ADMIN.* This is the scheme you added using the wizard.

> *Not USER_IS_ADMIN.* This scheme is also added automatically. It is the reverse of the scheme you just created. Whenever you create a new scheme, APEX will automatically create the reverse of the scheme for you. This makes it very easy to not only check that the user is an administrator, but also that the user is not an administrator.

Now the Create link should behave as it did before, appearing only to people who are administrators.

One big difference between using conditions and using authorization schemes is that you can easily reuse an authorization scheme with other page elements simply by selecting it from the drop-down list.

Any changes to the authorization scheme will automatically be reflected in any elements that use the scheme.

Protecting Your Resources

At first glance, it might look like you have succeeded in preventing nonadministrators from being able to create new records, since they can no longer access the Create button. However, it's important to note the distinction here between the following:

- Preventing the user from seeing the button

- Preventing the user from doing whatever clicking the button would have done

When users click the Create button, they are redirected to page 2 of the application, as shown in Figure 3-39, which is the page where they can create a new record. Also notice in Figure 3-40 that the cache is cleared for page 2. Any page items that are defined on page 2 will have their session state cleared, since you'd usually want the page to default to blank entries when you are creating a new record.

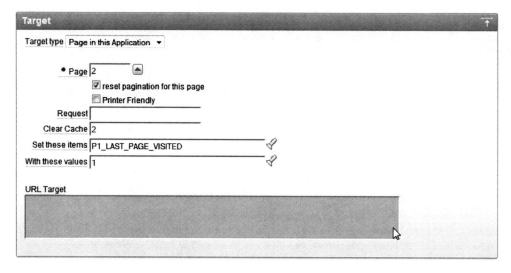

Figure 3-39. *The Create button redirects the user to page 2 in the application.*

So, what would happen if a nonadministrator tried to get to page 2 by typing that address into a browser? Well, that's easy to test. Simply change the page number specified in the URL of the browser to go to page 2 instead of page 1. In the browser, the URL will contain something like this:

```
http://127.0.0.1:7780/pls/apex/f?p=101:1:2357672961634263
```

where 101 is the application ID, and 1 is the page number. The long number after the page number is the session ID. Modify this URL as follows:

```
http://127.0.0.1:7780/pls/apex/f?p=101:2:2357672961634263
```

and then press the Enter/Return key to submit the URL request to the browser. You will see that a nonadministrator user can still access the page for creating new records, as shown in Figure 3-40.

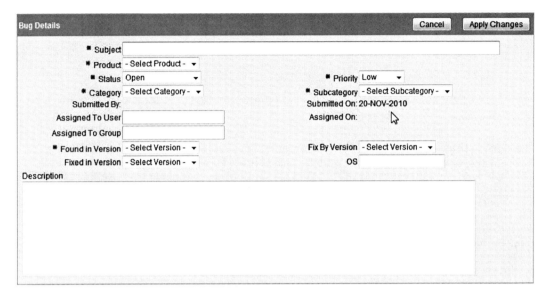

Figure 3-40. A nonadministrator is still able to access a page he should not be able to view.

This is where the simplicity and power of authorization schemes become very useful. You can apply the same USER_IS_ADMIN scheme to an entire page. To do so, edit page 2 of the application and go to the security settings, as shown in Figure 3-41.

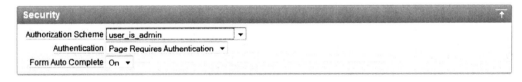

Figure 3-41. Setting the authorization scheme for the entire page

Note that the authorization scheme can work independently from any authentication settings you have made for the page. Here, you are not only saying that users need to be authenticated to view this page, but they also need to pass your authorization scheme check, and therefore they must be an administrator.

If you now repeat your test and modify the URL for a nonadministrator to navigate directly to page 2, you will see the error message shown in Figure 3-42.

Logout

 Error Sorry, only Administrators can do that

OK

Figure 3-42. *Your error message appears when a nonadministrator tries to access a page protected by an authorization scheme.*

To properly protect the resources in your application, make sure that when you are restricting the display of certain page elements, you also protect the resources for which those page elements are responsible. It's not enough to just hide all the links and buttons to a particular page, for example. Make sure you protect access to that page itself with an appropriate authorization scheme.

This applies equally to any processes your pages might execute as a result of a user action. For example, you could modify the PL/SQL page process that logs the search phrases so that it logs phrases only when the current user is an administrator by using the authorization scheme rather than using a condition. In this particular scenario, you would not get a warning message when nonadministrators perform a search (unlike when they try to access a page protected by the same authorization scheme), but the PL/SQL process would not be processed at all. By using the authorization scheme rather than a condition, you again have the benefit of being able to decide whether the scheme is checked on every page view or the cached value should be used.

To Cache or Not to Cache

Please excuse the corny title of this section, but it does describe the topic: deciding whether to evaluate authorization schemes on every page view or just once per session.

In this chapter's example, the USER_IS_ADMIN authorization scheme is evaluated only once per session. This means that the value is cached the first time it needs to be evaluated after a new session is established (which would usually occur after the user successfully authenticates to the application). So if a nonadministrator, such as the tim user, authenticates to the application, he will not see the Create link. But what if you modify that user so that he is now an administrator, as shown in Listing 3-7?

Listing 3-7. *Modifying the brian User to Be an Administrator*

```
apexdemo@10gR2> update user_repository

  2  set admin = 'Y'
  3  where username = 'brian';

1 row updated.

apexdemo@10gR2> commit;

Commit complete.
```

This user will still not see the Create button, even if he navigates away from the page and then returns to it. You would need to tell the user to log out and then back in again in order for his new administrator privileges to be recognized by the application. To avoid this, you could modify the authorization scheme so that it is evaluated on each page view. Then the next time the user performs an action that displays a page that references the authorization scheme, the authorization scheme will be reevaluated. In this case, the user's new administrator privileges would be recognized, so he would not need to log out and log back in.

As noted earlier, the downside to having authorization schemes reevaluated each time the page is displayed is performance. For example, imagine that your application has quite a large user repository and attracts perhaps 1,000 different users throughout the day, each viewing 10 different pages, each with a reference to your authorization scheme. That would mean that throughout the course of the day, your authorization scheme is evaluated around 10,000 times. Using once per session evaluation instead potentially reduces the number of queries the database needs to handle in a day by around 9,000 (to around 1,000 times a day—once for each user, assuming a user logs in for only a single session).

You might say, "So what? The query was running really quickly anyway!" Don't forget that anything you do in a multiple-user system can impact other sessions running in that database. So even if your query runs blisteringly fast, if you don't need to do it, then don't.

Your individual business requirements should determine whether every page view or once per session is best for that particular authorization scheme. In the example, promoting users to administrator status won't happen very often, so you don't need to reevaluate that check every time a page is viewed; once per session is a reasonable choice. Reevaluating your authorization schemes more often than necessary not only gives the database more unnecessary work to do, but may also negatively impact the impression your end users have of the application, if the pages take longer to refresh than they should.

Resetting the Caching

There is actually an alternative to making the user log out and then back in again when your authorization scheme is set to reevaluate once per user session. You can invalidate the caching of the authorization scheme values in the current APEX session with the following call:

```
apex_util.reset_authorizations;
```

This will force the authorization schemes to be evaluated again the next time they are referenced.

As an example, suppose you added a new Reset Auths button to the report page, and also added a new PL/SQL page process that makes a call to apex_util.reset_authorizations whenever the Reset Auths button is clicked. Now if the brian user (who is not an administrator) logs in to the application, he will see the screen shown in Figure 3-43. Notice that the report columns are still being hidden by conditions applied to the individual columns, rather than by the authorization scheme. Here, you are concerned only with the status of the Create button, since that page item is using the IS_ADMIN_USER authorization scheme.

BRIAN Logout
Bugs
Home
Bugs
Reset
Reset Auths
Search log
Go
* You have not entered a Search Phrase
Edit Bugid Reported Status Priority Description
1 27.01.06 Open High Pressing Cancel on the login screen gives an error
2 02.01.06 Closed High Logo occasionally does not appear
3 01.02.06 Open High Search doesn't return any results when nothing is entered

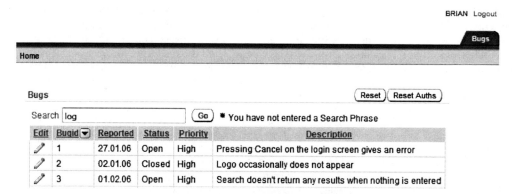

Figure 3-43. Nonadministrators can't see the Create button but can see the new Reset Auths button.

Now suppose you update the `user_repository` table to make the `brian` user an administrator (see Listing 3-7) while he is still logged in, and he navigates back to the report page. Figure 3-44 shows that the report columns will now be displayed (since they were being hidden by a condition, which does pick up the change to the `admin` flag for the user), but the Create button is still hidden, since the cached value for the authorization scheme is being used.

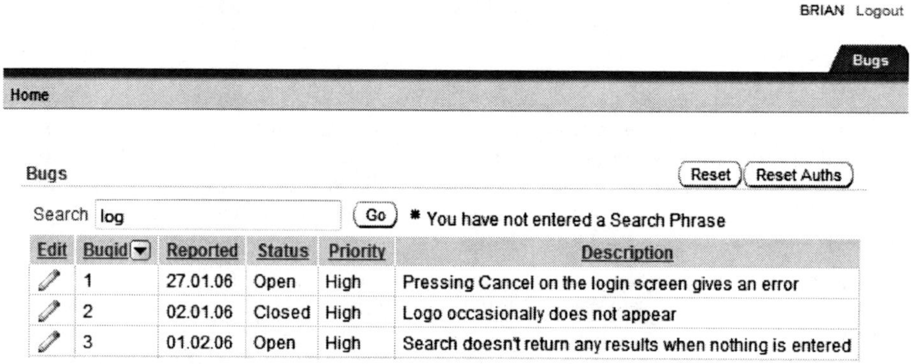

BRIAN Logout
Bugs
Home
Bugs
Reset
Reset Auths
Search log
Go
* You have not entered a Search Phrase
Edit Bugid Reported Status Priority Description
1 27.01.06 Open High Pressing Cancel on the login screen gives an error
2 02.01.06 Closed High Logo occasionally does not appear
3 01.02.06 Open High Search doesn't return any results when nothing is entered

Figure 3-44. The authorization scheme is still caching the old value.

If `brian` now clicks the Reset Auths button (which will call the `apex_util.reset_authorizations` routine), he is redirected back to the same page, and the authorization scheme value is reevaluated (having been invalidated by the call to `reset_authorizations`). Figure 3-45 shows that the Create button is now correctly displayed for the user.

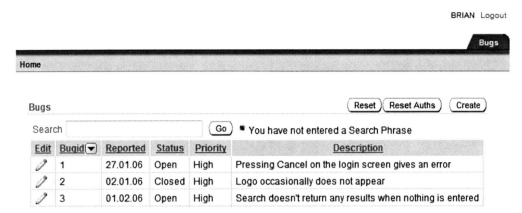

Figure 3-45. Calling apex_util.reset_authorizations forces the reevaluation.

Clearly, this is not a solution you'd use in your production applications, since it would be almost as inconvenient to have users click the Reset Auths button as it would to have them log out and then back in again.

However, you could make a call to the apex_util.reset_authorizations routine in other ways. It gives you many different alternatives to forcing the user to authenticate to the application again. For example, you could write a process that calls the reset_authorizations procedure only if *X* number of minutes have elapsed since the last time a call was made to it, or you could have a process that checks a table for a flag that determines whether the authorizations should be invalidated.

Summary

In this chapter, you learned about conditions and authorization schemes. Be sure that you understand the difference between the two. Use authorization schemes as a security mechanism to control access to different parts of your application. Use conditions to control the flow of processing, or to control the display of elements on a page when security is not an issue. For example, if you wish to display a certain button only on the first of the month, use a condition. But if you want to restrict access to that button to certain users, use an authorization scheme. Don't fall into the trap of enforcing security through conditions, because you might discover that your security is really an illusion. Review the section "Protecting Your Resources" if you have any doubts as to when to use conditions versus authorization schemes.

CHAPTER 4

Data Security

The previous chapter dealt with using conditional display and authorization schemes to control which data users can access and modify. However, even when you use both of these methods, users may still be able to gain access to data that they should not be able to view, or even worse, be able to modify or delete that data.

This chapter covers other methods, such as Session State Protection (SSP), you can use to help secure your application against potential misuse by a user (either intentionally or unintentionally). We will also look at using database features, such as Virtual Private Database (VPD), which is sometimes referred to as Fine-Grained Access Control (FGAC). Features such as VPD let you apply access controls at the database level, rather than at the application level.

URLs and Security

You will rarely need to construct URL syntax yourself, since APEX makes it easy to link to other pages and pass session information without manually constructing a URL. However, knowing exactly how a URL is built lets you see how someone could manipulate the URL to modify data or to access a part of your application he shouldn't be able to access.

Understanding the URL Syntax

One of the first things that users new to APEX often comment on is that the format of the URL seems a little untidy compared to other web development tools. For example, the following is a URL from the Buglist application:

```
http://127.0.0.1:8080/pls/apex/f?p=107:2:34396854152511::::P3_ID:2
```

At first glance, the URL seems difficult to decipher. However, the URL follows a structured syntax, which makes sense once you understand how it is constructed. The sample Buglist URL can be broken down into the following components:

`127.0.0.1`: The IP address of the server on which the web server is running. This could be a hostname instead.

`8080`: The port number on which the web server is listening.

`/pls`: Indicates that the request is to be handled by the `mod_plsql` handler.

`/apex`: The DAD name that you have specified in the configuration files. The DAD contains details about which database instance to connect to, as well as which user to connect as.

f?p=: Represents the core procedure that is called for APEX pages. The procedure is called f and contains a number of parameters. The sample URL passes only one parameter, called p.

107: The application ID that is being accessed.

2: The page number of the application.

34396854152511: The session number.

P3_ID: The name of a page item.
2: The value to which to set the associated page item.

The general format of the URL is as follows:

f?p=App:Page:Session:Request:Debug:ClearCache:itemNames:itemValues:PrinterFriendly

where:

App: The numeric application ID or alphanumeric application alias.

Page: The numeric page ID or alphanumeric page alias.

Session: The numeric session ID, which enables session state information to be maintained between page views by a user. The session ID can be referenced using the following syntax:

- Substitution string: &SESSION.

- PL/SQL: v('SESSION').

- Bind variable: :APP_SESSION.

Request: The value of the REQUEST session item, which can then be referenced during the accept phase of the page processing. For example, you can determine which button was pressed by referencing the value of REQUEST. You can reference REQUEST using the following syntax:

- Substitution string: &REQUEST.

- PL/SQL: v('REQUEST')

- Bind variable: :REQUEST

Debug: A flag to determine whether the page should be run in debug mode. It can be set to YES (to display the debugging details) or NO. You can reference the debug flag using the following syntax:

- Substitution string: &DEBUG.

- PL/SQL: v('DEBUG').

- Bind variable: :DEBUG.

ClearCache: Allows items in the session cache to be cleared (the values are set to NULL). The value depends on exactly what you wish to clear, such as:

- To clear cached items on an individual page, specify that page number.

- To clear cached items on multiple pages, specify the page numbers in a comma-separated format.

- To reset collections, specify individual collection names (or a comma-separated list of collection names).

- To reset the pagination on the requested page (if you wish to reset the pagination on a previously viewed report, for example), use the keyword RP.

- To clear the cache for all pages and all application items in the current application, use the keyword APP.

- To clear any items associated with all applications that have been used in the current session, use the keyword SESSION.

itemNames: A comma-separated list of item names that are used to set session state.

itemValues: A comma-separated list of item values that are used to set session state. These values are passed in the same order as the item names. You can't pass a value that includes a colon (since that would be parsed as a URL delimiter); you would need to escape the colon character or use an alternative character and then substitute it back for a colon in your code. You may pass a comma in the item value, but you must enclose the characters with backslashes, as in \Smith, Bob\.

PrinterFriendly: Specifies whether the page is being rendered in printer-friendly mode. If this value is set to YES, the page is rendered in printer-friendly mode. You can reference the value of PrinterFriendly in your page processing to determine which elements to display to make the page look better when printed.

Manipulating the URL

You might feel that the URL gives away too much information in the users' browser. In other words, since the URL displays some of the internal logic you're using (such as the item names), could malicious users exploit this to their advantage? The answer, unsurprisingly, is yes they could. As an example, let's take a look at the Buglist application again. Figure 4-1 shows the Update Bug screen.

▓ **Note** The part of the URL that specifies the port number (for example, port 8080) is easy to hide, as you will see in Chapter 15.

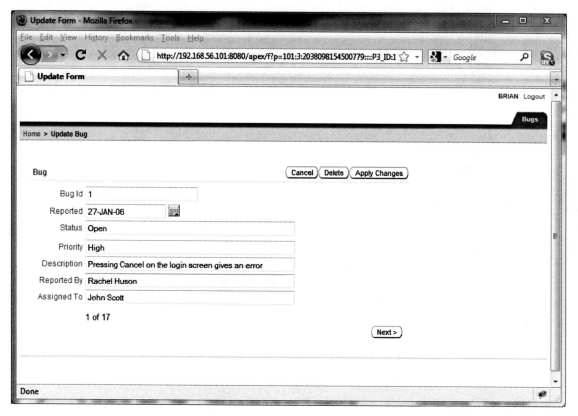

Figure 4-1. Updating a bug in the Buglist application

In this case, we're using the Embedded PL/SQL Gateway, so you don't see the /pls in the URL. Here's the URL that brought us to this page:

```
http://192.168.56.101:8080/apex/f?p=101:3:2038098154500779:::::P3_ID:1
```

Here, the itemNames parameter contains a single item (P3_ID), and the itemValues parameter contains a single value (1). In other words, when this page is called via that URL, the P3_ID page item will be set to a value of 1. The value of the P3_ID page item is used in the page to determine which record to retrieve and display to the user. Usually, you would want the user to go back to the previous page with the list of records and select a new one to edit. However, as you saw in the example of changing the page number in the URL in the previous chapter, it's possible for users to manipulate the URL directly. To test this with the P3_ID value, simply change the value of 1 to 2 and enter the new URL into the browser's address bar, as shown in Figure 4-2.

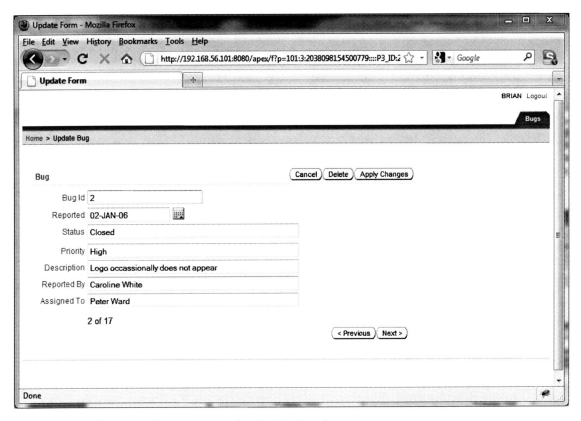

Figure 4-2. Modifying the URL directly to alter the P3_ID value

By manually setting the value of the P3_ID page item, you can retrieve a different record. In this example, URL manipulation lets you access records you were able to access anyway, so the fact that the user can modify the URL manually might not seem like all that big of a deal. However, if you make some changes to the Buglist application to make it a bit more realistic in terms of the different levels of data access that people might have, the potential issues related to URL manipulation should become a bit clearer.

First, instead of allowing the user to enter a free-format name into the Assigned To field, we'll make that field a list of people contained in the user_repository table. To do this, we'll create a new LOV that returns the list of users in the user_repository table, as shown in Figure 4-3. The query to use for the LOV is shown in Listing 4-1.

Figure 4-3. *Creating the LOV_USERS LOV*

Listing 4-1. *LOV Query to Return Usernames in the* user_repository *Table*

```
select
  initcap(forename) || ' ' || initcap(surname) as fullname,
  username as username
from
  user_repository
order by surname
```

■ **Note** Listing 4-1 uses the InitCap function here to format the forenames and surnames returned by the query. The InitCap function might not work nicely on all names (for example, the surname McMaster ends up being formatted as Mcmaster), so you probably want to take this into account in your own systems.

You can now change the P2_ASSIGNED_TO page item to be a select list, as shown in Figure 4-4, which is based on your new LOV, shown in Figure 4-5.

Figure 4-4. *Changing the* Assigned To *field to a select list*

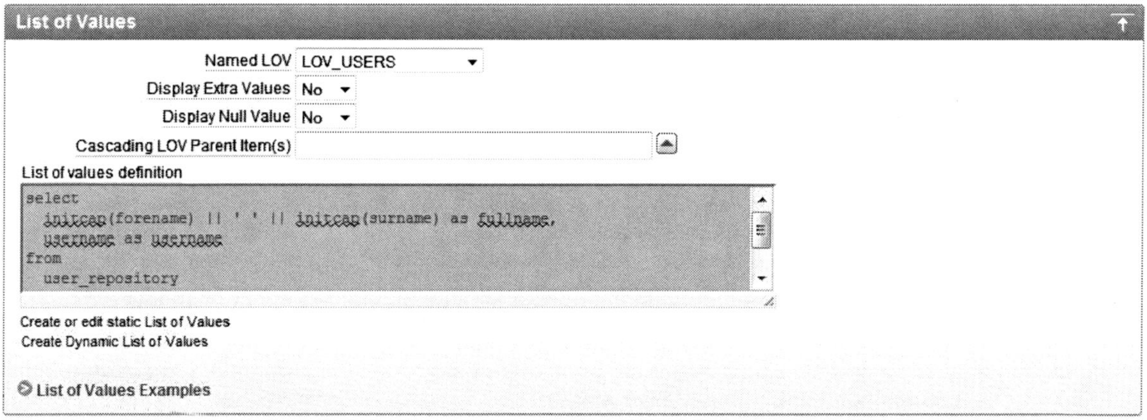

Figure 4-5. Basing the P3_ASSIGNED_TONAME page item on LOV_USERS

If you run the page again, you can see that the Assigned To field presents you with a list of users you can select from, as shown in Figure 4-6.

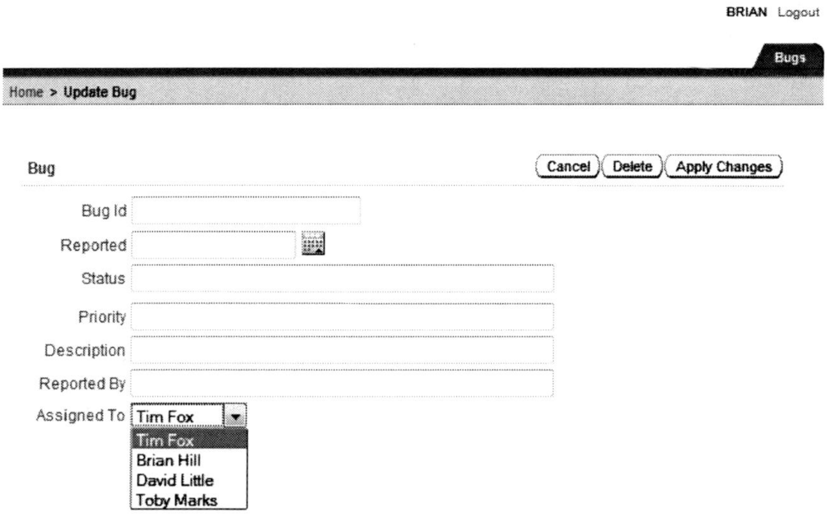

Figure 4-6. The list of users you can select from

The problem now is that in the buglist table, the assigned_toname field actually contains the old free-format text rather than the username from the LOV. Also, if you set a new Assigned To value from the Update Bug screen, the value shown in the report on the home page will be the username (see Figure 4-7), rather than the nicely formatted full name that appears in the select list. You could change the LOV so that it stores the nicely formatted name; however, you want it to store the username for a reason that will become clear in a moment.

Bugs   (Reset) (Reset Auths) (Create)

Search [   ] (Go) ■ You have not entered a Search Phrase [   ]

	Bug Id ▲	Reported	Status	Priority	Description	Reported By	Assigned To
✏	1	27-JAN-06	Open	High	Pressing Cancel on the login screen gives an error	Rachel Huson	John Scott
✏	2	02-JAN-06	Closed	High	Logo occassionally does not appear	Caroline White	Peter Ward
✏	3	01-FEB-06	Open	High	Search doesn't return any results when nothing is entered	Carl Watson	John Scott
✏	4	02-MAR-06	Open	Critical	Login doesn't work for user smithp	Laura Barnes	Mark Wilson
✏	5	02-MAR-06	Open	Low	Images don't look in the right positions	Lucy Scott	Steven Anderson
✏	6	02-MAY-06	Open	Medium	Pressing delete user gives permission denied error	Chris Donaldson	John Scott
✏	7	02-JUN-06	Open	High	Buttons don't work in firefox	Paul Mathews	Michael Stuart
✏	8	02-JUN-06	Closed	High	Pressing cancel on the login screen gives an error	Mark Lawson	Mark Wilson
✏	9	02-JUL-06	Open	High	Trying to add anew record gives an error	John Stevens	John Scott
✏	10	02-JUL-06	Open	Critical	The logout button doesn't close the browser	Steven Green	Steven Anderson
✏	11	02-AUG-06	Open	High	Javascript error on the profiles page	Mark Lawson	John Scott
✏	12	02-AUG-06	Open	Low	Text is too small on the home page	Carl Watson	John Scott
✏	13	02-SEP-06	Open	High	There is no way to tell who I'm logged in as	Caroline White	Paul Wilson
✏	14	02-SEP-06	Open	High	Customer details don't match the	Rachel Hudson	John Scott
✏	15	02-OCT-06	Open	Critical	Search results don't match the criteria	Laura Barnes	John Scott

Spread Sheet

row(s) 1 - 15 of 17 ▼ | Next ▶

Figure 4-7. Bug report showing the incorrect Assigned To value

You can display the correct value in the bug report by editing the Assigned To column in the report (the Column Attributes section of the report). Change the Display As field from Standard Report Column to "Display as Text (based on LOV, does not save state)," as shown in Figure 4-8, and then assign the LOV_USERS LOV that you created earlier.

Column Attributes   ⌃

Display As	Display as Text (based on LOV, does not save state) ▼
Number / Date Format	[ ] (▲)

Numeric format mask: 999G999G999G999G990
Graphical formatting for percentages, whole numbers between 0 and 100

Element Width	Number of Rows [ ]
Number of Columns (Radio Group)	[ ]
Element Attributes	[ ]
Element Option Attributes	[ ]

Figure 4-8. Changing the report Assigned To field to use the LOV

In the LOV attributes, set Display Extra Value to Yes, as shown in Figure 4-9. This means that the report will still display any names in the Assigned To column that don't also appear in the LOV. With this field set to No, the Assigned To column defaults to showing the first entry in the LOV, which is probably not desirable behavior in this case.

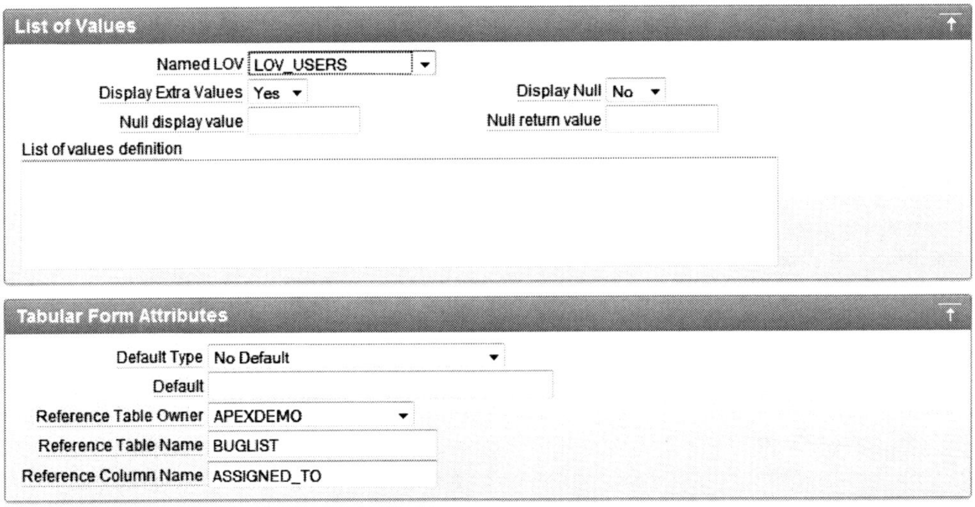

Figure 4-9. *Displaying values that don't appear in the LOV*

You have now changed the report so that it displays the full name of the user the record is assigned to (as it did before), while the Update Bug screen allows you to select a user from a list when assigning the bug. Now let's extend the example a bit more.

Suppose you want to implement a business rule that says that when users log in to the application, they can see only the bugs that are assigned to them. The exception is administrators, who are allowed to see all bugs. You can enforce this rule simply by modifying the query used for the report on the home page to take the logged-in username into account, as shown in Listing 4-2.

Listing 4-2. *Modified Report Query to Include Additional Restrictions*

```
select
  "ID",
  "BUGID",
  "REPORTED",
  "STATUS",
  "PRIORITY",
  "DESCRIPTION",
  "REPORTED_BY",
  "ASSIGNED_TO"
from
  "BUGLIST"
where
(
  instr(upper("STATUS"),
      upper(nvl(:P1_REPORT_SEARCH,"STATUS"))) > 0  or
  instr(upper("PRIORITY"),
      upper(nvl(:P1_REPORT_SEARCH,"PRIORITY"))) > 0  or
  instr(upper("DESCRIPTION"),
      upper(nvl(:P1_REPORT_SEARCH,"DESCRIPTION"))) > 0  or
```

145

```
instr(upper("REPORTED_BY"),
      upper(nvl(:P1_REPORT_SEARCH,"REPORTED_BY"))) > 0   or
instr(upper("ASSIGNED_TO"),
      upper(nvl(:P1_REPORT_SEARCH,"ASSIGNED_TO"))) > 0
) and (
  (upper(assigned_to) = :app_user)
  or
  exists (select 1 from user_repository
          where upper(username) = :app_user
          and admin = 'Y')
     )
```

Remember that the query in Listing 4-2 was generated by the application creation wizard. The reason for the references to instr is to allow the query to return the correct results if the user entered anything into the P1_REPORT_SEARCH field. You just need to add a where clause restriction, which checks if the uppercased ASSIGNED_TO column matches the currently logged-in username (remember that the :APP_USER bind variable will automatically be in uppercase, hence the need to uppercase the ASSIGNED_TO value). You also use an exists clause to check if the currently logged-in user is an administrator. If the logged-in user is an administrator, the query will return all records (that match the search criteria); otherwise, only records that are assigned to the user (and which match the search criteria) will be returned.

If you now run the application again while logged in as the user john (who is an administrator), you will see all the records. If you log in as the user brian (who is not an administrator), you will see only the records that have been assigned to that user, as shown in Figure 4-10.

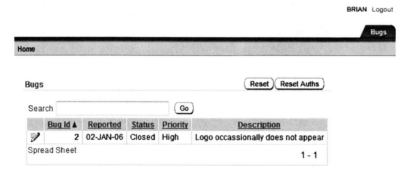

Figure 4-10. Report restricted to showing entries assigned to the logged-in user

So user brian can now see only the single record that has been assigned to him. If he chose to edit that record, he could actually assign it to someone else, and then he would not see any records in the report (until an administrator assigned some bugs to him). However, there is still a slight loophole in the Update Bug screen: the Next and Previous buttons allow the user to view records that aren't assigned to him. We could simply remove those buttons to solve that problem; however, for the moment, we will just ignore them.

The main point of this example is that it represents the way many people might implement security-access restrictions in their applications: restrict a set of records shown in a report and assume that any modification screens can be accessed only via a valid link from another screen. The flaw in this scheme is that knowledgeable users can manipulate the URL. For example, all brian needs to do is to change the link on the Update Bug screen and try setting the value of the P3_ID item to a different value, as shown in Figure 4-11. This user can completely bypass the restriction and access records assigned to other users. (The Assigned To field in Figure 4-11 shows Mark Wilson because it is pulling the record related to the value in the URL. This record is actually assigned to a user not listed in the LOV.

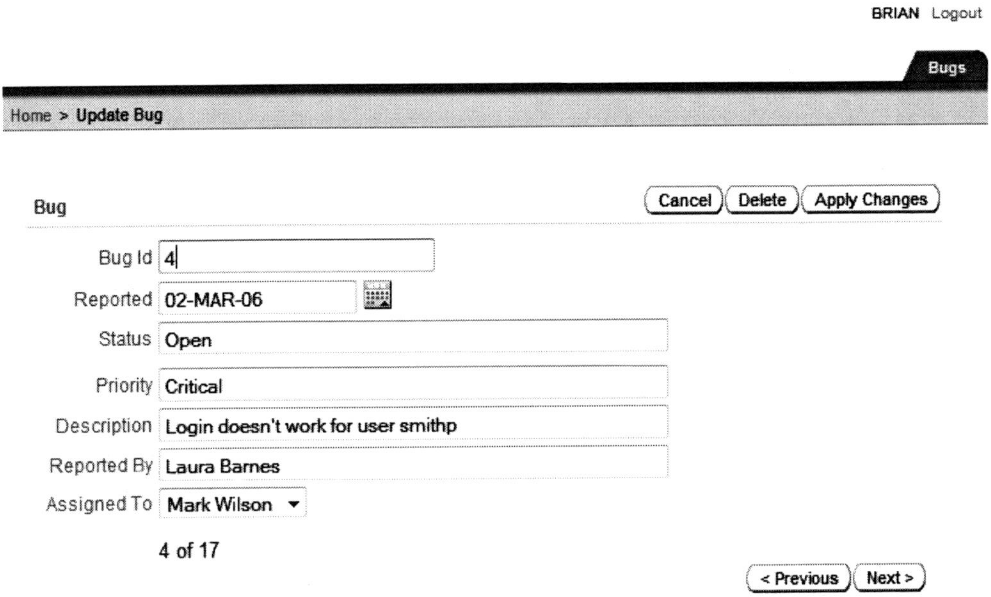

Figure 4-11. *URL manipulated to access other records*

You could just change the code you're using in the Update Bug screen to perform an additional check to determine whether the user should be able to access the record. While this could work, there is another way you can prevent this particular problem. This method is known as Session State Protection.

Session State Protection

Session State Protection (SSP) is a way of protecting the information stored in the user session from direct, unauthorized manipulation. In other words, you can detect whether a user has manipulated the URL in an attempt to access or modify a particular session item.

The default when you create a new application is for SSP to be disabled. When you enable SSP, the URLs that are used to navigate between pages in your application will also include checksums to prevent tampering with item values in session state.

There are very few reasons, other than for the simplest demonstration applications, why you wouldn't enable SSP in your applications, particularly if an application is going to be used to access confidential or valuable data. Using SSP is an extremely powerful way to protect your application against malicious (or even accidental) URL manipulation. As you will see, even just accepting the defaults provided by the wizard makes your application far more secure and resistant to manipulation. You should consider SSP, along with authentication and authorization schemes, as part of your core defenses in securing your application and data.

To take advantage of SSP, you need to enable the feature in your application, and then define which page and items you want to protect. You can define SSP against pages, page items, and application items.

Enabling Session State Protection

You can access the SSP settings for your application either via the Security Attributes section of the Application Attributes, as shown in Figure 4-12, or via the Session State Protection section of the Shared Components for your application, as shown in Figure 4-13. Clicking the Manage Session State Protection button in the Security Attributes section takes you to the same screen as the Shared Components Session State Protection screen (Figure 4-13). Here, you can access the SSP settings for particular pages, items, and application items directly, or you can access them via a wizard by clicking the Set Protection button.

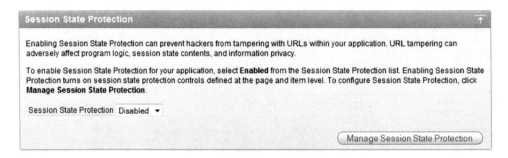

Figure 4-12. Accessing SSP from the Application Security Attributes

Figure 4-13. Accessing SSP from Shared Components

To enable SSP, click the Set Protection button. This takes you to the screen shown in Figure 4-14. From here, you can choose to disable, enable, or configure SSP. Choose Enable, and then confirm that choice, as shown in Figure 4-15.

Figure 4-14. Using the SSP wizard

Figure 4-15. Enabling SSP via the wizard

Well, that was quick and painless! So what has it done? If you log in again as brian and manipulate the URL on the Update Bug screen, you will see that you are still able to access records that user should not be able to access. This is because although you have enabled SSP, you haven't yet specified which items you want protected.

Configuring Session State Protection

To configure SSP, choose Configure in the wizard. You will see the screen shown in Figure 4-16.

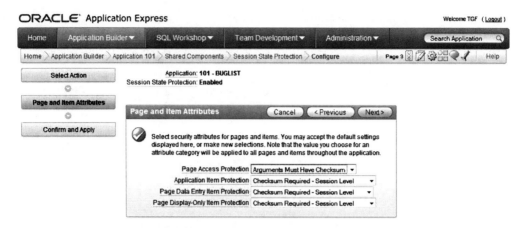

Figure 4-16. *Configuring SSP via the wizard*

This page allows you to define settings for page and item attributes. For now, just accept the default settings and apply the settings in the wizard.

Now the interesting part! Run the test as before (log in to the application as user brian and try to manipulate the URL on the Update Bug screen). Rather than being able to see records that you shouldn't be able to access, you will see a screen similar to Figure 4-17.

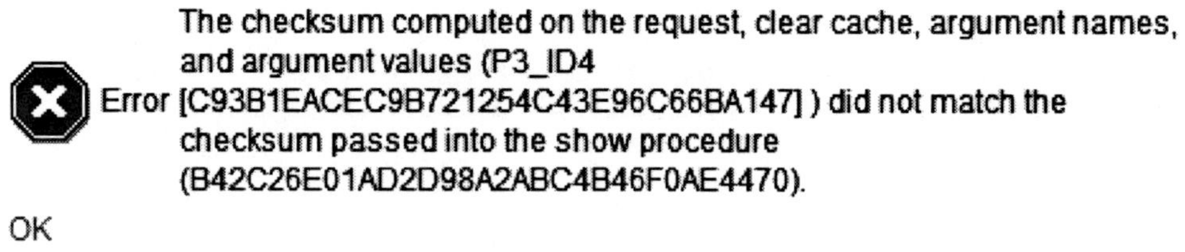

The checksum computed on the request, clear cache, argument names, and argument values (P3_ID4

Error [C93B1EACEC9B721254C43E96C66BA147]) did not match the checksum passed into the show procedure (B42C26E01AD2D98A2ABC4B46F0AE4470).

OK

Figure 4-17. *SSP issuing an error*

So what has happened here? If you examine the URL that was used, you'll see that an additional parameter has been added (the session ID is shortened to 123 here just for readability of the example):

```
f?p=101:3:10418706087826::::P3_ID:2&cs=3B42C26E01AD2D98A2ABC4B46F0AE4470
```

The cs parameter is the checksum, which is calculated based on the items and values that have been set by the application when building the URL. This checksum is then recalculated when the new page is being processed, and if the recalculated checksum does not match the checksum passed in the URL, an error is raised.

So, with very little effort, you have prevented users from being able to modify the URL to access records they shouldn't be able to access.

If you look back at the settings that were made for your application by the SSP wizard, you'll see that for the Update Bug screen, each page item is set to Checksum Required – Session Level, as shown in Figure 4-18. Therefore, when the user tries to modify the value of the P3_ID page item, which is protected by a checksum, the SSP functionality kicks in and issues the error you saw.

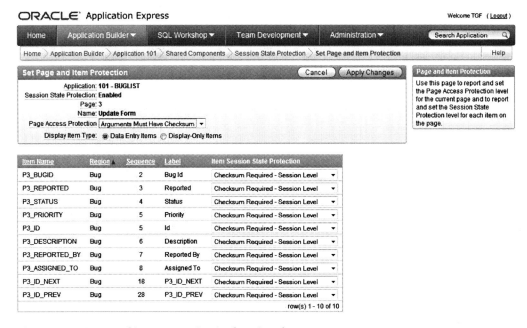

Figure 4-18. Page and item protection in the wizard

Now that you've seen how to protect your application from URL manipulation by using the defaults in the wizard, let's look at the four attribute categories you can protect with SSP:

- Page access

- Application item

- Page data entry item

- Page display-only item

Page Access Protection

Page access protection allows you to define SSP values for pages. You can select from the following values:

Unrestricted: The page can be requested directly using a URL, either with or without session state arguments (such as page items and values, cache clearing, and so on).

Arguments Must Have Checksum: If any arguments are passed in the URL, a corresponding checksum must also be provided.

No Arguments Allowed: The page can be requested via a URL, but no request, clear cache, or page item and values are allowed in the URL.

No URL Access: The page can't be accessed directly using a URL. The page may be accessed only as the target of a page branch, which does not perform a URL redirect.

In the example, the Update Bug screen was set to use Arguments Must Have Checksum; however, you can see how using the No Arguments Allowed or No URL Access settings could be extremely useful. For example, if you have a page in your application that you don't want users to be able to access directly—it should be accessible only via a page branch from another page—you could use the No URL Access setting for that particular page.

Application Item Protection

Application item protection allows you to define SSP values for application items. You can choose from the following values:

Unrestricted: The session state for the application item can be set by passing the item name and value via the URL or by posting it via a form. No checksum is passed in the URL.

Restricted: The session state for the application item may not be set from the browser. The session state for the application item can't be set via the URL or by being posted via a form. The only way to set the item value is through internal processes, computations, and so on. This is applicable only to items that can't be used as data-entry items and is always active, even if SSP is disabled. This setting can be used for application items and for pages items with any of the Display As types, such as the following:

- Display as Text (escape special characters, does not save state)

- Display as Text (does not save state)

- Display as Text (based on LOV, does not save state)

- Display as Text (based on PLSQL, does not save state)

- Text Field (Disabled, does not save state)

- Stop and Start HTML Table (Display label only)

Checksum Required – Application Level: The application item may be set via the URL only if the item name and value are accompanied by a checksum that is specific to the workspace and application; however, a user-level checksum or session-level checksum will also enable the application item to be set. This should be used when you want the item to be set via the URL by any user running the same application in the same workspace but using different sessions.

Checksum Required – User Level: Similar to the Application Level checksum in that the application item may be set via the URL as long as a checksum accompanies the item name and value; however, the checksum needs to be specific to the workspace, application, and user. A session-level checksum will also work, but an application-level checksum will not work. This should be used when you want to allow the item to be set via the URL where the checksum was generated by the same user running the same application in the same workspace but in a different session.

Checksum Required – Session Level: Similar to the User Level checksum in that the application item may be set via the URL only if a checksum accompanies the item name and value; however, the checksum must be specific to the current session. This should be used when you wish to allow the application item to be set by URLs only when the checksum was generated in the same session.

Which value to select for application-item protection depends on your particular situation. Many times, you may find that the default of using Checksum Required – Session Level is sufficient for your needs.

Page Data Entry Item Protection

Page data entry item protection allows you to define SSP values for page items that are used for data entry. The following values are available:

Unrestricted: The session state for the page item may be set by passing the item name and value via the URL or by being posted via a form. No checksum is required in the URL.

Checksum Required – Application Level: The session state for the page item can be set via the URL as long as the item name and value are accompanied by a checksum that is specific to the workspace and application. A user-level checksum or session-level checksum is also sufficient. This should be used when you want to allow the page item to be set by URLs that include a checksum generated by any user running the same application in the same workspace but in a different session.

Checksum Required – User Level: The session state for the page item can be set via the URL as long as the item name and value are accompanied by a checksum that is specific to the workspace, application, and user. A session-level checksum will also be sufficient. This should be used when you want to allow the page item to be set via a URL that includes a checksum that was generated by the same user running the same application in the same workspace but in a different session.

Checksum Required – Session Level: The session state for the page item can be set via the URL as long as the item name and value are accompanied by a checksum that is specific to the current session. This should be used when you want to allow the item to be set only by a URL that includes a checksum generated within the same session.

Page Display-Only Item Protection

Page display-only item protection allows you to define SSP values for page items that are used for display-only purposes. You can set the following values:

Unrestricted: The session state for the page item may be set by passing the item name and value via the URL or by being posted via a form. No checksum is required in the URL.

Restricted: The session state for the page item may not be set from browser, or via the URL or by being posted from a form. This should be used when you wish to prevent the page item from being set by anything other than internal processes, computations, and so on. This is always active, even if SSP is disabled. This can be used for any of the following Display As types:

- Display as Text (escape special characters, does not save state)
- Display as Text (does not save state)

- Display as Text (based on LOV, does not save state)

- Display as Text (based on PLSQL, does not save state)

- Text Field (Disabled, does not save state)

- Stop and Start HTML Table (Displays label only)

Checksum Required – Application Level: The session state for the page item may be set via the URL only if the item name and value are accompanied by a checksum that is specific to the workspace and application. A user-level or session-level checksum will also be sufficient. This should be used when you wish to allow the page item to be set by URLs that have a checksum that is generated by any user running the same application in the current workspace but in a different session.

Checksum Required – User Level: The session state for the page item may be set via the URL only if the item name and value are accompanied by a checksum that is specific to the workspace, application, and user. A session-level checksum will also be sufficient. You should use this when you want to allow the page item to be set via URLs that have a checksum that is generated by the same user running the same application in the same workspace but in a different session.

Checksum Required – Session Level: The session state for the page item may be set via the URL only if the item name and value are accompanied by a checksum that is specific to the current session. You should use this when you want to allow the page item to be set via URLs that have a checksum that was generated in the same session.

A Note About Bookmarks

You might be wondering how using SSP will affect users who have bookmarked a link to your application. The following situations apply:

- Any bookmarked links created after SSP was enabled will work if the bookmarked link contains a checksum.

- Any bookmarked links created before SSP was enabled will not work if the bookmarked link contains a checksum.

- SSP will not affect any bookmarks that do not contain checksums or that contain unnecessary checksums. The validity of the bookmarks will be determined by other criteria.

You can expire any bookmarks created before SSP was enabled, or expire any bookmarked URLs that contain previously generated checksums, by using the Expire Bookmarks button in the Session State Protection section of the application Security Attributes page.

Virtual Private Database

One of the benefits of using APEX to design and implement your applications is that you can implement access control policies at the database level rather than at the application level. If you are using the Enterprise Edition of the database, you can use the Virtual Private Database (VPD) feature (also known as Fine Grained Access Control, or FGAC).

In essence, VPD enables queries to be rewritten on the fly to include additional predicate information. The additional predicate information is determined from a security policy that you implement as a PL/SQL function; the function returns the additional predicate logic to be used in the where clause of the query. The security policy is then registered against the tables you wish to protect with VPD.

So why would you want to use this feature? Here are several reasons:

- It helps you separate security logic from application logic. By putting the security logic into the database, rather than in the application, you centralize the logic of how the underlying data should be accessed. This centralized logic can then easily be shared among different applications without you having to code additional logic into each application. In other words, since the security logic is implemented at the database level, it will occur transparently as far as the applications are concerned; users will be able to access only the data they are allowed to access.

- It increases the degree to which you can audit the data changes within your application. By using VPD, you can have a security policy (or set of policies) that present different views of the data depending on the logged-in user.

- It makes it far easier to incorporate changes to your security logic. Rather than needing to change your logic in multiple places in multiple applications, you just need to modify it at the database level (or, rather, in your security policy function).

- It can protect the data regardless of the method of access. In other words, if you implemented all of your security logic in your APEX application, you would also need to duplicate that logic in any Java applications that access the same data. Similarly, someone could just connect using SQL*Plus and modify the data directly, thereby circumventing the security logic of your application. By using the VPD functionality, you can protect the data no matter what application someone uses to connect to the database.

- It allows for easier maintenance. By using centralized security policies, which you can apply to many different tables, you decrease the amount of duplicate code you need to write and also make it far easier to modify that code later.

The point about protecting the data regardless of the method of access is a very important one. It's surprisingly common for people to modify data directly using tools such as SQL*Plus and TOAD, rather than using the in-house applications that were built specifically for the purpose. Using such tools circumvents any application, business, and security logic you've implemented in your application. By implementing as much logic as you can in the database, rather than in the application, no matter how a user modifies the data, you can still enforce the checks at the database level.

Implementing VPD

In the Buglist application, the list of bugs shown in the report is currently restricted by specifically including a where clause restriction in the query used in the report (see Listing 4-2). The query includes the predicate:

```
and (
    (upper(assigned_to) = :app_user)
    or
    exists (select 1 from user_repository
```

```
    where upper(username) = :app_user
    and admin = 'Y')
```

Imagine that a number of different applications—some written in APEX and others written in languages such as Java—query and operate on the data in this table. Each application that accesses the data in that table would also need to incorporate the same predicate; otherwise, the security logic would not be equivalent across all the different applications. Also, if you wanted to change the way the security logic was implemented, you would need to change it in each query in each application.

To demonstrate the point, let's create a new database user and give that user permission to select the data from the buglist table (the table queried in the report). Name the new database user brian, so that you can compare what happens when brian logs in to the Buglist application and runs the report versus what he can see when he logs in to the database as the brian user using SQL*Plus. As shown in Listing 4-3, create the brian user, then grant him create session permission so he can connect to the database and select permission on the buglist table in the APEXDEMO schema.

Listing 4-3. Creating the brian Database User

```
sys@DBTEST> create user brian identified by ardvark

  2  default tablespace users
  3  temporary tablespace temp;

User created.
sys@DBTEST> grant create session to brian;

Grant succeeded.
sys@DBTEST> grant select on apexdemo.buglist to brian;

Grant succeeded.
```

Now, using SQL*Plus, connect to the database as the brian user and query the buglist table.

```
brian@DBTEST> select count(*) from apexdemo.buglist;

  COUNT(*)
----------
        18
```

As you can see, brian can see every record in the table. However, you actually want him to be able to see only the records that have been assigned to him. To make that happen, you need to define your policy function.

Defining the Policy Function

The policy function needs to accept two VARCHAR parameters: one for the schema owner and the other for the object name. The function also needs to return a VARCHAR string, which is the string to be used in the new predicate. The function prototype should look like this:

```
function policy_function_name(owner in varchar2,
  object_name in varchar2) return varchar2
```

If you again connect as the APEXDEMO user in SQL*Plus (since you are protecting the data in that schema), you can create a simple function that returns the string you need, as shown in Listing 4-4.

Listing 4-4. Creating the Policy Function

```
apexdemo@DBTEST> create or replace function vpd_buglist(
  2     p_schema in varchar2 default null,
  3     p_object in varchar2 default null)
  4        return varchar2 as
  5   begin
  6     return '(
  7        upper(assigned_to) = nvl(v(''APP_USER''), USER)
  8        or
  9        exists (select 1 from user_repository
 10          where upper(username) = nvl(v(''APP_USER''), USER)
 11          and admin = ''Y''))';
 11   end;
 12   /
```

```
Function created.
```

This function simply returns a string, but notice that you must change the string slightly from the string you used in the original report query: instead of using :APP_USER to determine the username, you use nvl(v('APP_USER', USER). This is because :APP_USER will return only the username when the user has connected to the database via the APEX application. For the policy function to correctly determine the username when the user is connected via SQL*Plus (or some other application where the user connects as a database user), you need to use the USER function. The nvl(v('APP_USER'), USER) determines if the v('APP_USER') is a non-null value; that is, the user is connected via an APEX application. If so, you use the value returned by v('APP_USER'). If not, you use the value returned by USER.

Now that you've defined your policy function, you need to apply it to the buglist table, using the DBMS_RLS package. You use DBMS_RLS to link the policy you just defined to a particular schema object. First, grant the execute permission on DBMS_RLS to the APEXDEMO user:

```
sys@DBTEST> grant execute on dbms_rls to apexdemo;
```

```
Grant succeeded.
```

Next, connect again as the APEXDEMO user and add the policy against the buglist table, as shown in Listing 4-5.

Listing 4-5. Applying the Policy Using DBMS_RLS

```
apexdemo@DBTEST> begin
  2    dbms_rls.add_policy(
  3       object_schema => 'apexdemo',
  4       object_name => 'buglist',
  5       policy_name => 'Buglist Policy',
  6       function_schema => 'apexdemo',
  7       policy_function => 'vpd_buglist',
  8       statement_types => 'select');
  9  end;
 10  /

PL/SQL procedure successfully completed.
```

You apply the policy using the DBMS_RLS.ADD_POLICY procedure, which accepts a number of different parameters that allow you to define the schema and object name to which you wish to apply the policy, as well as the schema and function you wish to apply. Note that in this example, for simplicity, the policy function is defined in the same schema that contains the objects we're trying to protect. In practice, this is not recommended, as explained in the "VPD Best Practices" section later in this chapter. It's better and safer to define your policy functions in schemas separate from your data.

■ **Note** The RLS in DBMS_RLS stands for Row Level Security, which is where VPD and FGAC evolved from. You will often hear people referring to RLS, VPD, and FGAC interchangeably. All three acronyms essentially refer to the same sort of technique.

Now when you reconnect to the database as brian using SQL*Plus and query the buglist table in the APEXDEMO schema, you will see something interesting:

```
brian@DBTEST> select count(*) from apexdemo.buglist;

  COUNT(*)
----------
         1
```

You can see only one record now. To confirm that you're actually seeing records assigned to brian, select some columns from the table:

```
brian@DBTEST> select id, bugid, reported, status, assigned_to
  2    from apexdemo.buglist;
```

```
ID    BUGID REPORTED   STATUS          ASSIGNED_TO
----- ------ ---------  --------------- ----------------
  2        2 01-FEB-06 Open            brian
```

So, the policy function is being applied correctly if you connect via SQL*Plus. What about when you log in via your APEX application? Before trying that, you need to remove the predicate from the report query, as shown in Figure 4-19. Otherwise, you'll end up applying the predicate twice: once as part of the query and once due to the policy.

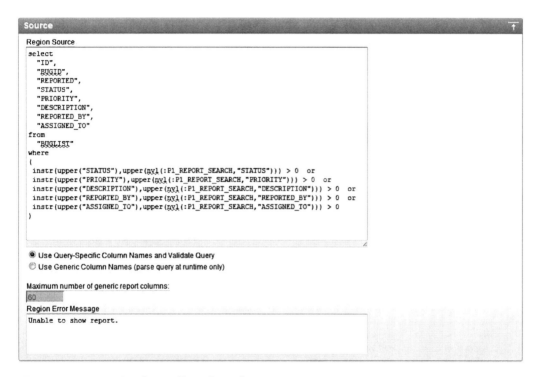

Figure 4-19. Removing the predicate from the report query

If you now run the application again and connect as the brian user (remember this is not the same as connecting as the brian database user), you see that the VPD policy is still being applied correctly, as shown in Figure 4-20.

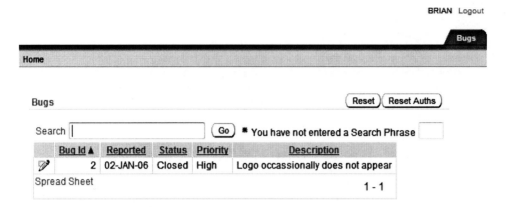

Figure 4-20. The VPD policy working through the application

Now connect to your application as the user john, who is an administrator. You will be able to view all of the records, as shown in Figure 4-21.

Figure 4-21. The application administrator can still see all the records.

If you edit one of these records and assign it to the brian user and then return to your SQL*Plus session and query the buglist table again, you will see that the new record is available:

```
brian@DBTEST> select id, bugid, reported, status, assigned_to

2    from apexdemo.buglist;

  ID  BUGID REPORTED  STATUS   ASSIGNED_TO
---- ------ --------- -------- ------------------------------
   2      2 02-JAN-06 Closed   brian
  11     11 02-AUG-06 Open     brian
```

So, no matter which application you use to modify the data, your policy function makes sure that other applications connected as that user see the correct data.

Closing the Loopholes

When you applied your policy function (Listing 4-5) to the table, you set the statement_types parameter to select. This means that the policy function will be applied only when a select statement is performed against the table. Since you granted only select permission to the brian user, that isn't an issue. But what would happen if brian also had delete and update permissions on the buglist table:

```
apexdemo@DBTEST> grant update, delete on buglist to brian;


Grant succeeded.
```

You can now connect as brian and see what happens when you try to delete a record from the buglist table:

```
brian@DBTEST> select count(*) from apexdemo.buglist;

  COUNT(*)
----------
         2

brian@DBTEST> delete from apexdemo.buglist;
18 rows deleted.

brian@DBTEST> select count(*) from apexdemo.buglist;
  COUNT(*)
----------
         0

brian@DBTEST> rollback;
Rollback complete.

brian@DBTEST> select count(*) from apexdemo.buglist;
  COUNT(*)
----------
         2
```

Well, clearly there's a bit of a problem here. brian is able to view only the 2 records assigned to him, which is correct; however, he is able to delete all 18 records in the table. Similarly, brian would be able to update all 18 records rather than just the 2 records assigned to him.

Fortunately, this loophole in permissions is easy to close. You can use the same policy function you created earlier and apply it to all select, update, and delete statements against the buglist table.

First, drop the existing policy, as shown in Listing 4-6.

Listing 4-6. Dropping the Existing Policy

```
apexdemo@DBTEST> begin
  2    dbms_rls.drop_policy(
  3      object_schema => 'apexdemo',
  4      object_name => 'buglist',
  5      policy_name => 'Buglist Policy');
  6  end;
  7  /

PL/SQL procedure successfully completed.
```

Then create the new policy against select, update, and delete statements, as shown in Listing 4-7.

Listing 4-7. Creating a New Select, Update, and Delete Policy

```
apexdemo@DBTEST> begin
  2    dbms_rls.add_policy(
  3      object_schema => 'apexdemo',
  4      object_name => 'buglist',
  5      policy_name => 'Buglist Policy',
  6      function_schema => 'apexdemo',
  7      policy_function => 'vpd_buglist',
  8      statement_types => 'select, update, delete');
  9  end;
 10  /

PL/SQL procedure successfully completed.
```

■ **Note** Instead of dropping the old policy and creating a new policy with the new statement_types parameter values, you could just create a new policy for the update and delete statements, or even create a separate policy for each type of operation. However, it's quite rare to want to give users different views of the data depending on whether they're performing an update, insert, select, or delete operation, so generally it's better to define a single policy that covers multiple statement types where appropriate.

You can now repeat the earlier experiment with the `brian` user and try to delete all the records from the `buglist` table:

```
brian@DBTEST> select count(*) from apexdemo.buglist;

  COUNT(*)
----------
         2

brian@DBTEST> delete from apexdemo.buglist;
2 rows deleted.

brian @DBTEST> rollback;
Rollback complete.

brian @DBTEST> update apexdemo.buglist set assigned_to = null;
2 rows updated.

brian @DBTEST> rollback;
Rollback complete.

brian @DBTEST> select count(*) from apexdemo.buglist;
  COUNT(*)
----------
         2
```

With the policy now also in effect against `update` and `delete` statements, the users have a unified view of the data and can perform Data Manipulation Language (DML) statements only against records that have been assigned to them. You could use a similar policy to control the inserts that a user is able to perform against the `buglist` table.

This policy is also being applied to the `APEXDEMO` user. If you connect as the `APEXDEMO` user and try to query the table, you will see this:

```
apexdemo@DBTEST> select count(*) from buglist;

  COUNT(*)
----------
         0
```

This is due to the fact that no records are assigned to the `APEXDEMO` user. If you want the `APEXDEMO` user to still be able to see all of the records, you can adapt the policy function to take this into account, as shown in Listing 4-8.

Listing 4-8. *Modified Policy to Take the* APEXDEMO *User into Account*

```
apexdemo@DBTEST> create or replace function vpd_buglist(
  2      p_schema in varchar2 default null,
  3      p_object in varchar2 default null)
  4        return varchar2 as
  5   begin
  6      if (USER = 'APEXDEMO') and (v('APP_USER') is null) then
  7        return '';
  8      else
  9      return '(
 10        upper(assigned_to) = nvl(v(''APP_USER''), USER)
 11        or
 12        exists (select 1 from user_repository
 13          where upper(username) = nvl(v(''APP_USER''), USER)
 14          and admin = ''Y''))';
 15      end if;
 16   end;
 17   /
```

Listing 4-8 just adds a check to determine if you're connected as the Oracle user APEXDEMO (and you're not running through the APEX application). If so, an empty string is returned to the predicate; that is, you will be able to see all of the records.

With just a few simple steps, you have restricted access to the data that a user is able to view and modify. Using VPD where appropriate can drastically simplify your application design and make it easier to maintain and evolve the security logic against all applications accessing a particular set of data.

Using Contexts with VPD

You have seen how you can easily create a policy function based on the username, since you can use nvl(v('APP_USER'), USER) to determine the username, regardless of how the user was connected to the database. But what if you want to use some other criteria? How could you do that so it would work in APEX, SQL*Plus, any Java applications, and so on? The answer lies in using *application contexts*, which allow you to set custom information linked to a particular session that can then be used in the VPD policy.

There are two types of contexts:

Application context: This type of context is private to a particular session and will expire once the session ends. An application context is useful in a stateless environment, where the session state needs to be reestablished each time the session reconnects. Application contexts are stored in the User Global Area (UGA).

Global application context: This sort of context can be shared across different sessions and will still exist after the session has ended. A global application context is not session-based and therefore allows you to maintain state information across multiple sessions. Global application contexts are stored in the System Global Area (SGA).

■ **Note** The difference between the two types of contexts can appear subtle at first; however, they both have their uses. For more information, refer to the "Implementing Application Context and Fine-Grained Access Control" section of the *Oracle Database Security Guide*.

Creating and Setting Application Contexts

When you use a tool such as SQL*Plus, you are already using contexts, because some have been set for you. For example, you can run the following query:

```
apexdemo@DBTEST> select sys_context('USERENV', 'SESSION_USER')

  2  from dual;

SYS_CONTEXT('USERENV','SESSION_USER')
----------------------------------------------
APEXDEMO
```

Here, you use the sys_context function to access the value of SESSION_USER parameter within the USERENV context namespace.

Other values are available within the USERENV namespace. Here's an example:

```
apexdemo@DBTEST> select sys_context('USERENV', 'MODULE')

  2  from dual;

SYS_CONTEXT('USERENV','MODULE')
----------------------------------------------
SQL*Plus
```

Querying the USERENV context namespace again, you retrieve the value of the MODULE parameter, which is set to the name of the application you are using to access the database—SQL*Plus, in this case.

By creating your own application context, you can set a parameter to a particular value and then reference that value in your VPD policy function. Listing 4-9 demonstrates creating an application context.

Listing 4-9. Creating an Application Context

```
apexdemo@DBTEST> create or replace context vpd_context

  2  using vpd_context_procedure;

Context created.
```

This creates the application context and binds it to a procedure called vpd_context_procedure, which we have yet to write. By binding the context to this procedure, you are effectively saying that only the vpd_context_procedure will be allowed to set values in the context. If you allowed anyone to modify the values stored in the context, they would be able to easily circumvent any logic that you use in your

VPD policy. The purpose of tying the context to a particular procedure is to ensure that the values set in the context can come from only your procedure.

As an example, let's extend the VPD policy so that users see only the bug records assigned to them (unless they are an administrator) *and* only those records in a particular state: Open or Closed.

First, create the vpd_context_procedure procedure, which will be used to set the context, as shown in Listing 4-10.

***Listing 4-10.** Creating the Procedure to Set the Context*

```
apexdemo@DBTEST> create or replace

  2  procedure vpd_context_procedure(
  3    p_status in varchar2 default null)
  4  as
  5    begin
  6      dbms_session.set_context('VPD_CONTEXT',
  7                               'STATUS',
  8                               p_status);
  9  end;
 10  /
```

This procedure accepts a single parameter, p_status. Then, in the dbms_session.set_context procedure, it sets the value of the STATUS parameter in the VPD_CONTEXT context to the value passed into the p_status parameter.

■ **Note** If you don't already have execute permission on the DBMS_SESSION package, you'll need to grant that permission before you are able to use the set_context packaged procedure.

You can now check that the vpd_context_procedure is successfully setting the context, as shown in Listing 4-11.

***Listing 4-11.** Verifying the Procedure Sets the Context Correctly*

```
apexdemo@DBTEST> select sys_context('VPD_CONTEXT', 'STATUS')

2  from dual;
SYS_CONTEXT('VPD_CONTEXT','STATUS')
--------------------------------------------

apexdemo@DBTEST> exec vpd_context_procedure(p_status => 'Open');
PL/SQL procedure successfully completed.
```

```
apexdemo@DBTEST> select sys_context('VPD_CONTEXT', 'STATUS')
2  from dual;
SYS_CONTEXT('VPD_CONTEXT','STATUS')
-------------------------------------------
Open
```

First, you query the value of the STATUS parameter in the VPD_CONTEXT context using the sys_context function to check that the context isn't set yet. Next, you call the vpd_context_procedure and pass in a string parameter. Then you query the STATUS parameter again and see that the context has been successfully set.

If you now disconnect from SQL*Plus, reconnect as the APEXDEMO user, and then run the query to check the value of the STATUS parameter in the VPD_CONTEXT, you will find that the value is empty. This is because the context was cleared when you terminated the session.

Now you can rewrite the VPD policy function to use the value that was set in the context, as shown in Listing 4-12.

Listing 4-12. Modified Policy Function to Use the Context Value

```
1  create or replace function vpd_buglist(
2      p_schema in varchar2 default null,
3      p_object in varchar2 default null)
4      return varchar2 as
5      begin
6        if (USER = 'APEXDEMO') and (v('APP_USER') is null) then
7          return '';
8        else
9          return '(
10            upper(assigned_to) = nvl(v(''APP_USER''), USER)
11            or
12            exists (select 1 from user_repository
13              where upper(username) = nvl(v(''APP_USER''), USER)
14              and admin = ''Y''))
15                and upper(status) =
16                  sys_context(''VPD_CONTEXT'', ''STATUS'')';
17        end if;
18      end;
```

```
Function created.
```

All you have done here is add an extra part to the predicate that compares the status column in the buglist table against the value stored in the STATUS parameter of the VPD_CONTEXT.

In order to try out the new policy function while connected as the brian user in SQL*Plus, you first need to grant execute rights on the vpd_context_procedure to brian:

```
apexdemo@DBTEST> grant execute on vpd_buglist to brian;
```

Now you can query the buglist table while connected as brian, and then set the application context and query the table again, as shown in Listing 4-13.

Listing 4-13. Using the Context Procedure to Affect the Policy

```
brian@DBTEST> exec apexdemo.vpd_context_procedure('Open');

PL/SQL procedure successfully completed.

brian@DBTEST> select count(*) from apexdemo.buglist;
  COUNT(*)
----------
         2

brian@DBTEST> exec apexdemo.vpd_context_procedure('Closed');
PL/SQL procedure successfully completed.

brian@DBTEST> select count(*) from apexdemo.buglist;
  COUNT(*)
----------
         0
```

If you use the vpd_context_procedure to set the STATUS parameter to a value of Open or Closed, that value will be used in the policy function and will affect the view of the data that the user is able to access.

Using Application Contexts in an APEX Environment

You have seen how you can use application contexts to influence the rules that are enforced by a VPD policy function. When you wish to use application contexts within the APEX environment, you need to be aware of an important factor:

The application context is valid only for the duration that the session is alive.

The architecture of the APEX environment is that the connection to the database is achieved through the use of the mod_plsql connection pooling. You therefore have no guarantee that the database session that was used to process your last page request will be the same database session that is used to perform your next page request. APEX (and mod_plsql) ensures that the session and state information are set up correctly for each of your page requests, whether or not you get the same underlying database session connection. However, reestablishing custom application contexts is not handled for you automatically, so you will need to make provisions to handle those yourself.

The easiest way to do this is to have a custom PL/SQL page process, or an application process that sets the value of the context on each page request. For example, in the Buglist application, you can change the report page so that it runs an anonymous PL/SQL block as a before header process, as shown in Figure 4-22, which simply executes the vpd_context_procedure and sets the parameter to Open. This way, the application context will be set to Open each time the page is executed.

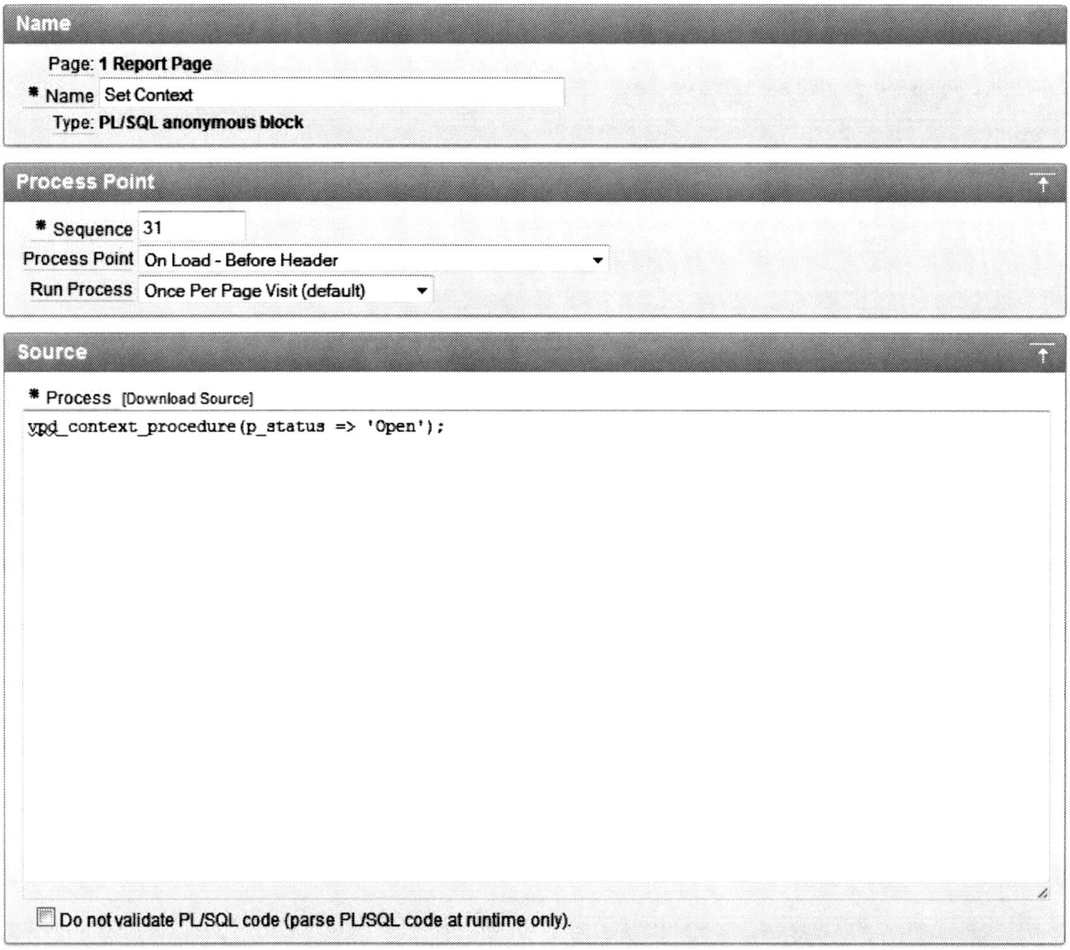

Name

Page: **1 Report Page**
* Name Set Context
Type: **PL/SQL anonymous block**

Process Point

* Sequence 31
Process Point On Load - Before Header
Run Process Once Per Page Visit (default)

Source

* Process [Download Source]

```
vpd_context_procedure(p_status => 'Open');
```

☐ Do not validate PL/SQL code (parse PL/SQL code at runtime only).

Figure 4-22. Using a PL/SQL block to set the application context

If you now run the report page, you will see that the report returns only records that are open and assigned to the brian user, as shown in Figure 4-23. If you click one of the records to edit it, you may get the error shown in Figure 4-24. This is because the database session used to process your page request might not be the same one that was used to process the report page; that is, the session does not have the context set. In this case, the automated row fetch process on the Update Bug page can't retrieve the record, and the policy is applied without a status for comparison. To fix this, you can create the same type of before header PL/SQL process that you have on the report page, or alternatively, create an application process that executes for every page in the application.

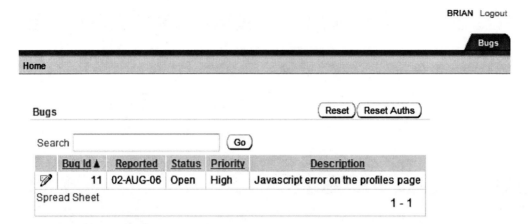

Figure 4-23. The report returns only open bugs.

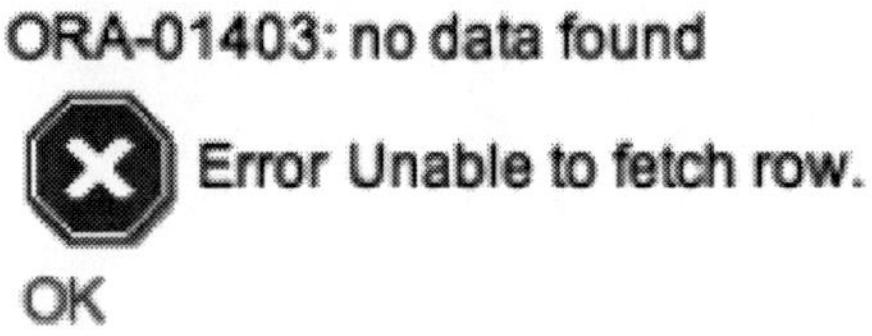

ORA-01403: no data found

❌ Error Unable to fetch row.

OK

Figure 4-24. Error returned when trying to edit a record

An alternative to using a page or application process to set the value stored in the context is to specify the PL/SQL in the security attributes of the application, as shown in Figure 4-25.

Figure 4-25. Setting a PL/SQL call to set the security context

Using Advanced VPD Features

So far, you have seen how you can limit the set of records returned by using VPD and a policy function, with the policy applied to the entire row. Other features of VPD allow you to apply the policy based on the columns the user is attempting to access. Here, we will look at a couple of advanced VPD features you may find useful in your applications.

Column-Level VPD Policy

Whereas your previous policy function applied to the entire row regardless of which columns the user was selecting, you can actually configure a policy that is applied only if the user is attempting to access certain columns.

As an example, let's set up the policy function so that the brian user is able to see all of the rows in the table unless he attempts to select the assigned_to field; in that case, he will be able to see only the rows assigned to him.

So, as before, you need to create a policy function and then link it to the table using the DBMS_RLS package. First, let's drop the old policy:

```
apexdemo@DBTEST> begin
  2     dbms_rls.drop_policy(object_name => 'buglist',
  3         policy_name => 'Buglist Policy');
  4   end;
  5   /

PL/SQL procedure successfully completed.
```

Now re-create the policy function as a much simpler one that just checks that the record is assigned to the user, as shown in Listing 4-14.

Listing 4-14. Creating the New Policy Function

```
apexdemo@DBTEST> create or replace function vpd_buglist(
  2     p_schema in varchar2 default null,
  3     p_object in varchar2 default null)
  4         return varchar2 as
  5   begin
  6     if (USER = 'APEXDEMO') and (v('APP_USER') is null) then
  7        return '';
  8     else
  9        return 'upper(assigned_to) = nvl(v(''APP_USER''), USER)';
 10     end if;
 11   end;
 12   /

Function created.
```

Like the previous policy function, this function checks to see if the user is connected as the Oracle user APEXDEMO. If so, it returns an empty string; otherwise, it returns a string that will compare the assigned_to column with the logged-in user, whether the user is logged in via an APEX application or as an Oracle user.

You can now apply the policy function using the DBMS_RLS.add_policy procedure, as shown in Listing 4-15.

Listing 4-15. *Applying the New Policy Function*

```
apexdemo@DBTEST> begin
  2   dbms_rls.add_policy(
  3     object_schema => 'apexdemo',
  4     object_name => 'buglist',
  5     policy_name => 'Buglist Policy',
  6     function_schema => 'apexdemo',
  7     policy_function => 'vpd_buglist',
  8     statement_types => 'select, update',
  9     sec_relevant_cols => 'assigned_to');
 10   end;
 11   /

PL/SQL procedure successfully completed.
```

Notice that this time, we used an additional parameter in the call to the add_policy procedure. By using the sec_relevant_cols parameter and setting the value to assigned_to, you are saying that you want the policy to be enforced only if the assigned_to column is in the DML statement that is being used against the table.

Now you can connect to the database via SQL*Plus as the brian user and check the effect of the new policy, as shown in Listing 4-16.

Listing 4-16. *Testing the New Policy*

```
-- perform a count of the records
brian@DBTEST> select count(*) from apexdemo.buglist;

  COUNT(*)
----------
         2
-- count using the bugid column
brian@DBTEST> select count(bugid) from apexdemo.buglist;

 COUNT(ID)
----------
        18
-- select using columns not part of the policy
brian@DBTEST> select bugid, reported, reported_by
  2   from apexdemo.buglist;
```

```
    BUGID REPORTED  REPORTED_BY
---------- --------- ------------------------------
         1 27-JAN-06 Rachel Hudson
         2 01-FEB-06 Caroline White
         3 02-AUG-06 Carl Watson
         4 03-FEB-06 Laura Barnes
         5 03-FEB-06 Lucy Scott
         6 05-FEB-06 Chris Donaldson
         7 06-FEB-06 Paul Matthews
         8 06-FEB-06 Mark Lawson
         9 07-FEB-06 John Stevens
        10 07-FEB-06 Steven Green
        11 08-FEB-06 Mark Lawson
        12 08-FEB-06 Carl Watson
        13 09-FEB-06 Caroline White
        14 09-DEC-05 Rachel Hudson
        15 10-FEB-06 Laura Barnes
        16 10-FEB-06 Carl Watson
        17 11-FEB-06 Paul Matthews
        18 11-FEB-06 John Scott

18 rows selected.
```

As you can see from Listing 4-16, if brian performs a select count(*) from the table, a result of 2 is returned. If he performs a select count(bugid), a result of 18 is returned. When brian queries the table without referencing the assigned_to column, he can see the data in all the columns he referenced from all 18 rows in the table. However, if the query references the assigned_to column, only the two records assigned to him are returned, as shown in Listing 4-17.

Listing 4-17. *Referencing the Column in the Query*

```
brian@DBTEST> select bugid, reported, assigned_to
  2  from apexdemo.buglist;

    BUGID REPORTED  ASSIGNED_TO
---------- --------- ------------------------------
         2 01-FEB-06 brian
         6 05-FEB-06 brian
```

At first glance, the difference between the way we used the VPD policy here and what we did earlier may seem quite subtle. Here, users are able to view data from all of the records unless they try to reference the column that is protected by your policy. In other words, any time they try to view data from the protected column, their view of the data is restricted to only those rows that the policy allows.

So you can expect this policy to also work just fine from your APEX application. If you run the application as it currently stands, since the report query references the assigned_to column (even though it is not being displayed in the report), the VPD policy restricts the rows to those that are assigned to brian, as shown in Figure 4-26.

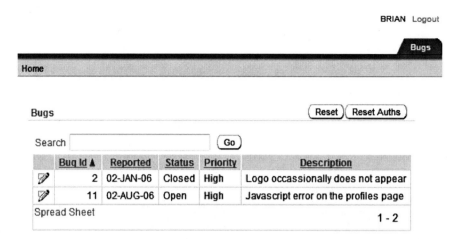

Figure 4-26. *Column-based VPD policy working in the application*

However, you can change the report query region source so that it no longer selects from the assigned_to column, as shown in Figure 4-27. If you now run the report again, something strange happens: you still get only the same two records returned. This is because, even though you are no longer selecting the assigned_to column in the query, you are referencing the column in the where clause. This illustrates the fact that the policy will be enforced if you reference the column in any part of the statement, even if you are not returning that column in the select statement.

Region Source

```
select
  "ID",
  "BUGID",
  "REPORTED",
  "STATUS",
  "PRIORITY",
  "DESCRIPTION",
  "REPORTED_BY"
from
  "BUGLIST"
where
(
  instr(upper("STATUS"),upper(nvl(:P1_REPORT_SEARCH,"STATUS"))) > 0  or
  instr(upper("PRIORITY"),upper(nvl(:P1_REPORT_SEARCH,"PRIORITY"))) > 0  or
  instr(upper("DESCRIPTION"),upper(nvl(:P1_REPORT_SEARCH,"DESCRIPTION"))) > 0  or
  instr(upper("REPORTED_BY"),upper(nvl(:P1_REPORT_SEARCH,"REPORTED_BY"))) > 0  or
  instr(upper("ASSIGNED_TO"),upper(nvl(:P1_REPORT_SEARCH,"ASSIGNED_TO"))) > 0
)
```

Figure 4-27. *Removing the assigned_to column from the select in the report query*

Once you completely remove the `assigned_to` column from the report query, all the rows will be returned by the query, as shown in Figure 4-28.

Figure 4-28. Column is not referenced, so all records are returned.

As you can see, column-based VPD is an extremely powerful piece of functionality that you can use to further secure data from users. If you need to secure your data like this, using a VPD policy is absolutely one of the best ways to do it, rather than coding the logic inside all your queries (inside all your applications).

Column Masking

So, now you can prevent users from seeing data in particular rows if they attempt to query a particular column that is protected by your policy. However, what if you want to allow users to still be able to see all of the rows but prevent them from seeing the data in a particular column? You can do that by using a technique called *column masking*.

Column masking allows you to display all the rows but mask (replace with `NULL`) the values of the specified columns for the restricted rows. This might sound complicated, but fortunately, it is incredibly simple to implement.

First, drop the existing policy:

```
apexdemo@DBTEST> begin
  2  dbms_rls.drop_policy(
  3    object_name => 'buglist',
  4    policy_name => 'Buglist Policy');
  5  end;
  6  /

PL/SQL procedure successfully completed.
```

Now re-create the policy, as shown in Listing 4-18.

Listing 4-18. *Re-creating the Policy to Use Column Masking*

```
apexdemo@DBTEST> begin
  2  dbms_rls.add_policy(
  3    object_schema => 'apexdemo',
  4    object_name => 'buglist',
  5    policy_name => 'Buglist Policy',
  6    function_schema => 'apexdemo',
  7    policy_function => 'vpd_buglist',
  8    statement_types => 'select',
  9    sec_relevant_cols => 'assigned_to',
 10    sec_relevant_cols_opt => DBMS_RLS.ALL_ROWS);
 11* end;

PL/SQL procedure successfully completed.
```

Note that, this time, you have included a new parameter, sec_relevant_cols_opt, setting the value to DBMS_RLS.ALL_ROWS, which is a constant defined in the DBMS_RLS package. The inclusion of this new parameter means that you want all of the rows returned from the VPD policy.

Now connect to SQL*Plus as the brian user and query the table again, as shown in Listing 4-19.

Listing 4-19. *Column Masking in Effect with the Policy*

```
brian@DBTEST> select bugid, reported, reported_by, assigned_to
  2  from apexdemo.buglist;

BUGID REPORTED  REPORTED_BY        ASSIGNED_TO
------ --------- ------------------ -------------
     1 27-JAN-06 Rachel Huson
     2 02-JAN-06 Caroline White     brian
     3 01-FEB-06 Carl Watson
     4 02-MAR-06 Laura Barnes
     5 02-MAR-06 Lucy Scott
     6 02-MAY-06 Chris Donaldson
     7 02-JUN-06 Paul Mathews
     8 02-JUN-06 Mark Lawson
     9 02-JUL-06 John Stevens
```

```
    10 02-JUL-06 Steven Green
    11 02-AUG-06 Mark Lawson       brian
    12 02-AUG-06 Carl Watson
    13 02-SEP-06 Caroline White
    14 02-SEP-06 Rachel Hudson
    15 02-OCT-06 Laura Barnes
    16 02-OCT-06 Carl Watson
    17 02-NOV-06 Paul Mathews

17 rows selected.
```

You can now see all of the rows, but you can't see the data in the `assigned_to` column if the record is not assigned to you. This behavior is obviously quite different from what happens when you use column-level VPD, so which one you use will be determined by your requirements.

The policy works with your applications. After you modify the report query to again select from the `assigned_to` column, you can test the results. Figure 4-29 shows the report you will see when logged in as `brian`.

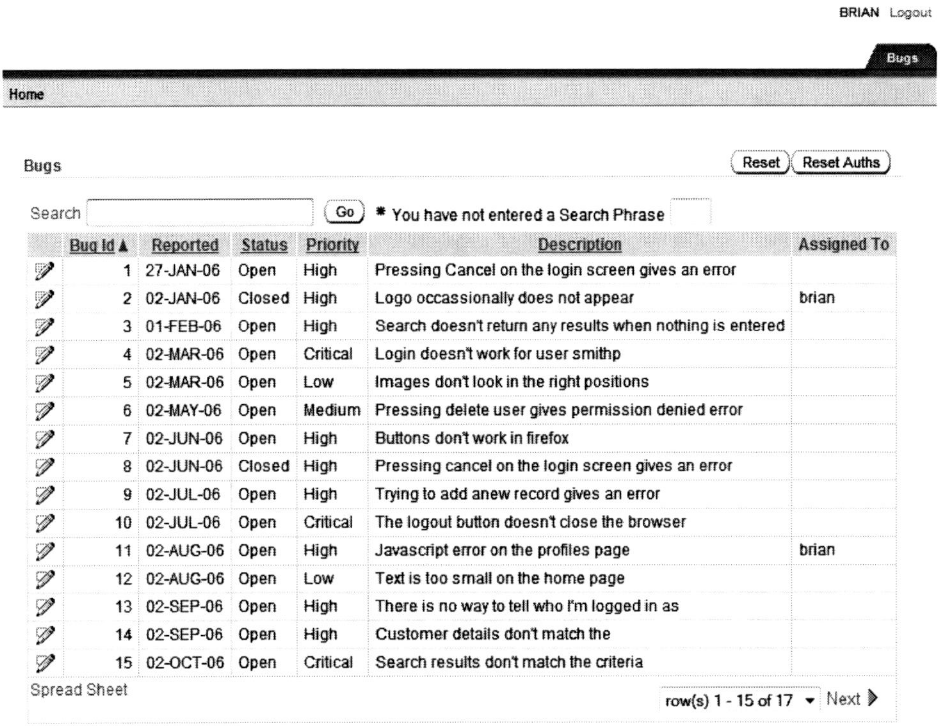

Bug Id	Reported	Status	Priority	Description	Assigned To
1	27-JAN-06	Open	High	Pressing Cancel on the login screen gives an error	
2	02-JAN-06	Closed	High	Logo occassionally does not appear	brian
3	01-FEB-06	Open	High	Search doesn't return any results when nothing is entered	
4	02-MAR-06	Open	Critical	Login doesn't work for user smithp	
5	02-MAR-06	Open	Low	Images don't look in the right positions	
6	02-MAY-06	Open	Medium	Pressing delete user gives permission denied error	
7	02-JUN-06	Open	High	Buttons don't work in firefox	
8	02-JUN-06	Closed	High	Pressing cancel on the login screen gives an error	
9	02-JUL-06	Open	High	Trying to add anew record gives an error	
10	02-JUL-06	Open	Critical	The logout button doesn't close the browser	
11	02-AUG-06	Open	High	Javascript error on the profiles page	brian
12	02-AUG-06	Open	Low	Text is too small on the home page	
13	02-SEP-06	Open	High	There is no way to tell who I'm logged in as	
14	02-SEP-06	Open	High	Customer details don't match the	
15	02-OCT-06	Open	Critical	Search results don't match the criteria	

***Figure 4-29.** Column masking in the application*

If you logged in to the application as a different user, you would still be able to see all the rows, but the `Assigned To` column would show only that data that is assigned to you.

As you can see, using VPD column-mask policies is an extremely powerful and flexible way to restrict the access users have to data. This technique might be useful in many different scenarios. For example, you might mask the salary field of an employee report so that employees are able to see only their own salary, while managers can see the salary of everyone who works for them.

A Note About Policy Function Types

You may be wondering when the policy function will be evaluated and whether you can control how often the policy function is executed in order to enhance performance. You can define your policy function to be of different types, depending on whether you want the output of your policy function to be cached. You can specify your policy function as one of five different types:

STATIC: The policy function is entirely static and will always return the same string. Therefore, the policy function output can be cached and reused repeatedly without having to reexecute the function.

SHARED_STATIC: The same as STATIC, but the resulting output can be applied across multiple objects that use the same policy function.

CONTEXT_SENSITIVE: This type is used whenever you use an application context. The policy function output can be cached and reused, and the function will be executed again only if the value of the application context is modified.

SHARED_CONTEXT_SENSITIVE: The same as CONTEXT_SENSITIVE, except the resulting output can be cached and applied to multiple objects that use the same policy function.
DYNAMIC: The policy function is executed every time. This is the default value. If your policy function is likely to be called many times and the output is not likely to change, you may benefit from using one of the other policy types that enables the output to be cached.

■ **Caution** Great care must be taken to use the correct policy type for your policy. For example, using a STATIC policy type could be disastrous for your application security if the policy should actually be evaluated dynamically.

You can define the policy type by using the policy_type parameter when you use the dbms_rls.add_policy procedure, as shown in Listing 4-20.

Listing 4-20. Defining the Policy Type

```
apexdemo@DBTEST> begin
  2   dbms_rls.add_policy(
  3     object_schema => 'apexdemo',
  4     object_name => 'buglist',
  5     policy_name => 'Buglist Policy',
  6     function_schema => 'apexdemo',
  7     policy_function => 'vpd_buglist',
  8     statement_types => 'select',
```

```
 9    policy_type => DBMS_RLS.DYNAMIC);
10  end;
11  /
```

PL/SQL procedure successfully completed.

VPD Best Practices

As noted earlier in this chapter, for simplicity, the VPD examples use an approach you will probably not want to take in your own production applications. Let's look back at a sample policy:

```
apexdemo@DBTEST> begin
 2      dbms_rls.add_policy(
 3        object_schema => 'apexdemo',
 4        object_name => 'buglist',
 5        policy_name => 'Buglist Policy',
 6        function_schema => 'apexdemo',
 7        policy_function => 'vpd_buglist',
 8        statement_types => 'select');
 9  end;
10  /
```

Notice that the object we were trying to protect (the buglist table) and the policy function that is used to protect it (vpd_buglist) are both contained in the same schema. This presents a potential risk for a production application, especially since the same schema is used as the working schema for the application. If malicious users found a way to run some SQL as the APEXDEMO user (perhaps by using a SQL-injection attack), they might be able to replace your policy function with one of their own, such as one that does not apply any additional predicate logic. They would then be able to gain full access to all the data.

To avoid this potential issue, you might wish to create the VPD policy functions in a separate schema entirely, so that one schema is used for your VPD security routines and the other schema is used for your data. You could then lock the account owning the schema in which you created the policy functions, making it much more difficult for malicious users to be able to modify the policy functions in some way.

Auditing

Here's a real-life incident to give you an idea of what can happen without auditing. A user had been training a new employee in how to use the in-house billing system. They had gone through all the different screens, creating new customers and orders, changing entries, deleting entries . . . the whole works. Unfortunately, the user had performed the entire training session while connected to the live system, rather than the test system, and only realized this after a good 30 minutes or so. This led to a frantic call to tech support to ask how to undo the changes they had made.

How did this happen? The user had two shortcuts on his desktop, both pointing to the same application but with a parameter in the shortcut determining whether the user connected to the test or live database. Rather than prominently displaying on screen which database the user was connected to, the database connection details were tucked away in a Help About type of pop-up window. On that day, the user accidentally started the application using the wrong shortcut and never thought to check the Help About pop-up window before making all of those database changes.

Even worse than not displaying the database connection prominently, the application used a common single account for every user, rather than using separate database accounts for logging in to the database. So, as far as the database was concerned, the same database user was performing all of the changes, since there was no way to tell users apart.

This real-life story illustrates two (or rather, at least two!) very important points:

- If you don't audit the users' actions, you will not be able to determine what they have done.

- If you use a common login for all users, you will not be able to track back changes to an individual person, even if you audit every action.

The purpose of this section is to demonstrate how you can very effectively audit the actions of users using your APEX application, as well as anyone accessing the data using another method.

Enabling Auditing

The previous sections covered how you can use the DBMS_RLS package to implement VPD policies that restrict the view of data that users will see. You might be thinking you could somehow use this to audit users' actions, perhaps by performing some logging inside the policy function. Or you might decide to create triggers on the table itself to perform some logging into another table whenever any DML is performed on that table. However, rather than reinventing the wheel, you can use the auditing functionality of the database to do this for you.

■ **Note** The auditing functionality described here assumes you are using the Enterprise Edition of the database. If you are just interested in "who did what," the Enterprise Edition of the database is not required. It is possible to implement auditing by using triggers or in some other appropriate method, but we recommend using a built-in auditing feature if possible.

You can use the DBMS_FGA package to enable auditing of user actions. The way you use this package is similar to the way you use the DBMS_RLS package.

As an example, let's audit all user actions against the buglist table. To do that, you add a policy (yes, another policy—this time an auditing policy), as shown in Listing 4-21. This needs to be performed by a DBA or another user who has rights to execute the DBMS_FGA package.

Listing 4-21. Creating an Audit Policy

```
system@DBTEST> begin
  2  dbms_fga.add_policy(
  3    object_schema => 'apexdemo',
  4    object_name => 'buglist',
  5    policy_name => 'Buglist audit',
  6    audit_condition => null,
  7    statement_types => 'select,insert,update,delete');
  8  end;
  9  /
```

```
PL/SQL procedure successfully completed.
```

As you can see, the syntax looks very similar to the syntax you used with the DBMS_RLS package. However, you don't need to write your own audit procedure, since that is done automatically for you. You have essentially said that you want to audit any select, insert, update, and delete statements against the buglist table in the APEXDEMO schema. One thing that might look a little strange is the audit_condition parameter being set to NULL. You can use the audit_condition parameter to specify a condition restricting the rows to be audited. Setting audit_condition to NULL causes auditing to occur for all rows.

If you now query the buglist table as the brian user from a SQL*Plus session, everything appears to work as you would expect:

```
brian@DBTEST> select count(*) from apexdemo.buglist;

  COUNT(*)
----------
         2
```

The user is not made aware that any form of auditing has taken place. However, an audit record has been placed in the audit table.

Viewing Audit Data

The audit information is accessible to a DBA via a view called dba_fga_audit_trail:

```
system@DBTEST> select session_id, db_user, object_schema,
  2  object_name, policy_name
  3  from dba_fga_audit_trail;

SESSION_ID DB_USER   OBJECT_SCHEMA   OBJECT_NAME     POLICY_NAME
---------- --------- --------------- --------------- -----------
      5005 BRIAN     APEXDEMO        BUGLIST         BUGLIST
```

You can tell from the audit log that the user brian accessed the buglist table in the APEXDEMO schema. However, even more information has been captured in the audit table. The definition of dba_fga_audit_trail, shown in Listing 4-22, shows all of the different types of information that is recorded.

Listing 4-22. Definition of dba_fga_audit_trail

```
system@DBTEST> desc dba_fga_audit_trail;
 Name                      Null?     Type
 ------------------------- --------- ----------
 SESSION_ID                NOT NULL  NUMBER
 TIMESTAMP                           DATE
 DB_USER                             VARCHAR2(30)
 OS_USER                             VARCHAR2(255)
 USERHOST                            VARCHAR2(128)
 CLIENT_ID                           VARCHAR2(64)
 EXT_NAME                            VARCHAR2(4000)
 OBJECT_SCHEMA                       VARCHAR2(30)
 OBJECT_NAME                         VARCHAR2(128)
 POLICY_NAME                         VARCHAR2(30)
 SCN                                 NUMBER
 SQL_TEXT                            NVARCHAR2(2000)
 SQL_BIND                            NVARCHAR2(2000)
 COMMENT$TEXT                        VARCHAR2(4000)
 STATEMENT_TYPE                      VARCHAR2(7)
 EXTENDED_TIMESTAMP                  TIMESTAMP(6) WITH TIME ZONE
 PROXY_SESSIONID                     NUMBER
 GLOBAL_UID                          VARCHAR2(32)
 INSTANCE_NUMBER                     NUMBER
 OS_PROCESS                          VARCHAR2(16)
 TRANSACTIONID                       RAW(8)
 STATEMENTID                         NUMBER
 ENTRYID                             NUMBER
```

You can see from the definition that the actual SQL text that was used should also have been captured, along with the statement type, the value of the system change number (SCN) when the statement occurred, and many other useful pieces of information that would help you to determine the entire environment when the statement occurred. Listing 4-23 shows examples of some of the data you will be able to find logged in the audit table.

Listing 4-23. Querying the dba_fga_audit_trail View

```
system@DBTEST> select sql_text from dba_fga_audit_trail;

SQL_TEXT
--------------------------------------------
select count(*) from apexdemo.buglist

system@DBTEST> select statement_type, extended_timestamp from dba_fga_audit_trail;

STATEME EXTENDED_TIMESTAMP
------- ---------------------------------------
SELECT  11-NOV-06 06.46.19.196957 PM +00:00
```

```
system@DBTEST> select db_user, os_user, userhost
  2* from dba_fga_audit_trail

DB_USER             OS_USER    USERHOST
------------------- ---------- --------------------
BRIAN               bhill      oim.enkitec.com
```

As you can see, the auditing facility works fantastically well and gives you a lot of information that helps to answer the three big questions: who, what, and when.

However, what happens if you access the table via your APEX application? Well, to demonstrate, run the report again, as shown in Figure 4-30.

Figure 4-30. Running the report with auditing enabled

Then query the audit table:

```
system@DBTEST> select session_id, db_user, statement_type
  2  from dba_fga_audit_trail;

SESSION_ID DB_USER                        STATEME
---------- ------------------------------ -------
  27020042 BRIAN                          SELECT
  24850031 ANONYMOUS                      SELECT
```

You can see the issue here: rather than auditing that user brian performed the action in the APEX application, it has been logged as being performed by the ANONYMOUS user. This is because ANONYMOUS is the user specified in the DAD.

So, after all we've said about not using a single account for logging in to the database, have we reached a roadblock in identifying which user performed the action in the APEX application? Well, as you might have guessed, we wouldn't have brought you this far if it wasn't possible to find out which user performed the action. The answer lies in the client_id column. Fortunately, the Oracle team behind APEX had the foresight to populate the client_id for you:

```
system@DBTEST> select db_user, client_id
  2  from dba_fga_audit_trail;

DB_USER             CLIENT_ID
------------------- ------------------------------
BRIAN
ANONYMOUS           BRIAN:6488441121768716
```

This is also an extremely good illustration of why it's important to instrument your code in the same way that the Oracle team has done by including the APEX session information in the client_id column. You never know when that information will be useful to someone else, and if you haven't made it possible for others to access that information, that lack could cause all sorts of unforeseen problems.

The client_id column not only contains the name of the user (brian) but also the session ID that was used (6488441121768716), so the format of the client_id value is user:session_id. Having this level of detail available to you from the audit log allows you to go back into the APEX instance management and drill down into the recent session information that matches the information from the client_id column, as shown in Figure 4-31. Then you can drill down into the session information, as shown in Figure 4-32.

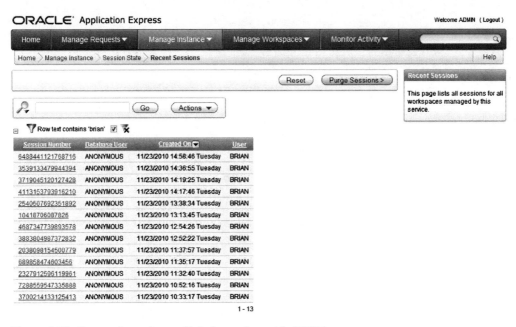

Figure 4-31. *Cross-referencing audit information with APEX logs*

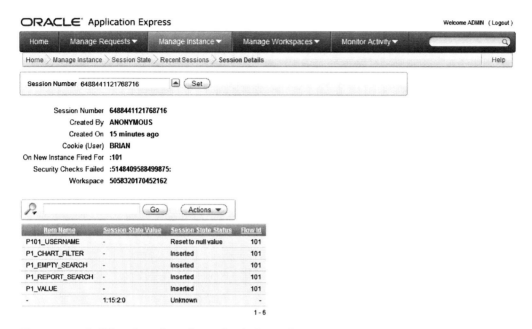

Figure 4-32. Drilling down into the session information

Summary

This chapter covered methods you can use to control the data your users can access and what actions they can perform on that data, while auditing the actions they perform.

It's extremely important to consider using features such as VPD and auditing in the early stages of application design. Although you can easily enable functionality such as auditing using the DBMS_FGA package later on, trying to retrofit VPD into an application when you have already written additional predicates for all your queries is a much bigger and more daunting task. There is often resistance to changing things once they are working—after all, who wants to risk being the one to break something that has worked for a long time? This is why you should consider the options you have available to you at the early stages of project design. Investigate the latest database features to see what they can do for you. Many people have written their own auditing solutions when they could have saved a lot of development time by using the built-in database features instead.

Take the time to think ahead when you're designing an application. Think about all the areas in which you can cut down on the amount of repetitive work you need to do. Using packages such as DBMS_RLS and DBMS_FGA means you don't have to reinvent the wheel to get the job done.

Navigation and Layout

An often overlooked area of application design is how users will navigate around the system. We typically give a lot of thought to how individual screens and pages will look; but, we don't always give the same amount of consideration to how the user will move among those pages. Why is this important? Well, if users find it difficult to navigate your application, they will quickly become frustrated with the application. Your application should have a navigation system that's easy to use and takes into account the areas users will access most frequently

APEX provides many components and methods that enable you to create different ways for users to navigate applications. However, there's no magic formula for determining which method or component will be most suitable for your particular situation—that's something you'll need to decide on a case-by-case basis.

This chapter covers some of the different tools Apex puts at your disposal for enabling navigation in your application. We'll concentrate here on using the built-in themes and templates. In Chapter 10, you'll see how you can modify these—and even create your own themes—to customize your application's look and feel, as well as its navigation system.

It is worth noting that in APEX 4.0, there are even more available themes and new features that can improve the user experience. We'll explore some of those features in this chapter.

Tabs

Tabs are an extremely simple yet efficient way of allowing users to navigate between different pages in your application. They are perhaps among the first navigation aids developers might choose to include, since APEX makes it extremely easy to implement them.

You can use two different types of tabs: standard and parent. Standard tabs are for applications that have only one level of tabs, with each tab associated with a particular page (although a tab can also be the current tab for many pages, as you'll see shortly). A parent tab, in contrast, acts as a container for a group of standard tabs. Using parent tabs, you can group standard tabs under a particular parent tab in order to define a more contextual list of tabs that is specific to the user's current task.

You can access the tabs used in your application in many different ways. For example, each page definition in the Application Builder contains a list of the tabs used on that page in the Shared Components section, as shown in Figure 5-1.

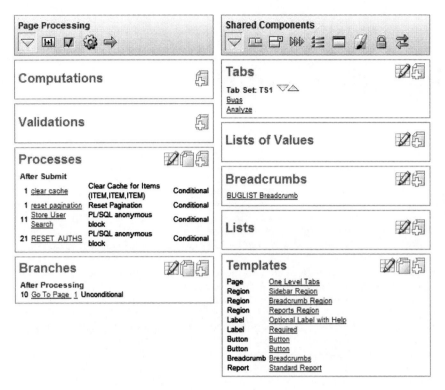

Figure 5-1. Tabs displayed in the Shared Components for the page definition

You can also view all of your application's tabs from the Shared Components section for the application, as shown in Figure 5-2. This screen is actually very comprehensive. It not only shows the tabs you've defined for the application, but also displays information about the definition of each individual tab.

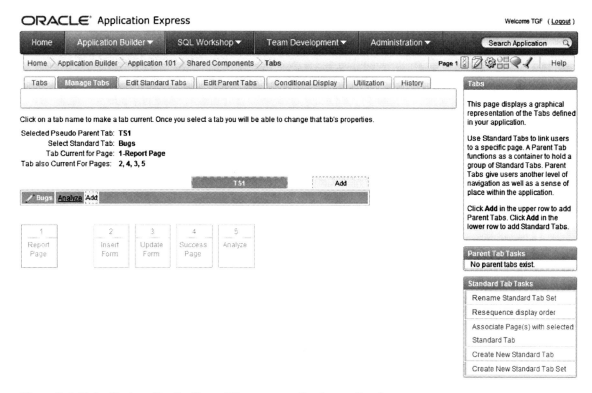

Figure 5-2. *Tabs displayed in the Shared Components for the application*

Understanding Tab States: Current and Noncurrent

In the example in Figure 5-2, notice that the tab has a single target, represented by the Tab Current for Page attribute—page 1 in this case. In other words, when the users click the tab, they will be taken to page 1. However, the tab can also be "current" for a number of pages, represented by the Tab Also Current for Pages attribute. In Figure 5-2, the tab is considered current for pages 2 through 5. So what does *current* actually mean?

A tab has two states: either current or noncurrent. The difference between current and noncurrent is quite a fluid one, in that you can customize your templates to have your own definitions, as you'll learn in Chapter 10. However, generally speaking, for the built-in themes and templates, a current tab reflects the fact that the user is currently on a page represented by that tab. In other words, the tab will appear to be different from the other tabs and, again generally, the tab will not be a clickable link. A noncurrent tab reflects the fact that the user can click the tab to navigate to a different page. Current tabs may use different images or colors so users can see at a glance where they are in the application. Exactly how the current and noncurrent states are implemented depends on the way the page template used for the page implements the standard tabs.

When users click a tab, they are taken to the page that's assigned as the current page for that tab (page 1 in the example), and the tab is considered the current tab. However, if the user is on one of the pages 2 through 5, the tab will also be considered the current one.

Using Standard Tabs

When an application uses a single level of tabs, they are standard tabs. The Buglist application has a standard tab set called TS1, as shown in Figure 5-3, which was created automatically when you created the application. All of the standard tabs belong to this tab set.

Figure 5-3. *The standard tab set in the Buglist application*

Figure 5-3 shows the definition of one of the tabs for the Buglist application. Here, you can define a single page for the page that will be linked to from this tab, as well as multiple entries in the Tab Also Current for Pages attribute, by specifying the individual page numbers separated by commas. You can also place the tab in another tab set, if one exists, by changing the Standard Tab Set attribute.

The tab attributes include both Tab Name and Tab Label. The Tab Name attribute is the name you'll use to refer to the tab within your application. The Tab Label attribute is the text that will appear on the tab when displayed to the user (if you customize the templates, you can display anything you like). You can actually do quite a few interesting things with the Tab Label attribute. The text doesn't need to be static and hard-coded. You can use substitution values in the Tab Label attribute, which will be replaced dynamically at runtime. For example, rather than setting the Tab Label attribute to `Edit Bug`, you could use `Edit Bug &BUG_NUMBER.`, which at runtime would show something like "Edit Bug 174," allowing users to see at a glance which bug they are editing.

Figure 5-4 shows some of the other attributes you can define for a particular standard tab. You can specify images to be used for the current and noncurrent states, as well as any additional image attributes. You can also link the tab to a parent tab set and define an authorization scheme for the tab.

Figure 5-4. Attributes of a standard tab

The Buglist application uses a page template called One Level Tabs. Figure 5-5 shows the definition of the Standard Tabs Attributes section of this template. We'll cover the details of page templates in Chapter 10; however, from Figure 5-5, you can see that the HTML used for current and noncurrent standard tabs is slightly different—the tabs use different images and different CSS classes for the Tab Label attribute. In this particular page template, the images used for the current and noncurrent tabs are hard-coded. However, if the template for your application uses the `#TAB_IMAGE#` substitution variable, then the values you entered for the image attributes shown in Figure 5-4 would be applied instead.

Figure 5-5. Page template definition for the standard tab attributes

By using authorization schemes with standard tabs, you can control whether a user can access a particular page through a tab. For example, if you implement the business requirement that only administrators should be able to access the Analyze page of your application, you can change the authorization scheme of the Analyze tab to use the USER_IS_ADMIN scheme you created earlier (in Chapter 4), as shown in Figure 5-6.

Figure 5-6. Using an authorization scheme with a standard tab

Now if you run the application while logged in as an administrator, you will see the Analyze tab, as shown in Figure 5-7. However, if you are logged in as a nonadministrator, you will not see that tab, as shown in Figure 5-8.

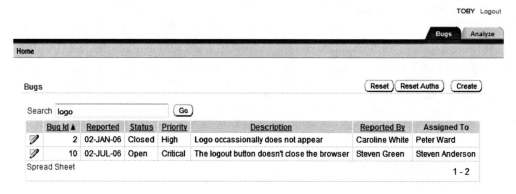

Figure 5-7. An administrator sees both tabs.

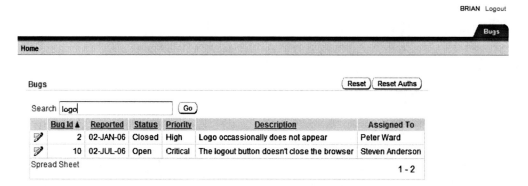

Figure 5-8. The Analyze tab is not displayed to nonadministrators.

▨ **Note** You might have expected to see an error displayed when the nonadministrator logged in, as shown in Figure 5-8. However, in this case, rather than the authorization scheme displaying an error, the tab is simply not displayed to anyone failing the authorization scheme logic, which is preferable behavior for navigation components such as tabs.

As you can see, using authorization schemes with standard tabs is an incredibly powerful way of customizing the navigation of your application dynamically at runtime depending on who is logged in (or any other criteria you prefer).

It is also possible to use conditions to determine whether a standard tab should be displayed, which gives even more flexibility to dynamically customize the navigation at runtime. We'll discuss how to define conditions for navigation in the "Navigation Bars" section later in this chapter.

Using Parent Tabs

In order to use parent tabs, you need to use a page template that supports them. Since the Buglist application currently uses One Level Tabs as the page template, you can't use parent tabs in it. Fortunately, this is quite easy to change. Just edit the page definition and select a page template that supports two levels of tabs, Two Level Tabs, as shown in Figure 5-9.

Now if you run the page again, it will look similar to Figure 5-10. Since you haven't defined a parent tab yet, the tab display is still much like it was before (aesthetics aside).

▨ **Note** If you used a different theme, you might see something very different from Figure 5-10, since each theme can display the tab layout in different ways. In fact, themes don't actually have to support displaying two levels of tabs.

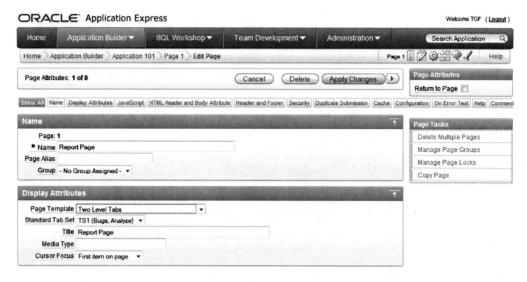

Figure 5-9. *Changing the Report page to use the Two Level Tabs template*

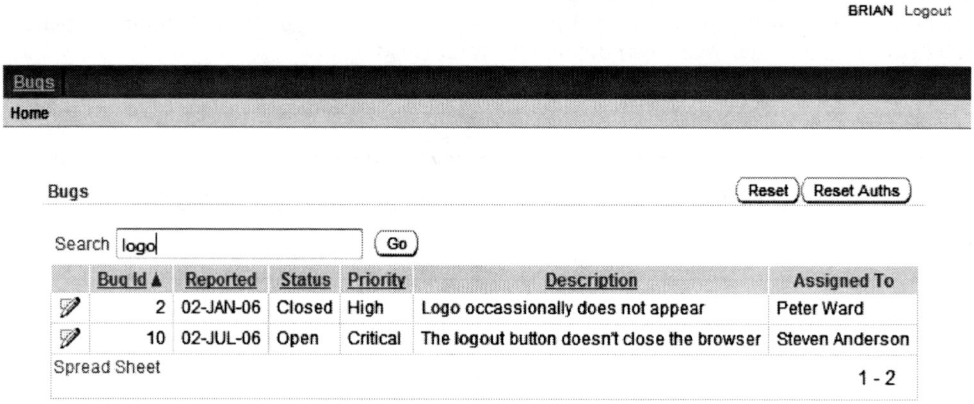

Figure 5-10. *The page using the Two Level Tabs page template*

As an example, let's create a new parent tab set called Bugtools, under which you'll group all of the bug-related standard tabs. To begin, click the Add link beside the TS1 tab set, as shown back in Figure 5-2. The link reads "Add," but if you hover your mouse over the link, the pop-up hint reads "Add New Parent Tab." This starts the parent tab creation wizard, as shown in Figure 5-11.

■ **Note** As with most APEX components, there are many different ways to reach the creation wizard for parent tabs, such as through the page definition or through the Shared Components section for the application. Look around the Application Builder to find all the different ways you can do tasks like this. You'll probably have a favorite way of doing these things, but it's always good to be able to find different routes since they might end up saving you more time (and make you more productive!).

Figure 5-11. Creating a parent tab

Give the parent tab a label and then assign a target page. You can also assign other attributes that will affect the session state when the user uses the tab, as shown in Figure 5-12.

Figure 5-12. Adding parent tab attributes

The attributes you can assign to parent tabs are similar to the usual settings you can make for page branches. You can specify a Request value, which can then be used within processes on the page to determine how the user arrived at that page. You can also clear session state from particular pages and assign values to items held in the session state. For now, simply make the tab take the user to page 1 and don't do anything with the session state. As you can see from Figure 5-13, the new parent tab you created has now replaced the TS1 tab set.

Now suppose you create a new page that displays some helpful information about the application. One of the options during page creation is to define whether a tab or parent tab should be reused or created for that particular page.

Figures 5-14 and 5-15 show how parent tabs can help to present different navigation choices to your users depending on which top-level parent tab they select. One tab shows a bug list; the other shows application help.

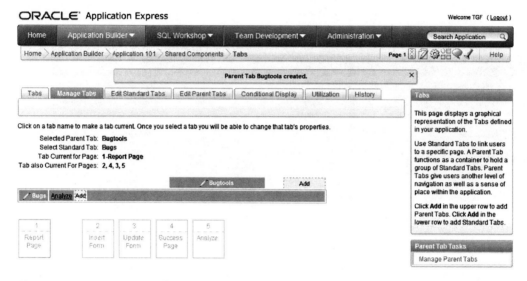

Figure 5-13. A new parent tab replaces the old TS1 tab set.

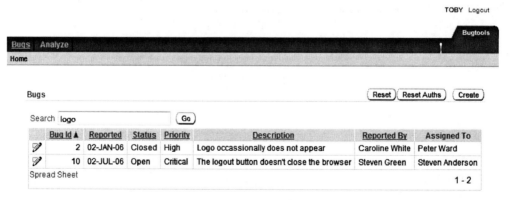

Figure 5-14. The Bugtools tab shows a list of tracked bugs.

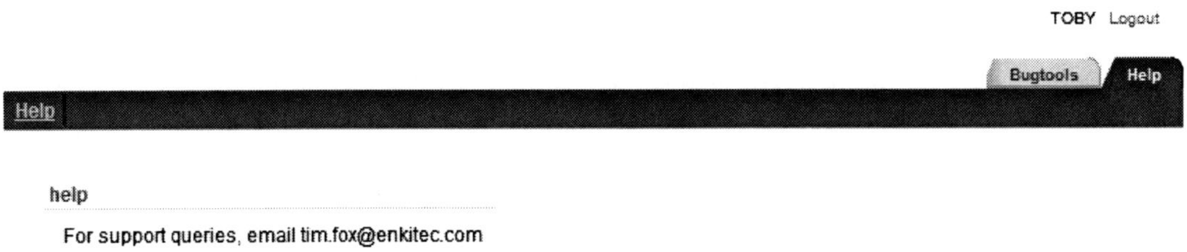

TOBY Logout

Bugtools | Help

Help

help

For support queries, email tim.fox@enkitec.com

Figure 5-15. The Help tab shows online help.

At first, getting parent tabs and two-level tabs working in your application can be quite confusing. Many people find that after they create parent tabs they are unable to get them to display in their application. This is usually because they don't understand how tab sets, parent tabs, and page templates work. If you are having problems getting your parent tabs to display, check whether you are using the correct parent tab set for that particular standard tab and also whether you have made the tab current for that page.

I find it very helpful to open two pages, one running the application and another running the APEX development environment. You can then make changes to the tabs or pages, then switch over to the running application and simply refresh the page to get the new code and test the functionality. Multi-tab browsers, like FireFox and IE8 make this really easy.

■ **Note** We encourage you to sit down and work through creating some parent tabs. Once you get the hang of this, it really isn't difficult, although it can seem that way when it is not working how you intended.

Navigation Bars

Like tabs, navigation bars can be an easy way to enable user navigation in your application. Unlike with tabs, though, an application may use only a single navigation bar. However, that navigation bar can contain multiple entries that are dynamically enabled and disabled at runtime.

If you look at the page template, you'll see #NAVIGATION_BAR# specified in the Body section (again, this depends on whether the page template and theme you are using support displaying a navigation bar). At runtime, the #NAVIGATION_BAR# is substituted for the actual HTML that represents the individual navigation bar entries.

Accessing Navigation Bar Entries

You can access the current navigation bar entries either through the Shared Components section of the application, as shown in Figure 5-16, or through the Navigation Bar section in the page definition.

Figure 5-16. Accessing navigation bar entries

The Buglist application currently has only a single navigation bar entry defined. This is the Logout entry, which produces the Logout link shown in the top-right corner of the page. Figure 5-17 shows the attributes for this Logout entry. As you can see, you can define an image and a target for the entry. In this case, the entry is using the special URL target of &LOGOUT_URL., which you can define within the authentication scheme for the application. For this application, the following target will be substituted:

```
wwv_flow_custom_auth_std.logout?p_this_flow=&APP_ID.&p_next_flow_page_sess=
&APP_ID.:1
```

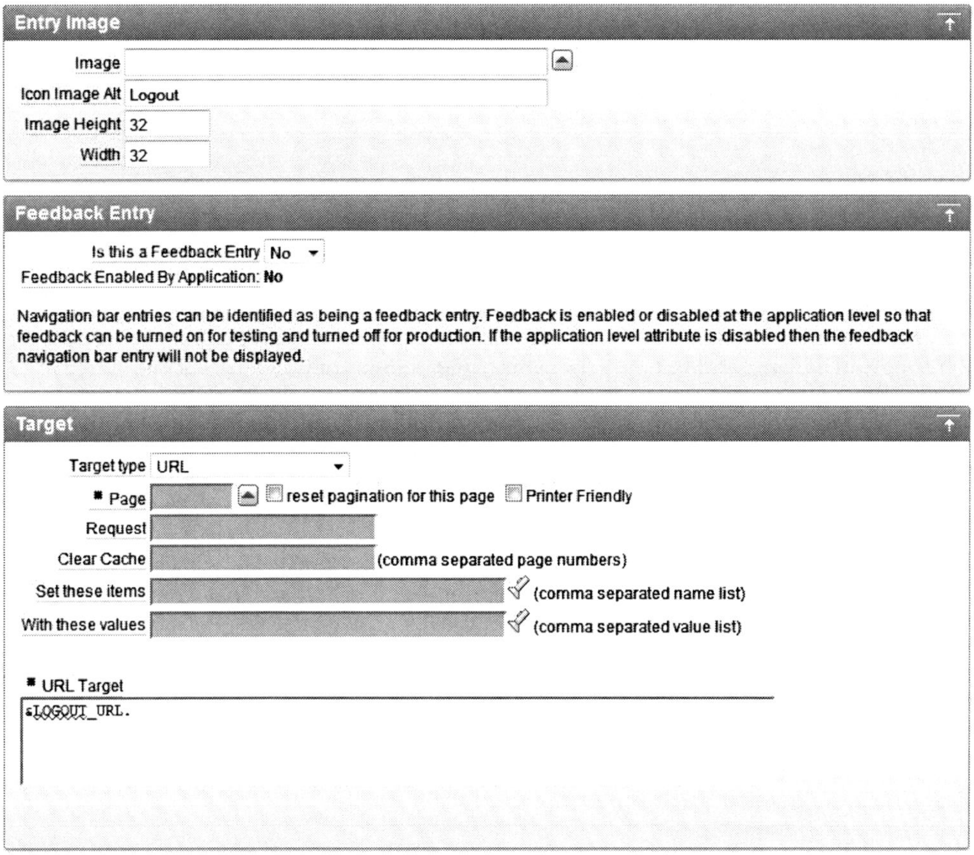

Figure 5-17. Attributes for the Logout navigation bar entry

This means that when the user clicks the Logout link, the standard `wwv_flow_custom_auth_std.logout` routine will be called, which performs some standard logout logic that you can use in your own applications. The parameters to the URL (which are used as parameters to the procedure) mean that users will be returned to page 1 in the application once they have successfully reauthenticated (remember that page 1 requires authentication).

Again, as with tabs, you can also use conditions with navigation bar entries, as shown in Figure 5-18. This example specifies that the navigation bar entry should be displayed only if the user is on page 1 or page 5.

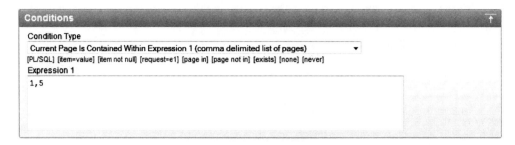

Figure 5-18. *The conditions for the Logout navigation bar entry*

Although navigation bar entries don't have the same capabilities as tabs in terms of being able to define current and noncurrent pages, you can use conditions to effectively mimic the same sort of behavior. For example, you can use the current page number or some other criteria to display different navigation bar entries.

Creating Navigation Bar Entries

Let's create a couple of new navigation bar entries: a simple Home entry to take users back to the first page of the application and a Help entry to open a pop-up Help window. Notice that when you create a navigation bar entry from scratch, you are asked whether this will navigate to a standard URL or to a Feedback page. As described in Chapter 1, Feedback pages are used to gather comments from users. For this exercise, we will use the URL method.

Create the Home entry as shown in Figure 5-19. To keep the example simple, just use a text link. However, you could quite easily use an image as well as or instead of the text. Add a simple condition, as shown in Figure 5-20, saying that the entry will not be displayed if users are already on the home page. Also, rather than using a URL target type, use a page in the application as the target, as shown in Figure 5-21.

Figure 5-19. *Creating the Home navigation bar entry*

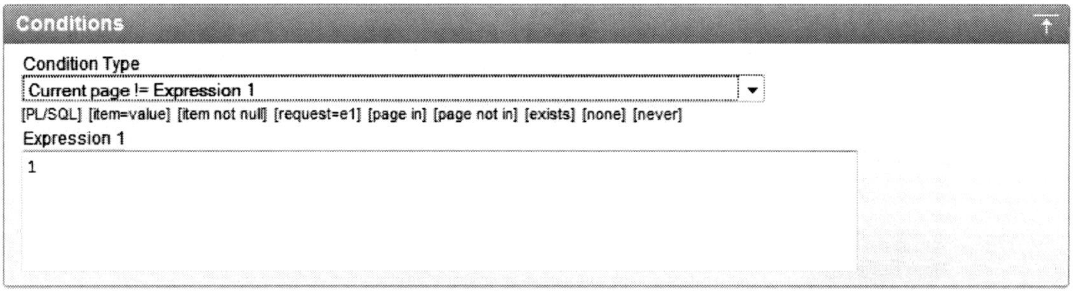

Conditions

Condition Type

Current page != Expression 1

[PL/SQL] [item=value] [item not null] [request=e1] [page in] [page not in] [exists] [none] [never]

Expression 1

1

Figure 5-20. Using a condition with the Home navigation bar entry

Target

Target type Page in this Application

* Page 1 ☐ reset pagination for this page ☐ Printer Friendly

Request

Clear Cache (comma separated page numbers)

Set these items (comma separated name list)

With these values (comma separated value list)

* URL Target

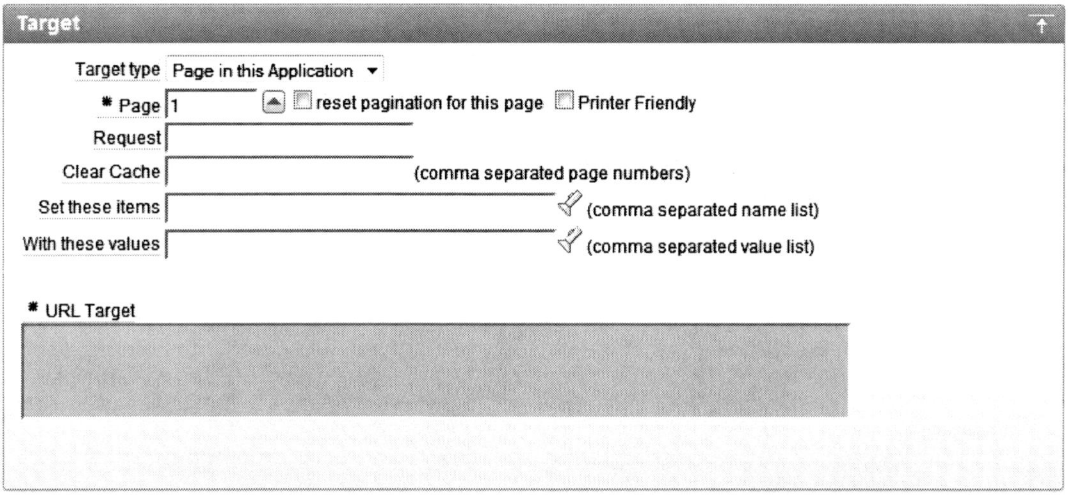

Figure 5-21. Specifying the page target for the Home navigation bar entry

If you run the page again, you'll see the new navigation bar entry displayed in the top-right corner, alongside the Logout link, as shown in Figure 5-22 (but remember that you won't see the new entry if you are already on page 1). Notice that the new Home link appears before the Logout link. That's because the Sequence attribute for the Home link is a numeric value that's less than the Sequence attribute value for the Logout link. The navigation bar entries are output in ascending order, so you can use the Sequence attribute to maintain a particular order among your entries.

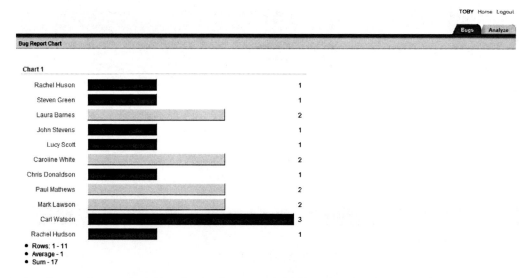

Figure 5-22. *The new Home navigation bar entry is displayed next to the Logout link.*

Now let's create the Help entry. This time, use a URL target, as shown in Figure 5-23. The URL target uses the following value:

```
javascript:popUp2('f?p=&APP_ID.:HELP:&SESSION.', 400, 400);
```

The `popUp2` JavaScript routine is one that is defined in the standard APEX JavaScript libraries, so you can use it in your own applications. The first parameter to the procedure is the URL you wish to open. Here, you're passing in the standard APEX URL `f?p` as well as some parameters to it that will take you to the Help page in the same application (note that here you're using the page alias `HELP`, rather than passing in a numeric page ID). The second and third parameters to the JavaScript routine are the width and the height of the pop-up window.

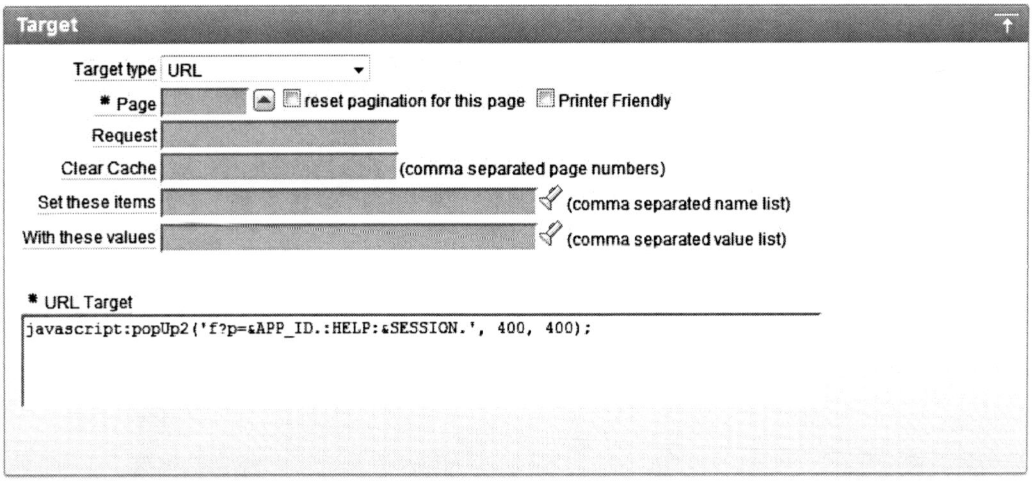

Figure 5-23. Creating the Help navigation bar entry

If you now rerun the page and click the Help link, you should see something similar to Figure 5-24. Note that the pop-up window is actually displaying the Help page as it would appear if you had navigated to it using the tabs; that is, you now have a pop-up window that also contains tabs and navigation bar entries. In a production application, most likely you wouldn't want to do this. Instead, you could define a very minimal page template specifically for your pop-up windows and use that. However, this example does demonstrate that you can easily add the ability to create a pop-up window from your navigation bar.

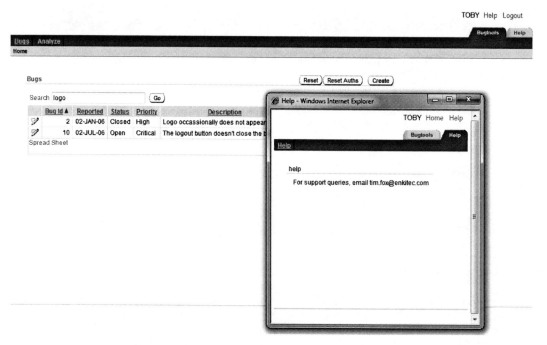

Figure 5-24. Displaying the pop-up Help window

Performing an Action on the Current Page

In some cases, you might want your navigation bar entry to take you back to perform an action on the current page. For example, you might want an entry to print the current page, to make the current page printer-friendly, or to reset the pagination on the current page. In this case, rather than hard-coding the page ID, you can use the substitution variable &APP_PAGE_ID., which will be replaced by the current page ID when you run the application. This way, the same navigation bar entry is able to work on multiple pages.

Figure 5-25 shows how to use &APP_PAGE_ID. to create a navigation bar entry that will put each page into Printer Friendly mode. Here, the page target specified is the &APP_PAGE_ID. substitution variable, and the Printer Friendly check box is selected. If you now run the application and click the Printer Friendly navigation bar entry, you will see a screen similar to Figure 5-26.

■ **Note** Make sure you add the period "." after the name of the &APP_PAGE_ID or you will get a nasty browser error that does not identify the root cause of the problem. You will not be able to see the entire substitution variable in the properties panel.

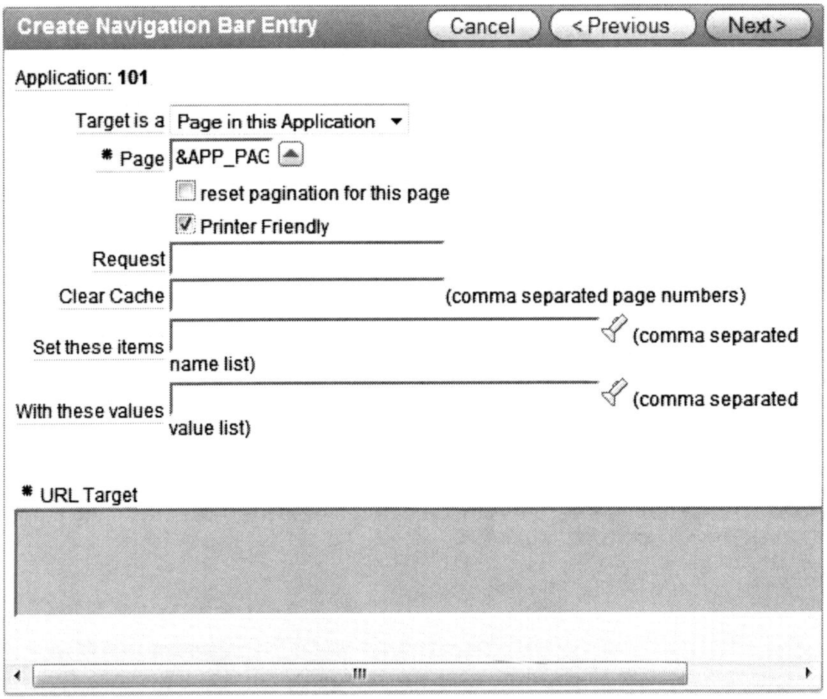

Figure 5-25. *Using the &APP_PAGE_ID. substitution variable to put the page in Printer Friendly mode*

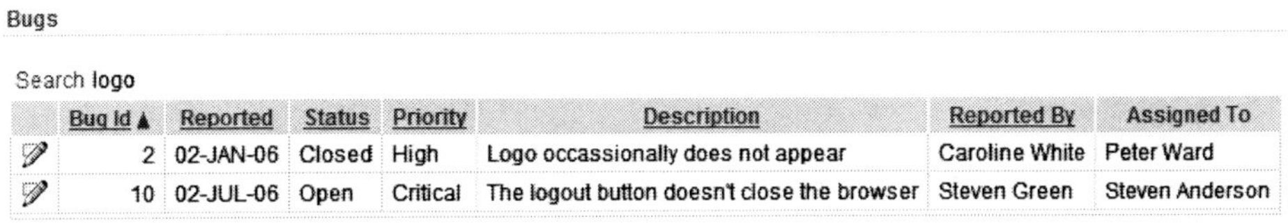
Bugs

Search logo

	Bug Id	Reported	Status	Priority	Description	Reported By	Assigned To
	2	02-JAN-06	Closed	High	Logo occassionally does not appear	Caroline White	Peter Ward
	10	02-JUL-06	Open	Critical	The logout button doesn't close the browser	Steven Green	Steven Anderson

Figure 5-26. *A page in Printer Friendly mode*

Note that there is no magic behind Printer Friendly mode. All it does is to make the page use a specific page template in which you can alter the layout of the page to be more suitable for printing. In this example, the template removed the navigation bars as well as the tabs and some of the form fields. You can completely customize the Printer Friendly template if you wish.

■ **Tip** Navigation bars may not suit all types of applications, but they do offer a very simple and quick way of defining a navigation system for your application. You may want to use navigation bars during the prototype phase of your application, while you're toying with different ideas for screen layouts.

Breadcrumbs

Breadcrumbs are yet another tool you can use to help users navigate your application. However, unlike most of the other navigation tools, breadcrumbs have a quite unique characteristic: they allow users to easily see their current position in the application relative to other areas of the application. Users can go back to previous locations in the application by following the breadcrumb trail created by their actions.

The Buglist application already has a breadcrumb menu, displayed just below the tabs, as shown in Figure 5-27. In this figure, the breadcrumb trail says the user is currently on the Analyze page and got to that page via the home page. Actually, the last part of the preceding sentence may or may not be true, since breadcrumbs allow for a great deal of flexibility in how you associate breadcrumb entries with each other. The way to read the breadcrumb trail in this case is that the user is able to go directly to the home page by clicking the Home link in the breadcrumb trail.

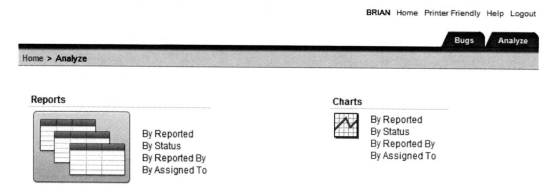

Figure 5-27. The breadcrumb trail shows the user is on the Analyze page.

An application can have multiple breadcrumbs defined and can display multiple breadcrumbs simultaneously. However, we suggest you use only one breadcrumb menu, perhaps two if necessary. Displaying more than two menus is rarely helpful and can actually make the task of navigating more confusing.

Accessing Breadcrumb Entries

You can view the breadcrumbs for your application from the Shared Components section, as shown in Figure 5-28, or via the page definition. If you select the Buglist breadcrumb, you also get a very useful outline of the breadcrumb entries, as shown in Figure 5-29.

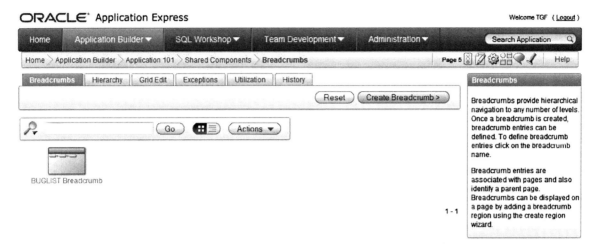

Figure 5-28. Breadcrumb defined for the application

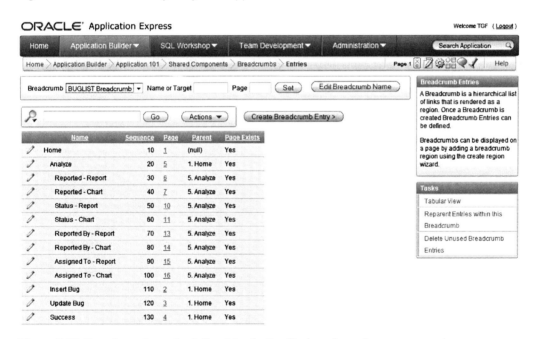

Figure 5-29. Breadcrumb entries defined for the Buglist breadcrumb

This outline view of the breadcrumb entries makes it easy to see how each breadcrumb entry relates to every other breadcrumb. For example, you can see that the root entry is Home, with four entries below it: Analyze, Insert Bug, Update Bug, and Success. The Analyze entry also contains a number of entries below it. You can also see that each breadcrumb entry corresponds to a particular page. This is similar to the way that tabs can be tied to a particular page; however, unlike a tab, a breadcrumb can relate to only an individual page.

Figure 5-30 shows some of the interesting attributes you can define for a breadcrumb entry:

Page: Specifies where the breadcrumb entry will appear. You can see that the Analyze breadcrumb entry is assigned to page 5, which means that the breadcrumb entry will be shown if you are on page 5.

Short Name and Long Name: Specifying a short name for the breadcrumb entry is mandatory. Optionally, you can also enter a long name. Depending on the theme and page template you use, the breadcrumb menu might use either the short name or the long name.

Parent Entry: Defines the parent breadcrumb entry that will appear with this breadcrumb entry. The parent for the Analyze breadcrumb is the Home breadcrumb, so if you are on page 5, you will see not only the Analyze breadcrumb, but also the Home breadcrumb. Similarly, if you have any other breadcrumbs that use the Analyze breadcrumb as their parent, the Analyze breadcrumb will also be displayed when you are on any of those pages. As mentioned earlier, the Home breadcrumb entry is the root entry, because it doesn't have a parent entry defined. There can be only one root breadcrumb entry in your breadcrumb trail.

Target: Assigns a target for the breadcrumb entry. In this case, the target is also page 5, so clicking the breadcrumb entry will take you to page 5. (Remember that the breadcrumb entry can also be displayed when the user is on a page other than page 5 if that page uses a breadcrumb that is a descendant of this breadcrumb.) You can also choose a page target different from the page used in the Breadcrumb section. Bear in mind that this may be confusing to users, since the page they branched to would not be the same as the page the breadcrumb links to; however, there may be cases where this is the behavior you want.

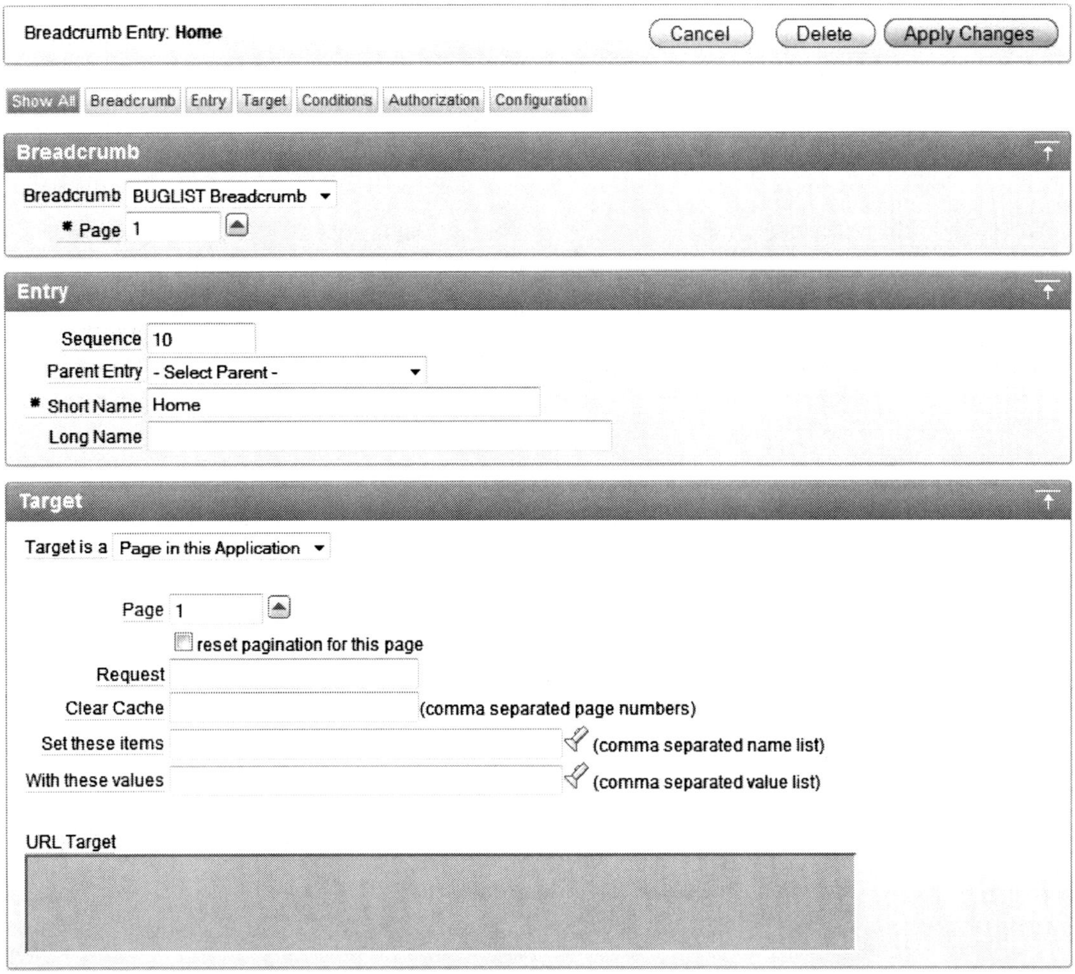

Breadcrumb Entry: **Home**		Cancel	Delete	Apply Changes

Show All | Breadcrumb | Entry | Target | Conditions | Authorization | Configuration

Breadcrumb

Breadcrumb BUGLIST Breadcrumb ▼
 * Page 1 ▲

Entry

Sequence 10
Parent Entry - Select Parent - ▼
 * Short Name Home
Long Name

Target

Target is a Page in this Application ▼

Page 1 ▲
  ☐ reset pagination for this page
Request
Clear Cache   (comma separated page numbers)
Set these items   ✎ (comma separated name list)
With these values   ✎ (comma separated value list)

URL Target

Figure 5-30. Breadcrumb entry attributes

Using Dynamic Breadcrumb Entries

As with some of the other navigation tools, you can use substitution variables with breadcrumb entries to enable them to display dynamic information at runtime. For example, if you want to modify the Update Bug breadcrumb entry to also display the number of the bug that is currently being edited, you could include the substitution variable P3_ID in the Short Name attribute for the breadcrumb, since this is the page item that represents the ID of the current bug, as shown in Figure 5-31. Then, when you edit a bug, the breadcrumb entry will also contain the bug ID, as shown in Figure 5-32.

This is a bit of a contrived example, since the bug ID might not be that useful in the breadcrumb entry. However, sometimes including dynamic information in the breadcrumb entry is a good idea. For example, imagine you are drilling down into a report of employees belonging to different departments. Once you select a department, you could filter the list of employees to show only those belonging to that particular department. You could show the department in the breadcrumb entry, so that users can easily see which department they are currently viewing.

■ **Note** Using substitution variables is not just limited to breadcrumb entries. You can use this technique in many different places to make your user interface much more dynamic and reflect at runtime what your users are actually doing.

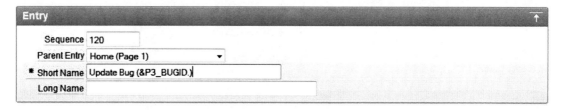

Figure 5-31. Using a substitution variable in the breadcrumb entry

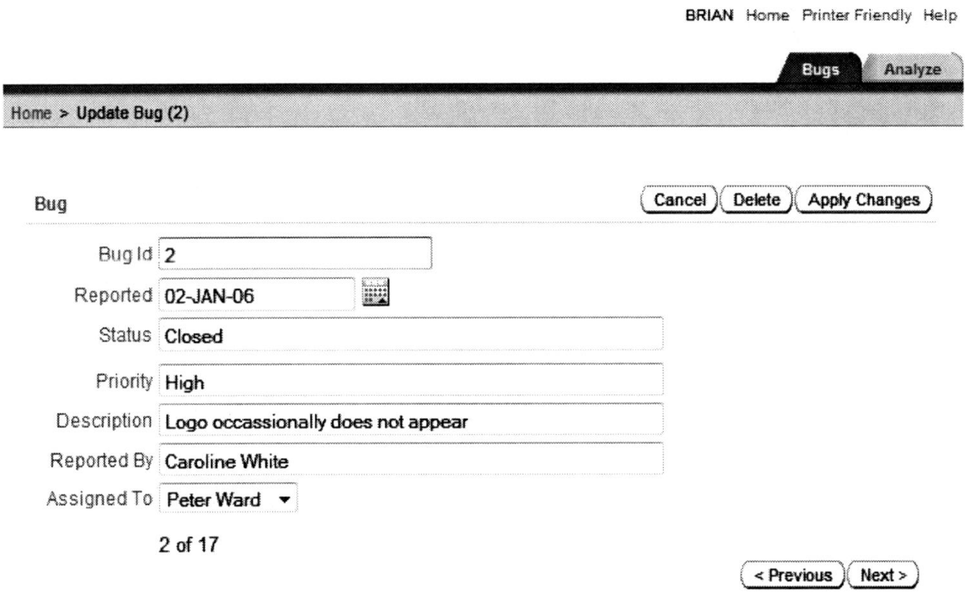

BRIAN Home Printer Friendly Help

| Bugs | Analyze |

Home > **Update Bug (2)**

Bug   (Cancel)(Delete)(Apply Changes)

Bug Id [2]

Reported [02-JAN-06] [▦]

Status [Closed]

Priority [High]

Description [Logo occassionally does not appear]

Reported By [Caroline White]

Assigned To [Peter Ward ▼]

2 of 17

(< Previous)(Next >)

Figure 5-32. The breadcrumb entry now displays the bug ID.

Displaying Breadcrumbs

To display your breadcrumb menu on a page, you must create a Breadcrumb region on that page, as shown in Figure 5-33. You can then select which breadcrumb menu you wish to use, as shown in Figure 5-34. The wizard allows you to create a new breadcrumb entry for the page and specify which breadcrumb entry should be the parent for the new entry, as shown in Figure 5-35. Figure 5-36 shows the page running after the new breadcrumb has been added.

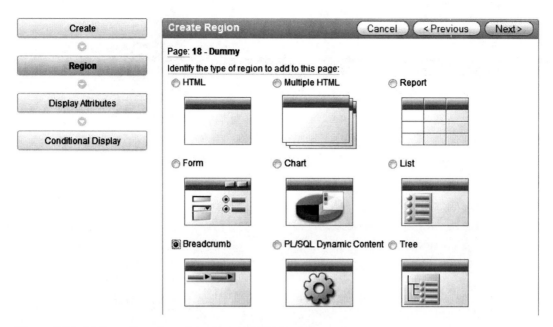

Figure 5-33. Adding a Breadcrumb region to the Help page

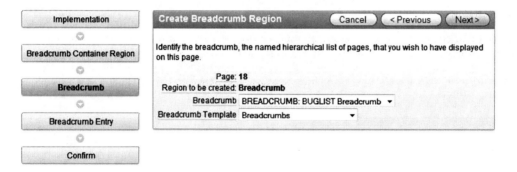

Figure 5-34. Selecting the breadcrumb to use in the region

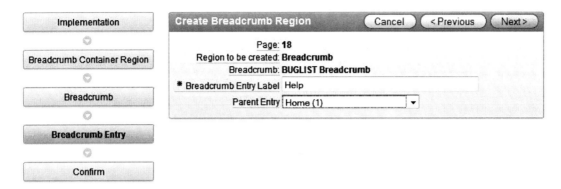

Figure 5-35. Defining the parent breadcrumb entry

Figure 5-36. New Breadcrumb region displayed on the page

You might be thinking that having to create a Breadcrumb region on each page is quite repetitive work and surely there must be an easier way to do it. You're absolutely right. An easier way to do it is by using page zero. As mentioned in Chapter 1, page zero is useful for displaying the same page element on all or multiple pages of your application; it's discussed in more detail later in this chapter.

Lists

Lists are another tool you can use to create a navigation aid in your application. Lists share many of the features of tabs, navigation bars, and breadcrumbs. They are extremely versatile—perhaps even more so than some of the other navigation tools.

Lists offer simplicity and ease of use, and you can use them to create many different types of navigation interfaces—with amazing results. Some great user interfaces are created using nothing more than some CSS and a list (for example, the APEX Evangelists site at http://apex-evangelists.com and the DG Tournament site at /www.dgtournament.com), so don't underestimate them. In fact, some developers opt to use a list where others would choose tabs.

Accessing List Entries

The Buglist application already contains a couple of lists, created automatically by the application creation wizard. The lists are visible on the Analyze page, as shown in Figure 5-37. One list shows the links for the reports, and the other displays the links available for charts. At first glance, the lists don't appear particularly exciting. In fact, they look like links, similar to the navigation bar entries.

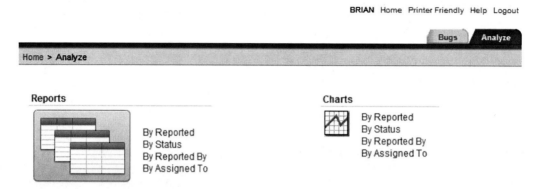

Figure 5-37. Lists as a navigation aid

The Lists section of the Shared Components shows the two lists that were created, as shown in Figure 5-38. If you examine the Charts list, you can see the individual list items, as shown in Figure 5-39.

The list entries look similar to the entries you can have in standard tabs or the navigation bar. You can give each list entry a target (where clicking the list entry will take the user), as well as define a condition for each. It's only when you view the individual attributes for a list entry that you can see the full range of available settings, as shown in Figures 5-40 and 5-41.

Figure 5-38. Lists available as shared components for the application

Figure 5-39. List entries in the Charts list

Figure 5-40. List entry attributes

Figure 5-41. More list entry attributes

In a way, lists combine the simplicity of navigation bar entries with the complexity of tabs. You can see from Figure 5-40 that you can build a hierarchy of list entries, with one entry being the parent of another. You can also define a target page for the list entry, as well as define the list of pages for which this list entry should be regarded as current, in much the same way as with tabs.

Currently, none of the Charts list entries has a parent defined, which is why they all appear at the same level in the list. You can easily change the parent entry for some of the entries, as shown in Figure 5-42. Here, the By Reported list entry is the parent of the By Status and By Report By list entries. However, if you ran the application again, you would not see any difference in the way the list entries are displayed on screen. This is because the template that is currently being used for the list does not take the hierarchy into account.

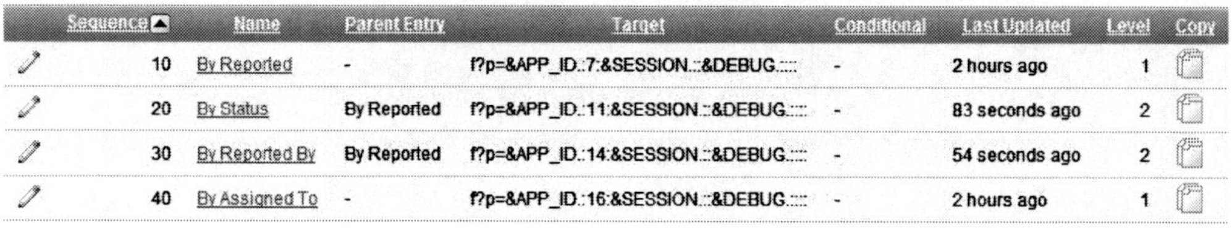

Sequence ▲	Name	Parent Entry	Target	Conditional	Last Updated	Level	Copy
10	By Reported	-	f?p=&APP_ID.:7:&SESSION.::&DEBUG.::::	-	2 hours ago	1	
20	By Status	By Reported	f?p=&APP_ID.:11:&SESSION.::&DEBUG.::::	-	83 seconds ago	2	
30	By Reported By	By Reported	f?p=&APP_ID.:14:&SESSION.::&DEBUG.::::	-	54 seconds ago	2	
40	By Assigned To	-	f?p=&APP_ID.:16:&SESSION.::&DEBUG.::::	-	2 hours ago	1	

Figure 5-42. List with an implied hierarchy

To show the hierarchy, you need to change the template from Vertical Unordered List without Bullet to another template, such as DHTML Tree, as shown in Figure 5-43. Now if you run the page, you should see the output shown in Figure 5-44. In this figure, we've expanded the list by clicking the plus sign (+) next to By Reported, which reveals the two items under it.

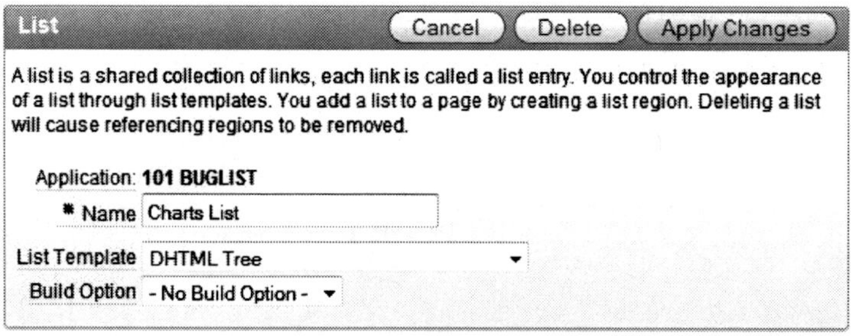

Figure 5-43. Changing the list template

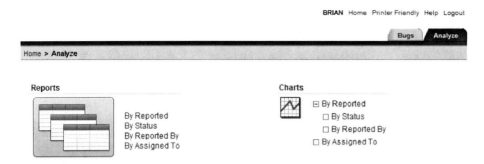

Figure 5-44. *The list is now displayed in a hierarchical manner.*

You can use other built-in templates to change the appearance of the list. By simply changing the template, you can change the list from being a vertical list to a horizontal list. You can also define images used with each list entry, or you could go for a completely DHTML menu. In fact, with APEX, you can have total control over the look of the list, since you can define your own list template. That way, you can create pretty much any sort of layout that is possible with HTML, CSS, and JavaScript.

Creating a Menu Using a List

So, how can you create a menu for your application using a list? You can do this by using the same principles as the two lists that were automatically created: add a new list and then create new list entries that link to particular pages. You can then display that list on each page, which will enable users to navigate to different pages.

Figure 5-45 shows the first step of creating a new list, using the Vertical Sidebar List template. (You can always change the list template later.) Next, create some simple list entry items for the list, as shown in Figure 5-46. These entries have been linked to the same pages you'd be able to navigate to using the tabs or links in the application.

Figure 5-45. *Creating a new list to use as a menu*

	Sequence ▲	Name	Parent Entry	Target	Conditional	Last Updated	Level	Copy
✎	10	Home	-	f?p=&APP_ID.:1:&SESSION.:	-	6 minutes ago	1	🗋
✎	20	Analysis	Home	f?p=&APP_ID.:5:&SESSION.::&DEBUG.:::	-	6 minutes ago	2	🗋
✎	30	Assigned To	Analysis	f?p=&APP_ID.:15:&SESSION.::&DEBUG.:::	-	5 minutes ago	3	🗋
✎	40	Reported By	Analysis	f?p=&APP_ID.:13:&SESSION.::&DEBUG.:::	-	1 seconds ago	3	🗋

Figure 5-46. Adding list entries

Now you need to display the list on the page, so create a new region on the home page as shown in Figure 5-47. This example uses the Sidebar Region for the template and also positions the display point of the region on the right side of the screen. The template for this region has been changed to Tree List (note that the template used for the region and the template used for the list are different types). If you now run the application and look at the home page, you'll see the list menu, as shown in Figure 5-48.

■ **Note** You'd probably expect a navigation menu to appear on the left side of the screen (well, people who read from left to right would expect that). However, in the page template used in this example, there is no suitable position on the left side. As you'll see in Chapter 10, you can modify the page template to position items wherever you desire.

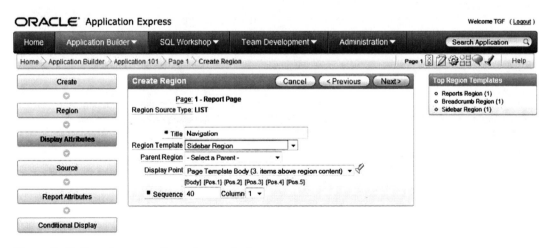

Figure 5-47. Creating a new list region on the home page

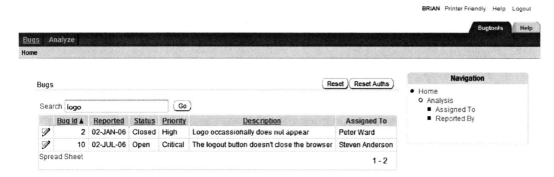

Figure 5-48. Displaying the navigation list

Clicking a list entry will take you to the relevant page. However, the menu is displayed only on the home page at the moment; if you click a link that takes you to another page, you won't be able to access the navigation list from there. As with breadcrumbs, you need to create a region on each individual page to display the list. And again, you can use page zero to achieve that in an efficient way.

As with tabs, you can also incorporate authorization schemes with individual list entries. For example, if you want to make sure that only administrators can access the Assigned To list entry, select the USER_IS_ADMIN authorization scheme you created in Chapter 4, as shown in Figure 5-49. If you now log in as a nonadministrator (using the jimb user, for example) and access the home page, you will no longer see the Assigned To list entry, as shown in Figure 5-50.

Figure 5-49. Adding an authorization scheme to a list item

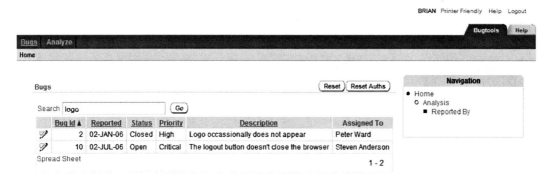

Figure 5-50. Nonadministrators will not see the Assigned To entry.

Notice that the hierarchy of the list items is still preserved, even though one of the items is no longer visible. You might be wondering what would happen if you applied the same authorization scheme check to the Analyze entry. As you can see in Figure 5-51, in that case, not only is the Analysis entry not visible, but you also can't see any entries that have the Analysis entry as their parent (and so on down the hierarchy chain).

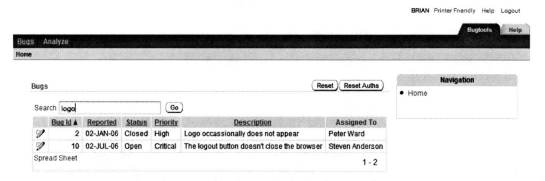

Figure 5-51. *Child entries are also hidden by authorization schemes.*

So, even though you haven't applied the authorization check to the Reported By list entry, the fact that you applied the authorization check to the parent item means that unauthorized users can't see any children of that parent item. This is an extremely powerful way of controlling access to a hierarchy.

Tracking Clicks on List Entries

Lists have a couple of features that can be extremely useful in certain circumstances. One is the ability to automatically count the number of times a user selects a particular list entry.

Through the attributes of each individual list entry, you can specify whether clicks on that entry should be counted, as well as a category for that click. By using categories, you can group different list entries for statistical purposes. For example, rather than counting individual clicks to both the By Reported By and By Assigned To entries, you might group both entries into an Analysis category. You might also enable the Home list entry for click counting and assign it a category of Home, as shown in Figure 5-52.

Figure 5-52. *Counting list entry clicks*

The clicks are counted internally through the `APEX_UTIL.COUNT_CLICK` procedure (or the shorthand notation Z), which will automatically log the clicks so you can view the results in the Administration section of your workspace. In the example in Figure 5-53, you can see that user `jimb` clicked two list items, both in the Home category (actually, he clicked the Home entry twice).

Note The click log isn't very detailed. For example, you can't see where the user was connecting from (his remote IP address) or what type of web browser he used. However, for simple logging purposes, the click log is definitely worth using.

Figure 5-53. Viewing external clicks in the Workspace Administration section

You can use this functionality when you want to keep a simple record of how your users navigate through your system. It can be very useful to know which areas of your application are the least or most used. Based on this information, you may want to adapt your application's design so that the most commonly used parts of the application are easy to access.

Using User-Defined Attributes for List Entries

So, what other tricks can you do with lists? The answer lies in the rather vaguely named User Defined Attributes section of the list entry, as shown in Figure 5-54.

Figure 5-54. The first three of the ten user-defined attributes you can add to a list item

What are these attributes for? As the name implies, they're for anything you would like. The key is understanding how the list template works. For example, the definition for the Tree List template shows that the same HTML is used to represent the list items, regardless of whether they are considered current, as shown in Figure 5-55.

Suppose you want to change the way each entry is displayed by wrapping each one in an HTML DIV section and using some CSS to specify what each DIV section should look like. The problem here is that using the standard attributes, you can differentiate between only a current and noncurrent entry, not between the different entries themselves. However, by using the user-defined attributes, you can change the look of individual entries. First, modify the HTML in the Template Definition section to wrap the entry in a DIV section:

```
<div id="#A01#"><li><a href="#LINK#">#TEXT#</a></li></div>
```

The substitution variable #A01# corresponds to the first user-defined attribute. Similarly, #A02# corresponds to the second user-defined attribute, #A03# to the third, and so on.

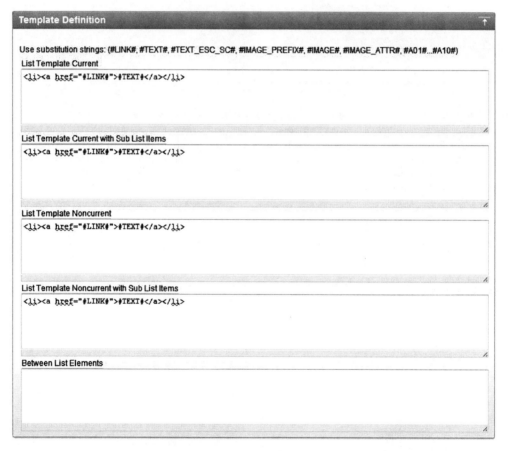

Figure 5-55. *Definition of the Tree List template*

Next, specify a value for the first user-defined attribute for the Home list entry, as shown in Figure 5-56.

Figure 5-56. Specifying a user-defined attribute

If you now run the application and view the HTML source code for the home page (you can usually do this via the View menu in your browser or by right-clicking the page and choosing View Source), you should see that the HTML generated for the Home list entry looks like this (with the code between the anchor tags omitted for brevity):

```
<div id="HOMEDIV"><li><a ...></a></li></div>
```

You can see that the DIV ID contains the substitution value that was specified in the User Defined Attributes section for the Home entry. Now you can implement your own CSS and then style each list entry in whatever way you desired.

Trees

Trees are typically used where you wish to represent hierarchical information. As you saw in the previous sections, you can create a menu system with a hierarchy, so you should be able to use a tree to display it.

So how would you go about creating a menu framework using a tree? As an example, let's mimic the menu created earlier using lists, this time using a table to specify the entries.

Creating a Table for the Tree Entries

First, create a simple table to hold the list of entries, as shown in Listing 5-1.

Listing 5-1. Creating a Table to Store the Tree Entries

```
apexdemo@DBTEST> create table tree_navigation(
  2  id number,
  3  parent_id number,
  4  title varchar2(30),
  5  link varchar2(60));

Table created.
```

The table is very simple, containing only four columns:

- The id column will contain a unique identifier for the entry.

- The parent_id column will refer to the ID of another entry if this entry has a parent. If parent_id is null, that entry will be considered to be the root node for the tree. There can be only a single root node.

- The title column will be the text displayed in the tree.

- The link column will enable you to direct users to another location if they click a particular tree node.

Next, insert some records that will mimic the same hierarchy used with the list earlier, as shown in Listing 5-2.

Listing 5-2. *Creating Data for the Tree Layout*

```
apexdemo@DBTEST> insert into tree_navigation

  2  values
  3  (1, null, 'Home', 'f?p=&APP_ID.:1:&SESSION.');

1 row created.

apexdemo@DBTEST> insert into tree_navigation
  2  values
  3  (2, 1, 'Analysis', 'f?p=&APP_ID.:5:&SESSION.');

1 row created.

apexdemo@DBTEST> insert into tree_navigation
  2  values
  3  (3, 2, 'Assigned To', 'f?p=&APP_ID.:13:&SESSION.');

1 row created.

apexdemo@DBTEST> insert into tree_navigation
  2  values
  3  (4, 2, 'Reported By', 'f?p=&APP_ID.:10:&SESSION.');

1 row created.

apexdemo@DBTEST> commit;

Commit complete.

apexdemo@DBTEST> select * from tree_navigation;

 ID  PARENT_ID TITLE          LINK
 --- ---------- -------------- ------------------------------
  1            Home           f?p=&APP_ID.:1:&SESSION.
  2          1 Analysis       f?p=&APP_ID.:5:&SESSION.
  3          2 Assigned To    f?p=&APP_ID.:13:&SESSION.
  4          2 Reported By    f?p=&APP_ID.:10:&SESSION.
```

Notice that the records use a link in the format of f?p, which allows you to refer to another page in the application. The benefit of doing it this way is that you can also specify links external to the application by using a fully qualified URL, such as http://www.google.com.

▪ **Note** This is a simple example for demonstration purposes. In practice, you'd probably want to use a sequence for the ID column, rather than manually inserting a value. Also, you'd need to ensure that there was only one entry in the table with a `parent_id` of null; that is, only one root node should be allowed. And, of course, in your production system, you would want to investigate some suitable indexes for a table like this!

Creating the Tree Component

Now you can create the tree component, as shown in Figure 5-57. By default, the tree creation wizard will create the tree on a new page. If you wish to place the tree on an existing page, change the Page Number attribute to the page you wish to use.

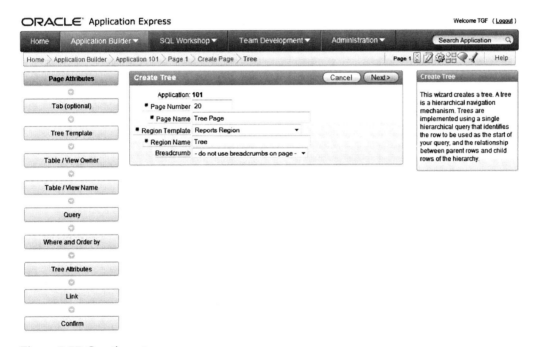

Figure 5-57. Creating a tree

APEX 4.0 lets you choose from three basic tree templates as shown in Figure 5-58. Choose the Classic style for this example.

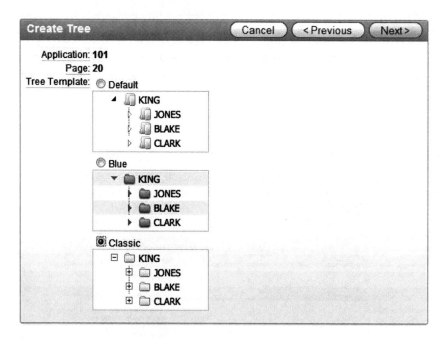

Figure 5-58. Selecting the tree template

You can choose to base the root node of your tree on a pop-up LOV, a SQL query, or a static item. Since this example stores the root node in the same table as the rest of the tree entries, choose to base it on a SQL query, as shown in Figure 5-59. The query for the root node is very simple:

```
select id from tree_navigation where parent_id is null
```

You could use some other criteria in your own applications, such as always giving the root node an ID of zero. However, in this example, the root node will have a null parent_id, so this simple query will work.

The wizard will then ask which schema and table should be used to create the tree. You will also need to specify which columns in that table to use, as shown in Figure 5-59. Also, as shown in the figure, choose to make the leaf node text a link by setting the Link Option attribute to Existing Application Item. This allows you to use the link column in the table.

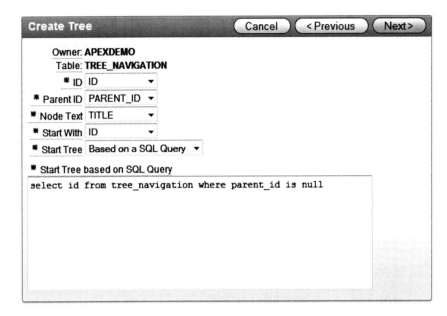

Figure 5-59. Selecting the tree attributes

If you now run the application, you should see a new Tree region on the page, as shown in Figure 5-60. If users click any of the tree entries, they will be taken to the page specified in the link column of the table.

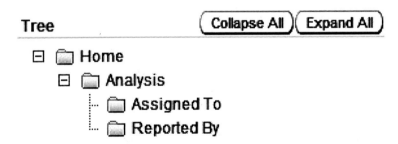

Figure 5-60. Tree region being driven from the table

Enabling and Disabling Tree Entries

You can extend this example to add the ability to enable and disable tree entries. As shown in Listing 5-3, add an enabled column to the table and update the Assigned To entry to be disabled.

Listing 5-3. Adding an Enabled Column to the Table

```
apexdemo@DBTEST> alter table tree_navigation
  2  add (enabled char(1) default 'Y');

Table altered.

apexdemo@DBTEST> update tree_navigation
  2  set enabled = 'N' where id = 3;

1 row updated.

apexdemo@DBTEST> commit;

Commit complete.

apexdemo@DBTEST> select * from tree_navigation;

 ID  PARENT_ID TITLE         LINK                             ENABLED
 --- --------- ------------- -------------------------------- -------
  1            Home          f?p=&APP_ID.:1:&SESSION.         Y
  2          1 Analysis      f?p=&APP_ID.:5:&SESSION.         Y
  3          2 Assigned To   f?p=&APP_ID.:13:&SESSION.        N
  4          2 Reported By   f?p=&APP_ID.:10:&SESSION.        Y
```

Now modify the tree query to use the new enabled column, as shown in Listing 5-4.

Listing 5-4. Adding a Restriction to the Tree Query

```
select "ID" id,
       "PARENT_ID" pid,
       "TITLE" name,
       "LINK" link,
       null a1,
       null a2
from "#OWNER#"."TREE_NAVIGATION"
```

If you run the application again, you will see that the Assigned To entry is no longer displayed in the tree, as shown in Figure 5-61. As with a list menu, if you disable an entry that also contains child nodes (for example, the Analysis entry), the child nodes will also be disabled. That means you won't see any child nodes that descend from the disabled node, even if those child nodes are not disabled themselves.

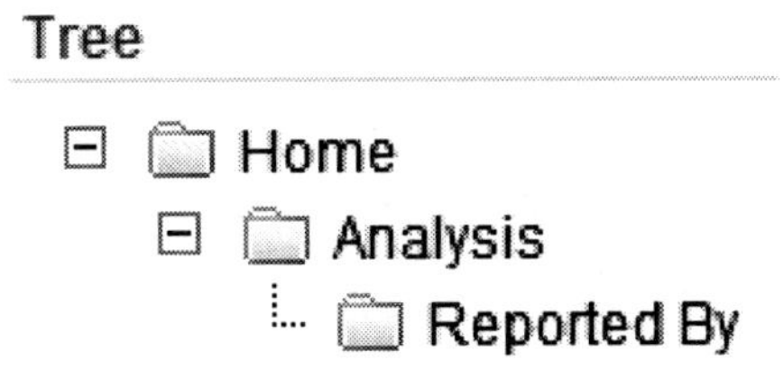

Tree

☐ 📁 Home
   ☐ 📁 Analysis
      ┊⋯ 📁 Reported By

Figure 5-61. Disabled entries do not appear in the tree.

■ **Tip** For another example of what you can do with trees, see Tony Jedlinski's excellent article "Build a Menu Framework." This article was published in the May/June 2006 edition of *Oracle Magazine* and is also available online (currently at www.oracle.com/technetwork/issue-archive/2006/06-may/o36apex-086847.html).

Page Zero

How does page zero relate to navigation? As you've learned in this chapter, breadcrumbs and lists (and trees, too) need to be created in a region on each page you wish to use them. Page zero is the solution to all that repetitive work.

You can think of page zero as a page with a very special purpose: to define elements that can appear on multiple pages within your application. In other words, if you define a region on page zero, that region can automatically appear on page 10 or page 15, even though you didn't specifically define the region on those pages. The previous sentence says "can appear" rather than "will appear," because you have complete control (through the use of conditional logic) over which pages anything you define on page zero will affect.

As an example, let's use page zero to make the navigation list you created earlier appear on every page, rather than just the home page.

Creating Page Zero

The first step is to create a page zero, since it isn't automatically created for you in your application. The page creation wizard includes a Page Zero option, as shown in Figure 5-62.

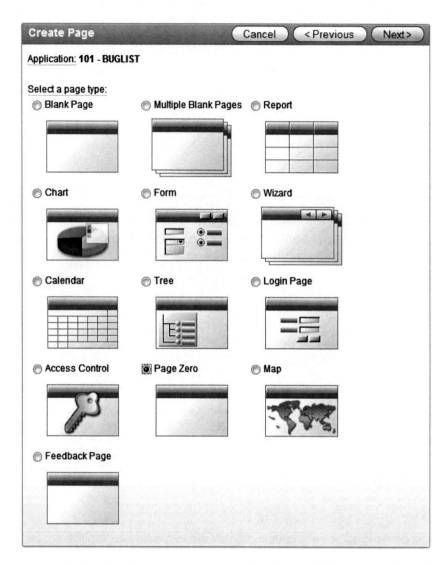

Figure 5-62. The Page Zero option appears at the bottom of the page creation wizard's choices for page type.

Once the wizard has completed, you should see your new page zero, as shown in Figure 5-63. As you can see, in the Application Builder, page zero looks quite different from other pages. Also, notice that it is not possible to run page zero directly.

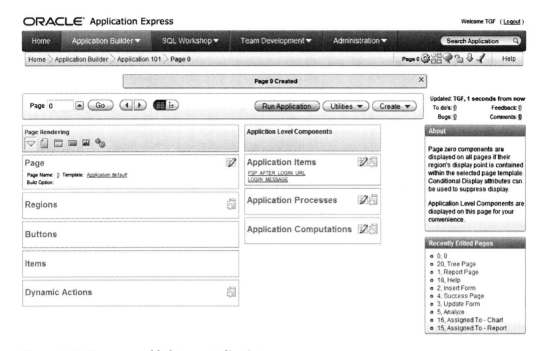

Figure 5-63. *Page zero added to an application*

Adding Regions to Page Zero

You can now create a new List region on page zero, as you did earlier for the home page, and use it for the navigation list you created in the previous section. If you run the application again, you'll see that the home page now contains two list menus, as shown in Figure 5-64.

Figure 5-64. *A List region defined on page zero appears on the Home page.*

One of the lists is due to the region defined on page zero, and the other list is due to the region defined on the home page. If you click the Analysis link in either list, you will see that the list defined on page zero also appears on the Analysis page, as shown in Figure 5-65.

Figure 5-65. A List region defined on page zero shows on every page.

The benefits of using page zero should now be obvious. By defining a single region on page zero, you can display the same navigation menu on every page of your application. This means that you have drastically reduced the number of bits of code you need to maintain. For example, if you want to move the list from the right side of the screen to the left, you need do that in only a single place, on page zero. If you had defined the menu individually on each page, you would need to change it in every individual place. Centralizing the code makes it far easier to adapt your application, and it also removes the possibility of forgetting to make a change somewhere.

But what if you want the menu to appear on only certain pages, rather than on every page? Well, once again, that's incredibly easy to do. You just use a condition in the region on page zero. Figure 5-66 shows using the "Current Page Is Contained Within Expression 1 (comma delimited list of pages)" condition to specify the list of pages on which the region should be displayed.

Conditions

Condition Type

Current Page Is Contained Within Expression 1 (comma delimited list of pages)   ▼

[PL/SQL] [item=value] [item not null] [request=e1] [page in] [page not in] [exists] [none] [never]

Expression 1

1,3,5,9

Figure 5-66. Using a condition to specify certain pages

Remember that you are limited only by your imagination here. You don't have to base the display on particular pages. Here are a few other possibilities:

- The condition could check the value of an application item.

- The condition could be based on the currently logged-in user.

- The condition could check the current time (imagine a system that displays a certain menu only during "out-of-office-hours" time).

- You could use some PL/SQL that queries a remote web server to determine if the menu should be shown.

Conditions allow amazing levels of control over your application. You can build some incredibly dynamic applications by using conditions within your navigational aids.

Layout

The built-in themes and templates allow you to position regions and page items in particular locations on the screen. Remember that you can create your own themes and templates, which allows you complete freedom to position your regions and items anywhere you desire. We will cover creating your own themes and templates in Chapter 10. Here, we'll concentrate on the mechanics of using the built-in ones.

Positioning Regions

Whenever you create a region on a page, you need to specify where you want the region to be positioned. In the Application Builder, you will see a drop-down list of all the currently available display points, as shown in Figure 5-67. These display points are defined in the current page template for the page.

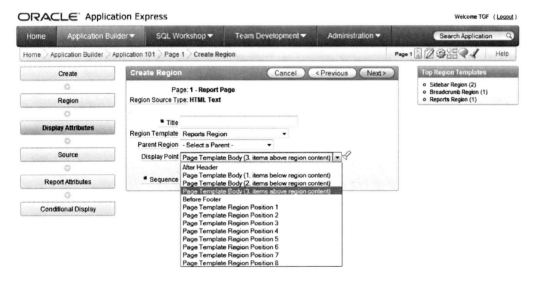

Figure 5-67. *List of currently available display points*

If you look at the page template (accessed from the Templates section of the Page Definition page of the Application Builder or from the Shared Components section, which shows all the templates), you'll see a lot of HTML in different sections, which is used to generate the page at runtime. For example, the HTML for the Footer section of the Two Level Tabs page template is shown in Figure 5-68.

Notice the substitution variable called #REGION_POSITION_05#. This corresponds to the Page Template Region Position 5 option in the Display Point drop-down list. The HTML used for the Body section of the page template contains other substitution variables, which correspond to the other available display points. The positions of these substitution variables in the page template determine exactly where the display points that you use for your regions will appear at runtime.

```
Footer
<hr />
<div class="t15customize">#CUSTOMIZE#</div>
<br />
#REGION_POSITION_05#
#FORM_CLOSE#
</body>
</html>
```

Figure 5-68. Footer section for a page template

Note that multiple regions can be contained in the same display point. In other words, you don't need to put each region into a different display point. The display point is effectively a container for your page regions, in the same way that the page itself is a container for different display points.

Fortunately, you don't need to keep checking the page template to see where each display point will end up being positioned. APEX makes it extremely easy to see how the display points will be displayed at runtime. Just click the small flashlight icon next to the Display Point drop-down list to see a pop-up window that shows a visual representation of the layout of the current page, as shown in Figure 5-69. For example, earlier in the chapter, you positioned the list menu in Region Position 3. From the pop-up layout window, you can see that Region Position 3 is on the right side of the screen.

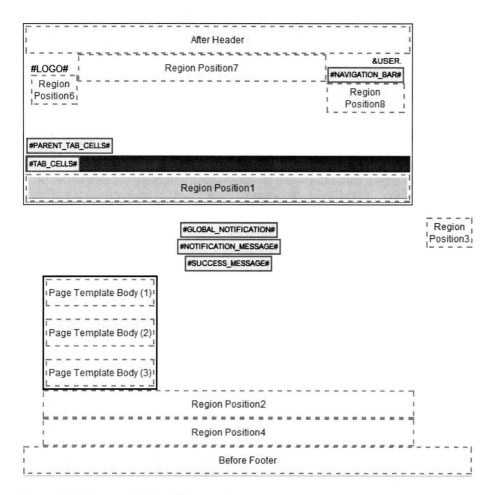

Figure 5-69. *Pop-up display of the page layout*

This pop-up representation of the page layout is completely dynamic. If you change the page template to move the region positions around, the pop-up will reflect the changed positions.

The position of these regions is entirely dependent on the page template (and therefore dependent on the theme you are using). If you change the theme (or template) the application is using, you may find your page regions appear in different positions. This gives you an extremely powerful way of completely changing the look and feel of your application, without having to manually reposition the page regions. However, there may be cases where you are using a display point in one page template (for example, #REGION_POSITION_05#) that does not appear in another page template, since not all the region positions must be specified in a template. In this situation, you would need to choose another display point for your page region from the ones that are available in the new template.

Since you can have multiple page regions within the same display point, the order in which those page regions appear on the page is determined from the Sequence attribute value that you specified for each region, as shown in Figure 5-70.

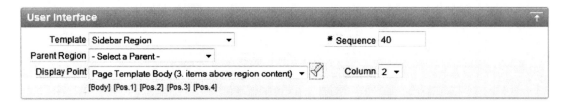

Figure 5-70. Sequence attribute for a page region

The example shows a Sequence attribute of 40, which means that the region would be rendered after any regions that have a Sequence attribute lower than 40, but before any regions that have a Sequence attribute greater than 40. This makes it very easy to change the order of your regions within the display point simply by changing the Sequence attribute.

Also notice in Figure 5-70 the attribute named Column. This is used where you want to display multiple regions at the same horizontal position in the same display point. So, for example, if you modify the list that is defined on page 1 to use column 2 (remembering that the list defined on page zero is using column 1), you will see the two lists displayed horizontally next to each other, as shown in Figure 5-71.

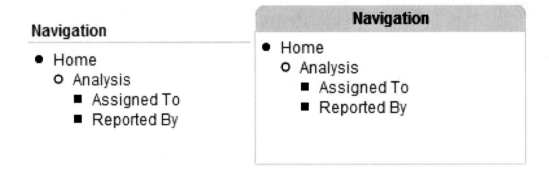

Figure 5-71. Lists displayed in columns

To implement the Column attribute, behind the scenes, APEX creates an HTML table for your regions and uses the Column value to position the region within that particular column.

By using the Sequence and Column values, you can position multiple regions within the same display points in whatever vertical and/or horizontal arrangement you wish.

Positioning Page Items

Page items are positioned within page regions (buttons can be placed in a particular page region position or among the region items, for example), in much the same way that you position page regions within pages. Figure 5-72 shows the page items defined on the Update Bug screen.

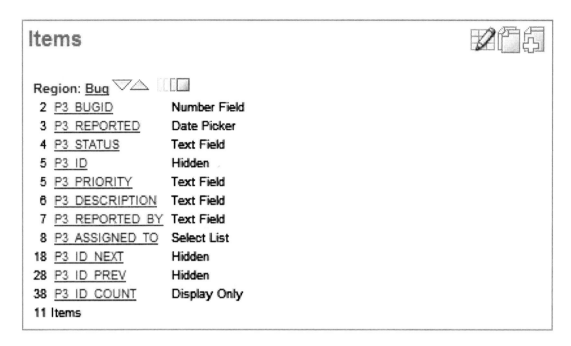

Figure 5-72. Page items displayed in order of sequence

In Figure 5-72, the sequence value of each item is displayed just to the left of the item name; for example, the P3_DESCRIPTION item has sequence 6. You can see that the page items use the sequence value to determine their order within the region.

You can also specify whether the page item should begin on a new line and field, as shown in Figure 5-73. The values that you select for these two attributes will determine how APEX displays the page item on the screen. Like the Column attribute for page regions, the Begin on New Line and Field attributes are used when APEX builds an HTML table to display the page items. If you select Yes for Begin on New Line, APEX will begin a new table row for your page item; otherwise, the item will be displayed horizontally after the previous page item. If you select Yes for the Field attribute, APEX will generate an HTML td tag (a new table column) in which to display your page item; otherwise, the page item will be displayed inside the same table column as the previous page item. Note that only certain combinations of Begin On New Line and Field are allowed: Yes/Yes, No/No, and No/Yes. You can't choose to begin on a new line without also creating a new field.

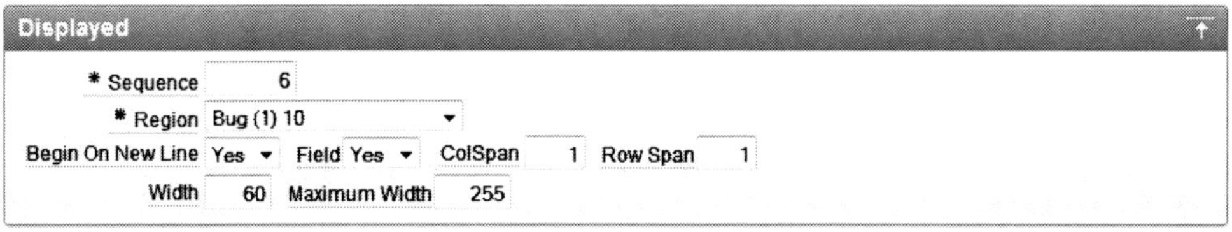

Figure 5-73. Display attributes for a page item

Drag-and-Drop Positioning

APEX 3.0 introduced drop-and-drop positioning for page items. This is a very slick and cool way to arrange your page items without needing to manually alter the sequence values and layout attributes.

To access the Drag and Drop Layout screen, click the small rectangular icon next to the up and down arrows in the Items section of your page. In Figure 5-72, you can see the icon just above the words "Number Field" to the right of P3_BUGID. A very useful feature is hiding behind this innocuous-looking icon.

Figure 5-74 shows the Drag and Drop Layout screen. All of the page items you have on your page will appear here. On this screen, you can drag the individual page items around and place them in new positions on the screen. You can also drag new page items onto the page and place them where you want them to appear. And you can remove page items by dragging and dropping them into the recycle bin at the bottom of the page.

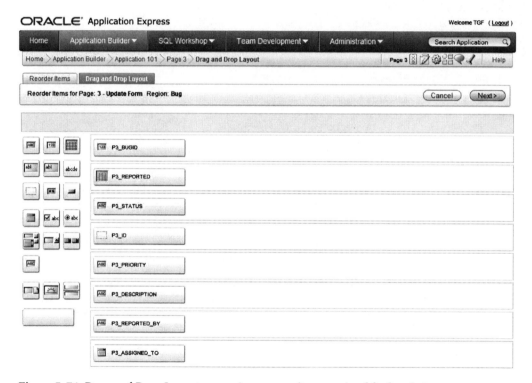

Figure 5-74. *Drag and Drop Layout screen (some page items omitted for brevity)*

This is a great new feature of APEX. It makes laying out your screen much easier, since you can see how it will look without having to run the application. Currently, drag-and-drop layout works on a per-region basis. A future release may extend this functionality to allow regions to be moved around using the same drag-and-drop method.

Summary

APEX supports several approaches to menus and layout. Tabs are commonly used on web pages, often to denote major sections within a site. APEX easily supports tabs. APEX also gives you the ability to create navigation bars for more detailed and granular navigation through a site. You can create navigation bar menus based on lists and trees that allow users to quickly navigate to specific pages. Breadcrumbs let you track a user's path through your site. Page zero and other layout-related features help you create and maintain a consistent look across all of your site's pages.

CHAPTER 6

Reports and Charts

Many applications need the ability to display information to the end user in the form of a report or a chart. Fortunately, APEX makes this extremely easy, allowing you to create reports and charts out of the box. APEX provides an assortment of ready-made report and chart types, and you can customize them in many ways. APEX 4 includes a new charting engine, AnyCharts 5.1, which improves rendering time, generates better graphics, and allows for greater customization.

Reports

You might think of reports as a simple way to present record information in a tabular format. You would certainly be correct, but reports are much more flexible than that. In APEX, you have complete control over how a report is processed and presented, which means that you can create some really advanced reports.

Looking at the home page of the Buglist application, you can see the report that was automatically created by the application creation wizard, as shown in Figure 6-1. This report has the same look and feel as the rest of our application because it is using a particular template. We will cover how to customize templates in general in Chapter 10. In this chapter, we will look at how you can modify the layout and look of reports specifically.

	Bug Id ▲	Reported	Status	Priority	Description	Reported By	Assigned To
✏	1	27-JAN-06	Open	High	Pressing Cancel on the login screen gives an error	Rachel Huson	John Scott
✏	2	02-JAN-06	Closed	High	Logo occassionally does not appear	Caroline White	Peter Ward
✏	3	01-FEB-06	Open	High	Search doesn't return any results when nothing is entered	Carl Watson	John Scott
✏	4	02-MAR-06	Open	Critical	Login doesn't work for user smithp	Laura Barnes	Mark Wilson
✏	5	02-MAR-06	Open	Low	Images don't look in the right positions	Lucy Scott	Steven Anderson
✏	6	02-MAY-06	Open	Medium	Pressing delete user gives permission denied error	Chris Donaldson	John Scott
✏	7	02-JUN-06	Open	High	Buttons don't work in firefox	Paul Mathews	Michael Stuart
✏	8	02-JUN-06	Closed	High	Pressing cancel on the login screen gives an error	Mark Lawson	Mark Wilson
✏	9	02-JUL-06	Open	High	Trying to add anew record gives an error	John Stevens	John Scott
✏	10	02-JUL-06	Open	Critical	The logout button doesn't close the browser	Steven Green	Steven Anderson
✏	11	02-AUG-06	Open	High	Javascript error on the profiles page	Mark Lawson	John Scott
✏	12	02-AUG-06	Open	Low	Text is too small on the home page	Carl Watson	John Scott
✏	13	02-SEP-06	Open	High	There is no way to tell who I'm logged in as	Caroline White	Paul Wilson
✏	14	02-SEP-06	Open	High	Customer details don't match the	Rachel Hudson	John Scott
✏	15	02-OCT-06	Open	Critical	Search results don't match the criteria	Laura Barnes	John Scott

Spread Sheet

row(s) 1 - 15 of 17 ▾   Next ▶

Figure 6-1. *Buglist report*

The code used as the region source for the report is quite a simple query, as shown in Listing 6-1.

Listing 6-1. *Buglist Report Region Source Query*

```
select
  "ID", "BUGID",
  "REPORTED","STATUS",
  "PRIORITY","DESCRIPTION",
  "REPORTED_BY", "ASSIGNED_TO"
 from    "BUGLIST"
where
(
 instr(upper("STATUS"),upper(nvl(:P1_REPORT_SEARCH,"STATUS"))) > 0  or
 instr(upper("PRIORITY"),upper(nvl(:P1_REPORT_SEARCH,"PRIORITY"))) > 0  or
 instr(upper("DESCRIPTION"),upper(nvl(:P1_REPORT_SEARCH,"DESCRIPTION"))) > 0  or
 instr(upper("REPORTED_BY"),upper(nvl(:P1_REPORT_SEARCH,"REPORTED_BY"))) > 0
)
```

The code in Listing 6-1 was generated automatically by the application creation wizard. Note that the query uses quotation marks (quotes) around the column names and the table name. Generally, it's a bad idea to use quotes like this, as it makes Oracle check the names in a case-sensitive manner. This means you must use quotes (and the correct case) when you later refer to that table or column. Without quotes, Oracle checks in uppercase so if you search for an unquoted lowercase "t," it is the same as searching for a quoted uppercase "T." Listing 6-2 demonstrates the effect of using quotes.

Listing 6-2. Effect of Using Quotation Marks

```
-- Create a table without quotes
apexdemo@DBTEST> create table upperCase(
  2   id number,
  3   data varchar2(20)
  4  );

Table created.

apexdemo@DBTEST> insert into upperCase
  2   (id, data)
  3   values
  4   (1, 'data 1');

1 row created.

-- Create a table with quotes
apexdemo@DBTEST> create table "MixedCase"(
  2   "Id" number,
  3   "Data" varchar2(20)
  4  );

Table created.

-- Can't insert into the table; we need to use quotes
apexdemo@DBTEST> insert into MixedCase
  2   (id, data)
  3   values
  4   (1, 'data 1');
insert into MixedCase
            *
ERROR at line 1:
ORA-00942: table or view does not exist

-- Using quotes, the insert works
apexdemo@DBTEST> insert into "MixedCase"
  2   ("Id", "Data")
  3   values
  4   (1, 'Data 1');

1 row created.

apexdemo@DBTEST> select * from upperCase;

        ID DATA
---------- --------------------
         1 data 1

apexdemo@DBTEST> select * from mixedcase;
```

```
select * from mixedcase
                *
ERROR at line 1:
ORA-00942: table or view does not exist
```

Creating tables with quoted names can lead to confusion. You'll find yourself trying to query a table that you know is there, but getting this error every time:

```
ORA-00942: table or view does not exist
```

When you get such an error, check carefully to be sure that the table name in your query matches the one used when the table was created. If the name is mixed-case or contains spaces or other unusual characters, you'll need to put that table name in quotes in your queries.

It's best practice not to use quotes in naming database tables, unless there's a very compelling reason to do so. Without them, you can write your SQL statements in whichever case you like, and they will work (where *work* is a relative term, of course).

Referring back to Listing 6-1, you can see that the query is selecting eight columns from the table, and uses the P1_REPORT_SEARCH page item to compare against the STATUS, PRIORITY, DESCRIPTION, and REPORTED_BY columns.

If you edit the Report region, you'll see that three tabs are available, as shown in Figure 6-2:

- The Region Definition tab allows you to modify the query itself, as well as adjust the positioning of the region and the other attributes that affect a page region, such as the conditional logic used to display it.

- The Report Attributes tab allows you to modify the attributes of the individual columns of the query used in the region definition, as shown in Figure 6-3.

- The Print Attributes tab allows you to control attributes relating to printing of the report, which we will cover in Chapter 9.

Figure 6-2. Editing a Report region

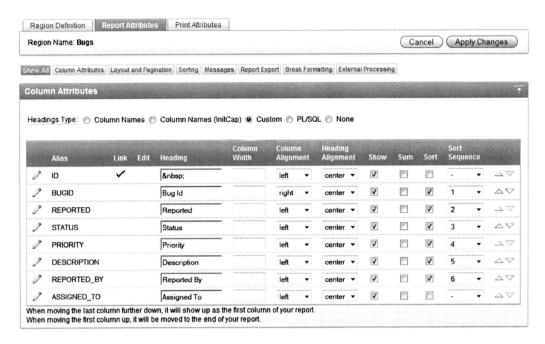

Figure 6-3. The Report Attributes tab

The Column Attributes section of the Report Attributes tab (Figure 6-3) lists each column selected in the query. Each column has a number of attributes, such as Column Alignment, Heading Alignment, Sort Sequence, and so on. You can also drill down even further; clicking the link next to each column name provides access to more of the column's attributes, as you will see later in this chapter.

From the Column Attributes section you can control a wide variety of report aspects, ranging from the report headers to how a column should be formatted and whether that column will be enabled as a link to some other page or external web site.

Report Headers

From Figures 6-1 and 6-3, you can see that the report uses the names of the columns as the column headings. Of course, as with most things in APEX, if you don't like using the column names this way, you can change it. The choices at the top of the Column Attributes section allow you to initial cap the column names, use custom headers, use a PL/SQL function, or not to display any headers (None).

Initial Capping

The Column Names (InitCap) choice uses the column names and also applies the InitCap function to them. InitCap is a simple function that changes the first letter of each word into uppercase and lowercases the subsequent letters of the word. For example, REPORTED becomes Reported. You might think that REPORTED_BY would become Reported_By, but APEX is a bit more sensible than that; it changes it to Reported By, substituting a space for the underscore character so that it looks nicer on the page.

Note that you can use the `InitCap` function in your own code, like this:

```
apexdemo@DBTEST> select
  2  initcap('REPORTED_BY') as colname
  3  from dual;

COLNAME
-----------
Reported_By
```

However, as you can see, the underscore remains. The translation of the underscore into a space is performed by some extra code in the APEX interface (presumably by using the Translate or Replace function), rather than being part of the InitCap code.

Custom Headings

You may want the heading names to be something else entirely, rather than based on the column names from the query itself. In that case, you would choose the Custom option at the top of the Column Attributes section. Then you can type anything you like into the Heading attribute for each column,

Custom Headings via a PL/SQL Function

One of the more interesting choices is to use the PL/SQL option to define the report's column headings. When you choose this option, you get an extra field in the Column Attributes section, where you can specify a function that will return the headings, as shown in Figure 6-4.

Figure 6-4. *Using PL/SQL to return heading names*

The PL/SQL function that you enter here needs to return a string containing the headings delimited by colons. As a simple example, you can enter the following code:

```
return 'ID:Bug Id:Reported:Status:Priority:Description:Reported By:Assigned To'
```

This function just returns a colon-delimited string, with each entry in the string corresponding to each column sequentially.

You can make this much more useful by returning a more generic list of headings. For example, let's say you want to store all the headings for your reports in a table so you can use them in various places throughout the application (for example, you might want to reuse them in an LOV). Listing 6-3 demonstrates creating such a table.

Listing 6-3. Creating and Populating the report_headings Table

```
apexdemo@DBTEST> create table report_headings(
  2   id number primary_key,
  3   table_name varchar2(200),
  4   heading_id number,
  5   heading_name varchar2(200)
  6  );

Table created.

apexdemo@DBTEST> insert into report_headings
  2   (id, table_name, heading_id, heading_name)
  3   values
  4   (1, 'BUGLIST', 1, 'Id');

1 row created.

apexdemo@DBTEST> insert into report_headings
  2   (id, table_name, heading_id, heading_name)
  3   values
  4   (2, 'BUGLIST', 2, 'Bug Id');

1 row created.

-- Extra rows added here

apexdemo@DBTEST> select * from report_headings;

        ID TABLE_NAME HEADING_ID HEADING_NAME
---------- ---------- ---------- --------------------
         1 BUGLIST             1 Id
         2 BUGLIST             2 Bug Id
         3 BUGLIST             3 Reported
         4 BUGLIST             4 Status
         5 BUGLIST             5 Priority
         6 BUGLIST             6 Description
         7 BUGLIST             7 Reported By
         8 BUGLIST             8 Assigned To

8 rows selected.
```

Listing 6-3 creates a table called report_headings to store the headings that should be used for each table. It then inserts a record for each heading for the buglist table. (Note that we've omitted some of the insert statements for brevity, but the final select statement shows the records that have been inserted.) The heading_id column allows you to order the way headings are listed for a particular table. You could use the id column, but using a separate column makes it easier to rearrange the heading order later.

Now you can create a packaged procedure that will, when a table name is passed into it as a parameter, return the colon-delimited list of headings that should be used, as shown in Listing 6-4.

Listing 6-4. Creating a PL/SQL Function to Return Headings

```
apexdemo@DBTEST> create or replace package pkg_report_headers as

  2  function get_headers(p_table in varchar2) return varchar2;
  3  end pkg_report_headers;
  4  /

Package created.

apexdemo@DBTEST> create or replace
2  package body pkg_report_headers as
3  function get_headers(p_table in varchar2) return varchar2 is
4    v_temp apex_application_global.vc_arr2;
5    begin
6      select heading_name bulk collect into v_temp
7      from   report_headings
8      where  table_name=p_table
9      order by heading_id;
10     return apex_util.table_to_string(v_temp, ':');
11   end;
12 end pkg_report_headers;

Package body created.
```

In the function definition, we declare a variable called v_temp as the type vc_arr2, which is defined in the wwv_flow_global package. The public synonym, apex_application_global, can be used to access this package:

```
v_temp apex_application_global.vc_arr2;
```

The vc_arr2 type is a PL/SQL associative array type that maps a binary integer to a varchar2. It is capable of holding an array of strings (you can look in the wwv_flow_global package to see the definition). We used a bulk collect statement instead of a cursor for loop to reduce network traffic. In a cursor for loop, a SQL statement is executed for each iteration of the loop. The bulk collect statement transfers groups of data in one round trip, which can significantly improve performance.

The rows in the report_headings table where the heading_name column matches the p_table input parameter are placed in the v_temp array:

```
select heading_name bulk collect into v_temp
from   report_headings
where  table_name=p_table
order by heading_id;
```

Once you've added all the heading names to the array, you use the apex_util.table_to_string function to return the array type as a string:

```
return apex_util.table_to_string(v_temp, ':');
```

Here, the second parameter to the `table_to_string` function is the character you wish to use as a delimiter in the returned string. The default character is actually the colon, so you don't need to specify it explicitly (we specified it for clarity here).

You can now test to check that the code works by calling the function via some SQL, as shown in Listing 6-5.

Listing 6-5. *Calling the Function via SQL*

```
apexdemo@DBTEST> select
  2   pkg_report_headers.get_headers('BUGLIST') as headings
  3   from dual;

HEADINGS
----------------------------------------------------------------------
Bug Id:Reported:Status:Priority:Description:Reported By:Assigned To:
```

So, with just a few lines of code, you are able to return a dynamic list of report headings. Using a bind variable in the call to pkg_report_headers.get_headers allows you to programmatically set or change the input parameter's value. Because the report we're dealing with is called BUGLIST, that's the value that will be sent unless you change it. You can plug this into your report by entering the following code in the "Function returning colon delimited headings" text box (Figure 6-4):

```
return pkg_report_headers.get_headers(:REPORT_NAME)
```

You can now dynamically update the report headings and have the changes immediately reflected in the report, as shown in Listing 6-6 and Figure 6-5.

Listing 6-6. *Updating the report_headings Table*

```
apexdemo@DBTEST> update report_headings
  2   set heading_name = 'Bug Status'
  3   where id = 4;

1 row updated.

apexdemo@DBTEST> commit;
Commit complete.
```

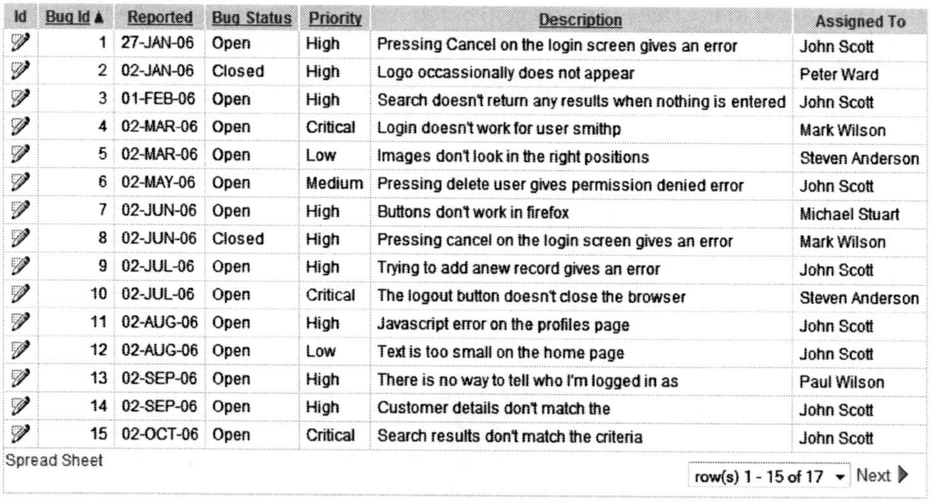

Id	Bug Id ▲	Reported	Bug Status	Priority	Description	Assigned To
🖉	1	27-JAN-06	Open	High	Pressing Cancel on the login screen gives an error	John Scott
🖉	2	02-JAN-06	Closed	High	Logo occassionally does not appear	Peter Ward
🖉	3	01-FEB-06	Open	High	Search doesn't return any results when nothing is entered	John Scott
🖉	4	02-MAR-06	Open	Critical	Login doesn't work for user smithp	Mark Wilson
🖉	5	02-MAR-06	Open	Low	Images don't look in the right positions	Steven Anderson
🖉	6	02-MAY-06	Open	Medium	Pressing delete user gives permission denied error	John Scott
🖉	7	02-JUN-06	Open	High	Buttons don't work in firefox	Michael Stuart
🖉	8	02-JUN-06	Closed	High	Pressing cancel on the login screen gives an error	Mark Wilson
🖉	9	02-JUL-06	Open	High	Trying to add anew record gives an error	John Scott
🖉	10	02-JUL-06	Open	Critical	The logout button doesn't close the browser	Steven Anderson
🖉	11	02-AUG-06	Open	High	Javascript error on the profiles page	John Scott
🖉	12	02-AUG-06	Open	Low	Text is too small on the home page	John Scott
🖉	13	02-SEP-06	Open	High	There is no way to tell who I'm logged in as	Paul Wilson
🖉	14	02-SEP-06	Open	High	Customer details don't match the	John Scott
🖉	15	02-OCT-06	Open	Critical	Search results don't match the criteria	John Scott

Spread Sheet

row(s) 1 - 15 of 17 ▾   Next ▶

Figure 6-5. Updated headings reflected in the report

You might be thinking that instead of using an array in the get_headers function, you could have just concatenated the headings together in a string. That's true. However, there are quite a few places in APEX where you will work with arrays and delimited strings (for example, when working with LOVs). If you're not already familiar with the table_to_string function and the corresponding string_to_table function, it's worth exploring them, because you'll find you use them more often as you become more experienced with APEX.

You might also have wondered about passing in a hard-coded value ('BUGLIST') for the p_table parameter of the function. You could instead pass in the value of a page item (for example, &P1_TABLE_NAME.) that represents the table you're using, which would allow the columns to be retrieved even more generically, if that's something that you'd like to try (sometimes there is such a thing as trying to make your code too generic).

As you can see, choosing the PL/SQL option for Headings Type is a powerful way to generate the heading names at runtime.

Named Columns vs. Generic Columns

You might have already noticed that when you define the region source query for your report, you have the option to use column names based on the query or to use generic column names, as shown in Figure 6-6.

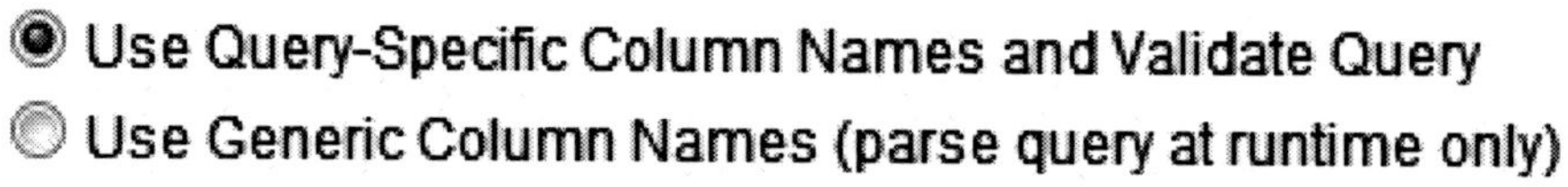

◉ Use Query-Specific Column Names and Validate Query
◯ Use Generic Column Names (parse query at runtime only)

Figure 6-6. Specifying the column names type

The default is the Use Query-Specific Column Names and Validate Query option. As the name implies, this means that when you enter your query and click the Apply button in the Application Builder, your query will be validated (checked to ensure it is syntactically correct and so on). In contrast, if you select the Use Generic Column Names (parse query at runtime only) option, the query will not be validated within the Application Builder when you hit the Apply button. Instead, it will be parsed at runtime, and you will not be forewarned if you've made a mistake in the query (such as incorrectly naming a column or table).

However, the difference between using named columns (as we'll refer to query-specific column names) and generic columns runs much deeper than just whether they are parsed and validated at design time. Both types serve a specific purpose, so one type may be more applicable to a particular situation than the other.

Generic Columns

When you choose the Use Generic Column Names option, you automatically lose the names of the columns in the Column Attributes section of the report, as shown in Figure 6-7. You can see that where the column names were defined by the query before, the columns are now named COL01, COL02 . . . all the way to COL60 (only the first six columns are shown in Figure 6-7).

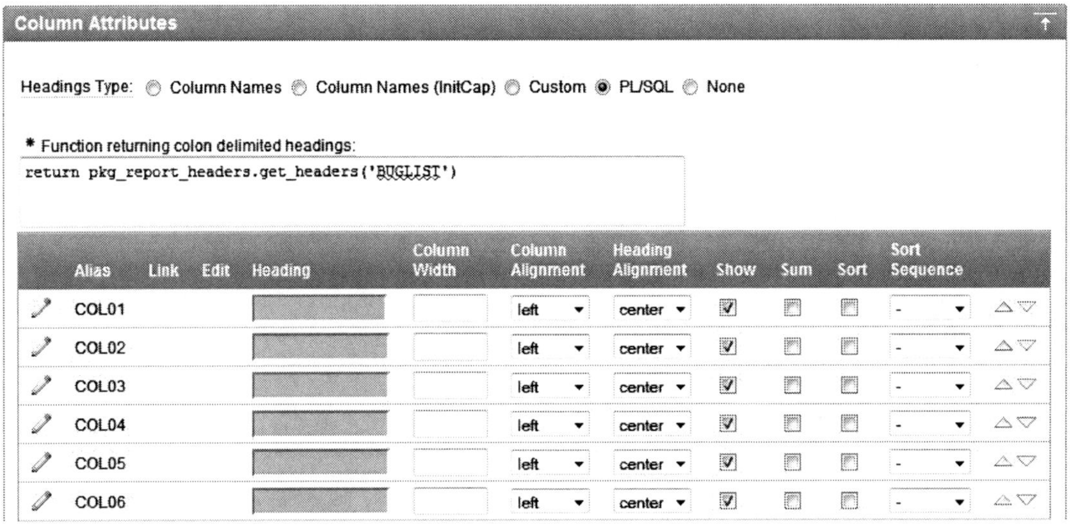

Figure 6-7. Using generic columns

You can actually control the number of generic columns by modifying the Maximum Number of Generic Report Columns value in the region source definition. The default value is 60. You can increase or decrease this number, depending on the number of columns you expect to return in your query.

So, why are generic columns useful and when would you choose to use them over named columns? Generic columns are handy when you have a report where each column will look more or less the same; that is, the structure of the report is fairly uniform, and you want to define that layout in a simple way that will be repeated across each of the columns defined for the report.

You can see the layout definitions in the templates. The Layout and Pagination section for the report definition shows that the report is using the Standard Report template, as shown in Figure 6-8.

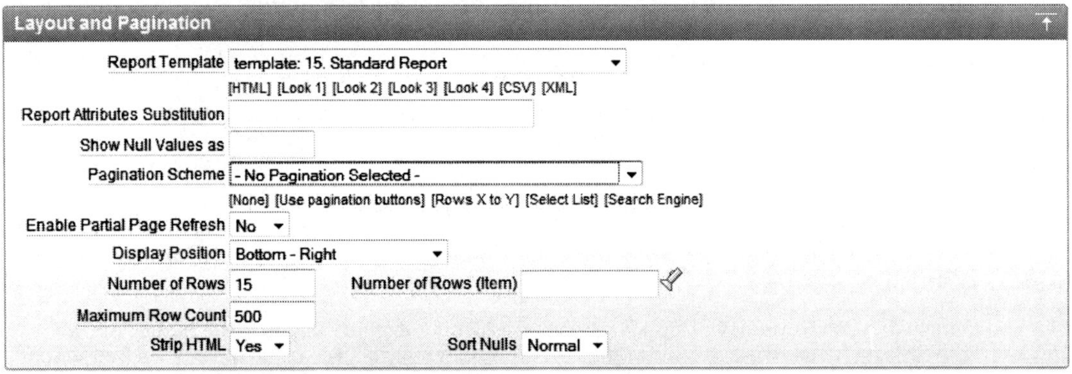

Figure 6-8. Layout and Pagination section for the report

You can examine the Standard Report template by clicking the link in the Templates section of the Page Definition section, which will list each type of template being used by the components on the page. The template defines different sections for particular parts of the report. The Column Heading template contains the following code:

```
<th class="t15header" #ALIGNMENT#>#COLUMN_HEADER#</th>
```

This code uses the standard HTML th element to create a table header tag and specifies a class attribute of t15header, which is defined within one of the CSS files included for the standard APEX templates. The substitution values of #ALIGNMENT# and #COLUMN_HEADER# pick up the value for the alignment assigned to each column header and the column header value itself.

The primary difference between generic columns and named columns is in the Column Templates section. For generic columns, the template contains this code:

```
<td class="t15data" #ALIGNMENT#>#COLUMN_VALUE#</td>
```

This looks similar to the Column Heading template, except that it uses the td element tag, a different CSS class, and the #COLUMN_VALUE# substitution variable. For every column of the report, this template substitutes the value of each column where the #COLUMN_VALUE# is specified. This is what we were referring to earlier when we said that generic columns are useful when you are not particularly concerned with the look of individual columns, but just want them all to be formatted in more or less the same way (using the same HTML markup and CSS class information).

You might also notice that you can control the template by assigning conditional logic, as shown in Figure 6-9. This example uses two different column templates. The first one encloses the #COLUMN_VALUE# in bold tags (<b> and </b>) if the PL/SQL expression:

```
'#PRIORITY#' = 'High'
```

evaluates to true. The other template displays the column value without the bold tags if the converse PL/SQL expression is true (that is, if the priority is not High).

Figure 6-9. Conditional logic in a generic column template

Now you might be surprised to see that even though you're using generic columns (COL01, COL02, and so on), you can use substitution strings such as #PRIORITY# to access the value of a particular column. Even though the template is being applied to each column, you are still able to evaluate particular columns for each row to which the template is being applied.

The end result of customizing the template in this way, if you hadn't guessed already, is that all the records that have a High priority are now displayed in bold, as shown in Figure 6-10.

Id	Bug Id	Reported	Bug Status	Priority	Description	Reported By	Assigned To
1	1	27-JAN-06	Open	High	Pressing Cancel on the login screen gives an error	Rachel Huson	John Scott
2	2	02-JAN-06	Closed	High	Logo occassionally does not appear	Caroline White	Peter Ward
3	3	01-FEB-06	Open	High	Search doesn't return any results when nothing is entered	Carl Watson	John Scott
4	4	02-MAR-06	Open	Critical	Login doesn't work for user smithp	Laura Barnes	Mark Wilson
5	5	02-MAR-06	Open	Low	Images don't look in the right positions	Lucy Scott	Steven Anderson
6	6	02-MAY-06	Open	Medium	Pressing delete user gives permission denied error	Chris Donaldson	John Scott
7	7	02-JUN-06	Open	High	Buttons don't work in firefox	Paul Mathews	Michael Stuart
8	8	02-JUN-06	Closed	High	Pressing cancel on the login screen gives an error	Mark Lawson	Mark Wilson
9	9	02-JUL-06	Open	High	Trying to add anew record gives an error	John Stevens	John Scott
10	10	02-JUL-06	Open	Critical	The logout button doesn't close the browser	Steven Green	Steven Anderson
11	11	02-AUG-06	Open	High	Javascript error on the profiles page	Mark Lawson	John Scott
12	12	02-AUG-06	Open	Low	Text is too small on the home page	Carl Watson	John Scott
13	13	02-SEP-06	Open	High	There is no way to tell who I'm logged in as	Caroline White	Paul Wilson
14	14	02-SEP-06	Open	High	Customer details don't match the	Rachel Hudson	John Scott
15	15	02-OCT-06	Open	Critical	Search results don't match the criteria	Laura Barnes	John Scott

Spread Sheet

Figure 6-10. Conditional template logic applied to the report

Three options are available for the conditions applied to the column templates:

- Use for Even Numbered Rows
- Use for Odd Numbered Rows
- Use Based on PL/SQL Expression

You can use the even and odd row options to make it easier to read the report by perhaps using a different CSS class to make alternate rows have a different background color. The PL/SQL expression option allows a great amount of flexibility to apply a different column template depending on specific criteria. Currently, the Application Builder allows you to specify up to four different column templates and associated conditions.

Named Columns

Using named columns with your reports gives you much more flexibility than generic columns afford. You can customize the layout of your report template to a much greater degree since, as the name implies, you can reference each column by name in the report template.

You can change the report query back to using the default Use Query-Specific Column Names and Validate Query option. However, the report will still be using a column-based template. To take advantage of named columns, you can create a new report template, as shown in Figure 6-11.

Figure 6-11. Creating a new report template

When you create a new report template from scratch, you are given the option of making it either a column template or a row template. This determines whether the report template can use generic columns or named columns; a report that uses named columns can use a row-based template.

When you create a row-based template, the definition of the template is slightly different from the definition for a column template, in that the template refers to the row rather than the column. By default, the row template contains a minimal amount of code, as shown in Figure 6-12.

Figure 6-12. Definition of a newly created row template

If you changed the report to use this new template and ran the page, you wouldn't see anything just yet, since the row template defines table rows and columns (using the tr and td elements), but there is no enclosing table element defined in the template yet (in this example anyway; yours may vary).

In Figure 6-12, you can also see that the template is using the substitution strings #1#, #2#, and so on. This is known as using *positional notation*; for example, #1# refers to the first column in the query.

To make this template a bit more visually pleasing, you can copy some of the CSS styling information that the Standard Report template uses. In the Row Template 1 box, use the following code:

```
<tr #HIGHLIGHT_ROW#>

<td class="t15data">#1#</td>
<td class="t15data">#2#</td>
<td class="t15data">#3#</td>
<td class="t15data">#4#</td>
```

```
<td class="t15data">#5#</td>
</tr>
```

Here, you're using the positional notation to show each of the first five columns and the same t15data CSS class that the Standard Report template uses for the columns.

Next, in the Before Rows section, add the following code:

```
<table class="t15standard" summary="Report">

<th class="t15header" #ALIGNMENT#>#1#</th>
<th class="t15header" #ALIGNMENT#>#2#</th>
<th class="t15header" #ALIGNMENT#>#3#</th>
<th class="t15header" #ALIGNMENT#>#4#</th>
<th class="t15header" #ALIGNMENT#>#5#</th>
```

Again, this is using the same sort of code that is used in the Standard Report template to create a table and then list each of the first five headings using positional notation.

Finally, in the After Rows section, use the following code:

```
<tr>

    <td colspan="99" class="t15afterrows">
        <span class="left">#EXTERNAL_LINK##CSV_LINK#</span>
        <table style="float:right;text-align:right;" summary="pagination">
            #PAGINATION#</table>
    </td>
</tr></table>
```

This was again taken verbatim from the Standard Report template. It simply inserts an extra area below the report that adds the ability to paginate the report and export it to a comma-separated values (CSV) format file.

If you save the template and run the report now, it will look exactly as it did before. The report template was changed, but the report is still using the Standard Reports template. The template setting needs to be changed to Buglist Report as shown in Figure 6-13.

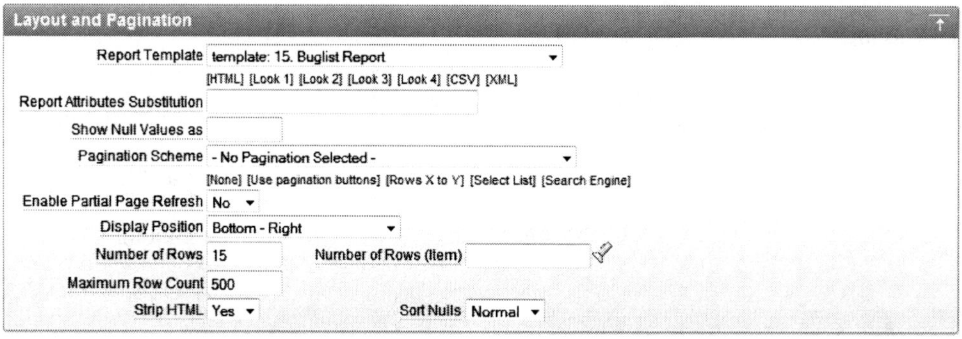

Figure 6-13. Selecting the Buglist Report template

If you now run the page, you should see the report looks pretty much as it did with the Standard Report region, although it is displaying only the first five columns of the query, as shown in Figure 6-14.

Id	Bug Id	Reported	Bug Status	Priority
1	1	27-JAN-06	Open	High
2	2	02-JAN-06	Closed	High
3	3	01-FEB-06	Open	High
4	4	02-MAR-06	Open	Critical
5	5	02-MAR-06	Open	Low
6	6	02-MAY-06	Open	Medium
7	7	02-JUN-06	Open	High
8	8	02-JUN-06	Closed	High
9	9	02-JUL-06	Open	High
10	10	02-JUL-06	Open	Critical
11	11	02-AUG-06	Open	High
12	12	02-AUG-06	Open	Low
13	13	02-SEP-06	Open	High
14	14	02-SEP-06	Open	High
15	15	02-OCT-06	Open	Critical

Spread
Sheet

Figure 6-14. Using the row-based template

As this point, you are probably wondering why you should go to the extra effort of using row-based templates when they end up looking the same as column-based templates. But in this template, you're still using positional-based notation. You have not yet taken advantage of the extra flexibility attained by referring to the columns by name.

In the original report, all the columns are in the same row. If a lot of data has been entered in the Description column, that could make the report difficult to read (perhaps making the report overly wide or limiting the amount of text that can be shown in the Description column). Wouldn't it be nice if you could make the Description column appear in a separate row below the main detail row of the record? Well, as you've no doubt guessed, you can accomplish this sort of layout by using row-based templates combined with named columns.

First, you need to convert the template to use the named columns rather than the positional notation. Change the Row Template 1 section to use the code shown in Listing 6-7.

Listing 6-7. Row Template Using Named Column Notation

```
<tr #HIGHLIGHT_ROW#>
  <td class="t15data">#ID#</td>
  <td class="t15data">#BUGID#</td>
  <td class="t15data">#REPORTED#</td>
  <td class="t15data">#STATUS#</td>
  <td class="t15data">#PRIORITY#</td>
  <td class="t15data">#DESCRIPTION#</td>
  <td class="t15data">#REPORTED_BY#</td>
  <td class="t15data">#ASSIGNED_TO#</td>
</tr>
```

This code adds the extra columns to the code. Note that in the query, you use the name of the actual column, rather than the heading name.

Also modify the Before Rows section to include the extra heading names, as shown in Listing 6-8.

Listing 6-8. Extra Heading Names in the Before Rows Template

```
<table class="t15standard" summary="Report">
  <th class="t15header" #ALIGNMENT#>#1#</th>
  <th class="t15header" #ALIGNMENT#>#2#</th>
  <th class="t15header" #ALIGNMENT#>#3#</th>
  <th class="t15header" #ALIGNMENT#>#4#</th>
  <th class="t15header" #ALIGNMENT#>#5#</th>
  <th class="t15header" #ALIGNMENT#>#6#</th>
  <th class="t15header" #ALIGNMENT#>#7#</th>
  <th class="t15header" #ALIGNMENT#>#8#</th>
```

Note that you could hard-code the names of the headings in the template. However, using positional notation gives you the ability to modify the headings using the options covered earlier in this chapter (such as via a PL/SQL function), without needing to modify the template again.

Now you should have a template that makes the report look exactly as it did before. Since you're now using named columns, you can modify the row template a bit more to move the Description column into a separate row, as shown in Listing 6-9.

Listing 6-9. Moving the Description Column into a Separate Row

```
<tr #HIGHLIGHT_ROW#>
  <td class="t15data">#ID#</td>
  <td class="t15data">#BUGID#</td>
  <td class="t15data">#REPORTED#</td>
  <td class="t15data">#STATUS#</td>
  <td class="t15data">#PRIORITY#</td>
  <td class="t15data">#REPORTED_BY#</td>
  <td class="t15data">#ASSIGNED_TO#</td>
</tr>
<tr>
```

```
    <td class="t15data" colspan="7">#DESCRIPTION#</td>
</tr>
```

This code creates another row below the original one and makes the Description column span the entire width of the row (by using the colspan attribute to make it span seven columns, which is the number of columns in the row above it). Since you have changed the order of the columns in the row, you also need to modify the Before Rows template, as shown in Listing 6-10.

Listing 6-10. Modified Before Rows Template

```
<table class="t15standard" summary="Report">

  <th class="t15header" #ALIGNMENT#>#1#</th>
  <th class="t15header" #ALIGNMENT#>#2#</th>
  <th class="t15header" #ALIGNMENT#>#3#</th>
  <th class="t15header" #ALIGNMENT#>#4#</th>
  <th class="t15header" #ALIGNMENT#>#5#</th>
  <th class="t15header" #ALIGNMENT#>#7#</th>
  <th class="t15header" #ALIGNMENT#>#8#</th>
```

The only change in Listing 6-10 is that you have removed the line that represented the heading for the Description column (which was column 6 in positional notation). When you mix positional notation with named notation, things can become confusing. It's not immediately apparent which positional element represents which column. If you probably won't want to later change the column headings in the report definition (or dynamically), you could hard-code them to make it easier to read and modify the template.

After these changes, the report looks like the one shown in Figure 6-15.

Id	Bug Id	Reported	Bug Status	Priority	Reported By	Assigned To
1	1	27-JAN-06	Open	High	Rachel Huson	John Scott
Pressing Cancel on the login screen gives an error						
2	2	02-JAN-06	Closed	High	Caroline White	Peter Ward
Logo occassionally does not appear						
3	3	01-FEB-06	Open	High	Carl Watson	John Scott
Search doesn't return any results when nothing is entered						
4	4	02-MAR-06	Open	Critical	Laura Barnes	Mark Wilson
Login doesn't work for user smithp						
5	5	02-MAR-06	Open	Low	Lucy Scott	Steven Anderson
Images don't look in the right positions						
6	6	02-MAY-06	Open	Medium	Chris Donaldson	John Scott

Figure 6-15. Using named columns to affect the layout

■ **Note** It is debatable whether the report in Figure 6-15 is actually any easier to read than it was before (in fact, you could argue that it's slightly more difficult to read, since the eye does not scan quite so easily across a nonuniform order like this). However, the point of this exercise is just to demonstrate how easily you can modify the layout of the report using named columns and templates. You could make this report easier to read by using a different CSS class for the Description column, so that the background of that column is a slightly different color.

We can extend this example a bit further, making it a little less cluttered and perhaps more useful to the end users. Imagine that the users want to see only the description from bugs that are still classified as Open. You can do this quite easily by using conditional logic with the row template, much as you saw with the earlier generic columns example. First, modify the row template to include an extra column before the Description, just to add some space and make it easier to read, as shown in Listing 6-11.

Listing 6-11. Inserting a Column Prior to Description

```
<tr #HIGHLIGHT_ROW#>

  <td class="t15data">#ID#</td>
  <td class="t15data">#BUGID#</td>
  <td class="t15data">#REPORTED#</td>
  <td class="t15data">#STATUS#</td>
  <td class="t15data">#PRIORITY#</td>
  <td class="t15data">#REPORTED_BY#</td>
  <td class="t15data">#ASSIGNED_TO#</td>
</tr>
<tr>
  <td class="t15data"></td>
  <td class="t15data" colspan="6">#DESCRIPTION#</td>
</tr>
```

Next, add a condition to this row template, which is a PL/SQL expression:

```
'#STATUS#' = 'Open'
```

This template will be used for records with an Open status. Listing 6-12 shows a second template to be used when the status is not Open (using the reverse PL/SQL expression logic). This second template does not display the Description column at all.

Listing 6-12. Row Template for Closed Bugs

```
<tr #HIGHLIGHT_ROW#>

  <td class="t15data">#ID#</td>
  <td class="t15data">#BUGID#</td>
  <td class="t15data">#REPORTED#</td>
  <td class="t15data">#STATUS#</td>
  <td class="t15data">#PRIORITY#</td>
  <td class="t15data">#REPORTED_BY#</td>
```

```
  <td class="t15data">#ASSIGNED_TO#</td>
</tr>
```

If you now run the report, it should look similar to Figure 6-16. Notice that where the bug is classified as Closed (Bug ID 2 in Figure 6-16), no description is shown underneath.

Id	Bug Id	Reported	Bug Status	Priority	Reported By	Assigned To
1	1	27-JAN-06	Open	High	Rachel Huson	John Scott
		Pressing Cancel on the login screen gives an error				
2	2	02-JAN-06	Closed	High	Caroline White	Peter Ward
3	3	01-FEB-06	Open	High	Carl Watson	John Scott
		Search doesn't return any results when nothing is entered				
4	4	02-MAR-06	Open	Critical	Laura Barnes	Mark Wilson
		Login doesn't work for user smithp				
5	5	02-MAR-06	Open	Low	Lucy Scott	Steven Anderson
		Images don't look in the right positions				
6	6	02-MAY-06	Open	Medium	Chris Donaldson	John Scott
		Pressing delete user gives permission denied error				

Figure 6-16. *Using conditional logic in a row template*

Row-based templates also allow you to use a number of conditional templates, based on even rows, odd rows, or PL/SQL expressions.

Named column templates are probably one of the most underused features of APEX. The amount of control and flexibility they give you is amazing. You can build some really complex-looking reports—ones that don't even look like standard tabular reports—by applying logic to vary how each individual row is represented in the report.

Report Pagination

When you define your report template, you can also specify a pagination scheme for the report (look back at Figure 6-8). APEX 3.0 currently supports the following pagination schemes:

- Row Ranges 1-15 16-30 (with set pagination)
- Row Ranges 1-15 16-30 in select list (with pagination)
- Row Ranges X to Y (no pagination)
- Row Ranges X to Y of Z (no pagination)
- Row Ranges X to Y of Z (with pagination)
- Search Engine 1,2,3,4 (set based pagination)
- Use Externally Created Pagination Buttons
- Row Ranges X to Y (with next and previous links)

Even though some of the schemes say no pagination, they still allow you to move through your report resultset in different ways.

Enabling pagination in your report and the type of pagination style you use can have an impact on the performance and usability of your report. To demonstrate the effect of the different pagination schemes, let's consider a report that returns a large number of rows. The report is based on a new table called big_emp. This table contains repeated records from the familiar emp table, as well as the same indexes, for a total of more than 114,000 records, as shown in Listing 6-13. You can use any large table to test pagination yourself, since the point is to see the differences when using the various pagination schemes with the same data.

Listing 6-13. Definition of the big_emp Table

```
apexdemo@DBTEST> desc big_emp;

Name          Null?     Type
------------- --------  ---------------
EMPNO         NOT NULL  NUMBER(4)
ENAME                   VARCHAR2(10)
JOB                     VARCHAR2(9)
MGR                     NUMBER(4)
HIREDATE                DATE
SAL                     NUMBER(7,2)
COMM                    NUMBER(7,2)
DEPTNO                  NUMBER(2)
apexdemo@DBTEST> select count(*) from big_emp;

  COUNT(*)
----------
    114688
```

For a quick test, let's just create a new page in the application (to be removed later), with a new SQL Report region, using the following SQL in the region source:

```
select

  empno, ename,
  job, mgr,
  hiredate, sal,
  comm, deptno
from
  big_emp
```

Now we need some way of measuring the relative performance of each of the pagination types. This could be done in various ways, such as by running the page in debug mode and examining the timings, or by generating a trace file for the page and examining it with TKProf. However, a much easier way (though not as accurate in granularity) is to use the substitution string #TIMING# within the footer of the Report region. Then APEX will substitute the string for the time (in seconds) that it took to render that particular region; in other words, how long it took to run the query and generate the report for those particular rows retrieved. Figure 6-17 shows the timing information being displayed below the report when using the Row Ranges 1-15 16-30 (with set pagination) scheme. Notice the information above the report that's new with APEX 4.0. The report is telling you that it's returning too many rows to be practical and asks that you apply some type of filter. This can easily be suppressed via the the Pagination section in the Report Attributes page.

■ **Tip** You can use the #TIMING# substitution string in any region type. It can be a great way to track down performance issues in your application, or even just to provide some visual feedback to your end users to let them know how quickly your pages are being generated.

This query returns more than 100,000 rows, please filter your data to ensure complete results.

Empno	Ename	Job	Mgr	Hiredate	Sal	Comm	Deptno
7369	SMITH	CLERK	7902	17-DEC-80	800	-	20
7499	ALLEN	SALESMAN	7698	20-FEB-81	1600	300	30
7521	WARD	SALESMAN	7698	22-FEB-81	1250	500	30
7566	JONES	MANAGER	7839	02-APR-81	2975	-	20
7654	MARTIN	SALESMAN	7698	28-SEP-81	1250	1400	30
7698	BLAKE	MANAGER	7839	01-MAY-81	2850	-	30
7782	CLARK	MANAGER	7839	09-JUN-81	2450	-	10
7788	SCOTT	ANALYST	7566	19-APR-87	3000	-	20
7839	KING	PRESIDENT	-	17-NOV-81	5000	-	10
7844	TURNER	SALESMAN	7698	08-SEP-81	1500	0	30
7876	ADAMS	CLERK	7788	23-MAY-87	1100	-	20
7900	JAMES	CLERK	7698	03-DEC-81	950	-	30
7902	FORD	ANALYST	7566	03-DEC-81	3000	-	20
7934	MILLER	CLERK	7782	23-JAN-82	1300	-	10
7521	WARD	SALESMAN	7698	22-FEB-81	1250	500	30

1 - 15 ▶

Timing : 0.35

Figure 6-17. Using the #TIMING# substitution string in a region

To benchmark the pagination types, we timed how long it took to retrieve the first set of results (records 1–15), and then how long it took to page to other results (records 61–75 and records 136–150). This process simulates a user paging through the resultset (although, typically, users might not move that many pages into the results). This test was with the report's Max Row Count set to 120,000, to allow paging to the end of the resultset (in practice, you wouldn't want to return this many rows, but this test is to illustrate the effect that the different pagination schemes have on performance). Table 6-1 shows the results.

Table 6-1. Pagination Style Benchmarks with a Max Row Count Setting of 120,000

Pagination Style	Rows 1–15	Rows 61–75	Rows 136–150
Row Ranges 1-15 16-30 (with set pagination)	13.21	13.36	15.99
Row Ranges X to Y of Z (with pagination)	13.20	14.90	15.20
Search Engine 1,2,3,4 (set-based pagination)	13.30	14.20	14.87
Row Ranges X to Y (with next and previous links)	0.21	0.26	0.28

■ **Note** We ran our test on relatively modest hardware. You might get much faster times for your tests. The point is to illustrate the relative differences between timings, not to see how fast you can make each pagination type.

You can see from Table 6-1 that there's a huge difference in performance between the pagination styles that had to keep track of the number of overall results (such as Row Ranges X to Y of Z) compared with the simple Row Ranges X to Y pagination type. Also, remember that for some of the pagination types, there is no quick way for the user to jump to a particular set of results, which means that the performance effect is cumulative (that is, if it takes 5 seconds per page, then it might take 25 seconds to reach the fifth page if the user can't skip ahead). These benchmarks illustrate that if you have a very large resultset, the type of pagination you select can significantly affect how usable your report is for the end users.

You can greatly improve the performance of your reports by keeping the Max Row Count setting to a sensible value (or even allowing the user to define it). We are all very familiar with the typical search engines available on the Internet today. When you search for something with these search engines, you usually get many hits, often running to many pages of results. Typically, you'll use only the first page or so of results, rather than going to the twentieth or fiftieth page (since the first results must be most relevant, right?). You can apply the same logic to your reports, showing, say, just the first 500 results. Table 6-2 shows the results of rerunning the same benchmark, but this time with the report's Max Row Count set to 500 (which is the default value if you don't specify one).

Table 6-2. Pagination Style Benchmarks with a Max Row Count Setting of 500

Pagination Style	Rows 1-15	Rows 61-75	Rows 136-150
Row Ranges 1-15 16-30 (with set pagination)	0.30	0.33	0.32

Row Ranges X to Y of Z (with pagination)	0.19	0.29	0.34
Search Engine 1,2,3,4 (set-based pagination)	0.28	0.31	0.31
Row Ranges X to Y (with next and previous links)	0.23	0.24	0.28

The results in Table 6-2 clearly show a dramatic improvement for those pagination types that provide feedback about the maximum number of rows returned. So, if your users can live without knowing that *XXX* number of results were returned, you might use this approach. Note that this might not be preferable in all cases, so you should use your judgment about where reducing the Max Row Count setting for the report might be appropriate.

Break Formatting

You can use break formatting to specify whether a particular column will repeat values across rows. For example, if the current record contains the same value for a particular column that the preceding row contained, you can suppress outputting the value to make the report slightly easier to read.

An example of a column for which you might not want to repeat values is one that shows the department number in an employee report. Using the employee report from the previous examples, rearrange the order to display the department number first. You can do this quite easily via the Column Attributes section, as shown in Figure 6-18.

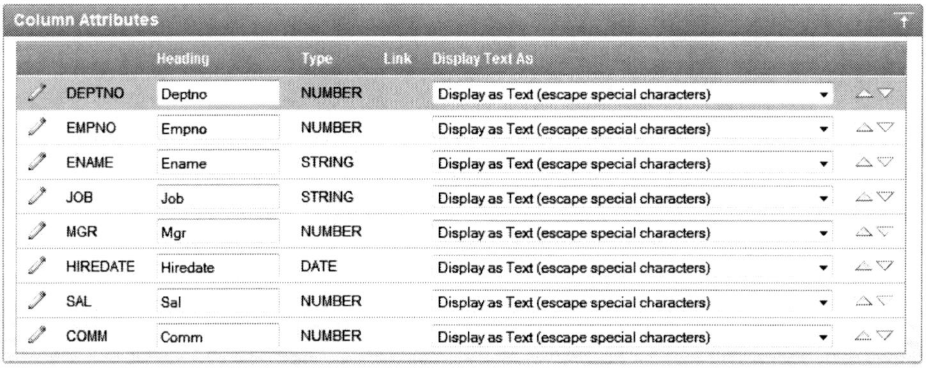

Figure 6-18. Rearranging columns in the Column Attributes section

Here, you can use the small up and down arrows to the right of the Sort Sequence select list to move the DEPTNO column so that it is the first column in the list of columns. When you use a column-based template, as discussed earlier in the chapter, you don't need to also modify the query to rearrange the column order in the report. When the template uses named columns, though, you do need to modify the template to rearrange the order.

■ **Note** In previous versions of APEX, each time you moved a column, you had to resubmit the page to the server to effect the change. Now, that work is performed via Ajax, and no full page refresh is required. This makes your application much more responsive, and it's quicker for users to make changes to their data.

Next, go to the Break Formatting section of the report, and you will see the options for breaks are First Column; First and Second Columns; and First, Second and Third columns. For this example, choose First Column. The resulting report is shown in Figure 6-19. It no longer shows repeated data for the DEPTNO column, so that it becomes much easier to visually group the data in the report.

Emps

DEPTNO▼	EMPNO	ENAME	JOB	MGR	HIREDATE	SAL	COMM
10	7782	CLARK	MANAGER	7839	09-JUN-81	2450	
	7839	KING	PRESIDENT		17-NOV-81	5000	
	7934	MILLER	CLERK	7782	23-JAN-82	1300	
20	7369	SMITH	CLERK	7902	17-DEC-80	800	
	7566	JONES	MANAGER	7839	02-APR-81	2975	
	7788	SCOTT	ANALYST	7566	19-APR-87	3000	
	7876	ADAMS	CLERK	7788	23-MAY-87	1100	
	7902	FORD	ANALYST	7566	03-DEC-81	3000	
30	7499	ALLEN	SALESMAN	7698	20-FEB-81	1600	300
	7521	WARD	SALESMAN	7698	22-FEB-81	1250	500
	7654	MARTIN	SALESMAN	7698	28-SEP-81	1250	1400
	7698	BLAKE	MANAGER	7839	01-MAY-81	2850	
	7844	TURNER	SALESMAN	7698	08-SEP-81	1500	0
	7900	JAMES	CLERK	7698	03-DEC-81	950	

1 - 14

Timing : 0.13

Figure 6-19. Using a report break to avoid repeated columns

As you can see in the Break Formatting section, some other interesting options are available for report breaks. One is to repeat the report headings whenever a break is performed, which makes it even easier to visually comprehend the data in the report. (Note that you'll need to make sure your returned data is ordered sensibly using order by so that the breaks can be performed.) You can also add some extra text before break columns or after. Figure 6-20 shows some extra tweaks to repeat the report heading whenever the DEPTNO value changes and to display the sum of the salary for that DEPTNO. Figure 6-21 shows how different the report looks with just a bit of work.

Of course, you should take advantage of break formatting only when it makes sense to do so with regard to both your business rules and the data you are displaying. Otherwise, the report can actually become more confusing to read.

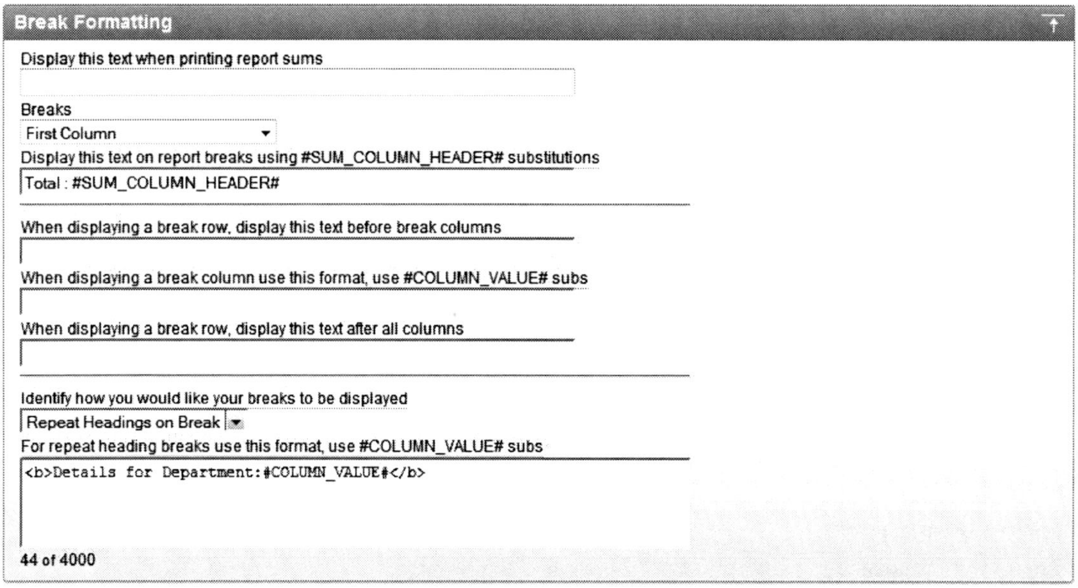

Break Formatting

Display this text when printing report sums

Breaks

First Column ▼

Display this text on report breaks using #SUM_COLUMN_HEADER# substitutions

Total : #SUM_COLUMN_HEADER#

When displaying a break row, display this text before break columns

When displaying a break column use this format, use #COLUMN_VALUE# subs

When displaying a break row, display this text after all columns

Identify how you would like your breaks to be displayed

Repeat Headings on Break ▼

For repeat heading breaks use this format, use #COLUMN_VALUE# subs

```
<b>Details for Department:#COLUMN_VALUE#</b>
```

44 of 4000

Figure 6-20. Customizing break formatting to display sums and headings

Details for Department : 10

Empno	Ename	Job	Mgr	Hiredate	Sal	Comm
7782	CLARK	MANAGER	7839	09.06.81	2450	
7839	KING	PRESIDENT		17.11.81	5000	
7934	MILLER	CLERK	7782	23.01.82	1300	
Total : Deptno					**8750**	

Details for Department : 20

Empno	Ename	Job	Mgr	Hiredate	Sal	Comm
7566	JONES	MANAGER	7839	02.04.81	2975	
7902	FORD	ANALYST	7566	03.12.81	3000	
7876	ADAMS	CLERK	7788	23.05.87	1100	
7369	SMITH	CLERK	7902	17.12.80	800	
7788	SCOTT	ANALYST	7566	19.04.87	3000	
Total : Deptno					**10875**	

Details for Department : 30

Empno	Ename	Job	Mgr	Hiredate	Sal	Comm
7521	WARD	SALESMAN	7698	22.02.81	1250	500
7844	TURNER	SALESMAN	7698	08.09.81	1500	0
7499	ALLEN	SALESMAN	7698	20.02.81	1600	300
7900	JAMES	CLERK	7698	03.12.81	950	
7698	BLAKE	MANAGER	7839	01.05.81	2850	
7654	MARTIN	SALESMAN	7698	28.09.81	1250	1400
Total : Deptno					**9400**	
report total:					**29025**	

1 - 14

Timing : 0.09

Figure 6-21. Report showing department breaks and sums

It is important to note that you could have achieved almost the same results had the report been built as an Interactive Report rather than in the Classic style. Using the Action button on an Interactive report, you can create control breaks on the fly. If you wanted specific text displayed on each break, though, you'd still have to do some work.

Column Formatting

You might think that formatting a report column refers only to things like controlling the currency symbol or perhaps setting the number of decimal places displayed in a numeric value. However, APEX allows a great deal of control over the column formats, so you can think of formatting as referring to the onscreen display of any type of data represented by your columns.

Number and Date Formatting

The Column Formatting section of the Column Attributes section for a report includes a Number/Date Format setting. As an example, the Buglist report currently displays the date that the bug was reported in the format DD-MON-YY. You can modify that by changing the formatting of the REPORTED column, as shown in Figure 6-22.

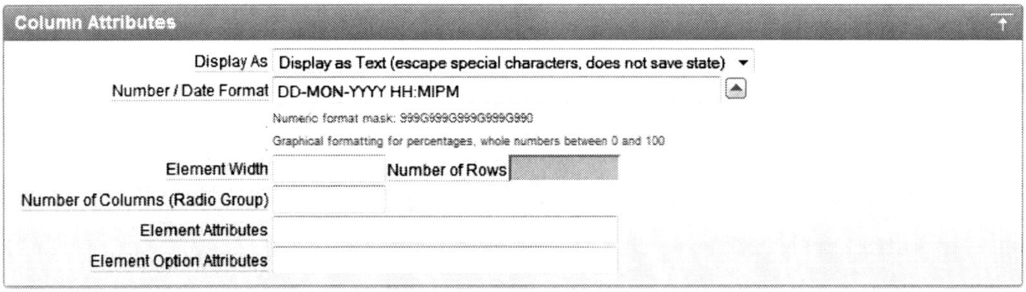

Figure 6-22. Modifying the date formatting for the REPORTED column

Figure 6-22 shows the Number/Date Format value for the REPORTED column changed to use DD-MON-YYYY HH:MIPM. This value was selected from the pop-up list for this field. The text field is a free-format field, so you can type anything into it, as long as the value makes sense for the particular field and is valid. For example, you will get strange results if you try to apply a date-format mask to a numeric column, or if you specify invalid characters in your date-format mask. Note that no validation of the input text takes place at design time; it is used only at runtime.

If you ran the report after making this change to the date format, you'd find that the REPORTED column now displays values such as 27-JAN-2006 12:00AM. In our example, all the times display as 12:00AM, since only a date (not a time component) was used when each record was created. Thus, the time defaults to 12:00AM.

Another interesting format mask for dates uses the keyword SINCE, which displays a text description of how long ago that date occurred. For example, you might see 6 months ago, 2 days ago, 8 minutes ago, and so on. This makes it much easier for the end users to immediately see how long ago an event occurred, rather than having to mentally calculate it themselves. Also, when you use the SINCE mask, the value is calculated each time it is used, so you'll see the age of the record increasing each time you view the report—for example, from 8 minutes ago to 9 minutes ago and so on.

CSS Classes

You can also assign particular CSS classes and styles to the column, For example, if you wanted to display the REPORTED field in bold, you could take advantage of the predefined CSS class called fielddatabold, which is defined in the standard APEX CSS files. All you would need to do is to enter the text fielddatabold into the CSS Class field in the Column Formatting section, and APEX would enclose your column data in an HTML span element and assign the class to it, as shown here:

```
<span class="fielddatabold">27-JAN-06</span>
```

Highlighted Words

You can also enter a comma-delimited list of words into the Highlight Words text field in the Column Formatting section, and APEX will automatically highlight any words that match the column data when you run the report. It does this by wrapping any matching words in an HTML span element and applying a CSS style to that span. For example, entering JAN in the Highlight Words field generates the following HTML (manually broken here):

```
<td class="t15data">27-
  <span style="font-weight: bold; color: red;">JAN</span>-06</td>
```

Although this built-in highlighting is great, considering you get it for free, you have no control over how the word is highlighted—you can't modify the CSS styling that is used. So unless you always want your words highlighted in bold red text, you might find this feature of limited use.

HTML Expressions

Perhaps the most interesting, yet often overlooked, part of the Column Formatting section is the HTML Expression text field. This is extremely powerful, since it allows you to essentially apply another template to the column.

As an example, let's imagine that you'd like the Buglist report to give the end users a quick way to e-mail the person who reported the bug. To do this, you could turn the REPORTED_BY column into a link that, when clicked, launches the default e-mail client and automatically fills in the e-mail address of the person who reported the bug. This is not quite as difficult as it might seem at first, but it does require changing the report a bit.

First, you need to modify the query used for the report so you can extract the e-mail address of the person who reported the bug. Recall that the query was originally as follows:

```
select
  "ID","BUGID",
  "REPORTED","STATUS",
  "PRIORITY","DESCRIPTION",
  "REPORTED_BY", "ASSIGNED_TO"
from
  "BUGLIST"
where
```

```
(
    ... where clause omitted
)
```

Currently, the users who reported bugs are not maintained in the user_repository table, so you wouldn't be able to get the e-mail address from there. (The reported_by field is actually a free-format field, so any name could be typed in it.) For this example, we have inserted records into the user_repository table to represent each person who has reported a bug, and also modified the bug-editing screens to allow only the reporting person to be selected from a list of people in the user_repository table. We will not show all the steps we performed, since they are not directly relevant to this example, but you can see the changes in the application export included with the downloadable code provided for this chapter.

You can now change the report query to extract the e-mail address from the user_repository table by performing a subquery, as shown in Listing 6-14.

Listing 6-14. Subquery to Extract E-Mail Addresses

```
SELECT
    bl.id,
    bl.bugid,
    bl.reported,
    bl.status,
    bl.priority,
    bl.description,
    bl.reported_by,
    bl.assigned_to,
    (select ur.email from user_repository ur
        where ur.username = bl.reported_by)
        as reported_email,
    (select initcap(ur2.forename) || ' ' || initcap(ur2.surname) from
        user_repository ur2 where ur2.username = bl.reported_by)
        as reported_full_name
FROM buglist bl
WHERE(
    ... where clause omitted
)
```

This query is essentially the same as before, except now the subquery looks up the e-mail address from the user_repository table and also generates the full name of the user by using the InitCap function to uppercase the forename and surname of the person who reported the bug, This is necessary because the reported_by field now contains the username of the user, rather than the free-format text it contained previously. Note also in Listing 6-14 that table aliases have been added to make it easier to remove any ambiguity about which table the columns reference.

If you now looked at the Report Attributes section, you would see the REPORTED_EMAIL and REPORTED_FULL_NAME columns added to the list. You could just modify your report template to display this new column, but it would be nice to use it in a link from the user's full name. To do that, enter the following code in the HTML Expression field for the REPORTED_BY column:

```
<a href="mailto:#REPORTED_EMAIL#">#REPORTED_FULL_NAME#</a>
```

Even though you place this code into the HTML Expression field for the REPORTED_BY column, you are actually referencing the two other columns you haven't directly used in the report. The code will generate an HTML a (anchor) element, with the special href attribute of mailto:, which most modern browsers recognize as meaning that the default mail client should be launched when the user clicks the link. You pass the value of the #REPORTED_EMAIL# column into the href, so that when the default mail client launches, it generates a new e-mail message and uses the value of the REPORTED_EMAIL column as the e-mail address to which to send the message. By using the REPORTED_FULL_NAME column value inside the HTML anchor, the text that is displayed for the link is the user's full name, rather than the login username, which you would have gotten if you had used #REPORTED_BY# instead.

But why use the REPORTED_BY column here, when it isn't actually displayed in the report? You could have just as easily shown the REPORTED_EMAIL column in the report, and used the same HTML expression to format it slightly differently. Well, that's a good question. Doing that would make it slightly less confusing when you return to this code in six months or so. However, doing it this way demonstrates that in the HTML expression, you can reference columns other than just the current one. This is what gives HTML expressions their power. Using them, you can completely transform the way a particular column is represented on the screen.

You can use HTML expressions in many different ways. Typical uses include making custom links (as in this example), generating the correct HTML for an image to be displayed, and linking in some custom JavaScript for that item.

One place you should definitely consider using HTML expressions is if you find yourself including HTML markup inside your queries. For example, rather than write code like this:

```
select
  name,
  '<img src="apexdemo.generate_image?p_file=' ||
    filename || '"</img"' as custom_image
from
custom_files
```

use code like this:

```
select
  name,
  filename as custom_image
from
  custom_files
```

then use an HTML expression to transform the custom_image column like this:

```
<img src="/apexdemo.generate_image?p_file=#CUSTOM_IMAGE#"></img>
```

We suggest doing it this way for two reasons:

Readability. Your code will be much more readable. It will be much easier to modify the second query than the first, since the extra text, and particularly the quotation marks, make the first query more difficult to read.

Performance: By minimizing (or better still, eliminating) the HTML markup in your queries, you make it possible for Oracle to reuse the same cached query used in different places in your application, even though the HTML expression might format the results differently. When you use the first query, you might need to have multiple versions of it throughout your application, if you want the resulting HTML to be displayed slightly differently.

It is definitely best practice to try to separate your queries from the display markup as much as you can, and using HTML expressions makes that task very easy indeed.

Columns as Links

APEX makes it easy to use the columns in your report as links, either to pages in the same application or to external URLs. In the previous example, in rewriting the query, the original column link for editing a bug (which was created by the application creation wizard) was lost. However, it is very easy to re-create that link.

All you need to do is decide which column you want to turn into a link and choose that column in the Column Attributes section of the Application Builder. Then you can access the Column Link section for that particular column, as shown in Figure 6-23.

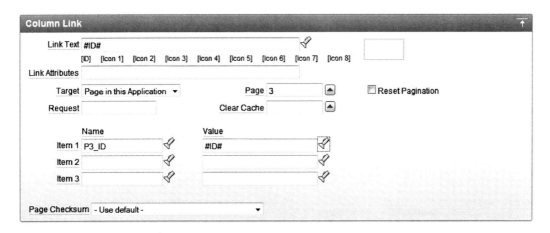

Figure 6-23. Column link attributes

As you can see from Figure 6-23, you can use substitution values in the link text. This example has #ID# as the link text, which means that you'll still be able to see the data in that column, but APEX will turn that text into a link for you. The target of this link is set to be another page in the application. You could also make the link an external URL, and then you'll be able to enter a URL.

When the target is another page in your application, you can set page items to certain values via the link that will be generated. This example sets the value of the P3_ID page item to the value represented by the substitution string #ID#. In other words, the value of that page item is set so that the page being linked to (page 3) is then able to retrieve the details about that particular record in a page process.

■ **Note** You might wonder what happens if you want to pass across more than three items in your link; for example, if you have a four-part primary key. There are all sorts of work-arounds for that, and two main schools of thought. One school of thought (the one we belong to) is that when you get to the stage where your primary keys become that complex, it is perhaps time to think about using surrogate primary keys (that is, a single value that uniquely identifies the record). If you use surrogate keys, you will be able to pass across the primary key, which the other page can then use to retrieve all of the details for that particular record. The other school of thought maintains that having three, four, five, or more components of the primary key is the correct way to go.

Charts

Like reports, charts are a great way to visually present information to the user. APEX provides built-in charting functionality and a wizard to help you create charts. However, unlike reports, charts usually make sense only for certain types of data (or, rather, to represent the relationships between certain types of data).

To add a chart, you can either create a chart on an existing page or on a new page. If you want to add a chart to an existing page, first create a new region and select a region type of chart. This will give you access to the chart creation wizard, where you can choose which type of chart you wish to create, as shown in Figure 6-24. To create a new page for your chart, choose Create Page from the Application Builder, and then select a page type of chart. This will also take you to the chart creation wizard.

Figure 6-24. Using the chart creation wizard

As you can see in Figure 6-24, two different types of charts are currently available in APEX:

HTML chart: This is the most basic, although still highly effective, charting method in APEX. It relies on nothing more than standard HTML to produce static charts. This type of chart does not require the end user to have anything other than a standard web browser, and should therefore work in the vast majority of cases (even on mobile devices).

Flash chart: This chart type was introduced in APEX 3.0. It uses the AnyChart Flash chart component, which is shipped as part of the APEX product, to produce animated, interactive Adobe Flash charts. To view the charts, the end user needs a web browser with Flash Player version 8 or higher installed (the installation of Flash Player can be easily automated as part of the Flash display itself).

In the previous version of APEX, a third chart type, Scalable Vector Graphics (SVG), was available. Although the SVG format is still supported in APEX 4.0, you can't create new SVG charts. If you upgrade an application that contains SVG charts, you can leave them alone or choose to upgrade them. The Region Definition for SVG charts contains a task named "Upgrade to New Flash Chart."

If you have an application that contains several SVG reports, you can upgrade the application to APEX 4.0 and convert all of the SVG charts at once as part of the upgrade.

The type of chart you use in your applications should be driven by two factors:

- How the end users will access the application. For example, if they will be using mobile devices (smart phones, PDAs, and so on), they may not be able to view SVG or Flash charts.

- The degree of interactivity with the data your users need. For example, the Flash chart allows much more interactivity than the standard HTML chart.

When you created the Buglist application, the application creation wizard automatically created charts (and reports) for you. Here, we will demonstrate how you can create your own charts, although obviously you can just modify the existing ones, too.

Chart Query Types

The basic format of the query to define the chart data is essentially the same for many chart types and styles. The standard format for the query is:

```
select
    <link>,
    <label>,
    <value>
from table
```

where `link` represents the link to use if the user clicks that particular data item in the chart, `label` represents the text to use as the label in the chart, and `value` represents the numeric value to use for the data point.

There are some exceptions to this general format. The following sections describe various chart types that require slight modifications of the general query format. Most of those are really subtypes of the Flash chart. We don't illustrate each subtype of chart (dial, range, candlestick, and so on) in this chapter, but we do list the query variations because that information may come in very handy down the road.

Dial Chart Syntax

When you use a dial chart, you use the following general syntax:

```
select
  <value>
  <maximum_value>
  [ , <low_value [ , <high_value> ]
from
  table
```

where `value` is the initial value for the data point, maximum value is the highest possible value allowed for the data point, and `low_value` and `high_value` are the historical low and high values (optional).

Multiple Series Syntax (Flash Charts Only)

Flash charts allow you to define multiple series to display in the chart. You can do this by entering additional series in the chart attributes, or you can list each series in a single query (if the data lends itself to being queried in that way). The following is the syntax for querying multiple series:

```
select
  link,
  label,
  series_1_value,
  series_2_value,
  [ , ...]
from
  table
```

where the values for the different series are determined from the column aliases you use.

Range Chart Syntax (Flash Charts Only)

If you use a range chart type in a Flash chart, you need to provide two different values for each bar:

```
select
  link,
  label,
  low_value,
  high_value
from
  table
```

Candlestick Chart Syntax (Flash Charts Only)

Candlestick charts require four different values for each data point: a value for `open`, `low`, `high`, and `close`.

```
select
  link,
  label,
```

```
  open,
  low,
  high,
  close
from
  table
```

Gantt Charts

Two types of Gantt charts are supported in APEX 4—Project and Resource. Both of these charts are used for project management and, to be used effectively, require a specific set of data. The query syntax describes what is necessary and is shown below:

Project Gantt chart syntax:

```
SELECT link, task_name, task_id, parent_task_id, actual_start_date, actual_end_date, progress
FROM   ...
```

Resource Gantt chart syntax

```
SELECT link, resource_id, resource_name, resource_parent_id, actual_start_date,
actual_end_date
FROM   ...
```

As you can see, these are fairly specialized reports, but if you are making use of the Team Development features of APEX 4.0, the data to support these reports will likely be available.

Flash Maps

Flash Maps are created using map files, which are included with APEX in conjunction with a query. The syntax of the query is basically the same for any map page, but what you include in the query has to match with the type of map you select. If you plan to use your own data to reference geographical information in a map, it must correspond to the region information associated with the map. If, for example, you want to show the population of Dallas County on a map of Texas, you need to have 'dallas' in your data as that is the lowest level of detail associated with state maps of the United States. The syntax used with maps is very simple, as shown here:

```
SELECT null link, region label, value Populations
FROM (
SELECT 'Florida' region, 18328340 value FROM dual
UNION ALL
SELECT 'Alaska' region, 686293 value FROM dual)
```

On a map of the United States, this query would result in Florida and Alaska being highlighted, with each displaying the label and value when the mouse is hovered over the region.

HTML Charts

Since we've already touched on the existence of HTML charts and Flash charts, it is important to define the distinctions between the two charting methods.

- HTML Charts
  - ○ Support only bar charts
  - ○ Limited interactivity, no animations
  - ○ Do not require a browser plugin to execute
- Flash Charts
  - ○ Support multiple chart types—bar, dial, pie, map, etc.
  - ○ High levels of interactivity—animations, region highlighting, etc
  - ○ Require the Flash browser plug-in

The charting examples here use a new page in the Buglist application to house the chart. Also, using the page creation wizard, we added a new tab called Charts to the tab set, for easy navigation to the new page (see Chapter 5 for details on adding tabs).

Suppose you want to see a chart of how many bugs were reported by each user. You can create a new HTML Chart region on the page and give it a title of Reported By. Now you need to provide the query to generate the chart. If you examine the definition of the buglist table, you can see that you can use a group by query against the REPORTED_BY field and perform a count on the returned records, as shown in Listing 6-15.

Listing 6-15. Using a Group By Query

```
apexdemo@DBTEST> desc buglist;
 Name              Null?    Type
 ---------------   -------- ------------
 ID                NOT NULL NUMBER
 BUGID                      NUMBER
 REPORTED                   DATE
 STATUS                     VARCHAR2(30)
 PRIORITY                   VARCHAR2(30)
 DESCRIPTION                VARCHAR2(255)
 REPORTED_BY                VARCHAR2(30)
 ASSIGNED_TO                VARCHAR2(30)

apexdemo@DBTEST> select
  2  reported_by, count(*)
  3  from buglist
  4  group by reported_by;

REPORTED_BY            COUNT(*)
--------------------  ----------
LScott                         1
SGreen                         1
PMathews                       2
LBarnes                        2
JStevens                       1
CWatson                        3
MLawson                        2
```

```
CDonaldson              1
RHudson                 1
RHuson                  1
CWhite                  2
```

However, rather than reporting the username, you want to show the forename and surname. To do this, you can adapt the query to perform a subquery against the user_repository table (or you could use a join if you prefer), as shown in Listing 6-16.

Listing 6-16. *Returning the Nicely Formatted Name*

apexdemo@DBTEST>

```
REPORTED BY          BUGCOUNT
-------------------- ----------
Lucy Scott              1
Steven Green            1
Paul Mathews            2
Laura Barnes            2
John Stevens            1
Carl Watson             3
Mark Lawson             2
Chris Donaldson         1
Rachel Hudson           1
Rachel Huson            1
Caroline White          2
```

You can now enter this query as the source for the chart. However, don't forget that you need to modify the query, since you must return a link, label, and value for each data point. At this stage, you do not want the data point to link to anything, so you can simply use NULL as the link, as shown in Listing 6-17.

Listing 6-17. *Modified Query to Use NULL as the Link*

```
apexdemo@DBTEST>  select
  2     null as link,
  3   (select ur.forename || ' ' || ur.surname
  4      from user_repository ur where
  5      ur.username = bl.reported_by) as label,
  6   count(*) as value
  7   from buglist bl
  8*  group by bl.reported_by;
apexdemo@DBTEST> /

LINK         LABEL                     VALUE
------------ -------------------- ----------
             Lucy   Scott               1
             Steven   Green             1
             Paul   Mathews             2
             Laura   Barnes            2
```

```
John    Stevens               1
Carl    Watson                3
Mark    Lawson                2
Chris   Donaldson             1
Rachel  Hudson                1
Rachel  Huson                 1
Caroline  White               2
```

In Listing 6-17, the columns aliases are modified to link, label, and value. You don't have to use these column aliases, strictly speaking, since it is the order of the columns that is important. However, using them makes debugging much easier—you can just run the query in SQL*Plus or SQL Workshop, and you'll be able to see immediately which columns are which.

If you run the page, you'll see a chart like the one shown in Figure 6-25. Note that the default is to assign random colors to each entry (which may not show up that well in the figure). The method used to assign the colors does show some intelligence, however. Rather than being completely random for each value, it uses the same color for repeated values (such as the entry for Carl Watson, since it reported three bugs) and also the same color for values that are near each other statistically (which may or may not be appropriate to your situation).

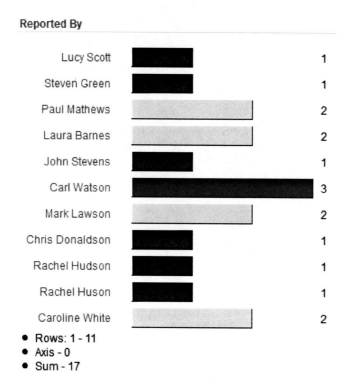

Reported By

Lucy Scott		1
Steven Green		1
Paul Mathews		2
Laura Barnes		2
John Stevens		1
Carl Watson		3
Mark Lawson		2
Chris Donaldson		1
Rachel Hudson		1
Rachel Huson		1
Caroline White		2

- Rows: 1 - 11
- Axis - 0
- Sum - 17

Figure 6-25. HTML chart showing number of bugs per reporter

Now, what if you wanted to make this chart a bit more useful and enable the user to quickly see the bugs reported by a particular person. You can do this by providing a link that goes from the chart back to the same page but sets the value of a hidden page item with the value of the person who was clicked.

First, create a hidden item on the page, which will be used to store the name. Let's call it P14_REPORTED_BY. Then create a Report region below the Chart region. This performs a query against the buglist table and displays any rows where the REPORTED_BY columns match the value of the P14_REPORTED_BY page item. Also add some conditional display logic so that the report does not display if the value of the P14_REPORTED_BY page item is NULL (for example, the first time the user views the page without having clicked an item in the chart).

In the report, the query would look like this:

```
select
    bugid, reported,
    status, priority,
    description, assigned_to
from
    buglist
where
    reported_by = :P14_REPORTED_BY
```

Note the use of the P14_REPORTED_BY page item in the query. You also need to modify the query used for the chart so that it includes a link. Recall the format of the standard APEX URL (discussed in Chapter 5). You can create a URL that links back to this same page (in the same application) and automatically sets the value of the P14_REPORTED_BY page item. To achieve that, you want a URL that looks similar to this (divided over two lines for readability):

```
http://server:port/DAD/f?p=APP:PAGE:SESSION::::
P14_REPORTED_BY:cwatson
```

Fortunately, rather than needing to worry about getting the correct values for the server name, port number (if not on the default port value of 80), and DAD, you can use a relative URL that will automatically use the values for the current page. You can also use the substitution strings APP_ID, APP_PAGE_ID, and APP_SESSION in the URL. So your URL now looks like this:

```
f?p=&APP_ID.:&APP_PAGE_ID.:&APP_SESSION.:::::P14_REPORTED_BY:
```

Notice how you can just use f?p to indicate the relative URL, rather than needing to specify everything from the http:// onwards. You can now replace the null as link part in the query with the code shown in Listing 6-18.

Listing 6-18. Querying Using a Link Back to the Same Page

```
select
    'f?p=&APP_ID.:&APP_PAGE_ID.:&APP_SESSION.:::::P14_REPORTED_BY:'
    || bl.reported_by as link,
    (select ur.forename || ' ' || ur.surname from user_repository ur
        where ur.username = bl.reported_by) as label,
    count(*) as value
from buglist bl
group by bl.reported_by
```

Running the page again and clicking one of the data points will show additional detail in the report section, as shown in Figure 6-26.

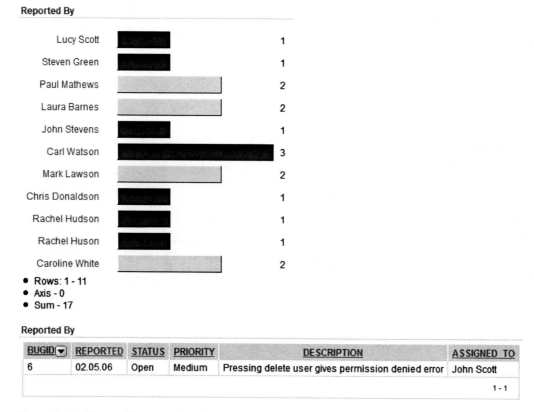

Reported By

BUGID▼	REPORTED	STATUS	PRIORITY	DESCRIPTION	ASSIGNED TO
6	02.05.06	Open	Medium	Pressing delete user gives permission denied error	John Scott
					1 - 1

Figure 6-26. *Chart with report detail*

In Figure 6-26, you can also see some summary details displayed in the chart, including the number of rows shown (1-11) and the sum of all the values displayed (17). If you look at the Chart Attributes section for the HTML chart, you'll see that you can include the following summary items:

- Number of data points

- Minimum value

- Average value

- First value

- Axis

- Maximum value

- Sum of all values

- Last value

In Figure 6-26, the Axis summary value is 0, which indicates that the base axis for this chart is 0. You can alter this by changing the value for the Axis setting in the Chart Attributes section. The valid Axis values are as follows:

- Average Value in Series

- First Value in Series

- Last Value in Series

- Maximum Value in Series

- Minimum Value in Series

- Zero

Changing the Axis setting allows you to create some interesting-looking charts. For example, if you wish to compare the values against some baseline, you can use the first value or last value. This makes it easy to see the values that are greater or lower than this baseline, since the values that are lower than the baseline will be seen extending in one direction, while the values that exceed the baseline will extend in the other direction, Note that we said "direction," rather than "left" or "right" in the previous sentence, because you can also modify the orientation of the chart between horizontal and vertical, which makes the baseline view just described perhaps even more visually useful.

HTML charts are quite basic when compared with the other two types of charts. However, they are very functional and are the most supported type of chart for your users (almost every browser type is able to display HTML charts). You may find that the lack of additional features is more than made up for by the fact that the chart will work out of the box for almost every user.

Flash Charts

Both APEX 3.x and 4.x support Flash-based charts, but version 4.x has the advantage of using a newer release the AnyChart product, version 5.1. The range of options presented by AnyChart is tremendous, and though we will only touch on certain features, covering all the possibilities is out of the scope of this book. To fully understand what you can do with charts in APEX 4, you have to experiment. You can access the AnyChart user guide at the `http://anychart.com/products/anychart/docs/users-guide/`. One thing to note is that not every type of AnyChart object is available in APEX. Only the Scatter (Marker) chart, for example, is available in APEX, though there are several other scatter chart types available in the full product.

Where Flash charts really shine is in the creation of dashboards. As every company becomes more data-hungry, the need for high-quality, usable reports grows. Given the amazing breadth of capabilities within AnyChart, you can easily create very high-quality visual representations of data with very little effort. Be careful in how you use some of the more obscure chart types (scatter, candlestick, etc.) as your users may not know how to read the chart. Just make sure you know your audience so you don't create overly complex, incomprehensible reports. One more thing to remember is to limit the use of animations in Flash Charts. While this feature does have a "wow factor," be conservative in where and how much you use it. If you build a dashboard, for example, you should probably limit animations as the motion can become annoying, especially if the page is refreshed frequently.

We built the dashboard shown in Figure 6-27 in about 30 minutes. It could have taken even less time, but it wouldn't have fit on the page as well as it does.

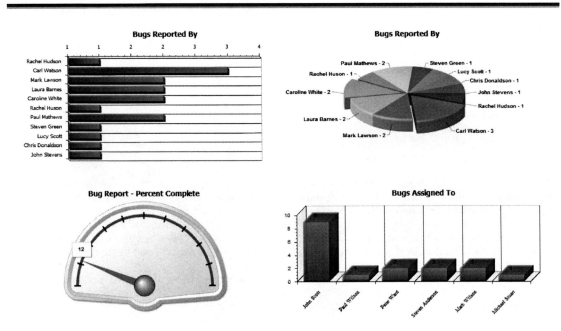

Figure 6-27. Buglist dashboard built with Flash charts

Some of the things we did to make this dashboard look the way it does are as follows:

1. The chart regions were all built without a template so that the line and title above the region wouldn't take up space.

2. The heights of all regions on the same row were set to make them appear to line up. I say "appear" because the height of a 3D Pie Chart and a Bar Chart don't look equal when they are next to each other (the pie chart looks shorter).

3. The x-axis labels on the 3D Column chart were rotated 45 degrees so that all the lables would be visible. If left horizontal, the label values would overlap and some of the text would not show up.

4. Two of the pie pieces were clicked to highlight them before this screen was captured.

In general, the process of creating Flash charts has not changed, but the number of options that can be applied to a report has increased in APEX 4.x. Table 6-3 lists the available chart types.

Table 6-3. Supported Chart Types

Type	Description
Column	Allows a single series, vertically oriented as a bar chart
Horizontal Bar	Allows a single series, horizontally oriented as a bar chart
Pie and Doughnut	Allows a single series, with each data point displayed as a slice in the pie
Scatter	Allows multiple series, vertically oriented and clustered by a common variable
Line	Allows multiple series, shows data over time compared to a single scale
Candlestick	Allows multiple series, shows the movement in the value of a data point over a specific time interval
Gauge	Allows multiple series, shows the value of datapoints in horizontal, vertical, or circular formats
Gantt	Allows single series, shows task duration and completion percentage

Figure 6-28 shows a Flash 3D Bar Chart based on the same query used for the HTML chart created in the previous section. This chart was no more difficult to create than the HTML version, but it is much more visually pleasing (although it's not as impressive in gray-scale). Adding one of the many animation features makes viewing reports almost fun (if that's possible).

The main consideration for using Flash reports is the requirement to install (or have) the Flash browser plug-in. Many corporations are becoming less open to installing any new software at the request of an application—especially automated installs as is the case with the Flash plug-in.

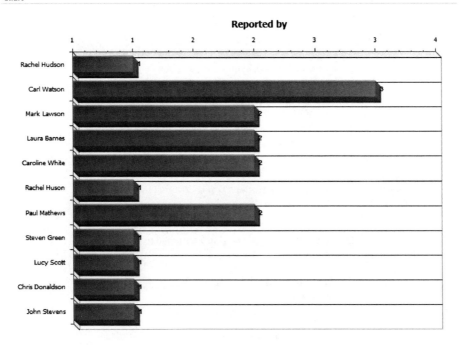

Figure 6-28. Flash 3D horizontal bar chart

Flash Maps

Another interesting new addition to Flash Charts is the Mapping feature, which allows you to use maps in your reports to display location-based information. You can display only those maps that are delivered with APEX 4.0 (there are more than 100). The lowest level of detail on each map is considered a "region." In the case of a map of Texas, available regions are counties and 3-digit zip codes. You can't drill down to a specific city with this level of detail. The page shown in Figure 6-29 contains a map of Texas with two counties, Tarrant and Dallas, highlighted. To make this work, the county names had to be known as they are stored in the map as the regions.

Map

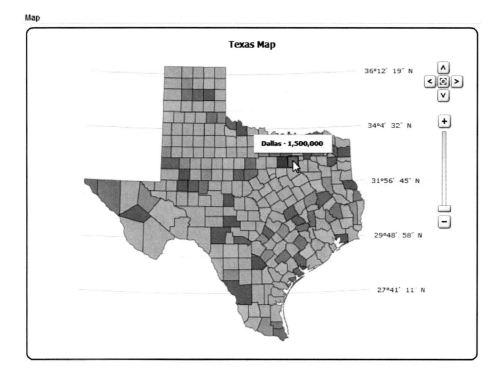

Figure 6-29. Flash Map using the state of Texas

Notice that when the mouse is hovered over Dallas County, the population value is shown. The query used to add this functionality is below:

```
select null as link, region Label, value Population
from
(
select 'Dallas' region, 1500000 as value from dual
UNION ALL
select 'Tarrant' region, 600000 as value from dual
)
```

As stated previously, the name of the county is synonymous with the region. When the county name is selected along with a value (population was used in this example), both are displayed upon hovering the mouse over the region.

Chart Localization

You can take advantage of CSS styling to display Flash charts in other languages. For example, the *Application Express User's Guide* suggests that to display the text in your chart in the Korean language, you can modify the CSS definitions for the text and tspan classes as follows:

```
text{font-family:Batang;fill:#000000;}
tspan{font-family:Batang;fill:#000000;}
```

Note that the charts are not automatically translated. You are simply modifying the font-family directive to use the correct font type, which can display the text in the correct format. It is still your responsibility to make sure the actual text is correct.

Asynchronous Updates

Flash charts provide a very handy feature called Asynchronous Updates, which automatically refreshes the chart at a specified interval and displays any changes in the underlying data. The Asynchronous Updates feature can be very useful for dashboard-type applications, where end users want to see constantly updated feedback about particular statistics without having to click a refresh button or resubmit the page.

To enable Asynchronous Updates, change the Asynchronous Updates setting to Yes and specify an Update Interval in seconds in the Refresh section of the Chart Attributes section.

If you use the Asynchronous Updates feature, be aware that any animation features you've used will also be executed as part of the refresh process.

Multiple Series

Using multiple series in your charts is no more difficult than using single series, although you need to take a bit of care that the data values you represent on the chart work well with each other. In other words, if you try to display multiple series in the same chart when there is no obvious correlation between the data in each series, you may end up making the chart more difficult to read.

Suppose you wish to modify the sample chart so that instead of just showing the number of bugs reported by people, it also shows the number of bugs assigned to people. You can do this by using a chart type that supports multiple series. Remember that you can't just change the chart type, so you need to delete the chart and create a new one (of another type).

For example, create a new Chart region type and select the Cluster Bar, Horizontal option, which enables you to specify multiple series. However, because you need to have a common link between the two series, you need to rewrite the previous SQL as shown in Listing 6-19, so that the chart shows all the users and the bugs reported by them, rather than just listing the users that have bugs assigned.

Listing 6-19. Modified Query to Show All Users, As Well As Bugs

```
select
  null as link,
  ur.username as label,
  (select count(*) from buglist bl
     where bl.reported_by = ur.username) as value
from user_repository ur
```

Note that this query is simplified a little by using NULL for the link, as well as by just using the username rather than concatenating the forename and surname. As before, you could provide a link to the same page, which generates a report showing the detail for a selected chart item.

If you look at the report attributes, you will see that this chart type has a Chart Series section, which allows you to add an extra series, as shown in Figure 6-30.

Figure 6-30. **Adding an extra series to a chart**

Add another series, but this time modify the query so that it returns the number of bugs assigned to people, as shown in Listing 6-20.

Listing 6-20. Query to Group Bugs by the assigned_to *Column*

```
select
  null as link,
  assigned_to as label,
  count(assigned_to)
from buglist bl
group by assigned_to
```

You can now see both series displayed in the same chart, as shown in Figure 6-31 (the color difference between the series may be difficult to make out in the screenshot).

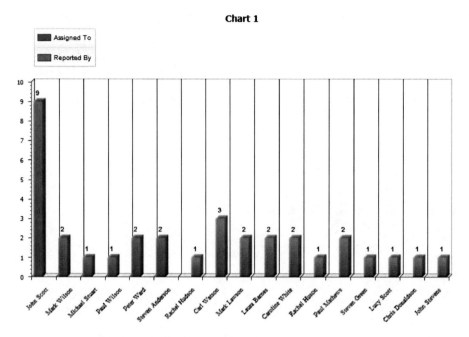

Figure 6-31. Using multiple series in a chart

Flash Chart XML Customization

You can further customize the look of Flash charts by modifying the XML used to generate those charts. The Chart XML section of the Chart Attributes section contains code similar to Listing 6-21.

Listing 6-21. XML Used by the Flash Chart

```
<?xml version = "1.0" encoding="utf-8" standalone = "yes"?>
<anychart>
  <settings>
    <animation enabled="false"/>
    <no_data show_waiting_animation="False">
      <label>
        <text></text>
        <font family="Verdana" bold="yes" size="10"/>
      </label>
    </no_data>
  </settings>
  <margin left="0" top="0" right="0" bottom="0" />
```

```
<charts>
  <chart plot_type="CategorizedBySeriesVertical" name="chart_5928617224245708">
    <chart_settings>
      <title text_align="Center" position="Top" >
        <text>Reported by</text>
        <font family="Tahoma" size="14" color="0x000000" />
      </title>
      <chart_background>
        <fill type="Solid" color="0xffffff" opacity="0" />
        <border enabled="false"/>
        <corners type="Square"/>
      </chart_background>
      <data_plot_background>

      </data_plot_background>
      <axes>
        <y_axis >
          <scale    mode="Stacked"    />
          <title enabled="false" />
          <labels enabled="true" position="Outside">
            <font family="Tahoma" size="10" color="0x000000" />
            <format><![CDATA[{%Value}
              {numDecimals:0,decimalSeparator:.,thousandsSeparator:\,}]]>
            </format>
          </labels>
          <major_grid enabled="False"/>
          <minor_grid enabled="False"/>
        </y_axis>
        <x_axis>
          <scale   mode="Stacked"     />
          <title enabled="false"/>
          <labels enabled="true" position="Outside">
            <font family="Tahoma" size="10" color="0x000000" />
          <format>
            <![CDATA[{%Value}
            {numDecimals:0,decimalSeparator:.,thousandsSeparator:\,}]]>
          </format>
```

```
        </labels>
        <major_grid enabled="True" interlaced="false">
            <line color="Black" />
        </major_grid>
         <minor_grid enabled="True">
        </minor_grid>
     </x_axis>
   </axes>
 </chart_settings>
 <data_plot_settings enable_3d_mode="true" >
   <bar_series style="Default">
     <tooltip_settings enabled="true">
       <format><![CDATA[{%Name}{enabled:False} -
        {%Value}
        {numDecimals:0,decimalSeparator:.,thousandsSeparator:\,}]]>
       </format>
       <font family="Tahoma" size="10" color="0x000000" />
         <position anchor="Float" valign="Top" padding="10" />
     </tooltip_settings>
     <label_settings enabled="true" mode="Outside" multi_line_align="Center">
        <format>
         <![CDATA[{%Value}
         {numDecimals:0,decimalSeparator:.,thousandsSeparator:\,}]]>
        </format>
       <background enabled="false"/>
       <position anchor="Center" valign="Center" halign="Center"/>
       <font family="Arial" size="10" color="0x000000" />
     </label_settings>
     <bar_style>
     </bar_style>
     <marker_settings enabled="True" >
       <marker type="None" />
     </marker_settings>
   </bar_series>
 </data_plot_settings>
```

```
#DATA#
    </chart>
  </charts>
```

```
</anychart>
```

As you can see in Listing 6-21, you can modify many options in the XML to affect how the chart will look and operate. Before doing so, read the documentation about the various options (and definitely make a backup of the current XML). As noted earlier, the Flash charts are produced with a third-party component, the AnyChart Flash chart component, which Oracle has licensed to ship with the APEX product. For more information and documentation about the various options, you can consult the original component documentation at www.anychart.com.

Generic Charting

You may want to have your chart use different SQL depending on certain criteria. For example, you might want to modify the where clause in the query, depending on what the user has selected from a list. You can do this in a couple of ways.

Function to Return the SQL

Generic charting is quite simple. Rather than defining the SQL in the Series Query section for the chart, you can change the Query Source Type setting from SQL Query to Function Returning SQL Query, and then write a query that returns the text to use for the SQL query, as shown in Listing 6-22.

Listing 6-22. Using a Function to Return the SQL

```
CREATE OR REPLACE FUNCTION generatequery(p_type IN VARCHAR2) RETURN VARCHAR2 IS v_sql
VARCHAR2(2000);

BEGIN
  v_sql := 'select id, name, salary from payroll where ';
  IF p_type IS NOT NULL THEN

    IF(p_type = 'DEPT') THEN
      v_sql := v_sql || ' and dept_name = v(''P1_SEARCH'')';
      ELSIF(p_type = 'MANAGER') THEN
        v_sql := v_sql || ' and manager = v(''P1_SEARCH'')';
      END IF;

  END IF;

  RETURN v_sql;
END;
```

This example passes in a parameter, p_type, to the function. This parameter is then used to determine whether to append an extra part to the where clause restriction, which compares the value of the P1_SEARCH page item against the dept_name column or the manager column.

Note that the v('ITEM') syntax is used in the function, rather than passing in the value of the search text and then concatenating it to the SQL like this:

```
v_sql := v_sql || ' and dept_name = ' || p_query_string;
```

Using this type of concatenation is extremely dangerous and makes your application susceptible to SQL-injection attacks. A malicious user could manipulate the value of the p_query_string parameter so that the string returned from the function contains some code you didn't anticipate (such as deleting from a table).

For performance reasons, you should use bind variable notation (:ITEM), rather than using the v('') function. We will come back to this issue of using bind variables in more detail in Chapter 14.

Pipelined Functions

Rather than using the Function Returning SQL Query option, an alternative way to achieve generic charting relies on a feature called *pipelined functions*. You know that the chart is expecting certain columns to be returned by the query, namely link, label, and value, like this:

```
select
  null as link, ename as label,  sal as value
from
  scott.emp
where
  deptno = :P101_DEPTNO
```

So you need a way of returning a link column, a label column, and a value column dynamically for each row of data. First, you need to create a type that will be used as the return type of your pipelined function; that is, this type will represent a single point on the chart:

```
create or replace type ty_chart_entry as object (

  link varchar2(60),
  label varchar2(60),
  value number
);
```

Next, create another type that is a collection of the ty_chart_entry type. This will effectively hold the table representing all the data points on the chart:

```
create or replace type tbl_chart_entry as table of ty_chart_entry;
```

Now you need to create the function itself, as shown in Listing 6-23.

Listing 6-23. Pipelined Function Definition

```
create or replace package chart_pkg

as
    function generate(p_type in varchar2)
      return tbl_chart_entry PIPELINED;
end;
```

```
create or replace package body chart_pkg as
  function generate(p_type in varchar2)
    return tbl_chart_entry PIPELINED is
  begin
    if (p_type = 'E') then
      for rec in (select ename, sal from emp) loop
        pipe row (ty_chart_entry(null, rec.ename, rec.sal));
      end loop;
    end if;
    if (p_type = 'D') then
      for rec in (select d.dname as name,
                     (select sum(e.sal) from emp e
                        where e.deptno = d.deptno) as sal
                     from dept d) loop
        pipe row (ty_chart_entry(null, rec.name, rec.sal));
      end loop;
    end if;
    return;
  end;
end;
```

Essentially, this function performs two entirely different queries depending on whether you pass in a 'D' (to query the dept table) or an 'E' (to query the emp table).

```
SQL> select count(*) from table(chart_pkg.generate('E'));

COUNT(*)
--------
14
SQL> select count(*) from table(chart_pkg.generate('D'));
COUNT(*)
--------

4
```

You can now create a new chart region on a page and add a select list (with submit) that returns 'E' or 'D', and use the value of this page item in the query, as shown here:

```
select
  link, label, value
from
  table(chart_pkg.generate(:P14_CHARTTYPE))
```

If you now run the page, you should see the different data, depending on what was chosen from the select list, as shown in Figures 6-32 and 6-33.

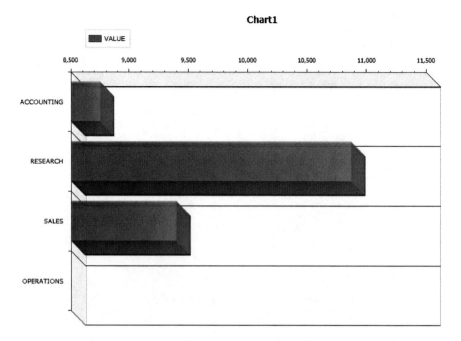

Figure 6-32. Querying the emp table with generic charting

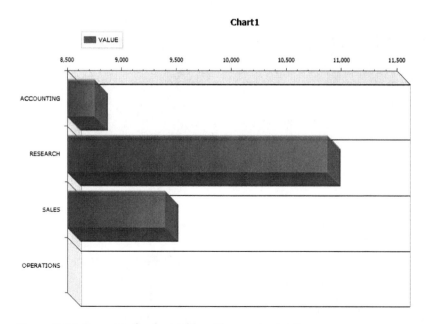

Figure 6-33. Querying the dept table with generic charting

You might find that you prefer the approach of using pipelined functions so that you don't risk producing dynamic SQL that could potentially be exploited via SQL injection. If there is a restricted set of queries that you want to enable the user to perform, using a pipelined function is an ideal way of providing that functionality.

Summary

This has been a long chapter, and it's long because APEX offers incredible power and flexibility in reporting and charting. Reporting gives you many options to use to effectively present data. You have control over page breaks, column formatting, and so on. You can even create reports in which each item links to pages on the Internet, or to other reports, forms, and so forth defined within APEX. For example, you could create a Buglist report in which clicking on a developer's name took you to a chart showing that developer's success rate in closing bugs on the first try.

Charting in APEX is a substantial topic in its own right, and we have only scratched the surface of what is available. While you can create basic, HTML-based charts, APEX also supports key industry standards such as SVG and Flash. Using those standards, you can provide elegant and highly effective charts and graphs to key decision-makers in your business. APEX's ability to link from reports to charts, combined with its support for industry standards makes APEX a highly effective reporting too

CHAPTER 7

Dynamic Actions

Dynamic Actions are a new feature of APEX 4.0 that allows you to implement Ajax functionality with minimal coding. To understand why Dynamic Actions are important, a little history of Ajax is in order. The name Ajax is an acronym for Asynchronous JavaScript and XML. It is more of a programming methodology than a new programming language. Prior to 1999 when Microsoft created the XMLHTTP ActiveX object, refreshing any content on a web page required a refresh of the entire page. The problem with full page refreshes was that if the user entered data before the refresh, the developer was often responsible for saving that data so that it reappeared after the new page was displayed. The drawback was that the developer needed to know something about all of the following technologies:

- XHTML

- The Document Object Model (DOM)

- CSS

- Use of the XMLHttpRequest object

- JavaScript

Using the XMLHTTP object, developers were able to make requests for data and update portions of a page without forcing a full page reload. Following Microsoft's lead, browsers like Mozilla, Safari, and Opera were quickly updated to support this functionality using a JavaScript object, as opposed to ActiveX, called XMLHttpRequest. Any browser that supports the XMLHttpRequest object can implement Ajax functionality, but browsers may not all work exactly the same way. Just because Microsoft has to be different, Internet Explorer versions 7 and 8 support both the ActiveX object as well as the XMLHttpRequest JavaScript Object.

Writing Ajax code manually required that all the nuances of the major browsers be accounted for. This required a significant amount of code just to make sure that applications would work across browsers. Although you can still write Ajax code in APEX, the good news is that you can add Ajax features to your APEX applications using Dynamic Actions via the same declarative methods you are accustomed to, and you don't have to worry about browser incompatibility.

APEX 4.0 offers two kinds of Dynamic Actions: Standard and Advanced. The Standard variety can be used only to show/hide/enable/disable items, while the Advanced type can handle just about anything you can do with Ajax. Standard Dynamic Actions are triggered by a value in an item, whereas Advanced Dynamic Actions can be executed by just about any type of activity. We will explore both types in this chapter along with a brief refresher on using Ajax in APEX, in case you find something that can't be done with Dynamic Actions.

Implementing a Dynamic Search

A common use for Ajax is to provide visual feedback on the web page while a user is typing something into a field. This approach is often used for search fields. The user begins typing into a search field, and the results corresponding to each letter the user types are dynamically displayed.

Consider the main screen of the Buglist application, which displays all of the bugs assigned to the currently logged-in user, as shown in Figure 7-1. Currently, the user can enter something into the search field and then click the Go button (or press Enter), and the report will be filtered to show only the matching records. It would be a nice touch if you could dynamically update the report as the user types into the search field. To do this, you can use Dynamic Actions. We'll set up a new page to show how this works.

First, create a new page containing an Interactive Report (page 41 in our application) using the default region template for the report. You need to ensure that the template contains the #REGION_STATIC_ID# substitution string or this example will not work. Most new templates do have this, but if you're using an older template you may have to switch to a newer one. We'll use the same SQL from the original report, as shown in Listing 7-1.

Listing 7-1. SQL Used in the New Search Page

```
select
  ID, BUGID,REPORTED,STATUS,PRIORITY,
  DESCRIPTION,REPORTED_BY,ASSIGNED_TO
from
  BUGLIST
where
(
 instr(upper("STATUS"),
   upper(nvl(:P41_SEARCH,"STATUS"))) > 0  or
 instr(upper("PRIORITY"),
   upper(nvl(:P41_SEARCH,"PRIORITY"))) > 0  or
 instr(upper("DESCRIPTION"),
   upper(nvl(:P41_SEARCH,"DESCRIPTION"))) > 0  or
 instr(upper("REPORTED_BY"),
   upper(nvl(:P41_SEARCH,"REPORTED_BY"))) > 0
)
```

For this example, we used the same Bread Crumbs and Tabs as before, so the report should look pretty much like the original, although this is an Interactive Report, whereas the original was Classic. If you run the new report, it should look like Figure 7-1.

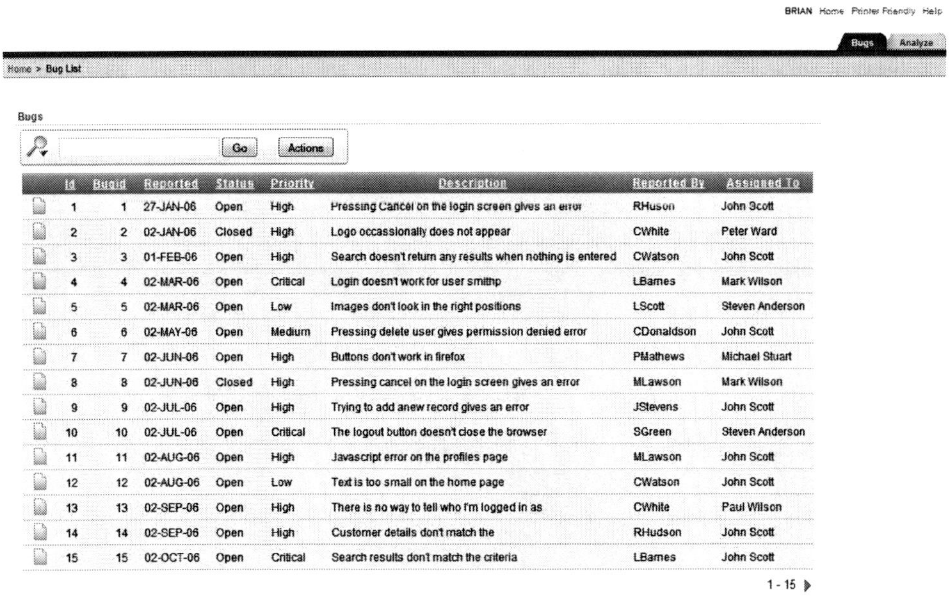

Figure 7-1. New report page

Now we need to make a few modifications to this page to enable the new search capability, but we will not be writing JavaScript. First on the list is removal of the built-in search bar. We need complete control over this input field so we'll add our own shortly. To remove the search bar, edit the page and locate the Report Attributes section. Set the "Include Search Bar" field to "No," as shown in Figure 7-2.

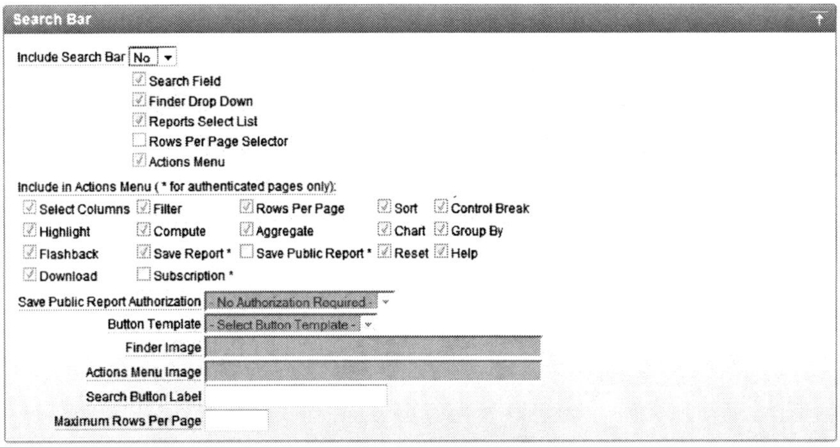

Figure 7-2. Disable Search Bar in new report

Now we have a report that has no search capability, so the next step is to add that functionality back. We accomplish this by adding an empty HTML region above the report and including a text field in this region to allow the user to enter a search. When adding the new region, set its Sequence to 5 so it shows up above the report. Then add a text field to the new region and give it a label like "Search" so the user will know what it's for. The name of this text item is important as it has to match the page item reference in the SQL from the report's Region Source. In our application, the text field is called P41_SEARCH. The page should now look like Figure 7-3.

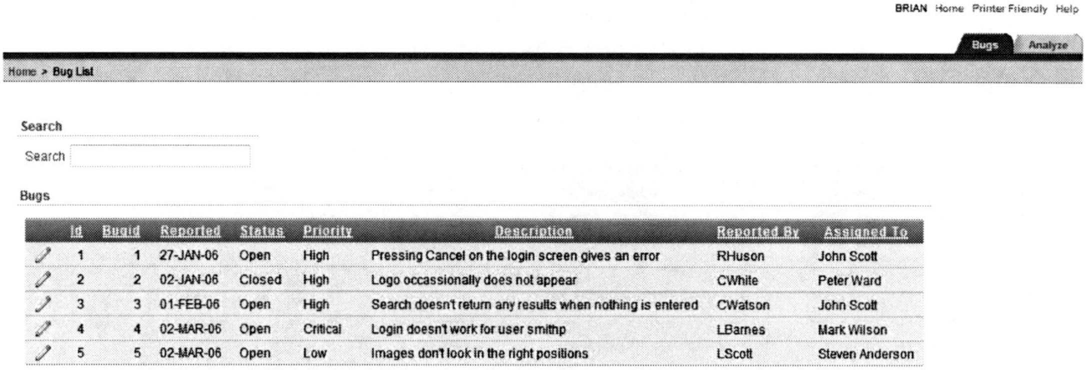

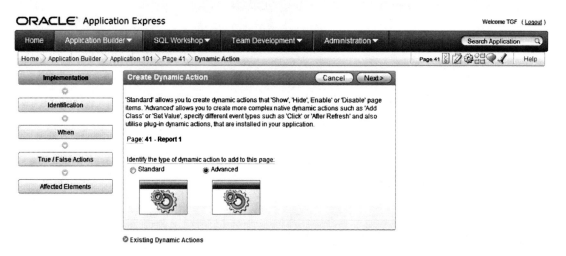

Figure 7-3. New report with search field

At this point, everything we've added to this page is out of the standard APEX bag of tricks. We have not modified any JavaScript, changed any templates, or written any non-standard SQL code in preparation for adding Ajax-like functionality. Now we'll add the Dynamic Action to enable not only search capability, but also character-by-character interactive search. We begin by creating a new Dynamic Action by clicking the "Create" icon in the new Dynamic Actions section of the page editor, as shown in Figure 7-4.

Figure 7-4. New Advanced Dynamic Action

In this case we used an Advanced Dynamic Action, as the Standard type can only handle show/hide/enable/disable (we'll get to those later). This new Dynamic Action is going to be used to refresh the report region based on what is entered in the Search field. You next have to give the Dynamic Action a name and a Sequence, just as in most other APEX controls, as shown in Figure 7-5. Because a Sequence is available for this type of object, you can probably infer that you can have multiple Dynamic Actions that operate on a field in a specific order. Powerful.

Figure 7-5. Naming the New Advanced Dynamic Action

It's in the next step that the fun begins. You are now able to identify the type of event that will trigger the Dynamic Action, as shown in Figure 7-6. This is the equivalent of writing JavaScript code to execute using onClick, onBlur, etc., but this takes only a single click. For our search field, we want each character entered to be used as input to the search and we don't want the user to have to click anything or tab out of the field to execute the search. The event type that matches this requirement best is Key Release since it will fire after each character is entered.

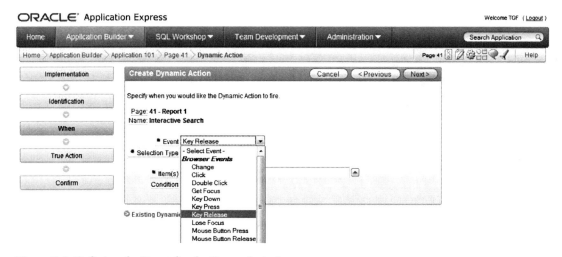

Figure 7-6. Defining the Event for the Dynamic Action

On this same page, we also identify the type of object that will trigger this Dynamic Action. There are several choices, listed as follows, along with an example:

- *Item*: P41_SEARCH

- *Region*: region name

- *DOM Object*: P41_SEARCH

- *jQuery Selector* : #P41_SEARCH

■ **Note** Outside of APEX, a jQuery selector to find the P41_SEARCH item looks like $('#P41_SEARCH'). When you set the Selection Type of a Dynamic Action to "jQuery Selector," you need only supply what would be inside the quote marks from the example, #P41_SEARCH. The function type, $(…) is implied. APEX won't tell you if you've entered an invalid jQuery selector, it just won't work.

In all cases, you are identifying some page item, but you have great flexibility in how it is identified. In this case, set the Selection Type to "Item" and then use the popup LOV to select your search field (again, P41_SEARCH in this example). You can also set a condition to determine when the Dynamic Action should fire, but for this example, accept the default "No condition" setting as shown in Figure 7-7.

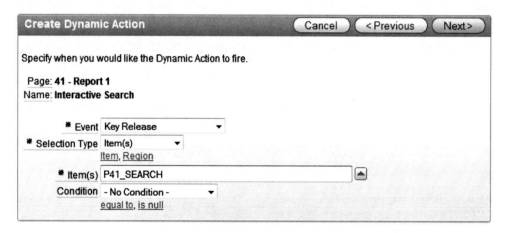

Figure 7-7. Defining the triggering item for the Dynamic Action

Once the triggering item has been defined, the next step is to define the "When Condition, " or what should happen as a result of the Dynamic Action being fired. In this step, shown in Figure 7-8, you select from a list of actions to perform. In this case, select "Refresh" since we want to refresh the report region as the user types in a search string. Also, uncheck the "Fire on Page Load" check box, as shown in Figure 7-9, because this will do just what it says. For our example, it would not be terrible for the Dynamic Action to execute when the page loads because the search field will be empty, which will cause all rows of the report to display. Since the report will do this on its own, we would just be forcing a second query for no benefit.

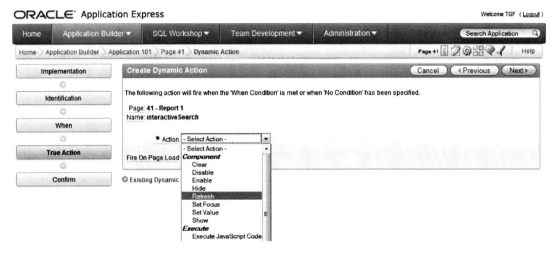

Figure 7-8. Defining the When Condition for the Dynamic Action

Notice that in this step, there is only one "When Condition" and that condition is considered to be true. In other words, we said that the triggering event was "Key Release" and there was no condition set on that event. Therefore this event will fire whenever a key is released in this field. Had we added a condition to the event, we would have to specify what happens if the condition is not met (we'll see this in the next example).

| Create Dynamic Action | Cancel | < Previous | Next > |

The following action will fire when the 'When Condition' is met or when 'No Condition' has been specified.

Page: 41 - Report 1
Name: interactiveSearch

＊ Action Refresh
          Disable, Enable, Show, Hide
Fire On Page Load ☐

Figure 7-9. Disable Fire on Page Load for the Dynamic Action

Now we know what the trigger is and what will happen when the Dynamic Action fires, but we have not defined what element will be affected. As you probably guessed, the last step allows you to do exactly that. Figure 7-10 shows the available element types. This screen has a two-step process built in where you select the object type and the corresponding element identifier. For this example, select "Region" and then the name of the report region.

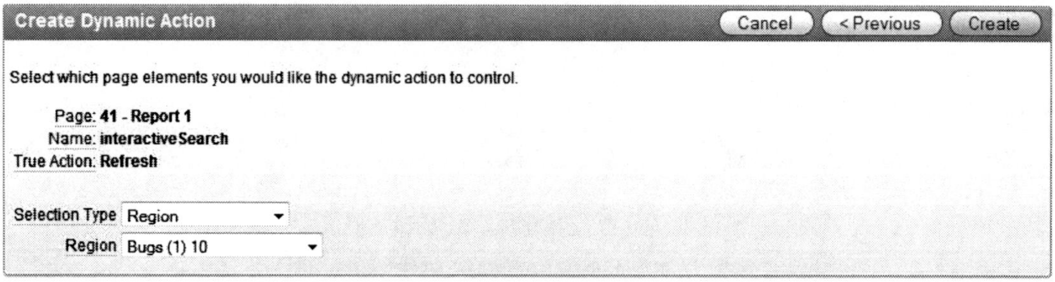

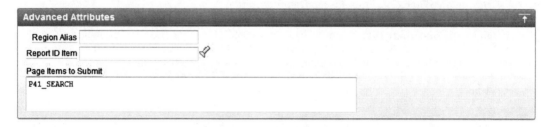

Figure 7-10. *Select the Element Affected by the Dynamic Action*

So that's it—sort of. If you run the report now, it will show up and when you type in the Search field you will see an indication that something is happening (in Firefox, a "busy" graphic will show up at the top of the page), but the search feature does not work. The last thing we need to do is tell the report to submit the P41_SEARCH field so that the session state will contain the values and the search can be executed. This is done on the Report Attributes page via the Advanced Attributes section, as shown in Figure 7-11. This is why it was important to note that the name of the search field must match the page item in the report's Region Source.

Figure 7-11. *Define the Page Item to Submit*

Now when you execute the report, searches will be executed as you type in the Search field, as shown in Figure 7-12. Awesome! And you didn't have to write a single line of JavaScript.

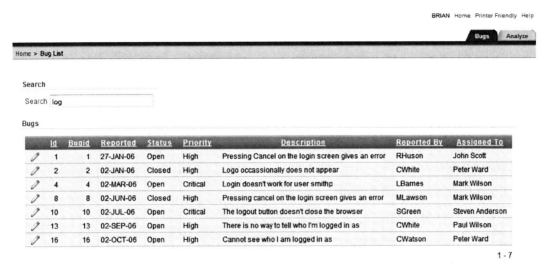

Figure 7-12. Interactive Search using Dynamic Actions

■ **Note** Now obviously it's very difficult to demonstrate just how cool a dynamic filtering report like this is with a static screenshot. We encourage you to try out the sample code to see how well it works at runtime and how useful it can be for end users.

Calling On Demand Processes

Prior to APEX 4.0, Calling On Demand Application Processes required knowledge of JavaScript and the `htmldb_get()` function to implement Ajax functionality. With the advent of Dynamic Actions, the process of calling On Demand processes has changed somewhat, but has also become easier. We'll use an earlier example from Chapter 3 to illustrate this point.

Understanding Your Choices

Remember that we created an Application Process that was fired on Submit to store the search values entered on the Buglist report. If we want to implement this feature in our new report, we can do so in (at least) two ways:

1. Create a JavaScript function that uses Ajax (`htmldb_get`) to call the existing Application Process. Then build a Dynamic Action that executes JavaScript to run our new function, which uses Ajax to call the Application Process.

2. Create a Dynamic Action that executes PL/SQL.

Option 2 is recommended. It will be much easier to accomplish and will directly associate the PL/SQL code with the Dynamic Action. If you are going to use the PL/SQL that was in the Application Process, you can remove the Application Process unless some other piece of code makes use of it. Since your existing Ajax code will continue to operate, leave it alone. For new, dynamic code, however, Dynamic Actions are strongly recommended as they are so easy to construct and maintain, and they encapsulate so much functionality.

Creating a Dynamic Action

Return back to our example. In our original search logger, we used the SQL shown in Listing 7-2 to record the user's input:

Listing 7-2. *SQL Used to Store Search Strings*

```
begin
  insert into user_searches
    (id, logged, username, search_phrase)
  values
    (search_seq.nextval, sysdate, :APP_USER, :USER_SEARCH_STRING);
end;
```

To implement the same functionality in our new page, we can use this same code to very quickly create a Dynamic Action that executes PL/SQL. There is one twist, however, since our new page has Interactive Search capability. We only want to store the final search value (log only the full string the user searched, not every letter keyed; for example capture the word *dog*, rather than capturing *d*, then *do*, then *dog*).

First, clear any previously logged searches so that we can easily check that the new functionality is working, as follows:

```
apexdemo@DBTEST> select count(*) from user_searches;
  COUNT(*)
----------
        15

apexdemo@DBTEST> delete from user_searches;
15 rows deleted.

SQL> commit;

Commit complete.
```

Next, create a new Dynamic Action on the page we created earlier in this chapter (page 41 in our application). We will again use an Advanced Dynamic Action as we need to execute a PL/SQL block. Since we already have the code from the On Demand Application Process, there is no need to open that object. Start by creating the Dynamic Action and giving it a name (we used "Log Searches"). In the second step, as shown in Figure 7-13, set the Event Type to "Lose Focus" so the Dynamic Action fires only when the user leaves the P41_SEARCH item, not on each keystroke. Again we will use the P41_SEARCH item as the trigger and this time we will set a condition that restricts the Dynamic Action from firing unless the user has entered something in the search field.

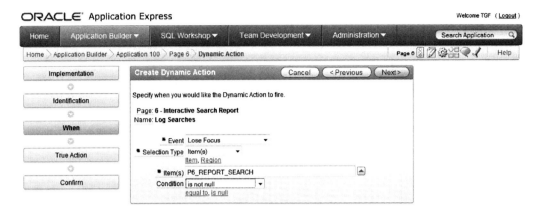

Figure 7-13. Specifying the Event for the Dynamic Action

In the next step, we set the Action of the When Condition to "Execute PL/SQL Code." Again the "Fire on Page Load" is disabled and the PL/SQL code from the original On Demand Application Process is copied in. Figure 7-14 shows the completed When Condition setup.

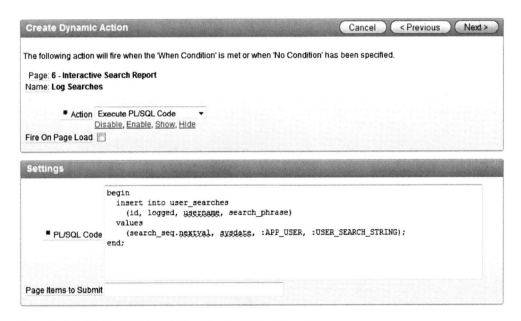

Figure 7-14. Setting the True Action for the When Condition

Defining the False Action is the next step, shown if Figure 7-15. Since we had a condition on the event, "is not null," we have to say what to do (if anything) when the value of the triggering item is null. Well, if the user does not enter anything in the Report Search item and tabs away, that's OK. Therefore we can leave the False Action of the When Condition set to "No False Action." One possible way to use the False Action is to ensure that the user enters data in a field before being allowed to tab out. At that point, you could pop up a JavaScript alert to tell the user what is wrong. For this example, it is not really appropriate, but would be in many other cases.

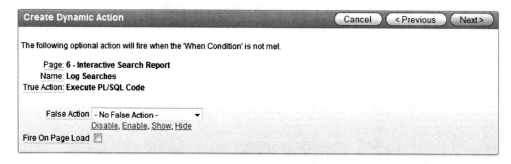

Figure 7-15. *Setting the False Action for the When Condition*

The final steps in the creation of the Log Searches Dynamic Action are to verify and commit the changes. You can now test the page by entering some text in the P41_REPORT_SEARCH item and tabbing away or clicking the mouse elsewhere on the form. If you then examine the user_searches table, you should see a record of all the user's search entries. Listing 7-3 shows an example.

Listing 7-3. *Viewing the Logged Searches*

```
SQL> select * from user_searches;

    ID LOGGED      USERNAME    SEARCH_PHRASE
------ ---------   ----------  --------------
  1703 26-DEC-10  BRIAN       customer
  1701 26-DEC-10  BRIAN       logo
  1702 26-DEC-10  BRIAN       cancel

3 rows selected.
```

As you can see, creating a Dynamic Action that provides the same functionality as an Ajax / On Demand Application Process is very quick and easy. If you know what you want to accomplish, creating a control like this can literally be done in five minutes or less.

Showing and Hiding Page Elements

Advanced Dynamic Actions give you the flexibility to manipulate almost any object on an APEX page. You can add content to empty sections of a page, for example, by populating an empty <DIV></DIV> tag set, or by hiding whole page sections until they are required. The reasons for implementing functionality such as this vary widely, but you should focus more on improving functionality than creating a "wow factor." One example we have used in the past is to show a report that allows the user to select a row to edit, and to pop up the edit form on the same page when a row is selected. This keeps the user on the same page during both searches and edits. In this section, we will explore using Advanced Dynamic Actions to hide and show elements on an APEX page.

Showing and Hiding Fields Using Advanced Dynamic Actions

One of the most popular uses for Ajax functionality is toggling the display of page elements. This can be done for a variety of reasons, but a major benefit is that a single screen can be used in multiple ways. For example, data can be shown or hidden based on the authorization level of the user. This is not just for individual fields, as entire sections of a page can be enabled/disabled at will. Both Standard and Advanced Dynamic Actions can be used to show/hide items, but if you want to use a button as a trigger, you have to use an Advanced Dynamic Action.

As an example, imagine that the Buglist application users frequently show other users the results of their searches, but they don't want to reveal the actual search text that was used (for whatever reason). Wouldn't it be nice if they were able to quickly hide the search field before they showed the page to someone else? Well as you've probably guessed, it is very easy to do that using Dynamic Actions.

To do this, we first create a new button for which the user can use to hide the search text. For a button to work in this context, it must be placed in a region position so that it can be assigned an ID using the button attributes field, as shown in Figure 7-16. We'll add this button at the top of the region so it stays in one place no matter how many records are displayed in the report.

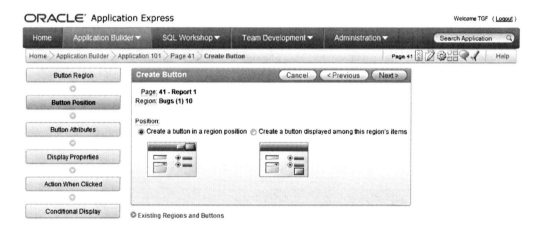

Figure 7-16. Creating a new button

Create this as an HTML button and assign an HTML Button Attribute to it, as shown in Figure 7-17. Buttons don't automatically get ID's like text items do, so we have to give it one. When you build the Dynamic Action on this button, you are required to provide an ID for the triggering object. Name this ID P41_BTN_HIDE_SEARCH so there is no question what this button is for. Your naming conventions may allow for a shorter name, but for this example we'll use very descriptive names.

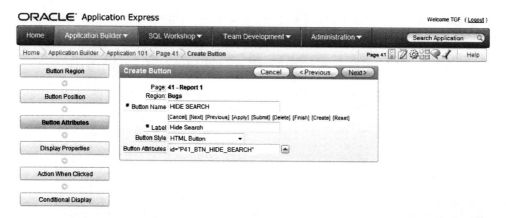

Figure 7-17. Assign button attributes

Assign this button to the top of the report region, and then set the button's Action to "Redirect to URL" as shown in Figure 7-18. Now we're going to use a little JavaScript magic to make our button's label change every time we click on it. We're doing this because we want the Dynamic Action to be able to hide as well as un-hide the Search region. For this to work, the Dynamic Action needs to know the state of the region—visible or hidden so it knows how to change the state. Because we're using a button, the only value we have to work with is the label. So the JavaScript we're adding, as follows, will change the label of the button to either "Hide Search" or "Show Search" each time it is clicked:

```
javascript:this.value=(this.value=='Hide Search') ? 'Show Search' : 'Hide Search';
```

This is a standard, "in line if" that says, "if the value of the button is 'Hide Search,' then set it to 'Show Search,' otherwise set it to 'Hide Search.'" Even though this button will not submit the page, uncheck the "Execute Validations" checkbox to reinforce that this is not a Submit button. Since this button is not going to have a condition, click "Create Button" to finish the process.

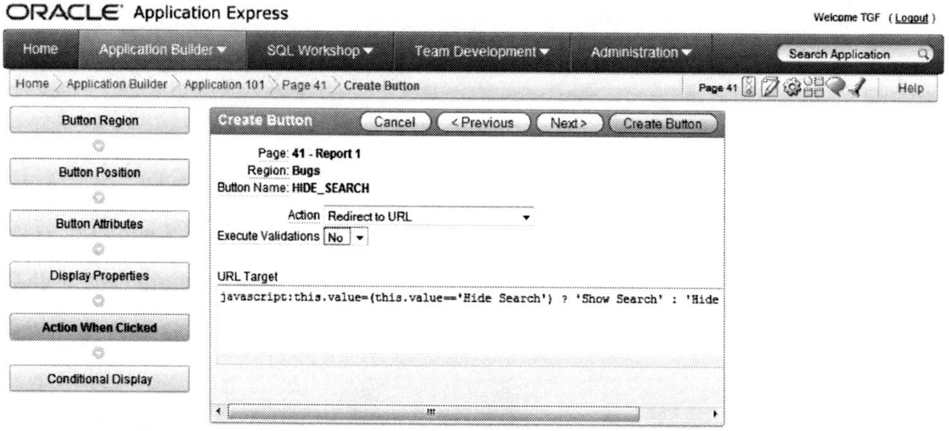

Figure 7-18. Set button action

Now when you run the report, you can see that the "Hide Search" button is positioned at the top of the Report region. If you click it a few times, as shown in Figures 7-19 and 7-20, you'll see that its label toggles between "Hide Search" and "Show Search" just like we need it to. It doesn't do anything else, though … yet!

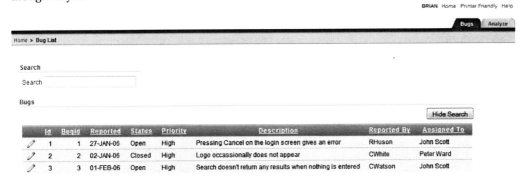

Figure 7-19. Button with "Hide Search" label

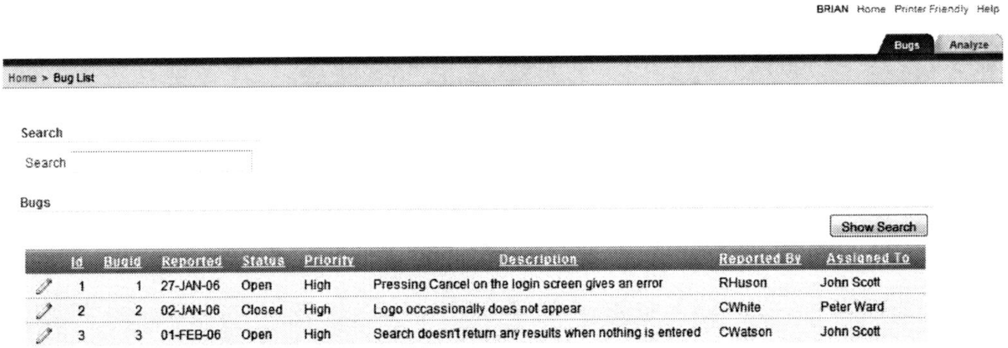

Figure 7-20. Button with "Show Search" label

Now comes the easy part, building the Dynamic Action. Remember that we want to hide the search criteria when the button has the label "Hide Search" and re-display it when the label is "Show Search." We could choose to hide only the P41_REPORT_SEARCH item, but that would leave the region title on the page, which would not look good. It would be better to hide the entire Search region, so that is exactly what we'll do (and it doesn't take any more effort than hiding a single field).

We start by creating an Advanced Dynamic Action because this will allow us to use a "click" action as the trigger. Remember that Standard Dynamic Actions are triggered by the value of an item, not an action like a button click. Figure 7-21 shows an Advanced Dynamic Action named "Hide Search." The sequence is not really important as all of the Dynamic Actions we have created are independent.

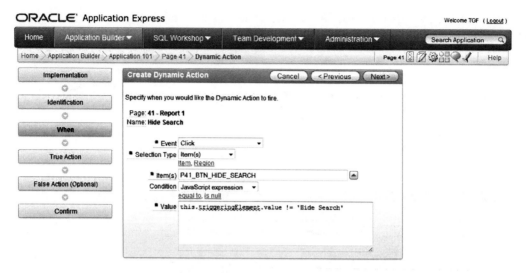

Figure 7-21. Hide Search Dynamic Action

Next we define the attributes of the When Action, as shown in Figure 7-22. The event we want to use is "Click" since we're using a button as the triggering element. We can use the Item Selection Type since we assigned an item ID to our HTML button. The Condition is set to evaluate a JavaScript expression that must evaluate to True or False. In a JavaScript expression, you have access to the following three types of information:

this.triggeringElement: A reference to the DOM object of the element that triggered the dynamic action.

this.browserEvent: The event object that triggered the event. Note: On load this will be equal to 'load'.

this.data: Optional additional data that can be passed from the event handler.

The triggering element we used was the P41_BTN_HIDE_SEARCH and as we know, the value of the button will either be "Hide Search" or "Show Search." So, the JavaScript expression we need is shown as follows:

```
this.triggeringElement.value != 'Hide Search'
```

Now, you may ask why the expression uses a "not equal to" operator, because this says that the Dynamic Action will fire when the value of the triggering button is not equal to "Hide Search." The reason for this is that the JavaScript used to change the button label fires before the Dynamic Action so that the label will be "Show Search" the first time the Dynamic Action is executed. Therefore, we're actually hiding the Search region when the label says "Show" and showing it when the label says "Hide."

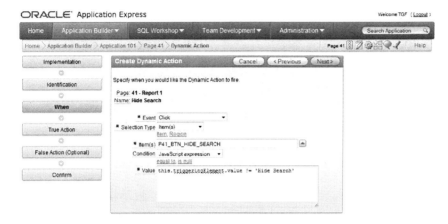

Figure 7-22. When Condition for the Dynamic Action

Setting the True action of the When Condition is next in the process, as shown in Figure 7-23. It is in this step that we define what happens when our JavaScript expression evaluates to True, which is, as you know, to hide the Search region. At this point, we can only set the action, but not the element that will be affected. That happens in the next step. Again, we disable "Fire on Page Load" because we only want the Dynamic Action to fire on a button click. Since we are hiding an entire region, the "Hide all items on the same line" setting is somewhat immaterial. We set it to "No" just for illustration purposes.

Figure 7-23. True Action for the When condition

When you identify a condition in a Dynamic Action, you will have to set a False Action for the corresponding True action. For this example, our False Action is to show the Search region. This step in the process has the same attributes as the True action and is shown in Figure 7-24.

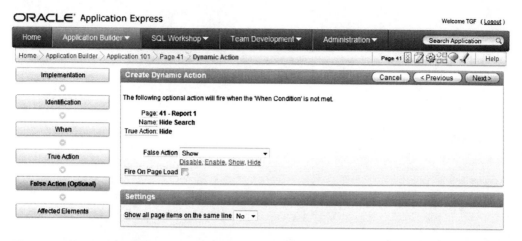

Figure 7-24. False Action for the When Condition

Finally, we set the identify the element, the Search region, that is affected by this Dynamic Action. When you click the "Create" button, shown in Figure 7-25, the Dynamic Action is created and ready to use. We now have a page with a new button with a dynamic label which, when clicked, causes a region to display or hide. With a few clicks and two JavaScript expressions, we created functionality that may have taken hours to create by coding Ajax manually.

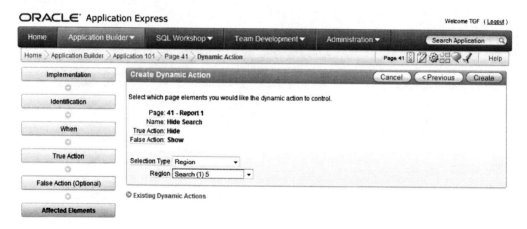

Figure 7-25. Affected Elements of the Dynamic Action

You can now test the page with the Dynamic Action enabled. In the last test, only the button's label changed, but now the label changes and the Search region is hidden and re-displayed. Figures 7-26 and 7-27 show the two states of this page. This button/toggle feature can be used in lots of places, so have fun and experiment.

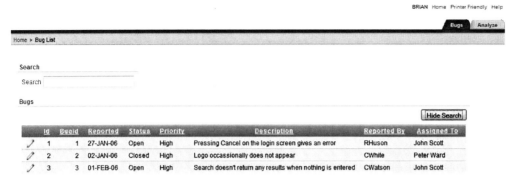

Figure 7-26. Buglist page with the Search Region displayed

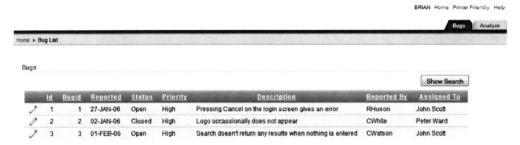

Figure 7-27. Buglist page with the Search Region hidden

Showing and Hiding Items Using Standard Dynamic Actions

In case you had forgotten, Standard Dynamic Actions are based on items and can only handle show/hide/enable/disable functions. They are easy and fast to create, while being more restrictive than Advanced Dynamic Actions. To see how Standard Dynamic Actions work, we'll modify the update form from the Buglist application so that the description field is hidden for bugs that have been closed. This may seem simplistic and a little impractical, but once you complete an exercise like this, you'll see how powerful this feature can be. A Standard Dynamic Action will be used to add this functionality.

First, if you don't already have a form with an interactive report on the Buglist table, create them (you have two minutes). Your Buglist update form should look something like Figure 7-28.

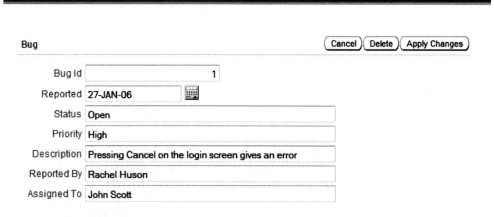

Figure 7-28. Buglist update form

To build the Standard Dynamic Action, edit the Buglist update form. Depending on the view setting (Component or Tree), you have two of the following options for creating a Dynamic Action:

1. On the Component View, the create Dynamic Action control is in the lower left quadrant of the screen. When you start from this point, the Dynamic Action can be created on any form element.

3. With the Tree view, you can right click on an item, PXX_STATUS, for example, and choose Create Dynamic Action.

This provides some insight into how Standard Dynamic Actions work. They are based on an item and will affect another element of the page. In Figure 7-29, we switched the edit view to "Tree" to show that the method for creating a Dynamic Action can initiated by right-clicking on the P40_STATUS item.

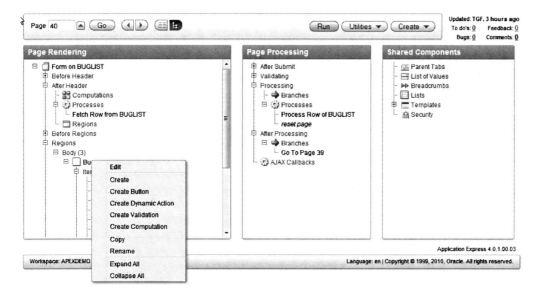

Figure 7-29. *Creating a Dynamic Action on P40_STATUS using the Tree View*

In the first step of the Dynamic Actions wizard, choose the Standard type as shown in Figure 7-30. The Standard variant has only the following four actions:

Show: The item displays when the event is true or No Condition is set

Hide: The item is hidden when the event is true or No Condition is set

Enable: The item is enabled when the event is true or No Condition is set

Disable: Disables the element. If the element is an item, it becomes non-editable and its value is not included if the form is submitted.

Create Opposite False Action: For the true action, create an equivalent false action. If the true action is set to Show, then a Hide action for the false condition would also be created.

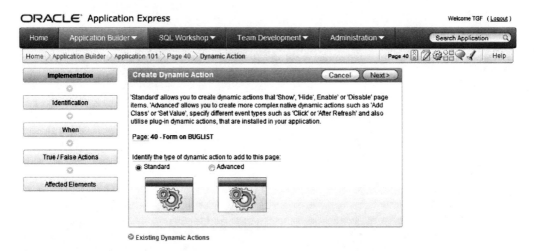

Figure 7-30. *Create a Standard Dynamic Action*

The next step is to identify the Dynamic Action. We recommend that you give each action a name that is somewhat descriptive of the function or the intended result. Since we are using this Dynamic Action to hide the description field, we called it "Hide Description." Figure 7-31 shows the identification process. Notice that there is a sequence number on Dynamic Actions just as with other elements. This allows you to create more than one Dynamic Action on an element and control the order of their execution.

Figure 7-31. *Identifying a Standard Dynamic Action*

At this point, you will define what causes the Dynamic Action to fire. Because we used the Tree view when creating the Dynamic Action on the P40_STATUS item, the item field was automatically populated with that value, as shown in Figure 7-32. You can also see the conditions that control whether or not the Dynamic Action fires. If we set the condition to "equal to" and the value to 'Closed', then we are saying, execute some action when the P40_STATUS item is equal to the string 'Closed'. At this point, we have not yet defined what the action will be.

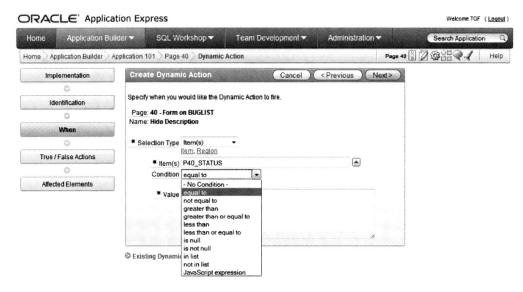

Figure 7-32. Setting the Dynamic Action condition

Now that the condition is set, the True Action, or what will happen when the condition is met, must be defined. Since we want to hide the Description field, the "Hide" option is checked, as shown in Figure 7-33. As a reminder, if you were building an Advanced Dynamic action, you would see several more actions to choose from in this step of the process. Up to this point, we have defined everything about the Dynamic Action with the exception of what element will be affected when it fires.

Figure 7-33. Setting the True Action

The last step in the process is to identify the element that will be hidden by the Dynamic Action. Depending on the "Selection Type" you choose, the options will be different. For this example, we chose "item" and then identified the P40_DESCRIPTION using the shuttle control, as shown in Figure 7-34.

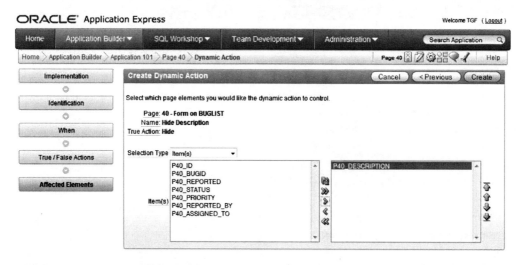

Figure 7-34. *Setting the Affected Elements*

Now when we run the page, we'll see differences in the display depending on the status. Figures 7-35 and 7-36 respectively show open and closed bugs. To really get a feel for this feature, just change the status (remember the spelling of 'Open') and tab out of the field.

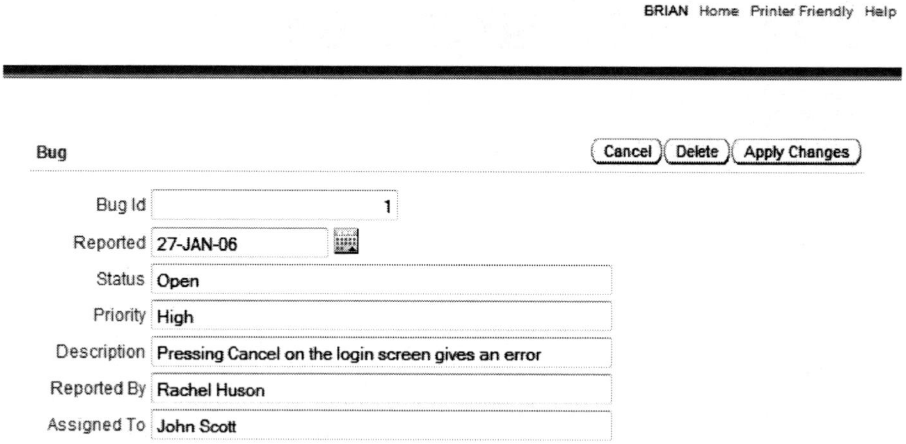

BRIAN Home Printer Friendly Help

Bug		Cancel Delete Apply Changes

Bug Id	1
Reported	27-JAN-06
Status	Open
Priority	High
Description	Pressing Cancel on the login screen gives an error
Reported By	Rachel Huson
Assigned To	John Scott

Figure 7-35. *Open bug with Description*

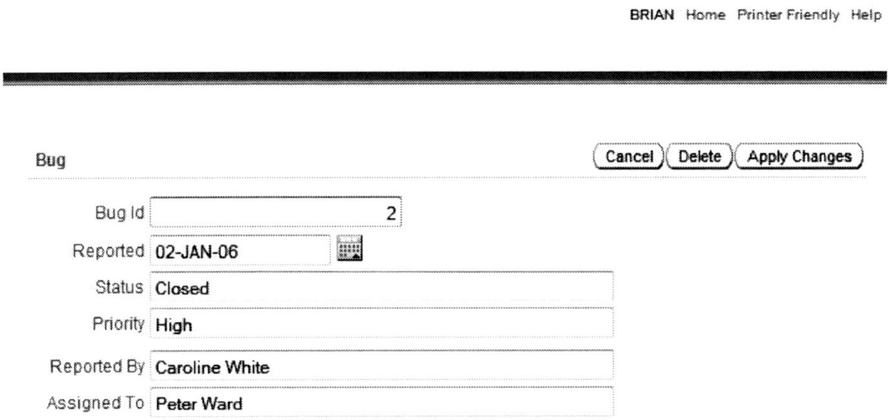
BRIAN Home Printer Friendly Help
Bug
Cancel
Delete
Apply Changes
Bug Id
2
Reported
02-JAN-06
Status
Closed
Priority
High
Reported By
Caroline White
Assigned To
Peter Ward

Figure 7-36. Closed bug with no Description

■ **Note** The Create Opposite False Action is important in this example. Since it was checked, the Dynamic Action fired when the value of `P40_STATUS` was changed to and from `'Open'`. If this option was unchecked, the description field would not be re-displayed if the status was changed back to `'Open'`. There may be cases when you want this behavior, so it is important to understand how Dynamic Actions are affected.

You may not have noticed, but during the creation of this Dynamic Action you were not able to set the event type that triggers the Dynamic Action. The default event type is "change" although there are many others to choose from. If you edit the new Dynamic Action, you can see the available event types, as shown in Figure 7-37. Changing the event to "click," for example, will cause the Dynamic Action to fire only after you click on `P40_STATUS` item. The condition is still the same so the form will not change unless the value of `P40_STATUS` is changed to `'Closed'`.

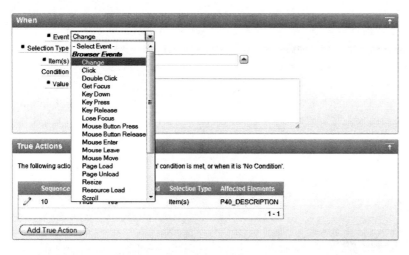

Figure 7-37. *Dynamic Action event choices*

If you edit the True Action by clicking on the Dynamic Action edit icon, as shown in Figure 7-38, you will see that you have more options for the Action than when the Dynamic Action was created. When you edit a Standard Dynamic Action, you basically have access to the functionality of Advanced Dynamic Actions and, as you may have guessed, you can turn a Standard Dynamic Action into an Advanced Dynamic Action. The reason for having a Standard Dynamic Action wizard is so that you can very quickly create hide/show/enable/disable functionality.

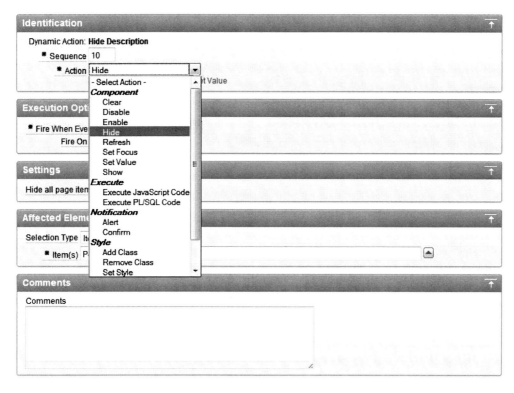

Figure 7-38. Dynamic Action choices

Showing and hiding elements dynamically are features that are used extensively in modern web applications. As you can see, Dynamic Actions can make this process extremely easy and will almost certainly expedite development where Ajax functionality is called for.

Ajax within APEX

Even though Dynamic Actions are very powerful and can replace a great deal of Ajax code, there may be an occasion where manually coding Ajax is required. The process of integrating Ajax and APEX has not changed from previous versions in that you still use the htmldb_get method to initiate the asynchronous process. We'll walk through the creation of a fairly simple Ajax process to give you a feel for how it works in relation to what we have just learned about Dynamic Actions. Following this exercise, you will likley begin using Dynamic Actions in favor of coding Ajax manually.

Working from the bottom up, we'll define what we want to run (some PL/SQL) and then build the supporting page and processes. To keep this simple while still illustrating the process, we'll create a page with a single button and an empty region that will be updated dynamically via an Ajax call. To call an anonymous PL/SQL block via Ajax, your code must be placed in an Application Process. Figure 7-39 shows the Application Process used to house the code to count the bugs with status = 'Open'. Notice that the htp.prn() procedure was used to produce the output in HTML. No HTML tags were added, but we could have, for example, added <TR><TD> tags to produce an HTML table. Also, the Process Point is set to On Demand so that this code is only executed when specifically called.

Figure 7-39. Application Process for use with Ajax call

Next, create a page that contains two regions. Region 1 will contain a single button object and Region 2 will be empty. When complete, the page should look like Figure 7-40.

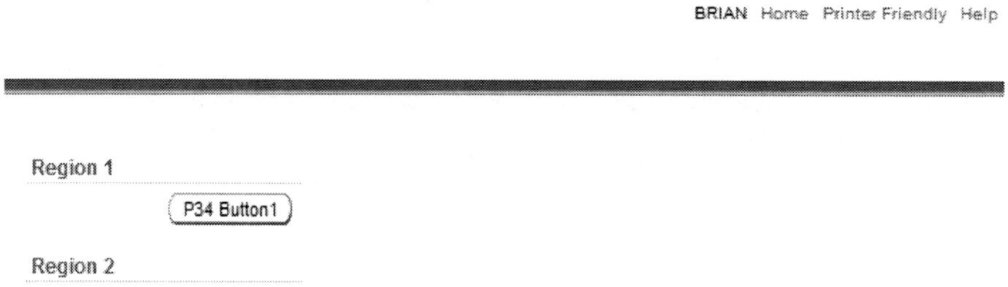

BRIAN   Home   Printer Friendly   Help

Region 1

(P34 Button1)

Region 2

Figure 7-40. Buglist update form

Since we're building an Ajax process, we need some JavaScript that will request some data from the server and then update the page. The JavaScript code must be placed in the HTML Header attribute of the page, as shown in Figure 7-41.

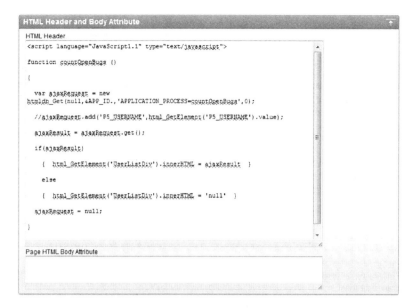

Figure 7-41. JavaScript code supporting the Ajax process

Listing 7-4 shows the complete text of the countOpenBugs JavaScript function. Up to line 6, everything is standard JavaScript.

Listing 7-4. countOpenBugs JavaScript function

```
1   <script language="JavaScript1.1" type="text/javascript">
2
3     function countOpenBugs ()
4
5     {
6
7       var ajaxRequest = new
        htmldb_Get(null,&APP_ID.,'APPLICATION_PROCESS=countOpenBugs',0);
8
9       ajaxResult = ajaxRequest.get();
10
11      if(ajaxResult)
12
13      {  html_GetElement('UserListDiv').innerHTML = ajaxResult  }
14
15      else
16
17      {  html_GetElement('UserListDiv').innerHTML = 'null'  }
18
19      ajaxRequest = null;
20
```

```
21   }
22
23 </script>
;
```

To understand what the htmldb_Get function does, take a look at its definition, as follows:

```
var ajaxRequest = new htmldb_Get(obj,flow,req,page,instance,proc,queryString);
```

The function accepts the following seven parameters and returns a result:

obj: This can be an HTML DOM element, a string, or null. It represents the element that the return result will update. You can pass in null if you want to retrieve the return result into a variable, rather than updating the DOM automatically. If you pass in a string, that string will be used to find an element in the DOM. For example, you can pass in P1_NAME to update the P1_NAME page item with the return result.

flow: This is a string that represents the application ID to which the Ajax call will be made. This should default to the current application (in APEX 3.0). In earlier versions, you should usually use html_GetElement('pFlowId').value to obtain the current application ID. p-FlowId is a DOM element stored in each page of your application.

req: This is a string (or null) that represents the request value for the Ajax call to an On Demand process (discussed in the next section). If you called an On Demand process, you would pass in a value like APPLICATION_PROCESS=getemployees, substituting the value of getemployees for the name of your On Demand process.

page: This is a string that represents the page in your application to which the Ajax XMLHttpRequest call should be made. For On Demand processes, you can define any page (since you will be passing APPLICATION_PROCESS=xyz in the req parameter). However, if you are using authentication in your application, the call will not succeed unless the user is already authenticated or the page you pass in is a public page. In APEX 3.0, the default is to use page 0 for this parameter. If you are retrieving content from a specific page (as opposed to calling an On Demand process), you should pass in the ID of the page that contains the content.

instance: This is a string that represents the APEX session ID. You should usually pass in null here, since the default behavior is for the session ID to be retrieved from the page. It is unlikely that you would ever need to use anything other than null here.

proc: This is a string that represents a procedure that you wish to call using the URL syntax. It is unlikely that you will ever need to pass anything in here.
queryString: This is a string that allows you to include extra query strings to the end of the URL passed in the proc parameter. Again, it is unlikely you will ever need to use this directly yourself.

So, let's look again at our usage of the htmldb_Get function:

```
var ajaxRequest = new
htmldb_Get(null,&APP_ID.,'APPLICATION_PROCESS=countOpenBugs',0);
```

When calling Application Processes, the notation is pretty simple. The only two pieces of information the htmldb_get function needs are the Application ID, provided by &APP_ID., and the identification of the Application Process. We passed null for the obj parameter since we are returning the results to the `ajaxRequest` variable. In line number 9, we are executing the asynchronous call to the Application Process. We then check the `ajaxRequest` variable to see if it contains data and, if so, we replace the contents of the `UserListDIV` with the data stored in the `ajaxRequest` variable using the code in line 13. This is accomplished using the `innerHTML` attribute of the DOM. What line 13 does is first locate the element called `UserListDiv` and, using the `innerHTML` attribute, replaces its contents. You will remember that when we created the page, the `UserListDIV` was empty. With this functionality, you can create entire pages dynamically and display them at will. While this is a powerful feature, you can see that there are several things you must understand to make this work. Before embarking on Ajax coding, make sure you can't use a Dynamic Action first.

OK, back to the example. Let's take a look at the page in the application builder. There is nothing special about Region 1, but there is a URL Target set on `P34_BUTTON1`, as shown in Figure 7-42, which directs the page to execute the `countOpenBugs` Application Process when the button is clicked.

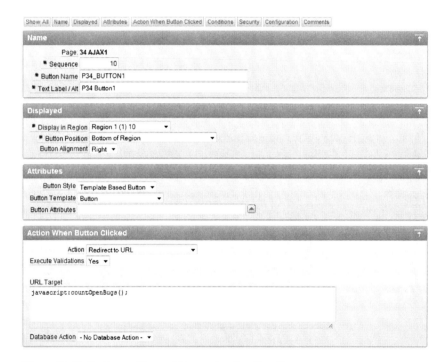

Figure 7-42. Button with a call to an Application Process

The button used to trigger the Ajax process exists in Region 1. Region 2, as shown in Figure 7-43, contains only `DIV` start and end tags in the region source. This `DIV` is named using the `"id=UserListDiv"` attribute so that it can be located by the Ajax process. As illustrated in Figure 7-42, the contents of this `DIV` will be replaced by the Ajax call.

We now have all the components built and can test the page. When the button is clicked, as shown in Figure 7-43, the Application Process counts the bugs and returns the result only, no items, no tags, just the value. If you want you can modify the Application Process so it returns the count inside of an HTML table or as the default value of a text item.

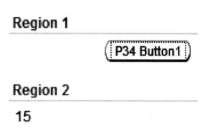

Figure 7-43. *Results of the Ajax call*

Summary

The goal of this chapter was to show the power of Dynamic Actions and how they can replace much of the manual Ajax coding you may have been doing in the past. We also included a brief discussion on how to invoke an Ajax process manually. In both cases, we have only scratched the surface of what you can do with Dynamic Actions and Ajax.

As we stated before, if you're planning to add dynamic functionality to your applications, try to do it first with Dynamic Actions, as it will almost certainly save you time and effort. You will likely see more consistency in your applications when using Dynamic Actions, since they are created declaratively and will be implemented consistently no matter who builds them (for the most part).

So, although you should not be afraid of adding dynamic features to your application, make sure that you're using it in the right places and for the right reasons. It's great to have a web site that makes people say "Oooooh!" But people can also quickly tire of an application if it seems that it places style over substance. At the end of the day, your application needs to be functional from the user's perspective. Using Dynamic Actions (and possibly Ajax) can help you to make your application more functional and responsive for the user.

Websheets

Websheets are intended to give users who have little or no SQL experience a way to create interactive, data-centric applications that allow users to share and update both structured and unstructured data. Users can create Data Grids, interactive reports, and text pages grouped into hierarchies with little or no coding. The Websheet application development environment operates more like a Wiki than a traditional Integrated Development Environment (IDE) in that users can assume the roles of consumers, contributors, or administrators.

You will quickly see that creating a Websheet is less like developing an application and more like using one. Features can be added on an ad hoc basis by authorized users and content can include both structured and unstructured data. While Websheets are intended to be built and used by non-developers, some of the features (and the ease with which they are created) will undoubtedly attract experienced developers as well.

In this chapter, we will re-build the Buglist application as a Websheet application to illustrate the power of Websheets. The Websheet application will contain many of the features of the original, some will be missing, and we will add some capabilities that would be difficult to implement in a traditional APEX application. We'll also explore some of the more Wiki-like features of Websheets.

Preparing for Websheet Development

Creating a Websheet application is as simple as logging in to APEX 4.0 as a developer, navigating to the Application Builder, and clicking the "Create" button. If you're using APEX 4.0 with an 11g database, you will have to do a little administrative work before creating your first Websheet application. The Websheet builder requires the application developer to have several specific privileges, but sadly, these privileges were not granted during the creation of the workspace. Listing 8-1 shows the privileges that must be manually granted to the default workspace schema prior to building a Websheet application (in our case, this schema is apexdemo). During the first execution of the Websheet application builder, you will also be asked to create several new database objects, but there is a wizard for that.

Listing 8-1. Websheet Developer Required Privileges

```
grant CREATE SESSION to apexdemo;
grant CREATE CLUSTER to apexdemo;
grant CREATE DIMENSION to apexdemo;
grant CREATE INDEXTYPE to apexdemo;
grant CREATE JOB to apexdemo;
grant CREATE MATERIALIZED VIEW to apexdemo;
grant CREATE OPERATOR to apexdemo;
```

```
grant CREATE PROCEDURE to apexdemo;
grant CREATE SEQUENCE to apexdemo;
grant CREATE SNAPSHOT to apexdemo;
grant CREATE SYNONYM to apexdemo;
grant CREATE TABLE to apexdemo;
grant CREATE TRIGGER to apexdemo;
grant CREATE TYPE to apexdemo;
grant CREATE VIEW to apexdemo;
```

You may find that your apexdemo schema has already been granted some of these privileges, but since all of these are required, it's recommend that you grant all of them as standard practice prior to beginning Websheet development. If you don't first run these grant statements, you will get most of the way through the initial setup of the development environment when you will get an insufficient privileges error message with no explanation as to the resolution.

To start the Websheet application builder, navigate to the standard Application Builder and click the "Create" button, as shown in Figure 8-1.

■ **Note** When you start development of a Websheet application, you log in to APEX 4.0 as a developer. Although a Websheet application will have an administrator, setup and configuration of the Websheet will be done using an APEX developer user.

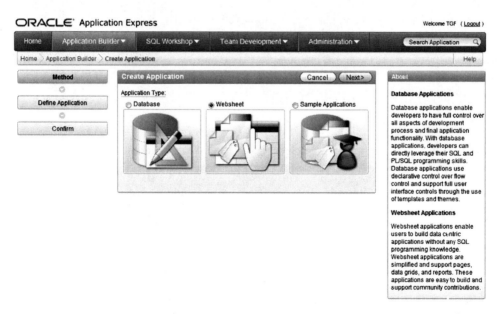

Figure 8-1. Creating a Websheet application

If this is your first time through the Websheet application builder wizard, you will be asked to create the required database objects as shown in Figure 8-2. You must click on the "Manage Websheet Database Objects" button, which will take you to the wizard that handles the requisite object creation. Figure 8-3 shows the first step in the process to create the new database objects.

Figure 8-2. Websheet application builder first run

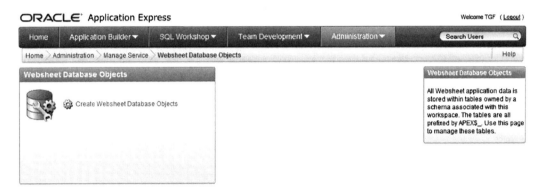

Figure 8-3. Wizard to create Websheet Database Objects

When you click the "Create Websheet Database Objects" link, the next page in the wizard allows you to select the schema in which the new Websheet database objects are created, as shown in Figure 8-4. As with the new privileges granted earlier, we chose the default schema for our workspace (apexdemo). If you did not properly grant the required privileges shown in Listing 8-1, you will see the "insufficient privileges" error when you attempt to create the new database objects.

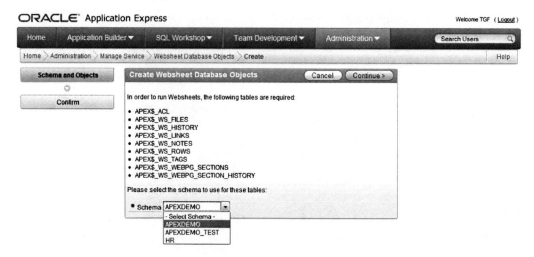

Figure 8-4. Select the Schema which will own the Websheet objects

After confirming and creating the new database objects, you will receive a notification that the objects were successfully created, as shown in Figure 8-5. At this same point, you will have the option to remove the database objects if, for example, you created them using the incorrect schema. You can also validate the objects but if they weren't valid, they would not have been created.

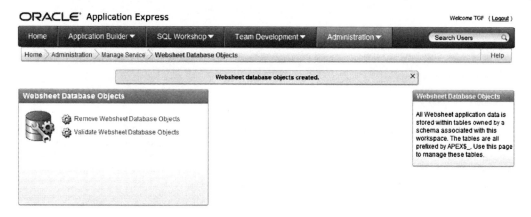

Figure 8-5. Websheet Database Object validation

Building a Websheet Application

Now that the housekeeping is done, we can actually create a Websheet application. For this example, we'll start by creating at Data Grid that is like an Interactive Report, but has several interesting new features. Following that we'll add some general content like reports and charts, and show how users can contribute content in a Wiki-like fashion. To get started, go back to the Application Builder and create a new Websheet Application. Since the environment now supports Websheet development, you will see the first (and only) page in the Create Websheet wizard, as shown in Figure 8-6.

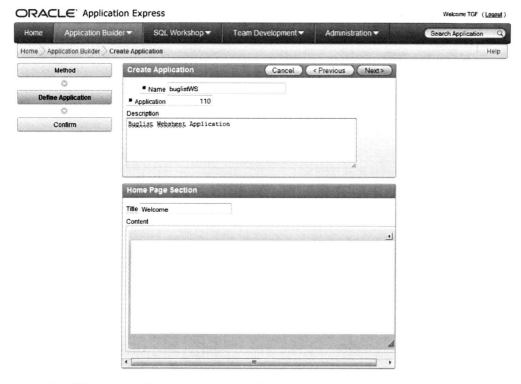

Figure 8-6. Websheet Application creation workflow

There is one more page in the creation workflow, but it is only a verification of what you just entered. That's it. Following successful creation of the Websheet, you'll see the page shown in Figure 8-7. Although it doesn't do anything just yet, remember that this is an application, not a new page or an extension to an existing application.

Figure 8-7. Websheet Application creation complete

Before anyone can access this new application, you will need to identify your user base. You can implement standard APEX authentication, LDAP, or custom authentication similar to that used in the original Buglist application. Since we want to re-build the Buglist application, we can use the same custom Authentication Scheme we used before (pkg_auth.authenticate). We have to do three things to make this work:

1. Add an administrator to the Access Control List

2. Identify the Authentication process we want to use

3. Identify the users who should have access to this Websheet via the Access Control List

Because we are going to re-build the Buglist application, we will use our custom Authentication scheme. By default, Websheets use the -BUILTIN- authentication process, so we need to change it. A requirement for changing the authentication scheme is that there must be a user in the Access Control List that is defined as an administrator. It doesn't really matter which user it is, but there has to be at least one.

The second step is pretty self-explanatory, but we will go into the details. Step three, however, needs a little explanation. You don't create new users via the Websheet Access Control List, you only add users who exist in some other user store (APEX default users, for example). Existing users will be able to log in to a Websheet, but unless they are in the Access Control List, they will immediately get an error message notifying them that they do not have access to the application. You'll see shortly that when we add users to the Access Control List, we are only prompted for the username and not the password. You can add any username to the Access Control List and you will not get an error because it will only be evaluated at login time.

Therefore, if you use the default APEX authentication scheme, only users in that store will have access to the Websheet. If you use a custom authentication scheme, as we will in this example, then you must add user names that exist in the custom user store (the user_repository table). What this means is that a Websheet using a custom authentication scheme will recognize the users assigned identified by that scheme, so you don't have to create new users, but you do have to say which users can access the Websheet.

So let's start by adding an administrator to the Access Control List. Navigate to the Application Properties page by clicking on the "Edit Properties" icon. In the Application Properties page, shown in Figure 8-8 and filtered to show the Authorization section, you have the ability to change the Access Control List type and to modify the Access Control List itself.

Figure 8-8. Websheet authentication

The Access Control List Type has two settings:

- *Default*: Authorization is based on APEX user role

- *Custom*: Authorization is based on the settings in the Access Control List

Because we're planning to use our custom authentication scheme and user store, choose "Custom" as the Access Control List Type. The "Access Control Roles" button provides a pop-up help window that describes what users can do once they authenticate to the Websheet. If you click on the "Edit Access Control List" the Access List management screen will be displayed as shown in Figure 8-9. Notice the "Create Entry" button.

Figure 8-9. Websheet Access Control List management screen

At this point, there are no entries in the Access Control List or they would be shown on this page. So you need to create an entry and the first one must be an administrator so we can change the authentication scheme. The Create Access Control List Entry screen, shown in Figure 8-10, allows us to identify the name of a user and the role this user will have. Remember that we are creating an entry in the Access Control List, not an APEX or custom user. This name will be used at login time along with a password that must exist in the specified user store, which is the reason the password is not required at this point. Go ahead and create two more users, as follows, one Reader and one Contributor, so that you have three total users in the Access Control List:

- Toby: Administrator

- Brian: Reader

- David: Contributor

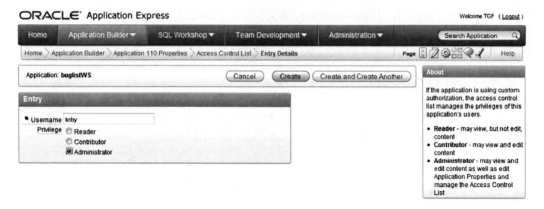

Figure 8-10. Create a Websheet admin user

You may recall that the user "toby" was an administrator in the original Buglist application, so we granted admin level privileges to the same user in the Websheet. Now that we have an administrator, we can navigate back to the Application Properties page and modify the Authentication Scheme. When you arrive at the Application Properties page, the default authentication scheme settings are displayed as. When you change to a custom authentication scheme, as shown in Figure 8-11, additional fields are displayed allowing you to identify the Authentication Function. Here we can identify the same function in the same manner used for the original Buglist application , return pkg_auth.authenticate. The Logout URL and the Invalid Session URL fields are set by default and don't need to be changed for this example. Once you apply the changes, you will be able to run the Buglist Websheet application.

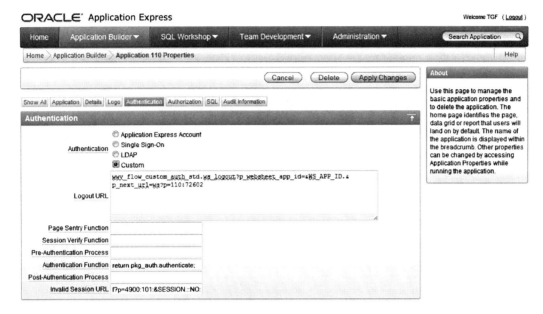

Figure 8-11. *Websheet authentication scheme*

Running a Websheet Application

OK, so we have created a Websheet and modified the authentication scheme, but the application doesn't do anything. That's because we haven't started "using" it yet. With Websheets, applications are intended to be built by users, not by developers. and they can evolve over time without intervention from the IT department. So let's start using the Buglist Websheet.

Logging In

First, let's log in to the Buglist Websheet as a Websheet administrator. You can get to the Websheet via the following URL or APEX Application Builder:

```
http://<server:port>/apex/ws?p=110:home
```

The differences in this URL from others we have seen in APEX are as follows:

- `ws`: identifies this application as a Websheet as opposed to a regular APEX app (which would use the 'f?p=' syntax)

- `p`: identifies the Application ID, in this case the Websheet Application ID is 110

- `home`: identifies the initial page to load

You will first see the Websheet standard login page as shown in Figure 8-12. On this page, the credentials fields are displayed along with a link back to the APEX 4.0 development environment (in case you need it). Log in to the application as the Websheet administrator. This is the user to which we granted the Administration role in the Websheet Access Control List.

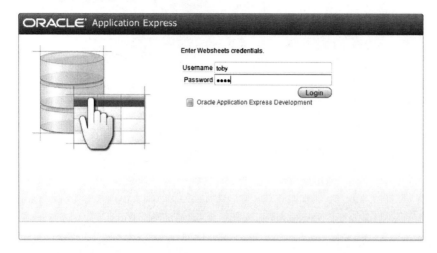

Figure 8-12. Websheet login screen

On the home page of the Buglist Websheet application, as shown in Figure 8-13, you can see the main menu, Page controls, and Annotation controls. Users will build their applications using these controls. Most of them are pretty self-explanatory, but they are not available to all users. Remember that there are three distinct roles that can be granted to a user in the Access Control List. Table 8-1 shows which controls are available based on role.

Figure 8-13. Websheet home page

Table 8-1. Features Available by Role

Main Menu	Administrator	Contributor	Reader
Administration	Yes	No	No
Page	Yes	Yes	Yes
Data	Yes	Yes	Yes
Page Controls	Yes	Yes	No
Annotations	Yes	Yes	No
Add	Yes	Yes	No
View	Yes	Yes	Yes

Building a Data Grid

Now that we are in the development environment, we can start actually building the Buglist application. We'll start just like we did in Chapter 3 by using the buglist.csv file as the source for our data, and we'll do this using a Websheet Data Grid. A Data Grid in a Websheet is nothing more than an interface to a table that allows you to define the interface and table "From Scratch" or as a "Copy and Paste." For non-developers, the Copy and Paste method will certainly be more attractive. To start the process, click the Data Grid icon on the home page, choose the "Copy and Paste" option, and navigate to the next step in the process. Although the title of the Data Grid Properties page says "Upload Spreadsheet," you can't actually do that. You have to open the buglist.csv file, copy the contents, and paste them into the appropriate section of the page as shown in Figure 8-14. You also have to give the Data Grid a name and an alias and decide if the column names are contained in row 1. If they're not, you can add them later.

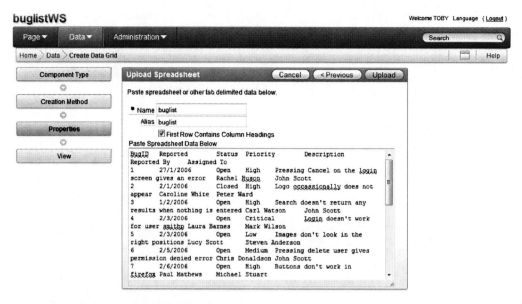

Figure 8-14. *Create a new Data Grid*

Pressing the "Upload" button completes the creation of the Data Grid and displays it, as shown in Figure 8-15.

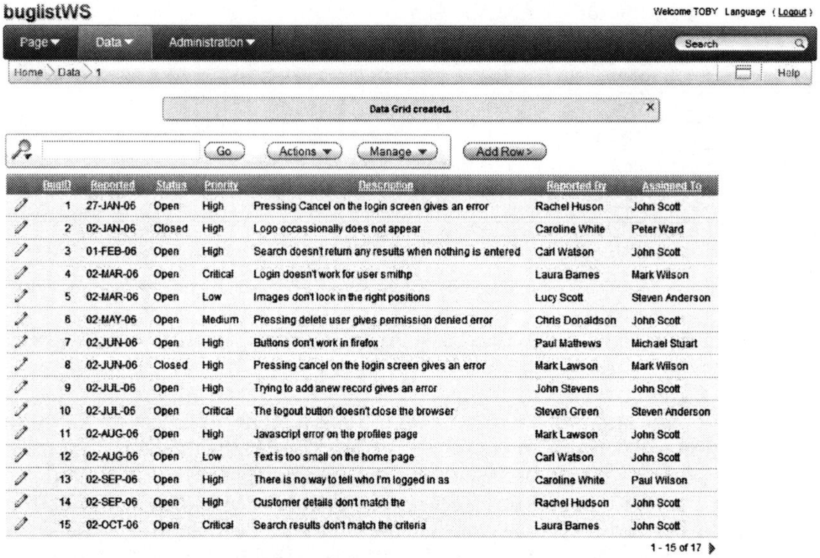

Figure 8-15. *Websheet Data Grid*

You may think this is a standard, interactive report, but you'd be wrong (sort of). There are some similarities to an Interactive Report in that the search bar and edit row functionality work just like an Interactive Report and all of the report manipulation features are there as well. The following is a list of features that are unique to a Websheet Data Grid:

- *Column Headings*: Clicking the column heading uncovers several features
  - Ascending / Descending sorts
  - Hide column
  - Control Break on Current Value
  - Column Value Search
  - Single-Click Search of existing values
  - Date ranges for date-based columns
- *Column Values*: Any column can be edited by clicking on it in the Data Grid
- *Add / Delete Rows*: Rows can be added or deleted using the Data Grid
  Add / Delete Columns: Columns can be added or deleted using the Data Grid

Clicking on a text-based column header produces the controls shown in Figure 8-16, while Figure 8-17 shows the controls associated with a date-based column. The values below the search field in the text-based column are pulled directly from the selected column. For date-based fields, the Websheet builds several date-related search values automatically. The user can perform a search on a column simply by clicking one of the auto-generated values. Hiding and showing columns is a feature that would require developer intervention in a standard APEX application. The Control Break icon is used to create a control break in the report using the values in the currently selected column. If you use any of these controls, you will notice the familiar report filters are displayed between the report search bar and the Data Grid.

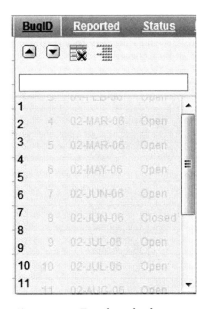

Figure 8-16. Text-based column controls

Figure 8-17. Date-based column controls

One of the best features of a Websheet Data Grid is in-line editing. A user can simply click on a value in any column and the column value transforms into an editable field. Figure 8-18 shows the Description field being edited. In this example, the edit icon (the pencil) is displayed while in-line editing is enabled. Having two paths to the Edit feature may be confusing for some users, so you may consider using one or the other. By default, all columns can be edited in-line, but this feature can be disabled by changing the Display Type column property to "Read Only," as we will see shortly.

buglistWS

Welcome DAVID Language (Logout)

| Page ▼ | Data ▼ | | | Search | | | 🔍 |

Home > Data > Buglist   Help

🔍▾ [   ] (Go) (Actions ▼) (Manage ▼)   (Add Row >)

☑		BugID	Reported	Status	Priority	Description	Reported By	Assigned To
☑	🖉	1	27-JAN-06	Open	High	Pressing Cancel on the login screen gives an error	Rachel Huson	John Scott
☑	🖉	2	02-JAN-06	Closed	High	Logo occassionally does not appear	Caroline White	Peter Ward
☐	🖉	3	01-FEB-06	Open	High	Search doesn't return any results when nothing is entered	Carl Watson	John Scott

Figure 8-18. In-line editing in a Websheet Data Grid

In order to edit the column properties, you must use the new "Manage" button on the Data Grid's search bar. The Properties tool, for example, is used to change the name and description of the Data Grid. The Toggle Checkboxes control enables and disables checkboxes on each row of the Data Grid. Once enabled, they can be used in conjunction with several of the Row controls to limit actions to specific rows. The Delete Data Grid and Copy functions work as expected, one deletes the Data Grid while the other copies the current Data Grid to another name.

Figures 8-19 and 8-20 show not only the list of tools available to manage the Data Grid as a whole, but also the Row and Column tools. The reason for drilling down on the Row and Column tools is that they contain several options for managing Row and Column properties, where the other tools very self-explanatory.

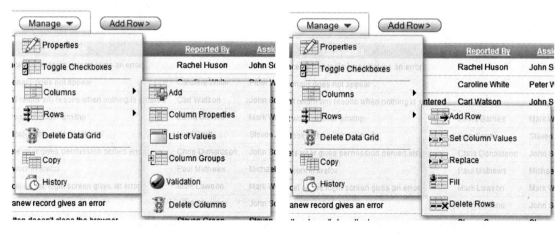

Figure 8-19. Data Grid Column tools   *Figure 8-20. Data Grid Row tools*

The Column Controls list is quite comprehensive. The ones that take the least explanation are the Add and Delete Column. Before discussing Column Properties, we need to look over the other three controls, as they are used in support of the Column Properties control.

- List of Values

- Column Groups

- Validations

The first control, shown in Figure 8-21, is used to create Lists of Values (LOV), which can be attached to any column, as we will see when we look at the Column Properties control. The interesting (or maybe disappointing) thing about this feature is that the LOV can only be based on a comma delimited list of static values. You cannot populate an LOV using a query. While this may be disappointing as a developer, the end user may have no SQL skills and allowing him to build dynamic LOVs may cause trouble.

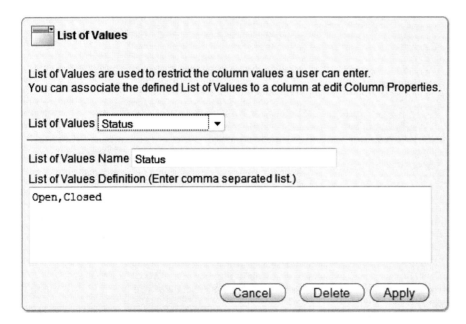

Figure 8-21. Data Grid List of Values

Next on the list is Column Groups, which are nothing more than a named group of columns. The effect of creating a Column Group is not seen on a report or Data Grid as you might expect. What they do is enable you to hide and show a set of columns by clicking an icon on an "add" or "edit" record page. Like LOV's, you create the Column Group here, as shown in Figure 8-22, and you apply it to the appropriate columns using the Column Properties control. Even after you assign a Column Group, you will not see the effect of grouping columns until you navigate to an "add" or "edit" record page.

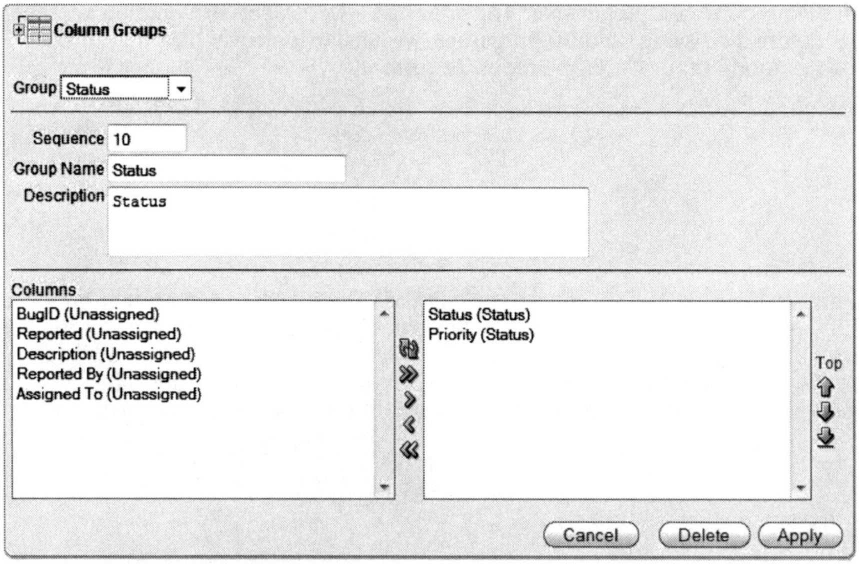

Figure 8-22. Data Grid Column Group

   The Validation control allows you to create rules that govern the type of data entered in any column of a Data Grid. Figure 8-23 shows the Validation types that are available by default. Because Validations can evaluate both column values directly or compare column values to an expression, Validations can be very comprehensive. We created a simple validation on the Description field, which ensures that the column value is not null.

   You can also create Validations that compare a column value to an Expression, which can basically be a text string. For example, if you wanted to restrict a field to a specific value (and you had not used a Select List), you can set the Validation Type to "Column Specified is contained in Expression," which will evaluate to true if the value of the column is contained anywhere within the expression. For example, if the Expression contained 'Open' and the column value was 'Open', the Validation would evaluate to true.

   Given that Validations that compare column values to Expressions only really work with single values in the Expression, use Select Lists where specific values are required. When Validations are more generic (null, not null, numeric, etc.) then Validations that do not look at Expressions work well.

   As you can see, not everything about Websheets is going to be end user–friendly. The way Validations work and the way the Types are defined can be confusing to a user who doesn't have much development experience.

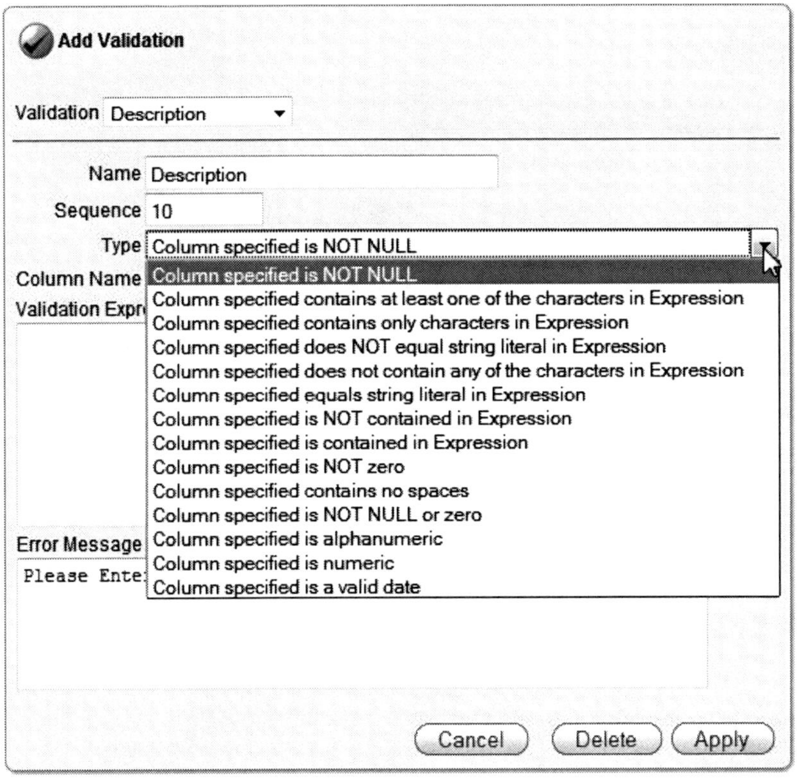

Figure 8-23. *Data Grid Validation Types*

The Row Tools are also interesting, although some of them are a little impractical. Figure 8-24 shows the controls available in a Websheet to manage data at a row level. The simple ones, Add Row and Delete Row, do exactly what they say they do. The Delete Rows control is useful in that it allows the user to mark records for deletion and then remove them all in one shot. Deleting rows in this manner requires that the Check Boxes in the Websheet be toggled on.

347

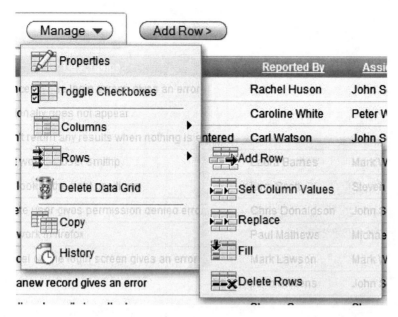

Figure 8-24. Data Grid Row controls

The other Row tools give you SQL-like capabilities in that you can modify multiple rows with one command. The Set Column Values control is interesting, but not overly practical for our Buglist application. This feature, shown in Figure 8-25, allows you to set a value in one or more rows very much like a simple update statement. You don't get to set a where clause, but you can specify either all rows, selected rows, or empty rows.

■ **Note** The row tools which modify data (set value, replace, and fill) will be restricted by any existing column level validations. If, for example, you try to set the value of a column in every row to NULL and there is a NOT NULL Validation on that column, the error message from the Validation will be displayed in the row control.

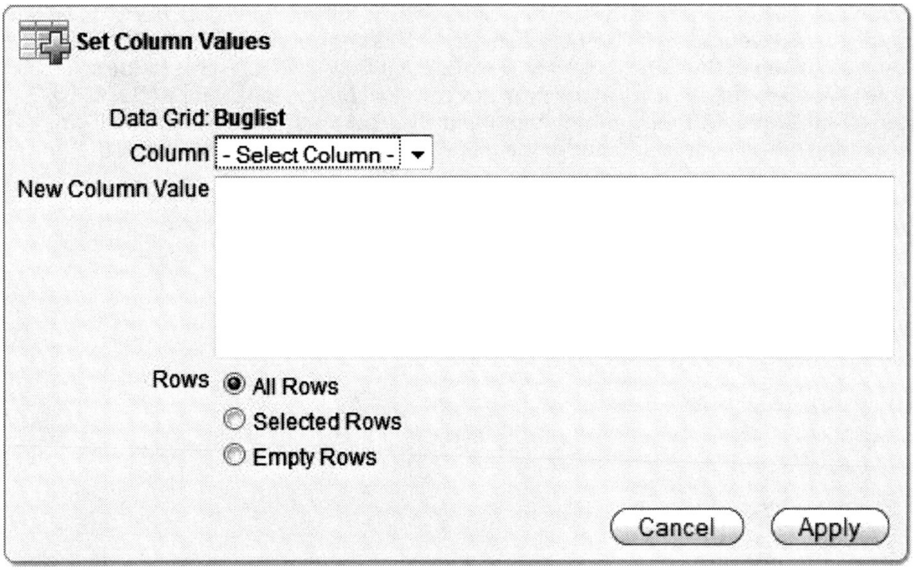

Figure 8-25. Data Grid Set Column Values control

The Replace row control can be very beneficial since it works like a Search and Replace feature in a text editor. You simply identify the column you want to update, the value to search for, and the value to replace when the search evaluates to true. As with the Set Column Values control, you can approximate a where clause using the All Rows or Selected Rows options. Figure 8-26 shows the Replace control.

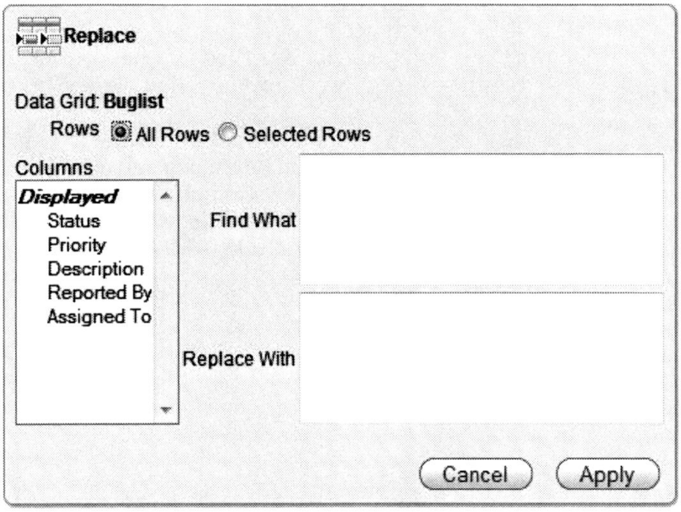

Figure 8-26. Data Grid Replace Values control

The last of the Row controls is the Fill feature. This enables you to fill columns that are set to NULL with the value from the row above where the NULL values start. This control does not take into account selected rows. It starts at the top of the table and scans down until it finds a NULL value in the selected column, backs up one row, takes the value from the previous row, and begins replacing NULL values with the new value in all subsequent. This does not mean that all NULL values will be replaced with a single value, but explaining the process is difficult so the following examples (Listings 8-2 and 8-3) have been created:

Listing 8-2. Table Before Being Filled

```
bug_id description
------ ----------------------------------
1      logo occasionally does not display
2
3
4      Buttons don't work in Firefox
5
```

Listing 8-3. Table After Being Filled

```
bug_id description
------ ----------------------------------
1      logo occasionally does not display
2      logo occasionally does not display
3      logo occasionally does not display
4      Buttons don't work in Firefox
5      Buttons don't work in Firefox
```

As you can see, the Fill process takes the last value prior to a NULL and uses that to fill the subsequent rows. When it encounters the next, NOT NULL value, it becomes the fill value for any additional rows that have NULL in the selected column. This process is not governed by what you can see on the page when you execute the Fill process, so this one can get away from you if don't know where all the NULL values exist.

Another very powerful feature of Data Grids is the ability to store Annotations (files, notes, links, and tags) in any row. The benefit of this feature is that a user could, for example, report a bug and attach either a screenshot or even a video capture of the error. They can also supply notes that allow them much more latitude in describing the error. The Data Grid does not include these objects by default, but the user can easily add them. Figure 8-27 shows the Edit screen for a row on a Data Grid.

Figure 8-27. *Data Grid Annotations*

As the user attaches objects to the Data Grid row, they are represented via additional sections in the Data Grid edit screen. Clicking on an attached file name or a link, as shown in Figure 8-28, immediately opens that object. Notes and Tags are displayed in line and can be viewed without navigating to another object or screen.

Figure 8-28. Data Grid Annotation view

As stated previously, Annotations are not included in Data Grids by default, but they can easily be displayed using the Select Column control on the Data Grid page. Figure 8-29 shows that the four columns for files, notes, links, and tags are actually available in any Data Grid, but are not automatically selected. We selected all four Annotation fields and added them to the Data Grid.

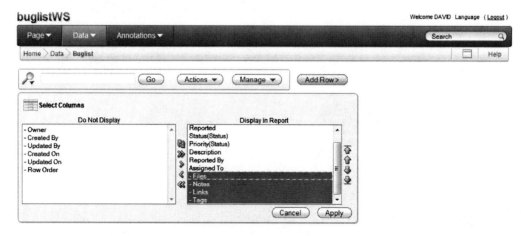

Figure 8-29. Data Grid Annotation field attributes

As soon as they are applied, the new columns appear and if any of the "new" columns contain data, icons show up to alert the user, as shown in Figure 8-30. All of the Annotation icons display pop-up text to help identify the contents and the user can click on any of them to go directly to the content (a file viewer for files, another browser window for a link, etc). This means that a Websheet provides limited document management capabilities.

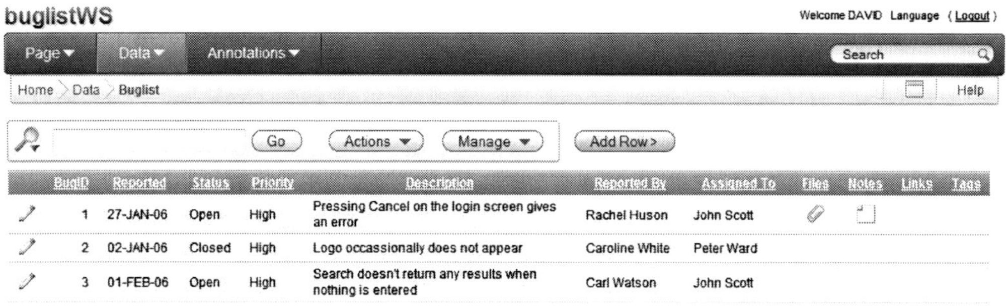

Figure 8-30. *Data Grid with Annotations*

Using the Buglist Websheet

Now that we know how to use Data Grids, arguably the most important feature of a Websheet, we can start using the Buglist application like a user would. Up to this point, we have been interacting with the Websheet as an administrator, so let's change roles to a Contributor. The Contributor user is David so we are logged in to the Websheet as this user. First, we need to navigate back to the Buglist Websheet home page as shown in Figure 8-31. The first thing you should note is that there are only two options in the main toolbar (Page and Data). The Administration option is gone due to the role of the current user. Also of interest is that the Data Grid we just created is not visible on the home page, which is standard behavior. Data Grids are objects that can either be accessed directly (via the Data option on the main toolbar) or by being added to a page.

In Figure 8-31, you can see that the content of the Welcome section has been modified. This section was added for us when we created the Websheet. By using the Edit link in this section, we change the title to "Buglist" and added the text, "This is the Buglist Websheet" into the Content text area.

Figure 8-31. *Buglist Websheet home page*

To make the Buglist Websheet provide the same functionality as the original application, we have to start building pages. The home page was added automatically when the Websheet was created, so we can use that as a starting place and begin adding content. If you want a new page, you click on (you guessed it) New Page. For this example, we'll add some content to the home page using the New Section control. The Create Section process, shown in Figure 8-32, requires that you decide what type of information the section will contain.

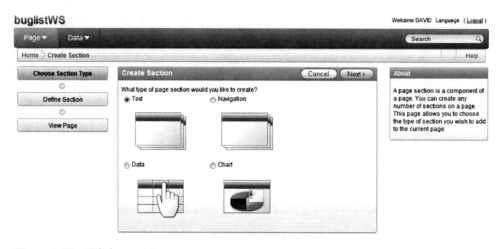

Figure 8-32. *Websheet section types*

Each section type has specific features. The following is a summary of what each type does:

- *Text*: The most flexible section type. Supports text, images, hyperlinks, SQL

- *Navigation*: Builds the Navigation tree for pages and sections

- *Data*: Makes Data Grids available

- *Chart*: Supports column, line, and pie charts

So, let's add the Buglist Data Grid we created to the home page so we can see the current list of bugs immediately when the application opens. This is done simply by choosing "Data" as the section type, selecting the appropriate Data Grid, and setting the title. The Create Data Section is shown in Figure 8-33. The Style selector, which has three settings, controls the look of the Data Grid but does not affect how it works.

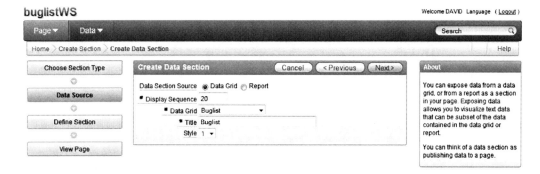

Figure 8-33. Adding a Data Section to a Websheet

When we created the Buglist Data Grid, we saw an object that looked like an interactive report, but it had lots of added functionality. When you finish adding Buglist Data Grid to the home page, as shown in Figure 8-34, you will see the data, but the Data Grid functionality is not available. The "Manage" button is not here, the headings are not clickable. This is basically just a report that can be used to search for and view data. To get back to the fully functional Data Grid, you have to click on the "Data" option in the main toolbar and click on the Data Grid you want to use.

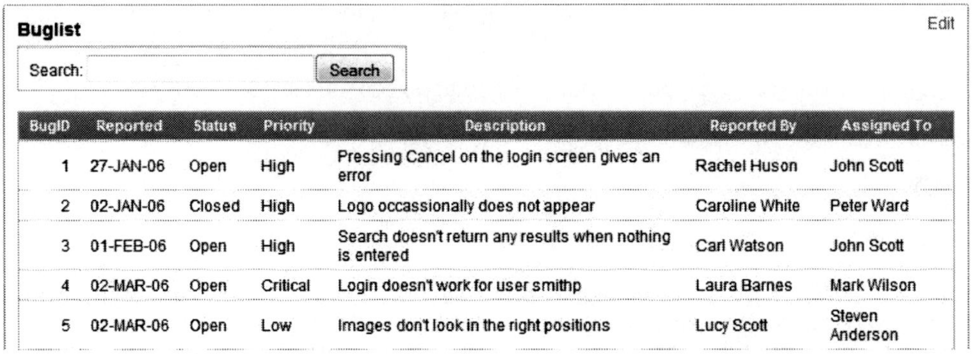

Buglist   Edit

Search: [   ] [Search]

BugID	Reported	Status	Priority	Description	Reported By	Assigned To
1	27-JAN-06	Open	High	Pressing Cancel on the login screen gives an error	Rachel Huson	John Scott
2	02-JAN-06	Closed	High	Logo occassionally does not appear	Caroline White	Peter Ward
3	01-FEB-06	Open	High	Search doesn't return any results when nothing is entered	Carl Watson	John Scott
4	02-MAR-06	Open	Critical	Login doesn't work for user smithp	Laura Barnes	Mark Wilson
5	02-MAR-06	Open	Low	Images don't look in the right positions	Lucy Scott	Steven Anderson

Figure 8-34. *Buglist Websheet home page*

■ **Note** Page sections in a Websheet occupy the entire width of the page, always. You cannot create sections next to each other, so Websheet pages can become very long, very quickly. To help this situation, a Navigation Section can be added, providing one-click navigation to both sections within pages and to other pages.

Another nice feature we had in the original Buglist application was a page containing graphical representations of our data. So let's add a graph, but place it on a new page. Clicking on the Add Page control opens the Create Page process, as shown in Figure 8-35, which allows us to name the page and create an initial section. If you would rather add all the sections manually, just make the section title blank, as we have done, and the page will be built with no sections. We also need to select the Parent page so that the Navigation control, which we will build shortly, will know how to get to this page.

Figure 8-35. *Websheet Create Page process*

We can now add a chart to the new Buglist Charts page by adding a new section and selecting Chart as the type. For this example, we chose to build a Column chart. In Figure 8-36, you can see that you have two choices for the source (or query) on which to base the chart. You must use a report or Data Grid that was previously created. Since we only have a Data Grid called Buglist, we chose that as the source. The Section Title will default to the name of the report or Data Grid, but you can change that as necessary.

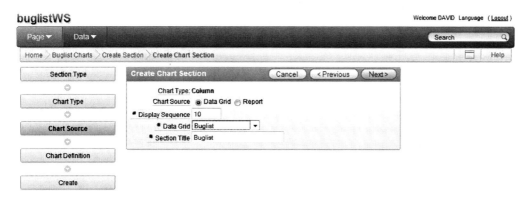

Figure 8-36. *Websheet Chart section creation*

Since you are using either a report or Data Grid as the source and both of those objects can have saved filters, you have the option of using either the default report or Data Grid settings or the saved filters. We did not create any filters on the Buglist Data Grid, so our only option was to select the Primary Report (Primary Default) setting, as shown in Figure 8-37.

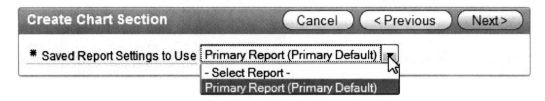

Figure 8-37. *Websheet Chart Source settings*

The final step in creating the column chart allows you to identify the things like axis labels, the type of functions to apply (sum, count, etc.), and the columns to which the functions are applied. For this example, we want to produce a count of bugs reported by person. Figure 8-38 shows the settings that will provide the desired result. The Chart Label identifies which will be used to produce the x-axis labels (the name of the person who reported the bug). The Axis Title for Label can be anything you want, but it should be something relevant to the chart.

The Chart Value field will list all of the numeric columns in the source query and allow you to perform functions on those values. In our Data Grid, the only numeric column is the bug_id, which is irrelevant to this chart, and since we are doing a COUNT, we don't need to identify a Chart Value. You can apply a sort on the Chart Value, the Chart Label, or use the default sort that was applied to the Data Grid. We left ours at the default sort.

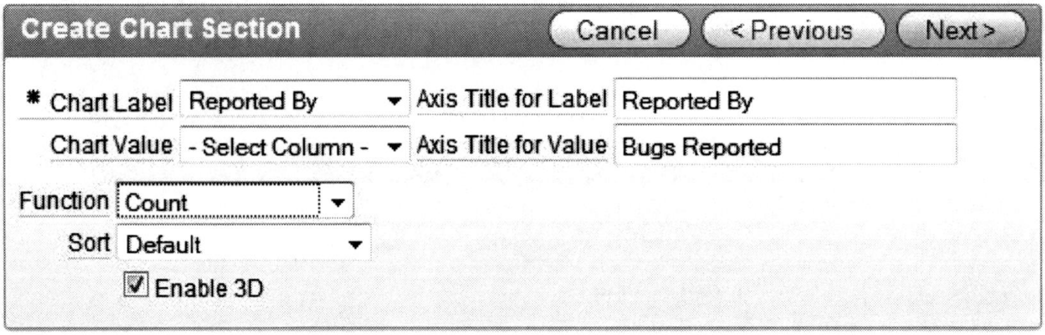

Figure 8-38. *Websheet Chart Label settings*

Following the verification step, the chart is produced in the new section, as shown in Figure 8-39. The chart has what we wanted on it, but there are a few things to note. First, not all of the Chart Labels (on the x-axis) are being displayed. This is default behavior as there is no way to fit all of the labels horizontally and there is no way to rotate the text of the labels. You can, however, see the label on each column by hovering the mouse as done in Figure 8-39. The units used to display the count on the y-axis is set to two decimals by default and you can't change that either. These may seem like shortcomings to a developer, but remember that this application is intended to be built by a user, so keeping it simple is the focus.

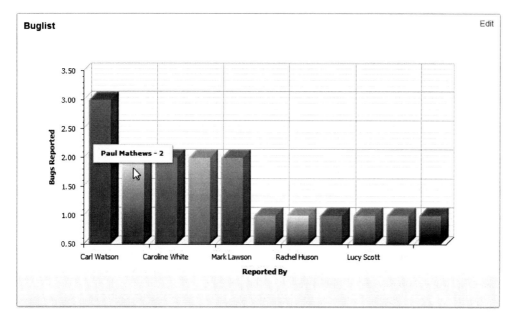

Figure 8-39. *Display Column Labels by hovering the mouse over a Column*

So we have a home page, a Data Grid, a column chart, and a custom authentication scheme. To put it all together, we only need to add one more thing: a Navigation Section. To do this, we'll have to add a new section to the home page between the Welcome and Buglist sections. Figure 8-40 shows the Navigation Section creation process. As noted earlier, you can add Navigation Sections for either sections or pages. Since our home page is not too long and we have a separate Chart page, we'll add a Page Navigation Section.

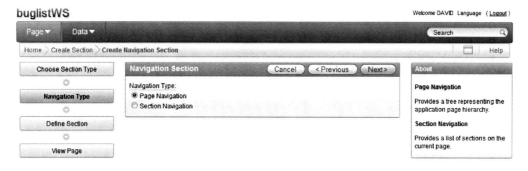

Figure 8-40. *Websheet Navigation Section Type*

You then just have to set the sequence of the Navigation Section so it fits where you want it and give it a title. You can also set a limit to the number of levels (shown as indentions on the Navigation tree) that the Navigation tree will display. If you go beyond this limit, users can always select a page individually using the Page selection on the main toolbar. Figure 8-41 shows the settings for our Page Navigation control.

Figure 8-41. Websheet Page Navigation settings

With all the pieces put together, the Buglist Websheet is a usable system. Figure 8-42 shows the finished product. Looking at it now, it would probably look better if the original Welcome section were removed so that the Navigation Section was at the top of the page.

Figure 8-42. Completed Websheet Application

Contributing Content to a Websheet

Although we have an application that works like the one we originally developed using standard APEX features, it can be changed by those who are using it, as opposed to just a few developers. Remember that all the work we did to create the Buglist Websheet was done as a Contributor. We only logged in as the administrator to create the Access Control List.

The most flexible content generator, and therefore the most difficult to use, is the Text Section. It's difficult because it is like an HTML development tool that allows you to build content and expects you to know the Websheet-specific syntax that is described very nicely in the Help system. To see the markup examples, simply edit one of the Text sections (the Welcome section, for example) and click the "Markup Syntax" in the middle-right of the screen. As you can see, using this content generator allows for coding that is somewhat contrary to the "Wiki-like" description we gave to Websheets at the beginning of the chapter. You can forego these features and just add text like you would on a Wiki, but this is APEX, which means you're only a few keystrokes away from the database —the features are there if you want to use them.

One of the more interesting types of Websheet Markup syntax is SQL. You can access data based on your privileges and your ability to write SQL. The markup is a little different than what a developer is used to and the output is better than you may expect. For example, you can enter a SQL statement in the Text section using the following syntax:

```
[[SQL: select * from buglist where priority = 'Critical' ]]
```

The double brackets ([[…]]) along with a prefix (SQL in this case) are a Websheet-only convention. The output generated by this SQL statement is more than just column headers and some data. It is actually formatted to look like an APEX report, as shown in Figure 8-43, and it comes with a search field! Just another example of Websheets doing something good for the non-developer. Remember that when we created a Data Grid and added it to a page section, it looked like the report we just created. When we created the report with a SQL statement, no Data Grid was created.

◼ **Note** Websheet Markup Syntax requires that the markup type, "SQL" for example, must be followed immediately by a colon (:). If you put a space between the prefix and the colon, the markup will not be interpreted and the Text Section tool will be re-displayed with your markup text highlighted in red. No error message will be displayed and if you click on the highlighted text, the Text Section editor will be re-opened, but without your statement. If you click the "Edit" link, your statement will be re-displayed so you can fix it.

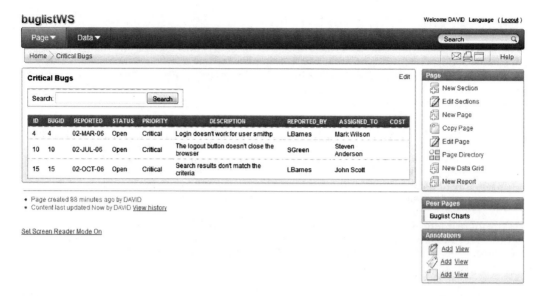

Figure 8-43. *Text Section based on SQL*

Now let's say that you want to put a logo on the home page. You have to first get the logo file into the Websheet application then include it in a page using a Text Section. The logical place to put the logo is in the Welcome section on the home page. Previously, we used the bug.jpg logo file so that all we needed to know was where that file was located to identify it for upload. To make the logo file available click the Add File icon. The Add File process, as shown Figure 8-44, will upload and make the file available to any page. The uploaded file can now be seen where it was uploaded in the "Files" menu at the bottom right of the page.

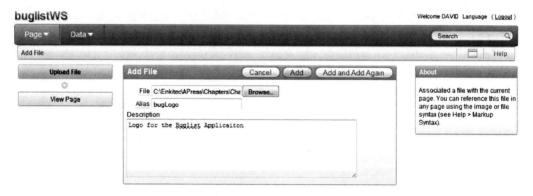

Figure 8-44. *Adding an Image file to a Websheet*

■ **Note** Any file you upload is available to any page in the Websheet application. If you are on the home page when you add a file, however, only the Home Page will show that the file exists. Also please note the "x" next to each uploaded file that is used as the delete mechanism. If you click this link, the file will be deleted without warning and all pages using the file will begin showing the link to the file instead of the contents. If you add the file back, the pages using the file will begin showing the content without being modified.

To add the bug.jpg file to the home page, edit the first section as shown in Figure 8-45, adding the reference to the bug.jpg image file. If you're not sure about the syntax to add an image, click on the Markup Syntax link to see examples. Notice that we set the width=100 attribute on our image tag. By doing this, the image is reduced in size proportionally, which makes it fit better in the application. Since our image has a white background, it won't look as nice as it could because the backgrounds of all sections are grey. To remedy this situation, you could use images (and image formats) that support transparent backgrounds.

Figure 8-45. Adding an Image to a Text section

So let's take a look at the semi-finished product. It is "semi" because a Websheet is never really finished. Users will continue to add content as long as the application is relevant. Figure 8-46 shows the Buglist Websheet application with the logo in the top section, a Navigation Section, and a report based on a Data Grid. All of this was done with very little coding. By virtue of adding a file to the Buglist

Websheet, a new option, Annotations, has been added to the main toolbar. Clicking this link will allow you to see files, tags, notes, and links that have been added to the application.

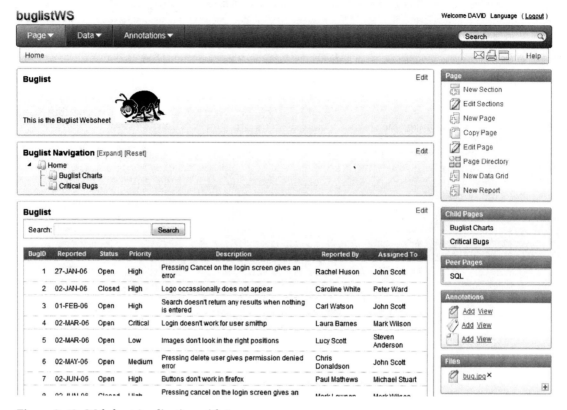

Figure 8-46. Websheet Application with Logo

The other Annotations you can add to your pages are Tags and Notes. Tags are used to describe the content of the page and operate like meta-tags in a standard HTML application. The benefit to using tags is that it makes your pages more searchable. Notes are just free text. Be aware that Notes and Tags are attached to the screen at the bottom right. There is no limit to the number of Notes and Tags you can create, so don't be surprised if pages get really long. Also, notes are deleted using the same mechanism as images and there is no warning that a Tag or Note is about to be deleted.

■ **Note** Since Notes are confined to a very small space on a page, you may consider creating a standard page called "Notes" and instruct your users to put their comments in new Text Sections so that they are easier to read.

So there you have it. A working application that required very little coding (although we did steal the authentication mechanism from the original system) and provides the functionality to support the bug tracking community. Along with standard application features, we also displayed the ability for users to add new pages, notes, charts, and more.

Summary

Websheets are designed for Web-based content sharing and are intended to be built and used by non-developers. The source of most Websheets will likely be spreadsheets, as the interface to import them is so straightforward. There are some areas, such as setting up authentication and the Access Control List, that will likely require some involvement of the IT guys, but mainly just for setup. Once the system is configured, though, the users should be able to take over and run with the application.

CHAPTER 9

Reporting and Printing

In versions of APEX prior to version 3.0, printing was often seen as one of the weakest areas. It has always been possible to use the print functionality of the browser to print the web page that is currently being viewed (for example, if it contains a report), and this sort of built-in browser functionality may be sufficient in many cases. However, if you require more complex printing or you wish to print only the report, rather than the entire content of the page, clearly you will need another solution.

APEX version 3.0 introduced printing functionality, a much-welcomed improvement (perhaps one of the key features that encouraged people to justify upgrading from an earlier version of APEX). However, the introduction of printing ability also introduces some new decisions that need to be made, and potentially some extra work in setting up a print server (also referred to as a *report server, print engine*, or *report engine*).

Choosing a Print Server

APEX 4.0 does not natively contain a printing engine. In other words, it is not APEX itself that generates a PDF for printing. Instead, APEX sends the data you wish to print to a separate system (the print server), which processes the data and produces the desired output, which is returned to APEX and then sent back to the user's browser. Figure 9-1 illustrates this process.

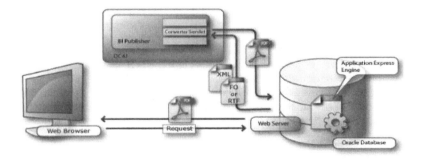

Figure 9-1. PDF files are generated by a server, and sent back to the client's web browser where they can be printed locally.

You may be thinking that it would be better if APEX itself contained everything it needs to produce the printed output. There are a few probable reasons why that is not the route the Oracle team took. First, building a print server that could run "inside" the database would be a big task (and a diversion from the core APEX development). Second, if the team did build a print server, it would likely be implemented partly in Java, which would make the solution unavailable to Oracle XE, which currently does not support Java inside the database. Third, Oracle already has an excellent, well-established report server called BI Publisher.

So, what the Oracle team has done is to allow you to point your APEX instance to a print server, and when a user chooses to print, the work is offloaded to that print server, rather than being handled internally by APEX.

However, very wisely, the Oracle team has not tied you into using Oracle BI Publisher. You can point at any print server, or rather, any print server that meets the requirements. Currently, you can use the following as a print server:

- Oracle BI Publisher

- Oracle Containers for Java EE (OC4J) with Apache FOP

- Any other Extensible Stylesheet Language Formatting Objects (XSL-FO) processing engine

Following are some of the factors involved in choosing a print server:

Cost: BI Publisher has a license cost. Apache FOP is free.

Ease of Use: BI Publisher has some additional features that make designing reports much easier than a basic FOP solution.

Availability: Do you already have one of the supported print servers configured and working?

For many individuals and small companies, BI Publisher is simply not an option due to the cost. Larger companies may already be using BI Publisher somewhere else in the organization, so they can use the existing BI Publisher report server.

You might look at the relative costs of BI Publisher and Apache FOP and assume that Apache FOP must be much more limited (more expensive is better, right?); however, that is very much untrue. BI Publisher, together with some of the plug-ins it provides, does make it incredible easy to visually design your reports. However, almost anything you can produce in BI Publisher can be produced using Apache FOP—it just might take more time and work. That additional effort adds up and represents a very real cost to your company. So, you'll need to find the sweet spot for your particular circumstances. Do you want to pay a lot of money for BI Publisher, but potentially save a lot of development costs when designing your reports? Or would you prefer to spend nothing (in theory) on the FOP solution, but potentially have higher development costs when designing your FOP-based reports?

Deciding where to run your print server is often a matter of policy. Since APEX runs in the database, there are no choices to make about where to run it. Many organizations, however, try to avoid running anything on the database hardware other than the Oracle binaries. For this reason, APEX architectures often include at least two computers. In most cases, a separate machine is used to host an Oracle HTTP server that acts as the HTTP listener for APEX. We often see the web-tier of the architecture being used to host the print servers along side of the HTTP server. Using the web layer of the architecture allows for enhancements like load balancing or introducing a firewall between the web and database layers. It is best to keep your print server close to the database server since there may be significant amounts of data passed between them.

Configuring APEX to Use a Print Server

If you open the Buglist report in the Buglist application and go to the Print Attributes section, as shown in Figure 9-2, you are warned that printing has not been enabled for the instance yet. Notice that you are able to change settings related to the print attributes (which are discussed in the "Configuring Some Simple Print Options" section a little later in the chapter); however, printing will not work.

Region Definition	Report Attributes	**Print Attributes**

Region Name: Bugs   (Cancel)   (Apply Changes)

Show All	Printing	Page Attributes	Page Header	Report Column Headings	Report Columns	Page Footer

Printing

Report printing is currently not available, there is no print server configured.

Enable Report Printing No ▾

Link Label Print

Response Header Report Settings ▾

View File As Attachment ▾   File Name

Output Format PDF   ▾   Item

Report Layout Default Report Layout ▾

Print Server Overwrite

Print URL f?p=&APP_ID.:1:&SESSION.:FLOW_XMLP_OUTPUT_R5086816524480250

Figure 9-2. The instance has not been configured for printing.

Once the instance administrator configures the instance for printing, the warning message shown in Figure 9-2 will disappear. Printing can effectively be performed by any application running in that instance (although you have the choice of whether to allow printing from individual reports in applications).

To configure APEX to use a print server, go into the administration interface, as shown in Figure 9-3. From there, choose Instance Settings to go to the Instance Settings window, as shown in Figure 9-4.

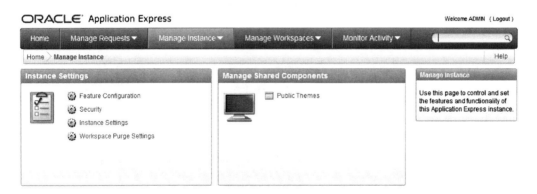

Figure 9-3. Instance administration interface

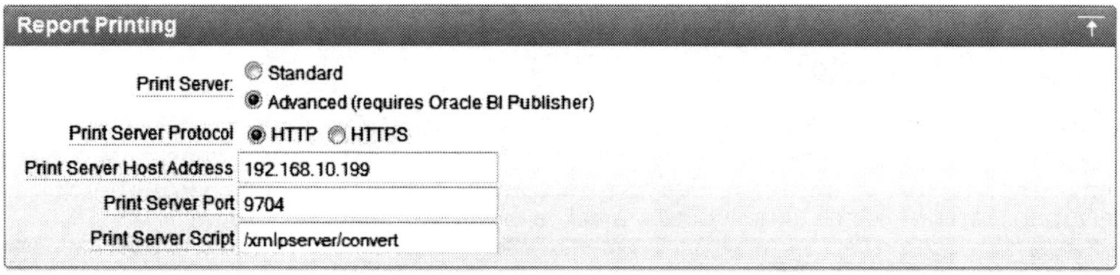

Figure 9-4. Instance Settings window

The settings required to configure a print server are as follows:

Print Server: Choose either Standard or Advanced. To use Advanced, you need to be using Oracle BI Publisher. Choose Standard for Apache FOP or another XSL-FO processing engine.

Print Server Protocol: Choose either HTTP or HTTPS. Bear in mind that data is transferred between the APEX instances and the print server, so if it's important that no one should be able to see that raw data on that particular part of the network, use HTTPS so that the data is transferred in an encrypted manner (this is the same as the HTTPS protocol used on secure web sites). But also bear in mind that the resulting PDF document will display the data in clear text.

Print Server Host Address: This is the hostname or IP address of where the print server is running (essentially, the address of the machine where the print server is installed).

Print Server Port: This is the port number on which the print server is running. Typically, for a default installation of BI Publisher, this is 9704. For Apache FOP, it is often 8080. However, this value can be anything, so make sure you find out from the person responsible for the print server on which port it is running.

Print Server Script: Think of this as the URL to which APEX sends the data to enable the print server to process the data and produce a report. Typically, for BI Publisher, this will be /xmlpserver/convert. For Apache FOP, it could be /cocoon/fop_post or something similar. Again, check with the person responsible for the print server to obtain the correct value to use.

That is all you need to do from the APEX side of things to enable printing from the entire APEX instance. These settings enable you to generate a printed report via the print server of your choice.

■ **Note** When the APEX instance administrator enters the values for the print server, there is no attempt to validate these settings. The only way you can test whether the settings are correct is to actually try to print something.

Printing Reports

We now have our print server installed and running, and the APEX instance configured to use the print server (see Figure 9-4). For this discussion, we'll use BI Publisher, but the basic procedures and options apply to Apache FOP as well.

You can connect to BI Publisher using a browser, entering a URL similar to `http://dbvm:9704/xmlpserver`. You'll see an administration login window, as shown in Figure 9-5.

■ **Note**   If you do not have BI Publisher installed in your environment, there is a wealth of information on the Oracle Technology Network at http://www.oracle.com/technetwork/middleware/bi-publisher/overview/index.html

---

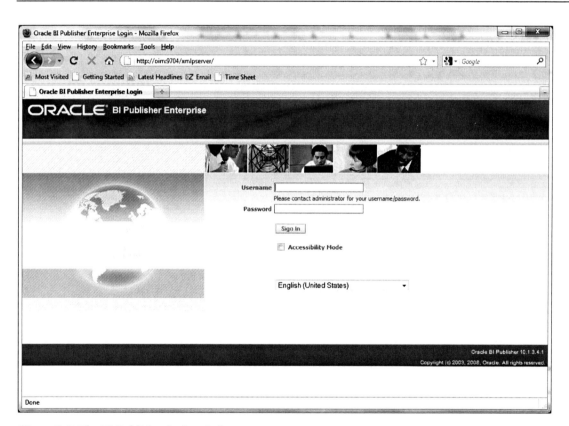

Figure 9-5. The BI Publisher login window

This is where you would log in to BI Publisher to use all its functionality as a separate product. With BI Publisher, you can create ad hoc reports, recurring reports, and scheduled reports that are generated at specific times (for example, month-end reports). You can schedule these reports to be e-mailed out to all department heads, or perhaps uploaded to a web server so that the latest sales figures are always available without having to manually create the reports. Here, we are dealing with only the APEX integration side of things.

From the APEX perspective, you don't actually need to log in to the BI Publisher web interface, as most printing tasks can be done from the APEX side. Parameters and settings are passed across to BI Publisher when the report is printed.

Enabling Printing for a Report

Let's take a simple example: we want to enable printing for the Buglist report on page 1 of the Buglist application. Figure 9-6 shows how easy it is to enable printing for that report. All we need to do is open that report, go to the Print Attributes section, and set Enable Report Printing to Yes, as shown in Figure 9-6. The only other change we made was to give a slightly more meaningful label for the link (changing it from "Print" to "Print Bugs").

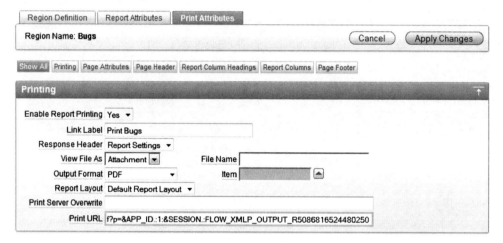

Figure 9-6. *Enabling printing for the Buglist report*

The settings in the Print Attributes section work as follows:

Enable Report Printing: Set it to Yes to enable printing from the report, or No to disable printing.

Link Label: The on-screen label used for the link to print the report.

Response Header: You can customize the response header sent back to the user's browser to enable items like the content disposition to be defined.

View File As: Allows you to specify whether the output should be opened directly in the browser window (Inline) or downloaded as an attachment (Attachment), which can then be opened automatically by whichever application is associated with that type of file.

File Name: Rather than using the generated file name based on the region name, you can specify a particular file name here.

Output Format: Allows you to produce output in different formats (we will look at this in more detail soon, in the section about setting basic print options).

Item: Allows you to specify the output type via an Item rather than specifying it in the Output Format setting.

Report Layout: Allows you to specify a particular report layout for the output.

Print Server Overwrite: Allows you to configure a different print server for this particular report, rather than using the default one defined for the entire instance.

Print URL: Allows you set a URL to use in a link or from a button to generate the report, rather than using the default link.

If you now run the application and view the Buglist report, you see the new Print Bugs link, as shown in Figure 9-7.

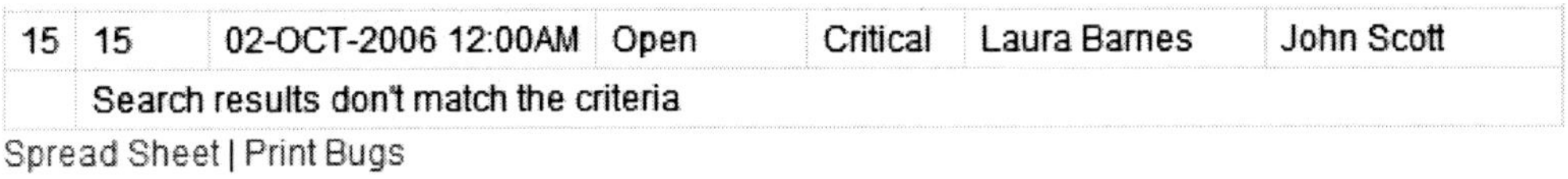

15	15	02-OCT-2006 12:00AM	Open		Critical	Laura Barnes	John Scott
	Search results don't match the criteria						

Spread Sheet | Print Bugs

Figure 9-7. Print link is enabled on the report.

If we examine the URL that the Print Bugs link goes to, we find the following:

```
http://dbvm:7780/pls/apex/f?p=103:1:970917396197354:
FLOW_XMLP_OUTPUT_R4238061396701896_en-us
```

Notice the `FLOW_XMLP_OUTPUT_R4238061396701896_en-us` value, which is passed as the request value. This enables APEX to handle the request correctly, passing the data from the on-screen report through to the print server (BI Publisher in this example) to create the PDF.

If you click the Print Bugs link, after a short delay, the PDF for the report should open in your browser, as shown in Figure 9-8.

Bug Id	Reported	Bug Status	Priority	Description	Reported By	Assigned To
1	27-JAN-2006 12:00AM	Open	High	Pressing Cancel on the login screen gives an error	Rachel Huson	John Scott
2	02-JAN-2006 12:00AM	Closed	High	Logo occassionally does not appear	Caroline White	Peter Ward
3	01-FEB-2006 12:00AM	Open	High	Search doesn't return any results when nothing is entered	Carl Watson	John Scott

Figure 9-8. Default PDF output for the Buglist report (using BI Publisher)

Once you have the PDF open in your browser, you can print the report by using your browser's print function, which will print to your local printer.

As you can see, the PDF in Figure 9-8 isn't exactly ideal in terms of layout or formatting. However, considering how little work we needed to do to get this PDF produced from our application, it is still very impressive. If you already have BI Publisher installed, configured, and working in your environment, and your APEX administrator has already configured the APEX instance for printing, then all you (as a developer) need to do is to switch on the Enable Report Printing option for the report, and that's it!

Troubleshooting Print Problems

One of the common problems people have with printing is that when they click the print link, the PDF fails to open in the browser. You might see an error something like the one shown in Figure 9-9.

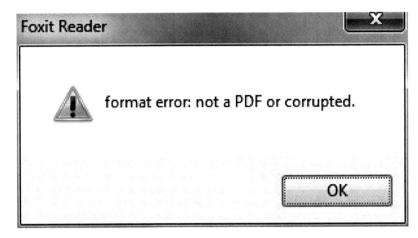

Figure 9-9. PDF fails to open.

In this example, we have deliberately stopped the print server. However, notice that as far as the end user is concerned, there is little explanation of why the PDF could not be opened.

A PDF can fail to be produced for many reasons: the print server not running, network and/or firewall issues, data-related problems, and so on. One technique that can be useful to try to diagnose this problem is, instead of trying to open the PDF automatically (and getting the error), to try saving the PDF to your disk first, and then opening the resulting file in a text editor. Look through the file to see if it sheds any light on the cause of the printing problem.

For example, rerunning the previous example but this time saving the file and then opening it in an editor, we can see the output shown in Listing 9-1.

Listing 9-1. Viewing the Contents of the Problem PDF File

```
<pre>report error:

ORA-20001: The printing engine could not be reached because either the URL
specified is incorrect or a proxy URL needs to be specified.</pre>
```

The reason the PDF could not be opened is now fairly obvious. The file is not a valid PDF file and instead contains an error message (from APEX) that the print engine could not be reached (since we stopped the print engine). However, some of the errors might not be quite so obvious. For example, we have occasionally had issues with unescaped characters in the data.

Also, let your print server administrator know about the problem. The administrator might be able to search through the print server log files, which can show if APEX and the print server are actually managing to communicate in the first place.

If you are using an 11gR1 or R2 database, you must run the SQL in Listing 9-2 as SYS in order to grant the appropriate privileges to local network resources:

Listing 9-2. Granting Privileges to Local Network Resources to Enable Printing in 11G Databases

```
DECLARE
  ACL_PATH  VARCHAR2(4000);
  ACL_ID    RAW(16);
```

```
BEGIN
  -- Look for the ACL currently assigned to 'localhost' and give APEX_040000
  -- the "connect" privilege if APEX_040000 does not have the privilege yet.
  SELECT ACL INTO ACL_PATH FROM DBA_NETWORK_ACLS
   WHERE HOST = 'localhost' AND LOWER_PORT IS NULL AND UPPER_PORT IS NULL;

  -- Before checking the privilege, ensure that the ACL is valid
  -- (for example, does not contain stale references to dropped users).
  -- If it does, the following exception will be raised:
  --
  -- ORA-44416: Invalid ACL: Unresolved principal 'APEX_040000'
  -- ORA-06512: at "XDB.DBMS_XDBZ", line ...
  --

  SELECT SYS_OP_R2O(extractValue(P.RES, '/Resource/XMLRef')) INTO ACL_ID
    FROM XDB.XDB$ACL A, PATH_VIEW P
   WHERE extractValue(P.RES, '/Resource/XMLRef') = REF(A) AND
         EQUALS_PATH(P.RES, ACL_PATH) = 1;

  DBMS_XDBZ.ValidateACL(ACL_ID);
   IF DBMS_NETWORK_ACL_ADMIN.CHECK_PRIVILEGE(ACL_PATH, 'APEX_040000',
     'connect') IS NULL THEN
     DBMS_NETWORK_ACL_ADMIN.ADD_PRIVILEGE(ACL_PATH,
     'APEX_040000', TRUE, 'connect');
   END IF;

EXCEPTION
  -- When no ACL has been assigned to 'localhost'.
  WHEN NO_DATA_FOUND THEN
  DBMS_NETWORK_ACL_ADMIN.CREATE_ACL('local-access-users.xml',
    'ACL that lets power users to connect to everywhere',
    'APEX_040000', TRUE, 'connect');
  DBMS_NETWORK_ACL_ADMIN.ASSIGN_ACL('local-access-users.xml','localhost');
END;
/
COMMIT;
```

You should also consider re-starting the BI Publisher server after making these changes in the database.

Configuring Some Simple Print Options

So far, we have managed to output a PDF version of the Buglist report using the default settings. Let's take a look at the other options available for the output format, page format, and report columns.

Choosing a Report Output Format

From the Print Attributes section of the report, you can choose to output the report in PDF, Word, Excel, HTML, or XML format, as shown in Figure 9-10.

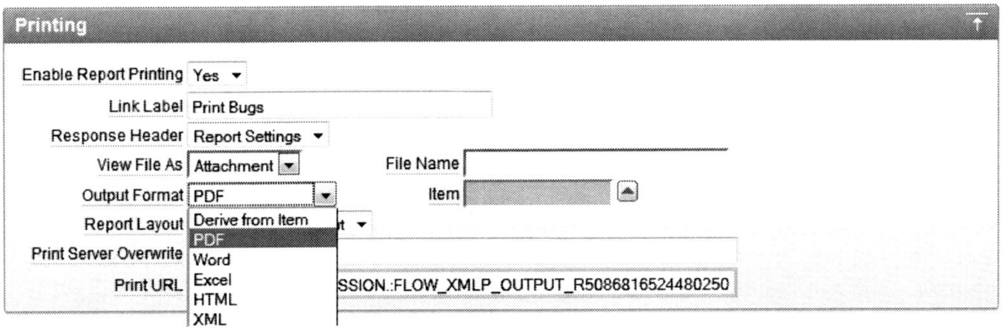

Figure 9-10. Available output formats

So rather than outputting in PDF format, the user might want to output the report in a format that can be easily used in Microsoft Word, for example. However, if we change the Output Format setting to Word, then it is set to output in Word for every user. We want the application to be a bit smarter (and more user-friendly) than that, and let the user specify the output format.

To allow users to select the output format, we add a new select list to the report, which lists each of the different output formats and the value we need to pass across to the print server (BI Publisher in this example) to produce the output in that particular format. We can create a static LOV for the select list, as shown in Figure 9-11.

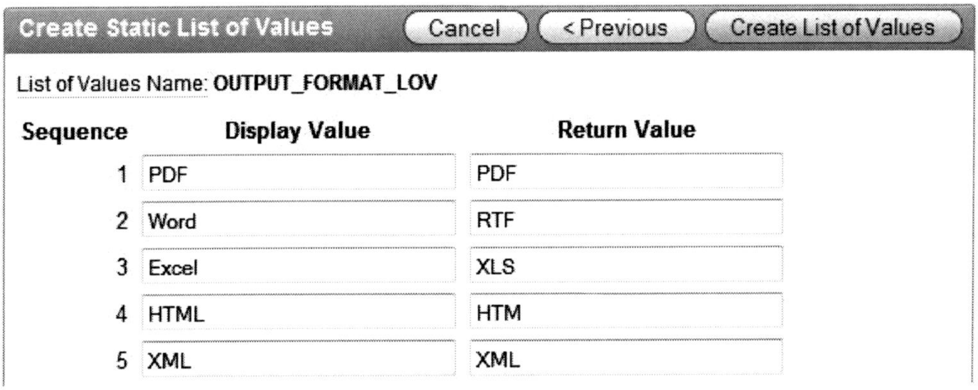

Figure 9-11. LOV for output formats

Notice the valid values for the return values in Figure 9-11 (PDF, RTF, XLS, HTML, and XML). Make sure you use these values; otherwise, you will not get the output in the desired format. Of course, you don't need to provide all of the output formats to the end users. You could just provide PDF and Word for example, or perhaps provide different formats to different users depending on their privileges.

We now need to change the Output Format setting to use the Derive From Item option, rather than one of the hard-coded options, and we specify the select list as the item from which to derive the output format. In this example, the select list is named P1_OUTPUT_FORMAT, as shown in Figure 9-12.

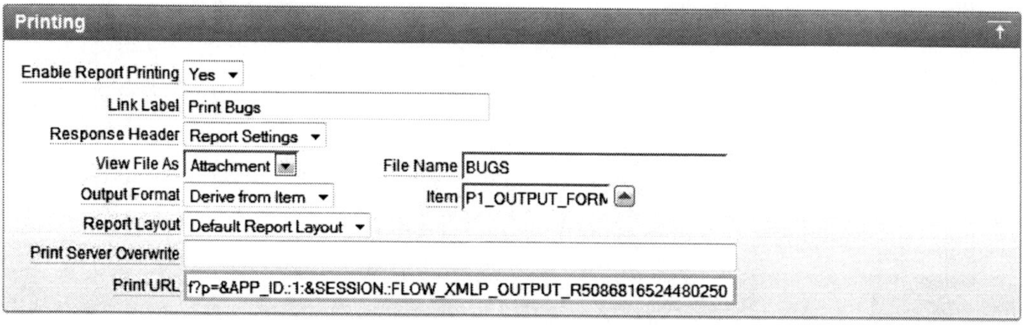

Figure 9-12. *Allowing dynamic output format*

We have also modified the File Name attribute in Figure 9-12 to be BUGS. This is actually the same name as the region itself (which would be used as a default), but we want to make sure the output is always called BUGS, even if we rename the region.

Setting Page Attributes

You can also modify the settings for the page attributes of the output, such as the paper size, orientation (landscape or portrait), borders, and so on. For our Buglist report, it makes sense to print the output in landscape format because we expect the rows to be wide.

Another interesting feature is the ability to define a page header and page footer for the output, as shown in Figure 9-13.

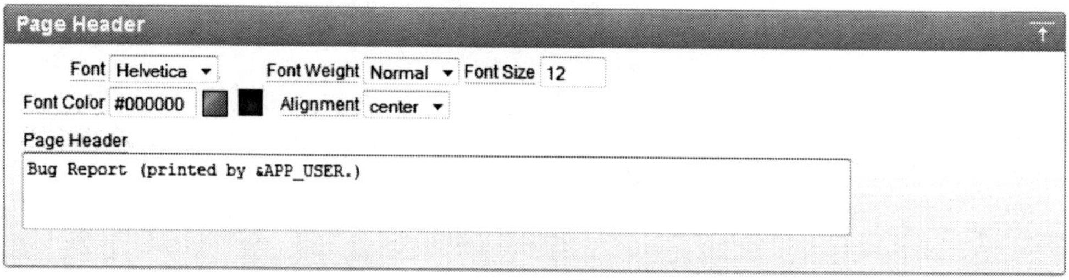

Figure 9-13. *Specifying a page header for the output*

A very nice feature of the Page Header and Page Footer options is that you can reference session state. For example, in Figure 9-13, we have used the value of the APP_USER session state to show the name of the user who produced the report. This could be very useful for auditing purposes. You could extend this simple example to reference a session state item that contains the current date and time, so that it is clear from the output when the report was produced (so that you can see whether the data is current).

▓ **Note** If the period following the APP_USER session state is omitted, the report will execute, but the output will be blank and no error message will be displayed. This detail is easy to miss and finding the solution to this issue can be maddening (based on personal experience) to say the least.

Selecting Columns

You can also define which columns should be included in the output. Why would you want to do this? Well, consider the case where you might want to display some sensitive information (such as customer bank account details) on the screen, but you don't want that information to be printed and taken off-site. Figure 9-14 shows the Report Columns section, where you can choose whether to include or exclude individual columns in the output. In this example, we have excluded the ID column from the output.

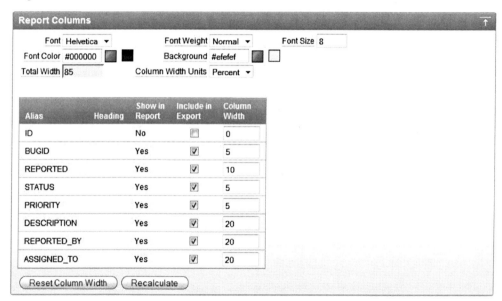

Figure 9-14. Including and excluding columns in the output

Notice that you can also change the width of each column in the output. The width is expressed as a percentage of the overall width. You can either specify the values for the widths yourself or use the Recalculate button to calculate the new values based on what you have entered.

Testing Print Settings

We have changed a number of settings in the report. Let's see the results. Figures 9-15 and 9-16 show the output in PDF and HTML format.

Bug Report (printed by BRIAN)

Bug Id	Reported	Bug Status	Prior ity	Description	Reported By	Assigned To
1	27-JAN-2006 12:00AM	Open	High	Pressing Cancel on the login screen gives an error	Rachel Huson	John Scott
2	02-JAN-2006 12:00AM	Close d	High	Logo occassionally does not appear	Caroline White	Peter Ward
3	01-FEB-2006 12:00AM	Open	High	Search doesn't return any results when nothing is entered	Carl Watson	John Scott

Figure 9-15. PDF output including header and custom column width

Bug Report (printed by BRIAN)

Bug Id	Reported	Bug Status	Priority	Description	Reported By	Assigned To
1	27-JAN-2006 12:00AM	Open	High	Pressing Cancel on the login screen gives an error	Rachel Huson	John Scott
2	02-JAN-2006 12:00AM	Closed	High	Logo occassionally does not appear	Caroline White	Peter Ward
3	01-FEB-2006 12:00AM	Open	High	Search doesn't return any results when nothing is entered	Carl Watson	John Scott

Figure 9-16. HTML output including header and custom column width

Notice how the HTML version isn't exactly the same as the PDF output. For example, the header isn't centered, and the width of the DESCRIPTION column doesn't seem to have honored the width percentage we specified. However, as a first attempt at producing the output in multiple formats, it's still impressive.

Creating Custom Report Layouts with BI Publisher

In the previous section, we used the default report layout for the output from our report. However, the real power of using BI Publisher with APEX is the ease with which you can create your own customized layouts for each report. Using the features of BI Publisher, you can create a number of different layouts for the report, and then specify which layout should be used.

Note that you can also use custom report layouts with Apache FOP. However, the way (and ease) in which those report layouts are created using the print servers is very different. Customizing report layouts with Apache FOP is discussed later in this chapter.

Installing the Client-Side Layout Tool

To create a new report layout, you use one of the best features of BI Publisher: the BI Publisher Desktop client-side tool for Microsoft Office. This separate client-side installation adds a plug-in to Microsoft Word. With this plug-in, you can design your report templates inside Word, just as you would design a regular Word document.

Figure 9-17 shows the plug-in installed into Word 2010. Notice the new Oracle BI Publisher menu option and the additional Data, Insert, Preview, Tools, and Help toolbar menus.

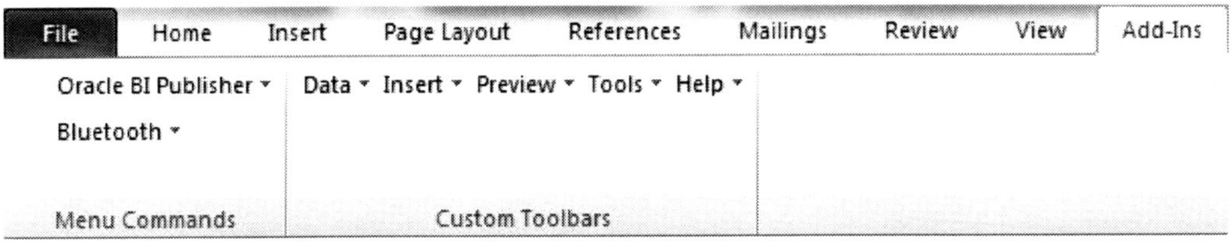

Figure 9-17. BI Publisher Desktop plug-in installed in Word

The BI Publisher Desktop can currently be downloaded from the BI Publisher section of the OTN web site at the following location:

```
http://www.oracle.com/technetwork/middleware/bi-publisher/downloads/index.html.
```

Once you have installed the BI Publisher Desktop tool (a very straightforward process of running the installation executable file, which walks you through a wizard), it should be integrated into Microsoft Word, as shown in Figure 9-17.

Creating a New Report Layout

As we mentioned earlier in the chapter, when the user chooses to print a report, APEX will send the data contained in that report to the print server, which is then responsible for generating the report. Whether you use BI Publisher or Apache FOP, the report data is sent in an XML format. Therefore, the report layout you use needs to operate on the data in an XML format.

Basically, the process of using your own report template breaks down into the following phases:

- Making BI Publisher Desktop aware of the columns that are available to use in the data that will be sent to the report server

- Designing the report layout in BI Publisher Desktop (really, in Word)

- Importing the new report layout back into APEX

- Using the new report layout for a particular report

Looking at our Buglist report (Figure 9-15), we can see that the standard rows/columns layout doesn't really make the report easy to read. It would be nice to be able to display the list of bugs in another way. Let's say that we want the details for each bug to be displayed in a more vertical format, like this

```
Reported By: ...

Status: ...
Priority:...

...
```

Creating a New Query

We begin to create our new report layout by first creating a new query. Go to Shared Components page, which has two options in the Reports section:

> *Report Queries*: Lets you define a query that can be used to produce a printable document. This option will also allow you to download the XML that the query would produce, which you can then use in the BI Publisher Desktop tool to manipulate the data.

> *Report Layouts*: Lets you upload a previously created report layout (without needing to define a particular query).

In this example, we want to create a report query based on the same query used in the Buglist report, so that we can get an XML representation of the data that is going to be sent to the print server. We need to use a query that gives us the same layout of data and includes the columns we want to use in the report layout. We also want to take into account whether the user has filtered the report in any way, since we want the printed report to reflect the same data that the on-screen report is displaying. So, we can create a new report query and use the same session state item.

Choose Report Queries to start the Create Report Query wizard, as shown in Figure 9-18 (depending on your version of APEX, the Create Report Query wizard may look slightly different). In Figure 9-18, we are basing the output format on an item (P1_OUTPUT), and we have included the P1_REPORT_SEARCH item session state. You can include as many session state items as you need here.

The next step in the wizard asks us to specify the query that is going to be used to generate the data. Listing 9-3 shows the query for the Buglist report (changed slightly to make it more readable—notice the ellipses in the subqueries).

Figure 9-18. Creating a new report query

Listing 9-3. Buglist Report Query

```
SELECT
  bl.id,
  bl.bugid,
  bl.reported,
  bl.status,
  bl.priority,
  bl.description,
  bl.reported_by,
  bl.assigned_to,
  bl.cost,
  (select ur.email from user_repository ur
     where ur.username = bl.reported_by)
    as reported_email,
  (select initcap(ur2.forename) || ' ' || initcap(ur2.surname) from
     user_repository ur2 where ur2.username = bl.reported_by)
    as reported_full_name
FROM buglist bl
WHERE
(
 instr(upper(bl.status),upper(nvl(:P1_REPORT_SEARCH,bl.status))) > 0  or
 instr(upper(bl.priority),upper(nvl(:P1_REPORT_SEARCH,bl.priority))) > 0  or
 instr(upper(bl.description),upper(nvl(:P1_REPORT_SEARCH,bl.description))) > 0  or
 instr(upper(bl.reported_by),upper(nvl(:P1_REPORT_SEARCH,bl.reported_by))) > 0
)
```

Notice that we are using the value of the P1_REPORT_SEARCH page item in the query in the predicate. The next screen in the wizard is shown in Figure 9-19. You can see that currently the report query contains a single query. You can add extra queries by clicking the Add Query button. This gives you the flexibility of creating a report that contains data from two unrelated queries.

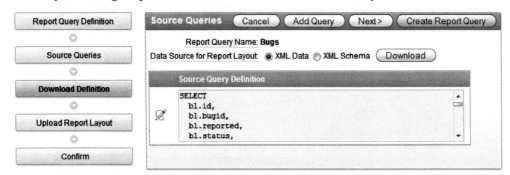

Figure 9-19. Source query definition

At this point, you can choose to create the report query. However, for this example, before we do that, we need to download the XML data from the query, because we are going to use that XML output to design our custom report layout.

Downloading the XML Data or Schema

You can choose to download the XML either as plain XML data or as an XML schema. The difference between the two choices is that the XML data file, as the name implies, contains the real data that is generated from running the query, while the XML schema file creates an XML document that details the definition of the XML document itself, without the data. The XML data will typically be much larger than the XML schema; however, the XML data has the benefit of allowing us to test the report layout in BI Publisher Desktop, since we'll have some data to display, so we'll choose this option for the example.

Listing 9-4 shows the format of the XML data file, and Listing 9-5 shows the format of the XML schema file. We have not reproduced the files in full, since they are quite large, but it can be helpful to see the content of these files to get an idea of how they differ.

Listing 9-4. XML Data File Content

```
<?xml version="1.0" encoding="UTF-8"?>
<DOCUMENT>
    <DATE>12/24/2010</DATE>
    <USER_NAME>TGF</USER_NAME>
    <APP_ID>101</APP_ID>
    <APP_NAME>Oracle APEX AppBuilder</APP_NAME>
    <TITLE>Bugs</TITLE>
    <P1_REPORT_SEARCH></P1_REPORT_SEARCH>
    <REGION ID="0">
        <ROWSET>
            <ROW>
                <ID>1</ID>
```

```
            <BUGID>1</BUGID>
            <REPORTED>01/27/2006</REPORTED>
            <STATUS>Open</STATUS>
            <PRIORITY>High</PRIORITY>
... rest of content omitted
```

Listing 9-5. XML Schema File Content

```
<?xml version="1.0" encoding="UTF-8"?>
<xs:schema xmlns:xs="http://www.w3.org/2001/XMLSchema">
  <xs:element name="DOCUMENT">
    <xs:complexType>
      <xs:sequence>
        <xs:element ref="DATE"/>
        <xs:element ref="USER_NAME"/>
        <xs:element ref="APP_ID"/>
        <xs:element ref="APP_NAME"/>
        <xs:element ref="TITLE"/>
        <xs:element ref="P1_REPORT_SEARCH"/>
        <xs:element ref="REGION"/>
      </xs:sequence>
    </xs:complexType>
  </xs:element>
  <xs:element name="DATE">
    <xs:simpleType>
      <xs:restriction base="xs:string"/>
    </xs:simpleType>
  </xs:element>
  <xs:element name="USER_NAME">
    <xs:simpleType>
      <xs:restriction base="xs:string"/>
    </xs:simpleType>
  </xs:element>
... rest of content omitted
```

Also notice in Listing 9-4 that the P1_REPORT_SEARCH session state item appears in the XML. This is why we needed to include this item when creating the report query. If we didn't, it would not be included in the data. (It could still be referenced from within the query inside APEX; it just would not be available in the report.)

After we download the XML data, we fire up Microsoft Word (which has the BI Publisher Desktop plug-in installed). We can now load the XML data into BI Publisher Desktop, as shown in Figure 9-20. After doing so, we'll get a message stating that the data has been loaded successfully.

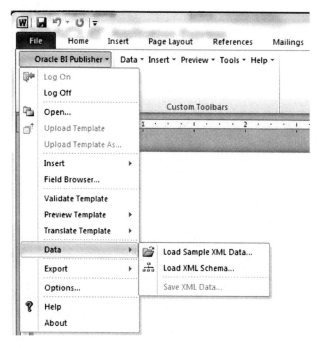

Figure 9-20. Loading the XML data

▪ **Note** If you get an error at this stage, it is likely due to a Java version mismatch. Consult the BI Publisher Desktop installation requirements document to find out whether your system meets the requirements.

Designing the Report Layout

Now the fun begins, as we begin designing the report layout. We can use basic Word functionality and create a page header to give the report a heading of "Bug Report." We could also include the current date and time if required, but we'll keep this layout simple.

We want to include each row in the XML data (that is, each bug) in the report. The BI Publisher Desktop tool contains some nice wizards that walk you through choosing the fields and data you want to include. We recommend using the wizards as much as possible to generate the code automatically. You can view that code to see how it works. Then, if desired, you can create fields manually or make adjustments if the wizards don't do precisely what you want.

For this example, we'll use the Table Wizard, as shown in Figure 9-21, and select the Free Form format.

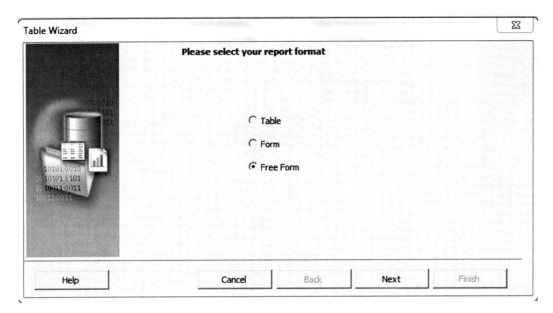

Figure 9-21. Creating a free-form report format

Next, we need to choose the grouping field, which refers to the repeating field in the data. The wizard gives us the following two choices (based on the data we loaded):

- Document/Region
- Document/Region/Rowset/Row

If you look back at the format of the XML data in Listing 9-4, you will see that each row is represented by the DOCUMENT/REGION/ROWSET/ROW element, so we select that as the grouping field.

Next, we need to select the fields that will be included in the report, as shown in Figure 9-22. And in the next step of the wizard, we can choose a field to sort the data by. In this case, it makes sense to sort the data by descending reported date.

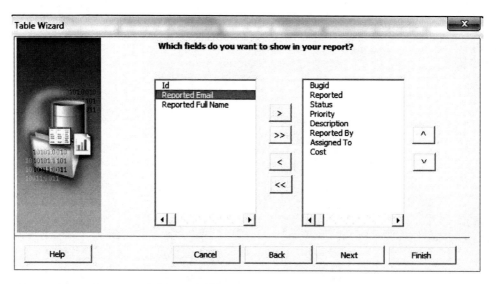

Figure 9-22. Selecting the fields to display in the report

Figure 9-23 shows the output of the wizard. You can see that all it does is insert form fields that represent the fields from the XML document. The Word document also includes a form field named F at the beginning and a form field named E at the end. These two form fields are there to allow the fields to be repeated for each record.

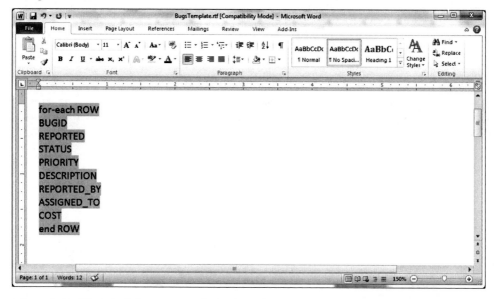

Figure 9-23. The Word document includes form fields

Testing the Report

Since we imported the XML data file into BI Publisher Desktop, we can now test the report from within the tool itself, without having to export the report layout into APEX. This is a quick way to prototype a report layout. We can even choose to preview the output in several different formats: PDF, HTML, Excel, and RTF (future versions of BI Publisher might support other formats).

Figure 9-24 shows the preview in PDF format. Admittedly, the layout isn't exactly pretty just yet, but it shows how easily we can control the positioning of the fields, as we now have a vertical style layout. Notice that the records run together with no spaces in between. As a quick exercise, go back to the Word document containing the template and add a blank line immediately before the "end ROW" field. When you preview the report again, you'll see that the records are separated by a blank line.

We could now make this report look a bit nicer by using standard Microsoft Word functionality. Figure 9-25 shows a new Word document containing a modified report layout. We created a table and positioned the XML elements for the columns (the form fields essentially) inside the table cells. We also assigned a contrasting table-shading color scheme to distinguish the definition of each individual bug.

If you previewed the report again, you would see a much more visually appealing report. However, let's continue and add a few other nice features before we finish with this report.

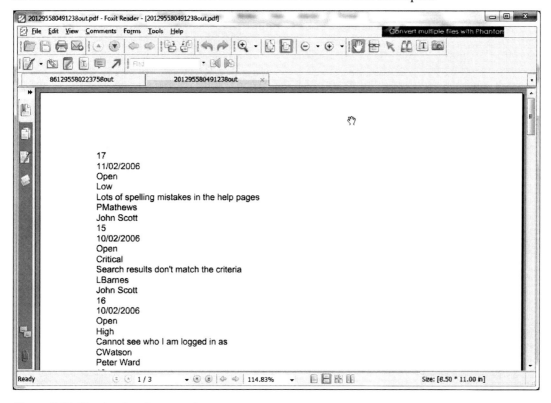

Figure 9-24. Previewing the report layout

Bug # : 17	Reported By : 11/02/2006
Status : Open	Priority : Low
Description : Lots of spelling mistakes in the help pages	
Reported by : PMathews	Assigned to : John Scott Cost :

Figure 9-25. Creating a nicer layout for the report

Showing the Search Criteria

Let's also include a line in the report that displays the search criteria that was used to generate the report. In the printed report, this will show whether the records were filtered. We can easily do this by adding an extra line at the top of the page that reads as follows:

```
Search Criteria: P1_REPORT_SEARCH
```

This would certainly meet the requirements; however, the line would be included in the report whether or not we actually provided a filter. So, if we simply ran the report and displayed all the records, we would have a line that read "Search Criteria:" at the top of the page. It would be nice to be able to suppress that line unless P1_REPORT_SEARCH actually contains a value, wouldn't it? Well, as you've guessed, we can do that!

To control whether the "Search Criteria" line is displayed, highlight it and choose the Insert Conditional Region menu option. This will allow us to specify a condition that is evaluated to determine whether to show that region, as shown in Figure 9-26.

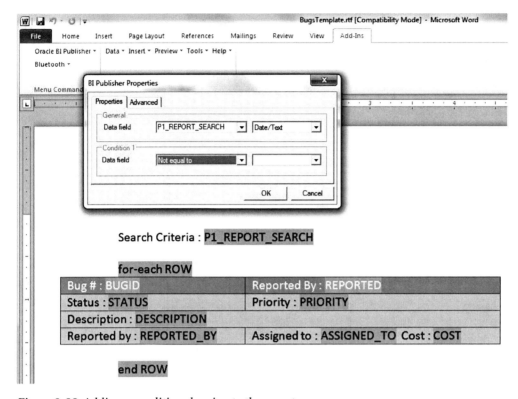

Figure 9-26. Adding a conditional region to the report

Essentially, the condition states that the entire "Search Criteria" line should be displayed only if the P1_REPORT_SEARCH field is not empty. As shown in Figure 9-26, the result of using the conditional region is that a new form field named C (for Condition) is placed before the "Search Criteria" text, with a closing form field of EC (for End Condition) placed after the P1_REPORT_SEARCH form field.

Once you become comfortable with how the form fields work, you can begin to create them manually. We can examine the code behind the conditional region we just added by highlighting the entire line and choosing Tools   Field Browser. This brings up a window that displays the form fields and the code behind each one, as in this example:

```
C                <?if:P1_REPORT_SEARCH!=''?>

P1_REPORT_SEARCH <?P1_REPORT_SEARCH?>
EC               <?end if?>
```

So, to create a conditional region, you could type the code that is behind the C form field, and use whatever logic you like in the condition. To display a particular XML element, for example, you could type the code <?ELEMENT?>.

Highlighting Priority Items

Another nice addition to the report would be to highlight any bugs that have a high priority. We can do this by using conditional formatting (as opposed to a conditional region). We select the PRIORITY form field and then choose Insert Conditional Format. This displays the Properties dialog box shown in Figure 9-27, which allows us to specify two conditions to allow the field to be formatted differently depending on the conditions.

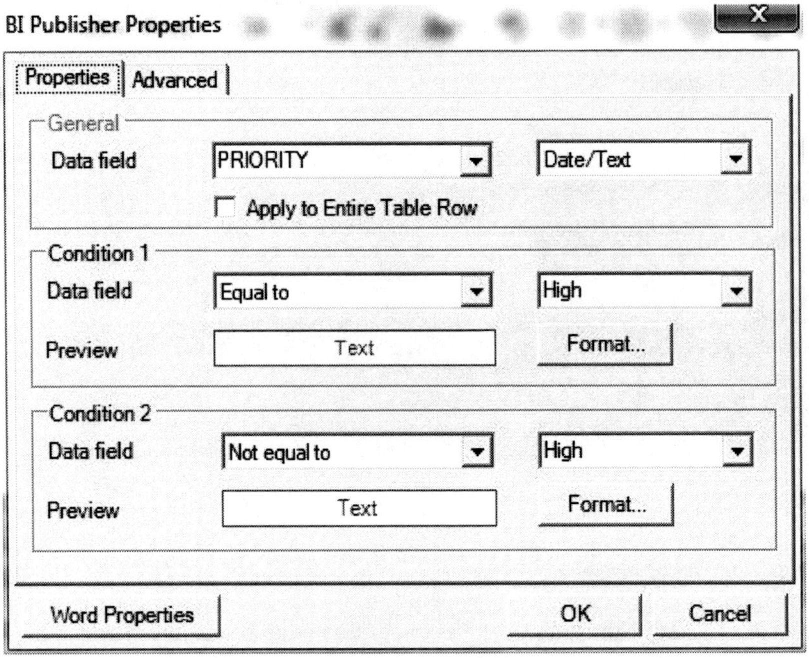

Figure 9-27. Adding conditional formatting to the report

If two conditions are not sufficient, you can use the Advanced tab to manually enter the code. Examining the code for this condition, we see the following (formatted here to make it easier to read; in the editor, it will most likely appear as one long line):

```
<?if:PRIORITY='High'?>

  <?attribute@incontext:color;'red'?>
<?end if?>
<?if:PRIORITY!='High'?>
  <?attribute@incontext:color;'green'?>
<?end if?>
```

Let's preview the report in BI Publisher Desktop. The results are as shown in Figure 9-28.

Bug # : 15	Reported By : 10/02/2006
Status : Open	Priority : Critical
Description : Search results don't match the criteria	
Reported by : LBarnes	Assigned to : John Scott Cost :

Bug # : 16	Reported By : 10/02/2006
Status : Open	Priority : High
Description : Cannot see who I am logged in as	
Reported by : CWatson	Assigned to : Peter Ward Cost :

Figure 9-28. Previewing the new report

Along with the priority being displayed in a different color depending on the condition we specified (which may not be apparent in the figure), notice that the line that specifies the search criteria is not present. This is because the XML data file that we loaded does not contain a value for the P1_REPORT_SEARCH session state item, as shown here (and in Listing 9-4):

```
<?xml version="1.0" encoding="UTF-8"?>

<DOCUMENT>
    <DATE>09-JUL-08</DATE>
    <USER_NAME>ADMIN</USER_NAME>
    <APP_ID>103</APP_ID>
    <APP_NAME>APEX - Application Builder</APP_NAME>
    <TITLE>Bugs</TITLE>
    <P1_REPORT_SEARCH></P1_REPORT_SEARCH>
    <REGION ID="0">
        <ROWSET>
... rest of listing omitted
```

However, when a user runs the real report through APEX, any value that is typed into the P1_REPORT_SEARCH field will be passed through in the XML data to BI Publisher, and then the conditional region should display.

Saving the New Layout for Later Use

So now that we have created the report layout, how do we use it in APEX? With BI Publisher, all we need to do is to save the Word document that we created as an RTF file. Note that no other format will work (so be careful not to accept the default Save As type of Word document). Once you have saved the layout as an RTF file, you can upload it into APEX to be used as a report layout.

If you recall, we left APEX back at the Create Report Query wizard (Figure 9-19). Now we return to APEX and go to the next page in the wizard, where we can choose to upload the new RTF, as shown in Figure 9-29.

Figure 9-29. Uploading the RTF report layout

Notice that for the Report Layout Source option, we have selected "Create file based report layout." The default option is "Use generic report layout," which is the original tabular layout.

Once we've uploaded the RTF layout, we get the option to test the report (which you should do). We also are provided with a URL that can be used from a link or button within the application to generate the report. In this case, the URL is as follows:

```
f?p=&APP_ID.:0:&SESSION_ID.:PRINT_REPORT=Bugs
```

Notice how the value for the REQUEST parameter in the URL uses the name of the report as a parameter to the PRINT_REPORT command.

We can now go back to the original Buglist report in the Buglist application and change the Report Layout setting from Default Report Layout to our new Bug layout. You will see all your custom report layouts in the drop-down list in the Print Attributes section.

Now run the application and type something into the search field to filter the records displayed in the report. Then click the Print Bugs link. The PDF version will display the same records as the on-screen report. Figure 9-30 shows an example of the report produced when we entered "error" in the search field. You can see that because we supplied a value for the P1_REPORT_SEARCH page item, the "Search Criteria" line is included in the report.

Bug # : 1	Reported By : 27-JAN-2006 12:00AM
Status : Open	Priority : High
Description : Pressing Cancel on the login screen gives an error	
Reported by : RHuson	Assigned to : John Scott Cost :

Bug # : 13	Reported By : 02-SEP-2006 12:00AM
Status : Open	Priority : High
Description : There is no way to tell who I'm logged in as	
Reported by : CWhite	Assigned to : Paul Wilson Cost :

Figure 9-30. Filtered PDF output

This quick example has illustrated just how easily you can create very advanced and dynamic reports using BI Publisher. However, before we finish this section on using BI Publisher, let's add a couple of other nice features just to show how powerful BI Publisher is.

Adding Graphics and Charts

One common requirement for printed reports is to include some sort of company logo on the report. This is actually pretty trivial to implement with BI Publisher Desktop. We can just insert a static logo in the Word document using the regular Insert ▸ Picture option in Word. For example, we inserted a regular GIF file with a ladybug (or ladybird, as we call them in the United Kingdom) image, to represent a bug logo for the report.

We can also add another really nice feature, which is to include a chart in the report that is created dynamically using the data from the report. To do this, from the Word document, choose Insert ▸ Chart, and then choose the columns to use in the axes. As an example, we added a chart showing the number of bugs per priority, as shown in Figure 9-31.

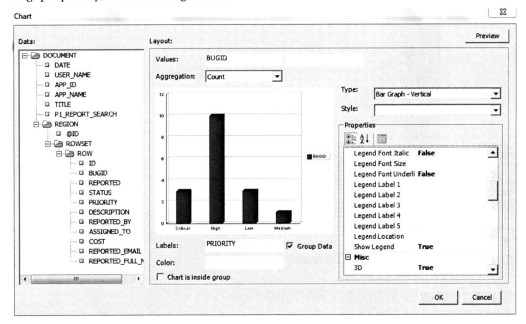

Figure 9-31. *Adding a chart to a report*

After you've added an image and/or a chart to your report, you can resave the RTF template and upload it again into APEX. Unfortunately, there is currently no option to replace an existing report layout, so you will need to delete the old report layout and create a new one. A side effect of that re-creation step is that any reports that used the old report layout will be "orphaned" from it and will resort to using the default report layout instead. So, make sure you go back and modify each report that needs to use the new layout.

Running the application again and generating the report results in a nice chart (and custom logo) at the end of the report, after the repeating rows, as shown in Figure 9-32.

As you've seen, using BI Publisher with APEX makes it very easy to create incredibly useful output formats for your end users. You can create some visually appealing reports (much better than the simple ones we have created for this demonstration) that show off the high-fidelity reporting capabilities of APEX.

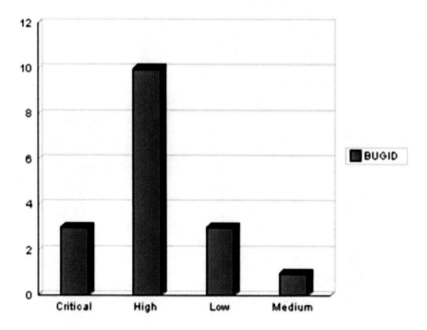

Figure 9-32. Including a chart and logo in the report

Generating Reports Through Apache FOP

The previous sections showed how easy it is to use BI Publisher as your print server. If you cannot use BI Publisher, your other option is Apache FOP or some other XSL-FO processing print server. As explained in the "Configuring APEX to Use a Report Server" section earlier in the chapter, to use Apache FOP, you must configure the APEX instance to use the FOP print server (choose Standard for the Print Server setting).

Installing Apache FOP

A couple of great resources walk you through setting up and configuring Apache Tomcat and Cocoon to enable PDF printing at no cost (other than your time, that is!).

- The PDF Printing section of the APEX OTN site, at
  www.oracle.com/technology/products/database/application_express/html/confi
  gure_printing.html. This details how to install and configure the supported
  Apache FOP that is bundled with the APEX installation itself.

- An entry in the blog of Carl Backstrom, one of the Oracle developers on the APEX
  team, at http://carlback.blogspot.com/2007/03/apex-cocoon-pdf-and-more.html.
  This demonstrates how to use another XSL-FO processing engine in a short video
  that walks you through the steps, and shows exactly which versions of the software
  you need to get up and running.

Here, we will briefly cover installing the supported Apache FOP engine supplied with APEX.

In the APEX installation file you downloaded (you still have a copy of that, right?), within the
utilities/fop directory, there is a Java WAR file named fop.war:

```
[oracle@db fop]$ pwd

/home/oracle/apex/utilities/fop

[oracle@db fop]$ ls -al
total 5580
drwxr-xr-x 2 oracle oinstall    4096 Jun  6 21:34 .
drwxr-xr-x 4 oracle oinstall    4096 Jun  6 21:34 ..
-r--r--r-- 1 oracle oinstall 5691921 Jun  6  2007 fop.war
```

You can load this WAR file into the OC4J container, which means you can load it into a tool like
Enterprise Manager or Application Server. In this example, we will load the WAR file into Enterprise
Manager.

First, connect to Enterprise Manager using the URL http://dbvm:8888/em/. Obviously, replace the
hostname (dbvm) and port number (8888) with those for your own environment.

Once you have logged in to the OC4J home page, click the Applications tab, choose the Deploy
button, and then specify the location of the WAR file. You have the option of loading the WAR file from
the local disk or from a location on the server (assuming you are not connected to the OC4J
administration control from the server itself). Figure 9-33 shows the settings we used on our local OC4J
server.

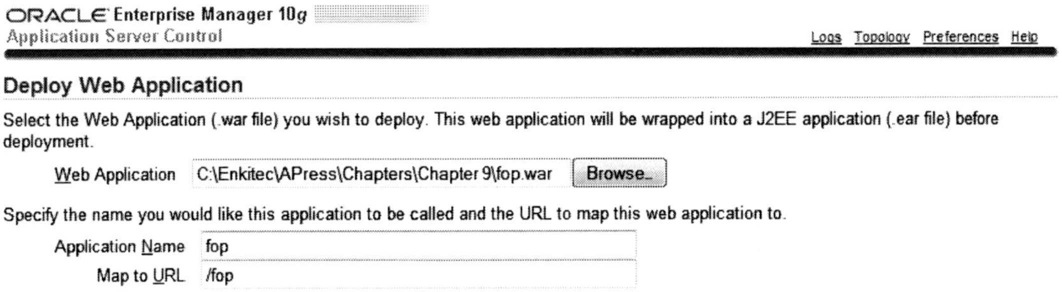

Figure 9-33. Loading the fop.war archive

397

On the following page in the wizard, you need to specify an application name (such as fop). Also, ensure the Context Root setting is cleared.

After you have completed all the steps (which are covered in the PDF Printing section of the guide on the APEX OTN site), the fop.war file should be successfully deployed to your OC4J container.

Creating a New Layout Using XSL-FO

You can print reports with Apache FOP as described in the "Printing Reports" section earlier in this chapter. For our Buglist report, we need to change the report layout back to the standard default layout, as shown in Figure 9-34, because the RTF layout we created in BI Publisher will not work with Apache FOP.

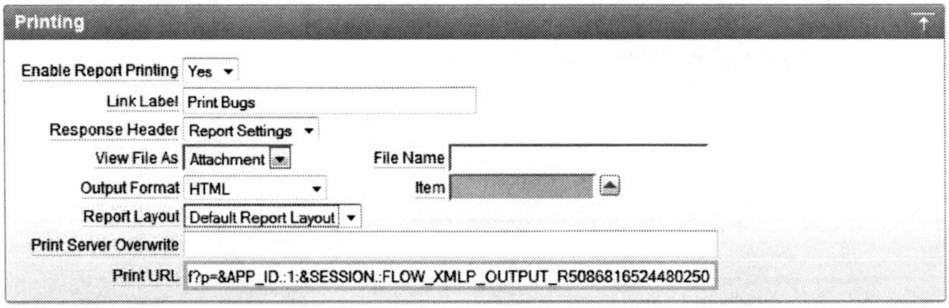

Figure 9-34. Using the default report layout for Apache FOP

When we print this report, we get a pretty basic layout, very similar to the first BI Publisher style layout shown earlier, as shown in Figure 9-35.

Bug Report (printed by BRIAN)

Bug Id	Reported	Bug Status	Priority	Description	Reported By	Assigned To
1	27-JAN-2006 12:00AM	Open	High	Pressing Cancel on the login screen gives an error	RHuson	John Scott
2	02-JAN-2006 12:00AM	Closed	High	Logo occassionally does not appear	CWhite	Peter Ward
3	01-FEB-2006 12:00AM	Open	High	Search doesn't return any results when nothing is entered	CWatson	John Scott
4	02-MAR-2006 12:00AM	Open	Critical	Login doesn't work for user smithp	LBarnes	Mark Wilson

Figure 9-35. The default report layout generated with Apache FOP

To understand how this report is being generated, we need to delve into the world of XSL-FO. Whereas with BI Publisher, you can design the report layout using Microsoft Word and the BI Publisher Desktop plug-in, with FOP, you need to design an XSL-FO template, which is used to generate the output. Essentially, the XSL-FO is an XSL document that is used to transform the XML data into the desired output format. It is the FOP engine that performs this transformation.

As you'll see, much more hands-on work is necessary to modify reports using XSL-FO as compared with using BI Publisher. The complexity of the XSL-FO is both a positive and a negative—you can alter any aspect of the output, but to do that, you need to learn the syntax and how XSL-FO works.

Using the Create Report Layout wizard, we'll create a new report layout for Apache FOP. Because we are using the standard print server, rather than the advanced (BI Publisher), we cannot choose the RTF format. Instead, we must choose the XSL-FO format.

As shown in Figure 9-36, the two choices for the layout type are Generic Columns, which means you refer to the columns by number, or Named Columns, which lets you reference the columns by name, similar to using the form fields in BI Publisher. Choosing Named Columns gives you more control; you'll know exactly what will be displayed where on the report. If you use Generic Columns, it's likely that, at some point, you'll end up having one column's data appear where you expected to see another column's data. (It's a similar situation to doing select * from table rather than listing the actual columns you want, as you can never guarantee the order they'll come out in unless you specifically list the order.)

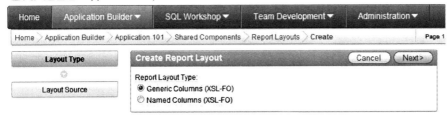

Figure 9-36. *Creating an Apache FOP report layout*

For this example, we'll choose Generic Columns, simply because that lets us see a sample of the XSL-FO code, as shown in Figure 9-37.

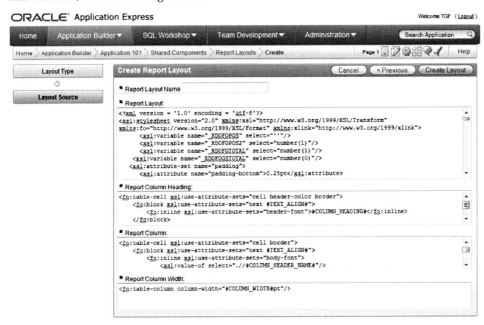

Figure 9-37. *Generic column XSL-FO code*

Understanding the XSL-FO Code

As we mentioned earlier, the layout code is actually an XSL document. It is broken into the following sections:

- The main code section contains the core code, which references each of the following sections.

- The report column heading section contains the code to display a heading for each column.

- The report column section contains the code to display each column.

- The report column width section is used to specify the width of columns.

■ **Tip** A great reference source for XSL-FO is available at www.w3schools.com/xslfo/default.asp.

In the main code section, we see code like the following:

```
<fo:table-header>

  <fo:table-row>
    #PRN_TEMPLATE_HEADER_ROW#
  </fo:table-row>
</fo:table-header>
<fo:table-body>
  <xsl:for-each select=".//ROW">
    <fo:table-row>
      #PRN_TEMPLATE_BODY_ROW#
    </fo:table-row>
  </xsl:for-each>
</fo:table-body>
```

This section is responsible for outputting the headers and detail for the records (in other words, this small section is responsible for the vast majority of what we see in the outputted PDF). Much of the rest of the main code is responsible for how the page is formatted and laid out (as opposed to displaying the actual data). Listing 9-6 shows some of that formatting and layout information.

Listing 9-6. Some XSL-FO Formatting and Layout Information

```
<xsl:attribute-set name="header-font">

  <xsl:attribute name="height">
    #HEADER_FONT_SIZE#pt
  </xsl:attribute>
  <xsl:attribute name="font-family">
    #HEADER_FONT_FAMILY#
  </xsl:attribute>
  <xsl:attribute name="white-space-collapse">
```

```
            false
    </xsl:attribute>
    <xsl:attribute name="font-size">
            #HEADER_FONT_SIZE#pt
    </xsl:attribute>
    <xsl:attribute name="font-weight">
            #HEADER_FONT_WEIGHT#
    </xsl:attribute>
</xsl:attribute-set>
```

Even if you're not familiar with XSL-FO (or with XSL), it should be reasonably obvious that the section of code in Listing 9-6 is responsible for the font settings for the header. Notice the references to things that look like APEX substitution strings, such as #HEADER_FONT_SIZE#. These values are actually passed across as the values you set in the Report Attributes section for your report.

Now let's take a look at the section responsible for the column headings, shown in Listing 9-7.

***Listing 9-7.** XSL-FO Section for Column Headings*

```
<fo:table-cell xsl:use-attribute-sets="cell header-color border">

  <fo:block xsl:use-attribute-sets="text #TEXT_ALIGN#">
    <fo:inline xsl:use-attribute-sets="header-font">
            #COLUMN_HEADING#
        </fo:inline>
  </fo:block>
</fo:table-cell>
```

The code in Listing 9-7 is remarkably short. This brevity really is one of the powers of XSL: a short code fragment can be used multiple times for many different data elements. This block of code is actually called as a result of the #PRN_TEMPLATE_HEADER_ROW# substitution variable we saw in the main block of code, or more precisely, this section of code is embedded into the main block of code as it is represented by the #PRN_TEMPLATE_HEADER_ROW# variable.

Formatting Report Headings

Let's try something relatively simple. We'll change the report headings so they're in italic and also use a red font. The way that we change the font for the heading is to add a font-style attribute to the column heading section of the XSL-FO (Listing 9-7). For example, the following column heading section uses font-style to ask for red, italic font:

```
<fo:table-cell xsl:use-attribute-sets="cell header-color border">

  <fo:block xsl:use-attribute-sets="text #TEXT_ALIGN#">
    <fo:inline xsl:use-attribute-sets="header-font"
      font-style="italic" color="red">
            #COLUMN_HEADING#
        </fo:inline>
  </fo:block>
</fo:table-cell>
```

We added font-style="italic" color="red" to the fo:inline section of the code. You might notice that this is very similar to what you would do in HTML to modify the text.

If you ran the application again, after assigning the new layout to the report, you would see that the headers are indeed in italics and use a red font. However, adding a font style in this way is really not the "correct" way to change font attributes, as we are not using pure XSL-FO.

Notice that in the fo:inline section, we state that for any following text, we want to use the values from the header-font declaration:

```
<fo:table-cell xsl:use-attribute-sets="cell header-color border">

  <fo:block xsl:use-attribute-sets="text #TEXT_ALIGN#">
    <fo:inline xsl:use-attribute-sets="header-font"
      font-style="italic" color="red">
          #COLUMN_HEADING#
        </fo:inline>
  </fo:block>
</fo:table-cell>
```

What we should really do is include our new formatting (italic and red) in the definition for the header-font section, which you saw in Listing 9-5. We can now modify that section of code, as shown in Listing 9-8.

Listing 9-8. *Modifying the XSLFO to Change the Font Style and Color*

```
<xsl:attribute-set name="header-font">

    <xsl:attribute name="height">
      #HEADER_FONT_SIZE#pt
    </xsl:attribute>
    <xsl:attribute name="font-family">
      #HEADER_FONT_FAMILY#
    </xsl:attribute>
    <xsl:attribute name="white-space-collapse">
          false
    </xsl:attribute>
    <xsl:attribute name="font-size">
          #HEADER_FONT_SIZE#pt
    </xsl:attribute>
    <xsl:attribute name="font-weight">
          #HEADER_FONT_WEIGHT#
    </xsl:attribute>
    <xsl:attribute name="font-style">
          italic
    </xsl:attribute>
    <xsl:attribute name="color">
          red
    </xsl:attribute>
</xsl:attribute-set>
```

Now if we run the report, we should again see the header font is in italics and the color of the header is red, as shown in Figure 9-38.

Bug Id	Reported	Bug Status	Priority	Description	Reported By	Assigned To
1	27-JAN-2006 12:00AM	Open	High	Pressing Cancel on the login screen gives an error	RHuson	John Scott
2	02-JAN-2006 12:00AM	Closed	High	Logo occassionally does not appear	CWhite	Peter Ward

Figure 9-38. *PDF showing XSL-FO changes*

Notice that the headings are not nicely lined up, due to some of the headers being wider than the columns are defined to be. We could modify the heading alignment and column widths, although we could also specify those items through the Report Columns section in the Report Attributes, as described earlier in the chapter. In fact, we could have also very easily changed the header color through the Report Column Headings section in the Report Attributes. However, we could not specify that the header should be in italics using that method. Italics need to be set manually in the XSL-FO code.

Highlighting Priority Items

As another example, let's say we want to highlight bugs that are a high priority. Looking at the code for the column template, we see the following:

```
<fo:table-cell xsl:use-attribute-sets="cell border">

    <fo:block xsl:use-attribute-sets="text #TEXT_ALIGN#">
        <fo:inline xsl:use-attribute-sets="body-font">
            <xsl:value-of select=".//#COLUMN_HEADER_NAME#"/>
        </fo:inline>
    </fo:block>
</fo:table-cell>
```

We have two choices here: we can explicitly check that we're processing the PRIORITY column and then check to see if the value is 'High', or we can just check to see if the value is 'High' (regardless of which column it is in). Since we are using the generic column layout rather than using named columns, it is much trickier to check specifically for the PRIORITY column. So, we'll go with the approach of displaying any column value that matches 'High' in red.

The xsl:choose syntax essentially allows us to perform an if-then-else operation in XSL.

```
<xsl:choose>

  <xsl:when ...>
        ...
  </xsl:when>
  <xsl:otherwise>
        ...
  </xsl:otherwise>
</xsl:choose>
```

We will use this syntax to check if the value of the current column is 'High' (and display it in red); otherwise, we display it normally. Replace the contents of the Column Template with the following code:

```
<xsl:choose>
  <xsl:when test=".//#COLUMN_HEADER_NAME#='High'">
    <fo:table-cell xsl:use-attribute-sets="cell border">
      <fo:block xsl:use-attribute-sets="text #TEXT_ALIGN#">
        <fo:inline xsl:use-attribute-sets="body-font-red" font-style="italic">
          <xsl:value-of select=".//#COLUMN_HEADER_NAME#"/>
        </fo:inline>
      </fo:block>
    </fo:table-cell>
  </xsl:when>
  <xsl:otherwise>
    <fo:table-cell xsl:use-attribute-sets="cell border">
      <fo:block xsl:use-attribute-sets="text #TEXT_ALIGN#">
        <fo:inline xsl:use-attribute-sets="body-font">
          <xsl:value-of select=".//#COLUMN_HEADER_NAME#"/>
        </fo:inline>
      </fo:block>
    </fo:table-cell>
  </xsl:otherwise>
</xsl:choose>
```

We use the xsl:choose construct to check the value of the current column in the data. The first case is when the column value does equal 'High'. Notice the parts we have highlighted. The first is where we test (using the test keyword) the current value of the column and compare it to a string. We have used the same notation for referring to the column value that was used in the original code.

```
.//#COLUMN_HEADER_NAME#
```

This allows us to reference the current XML element in the XML document that contains the data from the report.

Also notice that we changed the fo:inline statement to use the body-font-red attribute set, rather than the original body-font. This is because we need to display the value differently in both cases. So we need to add another attribute set to the main code. To do this, we simply copied the body-font attribute-set and added a color attribute to make the font appear in red.

:

```
<xsl:attribute-set name="body-font">

  <xsl:attribute name="height">
    12.0pt
  </xsl:attribute>
  <xsl:attribute name="font-family">
    #BODY_FONT_FAMILY#
  </xsl:attribute>
  <xsl:attribute name="white-space-collapse">
    false
  </xsl:attribute>
  <xsl:attribute name="font-size">
    #BODY_FONT_SIZE#pt
  </xsl:attribute>
  <xsl:attribute name="font-weight">
```

```
      #BODY_FONT_WEIGHT#
  </xsl:attribute>
</xsl:attribute-set>
<xsl:attribute-set name="body-font-red">
  <xsl:attribute name="height">
    12.0pt
  </xsl:attribute>
  <xsl:attribute name="font-family">
    #BODY_FONT_FAMILY#
  </xsl:attribute>
  <xsl:attribute name="white-space-collapse">
    false
  </xsl:attribute>
  <xsl:attribute name="font-size">
    #BODY_FONT_SIZE#pt
  </xsl:attribute>
  <xsl:attribute name="font-weight">
    #BODY_FONT_WEIGHT#
  </xsl:attribute>
  <xsl:attribute name="color">
    red
  </xsl:attribute>
```

. . . .

So to summarize, the column template will check the value of the current column. If it is equal to the string 'High', it will use the new body-font-red attribute-set; otherwise (if it is not equal to 'High'), it will use the original body-font attribute-set.

If we now run the report, we should see that any bugs with a priority of High have the PR-IORITY column marked in red (we've also used italics to make it more noticeable in the figure), as shown in Figure 9-39.

Bug Report (printed by BRIAN)

Bug id	Reported	Bug Status	Priority	Description	Reported By	Assigned To
1	27-JAN-2006 12:00AM	Open	*High*	Pressing Cancel on the login screen gives an error	RHuson	John Scott
2	02-JAN-2006 12:00AM	Closed	*High*	Logo occassionally does not appear	CWhite	Peter Ward
3	01-FEB-2006 12:00AM	Open	*High*	Search doesn't return any results when nothing is entered	CWatson	John Scott
4	02-MAR-2006 12:00AM	Open	Critical	Login doesn't work for user smithp	LBarnes	Mark Wilson
5	02-MAR-2006 12:00AM	Open	Low	Images don't look in the right positions	LScott	Steven Anderson

Figure 9-39. Highlighting High priority in red and italics

Adding Graphics to a Report

In the BI Publisher example, we included a static logo in the PDF. Let's see how we can achieve that in the XSL-FO–based layout.

To include the static logo, we need to do the following two things:

- Copy that image somewhere on the web server's file system so that it is accessible by the FOP engine.

- Reference the image as an external resource in the XSL-FO

To reference the image, we need to use an XSL-FO construct called `fo:external-graphic`, which we can use in a way similar to the image tag in HTML. For example, we can reference the image like this

```
<fo:external-graphic width="50px" height="50px"

    src='url("http://dbvm:7780/i/bug/bug.gif")'>
</fo:external-graphic>
```

In this example, the URL to the image is `http://dbvm:7780/i/bug/bug.gif`. We have also specified the width and height of the image so that it is scaled nicely on the resulting PDF.

Now we look through the main code and locate the section where the footer region of the PDF is processed.

```
<fo:static-content flow-name="region-footer">

   <fo:block xsl:use-attribute-sets="text footer">
     <fo:inline xsl:use-attribute-sets="body-font page-number">
        <fo:page-number/>
     </fo:inline>
   </fo:block>
   <fo:block xsl:use-attribute-sets="text text_2 #PAGE_FOOTER_ALIGNMENT#">
     <fo:inline xsl:use-attribute-sets="page-footer">#PAGE_FOOTER#</fo:inline>
   </fo:block>
</fo:static-content>
```

Notice that currently the footer displays just the page number (as indicated by the `fo:page-number` reference. We can change this to include the new `fo:external-graphic` construct.

```
<fo:static-content flow-name="region-footer">

  <fo:block xsl:use-attribute-sets="text footer">
    <fo:inline xsl:use-attribute-sets="body-font page-number">
      <fo:external-graphic width="50px" height="50px"
        src='url("http://dbvm:7780/i/bug/bug.gif")'/>
      <fo:page-number/>
    </fo:inline>
  </fo:block>
  <fo:block xsl:use-attribute-sets="text text_2 #PAGE_FOOTER_ALIGNMENT#">
    <fo:inline xsl:use-attribute-sets="page-footer">#PAGE_FOOTER#</fo:inline>
  </fo:block>
</fo:static-content>
```

If we now run the report again, we should see the logo appear in the footer area, as shown in Figure 9-40.

Figure 9-40. Including a custom image with XSL-FO

Our XSL-FO report is a simple example, which can easily be extended. For example, instead of using text for the priority, we could reference an image, or perhaps reference images that have been stored in the database (and made accessible via a URL, as discussed in the previous chapter).

Summary

Oracle's BI Publisher is an excellent product that makes it easy to build report formats for use in printing from APEX. BI Publisher is an enterprise product. If you work in a large organization, you may already have access to BI Publisher. Take advantage of that access if you can.

Good as it is, BI Publisher can sometimes be too costly or too complex to deploy for smaller organizations. In that case, look at a solution such as Apache FOP, which is based on XSL-FO. An XSL-FO solution is also extremely powerful and provides a good alternative to using BI Publisher, but requires more work on your side.

One final word on XSL-FO: a number of commercial products allow you to visually design XSL-FO templates, a bit like the BI Publisher Desktop product. We have tried a number of these products with mixed success; some are much easier to work with than others. Also, bear in mind that these are not APEX-specific tools and do require a learning curve of their own. And, in some cases, the XSL-FO produced by the tools did not work (that is, did not produce a PDF) when used with the `fop.war` shipped with APEX. So, we encourage you to test these products before purchasing (which is always wise to do with any software product!).

CHAPTER 10

Themes and Templates

Let's face it: most application developers are not graphic designers. Despite this fact, they frequently are tasked with making an application "look good." Oddly enough, you rarely hear about graphic designers being tasked with creating entity-relationship diagrams, tuning slow queries, and the like.

Good design is extremely difficult to create, yet amazingly simple to recognize. A well-designed site can exude a level of confidence to your users that will make them feel more confident about the quality of the goods or services that your site provides, even if it is nothing more than a simple department-level application. Unfortunately, it takes all of a second or two to realize whether or not a web site was professionally designed.

And while looks are not everything, they do make a lasting first impression on your users. You would be much less likely to provide personal information to or purchase something from a site riddled with spelling and grammar errors. Hackers know this, and so they go to great lengths to make phishing sites look identical to the sites that they are mimicking. This alone has caused many otherwise intelligent individuals to fall victim to credit card fraud and identity theft. While we surely do not endorse such behavior, the point is clear: looks do make a difference, for better or for worse.

Fortunately, not every site that you create needs to have an expensive, award-winning design. That would simply not be practical, necessary, or even possible. A good, achievable goal should be to make your applications look like you bought them from a vendor, rather than built them yourself.

APEX gives you a jump-start by providing 20 prebuilt sets of templates called *themes*. You can use any of these built-in themes in your applications with little to no modification. While these themes may not be revolutionary in terms of their design, they are more than adequate for most business and other applications. The new themes provided with APEX 4.0 provide a much more professional look and feel than those in previous versions.

This chapter will not teach you graphic design principles or how to become an expert in Photoshop, but it will outline some of the features in APEX that can help you, as a developer, make your application look professional, crisp, and clean.

Themes

The main user interface component that APEX provides is *themes*. Themes, an APEX shared component, are a logical collection of templates and their associated defaults. Themes have attributes, which dictate which templates are used as defaults for APEX regions and components. Aside from that, themes have little to no bearing on the actual user interface of an application. Templates, which will be discussed in more detail later in this chapter, control how an application looks and feels.

APEX 4.0 ships with 20 built-in, ready-to-use themes, as shown in Figure 10-1. Some are more professional-looking and better suited for business applications; others are designed to look more hip and modern. You can use any of these themes "as-is" in your own applications, or make modifications to a theme's corresponding templates to suit your specific needs.

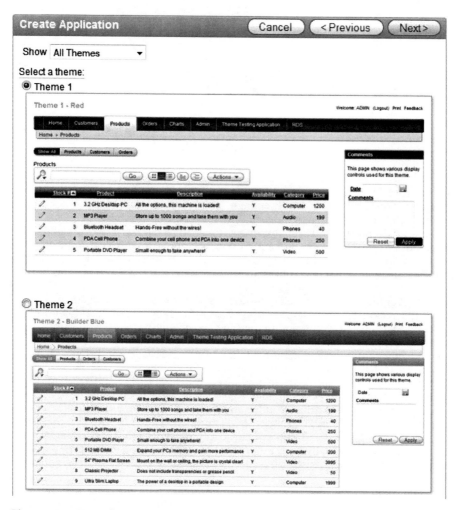

Figure 10-1. Two of APEX 4.0's 20 built-in themes

More often than not, developers tend to choose one of the built-in themes and make a few minor changes to it. They then use this slightly altered theme throughout all of their applications.

An APEX application can contain one or more themes. However, only one theme can be set to the current or active theme per application. Changing the current theme can be achieved only at design time by an APEX developer. Users of an application cannot elect to change themes during runtime. Although this is a limitation, it is unlikely that you will need more than one theme per application.

Associating a Theme with an Application

When creating an application, you have the following two ways to select which theme to associate with it:

- Copy a shared component from another application. Copying a theme from a shared component will create a copy of a theme from another application. The application that you are copying a theme from must also be in your workspace.

- Select a built-in theme. Creating a theme from a built-in theme will take a copy of one of the predefined themes and place it in your application.

If you want to create and reuse a single, consistent theme, you may want to consider using subscriptions, which are discussed in the "Template Subscriptions" section later in this chapter.

Copying a Theme

If you elect to copy a theme from another application, select Yes when prompted to Copy Shared Components from Another Application, and then select User Interface Themes, as shown in Figure 10-2.

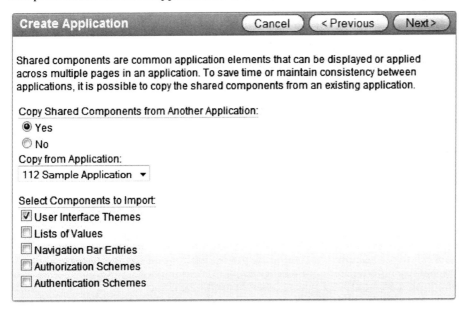

Figure 10-2. Copying a theme

On the next screen, you can select which theme to copy (if the application contains more than one) and whether to validate the theme, as shown in Figure 10-3. Validating the theme will inspect it to ensure that all template classes have been defined. Your choice of whether or not to validate the theme depends on how many and which types of templates you need.

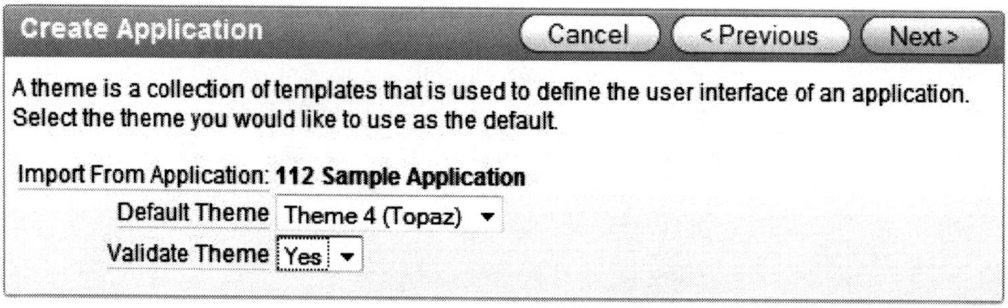

Figure 10-3. Selecting a default theme and validation rule

Choosing a Prebuilt Theme

If you choose to use a prebuilt theme, you will be prompted to select one of the 20 themes before completing the application-creation wizard.

When you choose a built-in theme, a copy of that theme will be added to your application. Any changes or modifications that you make to the templates in that theme will not be propagated back to the master copy of that theme. Thus, feel free to experiment with altering the templates of the built-in themes, as you can easily restore a clean copy of the original theme. You will always get a clean copy of a theme when adding it to your application.

■ **Note** In APEX 4.0, you can customize themes and add them to the available themes list.

Viewing Theme Details and Reports

Developers can control two major sections of a theme: the theme defaults and the associated templates. It may not be obvious that two different components of themes exist, as the default view for themes is set to Icons. In this view, shown in Figure 10-4, it is only possible to edit the associated templates that make up a theme. You will need to change to the Details view, as shown in Figure 10-5, in order to modify the default templates and other attributes of a theme.

Figure 10-4. The Icons view of themes in an application

Figure 10-5. The Details view of themes in an application

Once the report is switched to the Details view, clicking the name of the theme will display the theme defaults. Clicking the magnifying glass will display the templates that make up the theme. Not all of the template types are shown in the default report. If you click the Select Columns option under the Actions button, you can decide which template counts to add to the report as shown in Figure 10-6.

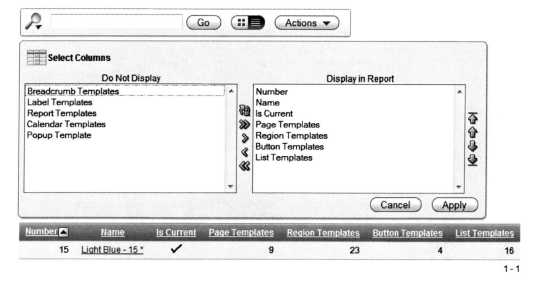

Figure 10-6. Modifying the templage count report for a theme.

Clicking the Reports tab allows you to see theme reports. The term *theme reports* is a bit misleading, as most of these reports focus on the contents of templates rather than the attributes of themes. Most theme reports can be applied to one specific theme or all themes in a given application.

Application Templates Report

The Application Templates report simply lists each template associated with a specific theme or with all themes in your application. Clicking any of the template names will bring you to the Template Details page, where you can make changes to the individual templates.

Theme Template Counts Report

Each template has the following two major attributes:

- The *template* column refers to the type of component that the template is used for (page, region, report, and so on).

- The *class* maps the template to common uses.

You'll learn more about template types and classes in the "Understanding Template Types and Classes" section later in this chapter.

The Theme Template Counts report displays every possible iteration of template types and classes with a count of each. If the Show Custom check box is checked, the report will also include all of the custom classes. None of the APEX built-in themes contain any templates associated with a "custom" class, so expect to see a 0 for the Template Count for any template that starts with "Custom" when viewing a report for a built-in theme.

File References Report

The File References report is aimed at making it easy to discern which files are referenced throughout the templates, shared components, and page components of an application. It allows the developer to search for a number of commonly used file extensions (`.gif`, `.jpeg`/`.jpg`, `.png`, `.js`, `.ico`, `.swf`, and `.css`) and identify which template, shared component, and/or page component references those types of files.

Files can be displayed with or without context.

Without Context: Only the file name and image are displayed. This will produce a list of distinct files used in your theme or themes. This option is useful for when you are moving an application from one server to another and need to also include all of the supporting files.

With Context: The component, theme, component name, and page are also displayed. This option will provide you with more details about each item. It is useful for locating or understanding where in an application a given file is referenced. This option could be used when you are considering removing an image and want to see which pages will be impacted, for example.

When using either option of this report, there is one thing to consider: it will not identify any files of any type that are generated as a result of a named PL/SQL program unit. You will need to search for files in your named PL/SQL program units—packages, procedures, and functions—separately.

Class References Report

The Class References report functions in almost the exact same manner as the File References report does, but locates Cascading Style Sheet (CSS) class references as opposed to file references.

As with the File References report, the Class References report does not search any named PL/SQL objects for CSS class definitions. It also does not search any CSS files that may be in the file system of the Apache webserver (if you are using a separate HTTP server).

This report searches for and identifies CSS classes, not the template classes that were previously mentioned. They are two very different and distinct constructs.

Template Substitution Strings Report

The Template Substitution Strings report will identify all possible, probable, and actual usages of substitution strings found in a given theme's templates. This report has limited practical use, as it attempts to combine possible values with actual values, and when used with the built-in themes, contains a lot of repetitive data.

Performing Theme Tasks

Situated on the right side of the Themes page is a group of tasks that can be performed on themes, as shown in Figure 10-7. Most of the theme tasks are self-explanatory.

Figure 10-7. Theme tasks

    Two of the tasks worth a bit of explanation are Import Theme and Export Theme. Themes, much like applications, can be exported and imported from one APEX application to another.

    Exporting a theme produces a SQL script that will contain all of the APEX API calls required in order to reconstruct the theme. When imported into a different APEX application, this file will run and rebuild the theme in that application. The file will not contain any of the CSS, JavaScript, or images in the file system that the theme references. If you are moving the theme to another instance of APEX, you will need to move any associated files in the file system or database separately.

    If you open the resulting SQL script that is exported and peruse through it, you will see the raw HTML that is used in the templates. Never edit and then import this file unless directed to do so by Oracle Support, as one typo can bring your entire application to a screeching and unpleasant halt.

Defining Theme Attributes

Themes have a few attributes that a developer can define during design time. Most of these attributes have to do with which template is mapped to which component.

    To access the attributes of a theme, simply click the name of a theme. You'll see a page with four sections: Name, Component Defaults, Region Defaults, and Calendar Icon Details.

Name

The simplest of the theme attributes, Name allows you to change the name of your theme. Only developers will see the name of a theme; end users will not see this value anywhere in an APEX application.

Component Defaults

The Component Defaults section, shown in Figure 10-8, allows you to specify a default template when new components are added to your application via the APEX wizards. Defaults that are assigned to APEX components can always be overridden when creating or modifying components in the Application Builder.

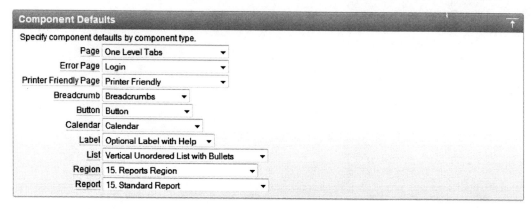

Figure 10-8. Mapping templates to components

Region Defaults

Similar to Component Defaults, the Region Defaults section, shown in Figure 10-9, allows you to specify which region templates to use when creating regions with the APEX wizards.

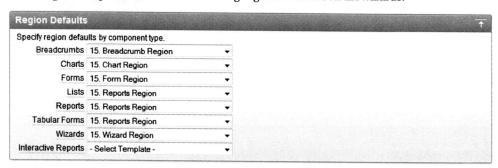

Figure 10-9. Specifying default region templates

APEX themes will have at least one region for each type of page component: report, form, chart, calendar, and so on. While this approach gives you maximum flexibility for your template design, it can add unnecessary complexity and actually make your application's user interface harder to manage.

In most applications, there is no difference between the appearances of region templates for charts, reports, forms, and calendars. In fact, you can assign the Chart Region template to a Form region and vice versa. No validations are performed when assigning templates to regions. Thus, there is little reason to have four separate templates—one for each component type. In fact, having four templates makes managing your templates four times as difficult.

You can consolidate even further by removing rarely used region templates from your theme. Some of the less popular region themes include all of the Alternative 1 regions, both Button regions, the Bracketed region, and both Wizard regions. See the "Removing Unused Templates" section later in this chapter for the case for getting rid of unused templates.

Calendar Icon Details

The Calendar Icon Details attribute allows you to change the default icon used when rendering a date-picker item. By default, the date picker will look something similar to the one shown in Figure 10-10 (results will vary based on which theme you use).

Figure 10-10. The default date picker

This option allows you to override the standard icon and use a custom image to represent a date picker. While this option is rarely used, it is nice to know that it does exist and where to find it.

Switching Themes

You can change or switch the current theme of your application at design time. In order to switch themes, the following two criteria must be met:

- You must have at least two themes installed in your application.

- The source theme must contain templates that correspond to the class of the templates in the target theme.

The first criterion is self-explanatory—without another theme, there is nothing to switch to. The second criterion means that both themes must contain corresponding classes in order to be "switchable." See the "Understanding Template Types and Classes" section later in the chapter for more information about template classes.

Templates

Almost every component in APEX has an associated template. The template's function is to provide the user interface for a specific component type when pages are rendered. Templates are mostly HTML, but also contain template-specific substitution strings or tokens that, during runtime, will be replaced with another template or the contents of its associated component. Templates may also contain references to static files, such as images, CSS files, and JavaScript libraries.

Removing Unused Templates

Most applications need only one or two of each template type. Keeping a large number of templates for each component type will only lead to inconsistencies, as developers will select templates that they feel look good rather than keeping to a standard. If there are only two region templates to choose from, for instance, the chance that a developer selects the proper one is 50%, versus a 10% chance when there are ten. By employing the "less is more" concept here, you can remove most of the templates from your theme, which will make your application look and feel more consistent from page to page.

Removing unnecessary templates also makes it easier to manage a theme. By default, APEX themes can have almost 70 templates. Thus, taking some time to remove what you do not think you will need will ultimately help keep your applications easier to manage.

You can use the reports on the Templates and Utilization subtabs, as described in the next section, to determine which templates are not being referenced in a specific application. Using this approach, you can trim the fat off your themes.

If you delete a template and want to get it back, you can simply create a new application based on the same built-in theme and copy it from there.

Viewing Template Information

When you click the magnifying glass next to the name of a theme (see Figure 10-4), you are technically now in the templates section of the APEX shared components. You will see a list of templates, in a report format, which correspond to the theme that you were just viewing. This page has four subtabs: Templates, Utilization, Subscriptions, and History.

Templates Subtab: Template Lists, Previews, and Tasks

By default, the Templates subtab, shown in Figure 10-11, lists only templates for the theme that you are viewing. By using the Theme select list, you can select a different theme (if one exists) or see all templates associated with any theme in your application.

	Template Name			Since	- All - ▾	
	Theme	- All - ▾		Referenced	All Templates ▾	
	Type	Page ▾		Subscribed	All Templates ▾	(Go)

Type	Name	References	Updated	Updated By	Subscribed	Default	Theme	Preview	Copy
Page	Login	2	5 weeks ago	tgf	-	-	15	▣	▢
	No Tabs	0	5 weeks ago	tgf	-	-	15	▣	▢
	No Tabs With Sidebar	0	5 weeks ago	tgf	-	-	15	▣	▢
	One Level Tabs	1	5 weeks ago	tgf	-	✓	15	▣	▢
	One Level Tabs with Sidebar	0	5 weeks ago	tgf	-	-	15	▣	▢
	Popup	0	5 weeks ago	tgf	-	-	15	▣	▢
	Printer Friendly	1	5 weeks ago	tgf	-	-	15	▣	▢
	Two Level Tabs	1	5 weeks ago	tgf	-	-	15	▣	▢
	Two Level Tabs with Side Bar	0	5 weeks ago	tgf	-	-	15	▣	▢
								row(s) 1 - 9 of 9	

Figure 10-11. The Templates subtab displaying only page templates. The default page template is indicated with a check mark.

You can further refine the report with the Show select list, which lets you select a template type. This select list will filter the report based on a specific template type: page, region, label, list, popup list of values, calendar, breadcrumb, button, or report. Using the Show select list comes in quite handy when editing a single type of template.

Another filter is the Referenced select list, which has three choices: All Templates, Templates Referenced, or Templates Not Referenced. This filter is particularly useful when determining which templates can be removed from your theme without impacting any existing pages.

Regardless of the filter settings, you can do one of three things with any template: preview it by clicking the stoplight icon, edit it by clicking its name, or copy it by clicking the copy icon.

Template Previews

Page, region, and report templates have an additional option: Preview. Clicking the preview icon, which will be available for only these three template types, will display a rough preview of what that template will look like when rendered in your application. This preview is intended to illustrate the structure of a template, rather than show exactly how it will appear in an application. There is no way to see how a template will really look aside from actually running it in an application.

The page template preview will give you an understanding of how the core structure of the page is designed by rendering all of the substitution strings and region positions found in a given page template. It will also attempt to lay out these items in the same way that the actual page template will place them. Some user interface components will be included, but most will not. Figure 10-12 shows an example of a Two Level Tabs Page template.

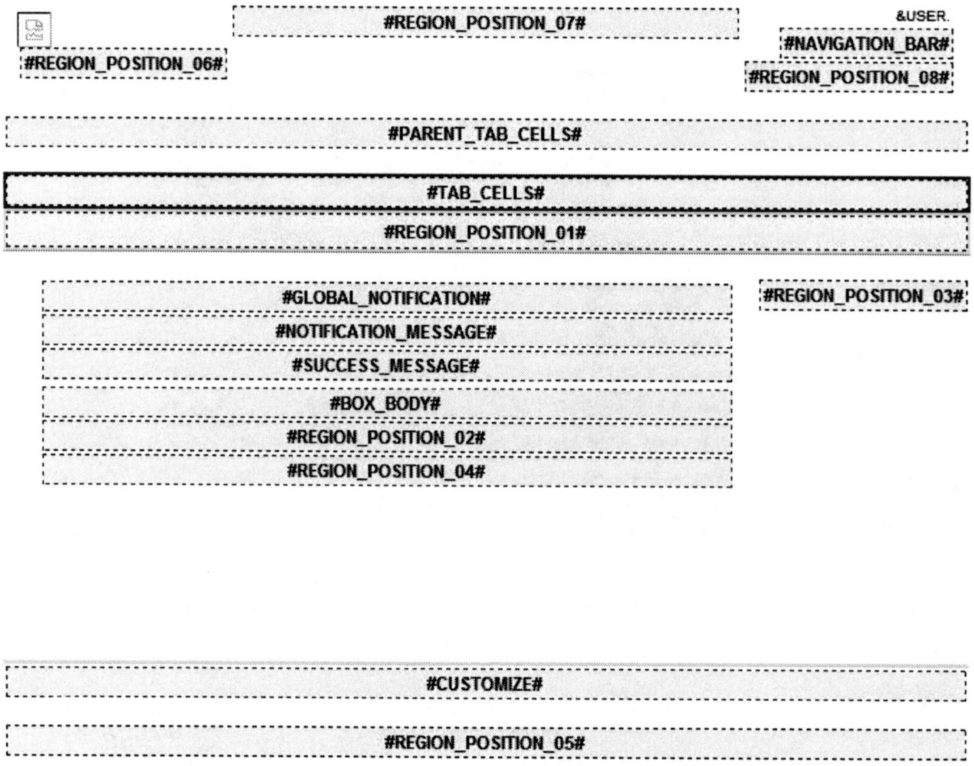

Figure 10-12. The preview of the Two Level Tabs Page template from Theme 12

Region template previews will render more information about a specific region template, but offer an even cruder view of how the template will look. In addition to the Title and Body tokens, each button position will be rendered as part of the preview. Immediately following the visual preview, a list of substitution strings and whether or not they are referenced is displayed. This list will give you a quick summary as to which button positions are referenced in the region template. Finally, the actual source of the region template is displayed on the page in a read-only fashion. Figure 10-13 shows an example of a Form Region template.

Template

```
Region TitleClosePreviousNextDeleteEditChangeCreateCreate2ExpandCopyHelp
Region Body
```

Template Substitution String References

Substitution	Referenced	From	Description
#TITLE#	Yes	Template	Region Title
#EDIT#	Yes	Template	Edit Button
#EXPAND#	Yes	Template	Expand Button
#CREATE#	Yes	Template	Create Button
#CREATE2#	Yes	Template	Create2 Button
#CLOSE#	Yes	Template	Close Button
#BODY#	Yes	Template	Region Body
#SUB_REGION_HEADERS#	No		Sub Region Headers
#SUB_REGIONS#	No		Sub Regions
#FORM_OPEN#	No		HTML Form Open
#FORM_CLOSE#	No		HTML Form Close
#HELP#	Yes	Template	Help Button
#DELETE#	Yes	Template	Delete Button
#COPY#	Yes	Template	Copy Button
#NEXT#	Yes	Template	Next Button
#PREVIOUS#	Yes	Template	Previous Button
#CHANGE#	Yes	Template	Change Button

Figure 10-13. The preview of the Form Region template from Theme 12

The report preview is perhaps the roughest of the bunch. Aside from where the report template is based on named or generic columns, only the core structure of how a report template will render is provided. Each preview uses only four columns when constructing the preview. As rough as this preview may be, it does give you an idea of the basic underlying table structure of a report template. Figure 10-14 shows an example of a Standard Report template preview.

Template Details

Name	Standard
Type	GENERIC_COLUMNS

Template Preview

COL1	COL2	COL3	COL4
1	[...]	[...]	23-OCT-07
2	[...]	[...]	23-OCT-07
3	[...]	[...]	23-OCT-07
4	[...]	[...]	23-OCT-07
5	[...]	[...]	23-OCT-07
6	[...]	[...]	23-OCT-07

Figure 10-14. The preview of the Standard Report template from Theme 12

Template Tasks

The Templates subtab also displays the Tasks region (it does not appear on the Utilization, Subscription, Publish or History subtabs), as shown in Figure 10-15. The Theme Reports option, will take you back to the associated reports for a given theme.

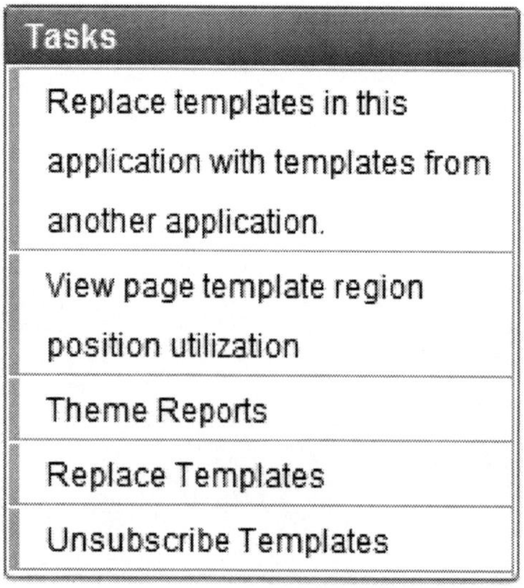

Figure 10-15. *Template tasks*

The other tasks are a bit more complex. "Replace templates in this application with templates from another application" does, well, just that. Instead of switching an entire theme, you may need to copy over some individual templates from one application to another. This item will facilitate such a copy. First, you will need to select the application from which you want to copy templates. Next, you can map which templates will be replaced with the new selections. Templates can simply be copied over or copied over and subscribed to (see the "Template Subscriptions" section later in this chapter).

The "View page template region position utilization" option displays a report of which region positions contain content based on page templates.

Utilization Subtab: Viewing Template References

The Utilization subtab, shown in Figure 10-16, gives you a slightly more detailed, but inconsistent, view of which templates are being used in your application. If a template is being referenced in your application, this subtab will display a count of how many times it is referenced. Some template types will provide a link to the page where the template is used; others will not. You can get a better view of which templates are being referenced from the Templates subtab.

Figure 10-16. *The Utilization report for page templates*

Subscriptions Subtab: Viewing Template Subscriptions

The Subscriptions subtab, shown in Figure 10-17, contains a report of which templates are subscribed from another application. Any or all subscriptions can be refreshed from this report by checking the corresponding template and clicking the Refresh Checked button. Subscriptions are discussed in more detail in the "Templates Subscriptions" section later in this chapter.

	Application	Type	Template	Copied From
☐	401	Page	Copy of Two Level Tabs with Side Bar	Application 400, Two Level Tabs with Side Bar
☐	401	Page	Copy of Login	Application 400, Login
☐	401	Page	Copy of No Tabs	Application 400, No Tabs
☐	401	Page	Copy of No Tabs with Side Bar	Application 400, No Tabs with Side Bar
☐	401	Page	Copy of One Level Tabs	Application 400, One Level Tabs
☐	401	Page	Copy of One Level Tabs with Side Bar	Application 400, One Level Tabs with Side Bar
☐	401	Page	Copy of Popup	Application 400, Popup
☐	401	Page	Copy of Printer Friendly	Application 400, Printer Friendly
☐	401	Page	Copy of Two Level Tabs	Application 400, Two Level Tabs

Figure 10-17. *The Subscription report for templates*

History Subtab: Viewing Historical Changes

For a historical view of who made the most recent modification to either page or region templates, take a look at the History subtab, shown in Figure 10-18. Historical changes for templates of other types are not tracked by APEX. This report will show only the last person to edit a specific template and how long ago that change occurred; specific changes and multiple edits are not tracked by APEX.

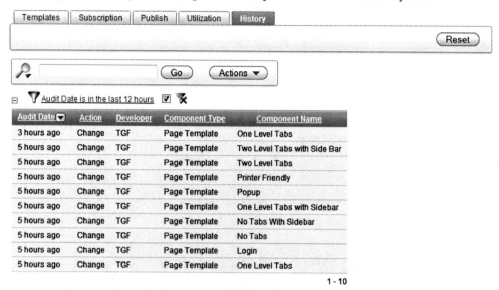

Figure 10-18. Recently updated page templates shown on the History subtab

Understanding Template Types and Classes

Templates themselves have two major attributes: types and classes. The *type* of a template refers to which APEX component it applies. When a template is created, the first option is to select the type. Currently you can choose from nine template types: page, region, report, label, list, button, breadcrumb, calendar, and popup. These are described in the "Choosing a Template Type" section later in this chapter. You cannot alter the type once the template is created, as the components of one type do not necessarily match those or another. For example, a page template makes up the structure of a page, whereas a breadcrumb template makes up the structure of a breadcrumb region, and thus the two cannot be interchanged.

Template *classes* are related to the template type. Each type has a predefined set of classes. Unlike types, classes can be changed after the template is created. Template classes are in no way whatsoever related to CSS classes.

The idea behind template classes is to streamline the ability to switch themes. If you have a region whose class is set to Report Region, then ideally, you would map it to a region of the same class in the destination theme when switching themes. Aside from mapping templates from one theme to another, template classes have little practical use. In fact, they can actually introduce some confusion.

As explained earlier, it is a good idea to delete any templates that you do not need. For example, if you have a region template whose class is set to Form Region, that region template can be associated with any type of region in APEX: form, chart, calendar, or otherwise. No validations or checks based on the template class occur when specifying a region's template.

Managing Template Files

Most templates will contain a mix of HTML and references to static files. Images and CSS files are used to create the user interface of an application. JavaScript libraries enhance the functionality. It is important to understand how each type of file is used and the best practices for managing them.

Images

In APEX, it is possible to upload and store images or CSS files in the database. While this method is convenient and simplifies deployment, it is not recommended in many cases, as it will potentially degrade the overall performance of your applications. If you are using the Embedded PL/SQL Gateway, the easiest way to handle images is to store them in the database. You can use the filesystem of the database server to store images, but you would have to build a custom PL/SQL procedure to access them.

When an image is uploaded to the database, it is stored as a Binary Large Object (BLOB) in a shared table called `WWV_FLOW_IMAGE_REPOSITORY`. This table is segmented so that files are secured from other workspaces. When accessing a file from this table, you can use either the `#WORKSPACE_IMAGE#` or `#APPLICATION_IMAGES#` syntax, depending on how the image was uploaded. When your page renders, APEX will translate either of those tokens with a call to the APEX function `wwv_flow_file_mgr.get_file`. This, in turn, will query the database for your file and then send it over the network to the client.

Images can be classified into two types based on their usage: template images and content, or "transactional," images. The type of images is based on how it is used; APEX makes no distinction between the two. Template images are those that make up the actual template of an application. Tab corners, logos, and images used to construct the borders of a region are good examples. Content images are those that are associated with an item in your data. A picture of a product is an excellent example of a content image.

Content images can be stored in the database, and in some cases, this is a better solution. This is because content images are not rendered on every page of an application; they are rendered only when requested. Think of a web site based on a catalog of music. Content images are rendered only as each user searches for different types of music and views album artwork. You will (or at least should) never have a single page that always renders all content images.

There is no simple metric that you can inspect to determine where to store content images. You can consider a number of variables, and then make an educated decision. If you anticipate a very high volume of transactions, you may want to consider storing your content images in the file system and storing a pointer to the corresponding image in the database. If a good portion of your target audience is connected via slower connections, the file system makes more sense as well, as each client will cache your images, so in the case of a repeat request, it will not need to query the database and send the image again.

On the other hand, if you anticipate a lower volume of transactions, and want to simplify the overall management of your site, you may opt to store content images in the database. This way, you will not need to rely on a system administrator to grant you access to the HTTP server. Also, when the DBA backs up your schema, all of the content images will also get backed up.

As an example, let's assume that you use a small image to make up the right corner of a noncurrent tab. Let's also assume that your application has five tabs, any four of which can be noncurrent. Thus, for each page in your application, you will need to render this image four times. If you have 100 users using your application, each with 20 page views, the procedure that calls the tab image stored in the database will be executed 8,000 times per day! (100 users × 20 page views × 4 tabs per page). A single week will yield 40,000 calls to the same procedure for the same image. Now what if you have a different image for the left side of a tab? Double the calls to the same procedure, for a new total of 80,000 executions per week—just for the tab images!

Still assuming that you get 2,000 page views per day, and adding the assumption that each tab image is 2KB to the equation, you will generate about an additional 16MB of network traffic per day, or almost 80MB per week! (2,000 page views × 4 tab images × 2KB each image). And again, this is just to render the tabs.

As if this isn't bad enough, the URL format that APEX uses with images stored in the database is executed as if it were a call to a procedure each time it is encountered. If we leave the browser to its own devices, it will never refer to its local image cache before pulling the image from the server for images stored in the database. For more details on static file storage, see the "Image, CSS, and JavaScript Storage" section coming up shortly.

■ **Note** Tyler Muth's blog describes a way around the image caching issue. If you believe that the lack of image caching is causing issues in your system, by all means check out his blog entry at

`http://tylermuth.wordpress.com/2008/02/04/image-caching-in-plsql-applications/`

Cascading Style Sheets

While HTML controls the structure of a page, CSS files are often used to control the user interface or style of a page. Think of HTML as the foundation, frames, and drywall, and CSS as the paint, trim, and carpeting.

It is a good idea to keep all styles in CSS files, and rely on HTML only for the core structure of a template. This will provide a few advantages. First, it will keep your HTML lean and easy to read. This will aid in the overall manageability of your applications. Second, keeping all style definitions in a CSS file is more efficient. Styles need to be defined in only a single place, and if a change is required, it can be quickly and immediately applied.

But perhaps the most important reason to put all style definitions in a CSS file is for Section 508 compliance. In the United States, the Rehabilitation Act was amended in 1998 to ensure that those with limited or no vision can still use computers as effectively as others. In a nutshell, this means that any web application needs to adhere to a set of standards that make it compatible with either high-contrast colors and large fonts and/or screen readers.

In either case, the necessary modifications require the separation of the structure of the user interface and the style. Thus, if you use CSS files to control the style, your application will be easier to make compliant with Section 508.

JavaScript Libraries

You may include JavaScript with an APEX application in a number of places: in a page header, as a static or dynamic region on a page, or in a static file referenced as part of the template. Typically, JavaScript libraries contain a number of functions that a developer can refer to from an APEX page, component, or item.

■ **Note** Including JavaScript libraries as part of a page template is a common practice that is not limited to just APEX. These libraries can help extend the functionality of your application by providing more interactive controls to the end user.

All APEX pages will automatically include five built-in JavaScript libraries: apex_4_0.js, apex_legacy_4_0.js, apex_widget_4_0.js, apex_dynamic_actions_4_0.js, and jquery-ui-1.8.custom.min.js. These libraries contain a number of prebuilt functions that are used in APEX itself, as well as in applications created by APEX. While most of these functions are undocumented, there are plans to provide more documentation in a future release of APEX. Should you wish to take advantage of some of these functions, it may be a good idea to copy them to a custom directory and then refer to them there. This will ensure that when the next release of APEX is applied and some of the functions are changed or removed, your applications will not be impacted.

Image, CSS, and JavaScript Storage

To investigate the impact of where files were stored, we created a simple APEX application with five tabs and pages, using Theme 12. We then copied this to a new application, where all references to the tab images stored in the file system were replaced with references to the exact same images stored in the database as shared components. Using Mozilla Firefox with the Firebug extension (www.getfirebug.com), we loaded each page with image timings enabled.

We performed the first test with the application whose images were stored in the database. The total time to render these images was 152 milliseconds (ms), as shown in Figure 10-19. What is more important to note is that only 2KB out of 8KB, or 25% of the images used, were retrieved from the cache. A full 75%, or 6KB, were retrieved from the database server. Of the 2KB retrieved from the cache, neither file was part of the changes we made to the templates—e.gif is the embedded edit link, and is burned into APEX, and ParentTabBase.gif is referred to in the associated CSS file.

■ **Note** In Firebug, light-gray bars indicate that the image was retrieved from the cache. Dark gray bars indicate that the image had to be retrieved from the server. See the "Tools for Working with Templates" section later in this chapter for more information about Firebug.

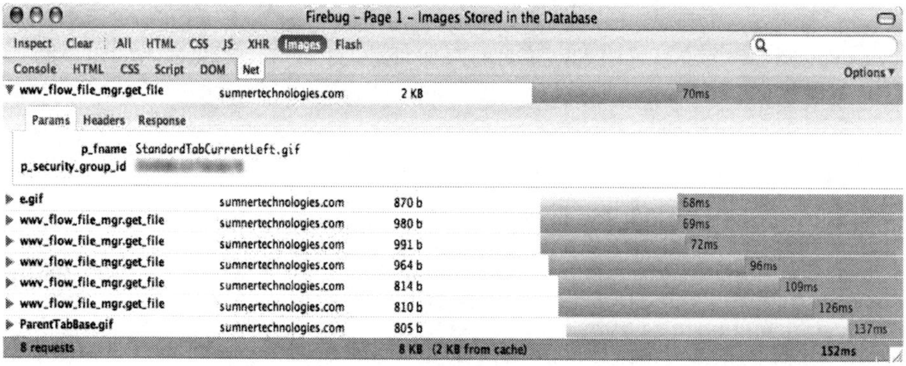

Figure 10-19. The results of loading templates images stored in the database

When we ran the same test on the application that stored its images in the file system, it took only 139 ms to render the images, as shown in Figure 10-20. In the grand scheme of things, this does not represent a significant savings. However, 100% of the images used were retrieved from the image cache! Not a single round-trip to the HTTP server or call to the database was necessary to render the images. This cost savings are drastic when the results are scaled up to more complex pages and/or more page views.

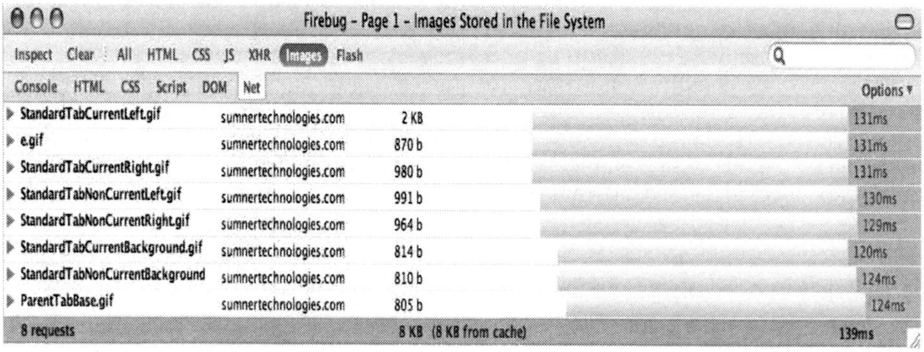

Figure 10-20. The results of loading templates images stored in the file system

The moral to this story is to put all images, CSS files, and JavaScript libraries that will be referred to frequently in the file system. The performance gain is far worth any extra effort required to manage these files.

Despite the obvious gains, there is one drawback to storing files—particularly CSS and JavaScript libraries—on the file system. When a change to a file is made, a browser may not immediately see that change, as it will refer to the cached version instead. In order to prevent this, you may want to append a version number to your CSS and JavaScript files. Each time you make a change to the file, change the name of the file to reflect a new version. This way, when a change is made, the browser will see a completely new file and always pull it from the server rather than use a cached version.

It is clear that storing files in the file system of the HTTP server is much more efficient than storing them in the database. But where on the HTTP server should these files be stored? One place that they should not be stored is the APEX images directory, commonly aliased as /i/. The files in /i/ are controlled by Oracle, and they can change or be renamed at any time. For example, suppose that you created a new CSS file called main.css and put it in the virtual directory /i/. Now suppose that Oracle releases the next version of APEX, and has decided to rename one of its CSS files to main.css. During the upgrade, you simply copy over the new images directory. All of a sudden, main.css is a completely different file, and your version is lost forever.

While copying your own files to /i/ is bad, referring to images, CSS files, or even JavaScript in /i/ can be equally as dangerous. If you have taken the time to examine the contents of the /i/ directory, you will have seen that it contains a wealth of images and JavaScript libraries. You may even be using some of these images and/or JavaScript libraries in your own applications. The danger in that is that if Oracle decides to change the contents of an image or JavaScript file, your application will also unintentionally change as well.

The recommended best practice for storing CSS, JavaScript, and images on the HTTP server is to use a completely different physical and virtual path. This way, your custom directory will be completely isolated from any changes that Oracle may decide to make, ensuring the integrity of your contents.

In keeping with APEX's tradition of simplicity, create a virtual directory called /c/, map that to a physical location on the HTTP server, and then upload your content there. Creating a new virtual directory is quite simple. All you need to do is add a single line to the httpd.conf file and restart the Apache server. For example, if you wanted to alias /c/ to the physical path /usr/local/custom_images, you would add the following line to your httpd.conf file and then restart Apache:

```
alias /c/ "/usr/local/custom_images/"
```

As simple and safe as this process is, you will typically run into resistance when you ask the system administrator to actually do it. Most system administrators don't like the idea of giving anyone access to anything. Thus, your challenge will be to convince the administrator that all you need is an operating system user that can read and write to a single directory, and do nothing else. Explain the savings in bandwidth that will be realized by moving images to the file system, citing the previously mentioned examples. Get the DBA's support, and approach the system administrator together as a united front. And if all else fails, find out her favorite restaurant, coffee spot, or retail store and include a gift card with your request.

Template Source

The template source is where you can put everything together to make up your user interface. Images, CSS files, JavaScript libraries, and HTML are all molded into a single place in the template itself. In addition to referencing content in the file system, all templates have a number of substitution strings or tokens that can also be embedded in the template source.

There is nothing special or proprietary about the HTML used in APEX templates. In fact, it may help you understand how templates are structured if you copy and paste the source of a template into an HTML editor. This will show you a rough representation of how the template will look when rendered in APEX.

Choosing a Template Type

Each template type is structured differently, based on its function. A button template, for instance, is much simpler than a page template. Here, we will examine each template type and describe some of the more common tokens used.

Breadcrumb Templates

Breadcrumbs were formerly called *menus* in previous versions of APEX. They are typically found at the top of the page and help facilitate navigation. Their name is derived from the Brothers Grimm fable *Hansel and Gretel*, where the main characters leave a trail of breadcrumbs to mark their way back home. Unlike the ones in the aforementioned fable, birds will typically not eat APEX breadcrumbs, so you can feel quite confident when using them in your application.

Breadcrumbs can be either current or noncurrent, and the structure of the template reflects that. The template provides attributes for some HTML to open and close the breadcrumb. Finally, there is a place to define which character or characters will be used to separate the breadcrumbs.

Most of the APEX themes will enclose the breadcrumb in a DIV region, thus using <div> for the region Before First attribute and </div> for the After Last attribute. If you are not comfortable with this approach, you could opt to use <table><tr> and </tr></table> in lieu of DIVs. Just remember to enclose the breadcrumb entry in a <td> and </td> if you elect to use HTML tables.

Although it is rare, sometimes a template will allow you to specify how an APEX component behaves. In the breadcrumb template, the Maximum Levels attribute is an example of this. Once the breadcrumb has expanded to this level, no additional levels will be rendered, no matter what. It is a good idea to keep this value artificially high, so you never accidentally run into this limitation.

In theory, the breadcrumb link attributes should render inside an anchor tag. However, it seems as if this functionality does not quite work. If you do need to define attributes of an anchor tag, you can simply do so directly in-line in the Current Page or Non-Current Page Breadcrumb Entry attribute.

#NAME# and #LINK# are the most commonly used tokens with breadcrumbs. Alternatively, you can also reference #LONG_NAME# to render the long name, as per the breadcrumb entry definition.

Button Templates

APEX supports three types of buttons: HTML, image, and template. It is best to create and stick to a single button template in your applications. HTML buttons will look different on different browsers and different operating systems, as illustrated in Figure 10-21. Using them will produce slightly different-looking user interfaces for each operating system and browser combination that your user base has. This can cause some pages to look different from how they were intended to appear and lead to confusion.

Figure 10-21. The same HTML button rendered in Internet Explorer 8, Firefox for Windows, Firefox for Linux

Using image buttons as your default button type should also be discouraged. Not only will they generate additional overhead that needs to be sent to each client, but they are also difficult to maintain. For example, if you have a button called "Save Changes" and want to change it to Apply Changes, you will need to re-create the image and upload it to the server. Any image that contains words is also not Section 508-compliant unless it has a corresponding title tag, so use image buttons with discretion.

Template-based buttons give you the best of both worlds. You can use CSS to create an attractive-looking button and also retain full control over what it says, changing it as often as you like. Creating a template-based button is quite straightforward, as it is the simplest type of template. You can change only a single region for a template-based button. Like breadcrumbs, buttons can be either DIV-based or table-based.

The #LINK# and #LABEL# tokens are the most important to note with buttons. #LINK# will be substituted to the button's corresponding link, if it has one. #LABEL# will contain the name of the button, per the APEX definition in your application.

A button template can be as simple as the one shown in Figure 10-22. All of the style for this button is defined in the CSS class called button-gray.

```
button.button-gray {
        background: url(../images/bt-gray-r.png) right no-repeat;
}
```

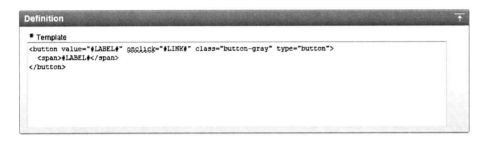

Figure 10-22. *A sample button template*

While all of that may seem like a foreign language, rest assured that a number of CSS editors are available, and they make editing CSS classes a breeze.

Region Templates

Region templates are twice as complex as button templates, meaning that they have two attributes that can be defined: the template itself and the HTML table attributes. Figure 10-23 shows an example of a region template.

```
Definition                                                                    ↑
Template
<table class="t15FormRegion" cellspacing="0"  border="0" summary="layout"
id="#REGION_STATIC_ID#" #REGION_ATTRIBUTES#>
<tr>
<td class="t15RegionHeader">#TITLE#</td>
<td align="right"
class="t15ButtonHolder">#CLOSE##PREVIOUS##NEXT##DELETE##EDIT##CHANGE##CREATE##CREA
TE2##EXPAND##COPY##HELP#</td>
</tr>
<tr class="t15Body">
<td colspan="2" class="t15Body">#BODY#</td>
</tr>
</table>
```

Figure 10-23. *A sample region template*

Region templates must at minimum contain a #BODY# token, which will be substituted with the contents of the region it is associated with: a calendar, report, form, chart, and so on. In addition to the #BODY# token, it is quite common to also incorporate a #TITLE# token in a region template. This will be replaced with the title of the region at runtime.

Most, but not all, regions will also contain a number of button positions. These button positions will be available when creating buttons that are bound to a region position. APEX has several predefined button position names. You cannot add your own to this list. Currently supported button positions are #CLOSE#,#PREVIOUS#,#NEXT#,#DELETE#,#EDIT#,#CHANGE#,#CREATE#,#CREATE2#,#EXPAND#,#COPY#, and #HELP# . Most regions from the APEX built-in themes will include most (or all) of these button positions.

Similar to template classes, the names of button positions do not necessarily need to represent their content. You can have a button called Create and assign it to the #HELP# position, as APEX does not check to see if the purpose of the button and button position match.

To keep things simple, it is not a bad idea to have only a couple button positions, and then rely on the sequences of individual buttons to control how they render on a page. This allows you to control button layout at the page level, rather than at the template level. It also offers more flexibility, as you can sequence buttons differently on a page-by-page basis, all with a single button template.

If you want to control the class of the items within a region, you can define it in the HTML table attributes. This class will then be applied to all items within a specific region.

Label Templates

Continuing with the trend of exponential complexity, label templates are twice as complex as region templates, with a total of four editable attributes. There are a pair of attributes for each label template itself and for the label template that displays when there is an error.

Unlike with button or region templates, you do not need to define a token for the content. There is no #LABEL# token, as APEX will automatically append that between the Before Label and After Label attributes.

Most of the prebuilt APEX themes have four types of label templates: Required, Optional, Required with Help, and Optional with Help. The Required and Optional label templates are the simpler types; clicking them will yield nothing. The Required with Help and Optional with Help label templates will open a pop-up window and display any help associated with their respective item. Figure 10-24 shows an example of a Required with Help label template.

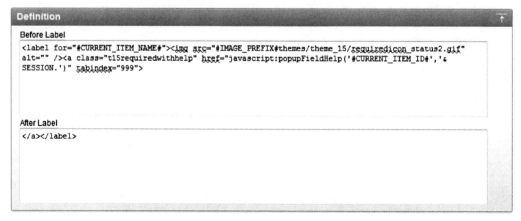

Figure 10-24. A sample Required with Help label template

In any case, it is a good idea to start any label template with the `<label>` tag. This will provide speech-based browsers with a concise label to read, rather than the often-cryptic item name. All item templates from the APEX built-in themes use the `<label>` tag.

For labels that provide item-level help, a JavaScript function is included as part of the template. The JavaScript `popupFieldHelp` function accepts two parameters: the current item ID, which is referred to with the token `#CURRENT_ITEM_ID#`, and the current application session. When called with these two parameters, a pop-up window that contains the item-level help will render.

When a validation throws an error that is associated with an item, the label template will use the On Error Before Label and On Error After Label attributes to render the item in question. The token `#ERROR_MESSAGE#` can be used in these attributes, and will be replaced with the error message of the validation that failed. Most prebuilt label templates simply use a different CSS class for the error attributes to render the label in red or a different color than the standard labels.

List Templates

Lists are one of the more complex templates, with 14 attributes to define. Fortunately, you will rarely need to define more than four or five of these attributes. APEX has the following two types of lists, as illustrated in Figure 10-25:

Flat: The flat list is the simpler of the two. It is nothing more than a list of items that, when rendered, will all be displayed, as long as each list entry's condition resolves to true. Most lists in APEX are flat lists.

Hierarchical: List entries in hierarchical lists are related to one another in a parent-child fashion. This definition is assigned when creating the list entries themselves. There is no setting or option for the list itself to make it a hierarchical list. As soon as the Parent List Entry attribute is set for at least one list entry, the list is considered hierarchical.

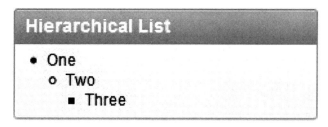

Figure 10-25. A hierarchical list and a flat list

The templates required for flat lists and hierarchical lists will vary. A flat list needs only the Template Definition section defined, whereas a hierarchical list will need both the Template Definition and the Sublist Entry sections defined. The only way to tell for certain which type of list is associated with a template is to edit the list template itself and inspect the Sublist attributes. As mentioned earlier in the chapter, the class of a template is designed to facilitate switching from one theme to another. Classes can be completely arbitrarily assigned and do not necessarily describe the template with which they are associated.

When creating a list, a list template must be associated with it. If the list being created will be hierarchical, be sure to select a hierarchical list template. If you do not, then when your list renders, you will see only the top-level list entries. If you are creating a flat list and select a hierarchical template, you will be OK in most cases, as the top level of the hierarchy is all that you will have defined. You can always override the list template when creating a list region in your application, as shown in Figure 10-26.

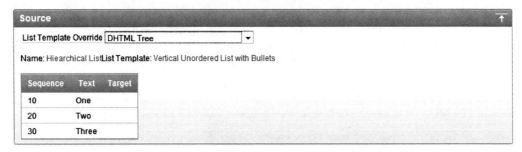

Figure 10-26. *Overriding the default list template when creating a list region*

List templates themselves are quite simple to understand. The list itself is sandwiched between two attributes: List Template Before Rows and List Template After Rows. In most cases, these two attributes are used to open an HTML list or table and then close it. Class definitions for the list itself can be included.

Once the list is opened, each list entry will then be rendered according to its sequence. If a list entry is the current entry, per its Current on Page attribute, then the List Template Current attribute will be used. Otherwise, the list entry will be rendered using the List Template Noncurrent attribute. Often, these two attributes are identical, except that the current entries are bolded. The substitution strings #LINK# and #TEXT# can be used to automatically generate the associated link and name of each list entry.

This is all that needs to be defined for a flat list. All of the remaining attributes for lists have to do with hierarchical lists. The hierarchical list templates included with APEX vary greatly as to how they render. Some will render all list items at once; others employ Dynamic HTML (DHTML) to provide an expand and contract function. In the simpler cases, the additional Subitem attributes are identical to the regular items. Others, such as the DHTML templates, are much more complex. If you need to create your own hierarchical list templates, it's best to begin with a copy of one of the built-in templates and modify that, rather than to start from scratch.

Page Templates

Page templates make up the foundation of the APEX template system. All other templates can map back to some portion of a page template. The three major classifications of page templates in APEX are no tabs, one level of tabs, and two levels of tabs. In addition to these three types, there are also specific page types for the login page and pop-up pages.

Page templates control more than their names may lead you to believe. In addition to storing the basic structure of the page, page templates also control the breadcrumbs, navigation bar, success and notification messages, error page, and both standard and parent tabs. At the bottom of every page template is a report of the associated substitution strings and whether or not they were referenced in this specific template.

The core structure of a page can be subdivided into three parts: the header, body, and footer. The header and body are required elements in a page template. The header portion of the page template is relatively constant in all APEX themes, as it is used to set up the default attributes of an APEX page and little else.

Page Header

The following in an example of a page header:

```
<html lang="&BROWSER_LANGUAGE." xmlns:htmldb="http://htmldb.oracle.com">

<head>
<title>#TITLE#</title>
<link rel="stylesheet" href="#IMAGE_PREFIX#themes/theme_1/theme_V3.css" type=
    "text/css" />
#HEAD#
</head>
<body #ONLOAD#>#FORM_OPEN#
```

The substitution string &BROWSER_LANGUAGE. will be replaced with the current language setting of your application. This tag will inform the browser which language the page will be rendered in so that it can act appropriately. The #TITLE# token will be replaced with the title of the page as defined in the application. Next, the style sheet for the theme is included. #IMAGE_PREFIX# will be replaced with the virtual path to APEX's image directory on the HTTP server. This parameter can be defined at the application level and rarely needs to be altered.

The #HEAD# tag will create a number of references to the required APEX JavaScript libraries and CSS files. If the #HEAD# tag is not included, your application may not function properly.

Inside the <body> tag, the #ONLOAD# token will be replaced with anything defined in a specific page's OnLoad region. Typically, this is used for JavaScript calls that need to execute as the page loads. Finally, #FORM_OPEN#—a required token—will open the HTML form that makes up the APEX page. Omitting #FORM_OPEN# from your page template will cause the loss of much or all of your application's functionality.

Page Body

Next is the body of a page. Technically, all that is required here is the #BOX_BODY# token, which will be replaced with the three fixed regions in APEX, Page Template Body 1 through 3. All of the other tokens are optional, but many are almost always used, as excluding them will limit the functionality of your APEX application.

Page Template Body 1 through 3 are fixed positions, in that they will all render stacked on top of one another. There is no way to alter this behavior. If you need a more flexible layout, you can use APEX's other fixed region positions—#REGION_POSITION_01# through #REGION_POSITION_08#—which can be added anywhere in the body template. Once added to a page template, any region on a page associated with that template can be assigned to these region positions. If only three are referenced in the template, only those three will be available when assigning regions to region positions. Repeating a region position definition in a page template is permitted, but be aware that the content will be rendered in each place the region position is defined in the template.

In the APEX built-in templates, some of the region positions have been assigned to specific purposes. #REGION_POSITION_01# is almost always used for the Breadcrumb region, #REGION_POSITION_02# is used for the Sidebar Content region, and #REGION_POSITION_03# is typically right-justified. If you need to repurpose any of these region positions for other needs, you can safely do so. However, be warned that if you do switch back to an APEX built-in theme, some of the components may not render in their intended positions.

The #LOGO# token will be replaced with a reference to the application's logo, per the application definition. #GLOBAL_NOTIFICATION#, #NOTIFICATION_MESSAGE#, and #SUCCESS_MESSAGE# will be replaced with the site's global notification message, any error messages or validation messages, and success messages, respectively. These three tokens usually appear consecutively in the body region of the page templates. Both the notification message and success message will actually be replaced with their corresponding regions in the page template. This allows the developer to incorporate some additional HTML or CSS references that can enhance the style of how these messages are rendered. For instance, it is common to render the notification message in a red font and the success message in a green font.

The #NAVIGATION_BAR# token will also be replaced with another template definition: Navigation Bar. This region is used to define the characteristics of the navigation bar itself, not each individual entry. When the navigation bar renders, it will replace the token #BAR_BODY# with an instantiation of the Navigation Bar Entry template for each item in the navigation bar. The Navigation Bar Entry template requires both a #LINK# and a #TEXT# token to render the corresponding link and name for each entry. Other tokens that can be used when specifying navigation bar entries include #IMAGE#, #WIDTH#, #HEIGHT#, and #ALT#. It's no coincidence that when defining navigation bar entries, the same attributes are available.

When placing regions on a page, one of the options is in which column to render the region. This allows you to place two regions next to one another, rather than on top of one another. When multiple columns are used, APEX will automatically manage the underlying HTML table structure required. As a developer, you can specify the options of that table in the Region Table attributes, as shown in Figure 10-27. You can specify attributes directly in the table tag, or you can include a class.

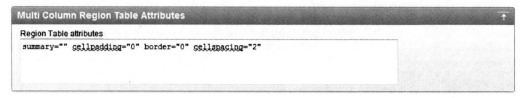

Figure 10-27. Developers can specify the table options for multi-column regions.

Page Tabs

Tabs are also part of the page template. Depending on which classification of page you are using, you will see one, two, or no references to the two tab tokens #PARENT_TAB_CELLS# and #TAB_CELLS#. When rendered, each of these tokens will be replaced with its corresponding current and noncurrent subtemplate entries.

Pages with two levels of tabs will naturally contain both tab tokens. Often, parent tabs are rendered above the standard tabs. Again, this is more of a de facto standard than anything else, and you can change this behavior if desired. However, if you decide to go with an unorthodox tab configuration, you may generate more confusion than its worth. Thus, it is advisable to adhere to this standard, especially for business applications.

Pages with only one level of tabs will contain only the #TAB_CELLS# token. When using one level of tabs, a virtual parent tab set is associated with all of the tabs. There is no need (or way) to render this tab set. Often, the user interface used for one level of tabs will resemble the parent tabs in two-level tab pages.

Pages with no tabs will not contain a reference to either tab token.

The standard and parent tab attributes subtemplates function identically. They differ only in which token they will replace when rendered. Each has two attributes: Current Tab and Non-current Tab. A number of tokens are available for both types of tabs. #TAB_LABEL# and #TAB_LINK# are two of the most common. It is also possible to refer to the image defined at the tab level with #TAB_IMAGE#.

In most cases, the current template will render the tab in a different color and/or style than the remainder of the table. For two levels of tabs, the current tab in the second level is typically bolded, and the noncurrent tabs are not. How to render current and noncurrent tabs is ultimately a decision that will be left up to the developer and/or graphic designer.

Error Page

Another attribute of a page template is the Error Page Template attribute. Each theme can have only a single error page, per the theme attributes, so it is necessary to define this section only for the page template that you designate as the error page. It is a good idea to have a separate page whose exclusive purpose is to serve as an application's error page.

Most of the APEX page templates contain rather Spartan-looking error messages. You will probably want to spend a few minutes to enhance this section to appear a bit more appealing. After all, most users will typically become more anxious when errors occur, so a friendly message with a number to call should ease their anxiety.

You can use the following four tokens in the error template:

#MESSAGE#: When #MESSAGE# renders, it will be replaced with the corresponding error message. It is a good idea to supplement this token with a phone number or contact person so that the user can report the error.

#BACK_LINK#: The #BACK_LINK# token will render a bit of JavaScript that will take the user back one page. #BACK_LINK# should always be included as part of an anchor tag, such as
`<a href="#BACK_LINK#">`.

#OK# and #RETURN_TO_APPLICATION#: These tokens are required only if you are translating your application to more than one language.

Report Templates

The report template is one of the most sophisticated template types in APEX. It is also one of the few template types that contain logic or business rules. Each report in APEX will have an associated report template. Keep in mind that each report is technically an APEX region, and thus will also have a region template associated with it. Think of the region template as the container for the report, and the report template as the rows and columns of the report itself.

You can choose from two main types of report templates: generic column and named column. Generic column report templates can be used for any query. Named column report templates include references to specific columns, and they can be used only with specific reports.

Generic Column Templates

Generic column templates or just column templates are the more common of the two template types. They can be used for any valid SQL report without any special provisions. In fact, all of the report templates that ship with APEX are generic column templates. The term *column template* is also used to describe generic column templates, because all columns will render from the same template.

When using a generic column template, think of it as a layered approach to building the report. First, the outermost layer needs to be defined. Then the definition of each row needs to be defined. Next, the headings are defined, and they typically have a slightly different look than the actual data. Finally, the cell or data elements are defined. You then zoom back out and define how to end each row and the actual table itself. It sounds more complex than it really is. Figure 10-28 shows an example of the Standard Report template from Theme 15. Notice that the Column Heading Template now includes both before and after column templates, new in APEX 4.0, along with the column heading template giving you even more control over the appearance of reports.

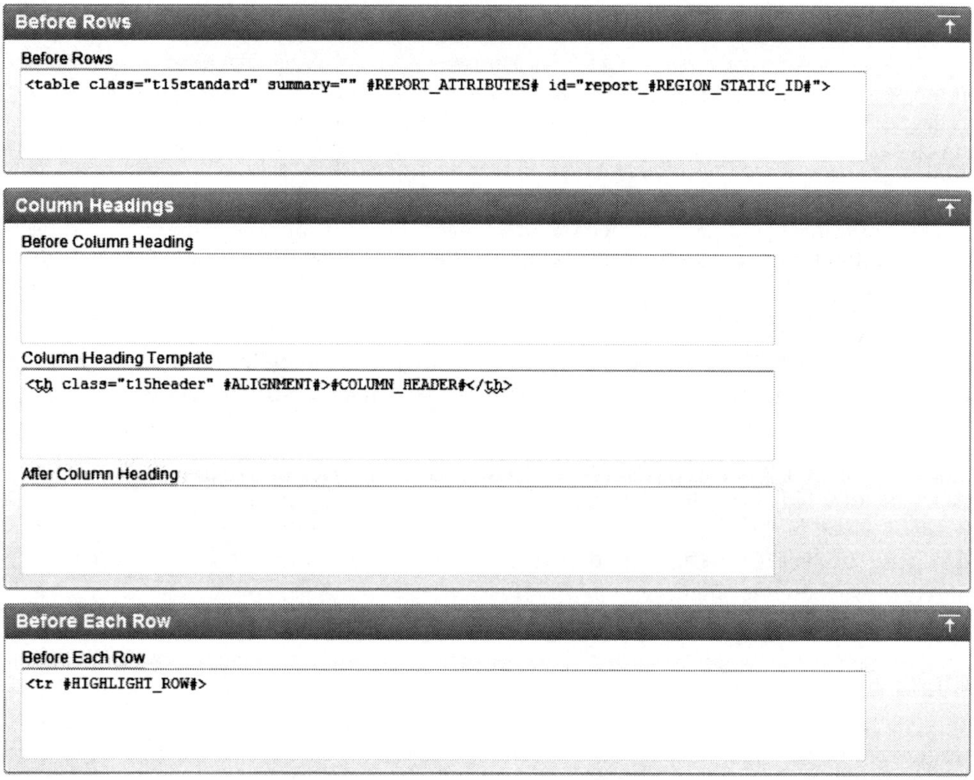

Before Rows

Before Rows

```
<table class="t15standard" summary="" #REPORT_ATTRIBUTES# id="report_#REGION_STATIC_ID#">
```

Column Headings

Before Column Heading

Column Heading Template

```
<th class="t15header" #ALIGNMENT#>#COLUMN_HEADER#</th>
```

After Column Heading

Before Each Row

Before Each Row

```
<tr #HIGHLIGHT_ROW#>
```

Figure 10-28. The Standard Report template from Theme 15

A report template in APEX is actually nothing more than an HTML table with its associated rows and columns, and some substitution strings or tokens. When this report is rendered, it will look something like Figure 10-29.

Buglist

ID	BUGID	REPORTED	STATUS	PRIORITY	DESCRIPTION	REPORTED_BY	ASSIGNED_TO	COST
1	1	27-JAN-06	Open	High	Pressing Cancel on the login screen gives an error	RHuson	John Scott	
2	2	02-JAN-06	Closed	High	Logo occassionally does not appear	CWhite	Peter Ward	
3	3	01-FEB-06	Open	High	Search doesn't return any results when nothing is entered	CWatson	John Scott	
4	4	02-MAR-06	Open	Critical	Login doesn't work for user smithp	LBarnes	Mark Wilson	
5	5	02-MAR-06	Open	Low	Images don't look in the right positions	LScott	Steven Anderson	
6	6	02-MAY-06	Open	Medium	Pressing delete user gives permission denied error	CDonaldson	John Scott	
7	7	02-JUN-06	Open	High	Buttons don't work in firefox	PMathews	Michael Stuart	
8	8	02-JUN-06	Closed	High	Pressing cancel on the login screen gives an error	MLawson	Mark Wilson	
9	9	02-JUL-06	Open	High	Trying to add anew record gives an error	JStevens	John Scott	
10	10	02-JUL-06	Open	Critical	The logout button doesn't close the browser	SGreen	Steven Anderson	
11	11	02-AUG-06	Open	High	Javascript error on the profiles page	MLawson	John Scott	
12	12	02-AUG-06	Open	Low	Text is too small on the home page	CWatson	John Scott	
13	13	02-SEP-06	Open	High	There is no way to tell who I'm logged in as	CWhite	Paul Wilson	
14	14	02-SEP-06	Open	High	Customer details don't match the	RHudson	John Scott	
15	15	02-OCT-06	Open	Critical	Search results don't match the criteria	LBarnes	John Scott	

row(s) 1 - 15 of 17 ▾ Next ▶

Figure 10-29. The Standard Report template rendered in an application

In the Before Rows attribute, an HTML table tag is opened. The only token used here is #REGION_STATIC_ID#, which is a unique internal ID that APEX will assign to this region. It is possible to use some other tokens, such as #TOP_PAGINATION# and even column names here.

Next, there is a separate attribute for the column headings. In many cases, the column headings will have a different font style and/or background color than the rest of the report. Including the #ALIGNMENT# token here will allow APEX to substitute the alignment setting defined in the report attributes. #COLUMN_HEADER# will be replaced with the formatted column header name, per the report attributes, whereas #COLUMN_HEADER_NAME# will represent the setting of the column alias. In the example in Figure 10-29, the #COLUMN_HEADER# for the first column would be Empno, and the #COLUMN_HEADER_NAME would be EMPNO.

The Before Each Row and After Each Row attributes denote the HTML used to open and close each row in a report. Often, they are simply set to <tr> and </tr>, respectively. Three possible tokens can be included at the Before Each Row level: #ROWNUM#, #COLCOUNT#, and #HIGHLIGHT_ROW#. The first two are used to assist in advanced page layout, but #HIGHLIGHT_ROW# is much simpler to understand. If included as part of the <tr> tag, #HIGHLIGHT_ROW# will automatically add some code to the report template that will change the color of the row that your mouse is hovering over to the color specified in the Background Color for Current Row attribute.

Each generic column report has four column templates. Only one is required for a report to render. The rest are there to facilitate some basic logic that can be embedded directly in the template. Three conditions are available for each column template: Use for Even Number Rows, Use for Odd Number Rows, and Use Based on a PL/SQL function. For example, if you changed the report shown in Figure 10-28 to use the Standard, Alternating Row Colors template, the column templates would look something like Figure 10-30.

Two column templates are defined: one is set to render for even rows, and the other is set to render for odd rows. The only difference between the two is the CSS class referenced: t13data versus t13altdata.

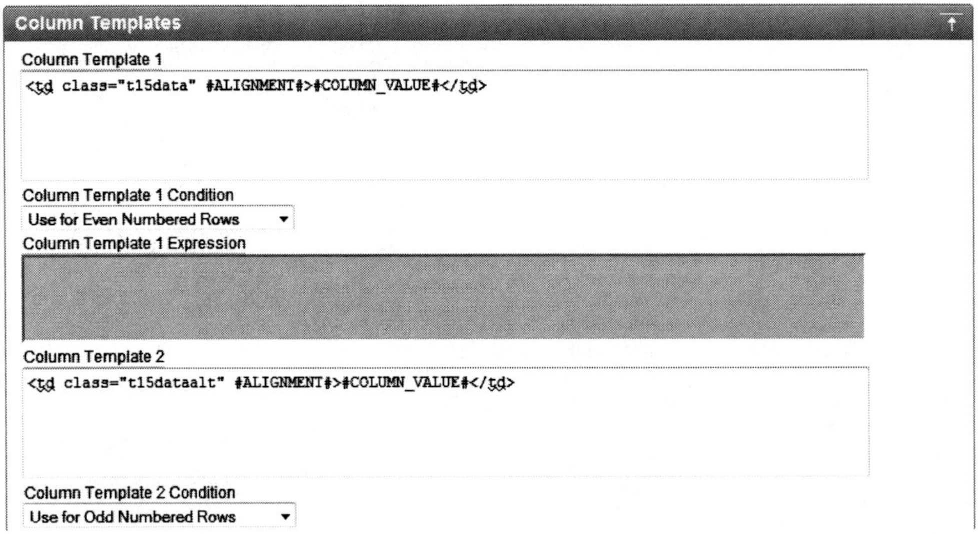

Figure 10-30. The column template for the Standard, Alternating Rows report template

When run, the rows in the report will alternate between the two CSS styles, which in this case, means alternating between a white and gray background, as shown in Figure 10-31.

Figure 10-31. A report with alternating column templates running

In addition to simple odd and even rows, a PL/SQL expression can be evaluated, and if it is true, a different column template can be used. Thus, you can inspect the value of a column, apply a function, and if the value meets some criteria, that row can be rendered in a different font, color, or style. In order for PL/SQL expressions in report templates to work, they must be applied before any odd/even conditions. Thus, if you were to use the Standard, Alternating Rows template, you would need to move the Odd and Even column templates from positions 1 and 2 to positions 2 and 3, and then use column template 1 for your PL/SQL function template, as shown in Figure 10-32.

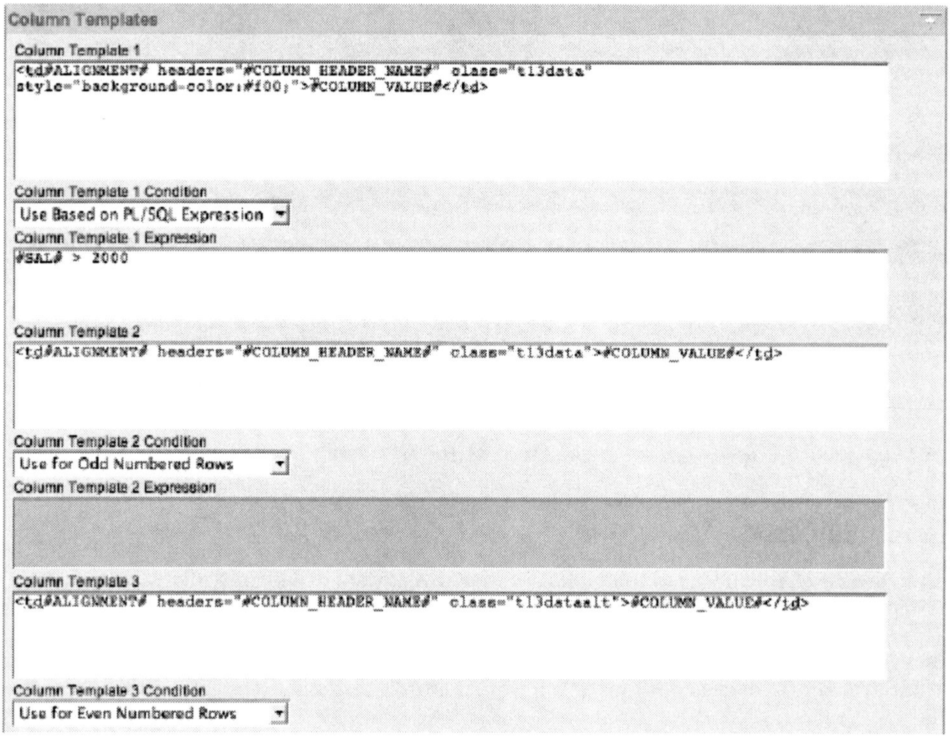

Figure 10-32. A column template that includes a PL/SQL expression

In the example in Figure 10-32, we made a slight modification to the first column template: we added the CSS style definition background-color:#f00;, which will render any row that meets the expression in red.

If the data type of the column being evaluated is CHAR, VARCHAR, or VARCHAR2, the column name and associated #s must be enclosed in single quotation marks. For all other types, the column need only be enclosed in #s without the additional single quotes. The name enclosed in #s must match the column name, or if used, the column alias. If COST were the column you were evaluating, the expression would look like this:

```
#COST# = 1000
```

When the report is run now, the row of any employee who has a salary of over 2,000 will be highlighted in red, as indicated in Figure 10-33.

Buglist

ID	BUGID	REPORTED	STATUS	PRIORITY	DESCRIPTION	REPORTED_BY	ASSIGNED_TO	COST
1	1	27-JAN-06	Open	High	Pressing Cancel on the login screen gives an error	RHuson	John Scott	
2	2	02-JAN-06	Closed	High	Logo occassionally does not appear	CWhite	Peter Ward	
3	3	01-FEB-06	Open	High	Search doesn't return any results when nothing is entered	CWatson	John Scott	
4	4	02-MAR-06	Open	Critical	Login doesn't work for user smithp	LBarnes	Mark Wilson	
5	5	02-MAR-06	Open	Low	Images don't look in the right positions	LScott	Steven Anderson	
6	6	02-MAY-06	Open	Medium	Pressing delete user gives permission denied error	CDonaldson	John Scott	
7	7	02-JUN-06	Open	High	Buttons don't work in firefox	PMathews	Michael Stuart	
8	8	02-JUN-06	Closed	High	Pressing cancel on the login screen gives an error	MLawson	Mark Wilson	
9	9	02-JUL-06	Open	High	Trying to add a new record gives an error	JStevens	John Scott	
10	10	02-JUL-06	Open	Critical	The logout button doesn't close the browser	SGreen	Steven Anderson	
11	11	02-AUG-06	Open	High	Javascript error on the profiles page	MLawson	John Scott	
12	12	02-AUG-06	Open	Low	Text is too small on the home page	CWatson	John Scott	
13	13	02-SEP-06	Open	High	There is no way to tell who I'm logged in as	CWhite	Paul Wilson	
14	14	02-SEP-06	Open	High	Customer details don't match the	RHudson	John Scott	
15	15	02-OCT-06	Open	Critical	Search results don't match the criteria	LBarnes	John Scott	

row(s) 1 - 15 of 17 ▾ Next ▶

Figure 10-33. All high priority, open bugs are highlighted in another color.

Named Column Templates

Named column reports are typically used to display a single row of data in a format other than row/column. They are mapped to a specific table or view, as the column names referenced are placed in the named column template itself. For this reason, none of the APEX built-in report templates are named column. Most of the report attributes, such as those for column-level sorting, column sums, and alignment, are not available in named column templates. All formatting should be done in the template definition itself.

A good example of when to use a named column template is when you need a formatted details view of a single record. You could use a read-only form to achieve the same goal, but using a named column template will give you much more flexibility in the design. In this template, you can use any HTML you like, and you do not need to worry about positioning and sequencing page items.

The structure of a named column report is very similar to that of a generic column report, with a few minor differences. Named column reports combine the Before Each Row, Column Template, and After Each Row attributes into a single attribute called Row Templates. The Row Templates attribute will contain the HTML required to render each specific column. This is in contrast to column templates, which define only a single column that will be used for all columns in a report.

Named column templates also have Column Headings, Before All Rows, and After All Rows attributes. Due to the nature of a named column template, these attributes are rarely used, as most of the HTML required for a named column template is typically found in the row template.

Like generic column templates, named column templates also have logic built in to them. You can define up to four row templates and elect to use them based on a PL/SQL expression or whether the row is an odd-numbered or even-numbered one. For most named column templates, this is not necessary, as only a single row of data is typically used.

When a new named column template is created, by default, APEX will seed Row Template 1, as shown in Figure 10-34.

Figure 10-34. *The default Row Template 1 for a new named column template*

This template definition is meant only as an example and will not actually work. Replace it with the HTML that you want to use with your report, referencing the specific column names that you have defined.

Using the example in the previous section, let's say that you want to create a nicely formatted view of a record from the BUGLIST table. In any HTML editor, create the layout that you want, using #COLUMN_NAME# substitution strings to represent where the data will go. The following is a quick example:

```
<table width="500" style="border:1px solid #333;background-color:#ddd;">
 <tr>
  <th>Reported:</th>
  <td>#REPORTED#</td>
  <th>Reported By:</th>
  <td>#REPORTED_BY#</td>
 </tr>
 <tr>
  <th>Status:</th>
  <td>#STATUS#</td>
  <th>Description:</th>
  <td>#DESCRIPTION#</td>
 </tr>
<table>
```

Next, simply cut and paste this HTML into the Row Template 1 of your named column page template, replacing anything that was there, and apply your changes. Run your application, and you should see something similar to Figure 10-35.

Report 1

Reported: 27-JAN-06	**Reported By:** RHuson
Status: Open	**Description:** Pressing Cancel on the login screen gives an error

Figure 10-35. *The results of the sample named column report template*

The format mask on the Salary column, which was defined as part of the report attributes, will still be applied to the report.

The possibilities of what you can do with a named column template are almost limitless. Nearly anything that works in HTML will work as part of a named column report template.

Pagination Template

All report templates, regardless of their type, contain a section to define the pagination style. More often than not, this is defined with only generic column templates, as named column templates typically are used for only a single row.

The pagination templates do not allow you to change the type of pagination method used, but rather to add some style to the pagination controls or change the text used when there are more records available.

By default, the pagination scheme Row Ranges X to Y (with next and previous links) will look something like what is shown in Figure 10-36. The corresponding Pagination subtemplate is quite sparse, with only a single element defined, as shown in Figure 10-37.

Buglist

ID	BUGID	REPORTED	STATUS	PRIORITY	DESCRIPTION	REPORTED_BY	ASSIGNED_TO	COST
1	1	27-JAN-06	Open	High	Pressing Cancel on the login screen gives an error	RHuson	John Scott	
2	2	02-JAN-06	Closed	High	Logo occassionally does not appear	CWhite	Peter Ward	
3	3	01-FEB-06	Open	High	Search doesn't return any results when nothing is entered	CWatson	John Scott	
4	4	02-MAR-06	Open	Critical	Login doesn't work for user smithp	LBarnes	Mark Wilson	
5	5	02-MAR-06	Open	Low	Images don't look in the right positions	LScott	Steven Anderson	
6	6	02-MAY-06	Open	Medium	Pressing delete user gives permission denied error	CDonaldson	John Scott	
7	7	02-JUN-06	Open	High	Buttons don't work in firefox	PMathews	Michael Stuart	
8	8	02-JUN-06	Closed	High	Pressing cancel on the login screen gives an error	MLawson	Mark Wilson	
9	9	02-JUL-06	Open	High	Trying to add anew record gives an error	JStevens	John Scott	
10	10	02-JUL-06	Open	Critical	The logout button doesn't close the browser	SGreen	Steven Anderson	
11	11	02-AUG-06	Open	High	Javascript error on the profiles page	MLawson	John Scott	
12	12	02-AUG-06	Open	Low	Text is too small on the home page	CWatson	John Scott	
13	13	02-SEP-06	Open	High	There is no way to tell who I'm logged in as	CWhite	Paul Wilson	
14	14	02-SEP-06	Open	High	Customer details don't match the	RHudson	John Scott	
15	15	02-OCT-06	Open	Critical	Search results don't match the criteria	LBarnes	John Scott	

row(s) 1 - 15 of 17 ▼ Next ▶

Figure 10-36. The Employees report with default pagination styles

Figure 10-37. The default Pagination subtemplate

Leaving an attribute of the Pagination subtemplate blank will cause the reporting engine to use the default settings. You do not need values in any of the attributes for pagination to work.

Figure 10-38 shows an example of adding some style to the Pagination subtemplate's first three attributes. When rerun, the report's pagination controls will be smaller, will not contain an image, and will say Next Page and Previous Page (as opposed to Next and Previous), as shown in Figure 10-39.

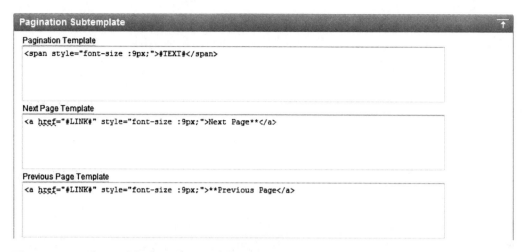

Figure 10-38. The modified Pagination subtemplate

Buglist

ID	BUGID	REPORTED	STATUS	PRIORITY	DESCRIPTION	REPORTED_BY	ASSIGNED_TO	COST
6	6	02-MAY-06	Open	Medium	Pressing delete user gives permission denied error	CDonaldson	John Scott	
7	7	02-JUN-06	Open	High	Buttons don't work in firefox	PMathews	Michael Stuart	
8	8	02-JUN-06	Closed	High	Pressing cancel on the login screen gives an error	MLawson	Mark Wilson	
9	9	02-JUL-06	Open	High	Trying to add anew record gives an error	JStevens	John Scott	
10	10	02-JUL-06	Open	Critical	The logout button doesn't close the browser	SGreen	Steven Anderson	

Previous Page row(s) 6 - 10 of 17 Next Page

Figure 10-39. The results of the Pagination Subtemplate modifications

Popup List of Values Templates

The popup list of values (LOV) template type is definitely the platypus of the bunch, as it contains a little bit of everything: icon definitions; attributes for a search field; button definitions; window attributes; pagination controls; and a header, body, and footer.

It also differs from the rest of the templates in that as a developer, you cannot manually assign this template to any APEX component. Rather, it will be used automatically each time an item type of popup LOV is added to an application. When using the APEX built-in themes, a popup LOV template will be automatically created. If you wish to customize a theme, you will need to alter the existing one, as you can have only one instance of the popup LOV template per theme.

No substitution strings or tokens are available in the popup LOV template. All items that need to be referenced will be done so automatically.

Most attributes of the popup LOV template are either self-explanatory or copies of attributes from other template types.

Calendar Templates

The calendar component has been greatly enhanced in APEX 3.0, with added support for weekly and daily views. All the calendar templates have attributes for each of the three different views, as the user interface of each will vary. Most built-in APEX themes come with three variations of calendar templates.

It is not advisable to create a calendar template from scratch. If you need a custom calendar template, it is best to copy a built-in one and modify that. Using this method will ensure that the core structure required remains in tact. When modifying a calendar template, you can add any number of styles to almost every facet of the calendar itself.

Calendars have a number of tokens that you can use to denote the day, day of week, and month. They are defined to the right of the calendar template attributes.

When customizing the look and feel of a calendar template, it is best to use CSS class definitions. This will help separate the structure of the calendar template from any of the styling that you add. Refer to any of the built-in APEX CSS files for some examples of how to use CSS definitions to control the look and feel of calendar templates.

Tree Templates

You won't find the templates used for rendering APEX trees with the rest of the templates. When a tree is created, the user is given the option to select one of the three templates. That template will be "burned in" to the definition of the tree itself. The tree templates are every bit as configurable as regular templates, but the tree lacks the centralized control of being a shared component.

Changing the structure of a tree template is not recommended, as it requires a number of images that are precisely created to line up with one another. Tree templates are also not scalable. Each time a new tree is created, the altered template will need to be applied by hand.

Template Subscriptions

APEX has a facility called *subscriptions*, which allows you to link shared components from one application to another using a publish/subscribe model. If the content of a component changes, the publisher can push the changes to the subscribers, or the subscribers can pull those changes from the publisher. Subscriptions work with a select number of APEX shared components: navigation bar items, authorization schemes, authentication schemes, LOVs, and of course, templates.

If you decide that you want to customize a built-in theme, or even create one from scratch, you may want to consider using template subscriptions. Using template subscriptions will allow you to create a master copy of your templates and subscribe to them from any other APEX application in your workspace. If you need to make changes to any of the templates, they can be applied to the master copy and published to all the subscribers. Subscriptions make managing APEX templates simple and straightforward.

Publish/subscribe is how the templates in APEX itself work. All of the templates are stored in a single application and then subscribed to from each component application (Application Builder, SQL Workshop, and so on). When Oracle wants to make a sweeping change in the user interface, the developers can do so in the master application and then publish the changes to all of the subscribers. This makes managing the user interface much simpler and more centralized, as it can be done in a single set of templates.

Setting up a common model for theme and template subscriptions is quite simple, and can save you countless hours should you need to rework or modify your user interface at a later date. We'll walk through an example here.

Setting Up a Theme Subscription System

To begin, create a new application and call it Theme Master. When prompted, select any theme (it doesn't matter which one you use for this example). This application will be the only place that any changes to templates are made. Now is also a good time to remove any unnecessary templates from your new theme, as discussed earlier in this chapter.

Next, create another new application from scratch and call it Theme Subscriber. When prompted to, select any theme. The theme selection here is even less important than with the Theme Master application, as you will be deleting it in favor of a subscribed copy to the first application.

In the Theme Subscriber application, navigate to the Shared Components section and select Themes. Create a new theme from scratch and give it any theme ID number and name, as shown in Figure 10-40.

Figure 10-40. Setting the theme ID number and name

Essentially, you have just created a theme without any templates, as shown in Figure 10-41. If you try to switch to your new theme, you will receive an error message that specifies which template classes do not exist in the target theme. In this case, none of the target template classes are found, and you cannot switch themes. If you edit the templates that make up your theme, there should be no rows.

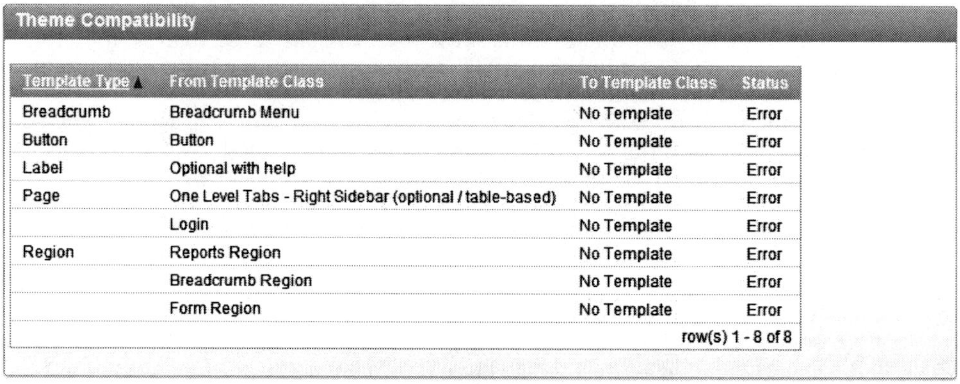

Theme Compatibility

Template Type ▲	From Template Class	To Template Class	Status
Breadcrumb	Breadcrumb Menu	No Template	Error
Button	Button	No Template	Error
Label	Optional with help	No Template	Error
Page	One Level Tabs - Right Sidebar (optional / table-based)	No Template	Error
	Login	No Template	Error
Region	Reports Region	No Template	Error
	Breadcrumb Region	No Template	Error
	Form Region	No Template	Error
		row(s) 1 - 8 of 8	

Figure 10-41. Switching to a theme without any templates defined

In Shared Components, navigate to the Templates section. Next, you will create subscriptions to all of the templates in your Theme Master application, as follows:

1. Click Create to add templates to the custom theme.

2. On the next page, select Page for the Template Type and click Next.

3. Set the value for Create Page From to As a Copy of an Existing Template, as shown in Figure 10-42, and then click Next.

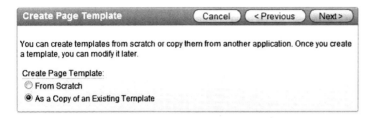

Figure 10-42. Creating a template as a copy of an existing one

4. Set the value of Copy From Application to the application that you created and called your Theme Master, as shown in Figure 10-43, and then click Next.

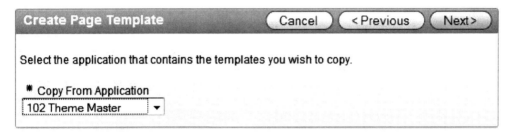

Figure 10-43. Selecting the source application for a template subscription

5. Set the Copy To Theme to your custom theme name, as shown in Figure 10-44, and then click Next.

Figure 10-44. Setting the source and destination when copying a template

6. You may want to change the name of each template to something other than Copy of Login. You can use any names, as long as they do not duplicate existing names. Replacing the "Copy of" with "Custom" or the name of your application/project/organization should suffice.

7. Determine which page templates you want to subscribe to by setting the Copy column to Copy and Subscribe, as shown in Figure 10-45. You do not necessarily need to subscribe to them all at this time, as you can create additional subscriptions later. The list of potential templates should already be trimmed to only what you think you will need. If additional templates are required, you can always add them to the master theme application and create a new subscription later on.

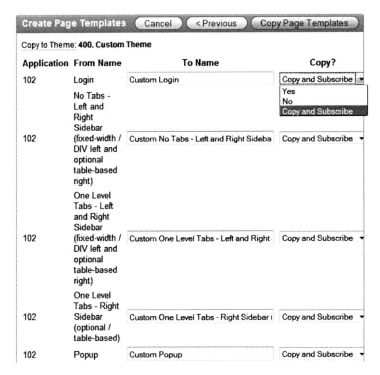

Figure 10-45. Selecting multiple templates to copy and subscribe to

8. When you have finalized your selection, click Copy Page Templates to create a subscription to the specified templates.

At this point, if you click the Subscription subtab, you should see all of the templates for which you just created subscriptions, as shown in Figure 10-46. It will also reference the master application of each template in the last column. From here, you can also refresh any one of the subscribed templates with the most recent copy of the associated master.

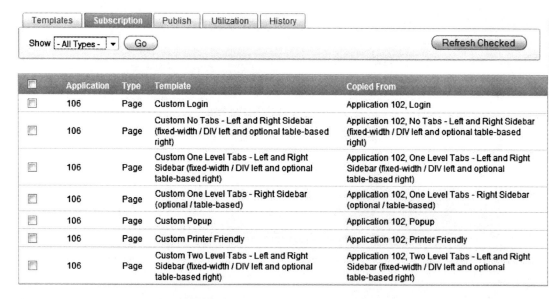

Figure 10-46. The Subscription subtab showing templates with subscriptions

To complete setting up the Theme Subscriber application, repeat this process for the remaining template types that you need in your theme. While this process is tedious, it is well worth the effort, as it will more than make up for the time you invested.

When you are finished setting up the Theme Subscriber application, the next step is to export your new theme. All subscriptions will be preserved when exporting themes, as long as they are imported back into the same workspace.

Once your theme is exported, you can reimport it into any other application in your workspace and switch to it, thus keeping all of your user interfaces consistent and subscribed to a central set of templates.

Refreshing Subscriptions

When changes need to be made to your templates, apply them to the master and then either push out to all of the subscriber applications or refresh them manually from each subscriber application, based on your needs.

In addition to being able to refresh templates from the Subscription subtab, you can refresh any template from the details page for that template, as shown in Figure 10-47. Simply navigate to the detail page of any template, and then in the Subscription section, click Refresh Template. A copy of the master template will be copied down to your subscribers, and all changes will be overwritten. You can also change which master template a subscriber points to from this page.

Subscription		
Reference Master Page Template From	102: Login (1)	⬆
Copied from Application : **102, Login**		
No templates subscribe to this template.		
		Refresh Template

Figure 10-47. Refreshing an individual template from its publisher

Tools for Working with Templates

A good carpenter is useless without his tools. The same holds true for the APEX developer, specifically when working with templates. It is critical to understand how to best use the tools that are available to you, as they will save you countless hours of time.

Tools come in a variety of shapes and sizes, and most important, cost. Going against common wisdom, in the world of software, the best tool is not always the most expensive tool. Most of the commonly used tools and utilities are open source, freeware, or relatively inexpensive.

If nothing else, download and use Firefox as your development browser. Firefox offers a wealth of plug-ins that are not available in Internet Explorer. These plug-ins add a number of essential bits of functionality to the browser; in come cases, making it feel more like a development tool. While the set of current popular add-ons will change over time, the following two are indispensable as of early 2008:

- Web Developer (`https://addons.mozilla.org/en-US/firefox/addon/60`) adds a toolbar with a variety of utilities and options. From viewing the borders of all HTML tables to viewing form details, the Web Developer add-on is essential when debugging template issues.

- Firebug (`https://addons.mozilla.org/en-US/firefox/addon/1843`) adds a powerful debugger to Firefox, which allows you to inspect and modify HTML, CSS files, and JavaScript libraries in-line on any web page. Once you use this add-on, you'll find it hard to believe that you lived without it.

Both add-ons are available free of charge and work with the latest release of Firefox. Firefox is also free, and you can download it from `www.mozilla.com`.

If you do choose to use Firefox as your development browser, be sure to test everything that you build in both Internet Explorer and Firefox. The majority of corporations, organizations, and the general public still use Internet Explorer as their standard browser. Be sure to ensure your applications work and look the same on both browsers.

Also, be aware of display size. Most developers have extra-large displays attached to their PCs. Most end users do not. Make sure that your applications fit into the de facto standard screen size of 1024×768 pixels. Some organizations are still using 800×600 pixel displays, so be sure to check your minimum screen size requirement. No one likes to use the horizontal scroll bars.

Summary

Creating an attractive user interface does not have to be hard. It is more important to standardize on a single, consistent design than to create a new, elaborate one. Err on the side of more consistency, rather than on the side of more sophistication. Keeping the design consistent will mask the fact that your single "application" may be a collection of several. Nothing screams mediocrity more than a suite of applications, each of which uses a completely different user interface or design.

APEX provides a robust, extensible framework for creating almost any user interface you desire. If a custom user interface is a requirement, seek the assistance of a graphic designer. You could spend a full week trying to figure out how to create a mask in Photoshop; a designer can crank out the entire set of templates in half as much time.

Contrary to the old adage, looks are everything, especially when your site is one of the first things your potential clients may see. Invest the time and energy required to make your APEX application look as good as it functions.

CHAPTER 11

Localization Issues

Since APEX is a web development environment, it allows your application to be accessed over an intranet or the Internet by a geographically diverse set of end users. These end users may cross geographical and language boundaries, which means that you may need to enable your application to be viewed in different languages. Fortunately, the APEX development team foresaw this requirement, and has provided a number of features to allow developers to create multilingual applications.

Now, not every application needs to handle different languages. Often, you can just ship an English version of the application. However, you can still take advantage of some localization-related features to make your application behave a bit nicer from the users' perspective, as you will see in this chapter.

Also, not only the application itself can benefit from being multilingual. Many people aren't aware that the Application Builder environment also provides the ability to be viewed in a number of different languages, potentially making development easier if English is not your first language.

ON THE VALUE OF LOCALIZATION

An editor on this book is a bicycle nut who spends far too much of his disposable income and time searching the Internet for good deals on bike parts. Chain Reaction Cycles, an online store based in the United Kingdom, is one of his go-to sources. He is comfortable ordering from this site because it localizes its pricing to appear in his native currency—American dollars. The site also computes shipping appropriate for the United States, as well as omitting the VAT taxes paid in Europe.

The editor recently visited another European site that implements localization only half way. This site asks him to input his country and then changes its catalog text to English, which is good, but then the site falls short by continuing to display pricing in Euros. The localization is half-hearted: getting the language right but the currency wrong.

Which store do you believe the bicycle-loving editor chooses to patronize? Of course, it's the store that does localization well. That store's good implementation inspires confidence that it is serious about selling to customers in the United States. The other store's half-hearted implementation inspires doubt. It's inconvenient too.

Localization matters. Those who localize correctly and wholeheartedly will win out over the lesser efforts. Our goal in this chapter is to help you be one of the winners.

Localizing Application Builder

Typically, when you install APEX, you will find that the Application Builder, SQL Workshop, and other user interfaces display in English, regardless of whether your operating system is set to use English as the primary language. In other words, even if your default locale is set to French, the APEX development environment (but not your applications) will be displayed in English. However, it is possible to have the development environment display in a number of different languages, depending on the default locale specified by the user's browser—that is, the default language setting of the browser used by the developer logging in to the development environment.

You can see which language is used when you connect to the Application Builder by looking in the lower-left section of the screen. For example, Figure 11-1 shows that the language is set to en-us (American English).

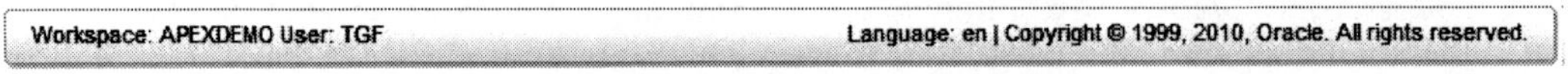

Workspace: APEXDEMO User: TGF   Language: en | Copyright © 1999, 2010, Oracle. All rights reserved.

Figure 11-1. Browser language set to en-us

Choosing a Language

Where you choose your browser's language depends on your browser and operating system. For example, suppose you use an Apple Mac and Firefox or Safari as your main browser (we can't recommend Firefox highly enough—it makes your development life easier). In Mac OS X, you can change the order of your preferred languages in the International section of System Settings, as shown in Figure 11-2. You can find the equivalent settings in Windows in the Control Panel.

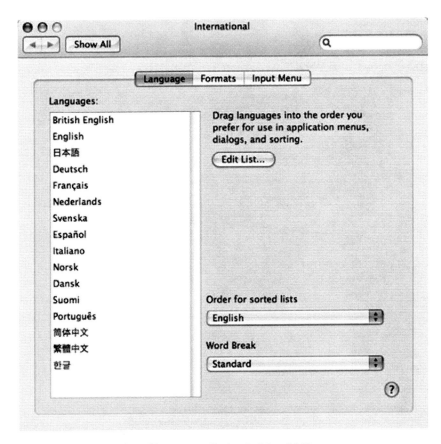

Figure 11-2. The preferred languages listing in Mac OS X

From here, you can rearrange the list to change your preferred language order. For example, you could move German (Deutsch) up to be your preferred language, as shown in Figure 11-3.

If you refresh the Application Builder page after changing your preferred language, you should see the browser language change from en-us to de, as shown in Figure 11-4.

However, at this point, all that has changed is the browser language string displayed in the Application Builder. The Application Builder itself (and SQL Workshop and other user interfaces) is still being displayed in English, not German as you might expect. This is because, by default, only the English translations are installed with APEX. If you want to display other languages, you need to manually install those language translations yourself.

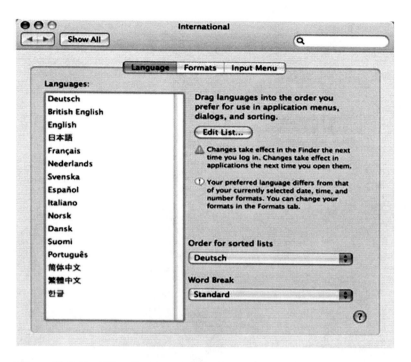

Figure 11-3. Enabling German as the primary language

Figure 11-4. Browser language now set to German (de)

Installing a Language File

You can see which languages are currently installed in APEX by logging into APEX as the instance administrator and navigating to Manage Service Installed Translations, as shown in Figure 11-5.

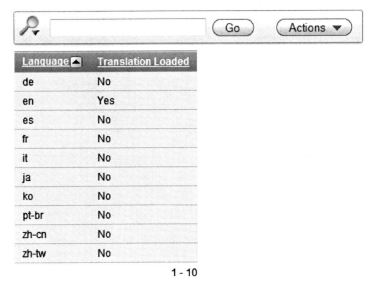

Figure 11-5. Viewing the installed languages for the instance

As you can see, the instance has only the en (English) language installed by default. So even if your browser language is set to German, APEX will determine that the German language is not installed and will fall back to showing the English translation instead.

So, how do you install the additional languages? Unfortunately, you can't just click and do it through a nice browser interface. You need to manually execute the SQL files yourself to load a specific language.

The SQL files that you need to load are part of the base APEX installation files as long as you download the apex_4.0.zip file. If you chose the apex_4.0_en.zip, the additional, non-English language files will not be available. If you did download the English-only file, you will have to download the apex_4.0.zip file as the files are not available separately. All you need to do in this case is unzip the file and change to the builder directory to locate the

Listing 11-1 shows a listing of the builder subdirectory in the directory where we downloaded APEX; in other words, if we downloaded and extracted APEX into the /tmp directory, it would be the /tmp/apex/builder directory.

Listing 11-1. Language Files in the builder Subdirectory

```
[oracle@oim builder]$ ls -al
total 64556
drwxr-xr-x 11 oracle dba     4096 Nov 19 13:25 .
drwxr-xr-x  8 oracle dba     4096 Mar  2 01:53 ..
drwxr-xr-x  2 oracle dba     4096 Nov 19 13:25 de
drwxr-xr-x  2 oracle dba     4096 Nov 19 13:25 es
```

```
-r--r--r--  1 oracle dba 35273236 Nov 19 13:25 f4000.sql
-r--r--r--  1 oracle dba  3197748 Nov 19 13:25 f4050.sql
-r--r--r--  1 oracle dba   129878 Nov 19 13:25 f4155.sql
-r--r--r--  1 oracle dba   837932 Nov 19 13:25 f4300.sql
-r--r--r--  1 oracle dba  3427440 Nov 19 13:25 f4350.sql
-r--r--r--  1 oracle dba  6376151 Nov 19 13:25 f4400.sql
-r--r--r--  1 oracle dba  2092367 Nov 19 13:25 f4411.sql
-r--r--r--  1 oracle dba  7305685 Nov 19 13:25 f4500.sql
-r--r--r--  1 oracle dba   185510 Nov 19 13:25 f4550.sql
-r--r--r--  1 oracle dba   985838 Nov 19 13:25 f4600.sql
-r--r--r--  1 oracle dba   181215 Nov 19 13:25 f4700.sql
-r--r--r--  1 oracle dba  2613201 Nov 19 13:25 f4800.sql
-r--r--r--  1 oracle dba  3328979 Nov 19 13:25 f4900.sql
drwxr-xr-x  2 oracle dba     4096 Nov 19 13:25 fr
drwxr-xr-x  2 oracle dba     4096 Nov 19 13:25 it
drwxr-xr-x  2 oracle dba     4096 Nov 19 13:25 ja
drwxr-xr-x  2 oracle dba     4096 Nov 19 13:25 ko
drwxr-xr-x  2 oracle dba     4096 Nov 19 13:25 pt-br
drwxr-xr-x  2 oracle dba     4096 Nov 19 13:25 zh-cn
drwxr-xr-x  2 oracle dba     4096 Nov 19 13:25 zh-tw
```

You may have noticed in Listing 11-1 that some of the SQL files relate to specific applications in APEX. For example, the f4500.sql file relates to the Application Builder application itself, and the f4050.sql file relates to the internal administration interface.

The important thing to notice in Listing 11-1 is that the directory contains a number of subdirectories, each corresponding to a particular language. For example, if you look inside the de subdirectory, you will see the SQL files that correspond to that language, as shown in Listing 11-2.

Listing 11-2. SQL Scripts to Install the German (de) Language

```
[oracle@oim de]$ ls -al
total 65088
drwxr-xr-x  2 oracle dba     4096 Nov 19 13:25 .
drwxr-xr-x 11 oracle dba     4096 Nov 19 13:25 ..
-r--r--r--  1 oracle dba 35691183 Nov 19 13:25 f4000_de.sql
-r--r--r--  1 oracle dba  3199609 Nov 19 13:25 f4050_de.sql
-r--r--r--  1 oracle dba   126568 Nov 19 13:25 f4155_de.sql
-r--r--r--  1 oracle dba   845207 Nov 19 13:25 f4300_de.sql
-r--r--r--  1 oracle dba  3409380 Nov 19 13:25 f4350_de.sql
-r--r--r--  1 oracle dba  6423183 Nov 19 13:25 f4400_de.sql
-r--r--r--  1 oracle dba  2143639 Nov 19 13:25 f4411_de.sql
-r--r--r--  1 oracle dba  7352214 Nov 19 13:25 f4500_de.sql
-r--r--r--  1 oracle dba   181763 Nov 19 13:25 f4550_de.sql
-r--r--r--  1 oracle dba   983752 Nov 19 13:25 f4600_de.sql
-r--r--r--  1 oracle dba   178292 Nov 19 13:25 f4700_de.sql
-r--r--r--  1 oracle dba  2621278 Nov 19 13:25 f4800_de.sql
-r--r--r--  1 oracle dba  3334726 Nov 19 13:25 f4900_de.sql
-r--r--r--  1 oracle dba     2868 Nov 19 13:25 load_de.sql
-r--r--r--  1 oracle dba      717 Nov 19 13:25 null1.sql
-r--r--r--  1 oracle dba     2005 Nov 19 13:25 rt_de.sql
-r--r--r--  1 oracle dba     2510 Nov 19 13:25 unload_de.sql
```

As you can see, the subdirectory contains a separate file for each application that makes up APEX. This allows you to have an English and a German version of the Application Builder, for example.

If you examine the load_de.sql file (or the equivalently named file for the other languages), you will find the beginning of the file contains some notes, which make a couple of very important points:

- It assumes the APEX owner.

- The NLS_LANG must be properly set in the environment prior to running this script; otherwise, character set conversion may take place. The character set portion of NLS_LANG must be set to AL32UTF8, as in AMERICAN_AMERICA.AL32UTF8.

The first point means that you need to load these scripts as the schema you installed APEX into (for example, the APEX_040000 schema), rather than your own application schema.

The second point is extremely important and is easy to overlook. If you fail to properly set the NLS_LANG environment variable before running the script, you may end up with some character set conversion, leading to corrupted characters being stored.

You can set the NLS_LANG environment variable using the export command in Linux/Unix, assuming you are using the Bash shell. If you are on a Windows system, you can use the SET command. Listing 11-3 shows the environment variable being set and then queried to check if it has been set correctly.

Listing 11-3. Setting the NLS_LANG Environment Variable

```
[oracle@oim de]$ export NLS_LANG=AMERICAN_AMERICA.AL32UTF8
[oracle@oim de]$ echo $NLS_LANG
AMERICAN_AMERICA.AL32UTF8
```

Next, to install the language translations, you need to connect via SQL*Plus (or some other tool if you prefer) as the APEX_040000 user and run the load_<language>.sql script. Since you don't normally log in to the database as APEX_040000, you can log in as another user and then alter the session to use the APEX_040000 schema. Listing 11-4 shows the session being altered, the load_de.sql script being run, and an abbreviated version of the script output.

Listing 11-4. Running the load_de.sql Script

```
SQL> alter session set current_schema=APEX_040000;

Session altered.

SQL> @load_de.sql
...LOTS OF OUTPUT REMOVED
...shared queries
...report layouts
...authentication schemes
......scheme 108165525079033088.4703
...done
Adjust instance settings

PL/SQL procedure successfully completed.
```

■ **Note** Depending on the speed of your machine, it may take a while to run this script. If you receive an error, or just wish to de-install a language, you can use the `unload_language.sql` script.

After installing the language file, if you again look at the Installed Translations section in the administration pages, you should see that the language was installed and is correctly detected. Figure 11-6 shows this section after running the `load_de.sql` script.

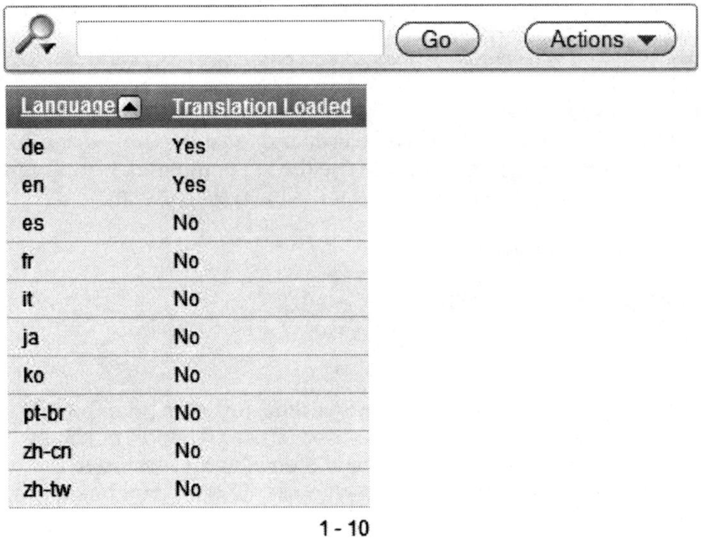

Language ▲	Translation Loaded
de	Yes
en	Yes
es	No
fr	No
it	No
ja	No
ko	No
pt-br	No
zh-cn	No
zh-tw	No

1 - 10

Figure 11-6. The German (de) language is now installed.

In earlier versions of APEX, you would have to change the preferred language of the browser to enable APEX builder page to display in a different language. In APEX 4.0, you don't have to change the browser settings to change languages. On the APEX home page, you will see a new sidebar menu called "Language," as shown in Figure 11-7, which displays all of the loaded translations. To change the language of the builder, simply click on German, or Deutsch, as in our example. The APEX home page, as shown in Figure 11-8, is now displayed in German. If you log out of APEX, you would see that even the APEX login page is displayed in German.

Figure 11-7. Application Builder page displayed in German

Figure 11-8. Application Builder page displayed in German

It is very much worthwhile to install the additional language translations reflecting the languages that your developers speak. This is particularly useful if you are running a public APEX instance that can be accessed by many developers around the world. It will present them with pages in their own language if that language is available; otherwise, it will fall back to using English.

Localizing Your Applications

The previous section described how to localize the Application Builder itself, but even if you don't need to localize the Application Builder (if all your developers are native English speakers, for example), you may still need to localize your own applications.

Obviously, it does not make sense to localize every single application, and it will very much depend on your own requirements (and resources) whether it makes sense to localize any given application. We won't get into a debate about whether it's sufficient to just use English and assume that all your site visitors will be able to understand it; however, there is often a benefit in including localization even if the end users also speak English. And remember that localization doesn't just mean the language that your applications are displayed in, but also refers to how numbers and currencies and dates and times are displayed. It also can mean application logic that is country-specific. So, by localizing your application, you are making it behave in the way that the end users expect it to behave, rather than forcing them to adopt a different style of working to fit in with your "hard-coded" (as far as they are concerned) ways of representing data.

A Simple Currency Example

Let's look at a simple example of how you can display currencies in your application in the locale of the end user. First, we need to introduce a currency field into the Buglist application. It's a bit of a contrived example, but we'll add a column to the `buglist` table called `cost`. In theory, this would allow a manager to assign an estimated cost to a reported bug that could then be used to prioritize and manage the bugs (as we said, it's a contrived example, but bear with us!).

We have also modified the report on the home page to include the Cost column in the report, and the Update Bug screen to allow the cost to be entered. We are not going to reproduce all the steps we performed, since by this point, you should be comfortable enough doing the work yourself. The end result is that if you enter a value for a cost against a bug and look at the report, you will see a page similar to Figure 11-9.

Id	Bug Id	Reported	Bug Status	Priority	Reported By	Assigned To	Cost
1	1	27-JAN-2006 12:00AM	Open	High	RHuson	John Scott	100.89
	Pressing Cancel on the login screen gives an error						
2	2	02-JAN-2006 12:00AM	Closed	High	CWhite	Peter Ward	
3	3	01-FEB-2006 12:00AM	Open	High	CWatson	John Scott	
	Search doesn't return any results when nothing is entered						
4	4	02-MAR-2006 12:00AM	Open	Critical	LBarnes	Mark Wilson	
	Login doesn't work for user smithp						
5	5	02-MAR-2006 12:00AM	Open	Low	LScott	Steven Anderson	
	Images don't look in the right positions						

Spread Sheet

Figure 11-9. *Retrieving a currency value in the report*

The currency value is being displayed in US dollars (USD) because we specified the following format mask for the Cost column in the report:

```
FML999G999G999G999G990D00
```

This mask will use the default currency symbol based on the NLS parameters for the session. In this case, the NLS parameters are being picked up from the setting in the DAD, typically `AMERICAN_AMERICA.UTF8`, which is why the dollar sign is displayed.

Now suppose that the application will be used exclusively in the United Kingdom, so we want to use pound sterling as the currency symbol. To use another currency symbol, we need to override the NLS setting each time we make a web request. We must do this each time because we want to make sure that the NLS setting is correct no matter which connection we get from the `mod_plsql` connection pool. In other words, if we just changed the setting when we authenticated to the application, we might get another connection from the connection pool that is still using the default NLS settings.

As explained in Chapter 4, the ideal place to make this sort of session setting is in the VPD section of the application security attributes. Any code that you place in the VPD section (or call from this setting) is executed each time you make a request.

You can add the following code to the VPD section to set the `NLS_TERRITORY` setting to United Kingdom:

```
BEGIN
  EXECUTE IMMEDIATE
    'ALTER SESSION SET NLS_TERRITORY="UNITED KINGDOM"';
END;
```

Note that you need to wrap `UNITED KINGDOM` in double quotes due to the space in the string.

If you now run the report page again, you should see that the Cost column uses the pound sign as the currency symbol, as shown in Figure 11-10.

Id	Bug Id	Reported	Bug Status	Priority	Reported By	Assigned To	Cost
1	1	27-JAN-2006 12:00AM	Open	High	RHuson	John Scott	£100.89
		Pressing Cancel on the login screen gives an error					
2	2	02-JAN-2006 12:00AM	Closed	High	CWhite	Peter Ward	
3	3	01-FEB-2006 12:00AM	Open	High	CWatson	John Scott	
		Search doesn't return any results when nothing is entered					
4	4	02-MAR-2006 12:00AM	Open	Critical	LBarnes	Mark Wilson	
		Login doesn't work for user smithp					
5	5	02-MAR-2006 12:00AM	Open	Low	LScott	Steven Anderson	
		Images don't look in the right positions					

Figure 11-10. Displaying the pound sign

Similarly, if you modify the `NLS_TERRITORY` setting in the VPD section to use Germany instead, as follows:

```
BEGIN
  EXECUTE IMMEDIATE 'ALTER SESSION SET NLS_TERRITORY="GERMANY"';
END;
```

you would see the euro symbol displayed, as shown in Figure 11-11.

Id	Bug Id	Reported	Bug Status	Priority	Reported By	Assigned To	Cost
1	1	27-JAN-2006 12:00AM	Open	High	RHuson	John Scott	€100,89
	Pressing Cancel on the login screen gives an error						
2	2	02-JAN-2006 12:00AM	Closed	High	CWhite	Peter Ward	
3	3	01-FEB-2006 12:00AM	Open	High	CWatson	John Scott	
	Search doesn't return any results when nothing is entered						
4	4	02-MAR-2006 12:00AM	Open	Critical	LBarnes	Mark Wilson	
	Login doesn't work for user smithp						
5	5	02-MAR-2006 12:00AM	Open	Low	LScott	Steven Anderson	

Figure 11-11. *Displaying the euro sign*

Notice that all we're doing here is displaying the cost using different currency symbols. We are not making any attempt to convert between currencies. In other words, if we are storing the currency as 100 USD but displaying it as 100 euros, our costs are going to be very wrong (unless, of course, the exchange rate changes such that 1 USD = 1 euro).

If you wanted to convert between currencies automatically, you would need to store the value in a fixed currency (for example, USD), and then maintain a table of exchange rates with which you could convert to the correct value depending on which NLS_TERRITORY setting you were using. (We'll leave the currency conversion as an exercise for the reader.) You could then modify this example so that rather than using a fixed NLS_TERRITORY setting in the VPD section, you instead picked up a setting specific for the user, as we'll demonstrate next.

User-Dependent Localization

In the previous example, we had one hard-coded NLS setting for all users. Now let's take a look at extending that simple example to allow for the end users being in different countries.

First, we need a way to store the NLS settings for each user. We could add an extra column to the user_repository table and then create a user profile type of page, where users can set their preferred time zone and region. However, we're going to keep this example simple, and just let users set the time zone on the report page. Then we will display the times according to the time zone they choose.

We've added a select list (called P1_TIMEZONE) to allow each user to select a time zone. We've created a new region on the right side of the page and added the select list to that region. The select list uses a query against a table called v$timezone_names:

```
select
  tzname||'-'||TZABBREV d,
  tzname r
from
  V$TIMEZONE_NAMES
```

The new select list is shown in Figure 11-12.

467

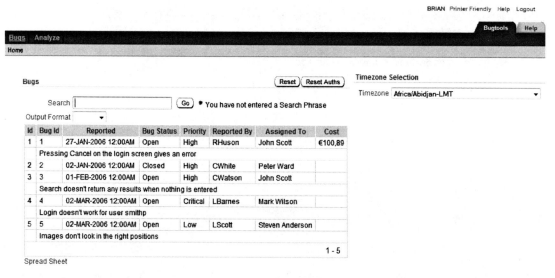

Figure 11-12. Selecting a time zone

If a user selects an entry from the P1_TIMEZONE select list, we need to use that value to modify the session time zone. We can do this by adding a before-header page process that executes the following block of code. To ensure that your code is protected against a SQL Injection hack (possible any time you use execute immediate) you first need to ensure that the value of :P1_TIMEZONE is actually a time zone. The code is as follows:

```
begin
  for cur in (select null from v$timezone_names
              where  tzname-:P1_TIMEZONE)
  loop
    alter session set time_zone = '''||:P1_TIMEZONE||'''');
  end loop;
end;
```

However, we need to ensure that this code is executed only when P1_TIMEZONE has a value; otherwise, the execute immediate statement will fail. We can use a Value of Item in Expression 1 Is NOT NULL condition on the new page process and use P1_TIMEZONE as the value of Expression 1.

We still will not see any visible difference in the report, even if we try selecting some different geographical time zones from the list. This is because the reported date stored against the bugs is just using a DATE data type. In order for our dates to be time zone-aware, we need to use a different data type. The data type we need to use depends on what we want to show. We have the following two main options:

TIMESTAMP WITH TIME ZONE: Allows you to store a timestamp using a particular time zone (defined from the client connection), preserving the time zone as part of the data for later reference.

TIMESTAMP WITH LOCAL TIME ZONE: Converts a timestamp to a baseline time zone (defined on the server), and then allows conversion of that timestamp upon retrieval for your particular session time zone. Columns of this type do not store any time zone information from the client; timestamps are stored in the local time zone, where *local* refers to the server itself.

The choice between which format you should use comes down to whether it's important to know the time zone with which the data was created. For example, if you need to know that a record was created with a timestamp of 9:00 a.m. in the US Eastern Time zone, you'll want to use TIMESTAMP WITH TIME ZONE to store that time zone. If you really don't care about the original time zone, you can use TIMESTAMP WITH LOCAL TIME ZONE to essentially convert all the date/time values into to the time zone of the server.

If you use the TIMESTAMP WITH TIME ZONE format, you can still convert between different time zones by using the built-in time zone functions. The following example finds the time zone offset between the local server time and a particular time zone. The offsets you see will depend on your time zone.

```
jes@DBTEST> SELECT TZ_OFFSET('Europe/London') from dual;

TZ_OFFSET
---------
+00:00

jes@DBTEST> select tz_offset('Australia/Darwin') from dual;

TZ_OFFSET
---------
+09:30
```

You can also convert between time zones.

```
1  select
2    systimestamp at time zone 'Asia/Singapore' as remote_time
3  from
4*   dual

REMOTE_TIME
---------------------------------------------
03-DEC-07 04.21.07.050327 PM ASIA/SINGAPORE
```

Here, we are converting the current time (as the server sees it) into the current time in a particular time zone (in this case Singapore, but you can use any valid time zone string). The syntax AT TIME ZONE looks a little strange at first, but it's an incredibly powerful way to easily convert time zone information to find out the date and time in one area relative to another. Obviously, you could adapt this code to use data stored in a table, rather than using the current server timestamp.

For our example, we will add a time zone-aware column to the buglist table and set it to use the TIMESTAMP WITH LOCAL TIME ZONE data type. Since we will set the value of this new column to the old reported column, and the reported column does not store any time zone information, it would not make sense to use the TIMESTAMP WITH TIME ZONE data type. Listing 11-5 shows the new column being added to the buglist table.

Listing 11-5. *Adding a Time Zone-Aware Column*

```
SQL> desc buglist;

Name                   Null?    Type
------------------     -------- --------------
ID                              NUMBER
BUGID                           NUMBER
REPORTED                        DATE
STATUS                          VARCHAR2(30)
PRIORITY                        VARCHAR2(30)
DESCRIPTION                     VARCHAR2(255)
REPORTED_BY                     VARCHAR2(30)
ASSIGNED_TO                     VARCHAR2(30)
COST                            NUMBER

SQL> alter table buglist
2   add (reported_ts timestamp with local time zone);
Table altered.

SQL> update buglist set reported_ts = reported;
19 rows updated.

SQL> commit;
Commit complete.
```

This might not seem like much of an improvement over the original DATE data type, but the following shows what happens if we query the data while changing our session time zone information:

```
1  select
2    to_char(reported_ts, 'dd/mm/yyyy hh24:mi:ss') as ts
3  from
4    buglist
5  where
6*   rownum < 5
SQL> /

TS
-------------------
27/01/2006 00:00:00
01/02/2006 00:00:00
02/08/2006 00:00:00
03/02/2006 00:00:00
```

So first, we see that the hour, minute, and second components are set to 00:00:00. Because when we originally created the data, we just specified a date for the reported field, without specifying a time, the time part has defaulted to midnight.

Now, the following shows what happens if we change our session time zone to be in a different part of the world:

```
SQL> alter session set time_zone = 'Australia/Darwin';

Session altered.

1  select
2    to_char(reported_ts, 'dd/mm/yyyy hh24:mi:ss') as ts
3  from
4    buglist
5  where
6*   rownum < 5
SQL> /

TS
-------------------
27/01/2006 15:30:00
01/02/2006 15:30:00
02/08/2006 15:30:00
03/02/2006 15:30:00
```

Notice how the time component has now changed to reflect the time difference between the server's (in this case, the server uses UTC) and the client's session time zone. Just to prove it, let's try another time zone.

```
SQL> alter session set time_zone = 'America/Los_Angeles';

Session altered.

1  select
2    to_char(reported_ts, 'dd/mm/yyyy hh24:mi:ss') as ts
3  from
4    buglist
5  where
6*   rownum < 5

TS
-------------------
26/01/2006 22:00:00
31/01/2006 22:00:00
01/08/2006 23:00:00
02/02/2006 22:00:00
```

Notice how not only are the times different, but the dates are also different to reflect the time zones. Also notice that for the 01/08/2006 date, the time is actually different from the other times, this is due to the daylight saving time switchover.

As you can see, displaying the dates and times in the local format that your end users would expect to see can make the data much more readable and immediately understandable. This way, they don't need to do time comparisons and conversions themselves.

We can now adapt the report to include the new `reported_ts` column (using a suitable format mask to display the column in *dd/mm/yyyy hh24:mi:ss* format), so that the user can select a time zone and have the dates and times correctly shown according to that particular time zone, as shown in Figure 11-13.

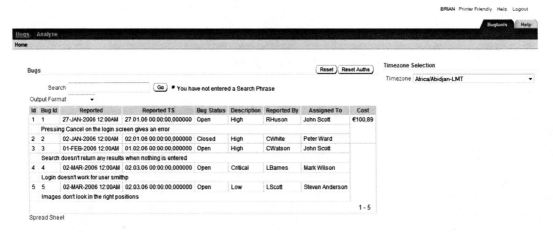

Figure 11-13. *Displaying time zone-aware columns in the report*

In a real-world situation, you would probably want to allow users to define their time zone, NLS territory, and so on in their profiles, and then set these settings in the VPD section of your application. However, this simple example shows just how powerful these relatively cheap-to-implement techniques can be.

NLS Parameters

The previous sections demonstrated how to set two session parameters that influence how data is displayed: `NLS_TERRITORY` and `TIME_ZONE`. Many more NLS parameters are available. You can use the `nls_session_parameters` view to see which settings are available (and their values) for your current session:

```
jes@DBTEST> select * from nls_session_parameters
```

```
PARAMETER                        VALUE
------------------------------   ------------------------------
NLS_LANGUAGE                     AMERICAN
NLS_TERRITORY                    AMERICA
NLS_CURRENCY                     $
NLS_ISO_CURRENCY                 AMERICA
NLS_NUMERIC_CHARACTERS           .,
NLS_CALENDAR                     GREGORIAN
NLS_DATE_FORMAT                  DD-MON-RR
NLS_DATE_LANGUAGE                AMERICAN
NLS_SORT                         BINARY
NLS_TIME_FORMAT                  HH.MI.SSXFF AM
```

```
NLS_TIMESTAMP_FORMAT          DD-MON-RR HH.MI.SSXFF AM
NLS_TIME_TZ_FORMAT            HH.MI.SSXFF AM TZR
NLS_TIMESTAMP_TZ_FORMAT       DD-MON-RR HH.MI.SSXFF AM TZR
NLS_DUAL_CURRENCY             $
NLS_COMP                      BINARY
NLS_LENGTH_SEMANTICS          BYTE
NLS_NCHAR_CONV_EXCP           FALSE
```

So, for example, you can use the NLS_TIME_FORMAT setting to modify the way that times are displayed to the user. Also, you can use the NLS_CURRENCY setting to modify the currency symbol that is used, rather than modifying the entire NLS_TERRITORY, which affects more than just the currency symbol.

Using these simple techniques, you can transform the way your application is perceived by end users.

■ **Tip** It is much more user-friendly to display dates and times in the end users' time zone, rather than forcing the users to manually calculate any offsets. Using the time zone data types requires very little extra coding. In fact, because they are still capable of storing regular dates, we almost always use the time zone data type rather than the plain-old timestamp data type. The advantage of this is that even if today we do not need to provide localized versions of our application, we can easily use the techniques described here to do so later.

Fully Translating Your Applications

The previous section demonstrated how you can easily localize dates and currencies in your application. But what if you want to provide a fully translated version of your application so that end users can access your site in their native language? Fortunately, the team behind APEX has made this a relatively straightforward process. And, obviously, you can combine this with the techniques shown previously to display dates and currencies in the correct format.

A core concept in the translation is that for each translated version of your application (for example Spanish, French, and so on), there is a *separate copy* of your application behind the scenes. In other words, you don't have one application that contains all the translations, but rather multiple applications. The user is taken to the correct application depending on the criteria you use to detect the language settings for that user.

Now, this multiple versions approach might sound like a huge overhead in terms of maintenance. For example, each time you change a piece of code in your application, do you need to also change it in every translated version of your application? Fortunately, that's not necessary. So if you have ten different translated versions of your application, you don't need to make the change in eleven (ten translations plus the original application) different applications. The mechanism for the translated application is much smarter than that.

Essentially, you can consider your original application as the master application, from which all the translated versions inherit the code, look and feel, logic, and so on. You never need to directly modify the translated versions. Instead, you modify the primary application and let those changes filter into the translated applications. In fact, you will not see those translated applications listed in the main Application Builder interface (to prevent you from editing them directly).

Defining the Primary Application Language and Derived From Language

The first step in providing a multilingual application is to decide what the primary language of your main application is going to be. You define this at the application level, in the Shared Components Edit Globalization Attributes section, as shown in Figure 11-14.

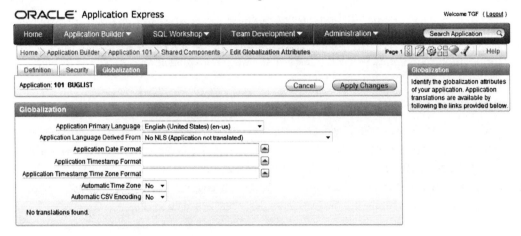

Figure 11-14. Defining the application's primary language

Why is it so important to define the primary language? Well, the APEX environment will use the Application Primary Language and Application Language Derived From settings to determine which application the end user should be directed to (remember that behind the scenes, there will be multiple applications—one for each translation).

In this example, we are telling APEX that the primary language of this application is en-us and that all users should always see the Application Primary Language version of the application (in this example, application 101). Even if we have translated versions of the application, every user would see the en-us version.

Since we wish users to see different translated versions of the application, we need to change the Application Language Derived From setting to something more appropriate. We have the following choices:

No NLS (Application not translated): This is used if you are not planning to translate the application at all (the primary application will always be used).

Use Application Primary Language: Very similar to the first option, except it allows you to use translated applications; however, all users will see the same translated application. For example, you can switch between English and Spanish, and all users will see the same change.

Browser (use browser language preference): This will use the end user's browser locale setting to determine the application's primary language. For example, if the user's browser is set to German, that user will see the German version of the application.

Application Preference (use FSP_LANGUAGE_PREFERENCE): This will use the value of the FSP_LANGUAGE_PREFERENCE application item, which can be set via the application using the APEX_UTIL.SET_PREFERENCE procedure. Since this is a user preference, the same setting will apply each time the user logs in to the application.

Item Preference: Similar to the Application Preference option (also uses FSP_LANGUAGE_PREFERENCE); however, this will be evaluated each time the user logs in to the application.

In this example, we are going to use the locale setting of the user's browser to determine the language to present. To that end, we need to change the Application Language Derived From setting to Browser, as shown in Figure 11-15.

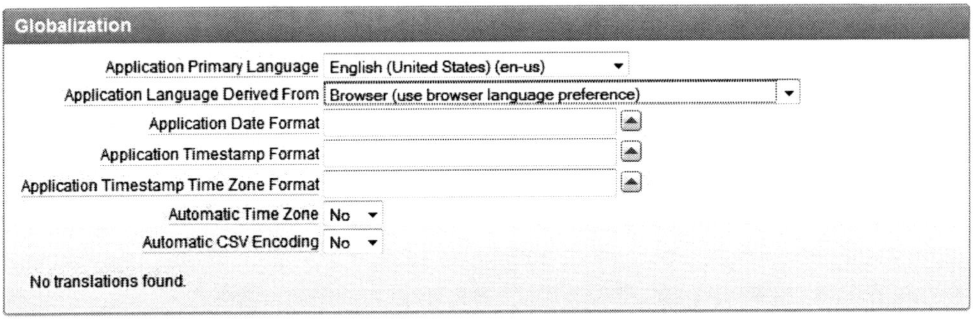

Figure 11-15. Using the browser language preferences

Now whenever the user connects to the application, APEX will automatically detect the browser language preference and will use that to determine which translated version of the application to show the user.

Creating Translated Versions of an Application

So, how do you create a translated version of the application? Like many things in APEX, it is done via the Shared Components section. Figure 11-16 shows the Translate Application wizard in that section.

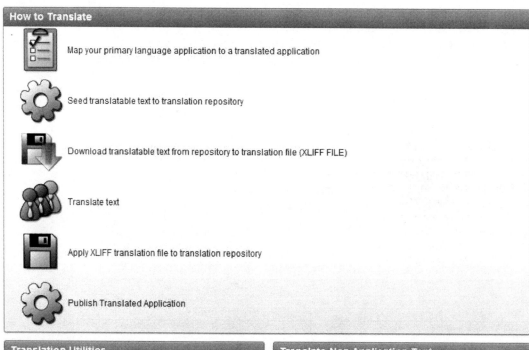

How to Translate

Map your primary language application to a translated application

Seed translatable text to translation repository

Download translatable text from repository to translation file (XLIFF FILE)

Translate text

Apply XLIFF translation file to translation repository

Publish Translated Application

Translation Utilities

- o Create and manage text messages
- o Manage Messages Repository
- o Manage Dynamic Translation Repository
- o Manually Edit Translation Repository
- o View Developer Log

Translate Non Application Text

- o Create and Manage messages callable from PL/SQL
- o Optionally translate messages which are used by PL/SQL procedures and functions.
- o Optionally identify any data that needs to be dynamically translated to support SQL based lists of values.

Figure 11-16. Translate Application wizard

As you can see from Figure 11-16, you need to go through a number of steps to turn your application into a multilingual one. You can simply click each link to go to the appropriate step in the wizard.

Mapping a Translation

The first step is to map your original primary language application to a translated application. You do this for every translated version of the application—the Spanish version, the French version, the German version, and so on.

This mapping allows APEX to create a new version of your application that corresponds to a particular language. The first time you do this, there will be no existing mappings. Figure 11-17 shows creating a new mapping.

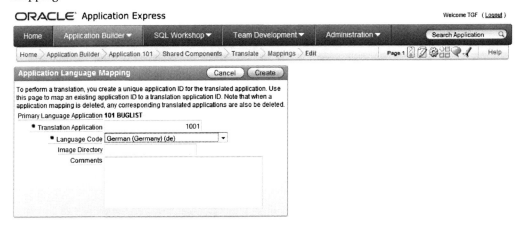

Figure 11-17. Defining a new application language mapping

Notice how you need to define an application ID for the mapping. This is the application ID that will be used for the behind-the-scenes application. You can pick any unused application ID that you like; however, there is one caveat that might seem a bit odd at first: you cannot use an application ID that ends in zero. For example, if you entered an ID of 10010, you would see the error message "Translation application ID must not end in zero."

The issue here is that APEX doesn't really use this as the application ID. Instead, this is used as the decimal portion of the application ID, with the original application ID used in front of the decimal point. In our example, the primary application has an ID of 101, so if we choose an ID of 1003 for the translated application, APEX will use the value of 101.1001 for the translated application. This is why you cannot use an ID that ends in zero: it would not be clear if 103.10010 referred to the ID of 10010 or 1001. This also explains why you don't see the translated applications in the traditional Application Builder interface.

For the mapping, you also choose the language that maps to this application ID. In the example in Figure 11-17, we are saying that when the language code is de, application 1003 should be used (or more precisely, application 101.1001 is used).

The end result of creating this mapping is nothing spectacular, as you can see in Figure 11-18. We created just one language mapping, but we could have created multiple mappings.

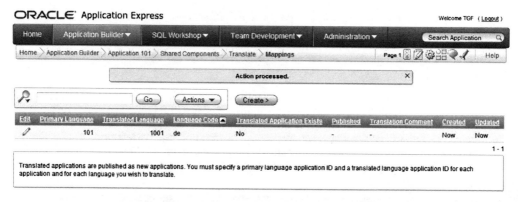

Figure 11-18. Translated application mapping

We now have a copy of the application that will be used if the user's browser is set to the de language code. However, we have not translated anything in the application yet, so the end user wouldn't see any difference (the text would still look like the original).

Seeding and Exporting the Translation Text

The first part of step 2 of the wizard lets you *seed* the translatable text, as shown in Figure 11-19. Here, you choose which language mapping you wish to use for your translation.

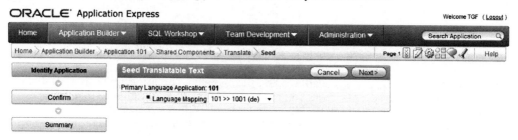

Figure 11-19. Seeding the translatable text

Seeding is the prerequisite for generating an XML Localization Interchange File Format (XLIFF) file. An XLIFF file contains all of the text in your original application and allows you to obtain the translations for the different language mappings you have created. XLIFF is an industry-standard file format that is used by many translation services to enable text in a document to be easily identified and isolated for translation purposes.

■ **Note** The XLIFF file doesn't contain everything that would be seen in the application, such as some error messages. Also, it does not contain any data from underlying tables. You need to handle these items yourself. Handling messages is described in the "Translating the Standard Messages" section later in this chapter.

It is important to realize that APEX does not have the facility to automatically translate your applications for you. It just enables you to easily generate a list of all the text (or much of it) used in your application, which you will then need to translate (either yourself or through a translation service). Figure 11-20 shows the result of the translation list generation.

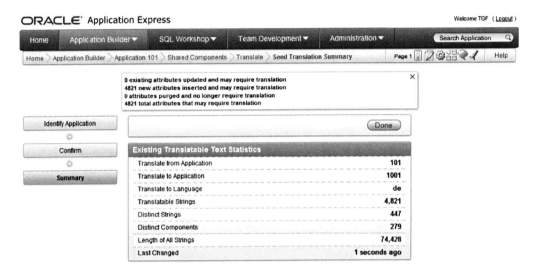

Figure 11-20. Translation List Generation

Once you have performed the seeding step, you can generate an XLIFF file, either for the entire application or for a specific page, as shown in Figure 11-21.

Figure 11-21. Generating XLIFF files

You can see in Figure 11-20 that you get some output from the seeding process that tells you the number of attributes (separate text strings) that might require translation (4821 in this example). The term *attribute* here refers to things like item labels, column headings, and so on.

You can also see in Figure 11-21 that you can either export all of the elements or export just those that require translation (if you've previously translated some, for example). The change in terminology between the word *element* and *attribute* can be a bit confusing, but essentially they're both referring to the individual pieces of text in the application.

So, let's take a look at a typical XLIFF file. The format of the XLIFF file follows a standard, so once you see how one XLIFF file works, you should understand how any XLIFF file works (regardless of the languages involved).

The header of the XLIFF file contains some comments that describe which application the file was produced for, the languages involved, and so on.

```
<?xml version="1.0" encoding="UTF-8"?>

<!--
  ******************
  ** Source      :  103
  ** Source Lang:  en-us
  ** Target      :  1003
  ** Target Lang:  de
  ** Page        :  1
  ** Filename:      f103_1003_p1_en-us_de.xlf
  ** Generated By: ADMIN
  ** Date:          03-DEC-2008 12:34:47
  ******************

-->
```

The rest of the file contains an XML document (all XLIFF files are XML documents that obey the XLIFF Document Type Definition) that describes the translatable text, as shown in Listing 11-6. For this example, we exported just a specific page (page 1), for the application mapping that we created earlier (103 >> 1003 (de)).

Listing 11-6. Exported XLIFF File for a Page

```
<?xml version="1.0" encoding="UTF-8"?>
<!--
    ******************
    ** Source      :  101
    ** Source Lang:  en-us
    ** Target      :  1001
    ** Target Lang:  de
    ** Page        :  1
    ** Filename:      f101_1001_p1_en-us_de.xlf
    ** Generated By: TGF
    ** Date:          03-MAR-2011 06:59:40
    ******************
  -->
<xliff version="1.0">
<file original="f101_1001_p1_en-us_de.xlf" source-language="en-us" target-language="de"
datatype="html">
<header></header>
<body>
<trans-unit id="S-5-1-101">
<source>Report Page</source>
<target>Report Page</target>
</trans-unit>

...
```

Note that we've included only the first lines of the XLIFF file in Listing 11-6. The actual file is more than 300 lines long, and that is just for one page, so you can imagine how big an XLIFF file for an entire application could be.

You can see that the file contains an XML fragment that describes each piece of text used in the application. (You don't really need to understand XML to see how this works; however, it does help if you have some XML knowledge.) For example, taking a snippet from Listing 11-6 (formatted as follows so it's easier to read):

```
<trans-unit id="S-5-1-101">

  <source>Report Page</source>
  <target>Report Page</target>
</trans-unit>
```

We have a section called trans-unit, which is our translation unit. Each unit has a unique ID (this allows APEX to associate a particular translation to the element in APEX). Inside each trans-unit section, we have the source text (the original text) and the target text (the translated version).

The interesting thing to note is that even if we use the exact same text in multiple places in the application, the XLIFF file will contain separate instances of that text. Take, for example, the "Report Page" text:

```
<trans-unit id="S-5-1-101">
<source>Report Page</source>
<target>Report Page</target>
</trans-unit>
<trans-unit id="S-5-1-101">
<source>Report Page</source>
<target>Report Page</target>
</trans-unit>
```

So even though the text is the same, each occurrence of the text is treated distinctly. You might think this is a bit wasteful. Why can't APEX just output the text once so that we would just translate it once? The reason is that it could be dangerous in certain circumstances to assume that just because the source text is the same, the target text will also be the same. Depending on your application, there might be other contextual information on the page, which means that given the same source text, you might want to provide different target text translations. By listing each occurrence of the text individually, APEX gives you the flexibility to either use the same translation or to provide a different one, depending on your exact situation.

The id attribute in the file also follows a standard convention. For the example, the id="S-5-1-101" breaks down as follows:

- The first part of the id is typically always S.

- The 5 is derived from the id column of the wwv_flow_translatable_cols$ table, which contains all translatable elements.

- The 1 comes from the translate_from_id column of the wwv_flow_translatable_text$ table (from step 2 in the wizard).

- The 101 is the application ID that is being translated.

So now we have the XLIFF file, and we need to translate the text in some way. As we mentioned earlier, you can either do it yourself (by using a standard text editor or a program that understands XLIFF files) or give the XLIFF file to another party to perform the translations for you. After you've translated the text, you will import the XLIFF file back into APEX. So, this is a three-step process, carried out as follows:

1. Export all the source and target text from APEX.

2. Modify the target text to whatever you choose (this is the manual process).

3. Import the source and target text back into APEX.

Translating Text

If you're going to translate the files yourself, you can use a regular text editor, as long as it can save in Unicode. For example, you could modify

```
<trans-unit id="S-14-4239963891701920-103">

    <source>Search</source>
    <target>Search</target>
</trans-unit>
```

so that it reads

```
<trans-unit id="S-14-4239963891701920-103">

    <source>Search</source>
    <target>Suche</target>
</trans-unit>
```

This method of using a plain text editor works very well. Actually, you can use good old Notepad on your Windows machine as it can store files in Unicode format. However, we highly recommend using a program that actually understands XLIFF format, which makes the process much easier. For example, the LocFactory Editor (www.triplespin.com/en/products/locfactoryeditor.html), a Mac OSX tool, lets you easily see how many translations you have left to do, as shown in Figure 11-22.

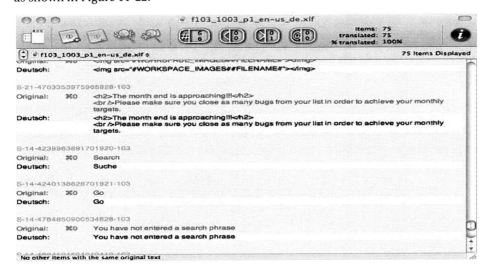

Figure 11-22. Using an XLIFF editor

After you provided the translations, you can resave the XLIFF file. You are then ready for the next step in the translation process, which is to import the XLIFF file back into APEX.

Applying Your Translation File and Publishing

After your XLIFF file is updated with translations, you move to step 4 of the wizard, as shown in Figure 11-23. (Note that we translated only one word in this example.)

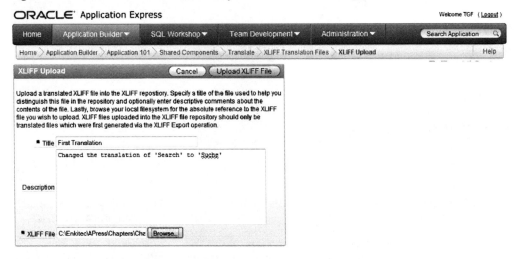

Figure 11-23. Importing the modified XLIFF file

Figure 11-23 shows the XLIFF file being uploaded. Note that we provide a title for the uploaded file so that we can identify the file to publish (which means to apply the XLIFF translation file to a particular translation mapping). Before you actually "publish" the application, you need to apply the translation using the link in the Tasks section, which is in the bottom right corner of the page, as shown in Figure 11-24.

■ **Note** Although it seems a little out of place, you must use the "Apply Translations" link before publishing the application. If you skip this step, the wizard will complete without issue, but your translations will not show up in the application.

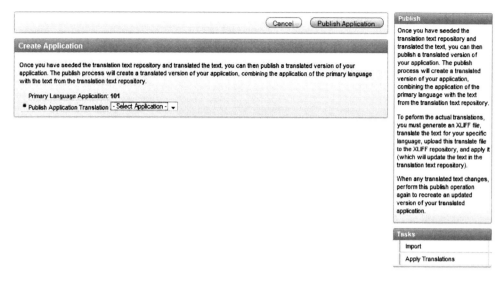

Figure 11-24. Apply Translation Link

The Apply Translations page, as shown in Figure 11-25, allows you to select the XLIFF file you just uploaded and to identify to which application translation it should be applied. In this example, the XLIFF file is called f101_1001_en_de.xlf and the application translation is labeled 101 >> 1001 (de). When you click the "Apply XLIFF Translation File" link, the translation is actually done.

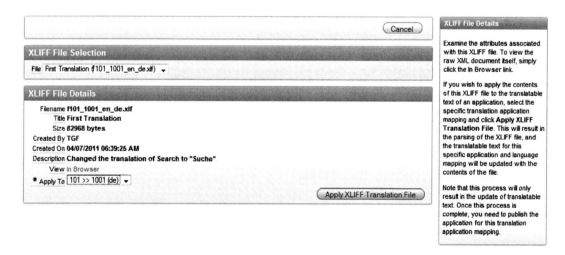

Figure 11-25. Apply Translations page

Following the translation, you are returned to the Publish Application page, as shown in Figure 11-26, where you once again set the Application Translation (101 >> 1001 (de)) and click the "Publish Application" button. This completes the overall translation process.

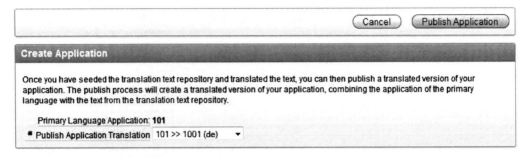

Figure 11-26. Applying the XLIFF translation file

Once you have applied the translation file, you can publish the new application with the click of a single button, and you're finished (well almost, you still need to test it)!

Testing the Translation

Now you can change the locale of your browser to test your translation. Depending on the browser you're using, you can either do this directly in the browser itself, independent of the locale of the operating system, or change the locale of the operating system, as described earlier in the chapter. Using Firefox, for example, you can simply go to the Advanced Section in Preferences and say that you want to use the German language as your primary language. Once you have done that, you can view the page and be presented with the new (behind-the-scenes) translated version of the application, which uses the word "Suche" instead of "Search."

Figure 11-27 shows both the translated version and the original version (which uses the primary application by default) for comparison.

Figure 11-27. Comparing the original and translated versions

Now, while Figure 11-23 may not be earth-shatteringly exciting, it does demonstrate the powerful functionality of APEX's built-in translation features. One of the major benefits is that you can easily separate the task of building the application from the task of translating it. You can concentrate on building an application in your own native language, and then at some future point, just export the XLIFF file and send it off to be translated by a third party. You are also free to extend your application to add more translated versions as and when you need them. In other words, you are not forced to pick which languages you want to support at a particular time; you can always go back and retro-translate applications you wrote months or years ago to support new end users' native languages.

Translating On the Fly

As you have seen, you can use XLIFF files to translate much of the text used in your applications. However, your application may have other text that you want to translate on the fly, particularly text that might follow a standard format but include some runtime parameters or contextual information.

For example, let's say that we want to present the users with an information panel that welcomes them to the Buglist application and also displays how many bugs they currently have assigned to them, something like this

```
Hello John, you have 4 bugs assigned to you.
```

We could do this in a number of ways, such as using label fields and then translating the fields using the XLIFF method, but this could get a little messy, since we would need to break up the string into the parts that are dynamic (John and 4) and the parts that are static.

An alternative method that is better suited in this case is to use the text message translation feature available in Shared Components, as shown in Figure 11-28. This feature allows you to define a substitution string, along with parameters if needed, and then to define for which language to use that substitution string. You can define multiple language versions of the same substitution string.

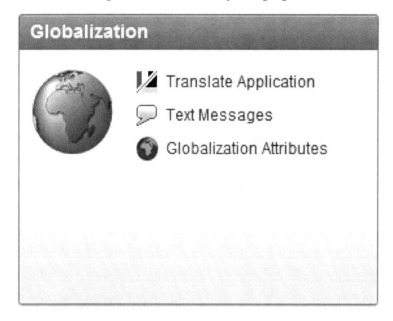

Figure 11-28. Text message translation

We begin by creating a new text message that contains the English version of the message, as shown in Figure 11-28.

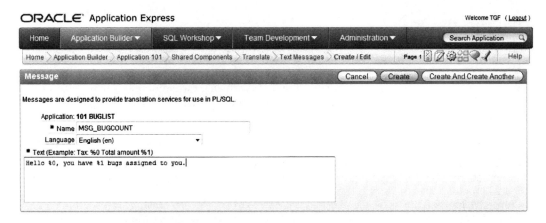

Figure 11-29. *Creating the US English bug count message*

Notice that in the message itself, we have used %0 and %1 to represent the username and number of bugs assigned to the person, respectively. You can use up to ten of these variables to represent dynamic values in the text. Also notice that we needed to define the language that this message represents.

Now we need to provide the translated version of this message (again, we'll use German, although obviously the same technique applies to any language). We create a new text message, define the language to be German, and use the following text:

```
Hallo %0, du hast %1 hervorragende wanzen.
```

Note that the purpose here is not to get an exact translation, but to show the principle. You could actually have an entirely different message for the translated version. It's also worth mentioning that you can swap the %0 and %1 for languages with different grammar. The most important thing is that the message name should match the original name that you created—MSG_BUGCOUNT in this example.

After you've created the message, you can reference it in your application from wherever you want the text (translated or default) to appear. To do that, you can use the APEX_LANG.MESSAGE routine in the APEX_LANG package, which contains many routines related to language translations. The APEX_LANG.MESSAGE routine has the following signature:

```
APEX_LANG.MESSAGE (

    p_name    IN    VARCHAR2 DEFAULT NULL,
    p0        IN    VARCHAR2 DEFAULT NULL,
    p1        IN    VARCHAR2 DEFAULT NULL,
    p2        IN    VARCHAR2 DEFAULT NULL,
    ...
    p9        IN    VARCHAR2 DEFAULT NULL,
    p_lang    IN    VARCHAR2 DEFAULT NULL)
    RETURN VARCHAR2;
```

The parameters to this routine are fairly self-explanatory, and are as follows:

- The p_name parameter is the name of the text message (which you just created).

- The p0 through p9 parameters are the values you can pass in, which are represented by %0 through %9 in the text.

- The p_lang parameter is the language you want obtain the text for (by default, this will be obtained through the language setting for the application).

The return result of the function is a string containing the text corresponding to the language (if you've defined text for the language parameter that is passed in) with any of the %0 . . . %9 strings replaced by the p0 . . . p9 parameters.

We can now create a new PL/SQL region on the page, which contains the following code:

```
htp.p(apex_lang.message(p_name => 'MSG_BUGCOUNT',

                    p0      => :APP_USER,
                    p1      => :P1_BUGCOUNT
));
```

We are using the htp.p procedure to output the return result of the APEX_LANG.MESSAGE function. Notice that we are using the APP_USER and P1_BUGCOUNT session state items to pass into the p0 and p1 parameters. (For the P1_BUGCOUNT item, you would just need to use a computation or default or other method to retrieve the number of bugs belonging to that user.)

Now if you run the application with your browser set to en-us, you should see the message displayed in the default language. If you set the browser language to German, you will see the translated version, as shown in Figure 11-30.

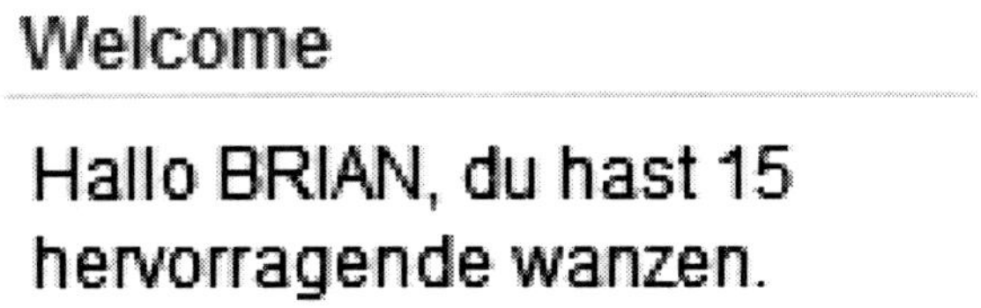

Welcome

Hallo BRIAN, du hast 15 hervorragende wanzen.

Figure 11-30. Displaying the translated text message

This is a very nice way of displaying very contextual and localized information to your end users. In a production system, you would probably want to cache this region to avoid the overhead of having to make the call to the APEX_LANG.MESSAGE routine until you really need to (for example, when the statuses of bugs are changed). You can also use the APEX_LANG.MESSAGE function in a SQL query to use data from the query to pass as the p0 . . . p9 parameters.

If that's not enough, how about another fairly common scenario? Currently in the Buglist application, we use a LOV to display the list of statuses that can be assigned to a bug. However, rather than displaying "Open" or "Closed," we would like to display localized text. We can define a dynamic translation that will be applied to the LOV.

First, we need to create a table to store the list of statuses (so we can use a dynamic LOV instead of a static one).

```
jes@DBTEST> create table tbl_status(
  2  id number,
  3  status varchar2(20));
```

```
Table created.

jes@DBTEST> insert into tbl_status (id, status)
  2  values (1, 'Open');
1 row created.

jes@DBTEST> insert into tbl_status (id, status)
  2  values (2, 'Closed');
1 row created.

jes@DBTEST> commit;
Commit complete.
```

Next, we set up the dynamic translations, where we must create a mapping between the data that will be returned from the table and a particular language translation. Figure 11-31 shows the dynamic translation for the text "Closed" into the German "Geschlossen" (again, the purpose is not to provide the most appropriate translation, just to show how you can do it).

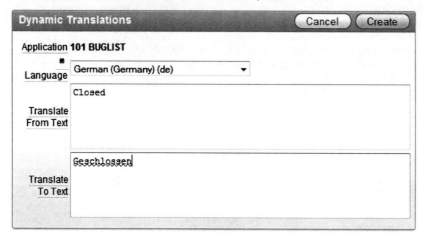

Figure 11-31. Creating a dynamic translation

Now we need to create the LOV using another method in the APEX_LANG package that will map the text used depending on the language. The code used in the LOV is shown in Listing 11-7.

Listing 11-7. Using Dynamic Translation

```
select
  apex_lang.lang(s.status) d,
  s.id r
from
  tbl_status s
order by d
```

Here, we use the WWV_FLOW_LANG.LANG function, passing in the value of the status column (Open or Closed). The LANG function then uses the dynamic translations we created earlier to retrieve the correct text based on the current language. The LANG function's signature is similar to that of the MESSAGE function (shown earlier):

```
FUNCTION LANG RETURNS VARCHAR2

Argument Name                    Type                 In/Out Default?
-----------------------------    -------------------  ------ --------
P_PRIMARY_TEXT_STRING            VARCHAR2             IN     DEFAULT
P0                               VARCHAR2             IN     DEFAULT
P1                               VARCHAR2             IN     DEFAULT
P2                               VARCHAR2             IN     DEFAULT
P3                               VARCHAR2             IN     DEFAULT
...
P9                               VARCHAR2             IN     DEFAULT
P_PRIMARY_LANGUAGE               VARCHAR2             IN     DEFAULT
```

Like the MESSAGE function, the LANG function allows you to pass in a parameter for the language to use, or else it defaults to the application language.

Now if you view the Buglist application using a German locale browser and look at the values in the status LOV, you should see the localized text, as shown in Figure 11-32.

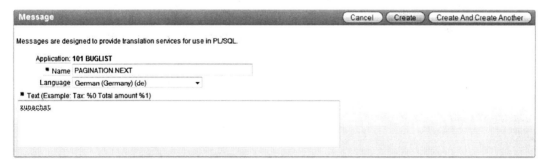

Figure 11-32. Dynamic translations in an LOV

In this fashion, you provide translations based on dynamic data, rather than static text. But obviously, you need to provide translations for the data you may wish to translate.

Translating the Standard Messages

As you've learned, you can use the XLIFF method to translate static text in your applications, and you can use routines in the APEX_LANG package to provide dynamic translations for other text. However, what about some of the built-in strings provided by APEX itself, which most applications will display?

For example, on the main page in the Buglist application, where we use a report to display the list of bugs, we have pagination enabled on the report. APEX uses some default text for the Next and Previous link labels. It would be very annoying if we translated every other part of the application and could not translate those messages, wouldn't it? Well, of course we can translate those messages. You do this using the same techniques already shown, but with a slight twist in that you need to know the correct syntax to translate a particular built-in message. The APEX help page lists the following built-in messages as translatable (search in the Managing Application Globalization section for the full list. as there are far too many to reproduce here):

- `FLOW.SINGLE_VALIDATION_ERROR - 1 error has occurred`

- `FLOW.VALIDATION_ERROR - %0 errors have occurred`

- `OUT_OF_RANGE - Invalid set of rows requested, the source data of the report has been modified`

- `PAGINATION.NEXT - Next`

- `PAGINATION.NEXT_SET - Next Set`

- `PAGINATION.PREVIOUS - Previous`

- `WWV_RENDER_REPORT3.SORT_BY_THIS_COLUMN - Sort by this column`

- `WWV_RENDER_REPORT3.X_Y_OF_MORE_THAN_Z - row(s) %0 - %1 of more than %2`

- `WWV_RENDER_REPORT3.X_Y_OF_Z - row(s)%0 - %1 of %2`

- `WWV_RENDER_REPORT3.X_Y_OF_Z_2 - %0 - %1 of %2`

To translate these messages, all you need to do is to create a new text message using the hard-coded string that represents the message for which you wish to provide a translation. Figure 11-33 shows an example for `PAGINATION.NEXT`.

Figure 11-33. Translating a standard message

You need to ensure you use the exact string name; otherwise, APEX will not find a match for it when it needs to display a standard message.

Now when you run the application, the standard Next link should be displayed with the relevant translation applied, as shown in Figure 11-34.

10-FEB-06 01.00.00,000000 AM	laura.barnes@foo.com	Laura Barnes

1 - 15 zunächst⊙

Figure 11-34. Displaying a translated standard message

Note that you can also use the variables %0, %1, and so on to allow dynamic values to be substituted at runtime, as in this example:

```
FLOW.VALIDATION_ERROR - %0 errors have occurred
```

This allows you to completely change the format of the error message, for example

```
There were %0 errors.
```

This also means that if you don't like the format of some of the standard messages, you can adapt them, even if you use the same language for the application.

Summary

Generally, you either need to localize your application or you don't. In other words, it is either a requirement of the application or people don't tend to do it. Obviously, if an application is an internal system that won't be exposed to nonnative language speakers (whatever that language is), you probably don't need to even think about localizing it. However, if you are designing commercial systems that can be accessed by a wide variety of people, there can be great benefits in providing localization features in the application. For one thing, it can bring a whole new set of potential customers to your application. Additionally, it can really help to cut down on support issues (in terms of nonnative speakers misunderstanding the text).

APEX provides a lot of different but related features to enable you to translate your entire application. You can use techniques such as NLS settings to customize the way that dates, currencies, and so on are displayed.

However, we do urge you to get the right people to help with the translations when localizing your application. For example, we know of one case where 99.9% of the translation was fine, but one sentence from the original English text had been translated out of context, leading to a completely different meaning in Russian. That one small translation error resulted in a real financial cost to the company concerned, as the text in question was part of a legally binding contract.

So, just because the technology makes it easy, don't cut corners on getting your translations done correctly! If it's critical to your business, do a double translation, whereby you have the original text translated to your target language, then give that translated text to another group to translate back to the original source language (to see if there has been any context lost along the way). Most commercial translation services provide these sorts of double-translation checks.

CHAPTER 12

Plug-ins

Plug-ins, new in APEX 4.0, allow you to extend the functionality of item types, region types, dynamic actions, and process types. The plug-in architecture includes a declarative development environment that lets you create custom versions of these built-in objects. For example, instead of using a standard select list or check box, you could build a "star rating" item that allows your user to provide feedback using a one-to-five star graphic. This new item type could then be used across all your applications.

While it was always possible to create custom functionality using tools like custom Ajax, the code could be located in multiple different places: inside the database, in JavaScript files, and so forth. You scan still use all the customization tools you are familiar with, but turning that code into a plug-in makes it much easier to use and manage since all of the code is contained in one object, your new type.

This new architecture also allows you to create plug-ins based on any jQuery component. The open source jQuery library is widely accepted and is loaded with useful JavaScript and Ajax functionality. Basing your plug-ins on existing jQuery functionality is a great way to add advanced features to your applications without generating mountains of new code manually.

In this chapter, we will explore the new world of plug-ins by creating a few from scratch while also reviewing some popular plug-ins that are available from the following online repositories:

- Oracle Applications Express Plug-ins page (www.oracle.com/technetwork/developer-tools/apex/application-express/apex-plug-ins-182042.html)

- APEX-PLUGIN.com (www.apex-plugin.com)

After seeing the number of plug-ins that are freely available, you may find yourself importing more plug-ins than you build. If you do build plug-ins of your own, you can use the downloadable ones as a guide and you can publish your own back to the online repositories. Think of this as a way to give a little back to your development community.

Creating Your First Plug-in

As with any development project, you first need to establish a goal; some new piece of functionality. Once the goal is defined, you can define the requirements to be mapped to your development framework. If your new functionality would be beneficial in other applications, you should consider creating it as a plug-in. Will it work as a plug-in? If your functionality is an extension of one of the standard types—item, region, process, dynamic action—then it is a candidate for making into a plug-in.

Running the APEX Plug-in Builder

The interface used to create APEX plug-ins is accessed under the Shared Components menu of the Application Builder. The plug-in builder interface is accessed via the Plug-ins link on the User Interface section. When you first enter the Plug-ins builder, as shown in Figure 12-1, you will notice that APEX 4.0 is delivered with no plug-ins. There is, however, a button on the page titled "View Plug-in Repository," which will direct you to a location on Oracle's corporate web site that houses plug-ins that are freely downloadable. We will explore this site later in this chapter, but for now we will focus on the mechanics of building a plug-in from scratch.

Figure 12-1. *Plug-ins builder home page*

We'll start by creating a simple item type plug-in, as it is the easiest to complete and illustrates most of the mechanics of the plug-in architecture. To create a plug-in of any kind, you have to first decide what its purpose will be. In this example, we'll create a text item that will require a value and will have a red background until a value is entered. After at least one character is entered in the field, the background will return to standard white. We'll call this plug-in requiredInColor.

To get started, we need to take a look at the plug-in builder. When you click on the Create button, the plug-in builder page is displayed as shown in Figure 12-2. We filled in the Name, Internal Name, and Type fields in the figure to illustrate how plug-ins should be named. Following are guidelines on plug-in naming best practices:

Name: The Name field will be used to identify the plug-in when adding them to pages using the standard builder pages. This name should be unique across your applications, but uniqueness is not required.

Internal Name: The Internal Name of a plug-in is used by APEX 4.0 to identify the plug-in and is never displayed. While the plug-in Name is not required to be unique, the Internal Name must be unique to your current application. Because plug-ins can be published to public repositories, it is recommended that their Internal Names be constructed so that they will be unique worldwide. For example: com.enkitec.requiredInColor.

These guidelines guarantee that your plug-in's name will not be a duplicate of one that you download from another site. They do not ensure that names for plug-ins you create are unique within your organization, so you'll have to manage that on your own. You'll notice that any plug-ins you download from Oracle's plug-in repository have names that are prefixed with com.oracle.apex.

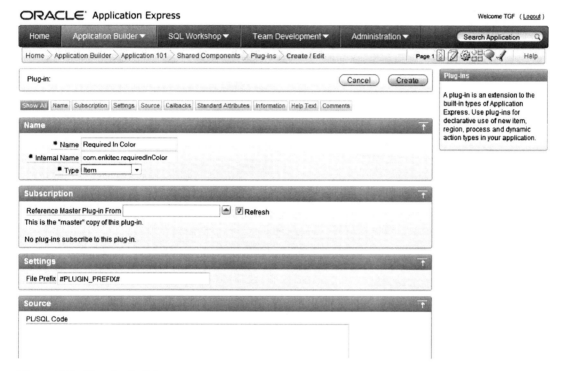

Figure 12-2. Plug-ins builder page

In the Subscription section of the plug-in builder, the Reference Master Plug-in From field allows you to use a copy of an existing plug-in by either entering the name or selecting it from a pop-up list of values. If you leave this field blank, by default the plug-in is considered a master. We will leave this field blank since we are creating a new plug-in.

The File Prefix, #PLUGIN_PREFIX#, is a virtual path that determines where any plug-in support files (like JavaScript files, CSS files, and so forth) will be stored. This prefix points to a location in the database. If you are using a separate HTTP server, you can get better performance if you store the supporting files there, as opposed to on the database. You can either create a new substitution string pointing to a new virtual directory or just use the #IMAGE_PREFIX# in place of the #PLUGIN_PREFIX#.

The next section, PL/SQL Code, is where the guts of the plug-in are built. This code is used to do the following:

- Render or display the plug-in

- Validate the plug-in

- Execute the plug-in

You can write your code as an anonymous PL/SQL block in the PL/SQL Code section. You can also create your code as a database package and refer to that package from a block in this section. You'll get better performance from the package-based approach.

Each plug-in type must implement a specific interface, known as a render function, which was standardized so that future APEX enhancements do not break existing plug-ins. Since we are talking about item type plug-ins, we'll first take a look at the item type render function shown in Listing 12-1.

Listing 12-1. Plug-in Render Function Interface

```
function <name of function> (
p_item                  in apex_plugin.t_page_item,
p_plugin                in apex_plugin.t_plugin,
p_value                 in varchar2,
p_is_readonly           in boolean,
p_is_printer_friendly in boolean )
return apex_plugin.t_page_item_render_result
```

■ **Note** The process for building plug-ins is not completely documented. In fact, you will not find the function definition from Listing 12-1 in any of the APEX 4.0 documentation. The only place to find information on how plug-ins are defined is by clicking on the "Render Function Name" in the Callbacks section of the Plug-in builder page.

The name of the function is not important, it just has to follow Listing 12-1's specification. The first two parameters in the render function are of type apex_plugin. The name apex_plugin is actually a synonym for the apex_040000.wwv_flow_plugin package. This record type contains attributes that allow you to control the operation of the item on which the plug-in is being built. The ID attribute, for example, is the HTML ID of the item that can be used in JavaScript to manipulate the Document Object Model (DOM). Listing 12-2 shows an excerpt from the wwv_flow_plugin package showing the definition of the t_page_item and t_plugin record types.

Listing 12-2. Plug-in Record Type Definitions

```
type t_page_item is record
(
    id                      number,
    name                    varchar2(255),
    label                   varchar2(4000),
    plain_label             varchar2(4000),
    format_mask             varchar2(255),
    is_required             boolean,
    lov_definition          varchar2(4000),
    lov_display_extra       boolean,
    lov_display_null        boolean,
    lov_null_text           varchar2(255),
    lov_null_value          varchar2(255),
```

```
    lov_cascade_parent_items    varchar2(255),
    ajax_items_to_submit        varchar2(255),
    ajax_optimize_refresh       boolean,
    element_width               number,
    element_max_length          number,
    element_height              number,
    element_attributes          varchar2(2000),
    element_option_attributes   varchar2(4000),
    escape_output               boolean,
    attribute_01                varchar2(32767),
    attribute_02                varchar2(32767),
    attribute_03                varchar2(32767),
    attribute_04                varchar2(32767),
    attribute_05                varchar2(32767),
    attribute_06                varchar2(32767),
    attribute_07                varchar2(32767),
    attribute_08                varchar2(32767),
    attribute_09                varchar2(32767),
    attribute_10                varchar2(32767)
)

type t_plugin is record
(
    name         varchar2(45),
    file_prefix  varchar2(4000),
    attribute_01 varchar2(32767),
    attribute_02 varchar2(32767),
    attribute_03 varchar2(32767),
    attribute_04 varchar2(32767),
    attribute_05 varchar2(32767),
    attribute_06 varchar2(32767),
    attribute_07 varchar2(32767),
    attribute_08 varchar2(32767),
    attribute_09 varchar2(32767),
    attribute_10 varchar2(32767)
)
```

As you can see in the t_page_item record, the name and ID of the item you are creating are available to you via this interface. When you want to operate on the value of your item type plug-in using JavaScript, you can pass the t_page_item.id to a JavaScript function and manipulate the DOM to control the appearance and utility of the item. You can also see that there are ten fields in both record types that start with "attribute." These are custom attributes that you can assign to your plug-in, which can be used to further define your item.

To define the features of your plug-in, you must construct a render function and, optionally, a validation function. The render function defines what the item will do and how it will be displayed. To protect against SQL injection attacks, a validation function should also be added, although it is not required. Listing 12-3 shows the contents of the PL/SQL code that implements our requiredInColor plug-in.

Listing 12-3. Plug-in PL/SQL Code

```
FUNCTION requiredInColor (
    p_item              in apex_plugin.t_page_item,
    p_plugin            in apex_plugin.t_plugin,
    p_value             in varchar2,
    p_is_readonly       in boolean,
    p_is_printer_friendly in boolean )
    RETURN apex_plugin.t_page_item_render_result
IS
    l_name varchar2(30);
    l_result        apex_plugin.t_page_item_render_result;
BEGIN
    IF p_is_readonly OR p_is_printer_friendly THEN
        APEX_PLUGIN_UTIL.print_hidden_if_readonly (
            p_item_name          => p_item.name,
            p_value              => p_value,
            p_is_readonly        => p_is_readonly,
            p_is_printer_friendly => p_is_printer_friendly );
        APEX_PLUGIN_UTIL.print_display_only (
            p_item_name       => p_item.name,
            p_display_value   => p_value,
            p_show_line_breaks => false,
            p_escape          => true,
            p_attributes      => p_item.element_attributes );
    ELSE
        l_name := APEX_PLUGIN.get_input_name_for_page_item(p_is_multi_value=>false);
        HTP.P('<input type="text" name="'||l_name||'" id="'||p_item.name||'"
'||'value="'||htf.escape_sc(p_value)||'" size="'||p_item.element_width||'"
'||'maxlength="'||p_item.element_max_length||'" '||p_item.element_attributes||'
onKeyUp="fldRequired('''||p_item.name||''')" />');
        APEX_JAVASCRIPT.add_library (p_name=> 'requiredInColor',p_directory =>
p_plugin.file_prefix,p_version => null );
    END IF;
    RETURN l_result;
END requiredInColor;
```

The code in Listing 12-3 adheres to the requirement shown in Listing 12-2. Following the declaration section, the first thing all plug-ins should do is detect whether the item has been identified as being read-only or printer-friendly. The l_name variable is used to store the name of the item on which the plug-in is based. To get the item name, the following function is called:

```
l_name := APEX_PLUGIN.get_input_name_for_page_item(p_is_multi_value=>false);
```

The call to this function includes a parameter, p_is_multi_value=>false. That parameter identifies the page item on which the plug-in is based as a single-value item. If the page item were a select list, for example, the value of the parameter would be set to true. The next two lines of code constitute most of the functionality of the plug-in. The line which begins with HTP.P actually renders the item as an HTML input item.

■ **Note** Because of the way single and double quote marks are used in PL/SQL, reading the code in Listing 12-3 is difficult at best. To make writing this code a little easier, use an HTML editor to build the code that you want and paste it in to the PL/SQL section of the plug-in builder. You can then modify the code one piece at a time replacing literals with the appropriate variables.

Notice that the value of the item, p_value, is being "escaped" using the htf.escape_sc() function, which changes values like "<" to "&lt." This function should always be used when passing values from an HTML page, as a malicious user can easily modify input values to submit SQL injection commands.

Paste Listing 12-3's code into the PL/SQL Code section of the plug-in builder and set the Render Function Name in the Callbacks section to the name of the render function from the PL/SQL code. If you forget this step, you will get an error saying that there is no render function for the plug-in when you run a page that contains the item-based plug-in. Figure 12-3 shows the populated PL/SQL Code section along with the correct setting for the Render Function Name.

Source

PL/SQL Code

```
function requiredInColor (
    p_item              in apex_plugin.t_page_item,
    p_plugin            in apex_plugin.t_plugin,
    p_value             in varchar2,
    p_is_readonly       in boolean,
    p_is_printer_friendly in boolean )
    return apex_plugin.t_page_item_render_result

is

    l_name varchar2(30);
```

☐ Do not validate PL/SQL code (parse PL/SQL code at runtime only).

Callbacks

Render Function Name	requiredInColor
AJAX Function Name	
Validation Function Name	

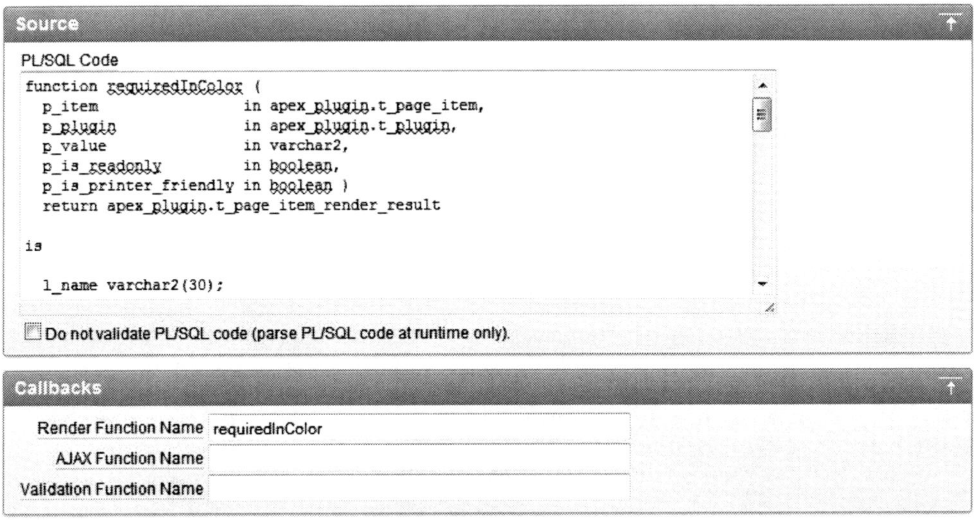

Figure 12-3. PL/SQL Code section of plug-in builder

Since we want to change the background color of the field as soon as a character is entered, the onKeyUp JavaScript function is called. You can see that the HTP.P function uses onKeyUp to call a JavaScript program called fldRequired. So where is this JavaScript? It's contained within an "included file" called requiredInColor.js that has to be uploaded to a location where APEX can find it.

To keep things simple, we used the #PLUGIN_PREFIX# substitution string so that uploaded files are stored in the database instead of on the HTTP server. The contents of the requiredInColor.js file are shown in Listing 12-4. The file has but one simple function: to change the color of the background of the item ID passed to it depending on whether any text has been entered. The background is set to #FEA5AD, which is a light red color when empty and white when populated. This file is uploaded using the Files section of the plug-in builder, as shown in Figure 12-4.

Listing 12-4. requiredInColor.js JavaScript File

```
function fldRequired(fldName)
{
  vValue = document.getElementById(fldName).value;
  if (!vValue)
    document.getElementById(fldName).style.background="#FEA5AD";
  else
    document.getElementById(fldName).style.background="#FFFFFF";
}
```

■ **Note** The "Files" section referred to in Figure 12-4 will not be visible until you create the plug-in.

Figure 12-4. File Upload section of plug-in builder

Once the JavaScript file is uploaded, the plug-in is ready to be used. Before moving on to using the new plug-in, it is important to discuss how you make changes to the uploaded JavaScript file. It is not as simple as making changes to the file and uploading it again, because APEX 4.0 does not allow the same file to be uploaded more than once. Instead, you have to delete the uploaded file and then re-upload it. While not insurmountable, the process is nothing short of annoying, as you must repeat the change/delete/upload cycle over and over while you're developing and testing your plug-in.

■ **Note** Since you are building standard JavaScript to support your plug-in, you can build a very simple HTML page that uses your JavaScript so that you can more easily troubleshoot the code. When you have it working, you can then go through the delete/upload cycle in the plug-in builder.

The last step in preparing the plug-in for use is to set the Standard Attributes. In this example, we only need to set the Is Visible Widget attribute, which tells APEX to display items based on this plug-in. If you want any plug-in to be visible, this attribute must be set. Figure 12-5 shows the Standard Attribute settings for this plug-in and the verification that our JavaScript file has been uploaded.

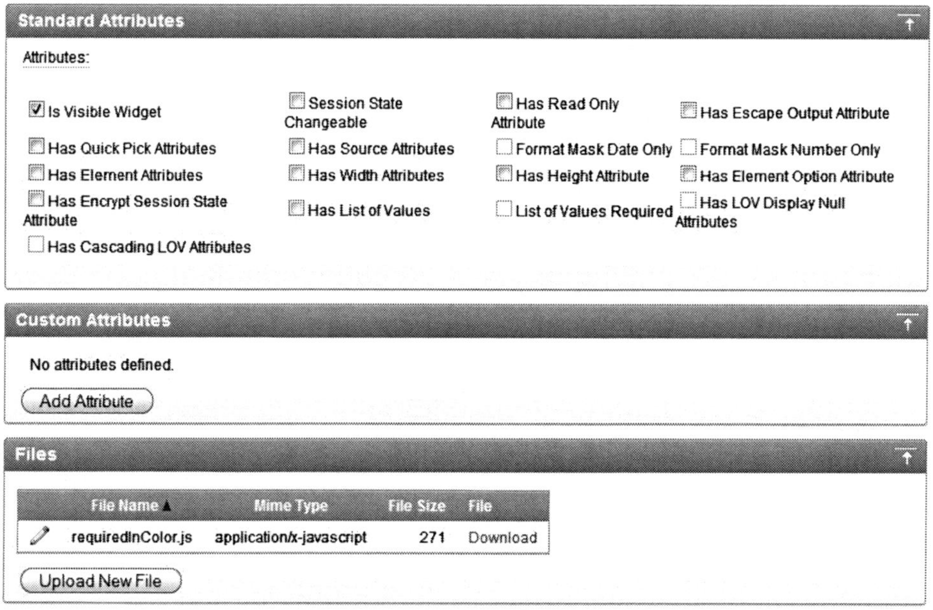

Figure 12-5. *Plug-in Standard Attributes*

Using Your New Plug-in

Now that your plug-in has been created, you can include it in any page in your application. It is important to note at this point that the plug-in you just created will only show up on the plug-in home page of the application where it was created. As discussed earlier in this chapter, existing plug-ins can be referenced in the Subscription section of the plug-in builder as opposed to being imported or re-created from scratch. Later in this chapter, we will cover sharing plug-ins by using the export and import features of the plug-in builder.

To test your new requiredInColor plug-in, you need to add it to a page. We modified an update form in the Buglist application. To add the new item type plug-in, edit the page (page 28 in our example) and create a new item. In Figure 12-6, the new item type is set to Plug-in.

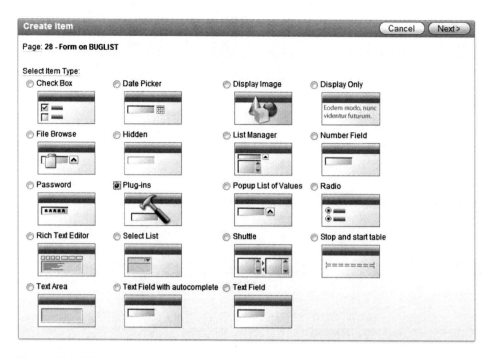

Figure 12-6. Creating item type plug-in

In the next step of the process, the installed plug-ins are displayed as shown in Figure 12-7. In our environment, you can see there are several available plug-ins and we have selected Required In Color. This is the name we assigned to our plug-in at the time it was created. The internal name (com.enkitec.requiredInColor) will never show up in a list of available items.

Figure 12-7. Select an existing item type plug-in

From this point on, the item creation process is the same as it would be if you were adding a standard, APEX text item. The only deviation, as we will see shortly, is if you have added custom attributes to your plug-in. In that case, you will have the opportunity to populate those new attributes during the item creation process. Our first plug-in does not contain custom attributes, so the creation process will be very familiar. In Figure 12-8, notice that we are naming the item as normal. The field name is defaulted with a value like P28_X and we modify it to read P28_REQUIRED.

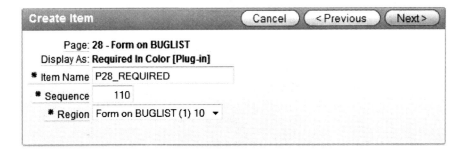

Figure 12-8. Name the new item type plug-in

To actually make this new plug-in-based item useful, we need to associate it with some database column. In the final step of the create item wizard, you would normally choose Database Column as the source type and some existing column as the source. Let's say we want to use this new item for the cost column to show that this column is required. If we assign it to the cost column now, we will get an error at runtime since there is already another item assigned to that column. So for now, leave the Source Type set to the default (Static Assignment), as shown in Figure 12-9. The item will be added to the page and will operate the way we want it to, but the values entered in this item will not be stored in the database.

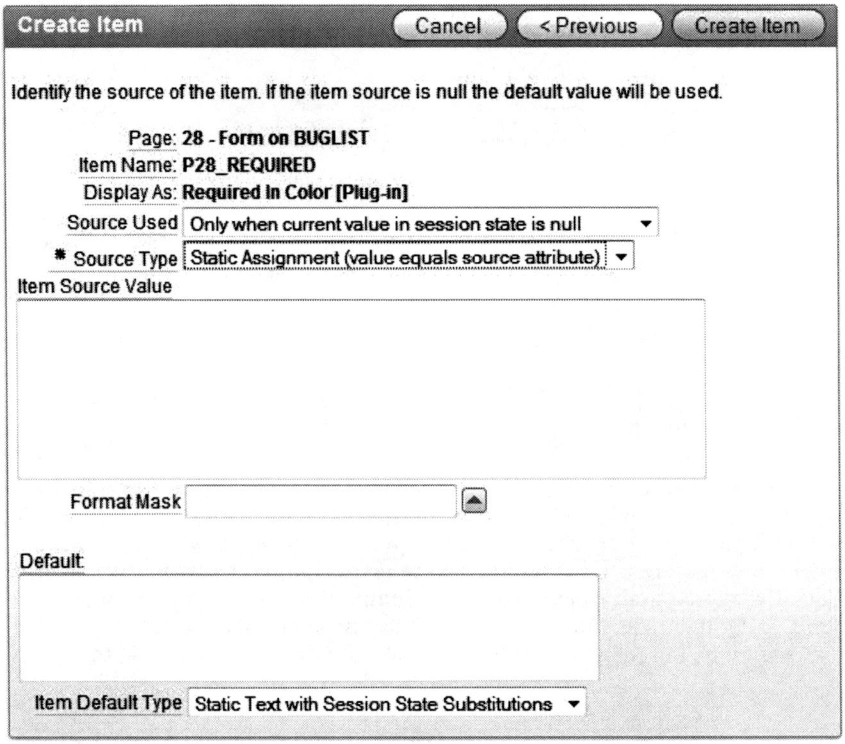

Figure 12-9. New item type plug-in, unpopulated

When you finish the creation process, run your page. In our case, this means executing a report and clicking the update icon to access the update form that contains our new item type plug-in. The update form, shown in Figure 12-10, contains our new, unpopulated field with a red background (you'll have to take our word for it since this page is monochrome).

The intention of this plug-in was to show the user that there is a field on the page that must contain a value. This is done visually by coloring the background of the page when the field is blank. When we enter a value, as shown in Figure 12-11, the characters show up and the background is changed back to standard white. Remember that our code only checks for a value, any value, and then changes the background color of the field. To make this plug-in more useful, you could further validate the input to ensure it meets the specifications of the system.

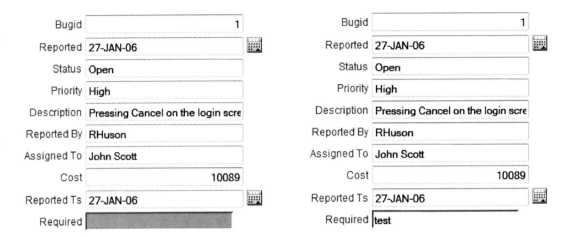

Figure 12-10. *New item type plug-in, unpopulated*   **Figure 12-11.** *New item type plug-in, populated*

The intention of this plug-in was to show the user that there is a field on the page that must contain a value. That is done visually by coloring the background of the page item when it is blank. When we enter a value, as shown in Figure 12-11, the characters show up and the background is changed back to standard white.

Remember that this new item doesn't really do anything other than rotate the color of the background. To make this new item actually useful, we need to associate it with a database column so that we can use it just like the current Cost item. To make this happen, a few simple steps are required:

1. Delete the current cost item from the page

2. Modify the P28_REQUIRED item, changing its name to P28_COST

3. Change the label to "Cost"

4. Change the Source Type to Database Column

5. Set the Item Source Value to the cost column

6. Re-position the new item, if you like

Now when you run the application and put a value in the Cost item, the value will be written to the database when you submit the form. If you do a little testing, you will notice that when the form containing the plug-in-based item displays a record that has a cost value, the item is displayed with a red background. The reason for this is simple. The render function we wrote executes the fldRequired JavaScript function using the onKeyUp event. This event will not be fired when the form is displayed, so we need to add some code that will execute our JavaScript function. Listing 12-5 shows the addition of the APEX_JAVASCRIPT.on_load_code function, which does just what you'd expect it to. The nice thing about this function is that it operates in conjunction with an onLoad script you may be using in the HTML Body of the form.

Listing 12-5. requiredInColor.js JavaScript File

```
function requiredInColor (
  p_item              in apex_plugin.t_page_item,
  p_plugin            in apex_plugin.t_plugin,
  p_value             in varchar2,
  p_is_readonly       in boolean,
  p_is_printer_friendly in boolean )
  return apex_plugin.t_page_item_render_result
is
  l_name varchar2(30);
  l_result        apex_plugin.t_page_item_render_result;

BEGIN
  IF p_is_readonly OR p_is_printer_friendly THEN
    APEX_PLUGIN_UTIL.print_hidden_if_readonly (
      p_item_name          => p_item.name,
      p_value              => p_value,
      p_is_readonly        => p_is_readonly,
      p_is_printer_friendly => p_is_printer_friendly );
    APEX_PLUGIN_UTIL.print_display_only (
      p_item_name        => p_item.name,
      p_display_value     => p_value,
      p_show_line_breaks => false,
      p_escape           => true,
      p_attributes       => p_item.element_attributes );
  ELSE
    l_name := APEX_PLUGIN.get_input_name_for_page_item(p_is_multi_value=>false);

    htp.p('<input type="text" name="'||l_name||'" id="'||p_item.name||'"
'||'value="'||htf.escape_sc(p_value)||'" size="'||p_item.element_width||'"
'||'maxlength="'||p_item.element_max_length||'" '||p_item.element_attributes||'
onKeyUp="fldRequired('''||p_item.name||''')"/>');

    APEX_JAVASCRIPT.add_library (p_name=> 'requiredInColor',p_directory =>
p_plugin.file_prefix,p_version => null );

    APEX_JAVASCRIPT.add_onload_code (p_code => ' fldRequired('''||p_item.name||''')');

  END IF;
  RETURN l_result;
END requiredInColor;
```

Replace the code in the PL/SQL section of the Required In Color plug-in and execute the page again. You can see that the Cost item is displayed with a white background for records that contain a Cost value. There is still much more you could do with this item. Adding real validation code to ensure that a value is entered and it is within specifications, for example, would be easy to do and you should be able to do that on your own.

Using Custom Attributes

Custom attributes are used to store metadata that can be added to any plug-in type. When adding a plug-in-based item to a page, you will be presented a prompt for each custom attribute attached to the type. You can assign up to ten custom attributes per plug-in, which allows for a great deal of flexibility. To keep things simple, we will assign a custom attribute to the Required In Color plug-in, which allows the developer to choose the color of the background of this item. We could add two attributes to control both the populated and unpopulated colors, but the mechanics are identical so we will stick with one in the interest of brevity.

The process of adding attributes is very simple. You navigate to the plug-in home page and edit the Required In Color plug-in. You'll notice that the Custom Attributes section reports that there are no attributes defined for this plug-in. Clicking the Add Attribute button displays the Edit Attribute page, as shown in Figure 12-12.

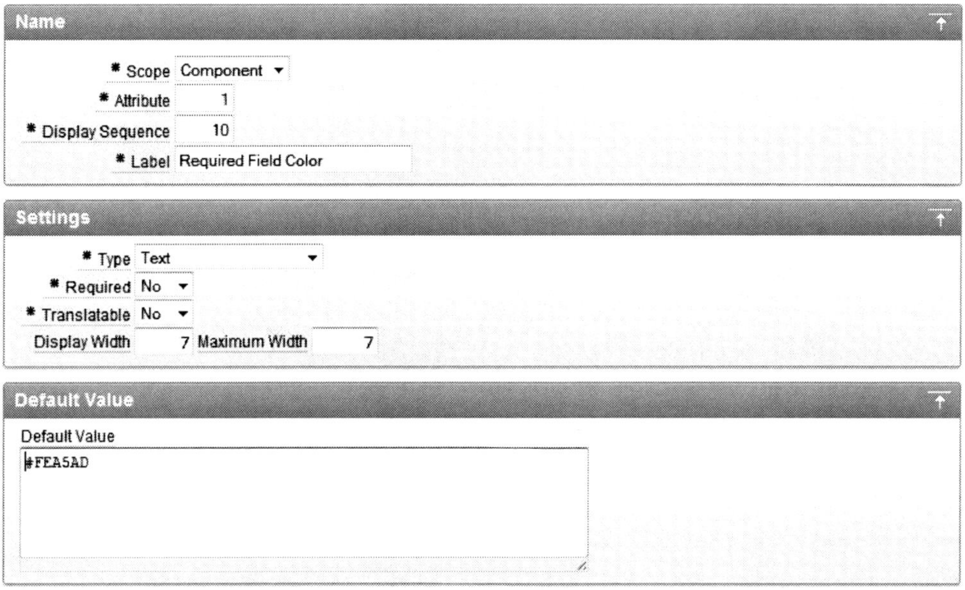

Figure 12-12. Edit Attribute page

Starting at the top of the Attribute definition, the Scope of the attribute refers to how the attribute can be used once the plug-in has been created. The Scope has two settings: Component and Application. If we set it to Application, then the developer using this plug-in would only be able to set the value of this attribute one time for the entire application. Using the Component settings allows for this attribute to be defined each time the plug-in is used.

The Attribute field is set to a numeric value that will be used to identify the attribute in code. The Display Sequence determines the order in which the Attributes are displayed in the APEX Builder and the Label is used to describe the attribute. We set the label to "Required Field Color."

The Settings section allows you to define the method the developer will use to set the value of the attribute. As you can see in Figure 12-13, there are several options from which to choose. For this example, we will use the Text type, as we want the developer to be able to enter a color value. We set the default value to #FEA5AD, so the text item's background will be rendered in color even if the developer forgets to set the value. You can see the definitions of the other settings by clicking on their labels.

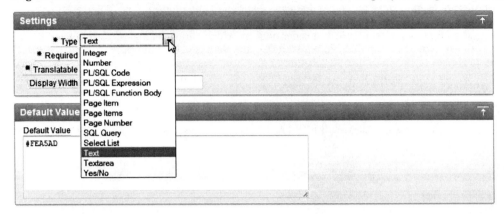

Figure 12-13. Attribute type selection

The Conditions and Help Text settings are the same as with other APEX objects. For this example, we left them blank and clicked the Create button to finish the Attribute creation process. So now we have a custom attribute, but it doesn't change anything because our code doesn't know about it. You can set the value of this attribute by editing the item that is based on this plug-in, as shown in Figure 12-14.

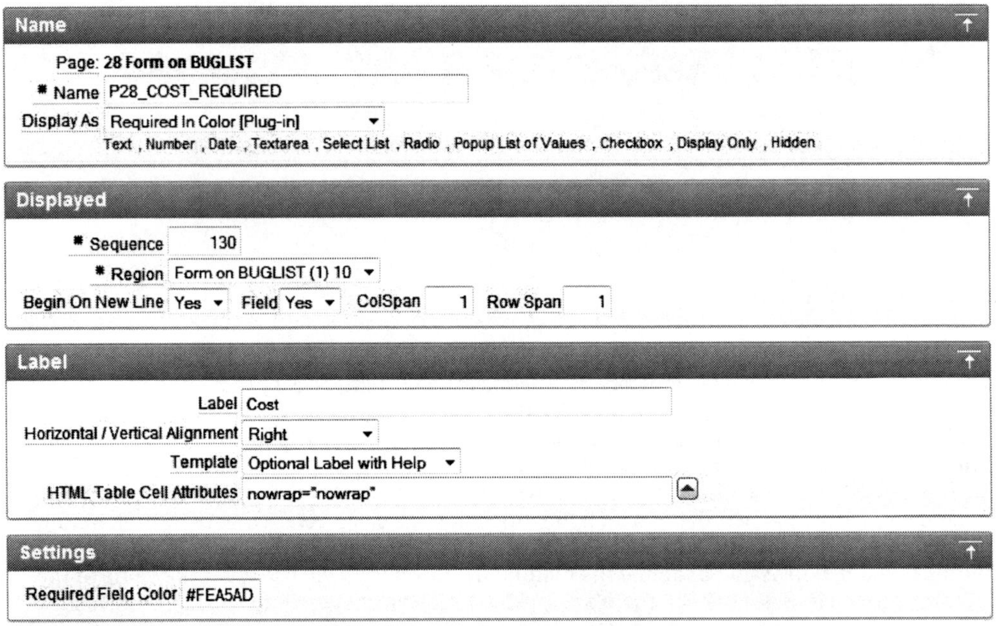

Figure 12-14. Item edit page

Your plug-in's custom attribute (or attributes) now show up in their own section on the item edit page called "Settings." For plug-ins with no custom attributes, the Settings section will not be displayed. You can see the default value that was set when the custom attribute was created, but you can change it to any value you like (just make sure it is a valid HTML color). To include our new attribute in the action, we have to make some code changes. First, we need to change the plug-in's PL/SQL code so that it has access to the attribute's value. Then we will modify the requiredInColor.js JavaScript file to use the new attribute value to paint the background of the item. Listing 12-6 shows the changes we made to the PL/SQL code. A new variable, l_background, is used to store the value of the single, custom attribute we added to the plug-in. We used the following declaration to gain access to the attribute's value:

```
l_background apex_application_page_items.attribute_01%type := p_item.attribute_01
```

When the l_background variable was defined, we had to know that the attribute used to store the background color was attribute number 1 because we can't refer to it by name. This was easy in our example since we only have one, but if you had multiple custom attributes on the plug-in, you would have to be sure about which ones you were using.

We also had to change the calls to htp.p and the APEX_JAVASCRIPT.add_onload_code to include the l_background parameter in when the fldRequired JavaScript function is called.

▪ **Note** When you're making changes to HTML code within the PL/SQL section, it can be excruciatingly difficult to get the single and double quotes right. A trick we use is to cut a piece of the code out and modify it slightly so that it can be executed in a simple, "select <some HTTP> from dual" statement in SQL*Plus. Once you see what the output looks like, you can change it a little at a time to make sure you have it right.

Listing 12-6. Plug-in PL/SQL Code Modified to Use Custom Attributes

```
function requiredInColor (
  p_item               in apex_plugin.t_page_item,
  p_plugin             in apex_plugin.t_plugin,
  p_value              in varchar2,
  p_is_readonly        in boolean,
  p_is_printer_friendly in boolean )
  return apex_plugin.t_page_item_render_result
is
  l_name varchar2(30);
  l_result       apex_plugin.t_page_item_render_result;
  l_background   apex_application_page_items.attribute_01%type := p_item.attribute_01;
BEGIN
  IF p_is_readonly OR p_is_printer_friendly THEN
    APEX_PLUGIN_UTIL.print_hidden_if_readonly (
      p_item_name          => p_item.name,
      p_value              => p_value,
      p_is_readonly        => p_is_readonly,
      p_is_printer_friendly => p_is_printer_friendly );
    APEX_PLUGIN_UTIL.print_display_only (
```

```
          p_item_name          => p_item.name,
          p_display_value      => p_value,
          p_show_line_breaks => false,
          p_escape             => true,
          p_attributes         => p_item.element_attributes );
    ELSE
      l_name := APEX_PLUGIN.get_input_name_for_page_item(p_is_multi_value=>false);

      htp.p('<input type="text" name="'||l_name||'" id="'||p_item.name||'"
'||'value="'||htf.escape_sc(p_value)||'" size="'||p_item.element_width||'"
'||'maxlength="'||p_item.element_max_length||'" '||p_item.element_attributes||'
onKeyUp="fldRequired('''||p_item.name||''','''||l_background||''')"/>');

      APEX_JAVASCRIPT.add_library (p_name=> 'requiredInColor',p_directory =>
p_plugin.file_prefix,p_version => null );

          APEX_JAVASCRIPT.add_onload_code (p_code => '
fldRequired("'||p_item.name||'","'||l_background||'")');

  END IF;

  RETURN l_result;

END requiredInColor;
```

To round out the changes related to our custom attribute, we need to modify the requiredInColor.js file, as it needs to receive two parameters instead of one. All we need to do is add a parameter, bkgColor, in the declaration of the fldRequired function and then use that variable name to color the item's background when it's empty. The new code is shown in Listing 12-7.

Listing 12-7. requiredInColor JavaScript Modified to Use Custom Attributes

```
function fldRequired(fldName,bkgColor)
{
  vValue = document.getElementById(fldName).value;
  if (!vValue)
  {
    document.getElementById(fldName).style.background=bkgColor;
  }
  else
  {
    document.getElementById(fldName).style.background="#FFFFFF";
  }
}
```

We're not done just yet, however. Remember that we have to upload the requiredInColor.js file so the plug-in has access to our changes. If a file with this name is already associated with the plug-in (which it is), we must first delete it as APEX 4.0 does not allow you implicitly replace an uploaded file. Using the edit plug-in page as shown in Figure 12-15, you must edit the existing requiredInColor file so you can delete it; then upload it again so our new changes are available.

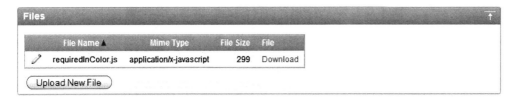

Figure 12-15. Item edit page

Once you apply the changes to the plug-in, you can execute your form. It should look just like it did before because the default value of the plug-in's attribute is the same. Try modifying the value of the "Required Field Color" setting on the P28_COST_REQUIRED item to some other color. Figure 12-16 shows our attribute being changed to yellow.

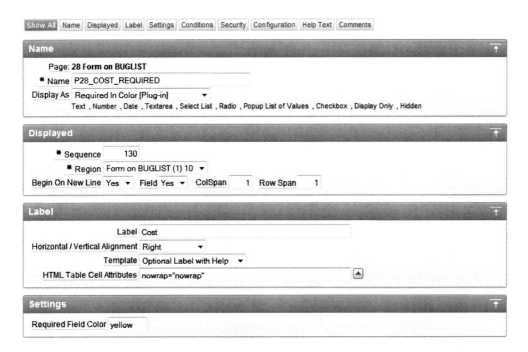

Figure 12-16. Custom Attribute setting changed

When you execute the page now, as shown in Figure 12-17, the Cost item's background is yellow when the value is null. You may have to back out the existing value to see the color change. Since we're talking in black and white, you'll have to take our word for it.

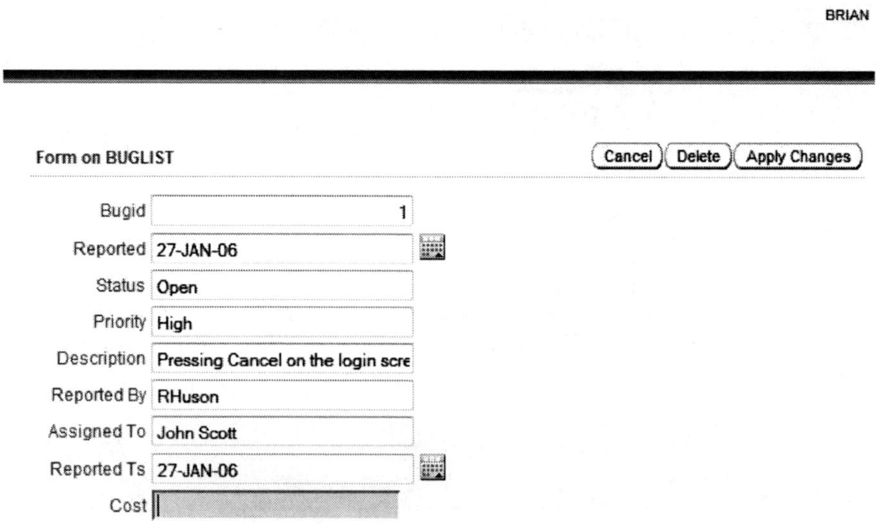

Form on BUGLIST   (Cancel)(Delete)(Apply Changes)

Bugid | 1
Reported | 27-JAN-06
Status | Open
Priority | High
Description | Pressing Cancel on the login scre
Reported By | RHuson
Assigned To | John Scott
Reported Ts | 27-JAN-06
Cost |

Figure 12-17. Custom Attribute setting changed

The functionality we created with this plug-in was pretty simple, but it took quite a bit of work to get it done. Now that it's done, though, it can be used everywhere and made available to fellow APEX developers worldwide.

■ **Note** Once you create an object that is based on a plug-in, you will not be able to delete the plug-in. This makes sense since the items using the plug-in would cease to operate if you delete it. This can be confusing, however, since the Delete button does not show up on the Edit Plug-in page if the plug-in is in use. To quickly locate the where the plug-in is use, you can view the plug-in Utilization report.

Exporting Plug-ins

When plug-ins are created, they are visible only to the application in which they were created. To make your plug-ins available to other applications, they must be exported and subsequently imported into other applications. If you choose to share your plug-ins with the APEX developer community, you would export them and upload them to an APEX plug-in repository, like the following:

- Oracle Applications Express Plug-ins page (www.oracle.com/technetwork/developer-tools/apex/application-express/apex-plug-ins-182042.html)

- APEX-PLUGIN.com (www.apex-plugin.com)

There are three ways to export plug-ins, but only one of them works. Following is the one approach that works:

- Exporting a plug-in from within the application in which it was created

However, the following two approaches do not work:

- Exporting a plug-in from the Application Builder home page

- Exporting a plug-in from an application other than where it was created

That only one approach works can be confusing since all three processes force you to select the application from which to export the plug-in (as we will see shortly), even if you are in the application where the plug-in was created. All three of the plug-in export processes will tell you that your plug-in was successfully exported, but you may not realize that the promise is false until you try to import the plug-in. The two processes that don't work generate an invalid export file. This is likely a bug that will be corrected in a later version of APEX 4.0. For now, just use the export plug-in feature inside your application.

So, to perform a successful plug-in export, navigate to the Plug-ins home page in the Shared Components section of the application in which you created the plug-in. Figure 12-18 shows the plug-ins home page for Application 101 and the "Export Plug-in" link in the Tasks region.

Figure 12-18. Export Plug-in Task on Plug-in home page

Notice that the plug-in we want to export, Required in Color, exists in this application. To start the actual export process, you click on the Export Plug-in link in the Tasks window. In Figure 12-19, you can see that even though you are editing the application that contains the Required in Color plug-in, you are still required to select the application that contains the plug-in you want to export.

Figure 12-19. Set Application step in the Export Plug-in process

Clicking the Set Application button takes you to the next step in the process where you can select the plug-in. Figure 12-20 shows that you can select both the plug-in to export as well as the file format (UNIX or DOS) to create. We selected the requiredInColor plug-in and set the File Format to UNIX. The character set of the export file defaults to that of the application.

Figure 12-20. Select the Plug-in to Export and the File Format to use

To complete the export plug-in process, press the Export Plug-in button. The interesting thing about this step is that APEX does not store an output file for you. Instead, it creates an export file on the fly, which is downloaded to your browser, as shown in Figure 12-21. You can either open the file or save it to your file system. The point of this exercise is to make the plug-in available to other applications, so you should save it. Listing 12-8 shows the valid file created during the export process. Notice that it is a SQL file that you could execute in SQL*Plus.

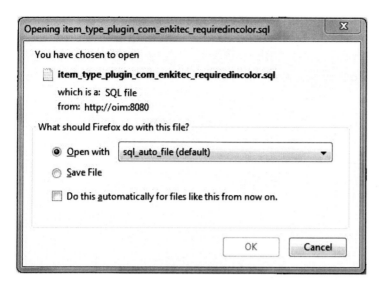

Figure 12-21. Browser download window for Plug-in Export

Listing 12-8. Exported Plug-in File

```
set define off
set verify off
set serveroutput on size 1000000
set feedback off
WHENEVER SQLERROR EXIT SQL.SQLCODE ROLLBACK
begin wwv_flow.g_import_in_progress := true; end;
/
--       AAAA        PPPPP    EEEEEE  XX        XX
--       AA  AA      PP  PP   EE        XX    XX
--      AA    AA     PP  PP   EE          XX XX
--     AAAAAAAAAA    PPPPP    EEEE        XXXX
--     AA        AA  PP       EE          XX XX
--     AA        AA  PP       EE        XX    XX
--     AA        AA  PP       EEEEEE  XX        XX
prompt   Set Credentials...
begin
   -- Assumes you are running the script connected to SQL*Plus as the Oracle user APEX_040000
or as the owner (parsing schema) of the application.
wwv_flow_api.set_security_group_id(p_security_group_id=>nvl(wwv_flow_application_install.get_w
orkspace_id,1280317158978593));
end;
/
begin wwv_flow.g_import_in_progress := true; end;
/
begin
```

```
select value into wwv_flow_api.g_nls_numeric_chars from nls_session_parameters where
parameter='NLS_NUMERIC_CHARACTERS';
end;
/
begin execute immediate 'alter session set nls_numeric_characters=''.,''';
end;
/
begin wwv_flow.g_browser_language := 'en'; end;
/
prompt  Check Compatibility...
begin
-- This date identifies the minimum version required to import this file.
wwv_flow_api.set_version(p_version_yyyy_mm_dd=>'2010.05.13')
end;
/
prompt  Set Application ID...
begin
   -- SET APPLICATION ID
   wwv_flow.g_flow_id := nvl(wwv_flow_application_install.get_application_id,101);
   wwv_flow_api.g_id_offset := nvl(wwv_flow_application_install.get_offset,0);
null;
end;
/
prompt  ...plugins
--
--application/shared_components/plugins/item_type/com_enkitec_requiredincolor
begin
wwv_flow_api.create_plugin (
  p_id => 9050220872125872 + wwv_flow_api.g_id_offset
 ,p_flow_id => wwv_flow.g_flow_id
 ,p_plugin_type => 'ITEM TYPE'
 ,p_name => 'COM.ENKITEC.REQUIREDINCOLOR'
 ,p_display_name => 'Required In Color'
 ,p_image_prefix => '#PLUGIN_PREFIX#'
 ,p_plsql_code =>
'function requiredInColor ('||chr(10)||
'   p_item               in apex_plugin.t_page_item,'||chr(10)||
'   p_plugin             in apex_plugin.t_plugin,'||chr(10)||
'   p_value              in varchar2,'||chr(10)||
'   p_is_readonly        in boolean,'||chr(10)||
'   p_is_printer_friendly in boolean )'||chr(10)||
'   return apex_plugin.t_page_item_render_result'||chr(10)||
''||chr(10)||
'is'||chr(10)||
''||chr(10)||
'   l_name varchar2(30);'||chr(10)||
''||chr(10)||
'   l_result        apex_plugin.t_page_item_render_result;'||chr(10)||
''||chr(10)||
'   l_background   apex_applicati'||
'on_page_items.attribute_01%type := p_item.attribute_01;'||chr(10)||
''||chr(10)||
```

```
'BEGIN'||chr(10)||
''||chr(10)||
'  IF p_is_readonly OR p_is_printer_friendly THEN'||chr(10)||
'       '||chr(10)||
'    APEX_PLUGIN_UTIL.print_hidden_if_readonly ('||chr(10)||
'      p_item_name              => p_item.name,'||chr(10)||
'      p_value                  => p_value,'||chr(10)||
'      p_is_readonly            => p_is_readonly,'||chr(10)||
'      p_is_printer_friendly => p_is_printer_friendly );'||chr(10)||
''||chr(10)||
'    APEX_PLUGIN_UTIL.print_display_only ('||chr(10)||
' '||
'    p_item_name            => p_item.name,'||chr(10)||
'    p_display_value     => p_value,'||chr(10)||
'    p_show_line_breaks => false,'||chr(10)||
'    p_escape            => true,'||chr(10)||
'    p_attributes        => p_item.element_attributes );'||chr(10)||
'      '||chr(10)||
'  ELSE'||chr(10)||
''||chr(10)||
'    l_name := APEX_PLUGIN.get_input_name_for_page_item(p_is_multi_value=>false);'||chr(10)||
''||chr(10)||
'    htp.p(''<input type="text" name="''||l_name||''" id="''||p_item.name||''"
''||''value="''||htf.escape_sc('||
'p_value)||''" size="''||p_item.element_width||''"
''||''maxlength="''||p_item.element_max_length||''" ''||p_item.element_attributes||''
onKeyUp="fldRequired(''''''||p_item.name||'''''',''''''||l_background||'''''')"/>'');'||chr(10
)||
''||chr(10)||
'    APEX_JAVASCRIPT.add_library (p_name=> ''requiredInColor'',p_directory =>
p_plugin.file_prefix,p_version => null );'||chr(10)||
''||chr(10)||
'    APEX_JAVASCRIPT.add_onload_code (p_code => '' fldRequired("''||p_item.name||''",''||
'"''||l_background||''")'');'||chr(10)||
'    '||chr(10)||
''||chr(10)||
'  END IF;'||chr(10)||
''||chr(10)||
'  RETURN l_result;'||chr(10)||
''||chr(10)||
'END requiredInColor;'
 ,p_render_function => 'requiredInColor'
 ,p_standard_attributes => 'VISIBLE'
 ,p_help_text => '<br />'||chr(10)||
''
 ,p_version_identifier => '1.0'
  );
wwv_flow_api.create_plugin_attribute (
  p_id => 9198214807522510 + wwv_flow_api.g_id_offset
 ,p_flow_id => wwv_flow.g_flow_id
 ,p_plugin_id => 9050220872125872 + wwv_flow_api.g_id_offset
```

```
   ,p_attribute_scope => 'COMPONENT'
   ,p_attribute_sequence => 1
   ,p_display_sequence => 10
   ,p_prompt => 'Required Field Color'
   ,p_attribute_type => 'TEXT'
   ,p_is_required => false
   ,p_default_value => '#FEA5AD'
   ,p_display_length => 7
   ,p_max_length => 7
   ,p_is_translatable => false
   );
null;

end;
/
begin
wwv_flow_api.g_varchar2_table := wwv_flow_api.empty_varchar2_table;
wwv_flow_api.g_varchar2_table(1) :=
'66756E6374696F6E20666C64526571756972656428666C644E616D652C626B67436F6C6F72290D0A7B0D0A0D0A616
C65727428626B67436F6C6F72293B0D0A0D0A20207656616C7565203D20646F63756D656E742E676574456C656D656
E744279496428';
wwv_flow_api.g_varchar2_table(2) :=
'666C644E616D65292E76616C75653B0D0A0D0A202069662028217656616C7565290D0A20207B0D0A20202020646F
3756D656E742E676574456C656D656E744279496428666C644E616D6529E7374796C652E6261636B67726F756E643
D626B67436F6C';
wwv_flow_api.g_varchar2_table(3) :=
'6F723B0D0A20207D0D0A2020656C73650D0A20207B0D0A20202020646F63756D656E742E676574456C656D656E744
279496428666C644E616D6529E7374796C652E6261636B67726F756E643D2223464646464646223B0D0A20207D0D0
A0D0A7D0D0A';
null;
end;
/
begin
wwv_flow_api.create_plugin_file (
  p_id => 9186432599158222 + wwv_flow_api.g_id_offset
 ,p_flow_id => wwv_flow.g_flow_id
 ,p_plugin_id => 9050220872125872 + wwv_flow_api.g_id_offset
 ,p_file_name => 'requiredInColor.js'
 ,p_mime_type => 'application/x-javascript'
 ,p_file_content => wwv_flow_api.g_varchar2_table
  );
null;
end;
/
commit;
begin
execute immediate 'begin dbms_session.set_nls( param => ''NLS_NUMERIC_CHARACTERS'', value =>
'''''''' || replace(wwv_flow_api.g_nls_numeric_chars,'''''''',''''''''.'') || '''''''');
end;';
end;
/
```

```
set verify on
set feedback on
prompt  ...done
```

As you can see in Listing 12-8, the plug-in export file contains everything required to rebuild your plug-in in another application, including your JavaScript function. Now, all you have to do is import this plug-in into another application (discussed in the next section) or push it up to one of the public, plug-in repositories.

Importing Plug-ins

One of us had a high school chemistry teacher who would not let students use their TI-30 calculators until they could pass a test with a slide rule. While at first this seemed ridiculous, in the end, the additional knowledge was a tremendous help in problem solving. What we just went through (building a plug-in from scratch) was the equivalent of using a slide rule in chemistry class. Although we didn't cover every variation of plug-in development, you've seen the steps required to build one and you have a working example.

When you start thinking about building plug-ins, we highly recommend that you first search the plug-in repositories to see if the capability you need has already been created. While plug-ins are relatively new, there is already a developer community that is building plug-ins and publishing them for anyone to use, free of charge. In many cases, plug-in developers are wrapping jQuery features in APEX plug-in code, taking advantage of jQuery's vast array of features. If you don't already know about jQuery, it's worth a serious look. In general, jQuery is an open source, JavaScript library that enables an amazing array of client-side features with very little coding. Although jQuery is based on JavaScript, it has its own scripting language so there is a learning curve involved. Thanks to the APEX development community, many of the most popular jQuery features have been used to create APEX plug-ins and published so you can use them in your applications. The two main repositories can be found at these locations:

- Oracle Applications Express Plug-ins page (`www.oracle.com/technetwork/developer-tools/apex/application-express/apex-plug-ins-182042.html`)

- APEX-PLUGIN.com (`www.apex-plugin.com`)

Now, instead of building JavaScript, jQuery, or Ajax into your pages manually, you can simply import existing plug-ins that utilize the standardized APEX plug-in interface. If you find a plug-in that almost fits your requirements but not exactly, you can extend an imported plug-in to get exactly what you need. As an added bonus, you can potentially save a lot of time and you may learn a great deal by reviewing code that someone else wrote. We will explore these capabilities by downloading and importing a plug-in from Oracle's repository on the Internet.

In keeping with the Buglist application development process, I wanted to demonstrate a useful jQuery plug-in that would benefit the application. I settled on using the jQuery Star Rating plug-in to allow user feedback on the Edit Bug page. Although I've never seen a bug tracking system that allows the user to rate the development team's ability to address issues, I think it's a good idea.

What this control does is allow the user to hover the mouse over a line of stars and click one of them to represent a 1 out of 9 rating. By default, this control produces a 9-star rating, but by using one of the plug-in's custom attributes, you can choose how many stars should be displayed. The result of using the star rating is an integer between 0 and the number of stars selected. To make this plug-in useful to our application, we'll have to add a column to the Buglist table to store the rating value.

```
apexdemo@10gR2> alter table buglist add (rating number);
Table altered.
```

We'll start the import process by downloading the Star Rating plug-in from Oracle's Plug-in Repository. You can quickly navigate to this page using the "View Plug-in Repository" button on the Plug-in home page. Figure 12-22 shows the repository page from which you can download the Star Rating plug-in.

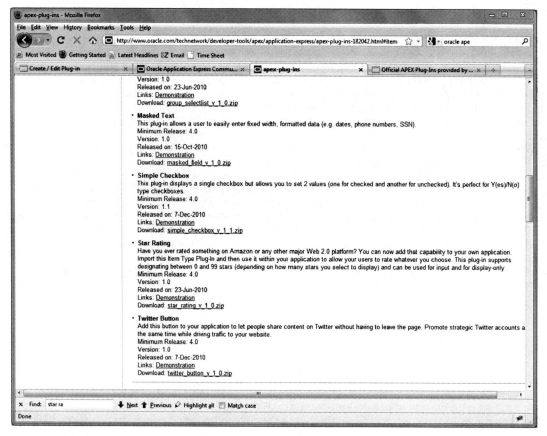

Figure 12-22. *Downloading the Star Rating plug-in*

The plug-in is downloaded as a ZIP file, the contents of which are shown in Figure 12-23. The file ending in .sql contains the APEX code related to the exported plug-in. The sub-directories, server, and source contain supporting files like Cascading Style Sheets, JavaScript, jQuery code, and so forth. Not all plug-ins will have this structure, but all of them will have a ".sql" file.

Name	Date modified	Type	Size
📁 server	3/20/2011 11:59 PM	File folder	
📁 source	3/20/2011 11:59 PM	File folder	
📄 item_type_plugin_com_oracle_apex_star_rating.sql	3/20/2011 11:59 PM	SQL File	35 KB
📄 readme.txt	3/20/2011 11:59 PM	Text Document	5 KB

Figure 12-23. Contents of the Star Rating plug-in ZIP file

To import the plug-in, you can use the Import feature either at the Application Builder home page or via the Plug-in button on the Plug-in home page. The import process is the same regardless of where you start. In Figure 12-24, the downloaded Star Rating plug-in is selected in the Import wizard. If you start from the Plug-in home page, the file type will be set to Plug-in by default, otherwise you need to set it. The character sets defaults to that of the exported plug-in, but it is recommended that Unicode UTF-8 is used, as this will cover the use of both single and multi-byte character sets.

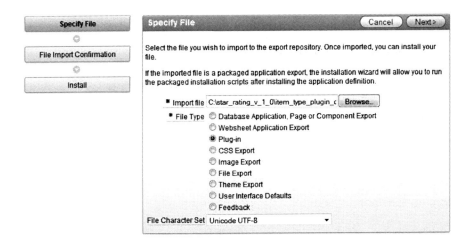

Figure 12-24. Importing the Star Rating plug-in

All that's left to do in the import process is to identify in which application this plug-in will be used. In our example, we chose application 101 BUGLIST. The result of the installation step is that you are presented with the Edit Plug-ins page populated with the details of the Star Rating, as shown in Figure 12-25. You still have to Apply Changes to finalize the import process.

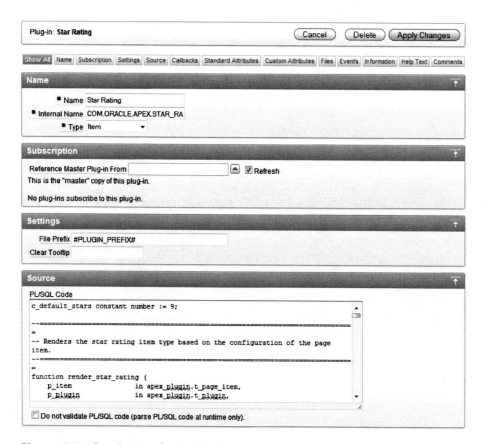

Figure 12-25. Star Rating plug-in details

Your imported plug-in is now ready to use. As discussed previously, we will add the Star Rating plug-in to the Edit Bug page so that the user can rate the developers (what a concept). You add the Star Rating to your page as an Item of type Plug-in. Aside from the normal item attributes, you get to set the number of stars you want in your rating, as shown in Figure 12-26. The default is 9, but of course you can change the plug-in so that it defaults to whatever number you want. For this example, we set the value to 5.

Figure 12-26. Star Rating plug-in Custom Attributes

The final step in implementing the Star Rating plug-in is to identify the source for the P29_RATING item. We created a column in the Buglist table called RATING, so we set the source type to database column and the Database Column Name to RATING, leaving all other attributes at their default value. Now when we run the Edit Bug page, the Rating (or Star Rating to be exact) is shown below the Cost item (our built-from-scratch plug-in). As you can see in Figure 12-27, the user can easily set and view the rating given to this particular bug.

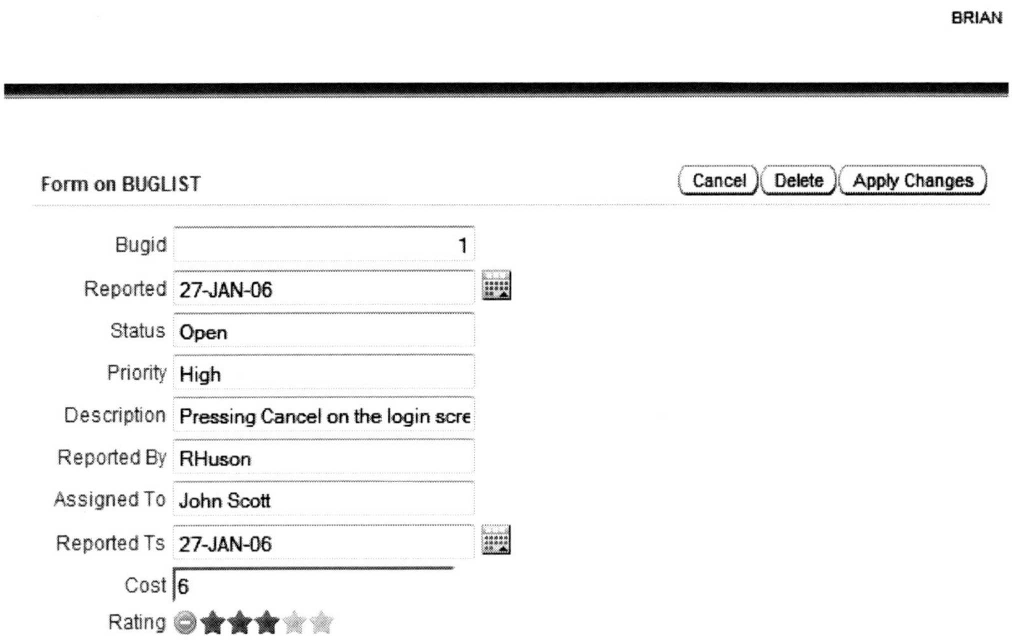

BRIAN

Figure 12-27. Edit Bug page with Star Rating plug-in

That was pretty easy, especially when compared to creating a simple plug-in from scratch. The simplicity of using this plug-in is a little deceiving in that the developer of the APEX plug-in had to know how to use the jQuery Star Rating feature and also how to wrap it in an APEX plug-in. We didn't show the text of the PL/SQL Code used to build this plug-in, as there just isn't enough space in this book to cover everything that's going on—including how jQuery itself works. Since the source of this plug-in is freely available, we encourage you to evaluate it, download, it and get to know it better my making some changes to it. If you can improve it significantly, maybe you can upload it to the repository so others can get the benefit as well.

You can also test the import process using the Required in Color plug-in we exported in the last section. The process will be the same as the Star Rating plug-in, except that the Required in Color plug-in does not have some of the attributes used in the Star Rating. Simply follow the steps in the import process and the import will be successful.

Summary

Plug-ins are a powerful new tool that should be exploited to the fullest. The modularization and standardization created by the plug-in architecture allow, for the first time, easy sharing of standard APEX building blocks. While it was always possible to build client-side code using JavaScript, sharing that code between pages or applications was a much more manual process.

The capabilities afforded by plug-ins is really only limited by a developer's desire (and maybe time and money). We didn't get into details on how to create process type, dynamic action, or region type plug-ins given that we only have one chapter to devote to the subject. We suggest that you go to Oracle's Plug-in repository and try them all out. If you find something useful, use it. If you can improve on it, do so and then give it back to the community.

In our description of the relative difficulty in creating plug-ins from scratch, we were certainly not suggesting that you never do it. What we were saying is that before you write some new, custom functionality, it may be well worth your time to scan the public, plug-in resources to see if what you are planning to do has already been done. Given the popularity and tremendous capability of the jQuery package, you will see more and more jQuery-based plug-ins pop up in the future.

Web Services

The term *web service* refers to a web-accessible application that performs some action based on a request from a client. For these entities to communicate, an agreed upon language, or communication protocol, must be used. The first web services used the Simple Object Access Protocol (SOAP), which is an XML-based messaging protocol. Although SOAP is effective, it is often perceived as being a heavy-weight and difficult to use.

The Representational State Transfer (REST) architecture, created by Roy Fielding in 2000, is a specification for building web services that is much simpler than SOAP. Both concepts have their pros and cons, but REST is emerging as the more popular of the two—as evidenced by its adoption by Yahoo, Facebook, and others. In addition, REST has become an integral component of Java starting with Java 6.

In APEX 4.0, you now have wizards for creating web service references for both SOAP and REST-based web services. Prior versions of APEX supported only SOAP web services. It is important to note that the APEX wizards build web service clients, not the actual web services. You either need a WSDL file to access a SOAP web service or knowledge of the input requirements for a RESTful web service.

In this chapter, we will work with both SOAP and RESTful web services, some of which are publicly available and some we will build on our own. We'll also explore the many APEX objects that can be based on web services, including Forms, Reports, and Processes.

Creating a Native Database Web Service

We will first take a look at SOAP web services from both the client and service perspective. The Oracle Database itself is a great resource for learning about web services since you can easily expose a stored procedure or function as a SOAP web service. Oracle calls this ability to expose stored procedures Native Database Web Services. The XML DB feature of the database can be used to store and manipulate native XML data, but it also allows you to expose procedures and functions as web services and lets you call them using HTTP. Actually, the XML DB feature is used to implement the Embedded PL/SQL Gateway used to access APEX. After we create our web service in the database, we'll use APEX to create a web service reference to consume it.

We could have just chosen to demonstrate how APEX works using an Amazon or Yahoo web service, but then you would only see how APEX is used to build a client. Without some understanding of web services in general, you may not understand what is happening in APEX. You will learn a great deal more by building your own web service as opposed to just using an existing one. When we're finished with these examples, you should feel comfortable utilizing any web service whether SOAP- or REST-based.

Before we start coding, we need to enable Native Database Web Services in the 11g database. The first order of business is to enable the HTTP listener that is built in to the database. The script in Listing 13-1 shows how to evaluate the current HTTP port setting and then how to set it. The HTTP port is considered disabled if it is set to zero. You can choose any port number you like, but using 8080 is recommended as it is universally recognized as a non-production, HTTP port. Some operating systems like Linux / Unix will restrict the use of port numbers below 1024.

Listing 13-1. Set the XML Database HTTP Listener Port

```
SQL> CONN sys/password@db11g AS SYSDBA

SQL> SELECT dbms_xdb.gethttpport FROM dual;

GETHTTPPORT
-----------
          0

SQL> EXEC dbms_xdb.sethttpport(8080);

PL/SQL procedure successfully completed.

SQL>
```

At this point, you can access database resources via browser at the port you set for the XDB HTTP listener. Use the URL shown in Listing 13-2 to access the XML Database root replacing the <host:port> label with your values.

Listing 13-2. Access the XDB Root Directory

```
http://<host:port>/
```

Index of /

Name	Last modified	Size
OLAP_XDS/	Mon, 03 Jan 2011 17:23:21 GMT	-
images/	Sat, 15 Aug 2009 00:49:30 GMT	-
olap_data_security/	Sat, 15 Aug 2009 00:35:56 GMT	-
public/	Sat, 15 Aug 2009 00:30:14 GMT	-
sys/	Sat, 15 Aug 2009 00:31:15 GMT	-
xdbconfig.xml	Sun, 10 Apr 2011 20:05:55 GMT	0
xds/	Sat, 15 Aug 2009 00:35:56 GMT	-

The script in Listing 13-3 is used to create a servlet in the database, called orawsv, which enables database-stored procedures and functions to be called via HTTP. When you call a database resource via this servlet, it will create a Web Services Description Language (WSDL) file for the object you are calling. The WSDL file is used by the web service client to identify how the web service is to be used. In short, the WSDL file shows the inputs required to use the web service and the output it will generate. The format of the WSDL file is based on a W3C standard, so automating its creation is pretty easy. When you use APEX to consume a web service, however, you may never see the WSDL file as it is used behind the scenes.

Listing 13-3. Create the orawsv Servlet

```
CONN sys/password@db11g AS SYSDBA

DECLARE
  l_servlet_name VARCHAR2(32) := 'orawsv';
BEGIN
  DBMS_XDB.deleteServletMapping(l_servlet_name);

  DBMS_XDB.deleteServlet(l_servlet_name);

  DBMS_XDB.addServlet(
    name     => l_servlet_name,
    language => 'C',
    dispname => 'Oracle Query Web Service',
    descript => 'Servlet for issuing queries as a Web Service',
    schema   => 'XDB');

  DBMS_XDB.addServletSecRole(
    servname => l_servlet_name,
    rolename => 'XDB_WEBSERVICES',
    rolelink => 'XDB_WEBSERVICES');

  DBMS_XDB.addServletMapping(
    pattern => '/orawsv/*',
    name    => l_servlet_name);
END;
/
```

After creating the servlet in Listing 13-3, you can verify that it was done correctly using the script shown in Listing 13-4. The Result Sequence, the output of the XQuery script, is used to show that the servlet was created correctly and which role is required to execute it.

Listing 13-4. Verify Creation of the orawsv Servlet

```
SET LONG 10000
XQUERY declare default element namespace "http://xmlns.oracle.com/xdb/xdbconfig.xsd"; (: :)
       (: This path is split over two lines for documentation purposes only.
          The path should actually be a single long line. :)
       for $doc in fn:doc("/xdbconfig.xml")/xdbconfig/sysconfig/protocolconfig/httpconfig/
        webappconfig/servletconfig/servlet-list/servlet[servlet-name='orawsv']
       return $doc
/

Result Sequence
-------------------------------------------------------------------------
<servlet xmlns="http://xmlns.oracle.com/xdb/xdbconfig.xsd">
  <servlet-name>orawsv</servlet-name>
  <servlet-language>C</servlet-language>
  <display-name>Oracle Query Web Service</display-name>
  <description>Servlet for issuing queries as a Web Service</description>
  <servlet-schema>XDB</servlet-schema>
  <security-role-ref>
    <description/>
    <role-name>XDB_WEBSERVICES</role-name>
    <role-link>XDB_WEBSERVICES</role-link>
  </security-role-ref>
</servlet>
```

Now that we have an HTTP listener and a servlet, we can call a stored procedure or function as a web service. Using the Buglist table, we'll create a simple package / function that will return the number of bugs based on the priority. While such a function may not be the best functional example of a web service, creating and invoking it will illustrate the process and give you a simple base from which to build. Listing 13-5 shows the creation of the BUGTYPE package and package body.

Listing 13-5. BUGTYPE Package

```
create or replace
package bugType as
  function bugTypeCount(bugType in out varchar2) return number;
end bugType;
/

create or replace
package body bugType as
  function bugTypeCount(bugType in out varchar2)
  return number
  is
    bugCount number;
  begin
    select count(bugid) into bugCount
    from   buglist
    where  priority = bugType;
```

```
      return bugCount;
   end;
end bugType;
/
```

The last step related to the creation of the Native Database Web Service is to grant the appropriate roles to the user who owns the web service resource, as shown in Listing 13-6. Granting the role XDB_WEBSERVICES_WITH_PUBLIC is optional as this allows the user to access any PUBLIC database object via web service. For testing, it doesn't really matter which schema(s) you use, but when you start implementing XML Database web services in production, you may want to limit the number of web service object owners so you can more easily manage security.

Listing 13-6. Grant Appropriate Roles to Web Service Object Owner

```
SQL> CONN SYS AS SYSDBA
SQL> GRANT XDB_WEBSERVICES TO apexdemo;
SQL> GRANT XDB_WEBSERVICES_OVER_HTTP TO apexdemo;
SQL> GRANT XDB_WEBSERVICES_WITH_PUBLIC TO apexdemo;
```

To test the configuration, you can now turn to your browser. As discussed previously, the orawsv servlet will create a WSDL file for you automatically. You can generate the WSDL file in your browser by going to one of the following URLs:

For packaged procedures or functions:

```
http://<host:port>/orawsv/<USER>/<PACKAGE>/<PROC or FUNC>?wsdl
```

For regular procedures or functions:

```
http://<host:port>/orawsv/<USER>/<PROC or FUNC>?wsdl
```

Note that your user name, package name, and procedure or function name must be in uppercase in the URL. If you forget this detail, you will get back a generic error message with no explanation as to the issue. If you get the URL right and the configuration is all correct, your browser will display the WSDL file, which looks like the one in Listing 13-7.

Listing 13-7. WSDL File Generated by orawsv Servlet

```
- <definitions name="BUGTYPECOUNT"
targetNamespace="http://xmlns.oracle.com/orawsv/INSTRUCTOR/BUGTYPE/BUGTYPECOUNT"
xmlns="http://schemas.xmlsoap.org/wsdl/"
xmlns:tns="http://xmlns.oracle.com/orawsv/INSTRUCTOR/BUGTYPE/BUGTYPECOUNT"
xmlns:xsd="http://www.w3.org/2001/XMLSchema"
xmlns:soap="http://schemas.xmlsoap.org/wsdl/soap/">
- <types>
- <xsd:schema targetNamespace="http://xmlns.oracle.com/orawsv/INSTRUCTOR/BUGTYPE/BUGTYPECOUNT"
elementFormDefault="qualified">
- <xsd:element name="SNUMBER-BUGTYPECOUNTInput">

- <xsd:complexType>
- <xsd:sequence>
```

```
            <xsd:element name="BUGTYPE-VARCHAR2-INOUT" type="xsd:string" />
            </xsd:sequence>
            </xsd:complexType>
            </xsd:element>

        -   <xsd:element name="BUGTYPECOUNTOutput">

        -   <xsd:complexType>

        -   <xsd:sequence>
            <xsd:element name="RETURN" type="xsd:double" />
            <xsd:element name="BUGTYPE" type="xsd:string" />
            </xsd:sequence>
            </xsd:complexType>
            </xsd:element>
            </xsd:schema>
            </types>

        -   <message name="BUGTYPECOUNTInputMessage">
            <part name="parameters" element="tns:SNUMBER-BUGTYPECOUNTInput" />
            </message>

        -   <message name="BUGTYPECOUNTOutputMessage">
            <part name="parameters" element="tns:BUGTYPECOUNTOutput" />
            </message>

        -   <portType name="BUGTYPECOUNTPortType">

        -   <operation name="BUGTYPECOUNT">
            <input message="tns:BUGTYPECOUNTInputMessage" />
            <output message="tns:BUGTYPECOUNTOutputMessage" />
            </operation>
            </portType>

        -   <binding name="BUGTYPECOUNTBinding" type="tns:BUGTYPECOUNTPortType">
            <soap:binding style="document" transport="http://schemas.xmlsoap.org/soap/http" />

        -   <operation name="BUGTYPECOUNT">
            <soap:operation soapAction="BUGTYPECOUNT" />

        -   <input>
            <soap:body parts="parameters" use="literal" />
            </input>

        -   <output>
            <soap:body parts="parameters" use="literal" />
            </output>
            </operation>
            </binding>
        -   <service name="BUGTYPECOUNTService">
            <documentation>Oracle Web Service</documentation>
        -   <port name="BUGTYPECOUNTPort" binding="tns:BUGTYPECOUNTBinding">
```

```
<soap:address location="http://oim:8080/orawsv/INSTRUCTOR/BUGTYPE/BUGTYPECOUNT" />
</port>
</service>
</definitions>
```

We won't go into much detail about what is in the WSDL file other than to say that it follows the W3C standards for WSDL 1.1 documents. The important things to note are the inputs and outputs (highlighted in Listing 13-7). The nice thing about WSDL-based web services is that the WSDL file is generated automatically and most web service development tools will automatically build the code necessary to call the web service. APEX is no exception. You don't really need to see the WSDL file in order to use the web service in APEX.

Creating a WSDL-based Web Service Reference in APEX

Having verified that our Native Database Web Service exists, we can now use that resource in an APEX application. You start the process by accessing the Web Service References menu in Shared Components, which brings up the Web Service References home page shown in Figure 13-1.

Figure 13-1. Web service reference home page

When you click the Create button you will be presented with three options for creating a web service: REST, Based on WSDL, and Manual. Since we will first use our Native Database Web Service, which is WSDL-based, choose "Based on WSDL" and click Next.

Figure 13-2. Web service type selection

You now have the option to search the Universal Description, Discovery and Integration Registry (UDDI) to find a WSDL file. A UDDI registry is a directory service that allows organizations to register their identities and search for other registered businesses. Not only can you locate information about companies in a UDDI, but also the web services they choose to make public. Since we created our own web service, we will not use the UDDI registry and so the radio button shown in Figure 13-3 can be set to No.

Figure 13-3. Bypass the UDDI registry search

Previously, we viewed the WSDL file for our web service, which was generated automatically by the database. We will use that same syntax to identify the web service we want to use in APEX, as shown in Figure 13-4. APEX uses the information is the WSDL file to build the input to the web service automatically. You may never actually see the SOAP request unless you build the Web Service Reference manually. If you choose to do the work yourself, the SOAP request must be formatted as follows:

```
<?xml version="1.0" encoding="UTF-8"?>
<soap:Envelope xmlns:soap="http://schemas.xmlsoap.org/soap/envelope/"
xmlns:tns="http://oim:8080/APEXDEMO/BUGTYPECOUNT"
xmlns:xs="http://www.w3.org/2001/XMLSchema">
   <soap:Body>
      <tns:BUGTYPECOUNT>
         <tns:bugType>#ZIP#</tns:bugType>
      </tns:BUGTYPECOUNT>
   </soap:Body>
</soap:Envelope>
```

■ **Note** The main difference between WSDL-based web services and RESTful web services are that RESTful web services do not require a SOAP request. Input parameters are provided to a RESTful web service directly in the URL.

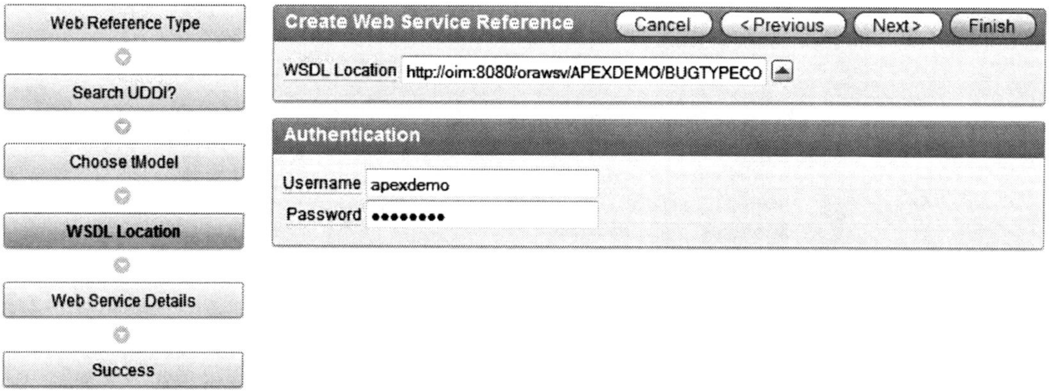

Figure 13-4. Identify the WSDL file

The username and password fields must be populated using the web service owner's database credentials. While it is possible to allow anonymous HTTP access to the database via the XML DB listener, Native Database Web Services require authentication. If you omit the username and password, APEX will display the error message shown in Figure 13-5, which does not accurately describe the issue. It should notify you that the username and password are required for this web service, but it doesn't, which can leave you scratching your head and searching for a solution. If you do supply an invalid username and/or password, the error message will report the issue correctly.

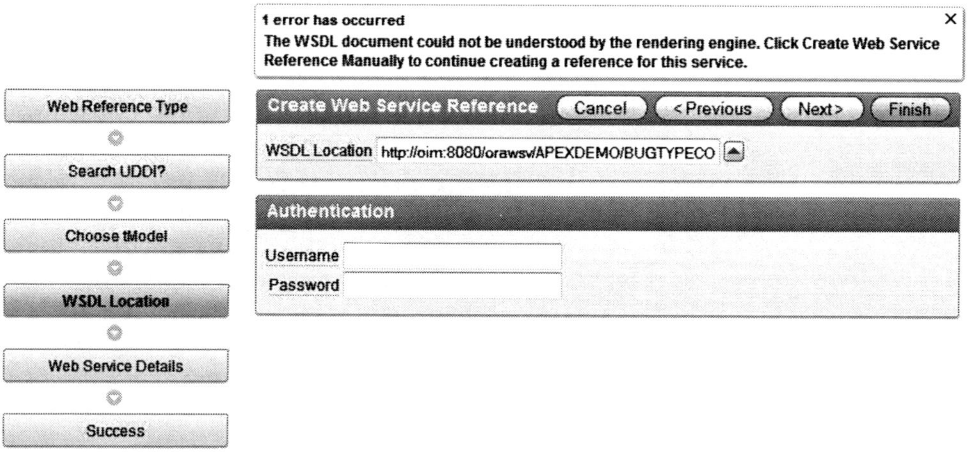

Figure 13-5. Error message if username and password are blank

If you provide the correct inputs, the last step is to verify the settings and select whether or not the web service requires basic authentication. In the case of Native Database Web Services, basic authentication is required. What this means is that the username and password must be included in the

SOAP request to this web service. APEX will help you with this also, as we will see shortly. The verification page should look like Figure 13-6.

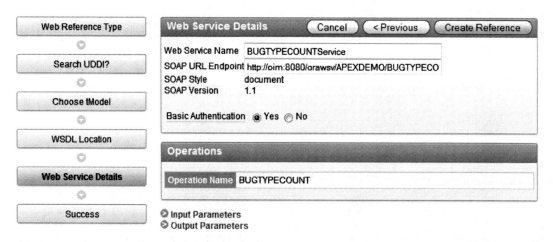

Figure 13-6. Web service verification page

When you click the Create Reference button, the web service reference is saved and a new wizard is started (see Figure 13-7), which assists you in using the new object on an APEX page. The best way to test your web service is to select the option that creates a form and a report on the web service. This will generate one page with a Form region containing the input items and a Report region that will display the output from the web service.

Figure 13-7. Web service page creation wizard

The first step in the new wizard, shown in Figure 13-8, allows you to select a web service reference to use in your new page. In our case, there is only one web service reference: the one we just created. Once you select the service, the remaining steps in the wizard guide you through the familiar process of building regions, items, and a report.

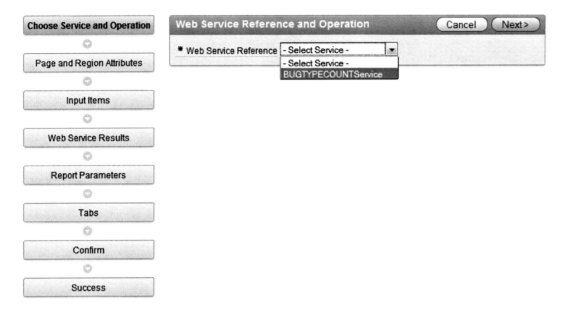

Figure 13-8. *Web service reference selection for new page*

Following the selection of the web service reference, Figure 13-9 shows that you can select any operation that is included in the web service. In our example, there is only one operation available, but we could have added more by basing the web service on a package and adding multiple functions.

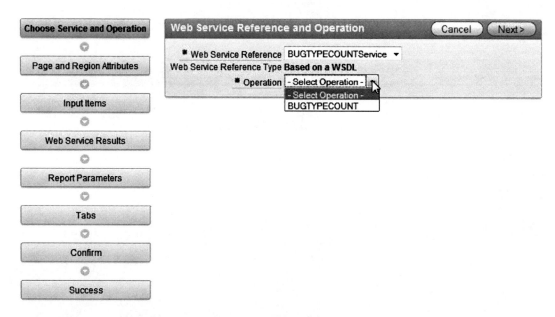

Figure 13-9. Selection of the web service reference operation

The wizard will now create a new page to house the web service reference. You can change the characteristics of the page, as shown in Figure 13-10, to suit your needs. As you can see from the workflow steps on the left side of the page, this is a relatively lengthy process with a few steps that you don't normally see during page creation. We intentionally left Breadcrumbs and Tabs out of this page to keep it simple.

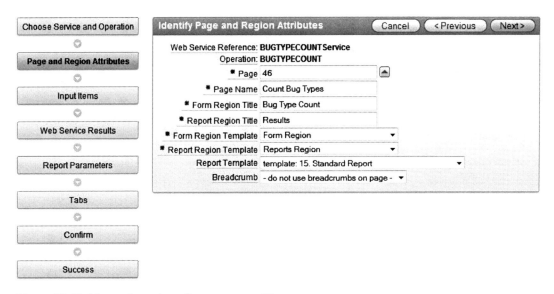

Figure 13-10. New web service reference page settings

The wizard next creates a page item that will be used to pass the input value to the web service. In web service lingo, this item is used to populate the input value in the SOAP envelope. Of course you won't see the SOAP envelope, which is one of the benefits of the web service architecture. Since APEX is enabling the web service behind the scenes, it uses web service lingo to name the input field. You can see how APEX sets the item name and label and how we changed it to make it more user-friendly in the following:

```
Default Item Name                 Default Item Label
-------------------------------   ----------------------------
P46_BUGTYPE-VARCHAR2-INOUT        Bugtype-Varchar2-Inout

Our Item Name                     Our Item Label
-------------------------------   ----------------------------
P46_WS_INPUT                      Priority
```

We changed the item name to show what functions as the input to the web service. For the item label, we set it to show that the input value must be the priority that you want to count. When the page is built, your user will appreciate these changes. Figure 13-11 shows the page that you set these values. There is also a "create" field that can be set to either "yes" or "no." In this example, we have only one input value so you must set this value to "yes." If you have a web service with multiple input values, you may want to set some or all of the "create" attributes to no and display them programmatically.

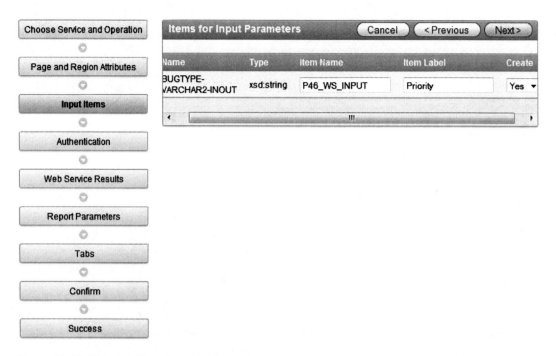

Figure 13-11. Naming the web service input item

Since Native Database Web Services require authentication, the next step of the process allows you to define item names and labels for the web service authentication parameters. In Figure 13-12, notice that we used the settings for the authentication items that APEX generated for us.

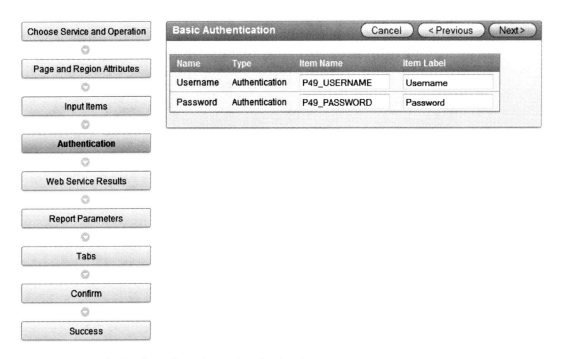

| | Choose Service and Operation |
| Page and Region Attributes |
| Input Items |
| **Authentication** |
| Web Service Results |
| Report Parameters |
| Tabs |
| Confirm |
| Success |

Basic Authentication   Cancel   < Previous   Next >

Name	Type	Item Name	Item Label
Username	Authentication	P49_USERNAME	Username
Password	Authentication	P49_PASSWORD	Password

Figure 13-12. Defining the web service authentication items

Next, we are required to define an APEX Collection, as shown in Figure 13-13, in which to store the results of the web service. Collections are used since a web service may return more than one value and you will need access to all of them. In addition, the report that is created as part of this process will use the collection as its data source. You must also select the " Result Tree to Report On." What this refers to is the component of the web service output that you want to include in the report. Since we are returning a single value, the wizard shows only one radio button (which is required) for the BUGTYPECOUNTOutput tag in the WSDL file.

Figure 13-13. Identifying the collection to store the web service output

We are now at the point where the report is defined. Remember way back at the beginning of this process we elected to create a Form and a Report? The report will display the output of our web service. The Form definition is basically done and now we have to decide what to display on the report. Figure 13-14 shows the available report parameters based on what APEX found in the WSDL file. The RETURN item is the return value from the web service while the BUGTYPE item is the value that you sent to the web service. For this example, we would recommend selecting both items so you can see the value of the Priority along with the number of bugs with this designation.

■ **Note** The position of the buttons partially atop the "Result Parameters to Display" titlebar is not a misprint. That is exactly how this page is rendered by APEX no matter how wide you make the page.

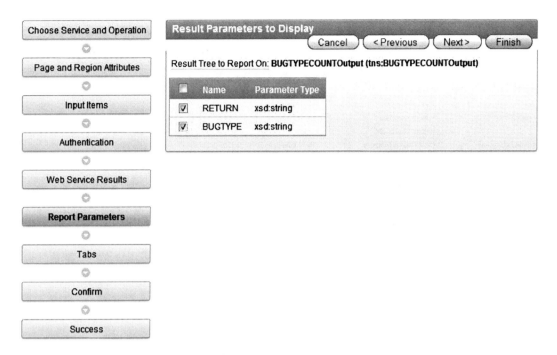

Figure 13-14. *Setting web service report parameters*

As stated earlier, we omitted Breadcrumbs and Tabs to keep the page simple. The last step, then, is to confirm the settings of the Form and Report built on your web service, as shown in Figure 13-15. If everything is correct, click the "Create Form and Report" button to take the next step towards seeing your web service in action.

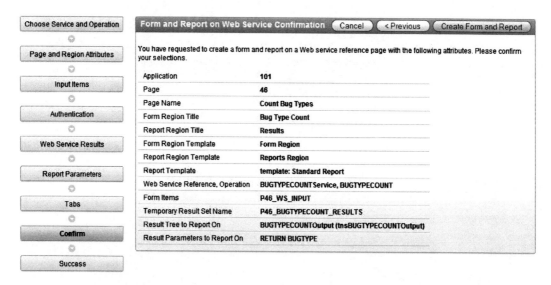

Figure 13-15. Setting web service report parameters

In the final step of this wizard (finally), APEX builds the page for you, tells you that everything was created successfully, and provides a "Run Page" button that takes you directly to the page so that you can test it. Figure 13-16 shows the new page as it is initially displayed. You will have to supply a valid user ID and password along with a priority (Critical, for example). Earlier we granted access to our web service to the database user apexdemo, so this is the only user who can exercise this web service.

BRIAN

Bug Type Count   (Submit)

    Username | apexdemo
    Password | ••••••••
    Priority |

Results

No data found.

Figure 13-16. Setting web service report parameters

When you enter a valid value for the priority and press the Submit button, the web service is called and the fruits of all our labor are revealed. In Figure 13-17, you see that the report region is populated showing the value we sent to the web service and returned value.

BRIAN

Bug Type Count   (Submit)

Username	apexdemo
Password	••••••••
Priority	Critical

Results

RETURN	BUGTYPE
3	Critical
	1 - 1

Figure 13-17. *Web service results*

If you need to make changes to the configuration of the web service, we recommend that you delete it and re-create it. You need to edit the web service reference you just created to understand why this is true. If you go back to the Web Services Reference section of Shared Components, you will now see an icon for your web service reference. When you click on the icon, you will see a single page like the one shown in Figure 13-18. There is no wizard to assist you in changing the settings of the web service reference. If, for example, you need to change the username and password for the web service, you will have to delete and re-add the web service reference.

You can, however, make changes to anything else about the page in the normal fashion. You can do things like change the order of the fields in the results report, modify labels, add other objects, and so forth. The web service configuration is really only tied to the action triggered by the Submit button. Now that you have a web service saved in the system, you can also go to the home of any application and add a form based on the web service and APEX will present you with the same wizard we just used in this example.

Figure 13-18. *Web serivce results*

Creating a RESTful Web Service

As discussed in the opening paragraphs of this chapter, RESTful web services are gaining in popularity since they are simpler to implement and use than their WSDL-based counterparts. The REST architecture operates very much like a standard HTML page in that a call is made to a RESTful web service using HTTP with one of four specific verbs : GET, POST, PUT, or DELETE. You probably recognize the first two as being the same methods you would use in an HTML form. The last two, PUT and DELETE, are not normally used in HTML forms.

To understand the REST concept and how these HTTP verbs are used, think of a standard APEX form that supports Create, Retrieve, Update, and Delete activities (commonly called a CRUD form). The REST architecture maps CRUD operations to HTTP verbs in the following manner:

REST Create	-	HTTP POST
REST Retrieve	-	HTTP GET
REST Update	-	HTTP PUT
REST Delete	-	HTTP DELETE

If you wanted to update a record via a RESTful web service, you would call the service at its URL, or endpoint, which would look something like this:

```
http://<server:port>/<service>
```

The RESTful web service would need to know how and where to perform its operation. The "how" is represented by the HTTP verb sent to the service. In an update, the verb passed to the web service would be PUT. To define "where" this operation should take place, the ID of the record to be updated would be sent in the URL like this:

```
http://<server:port>/<service>/<id>
```

Just by looking at the URL, you can't infer the purpose of this web service call since the HTTP verb cannot be seen. The RESTful web service in this example could be a Java servlet that performs a CRUD action based on the HTTP verb sent to it. If the HTTP verb was DELETE, then the <id> would tell the web service which record, for example, to delete. Notice that there was no mention of XML or WSDL. This is why people are starting to warm up to RESTful web services. It looks a lot like standard HTML, which means there's not much new stuff to learn and the web service itself does not have to follow a rigid standard. Although it looks as if you could call a RESTful web service with a standard HTML form in a browser, you can only send HTTP POST and GET verbs from a browser-based form. Therefore, you need a separate tool (client program) that can generate any of the four HTTP verbs.

To demonstrate the creation of a RESTful web service, it would be nice to be able to use the database server like we did for the WSDL-based variety, but Oracle only supports WSDL type Native Database Web Services. Another way to create a RESTful service would be to set up a Java application server, but that is outside the scope of this book. So, what do we do? We use APEX 4.0, which now allows you to create a RESTful web service out of any existing APEX report.

The first order of business, however, is to enable RESTful access to an APEX 4.0 instance. This can only be done via the APEX Administration interface. On the Mange Instance page, the Instance Settings section contains a link called "Security" that takes you to the page shown in Figure 13-19. The Allow RESTful Access setting is set to "No" by default so just set it to "Yes" and apply the changes. You can then log out of the Administration interface.

■ **Note** If you have never been to the administration page in Figure 13-19, you will be prompted to set the "Maximum Login Failures Allowed" and "Account Password Lifetime" attributes even if the "Require User Account Expiration and Locking" attribute is set to "no." You must provide positive integer values for both attributes, but the resulting behavior will still depend on the "Require User Account Expiration and Locking" setting.

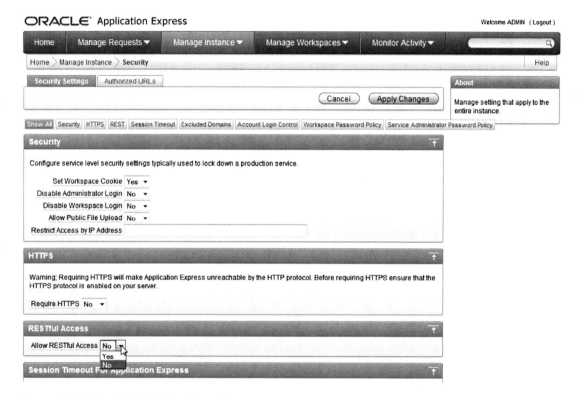

Figure 13-19. Enable RESTful web service access

We want to keep this example nice and clean so we created a standard, interactive report on the Buglist table to use as our RESTful web service. We created the report on a new page because one of the requirements of exposing a report as a RESTful web service is that the page that contains the report must be made public, as shown in Figure 13-20.

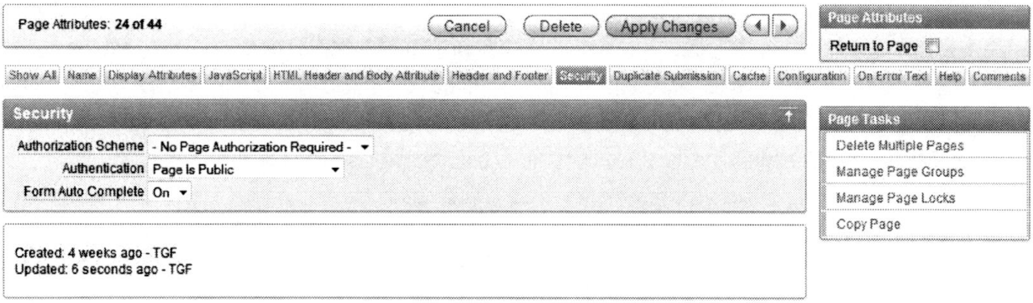

Figure 13-20. *Making the RESTful web service page public*

Navigate back to the Page Definition of the page you're using for your RESTful web service and click on the region that contains the report you want to expose. Click on the region name that contains the report and view the attributes section of the Report Definition page, as shown in Figure 13-21. Change the "Enable RESTful access" attribute to "Yes." When you enable RESTful access, you also have to set a Static ID for the report object. The Static ID will be used when calling the report as a web service. Apply these changes, which will take you back to the edit report page.

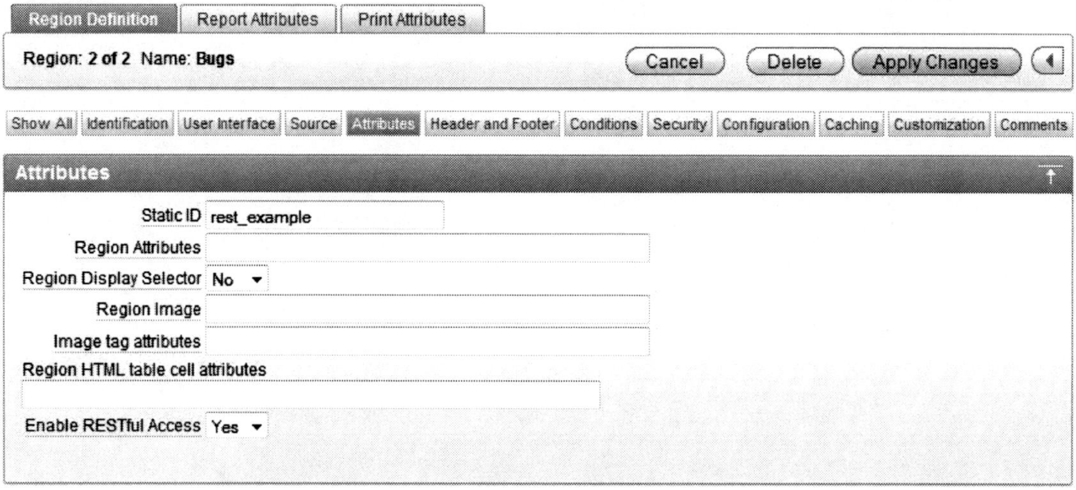

Figure 13-21. *Making the RESTful web service page public*

If you navigate back to the report region you were just on and view the region definition attributes, you'll see that APEX has generated some very important information regarding your RESTful web service. Figure 13-22 shows that the bottom of the Attributes section now contains the actual URL that you, or anyone else, can use to access your report via a web service call. APEX even labels the URL as "REST Access URL" to ensure you know what it's for.

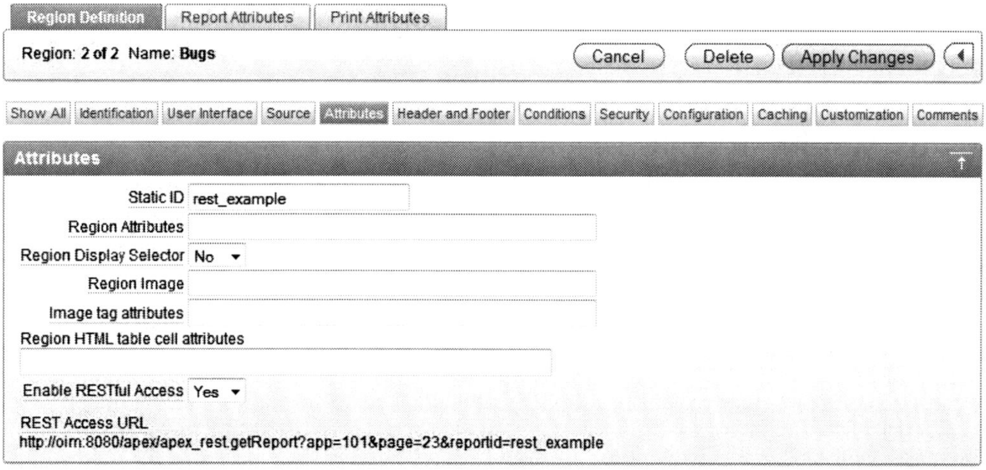

Figure 13-22. Rest Access URL generated automatically

The result of accessing this URL is shown in Listing 13-8. It is a very readable XML document containing a `<ROWSET>` tag that signifies that a bunch of rows will follow along with multiple `<ROW></ROW>` tags that contain your data by row. Your client is now free to format that data in any way they see fit.

Listing 13-8. XML Result of a Call to a Report Exposed as a RESTful Web Service

```
<ROWSET>
  <ROW>
    <ID>1</ID>
    <BUGID>1</BUGID>
    <REPORTED>27.01.06</REPORTED>
    <STATUS>Open</STATUS>
    <PRIORITY>High</PRIORITY>
    <DESCRIPTION>Pressing Cancel on the login screen gives an error</DESCRIPTION>
    <REPORTED_BY>RHuson</REPORTED_BY>
    <ASSIGNED_TO>John Scott</ASSIGNED_TO>
  </ROW>
  <ROW>
    <ID>2</ID>
    <BUGID>2</BUGID>
    <REPORTED>02.01.06</REPORTED>
    <STATUS>Closed</STATUS>
    <PRIORITY>High</PRIORITY>
    <DESCRIPTION>Logo occasionally does not appear</DESCRIPTION>
    <REPORTED_BY>CWhite</REPORTED_BY>
    <ASSIGNED_TO>Peter Ward</ASSIGNED_TO>
  </ROW>
...
</ROWSET>
```

While the foregoing is a great way to demonstrate a RESTful web service and also to make your application more accessible to others, it doesn't really benefit your application. To do that, we would need to call an external, RESTful web service.

Invoking an External Service

As mentioned before, organizations like Yahoo and Amazon have made RESTful web services available to the public so we can use one of those as an example. Since APEX does not allow you to declaratively build a RESTful web service, we won't go into detail about how the web services work, just how to use them.

We'll use Yahoo's RESTful web service for mapping to illustrate how APEX handles external web services. The prerequisite to running this example is to get a Yahoo Application ID. Yahoo requires that you identify how you're going to use their web service, but they ask only for minimal information before creating an application ID. You'll have to supply the application ID in all calls to the Yahoo RESTful web service. We'll create a page item for the application ID and make it visible, but once you get the process working you can make it invisible and default the value, since it is not important that the user see the application ID. The Yahoo page you use to start the application ID creation process is at the following location:

```
https://developer.yahoo.com/maps/rest/V1/
```

Click the "get an application ID" link to display the page that actually generates the application ID, as shown in Figure 13-23. If you don't have a Yahoo account, you will be asked to create one. Once you arrive at the Developer Registration page, fill it out so it looks something like Figure 13-23.

▥ **Note** Once you receive the application ID from Yahoo, we recommend that you copy and paste it into a document on your computer so it is easy to find if you need it again. Otherwise you will have to go back to Yahoo, login, and look around to find your application ID.

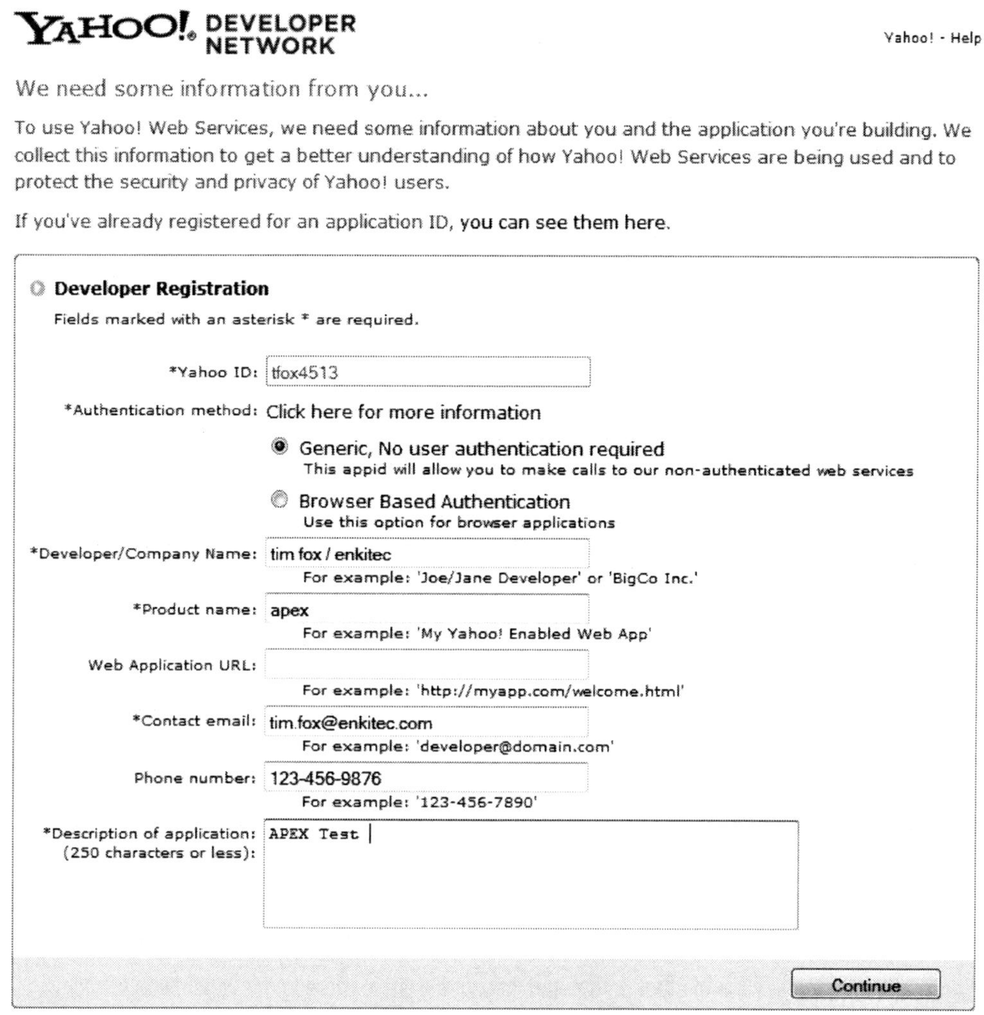

Yahoo! - Help

We need some information from you...

To use Yahoo! Web Services, we need some information about you and the application you're building. We collect this information to get a better understanding of how Yahoo! Web Services are being used and to protect the security and privacy of Yahoo! users.

If you've already registered for an application ID, **you can see them here.**

◎ **Developer Registration**

Fields marked with an asterisk * are required.

*Yahoo ID: | tfox4513

*Authentication method: Click here for more information

◉ Generic, No user authentication required
This appid will allow you to make calls to our non-authenticated web services

◎ Browser Based Authentication
Use this option for browser applications

*Developer/Company Name: | tim fox / enkitec
For example: 'Joe/Jane Developer' or 'BigCo Inc.'

*Product name: | apex
For example: 'My Yahoo! Enabled Web App'

Web Application URL: |
For example: 'http://myapp.com/welcome.html'

*Contact email: | tim.fox@enkitec.com
For example: 'developer@domain.com'

Phone number: | 123-456-9876
For example: '123-456-7890'

*Description of application: | APEX Test |
(250 characters or less):

[Continue]

Figure 13-23. Yahoo developer network registration

The next page will contain the application ID, which you should copy and store on your computer because you will need to enter it when you run your new page. Back in APEX, navigate to the Shared Components home page and click on "Web Service Reference," then click the Create button. For this example, you will choose the "REST" radio button, which will start the "REST Web Service Details" wizard as shown in Figure 13-24. The values you need to enter are as follows:

Name   : Name of the REST web service reference

URL   : The URL end point of the RESTful web service. If we didn't give you the URL, you could look it up yourself on Yahoo by searching for "REST web services."

https://developer.yahoo.com/maps/rest/V1/

The HTTP Method setting of "Get" denotes a read operation, which is what we want and this web service does not require username/password authentication, so leave that set at "No." We don't need to add REST HTTP Headers, so leave that blank as well.

Figure 13-24. REST web service wizard

We now need to identify the input parameters to the Yahoo web service. Figure 13-25 shows that we need to supply the application ID along with a location like a street address. Both inputs will string types.

■ **Note** Pay close attention to the case of input parameters because case matters to the Yahoo web service. These parameters will be included in the URL so if you get the case wrong, the web service will not return the expected results and it can be very difficult to figure out why.

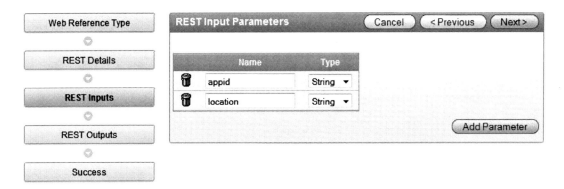

Figure 13-25. RESTful web service input parameters

The final step in the RESTful web service reference creation is shown in Figure 13-26. Here you identify where the results of the web service call are found and the type of the parameter that contains the results. The Yahoo page where we went to start the developer registration (https://developer.yahoo.com/maps/rest/V1/) tells you what the inputs and outputs look like and even shows some example code. The parameter name that is set to "URL" is just a name, but Yahoo tells you that the return value from the map API web service is a URL pointing to the image of the map you requested. The path setting of "/text()" will be explained shortly.

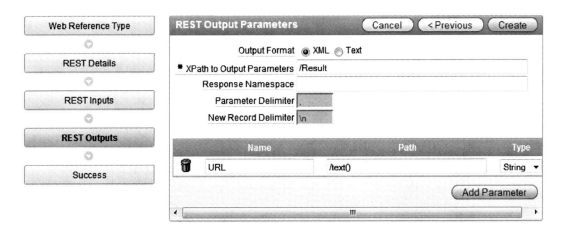

Figure 13-26. Return value setup for RESTful web service

After you click the "Create" button, a new wizard will launch, which allows you to create a form on the web service reference. Choose the "Create Form and Report on Web Service" radio button to continue. On the first step of the Form and Report creation wizard, choose the web service reference we just created (Yahoo Map REST), and the corresponding "Operation," which is populated based on the construction of the web service. There is only one operation (doREST), so select that value and click Next. The only two values you need to change on this page are the Form and Report region titles, as shown in Figure 13-27.

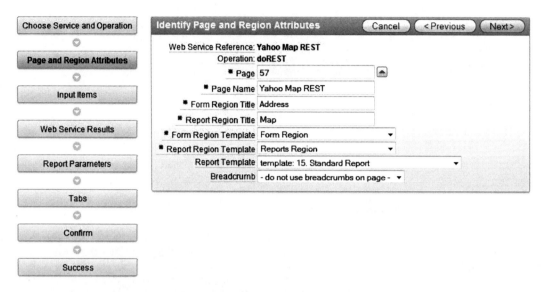

Figure 13-27. Form and Report settings for RESTful web service

You then set the labels for the input parameters that will show up on the form. The only thing we need to do here is change the labels so they're a little more user friendly. Figure 13-28 shows the parameter settings. The original label for the appid field was "appid" and we changed it to "Application Id."

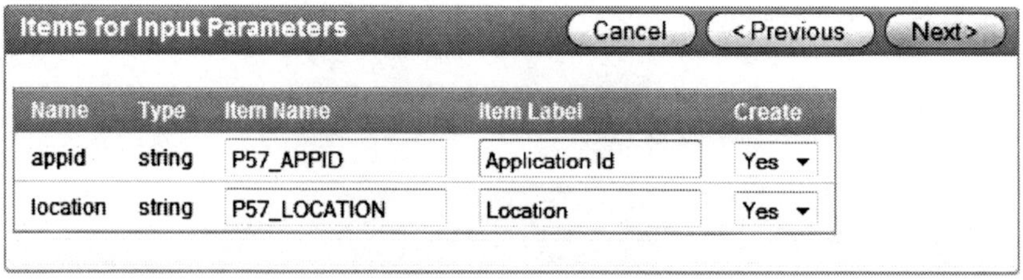

Name	Type	Item Name	Item Label	Create
appid	string	P57_APPID	Application Id	Yes ▾
location	string	P57_LOCATION	Location	Yes ▾

Figure 13-28. Form fields to call Yahoo web service

Now we have to define where to store the return value from the Yahoo web service. Thankfully, APEX does this for us by creating an APEX Collection and pulling the output parameter we set during the creation of the REST web service reference. All there is to do here is to tell APEX to display the output parameter (called URL) on the form, as shown in Figure 13-29. Of course you can change the name of the APEX collection, but we would only do this to adhere to some pre-defined standard.

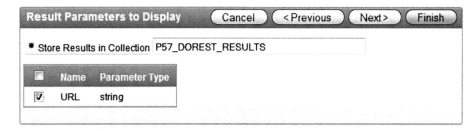

Figure 13-29. Set the web service output parameters to display

At this point, the Form and Report are ready to go. You can click Finish now and run the page that is shown in Figure 13-30. Notice that we have entered the application ID obtained from Yahoo and an address to place on a map. What we got back was not an image, but a URL to the image we want, so there's one more little change to make so that we render the image at that URL instead of displaying the text.

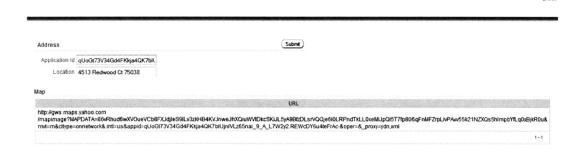

Figure 13-30. Form to call the Yahoo Map web service

Edit the page containing the Yahoo map and click on the "Report" link of the Map region. This will take you to the Report Attributes page, as shown in Figure 13-31. We need to edit the URL column of the report, so click on the edit link next to "URL," which is the only column in the report.

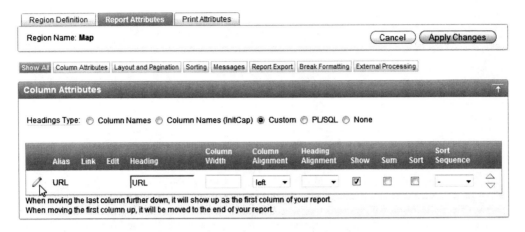

Figure 13-31. Web service report attributes

We will now simply modify the HTML Expression for this report column. Currently, there is no HTML expression, so we will tell this report column to display an image using the URL returned from the Yahoo web service. This is done simply by using a substitution, `<img src="#URL#"/>`, as shown in Figure 13-32.

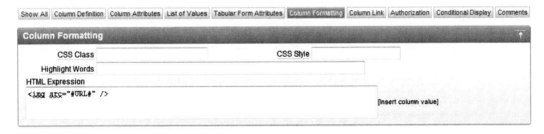

Figure 13-32. Changing the HTML expression for the web service report

After applying the changes and running the page again, you should see the address you entered, as shown in Figure 13-33, identified by a red star on a graphical Yahoo map. You'll just have to trust us on the red star thing, or you can go to Yahoo and enter the same address to ensure you're getting exactly the same information directly from Yahoo maps as you are from your web service call.

Address   (Submit)

Application Id qUoGt73V34Gd4FKkja4QK7bIUjnI\

Location 5605 N MacArthur Blvd Irving TX 7!

Map

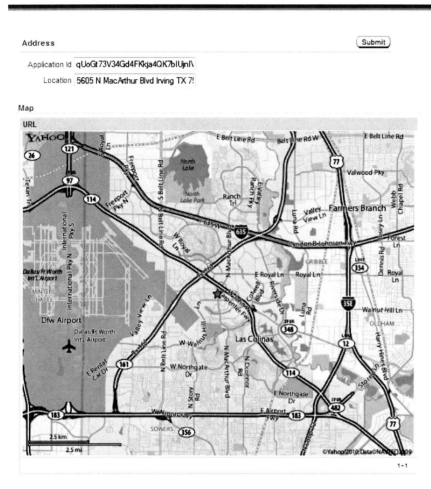

Figure 13-33. *Graphical map display as a result of a RESTful web service call*

Summary

Web services, in their many forms, have been around for more than ten years and they still haven't gained the widespread acceptance that many people thought they would. There are now several tools available that assist in implementing Service Oriented Architectures (SOA) or Enterprise Service Buses (ESB), but they all require heavy investments in capital as well as manpower.

Using what we have learned in this chapter, you can begin using web services in both a budget- and developer-friendly way. We described how to expose any Oracle stored procedure or function as a WSDL web service and how to use the Oracle database server itself in place of an application server. Both of these features greatly simplify entry into the realm of web services. Since APEX does not let you declaratively build either RESTful or WSDL web services, we did not delve into the details of building server components. If your organization is moving towards a SOA implementation, there will likely be a team dedicated to building web services that you now know how to consume with APEX.

As with plug-ins described in the previous chapter, we encourage you to look for web services, both internal as well as external, which can improve the usability of your applications while also injecting standardization into your development efforts.

Performance and Scalability

Quite often, we tend to think of performance and scalability in terms of optimizing large systems to cope with huge numbers of end users. However, that is only one side of it. Often, even the most modest of systems can benefit from considering performance and potential scalability in their design.

Performance and scalability can be measured in many different ways. For example, for one application, they might be measured as the number of end users who can simultaneously enter data into a data-entry screen. For another application, they might be measured by the number of end users who are able to run a report simultaneously. At another site, they might simply be measured by the number of end users who are able to browse through mainly read-only pages in the application. While there are many different ways in which you can measure these metrics, ultimately, it comes down to simply getting the best out of your available resources—the CPU, disks, network, and so on.

Most people realize that if their application is able to scale, it will be able to support more users as it grows. However, another advantage is that since your application is designed to scale, you will be able to run it on far more modest hardware than if it had not been designed to scale.

There are many different areas in which you can design your application to enable it to scale better, ranging from the way that you use SQL and PL/SQL, to changes you can make to your infrastructure (such as web server settings and network settings). In this chapter, we will cover APEX-specific features, tweaks, and techniques that can help your application scale. We will also cover a few PL/SQL and SQL details specific to APEX applications. These techniques can have dramatic effects, and we encourage you to investigate them in your own environment (testing them first, of course!).

Diagnosing Performance Problems

It's often the case that applications are moved into production without any consideration of their performance. If your database is running 10, 30, 100, or more different applications that have been developed with this mindset, then no one has considered the impact that their system might have on other (already running) systems. The end result of this is that one day your application may suddenly start to develop performance problems. Then you're in the position of trying to diagnose performance problems and come up with quick fixes, or possibly having to redesign complete sections of your code and application.

This is a bit of a chicken-and-egg situation here. We advocate designing and building your application with scalability and performance already in mind. So, with that said, why would we start by discussing how to diagnose performance problems, rather than just showing you how to write good, scalable applications in this first place?

Unfortunately, there is no easy, three-step process for writing scalable applications that will cover every possible scenario. Writing a scalable application is more of an iterative approach, whereby you test individual components of your application as you design them and check to see whether they meet the requirements. So, you need to know how to determine if components meet specific requirements, which you can do by using the facilities of the APEX environment.

The real core of the problem is this: how do you define a "performance problem"? Ideally, that should be defined within the business requirements early on in the project. For example, you might have requirements such as "No page should take longer than 5 seconds to render," or "Reports should always be returned in 3 seconds or less, unless it is the month-end run—in which case, 20 seconds is an acceptable return time."

It is not always worthwhile trying to shave off another 0.01 second from your query if it runs in 1 second and your users are perfectly happy with the performance. You need to know what the specific boundaries are in your specific case. You may have some users who get impatient waiting 6.5 seconds for a report to render and another user who is quite happy with that amount of time, but you need to define somewhere what an acceptable metric is as far as the business requirements are concerned.

Statements such as "It's running slowly" are not that useful, since you need to be able to compare "slowly" against something. A user who thinks something is running slowly today might be comparing its performance to yesterday, when it actually ran faster than it usually does (and today it is running at "normal" speed).

So, you need a *baseline* with which to compare your metrics. Fortunately, APEX gives us access to information that is useful in establishing these baselines for our application (and the pages and regions within it).

Viewing Application Reports

Within the Application Builder interface, you can view reports about the performance of the pages within your application. If you're familiar with the Application Reports section of pre-APEX 4.0 versions, you will find that some of the report names have changed, but there are more ways to evaluate your application's performance than ever before.

From the Administration home page, shown in Figure 14-1, you have access to two very useful dashboards: Monitor Activity and Dashboard. The names probably could have been a little more explanatory, but you'll get used to them in no time. The Monitor Activity icon takes you to the complete list of monitoring reports (many of which are new or have new formats), while the Dashboard icon gives you quick views of several aspects of APEX 4.0 performance levels. Notice that the menu at the bottom right quadrant of the page also gives you direct access to each component of the Dashboard, but not to the Monitor Activity features. Once you are in the Dashboard, you'll notice that the Performance tab contains a button that takes you to the Monitor Activity page.

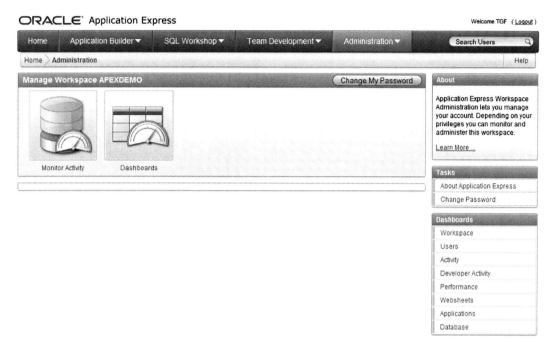

Figure 14-1. *Application activity reports*

Page Performance Reports

We'll first take a look at the Dashboard, which gives you a quick overview of the entire APEX environment along with some specific page performance statistics. When you enter the Dashboard, click on the Performance tab to view the main Page Performance report. This report is a slightly simplified version of the Page Performance report from earlier versions of APEX, but it still gives you the performance information you need at quick glance. In Figure 14-2, you'll see the Performance report set to display one day's worth of information. As with most APEX performance reports, you can change this filter to show statistics anywhere from the last ten seconds to the previous four days. This report shows an overall view of how each page in your application (which has been viewed) is performing in terms of how long it took to process and render that page.

Many different reports are available to give you detailed information about your application, as shown in Figure 14-1. You will find some of these reports more useful than others, so it is worth familiarizing yourself with the information that each report provides.

We'll look at a couple of application reports next.

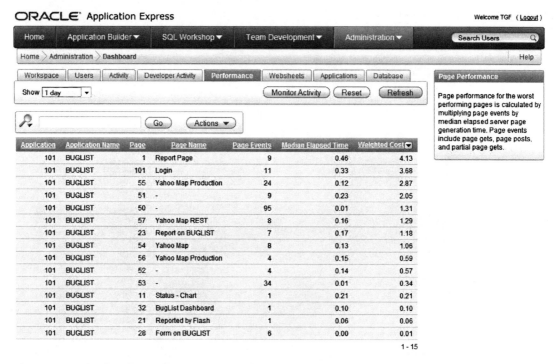

Figure 14-2. Viewing the application Page Performance report

In the Page Performance report, you can see that it's sorted this report to show the slowest pages first, as measured by Median Elapsed Time. You can also see a figure for the *Weighted*, which is calculated by multiplying the page events by the rendering time. In the example in Figure 14-2, the weight of page 1 is 4.13. This is basically a gauge of how much work is being done by a page.

The incredible useful aspect of this report (along with most other performance reports) is that the statistics for each page are being stored historically, so you can compare the figures you got today with the averages achieved historically. For example, if you compare the figures from today with the figures over the past four weeks, you might find that the report page takes on average around 0.3 seconds. This indicates that the figures for today are perfectly within what you might define as normal operating limits.

However, sometimes you need to be cautious about looking at averages, since they might mask anomalous behavior if you are looking over a long time period. For example, if you have 1,000 page views, and 999 of those views took 0.1 second but the last view took 30 seconds, then your average page view time over those 1,000 requests would come out at around 0.1299 second (129.9 seconds for all 1,000 requests). So, at first glance the response time looks good, at less than 0.2 second. However, the poor person who had to sit and wait 30 seconds for a page that usually returns in around a tenth of a second would probably disagree with your analysis. This is where you can use the weight value to determine where the average page timing lies in terms of all the page views. In the example, the weight of our 1,000 page views would be 129.9 seconds. If we compare this to the average (0.1299), we would expect the weight to be around 100 seconds (0.1 second per page), so we can see that the weight is around 30 seconds higher, indicating a potential problem.

So, do be careful when looking at averages over too long a time window, because any anomalous timings will be diluted. Typically, you will compare the timings within the past 7 days, or perhaps the last

14 days. If you're comparing longer periods than that, you will need to remember to factor in everything that may have impacted the timings. For example, you might have changed a piece of code three weeks ago that drastically altered the subsequent timings, or you might have doubled the amount of RAM in the server a month ago, or you might have changed the database configuration last week. Remember that comparisons are useful only if you're absolutely sure about what you're comparing (and that it makes sense to compare them in the first place!).

Page Views by View Report

As well as the averaged times in the composite Page Performance report, you can actually drill down into individual page views using the Page Views by View report on the Monitor Activity page. To get to this report, which is shown in Figure 14-3, simply click on the Monitor Activity button or go back to the Administration home page and click on the Monitor Activity icon. In the Page Views by View report, you can see, retrospectively, exactly how long individual pages took to process and render.

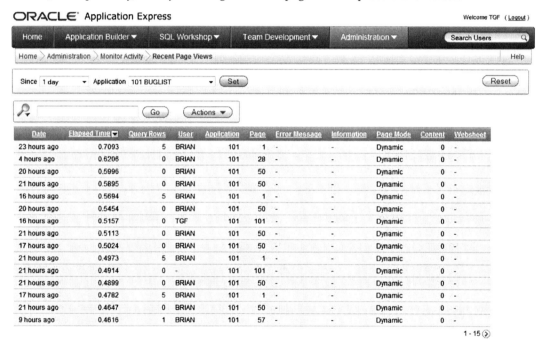

Figure 14-3. Page Views by View report

In the example in Figure 14-3, you can see that 23 hours ago, the brian user viewed page 1, and it took 0.7093 seconds to process and render. This sort of information is invaluable when it comes to diagnosing performance problems with your application. In many other development environments, when a user calls the help desk and says, "It took ages to run the XYZ report," unless you have put in your own custom code to time those pages and processes, you're not going to be able to view the timings that occurred when the user ran the report. However, with APEX, by default, every time users interact with your application, statistics are being recorded about how long those actions took to occur.

Now, you might be thinking, "Wow, clearly that logging adds overhead. Can I make my application run even faster if I disable that sort of logging?" Yes, the logging adds some slight overhead, but the benefit of this logging more than outweighs the overhead. Your users will definitely not notice the slight millisecond decrease in the time it takes to process the page if you were to disable this logging. They would almost certainly notice the extra amount of time it takes to diagnose performance problems if you were to try to do it without being able to access these statistics.

The Page Views by Views report contains a number of useful columns. Along with the application, page, user, timestamp, and elapsed time, it offers the following information:

Query Rows: This represents the number of report rows processed on the page. This information can be useful when comparing timings for a page that contains reports that are returning different numbers of rows, indicating perhaps a different dynamic query being used, search criteria, where clause restriction, and so on.

Error Message: This shows any error message that was generated as a result of the page being processed.

Page Mode: This shows whether the page was generated dynamically or a cached version of the page could be used. (We'll cover caching in the "Making Your Applications More Scalable" section later in the chapter.)

There are few more valuable statistics that can be used in performance tuning, but they are not included in the Page Views by View report by default. You can add these columns to the report using the Select Columns option under the report's Action button.

Session: This is the session ID used by the user when the page was processed. This information can be useful when referring to other reports to follow exactly what a user did in a particular session.

Think Time: Don't confuse this with how long it took to produce the page. This value is actually the duration between the user performing an action and the next action. In other words, if the user views a page and then spends 30 seconds before clicking a button, then the think time would be 30 seconds for the prior page. If you look at the values shown in Figure 14-3, you can see that the think time roughly corresponds to the time difference between one action and the previous one.

Cached Regions. This indicates the number of cached regions that were used when generating the page. If all of the regions were generated dynamically, you will see a 0 in this column

You can see the new columns in the Page Views by View report in Figure 14-4. Since we are not dealing with a Websheet application, we also removed the Websheet column to help contain the width of this report.

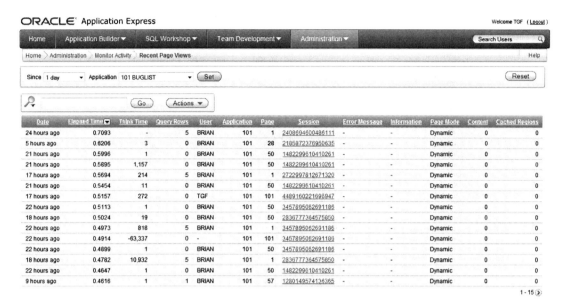

Figure 14-4. Modified Page Views by View report

As mentioned earlier, you need to be careful about comparing like with like when you compare timings. The Page Views by Views report enables you to determine whether the pages and regions were generated in the same way (that is, dynamically or cached), whether the report returned similar numbers of rows, and so on.

You can also filter the Page Views by Views report for a particular user or session. This means that if user Bob calls the help desk to say that the application is running slowly, you can quickly refine the resultset to view the timings for the current session that Bob is using. You can also use those timings to compare against historical values or against timings that another user is currently experiencing. In this way, you can hone in on whether it is the entire system that is experiencing a performance issue or something particular to Bob's session (or even whether there is an issue at all as far as the APEX infrastructure is concerned).

These are just a couple of the APEX reports that give you information related to performance. As you've seen, they contain useful timing information. Now we will show how easily you can get information about the page timings from your application.

Archived Log Timing Information

When you and your end users access your application, the timing details are stored in some internal tables and made available to you via some views. Two different tables are used to store the timing information: wwv_flow_activity_log1$ and wwv_flow_activity_log2$. These two tables are identical to each other; however, they are used alternately to store the past 14 days' worth of data. After 14 days, a log switch occurs and the contents of the other table are truncated, and that table is used to store the current details (with the original table now used to store the previous 14 days' worth of data).

The alternation of tables every 14 days means that at any point in time, you have access to up to the past 28 days' worth of data, with each table holding a window of up to 14 days' data. Whenever a log switch occurs, you will lose the data that was currently being held in that table.

■ **Note** Some of the APEX reports give you the option to view historical data older than 28 days. However, these reports will actually just show you the results up to 28 days, since any data held before that cutoff point has subsequently been discarded.

The reports typically use the wwv_flow_activity_log and wwv_flow_user_activity_log views, which collate (and union) the data in both the wwv_flow_activity_log1$ and wwv_flow_activity_log2$ underlying tables. Listing 14-1 shows the definition of the wwv_flow_activity_log1$ table (which, of course, is identical to that of the wwv_flow_activity_log2$ table).

Listing 14-1. Definition of the wwv_flow_activity_log1$ Table

```
apex_040000@DBTEST> desc wwv_flow_activity_log1$;
```

Name	Null	Type
TIME_STAMP	NOT NULL	DATE
COMPONENT_TYPE		VARCHAR2(255)
COMPONENT_NAME		VARCHAR2(255)
COMPONENT_ATTRIBUTE		VARCHAR2(4000)
INFORMATION		VARCHAR2(4000)
ELAP		NUMBER
NUM_ROWS		NUMBER
USERID		VARCHAR2(255)
IP_ADDRESS		VARCHAR2(4000)
USER_AGENT		VARCHAR2(4000)
FLOW_ID		NUMBER
STEP_ID		NUMBER
SESSION_ID		NUMBER
SECURITY_GROUP_ID	NOT NULL	NUMBER
SQLERRM		VARCHAR2(4000)
SQLERRM_COMPONENT_TYPE		VARCHAR2(255)
SQLERRM_COMPONENT_NAME		VARCHAR2(255)
PAGE_MODE		VARCHAR2(1)
CACHED_REGIONS		NUMBER
CONTENT_LENGTH		NUMBER
APPLICATION_INFO		VARCHAR2(4000)
WORKSHEET_ID		NUMBER
IR_SEARCH		VARCHAR2(4000)
IR_REPORT_ID		NUMBER
WEBSHEET_ID		NUMBER
WEBPAGE_ID		NUMBER
DATAGRID_ID		NUMBER

You can see that the columns in this table match up to some of the columns in the reports covered in the previous sections. For example, the NUM_ROWS column contains the number of report rows for that page view, and the ELAP column contains the elapsed time for that page.

The `wwv_flow_activity_log` and `wwv_flow_user_activity_log` views look very similar to Listing 14-1 (with only a different column or two). However, the APEX Dictionary provides another way to see this information, via a view called `apex_workspace_activity_log`, as shown in Listing 14-2.

Listing 14-2. Definition of the apex_workspace_activity_log View

```
apexdemo@DBTEST> desc APEX_WORKSPACE_ACTIVITY_LOG;
```

Name	Null	Type
WORKSPACE	NOT NULL	VARCHAR2(255)
APEX_USER		VARCHAR2(255)
APPLICATION_ID		NUMBER
APPLICATION_NAME		VARCHAR2(255)
APPLICATION_SCHEMA_OWNER		VARCHAR2(30)
PAGE_ID		NUMBER
PAGE_NAME		VARCHAR2(255)
VIEW_DATE		DATE
THINK_TIME		NUMBER
SECONDS_AGO		NUMBER
LOG_CONTEXT		VARCHAR2(4000)
ELAPSED_TIME		NUMBER
ROWS_QUERIED		NUMBER
IP_ADDRESS		VARCHAR2(4000)
AGENT		VARCHAR2(4000)
APEX_SESSION_ID		NUMBER
ERROR_MESSAGE		VARCHAR2(4000)
ERROR_ON_COMPONENT_TYPE		VARCHAR2(255)
ERROR_ON_COMPONENT_NAME		VARCHAR2(255)
PAGE_VIEW_MODE		VARCHAR2(15)
APPLICATION_INFO		VARCHAR2(4000)
INTERACTIVE_REPORT_ID		NUMBER
IR_SAVED_REPORT_ID		NUMBER
IR_SEARCH		VARCHAR2(4000)
WS_APPLICATION_ID		NUMBER
WS_PAGE_ID		NUMBER
WS_DATAGRID_ID		NUMBER
CONTENT_LENGTH		NUMBER
REGIONS_FROM_CACHE		NUMBER
WORKSPACE_ID		NUMBER

This view is the way that you would query the data about your applications from within the applications themselves. This can be a very useful function to give to your end users, or perhaps an administrator-level account in the application, so you no longer need to log in to the development environment to obtain these statistics.

For example, you can query the page timings for a particular application from within SQL*Plus, as long as you are connected to the schema associated with the workspace that the application resides in (otherwise, the view would not allow you to see the data for that particular application). Listing 14-3 shows a query to obtain the average page time for pages accessed in application 101.

Listing 14-3. Querying Page Timings from the apex_workspace_activity_log View

```
apexdemo@DBTEST> select

  2  page_id,
  3  avg(elapsed_time)
  4  from apex_workspace_activity_log
  5  where application_id = 101
  6  group by page_id;

  PAGE_ID AVG(ELAPSED_TIME)
---------- -----------------
        1              .552
        2              .034
        3              .309
       11              .207
       17              .208
       19              .270

6 rows selected.
```

As we've discussed, this view will show only data going back a maximum of 28 days. However, you could create a separate table based on this view to archive the current information, as shown in Listing 14-4.

Listing 14-4. Archiving Data from the apex_workspace_activity_log View

```
apexdemo@DBTEST> create table apex_custom_log

  2  as select * from apex_workspace_activity_log;

Table created.

apexdemo@DBTEST> select count(*) from apex_custom_log;

  COUNT(*)
----------
        71
```

You could then copy records from this view at periodic intervals. For example, you can insert any entries that were created the previous day into your historic table, as shown in Listing 14-5.

Listing 14-5. Archiving the Previous Day's Data

```
apexdemo@DBTEST> insert into apex_custom_log

  2  (select * from apex_workspace_activity_log
  3    where trunc(view_date) = trunc(sysdate) - 1);

17 rows created.
```

Then in any custom queries against the apex_custom_log, you could just query records that have been created today and union those records with the historical records (thereby making sure you don't include duplicates from records already archived), as shown in Listing 14-6.

Listing 14-6. Querying from the Custom Historic Table

```
apexdemo@DBTEST>select
  2    page_id,
  3    sum(elapsed_time)
  4  from (select * from apex_workspace_activity_log
  5            where trunc(view_date) = trunc(sysdate)
  6        union
  7          select * from apex_custom_log)
  8  where application_id = 101
  9  group by page_id

   PAGE_ID SUM(ELAPSED_TIME)
---------- -----------------
         1              4.09
         3               .88
         5               .51
        19               .93
        24               .48
       101               .54

6 rows selected.
```

Depending on the amount of data you store in your historic data tables, the query shown in Listing 14-6 might be far from optimal. You might rewrite the query to include the restrictions on application ID in the subquery to avoid returning records from the union that you're no longer going to use, as follows:

```
6  union
7    select * from apex_custom_log where application_id = 108
```

Remember that you might need to tune the queries that are going to help you to tune other queries!

Automated Statistic Threshold Notification

This section has a rather grand title, but really all it means is coming up with a method to proactively warn you if some page views are taking longer than your business requirements specify that they should. Rather than waiting for your users to tell you about a slow-running page, wouldn't it be nice to have the application notify you itself?

As you've seen, all of the necessary data is already there. You just need to come up with a way to have the application notify you, rather than generating the reports yourself.

Listing 14-7 shows a packaged procedure that will check the elapsed times for any applications in the workspace that have the same schema defined as the schema in which you create the package. Remember that when you create a workspace in APEX, you link it to a primary schema that is then used as the parsing schema (you can add other schemas after you have created the workspace). In order to be able to view applications that were created in a particular workspace, you need to create this package in the same schema that you used when you created the workspace.

Listing 14-7. Pkg_monitor to Check Elapsed Times

```
CREATE OR REPLACE PACKAGE pkg_monitor AS

 PROCEDURE CheckElapsed(p_Elapsed in number,
                        p_ToEmail in varchar2);

END pkg_monitor;


CREATE OR REPLACE PACKAGE BODY PKG_MONITOR AS

  PROCEDURE CheckElapsed(p_Elapsed in number,
                         p_ToEmail in varchar2) IS
    v_text clob;
  BEGIN
    wwv_flow_api.SET_SECURITY_GROUP_ID;
    for x in (select
                    application_id,
                    page_id,
                    elapsed_time
              from
                    apex_workspace_activity_log
              where
                    elapsed_time > p_Elapsed
              order by
                    elapsed_time desc) loop
      v_text := v_text || 'Application: ' || x.application_id;
      v_text := v_text || ' Page Id: ' || x.page_id;
      v_text := v_text || ' Elapsed Time: ' || x.elapsed_time;
      v_text := v_text || utl_tcp.crlf;
    end loop;

    apex_mail.SEND(p_to => p_ToEmail,
                   p_from => 'alerts@yourdb',
                   p_body => v_text,
                   p_subj => 'Elapsed Time Metric Warning');
    apex_mail.push_queue('localhost', 25);
  END CheckElapsed;
END pkg_monitor;
```

Listing 14-8 shows the code being executed.

Listing 14-8. Executing the Monitoring Code

```
apexdemo@DBTEST> exec pkg_monitor.checkelapsed(p_Elapsed => 3,

2  p_ToEmail => tim.fox@enkitec.com);
```

Pushing email: 11990304546358254

Pushed email: 11990304546358254

PL/SQL procedure successfully completed.

And the following is the resulting e-mail body:

Application: 108   Page Id: 1 Elapsed Time: 4.56
Application: 108   Page Id: 4 Elapsed Time: 3.58

You can see that Listing 14-8 calls the procedure and passes 3 in the p_Elapsed parameter. In other words, we want to see which pages took longer than 3 seconds to process and render. The results show that pages 1 and 4 in application 101 took 4.56 seconds and 3.58 seconds, respectively (for a particular session view). Clearly, you can easily add other useful information in the e-mail, such as the session information, and the timestamp and user information of when that page view occurred.

Now let's go over the code for the procedure in Listing 14-7, beginning with the following line:

```
wwv_flow_api.SET_SECURITY_GROUP_ID;
```

The call to the SET_SECURITY_GROUP_ID procedure (which is defined in the WWV_FLOW_API package) is necessary because we are running this procedure from SQL*Plus, not from within the APEX environment. If we omitted this procedure and tried to call the packaged procedure, we would get the following error:

```
apexdemo@DBTEST> exec pkg_monitor.checkelapsed(p_Elapsed => 3,

2  p_ToEmail => 'jes@shellprompt.net');

ERROR at line 1:
ORA-20001: This procedure must be invoked from within an application session.
ORA-06512: at "FLOWS_030000.WWV_FLOW_MAIL", line 165
ORA-06512: at "FLOWS_030000.WWV_FLOW_MAIL", line 195
ORA-06512: at "APEXDEMO.PKG_MONITOR", line 15
ORA-06512: at line 1
```

■ **Note** The error message actually refers to the APEX_040000.WWV_FLOW_MAIL package, since the apex_mail package is just a synonym. Fortunately, the word mail appears, so we have enough information to work out that the issue is with the call to the mail package.

So, the call to wwv_flow_api.SET_SECURITY_GROUP_ID is necessary to ensure that the correct APEX environment has been set up within the procedure to allow us to call the APEX_MAIL package later on. If you didn't wish to do it this way, you could use the UTL_MAIL package instead of the APEX_MAIL package. The UTL_MAIL package is a standard package that does not rely on the APEX environment to work. However, the APEX_MAIL package is easier to work with, so you may find it easier to set up the correct environment and then use the standard APEX routines. Many companies disable all database packages that start with UTL so if you try to use UTL_MAIL and it fails, check to see if it is disabled.

The next section of code sets up a cursor loop that enables us to loop through the records in the apex_workspace_activity_log table and find any records where the elapsed time is greater than the value of the parameter p_Elapsed.

```
for x in (select

            application_id,
            page_id,
            elapsed_time
        from
            apex_workspace_activity_log
        where
            elapsed_time > p_Elapsed
        order by
            elapsed_time desc) loop
...
end loop
```

In this example, we are searching all the records. You could modify this to just show any records that exceed that elapsed time that have occurred in the past 15 minutes, or whatever interval you prefer. You could then run the procedure at periodic intervals via a job. For example, you could run the procedure every 15 minutes and report on any records within the last 15 minutes.

Inside the cursor loop, we build up a Character Large Object (CLOB) by concatenating values from the returned rows, as follows:

```
v_text := v_text || 'Application: ' || x.application_id;

v_text := v_text || ' Page Id: ' || x.page_id;
v_text := v_text || ' Elapsed Time: ' || x.elapsed_time;
v_text := v_text || utl_tcp.crlf;
```

Here, we use x.application_id to refer to the application_id column returned by the cursor loop (defined as x). The utl_tcp.crlf reference at the end is there to append a carriage return/line feed to the e-mail (to start a new line for each row in the loop).

The final section of the code uses the apex_mail.send procedure to place the e-mail in the mail queue (inside the APEX mail queue). We then use the apex_mail.push_queue procedure to force the queue to be pushed. If you omitted this call, the e-mail messages would be pushed out when the scheduled mail job that is installed when you install APEX runs (typically, every 10 or 15 minutes, depending on your configuration). However, we prefer to push these types of messages out manually, so that they are delivered immediately.

```
apex_mail.SEND(p_to => p_ToEmail,

            p_from => 'alerts@yourdb',
            p_body => v_text,
            p_subj => 'Elapsed Time Metric Warning');
apex_mail.push_queue('localhost', 25);
```

In the push_queue call, we use the value of localhost for the mail server name and 25 as the port number (this is the default port for an SMTP mail server). In your own configuration, you may need to use a different address if you do not have a mail server running on the same machine as the database (since localhost refers to the machine the database is on, which is not necessarily the same as the machine the web server is running on).

This example demonstrated how, with very little work, you can have statistics about the performance of your applications e-mailed to you. As mentioned earlier, you can easily extend this simple example to give you all sorts of extra details. The following are just a few other ways you could extend this example:

- Add links into the e-mail that will take you to the relevant report details inside the Application Builder.

- Schedule this procedure to run as a job (using DBMS_SCHEDULER or DBMS_JOB), which will silently run behind the scenes and send you e-mail messages whenever anything crosses your threshold of acceptable timings.

- Parameterize the procedure more, so that rather than checking every application (and page), it uses another parameter table. That way, you could specify exactly which applications (and pages) you're interested in knowing about.

- Have different thresholds for different pages, or perhaps even different thresholds for different times of the day. For example, during peak hours, reports might need to run in less than 3 seconds, but on weekends, when you view the whole weeks' worth of data, it might be sufficient to run within 10 seconds.

You can see just how useful this sort of automated statistics collection can be in detecting performance problems with your application.

The application reports offer a way to examine the (historical) timing information behind your page requests and views. You can also view the current timings behind page views directly from the application itself by running your application in debug mode, as discussed next.

Using Debug Mode

One way to enable debug mode is to use the Developer toolbar, which is visible if you are running your application while logged into the Application Builder interface, as shown in Figure 14-5.

Figure 14-5. Accessing debug mode from the Developer toolbar

Another way to access debug mode is by modifying the URL used for the application page view to set the Debug flag to YES in the f?p syntax. Remember that the f?p syntax is as follows:

```
f?p=App:Page:Session:Request:Debug:ClearCache:itemNames:itemValues: PrinterFriendly
```

To enable debug mode, set the fifth parameter to YES (remembering that in APEX, the parameters in the URL are colon-delimited), as follows:

```
f?p=101:1:&APP_SESSION.::YES
```

After clicking Debug on the Developer toolbar in the Application Builder interface or modifying the URL with the Debug parameter, you won't see any differences on the screen, but the Debug button label will change to "No Debug" as shown in Figure 14-6. As long as the button reads "No Debug," APEX is collecting debug information. The collection process stops when you either click the No Debug button or when you exit the application.

Figure 14-6. Active debug session

After turning off the debugger, you can view the debug information by clicking the View Debug button. The resulting page is shown in Figure 14-7 provides a great deal of information about what it takes to render this page. The graphic at the top of the page has a column that equates to each row in the debug report and is intended to help you locate the slowest steps. If you click on any of the columns in the graph, you are immediately taken to the corresponding row in the report so you can address the issue if necessary.

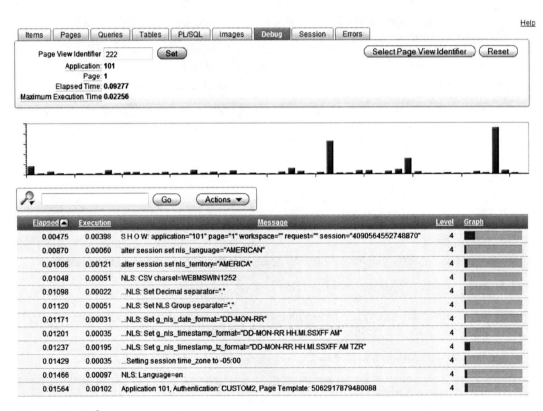

Figure 14-7. Debug report

A huge amount of information is made available when running in debug mode. Starting with the header information in Figure 14-7, you can see that it shows you exactly what is happening within the

APEX environment as that page is being processed. For example, you can see information about the National Language Support (NLS) settings of the database session configured in the DAD.

The values on the left are the timings between elements. Here, you can see that almost no measurable time (in the units we're working with, which are hundredths of seconds) was spent processing the two alter session statements. The timing figures are the cumulative time that has passed, If you look a bit further down, you see the lines shown in Figure 14-8.

| 0.00548 | 0.00083 | alter session set nls_language="AMERICAN" | 4 |
| 0.00628 | 0.00027 | alter session set nls_territory="AMERICA" | 4 |

Figure 14-8. Alter session timings

A nice feature of the APEX 4.0 debug report is that the execution time of each step is included in the Execution column. You no longer have to calculate the execution time using the Elapsed times. For example, you can see in the following line (see Figure 14-9) that the time required to loop through the rows of the report was 0.00754 seconds.

| 0.05667 | 0.00754 | rows loop: 15 row(s) | 4 |

Figure 14-9. Timing of one execution step in the debug information

Figure 14-10 shows the end of the timing information (not shown in Figure 14-7) that gives you the overall, elapsed time to render this page.

0.06786	0.00039	Computation point: After Footer	4
0.06820	0.02256	Processing point: After Footer	4
0.09080	0.00167	Log Activity:	4
0.09243	0.00035	v$sesstat.statistic# = 436: execute count=2	4
0.09277	-	End Show Page	4

Figure 14-10. Last rows of debug report showing complete elapsed time for page rendering

This indicates that it took a total of 0.9277 second to display this page. In this information, you can also see a complete breakdown of how long it took to process every region and item on the page. This makes it easy to determine which parts of the page are taking the most time to render.

■ **Note** This test was done on a test system that's not particularly fast, but the page shown in the debug report had been accessed several times prior to generating the report. As with any Oracle-based application, you may find that the first time you access an application, it is slower than the subsequent operations. This may be due to the fact that your SQL may not be in the shared pool and therefore needs to be hard-parsed, which takes time. You may also have to wait for connections to be established by the connection pool or to pull your data off disk if it is not in the database's butter cache. It might seem strange, but sometimes using the system more frequently could actually make it perform a bit better (but don't quote us on that)!

Running your page in debug mode will also let you check the assignments made to your page items, as well as bind values assigned to query. For example, if you enter the word john into the search field on that page and run the page in debug mode, you would see output similar to that shown in Figure 14-11.

0.06340	0.00166	show report	4	
0.06506	0.00026	determine column headings	4	
0.06531	0.00096	activate sort	4	
0.06627	0.00408	parse query as: APEXDEMO	4	
0.07038	0.00101	binding: ":P1_REPORT_SEARCH"="P1_REPORT_SEARCH" value="john"	4	
0.07137	0.00040	print column headings	4	
0.07177	0.01313	rows loop: 15 row(s)	4	

Figure 14-11. Debug report showing bind variable usage

Here, you can see that the query is being parsed as the APEXDEMO user (which in itself is very useful information, as sometimes you might assume that you're querying an object in one schema when, in fact, you're querying another schema due to synonyms or some other factor). You then see information about the bind variables used in the query in the report. Remember that the query was as follows:

```
select
  ID,BUGID,
  REPORTED,STATUS,
  PRIORITY,DESCRIPTION,
  REPORTED_BY, ASSIGNED_TO,
  (select ur.email
   from
     user_repository ur
   where
     ur.username = bl.reported_by
  ) as reported_email,
  (select initcap(ur.forename) || ' ' || initcap(ur.surname)
   from
     user_repository ur
   where
     ur.username = bl.reported_by
  ) as reported_full_name
 from    BUGLIST bl
where
(
 instr(upper(STATUS),upper(nvl(:P1_REPORT_SEARCH,STATUS))) > 0  or
 ... extra code removed...
)
```

Note the use of the P1_REPORT_SEARCH page item in the query. This is actually used as a bind variable. Looking again at the debug information, you see the following line:

```
":P1_REPORT_SEARCH"="P1_REPORT_SEARCH" value="john"
```

Here, you can clearly see that the bind variable in the query (:P1_REPORT_SEARCH) is using the value of the P1_REPORT_SEARCH page item, which has a value of john. If you are having unexpected results with any queries, you can use debug mode to do an end-to-end check to make sure that the values entered into fields are ending up being the right values used as bind variables in the queries.

You can also take advantage of debug mode to do conditional processing in your application. For example, you could create a new PL/SQL region on the page with the following code:

```
htp.p('Current System time is: '
  || to_char(SYSDATE, 'dd/mm/yyyy hh:mi:ss'));
```

This simply uses the htp.p procedure to output a string containing the current time to the page. If you want to show this only when you are running the page in debug mode, you can add the following PL/SQL expression condition to the region:

```
v('DEBUG') = 'YES'
```

The built-in debug information is very comprehensive, but by using techniques like this, you can extend it to include whatever custom information is useful to you. For example, you might find it useful to use some of the logic shown earlier to create a footer region that displays the timings of the last ten page views of this page so that you can easily compare the current time with historical times just from a single debug page.

To disable debug mode, just modify the URL to remove the YES value in the Debug parameter position, or click the No Debug link on the Developer toolbar if you're logged in to the Application Builder.

Using debug mode enables you to see information about your application within the APEX environment. Now let's look at another way to get information about how your application is performing: SQL tracing.

Using SQL Tracing and TKProf

Using SQL tracing allows you to see how your SQL and PL/SQL is being handled as far as the database is concerned (as a generalization). SQL tracing gives you more detail at the SQL and PL/SQL level, but you won't get all of the APEX-specific information that debug mode provides. Debug mode and SQL tracing serve very different purposes, and they both should be considered tools to use when trying to diagnose performance issues and problems.

Enabling SQL Tracing

As with debug mode, you can enable SQL tracing by adding an extra parameter to the URL, as follows:

```
http:/.../f?p=101:1&p_trace=YES
```

Note that you use the ampersand (&) here to specify the additional parameter, rather than the usual APEX convention of colon-delimited parameters.

When you add this parameter to your URL and press Enter in your browser, you will see the page refresh, but you will not see any difference in the page itself. This is because, unlike debug mode, SQL tracing produces a separate file containing the trace information. The trace file will correspond to the database session that was used to generate the page. You will need to submit the page with p_trace=YES set in the URL for each page that you wish to trace.

Finding the Trace Information

The location of this trace information is defined at the database level. To find out where this is, you need to connect to the database via SQL*Plus as a privileged user and type the following statement:

```
dba@DBTEST> show parameter USER_DUMP_DEST
```

You will see something like the following:

```
NAME              TYPE              VALUE
----------------- ----------------- -------------------------------------------
user_dump_dest    string            /opt/oracle/diag/rdbms/orcl/orcl/trace
```

The VALUE column shows the path to the trace file. Notice that this trace directory looks different from the one used in 10g. Once you navigate to the correct directory, you will probably find that it contains a lot of files. However, unless your users are in the habit of creating a lot of trace files, the one you want will probably be the latest file in that directory. Another way to check is to search through the files for the session ID that was used. In the example, the following URL was used to generate the trace file (omitting the host, port, and DAD part to make the URL more readable):

```
http://.../f?p=108:1:3690590133226902::&p_Trace=YES
```

You could search through the trace files for the session ID (3690590133226902 in this example) using the following Unix command:

```
jes@pb(udump)$ grep -l "3690590133226902" *
dbtest_ora_962.trc
```

The part in bold is just the prompt, which shows that we're logged in as the jes user (the machine name is pb) and currently in the udump directory. You use the grep command to search through all the files in that directory, with the –l parameter to show just the file name that matches (rather than showing the actual text matches in the file). In this example, the file that was generated is called dbtest_ora_962.trc.

Processing and Interpreting Trace Information

The raw trace files themselves can be very useful. However, rather than look through the raw trace file, you can run it through a utility called TKProf, which will produce a summary of the information. The file is summarized, but you still get a huge amount of detail.

To use TKProf, run the tkprof command, passing it the name of the raw trace file as the input and a name for the output file (output.trc in this example), as follows:

```
jes@pb(udump)$ tkprof dbtest_ora_962.trc output.trc

...some header output omitted
jes@pb(udump)$ls -al output.trc
-rw-r--r--   1 oracle  oinstall  111506 Jan 24 11:40 output.trc
```

The utility will output some version information (which we've omitted here) and will then generate the output file you specified. Listing 14-9 shows an example of the beginning of the output file generated by tkprof.

Listing 14-9. *Header Information in a SQL Trace File*

```
Trace file: dbtest_ora_962.trc

Sort options: default

********************************************************
count    = number of times OCI procedure was executed
cpu      = cpu time in seconds executing
elapsed  = elapsed time in seconds executing
disk     = number of physical reads of buffers from disk
query    = number of buffers gotten for consistent read
current  = number of buffers gotten in current mode (usually for update)
rows     = number of rows processed by the fetch or execute call
********************************************************

ALTER SESSION SET EVENTS '10046 TRACE NAME CONTEXT FOREVER, LEVEL 12'


call     count       cpu  elapsed  disk  query   current   rows
-------  ------  --------  --------  -----  ------  ---------  -----
Parse         0      0.00      0.00      0       0          0      0
Execute       1      0.00      0.03      0       3          0      0
Fetch         0      0.00      0.00      0       0          0      0
-------  ------  --------  -------  -----  ------  ---------  -----
total         1      0.00      0.03      0       3          0      0
```

The beginning of the file gives you some information about what the various columns and fields used in the report represent. You then see the first command that was executed within the following traced session:

```
ALTER SESSION SET EVENTS '10046 TRACE NAME CONTEXT FOREVER, LEVEL 12'
```

This command is the one that actually caused the session to produce the trace file (hence it is the first one to be traced). After this command, you see details about what happened when that command was processed. If you search through this file for the code used in the report (the query against the buglist table), you will find a section similar to Listing 14-10 (with some of the query omitted for brevity, but the entire query text is contained within the TKProf report and the corresponding raw trace file).

Listing 14-10. *TKProf Report Section for the Report Query*

```
select ID,BUGID,...

 from   BUGLIST bl
where
(
```

```
                instr(upper(STATUS),upper(nvl(:P1_REPORT_SEARCH,STATUS)))) > 0  or
        ...
        )

        call     count       cpu    elapsed  disk   query  current   rows
        -------  ------  --------  ----------  -----  -------  --------  -----
        Parse        1      0.00        0.00      0        0         0      0
        Execute      1      0.00        0.00      0        0         0      0
        Fetch        3      0.00        0.00      0       10         0      2
        -------  ------  --------  ----------  -----  -------  --------  -----
        total        5      0.00        0.00      0       10         0      2

        Misses in library cache during parse: 0
        Optimizer mode: ALL_ROWS
        Parsing user id: 72      (recursive depth: 1)
```

Many of the timing values here are 0. This is because the query itself is not a particular demanding one in terms of CPU or logical/physical I/O, and in the resolution that we're measuring (hundredths of seconds), they simply do not register.

You can see that the parse count for the query was 1, which means that it is the first time the query was parsed in this session. However, notice that the "Misses in library cache during parse" value is 0. This means that the parse was a soft parse, as the database was able to use a query that had already been parsed and was being held in the cache. You can also see that the query was executed once (the execute count), and that 10 logical I/Os (in the query column) were performed to retrieve 2 rows.

You might notice that you can't see the value that was used for the bind variable in the TKProf report. For that information, you need to look in the raw trace file (remember that TKProf produces a summarized report).

In the raw trace file, you will see that APEX actually *identifies itself* when running code in the database. The following is a section in the raw trace file:

```
*** ACTION NAME:(PAGE 1) 2007-01-24 11:19:51.095

*** MODULE NAME:(APEX:APPLICATION 108) 2007-01-24 11:19:51.095
*** CLIENT ID:(JOHN:3690590133226902) 2007-01-24 11:19:51.095
```

APEX uses the DBMS_APPLICATION_INFO package so that it can define the module name (to identify the application), the action name (to identify the page in the application), and the client ID (which shows you the application username and session ID). This is incredibly useful information, as it allows you to track a trace file back to a particular user's session.

As you've seen, generating a trace file will enable you to find the queries and PL/SQL that are consuming the most resources in your application.

Giving Timing Information to the Users

You've seen how you can determine retrospective timing information by using the application reports and also get current information using debug mode and SQL tracing. You might find it useful to also give your users some easily identifiable feedback about how quickly (or slowly!) the page or region is taking to render.

You can do this quite easily by using the #TIMING# substitution string in your page. For example, in the region footer for the report, you could enter some text and reference the substitution string, as shown in Figure 14-12.

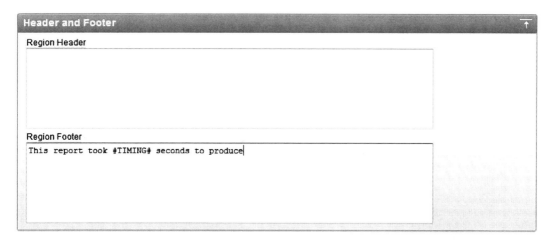

Figure 14-12. Referencing #TIMING# in the report footer

When the users run the page, they will see the time it took to generate the report below the report, as shown in Figure 14-13. Now if this report suddenly takes more time to produce, the users will not just be able to tell you that it was slower, but they also can report exactly how much slower.

Search logo

Bugs

(Go)

BUGID ▼	REPORTED	STATUS	PRIORITY	REPORTED BY	ASSIGNED TO	DESCRIPTION
2	2	02-JAN-2006	Closed	High	CWhite	Peter Ward
Logo occasionally does not appear						
10	10	02-JUL-2006	Open	Critical	SGreen	Steven Anderson
The logout button doesn't close the browser						
						1 - 2

This report took 0.01 seconds to produce

Figure 14-13. Timing information shown below the report

It might be overkill to include this sort of information on every region on your page (in fact, it would look horrid and would waste a lot of screen real estate), but you might want to consider adding it for certain important regions.

Making Your Applications More Scalable

In the previous section, we covered how you can detect and diagnose performance issues. In this section, we will look at some of the ways that you can make your applications more scalable. These techniques include image caching, page and region caching, and HTTP compression. This cannot by any means be considered an exhaustive list (since there are almost an infinite number of ways you could code your applications), but their use can greatly enhance the scalability of your applications.

Image Caching Revisited

We touched on image caching in Chapter 1, but we wanted to reiterate just how important image (and other file) caching can be in making your application more scalable. Remember that every time the user's browser must request a file, it means the following:

- A request is made to the web server.

- A request might be made to the database via the mod_plsql handler.

We say "might be made to the database," because you might be requesting one of the JavaScript files or image files that reside on the file system of the machine running the web server. Usually, files that are stored on the file system are handled correctly by the web server in terms of being able to add the proper expiry header information to the web request so that the browser is able to cache the file in its own local browser cache. However, as discussed in Chapter 1, expiry information is not added when you store images and files in the default APEX file repository. So, if you are referencing files that are stored in this location (using APP_IMAGES, WORKSPACE_IMAGES substitution strings, for example), then you are potentially making your end users' browsers request those resources every single time they access the page, even though the resource may not have changed.

When people start to see their database or web server struggling to cope with the demand, they often have the knee-jerk reaction to throw more resources at it (add more RAM to the machine, install faster disks, upgrade the machine completely, and so on). However, sometimes you need to step back and check whether the problem is due to your implementation rather than the infrastructure. In many cases, the problem is that the application has been designed so that it doesn't scale, rather than that the application has scaled better than the hardware and infrastructure allow.

Using the techniques discussed in Chapter 1, you can use cached images and other resources in your application. If the browser can use the cached resource, it will not need to make a request to the web server. Correspondingly, you will not incur that potential hit against the database—not only do you free up the web server, but you also free up the database.

This really isn't about not using your web server or database. It is about being smart about working out what you really need to request. If you can avoid making unnecessary requests, then you free up the web server and database to support many more requests for things that really are needed. Ultimately, you may be able to support far more end users with fewer hardware requirements.

Page and Region Caching

With APEX 4.0, you can opt to cache the output result for a page or region and then use that cached result for subsequent requests, rather than generating the page or region dynamically each time it is requested.

As you know, whenever you visit a page in an APEX application, all of the regions in that page are dynamically processed, and the results are returned to your browser. However, you might have some static content that does not change or does not change that often (where *often* is a relative term, of course).

For example, in the Buglist application, when users first land on the Buglist page, they are shown all the records in the report (or rather the number of records we allow with the pagination), as shown in Figure 14-14. This means that every time someone navigates to this page, that report is being generated (and therefore the underlying query is being executed), whether or not the user uses that report. Some users may immediately enter some search criteria, in which case, they did not need the unfiltered report query to have already been executed. It would be extremely useful to avoid running that query each time the user navigates to the page, and instead run it only when necessary. Fortunately, this is exactly what region caching allows us to do.

Search [   ] * You have not entered a search phrase

Bugs

(Go)

BUGID ▼	REPORTED	STATUS	PRIORITY	REPORTED BY	ASSIGNED TO	DESCRIPTION
1	1	27-JAN-2006	Open	High	RHuson	John Scott
Pressing Cancel on the login screen gives an error						
2	2	02-JAN-2006	Closed	High	CWhite	Peter Ward
Logo occasionally does not appear						
3	3	01-FEB-2006	Open	High	CWatson	John Scott
Search doesn't return any results when nothing is entered						
4	4	02-MAR-2006	Open	Critical	LBarnes	Mark Wilson
Login doesn't work for user smithp						
5	5	02-MAR-2006	Open	Low	LScott	Steven Anderson
Images don't look in the right positions						
6	6	02-MAY-2006	Open	Medium	CDonaldson	John Scott
Pressing delete user gives permission denied error						
7	7	02-JUN-2006	Open	High	PMathews	Michael Stuart
Buttons don't work in firefox						
8	8	02-JUN-2006	Closed	High	MLawson	Mark Wilson
Pressing cancel on the login screen gives an error						
9	9	02-JUL-2006	Open	High	JStevens	John Scott
Trying to add anew record gives an error						
10	10	02-JUL-2006	Open	Critical	SGreen	Steven Anderson
The logout button doesn't close the browser						

1 - 10

This report took 0.48 seconds to produce

Figure 14-14. *Report region showing all dynamically generated content*

Figure 14-15 shows the Caching section for the report region we use for that Buglist report. Three Caching settings are available as follows:

- *Not Cached*: The region is generated dynamically each time it is needed. This is the default.

- *Cached*: The region is cached independently of which user is being used.

- *Cached by User*: The region is cached for a particular user.

Figure 14-15. Caching options at the region level

In addition to region caching, you can also cache at the page level. This is very similar to enabling caching at the region level, as shown in Figure 14-16.

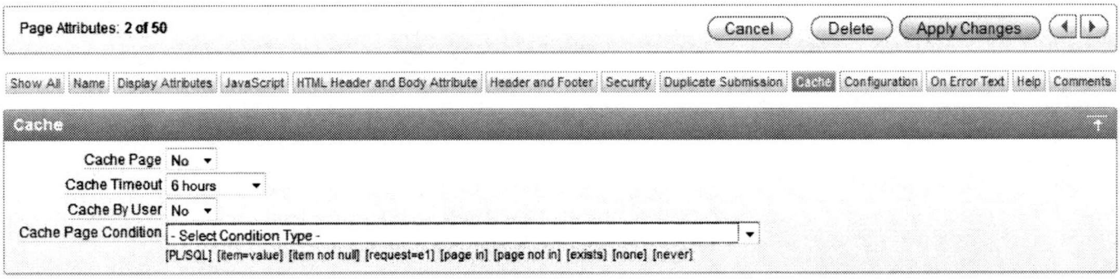

Figure 14-16. Caching options at the page level

In the Buglist report region Caching section, if you set the Caching value to Cached and navigate back and forward to the page (to make sure you get the cached version), you should see something like Figure 14-17. You get the same report, but compare the timing information at the bottom of the screen to the original version (Figure 14-14). Before you enabled caching, the line read as follows:

```
This report took 0.48 seconds to produce.
```

After enabling region caching, you see the following:

```
This report took 0.10 seconds to produce.
```

Search [   ] * You have not entered a search phrase

Bugs

(Go)

BUGID▼	REPORTED	STATUS	PRIORITY	REPORTED BY	ASSIGNED TO	DESCRIPTION
1	1	27-JAN-2006	Open	High	RHuson	John Scott
Pressing Cancel on the login screen gives an error						
2	2	02-JAN-2006	Closed	High	CWhite	Peter Ward
Logo occasionally does not appear						
3	3	01-FEB-2006	Open	High	CWatson	John Scott
Search doesn't return any results when nothing is entered						
4	4	02-MAR-2006	Open	Critical	LBarnes	Mark Wilson
Login doesn't work for user smithp						
5	5	02-MAR-2006	Open	Low	LScott	Steven Anderson
Images don't look in the right positions						
6	6	02-MAY-2006	Open	Medium	CDonaldson	John Scott
Pressing delete user gives permission denied error						
7	7	02-JUN-2006	Open	High	PMathews	Michael Stuart
Buttons don't work in firefox						
8	8	02-JUN-2006	Closed	High	MLawson	Mark Wilson
Pressing cancel on the login screen gives an error						
9	9	02-JUL-2006	Open	High	JStevens	John Scott
Trying to add anew record gives an error						
10	10	02-JUL-2006	Open	Critical	SGreen	Steven Anderson
The logout button doesn't close the browser						

1 - 10

This report took 0.10 seconds to produce

Figure 14-17. Report with region caching enabled

This means that it took 0.38 second less time to use the cached version of the region than processing it dynamically. In other words, the cached version took between a third and a half the time compared to the dynamic version. Note that we tested these timings over several page views, and these numbers were quite representative of the time savings of using the cached version.

The Caching section for the report (Figure 14-15) also offers a setting called Timeout Cache After, which lets you specify how long that cached region should be considered valid. You can choose from a number of different settings, ranging from as short as 10 seconds, through 1 minute, 10 minutes, hours, days, weeks, or even a year. This level of granular cache expiry means you can specify a value that is relevant to your exact situation. If your system is used by a lot of people and the data does not tend to change that often (people are mainly viewing information that is quite static, perhaps updated overnight by a batch process), you might set a Timeout Cache After value of 1 hour or 6 hours. Then when users visit the page each day, you would not need to query the underlying tables, since the data would not have changed since the previous business day.

Alternatively, you might have a system with a large number of end users, where the existing data is changed often and new records are frequently created throughout the day. In this situation, you might choose an extremely short Timeout Cache After value of 10 seconds or 30 seconds. Then if users navigated to a different page and then went back to the original report page within 30 seconds, they would see the cached version. After the 30-second period has elapsed though, the region would be generated dynamically, and the users would see any data that had been added or modified.

Also, rather than simply defining a page or region as either cached or not cached, you can define some conditional logic to determine whether the cached version should be used at run-time or whether a dynamic version should be used. Using conditional logic with your caching mechanisms allows you to be extremely flexible and creative about when the cached versions should be used. For example, you could set the Timeout Cache After value to a very long value (say hours or days), but use some conditional logic to trigger when the dynamic content should be used to obtain the latest results.

Page and region caching are extremely useful when you have large numbers of users. Imagine 200 end users who all navigate between two pages most of the day. If each user navigates to a page containing a report (like our Buglist report) say 30 times an hour, that means that page will be viewed around 48,000 times each day. Without caching, the underlying query behind that report would be executed at least 48,000 times a day (more if the users enter search criteria or the like). Imagine now that you enable caching with a 5-minute expiry. The users visit the page 30 times each hour (on average), which means they visit the page every 2 minutes or so, so there is an extremely high chance that you would be able to use the cached version rather than running the query each time. You might find that rather than the query being executed 48,000 times a day, it executes 1,000 times, which is potentially a huge savings in database resources. If you told your DBA that you could decrease the number of queries by an order of magnitude, he would undoubtedly love you all the more for it.

To illustrate just how much you can improve performance from your users' perspective, let's suppose that we created another report region on the page, which queries the all_objects view as follows:

```
select
  owner, object_name
from
  all_objects
```

On our test system, this returns around 72,000 objects, so we set the Max Row Count for the report to 75,000 (otherwise, it would report on only the first 500 rows, by default, as you saw in Chapter 6). We also modify the pagination scheme for the report so that it uses the Row Ranges X to Y to Z (with pagination) option. As you saw in Chapter 6, this scheme shows the total number of rows returned, and it is one of the worst performing pagination schemes. We have added the same type of footer text used earlier to the report region to display the timing information.

As shown in Figure 14-18, it takes more than 3 seconds to generate this report. Remember that this is a 5-second (or more) overhead every time we navigate to this page. Navigate back and forward to this page a number of times, and you certainly begin to feel how slow the page is to render. If you navigated to this page 100 times a day, you would spend more than 500 seconds a day waiting for that region to render. That is more than 8 minutes a day wasted just sitting and waiting (and scale that up if you have a lot of users doing the same thing).

All Objects

OWNER▼	OBJECT_NAME
APEXDEMO	BUGLIST_TABTEST_SEQ
APEXDEMO	bi_BUGLIST_TABTEST
APEXDEMO	EBA_BT_SEQ
APEXDEMO	EBA_BT_USER
APEXDEMO	EBA_BT_USER_PK
APEXDEMO	EBA_BT_USER_UK
APEXDEMO	BIU_EBA_BT_USER
APEXDEMO	EBA_BT_GROUP
APEXDEMO	EBA_BT_GROUP_PK
APEXDEMO	EBA_BT_GROUP_UK
APEXDEMO	BIU_EBA_BT_GROUP
APEXDEMO	EBA_BT_USER_GROUP
APEXDEMO	EBA_BT_USER_GROUP_PK
APEXDEMO	BIU_EBA_BT_USER_GROUP
APEXDEMO	EBA_BT_URGENCY

row(s) 1 - 15 of 72477 Next Page**

This report took 3.98 seconds to produce

Figure 14-18. Querying all_objects with no caching

Now, let's enable caching for that region. Then the first time you visit the page, you have to wait the 5 or more seconds for the region to render. On subsequent visits to the page, it is rendered much faster (in around 0.3 second).

You can use the application reports that we looked at earlier in the chapter to see which pages and regions are currently cached in your application. For example, Figure 14-19 shows the Cached Regions report. Here, you can see that the All_objects region has another 555 seconds before it is expired (it has existed for 45 seconds, so we know that it was set to expire after 555 + 45 = 600 seconds, or 10 minutes). You can also see the size of the region (3,470 characters), as well as when the region was cached, the method of caching, and which use caused the region to be cached. From this report, you can also manually purge expired and checked regions to force them to be removed from the cache.

Figure 14-19. Viewing the Cached Regions report

You can enable caching at the region level for any type of region, such as report regions, PL/SQL regions, HTML regions, and so on. However, you need to consider which regions it makes sense to cache. Obviously, it would be counterproductive to cache content for long periods if your users wish to see the most current information. On the other hand, it would not make sense to dynamically generate content that does not change that often. For example, if you have an HTML region that contains static text that changes very infrequently, you would probably benefit from caching that region.

Using region and page caching appropriately in your application can have a great effect on the response time of the application from the users' perspective, and also decrease the resource requirements for your application from the database's perspective.

Now that you've seen how to use image, region, and page caching to avoid repeatedly transferring the same content, let's look at another way to make your application more scalable: by reducing the size of the HTML output, the CSS files, and JavaScript files to reduce the time it takes to download them.

HTTP Compression

HTTP compression allows you to compress the web server response before sending it to the user's browser. When the user's browser receives the compressed response, the browser decompresses it before displaying the result. All of this happens transparently as far as the end user is concerned.

The main aim in compressing the web server response is to reduce the size of the information that needs to be sent to the browser. Certain items will be more compressible than others. For example, raw HTML is usually very compressible, as are CSS files. However, compressing images such as JPEGs will usually result in a poor compression ratio, because the JPEG format has already optimized the size of the file to a high degree. In some rare cases, you can actually end up with a file that is bigger after compression than it was before. It is important to compress only items that will result in good compression ratios, rather than trying to compress everything for the sake of it. Also, be aware that the compression process itself incurs an overhead, since it involves using processor and memory resources on your web server. Therefore, you need to ensure that your web server is able to handle the extra processing requirements.

By using page compression, you can achieve the following three areas of improvement:

- The bandwidth requirements are reduced (less information is transferred to the user).

- The pages load faster from the users' perspective (they don't need to wait as long for the information to be transferred, since there is less of it).

- Your web server may able to handle a greater number of requests (it is transferring less information per request; therefore, it can service more requests over the same period of time).

You may be wondering why it's necessary to compress the content. After all, the speed of Internet connections is getting faster and faster, and broadband connections have become affordable for many home users. But while connection speeds have increased, so has the complexity of web sites. They can quite often contain references to images, Flash movies, CSS files, JavaScript files, and so on. So before you can view the web page, you need to wait for your browser to request the original page, along with any linked files. Using compression, you can reduce this wait time.

By default, the supplied Oracle HTTP Server (OHS) does not have any form of compression enabled. To take advantage of HTTP compression, you can use an Apache module, either `mod_gzip` (for Apache 1) or `mod_deflate` (for Apache 2). OHS is based on Apache 1, so to enable compression on that web server, you need to use `mod_gzip`. If you use an Apache 2 server to proxy requests to OHS, you may wish to use `mod_deflate` on that Apache 2 server to enable compression.

■ **Note** Apache modules are essentially plug-ins that you can use to modify the way that Apache works. There are many different Apache modules available, for all sorts of different purposes.

Note that in Oracle Database XE and now Oracle Database 11*g*, you can use the embedded PL/SQL gateway (DBMS_EPG), which will handle web requests, rather than requiring an external web server (OHS). However, the embedded PL/SQL gateway will not handle HTTP compression. In order to take advantage of this great feature, you can use another Apache server to proxy requests to the embedded PL/SQL gateway (you will see how to proxy requests in Chapter 15). So even if you're using the embedded PL/SQL gateway, you should still consider using HTTP compression to help allow your application to scale.

Examining HTTP Headers

Whenever a browser makes a request to a web server, the browser will send a number of HTTP request headers, which tell the web server what information the browser is requesting, along with information about the capabilities of the browser.

To examine the HTTP headers, we use a tool that is part of the libwww-perl (LWP) collection. You can easily install this collection of tools if you have Perl installed. The tools allow you to easily construct web requests and examine the responses using Perl scripting and command-line tools. One of the tools available in LWP is the GET command, which allows you to construct a URL request from the command line, as shown in Listing 14-11.

Listing 14-11. LWP GET Command Usage

```
[jes@pb tmp]$ GET

Usage: GET [-options] <url>...
    -m <method>   use method for the request (default is 'GET')
    -f            make request even if GET believes method is illegal
    -b <base>     Use the specified URL as base
    -t <timeout>  Set timeout value
    -i <time>     Set the If-Modified-Since header on the request
    -c <conttype> use this content-type for POST, PUT, CHECKIN
    -a            Use text mode for content I/O
    -p <proxyurl> use this as a proxy
    -P            don't load proxy settings from environment
    -H <header>   send this HTTP header (you can specify several)
    -u            Display method and URL before any response
    -U            Display request headers (implies -u)
    -s            Display response status code
    -S            Display response status chain
    -e            Display response headers
    -d            Do not display content
    -o <format>   Process HTML content in various ways
    -v            Show program version
    -h            Print this message
    -x            Extra debugging output
```

Listing 14-12 shows an example of a command-line request to the Google web site (we show only the first ten lines of output by piping the output of the GET command through the head command).

Listing 14-12. Request to the Google Home Page

```
[jes@pb tmp]$ GET www.google.com | head -n10

<html><head><meta http-equiv="content-type" content="text/html;
charset=ISO-8859-1"><title>Google</title><style><!--
body,td,a,p,.h{font-family:arial,sans-serif}
.h{font-size:20px}
.h{color:#3366cc}
.q{color:#00c}
--></style>
<script>
<!--
function sf(){document.f.q.focus();}
// -->
```

The output from the GET command is the actual content response from the remote web server. We can use this command to request the static apex_logo.gif file from our APEX installation, as shown in Listing 14-13.

Listing 14-13. Requesting the APEX Logo Image

```
[jes@pb tmp]$ GET -d -e "http://127.0.0.1/i/htmldb/apex_logo.gif"

Cache-Control: max-age=1296000
Connection: close
Date: Sun, 18 Feb 2007 14:13:41 GMT
Accept-Ranges: bytes
ETag: "1b0e73-cbf-44f7bb16"
Server: Oracle-Application-Server-10g/9.0.4.0.0 Oracle-HTTP-Server
Content-Length: 3263
Content-Type: image/gif
Expires: Fri, 16 Mar 2007 08:10:10 GMT
Last-Modified: Fri, 01 Sep 2006 04:46:14 GMT
Client-Response-Num: 1
```

This example uses the -d and -e arguments to the GET command so that the contents of the image file are not displayed (since it is just binary, it wouldn't make sense to display it). The HTTP response headers show information about the resource that was requested.

If we request the Google home page using the GET tool, we see the output in Listing 14-14.

Listing 14-14. Request Header Sent in a URL Request

```
[jes@pb tmp]$ GET -d -U -e www.google.com

GET http://www.google.com/
User-Agent: lwp-request/2.07
```

```
Cache-Control: private

Date: Sun, 18 Feb 2007 21:12:03 GMT
Server: GWS/2.1
Content-Type: text/html
Content-Type: text/html; charset=ISO-8859-1
Client-Response-Num: 1
Client-Transfer-Encoding: chunked
Set-Cookie: PREF=ID=506820471aef2070:TM=1172783523:LM=1172783523:S=iVgPJnGJwayhONgz;
expires=Sun, 17-Jan-2038 19:14:07 GMT; path=/; domain=.google.com
Title: Google
```

This example uses the -U parameter to display the request headers (highlighted in bold).

The command-line GET tool sends very few headers by default—nowhere near the amount of information that the average browser will send. However, it is sufficient information for the web server to process the request. The User-Agent header can be used by the web server to identify what sort of web browser is making the request.

If you have one of the compression modules loaded in your web server, when the web server receives a request, it will examine the request headers to see whether the browser supports handling compressed content. If the browser does support compressed content, the web server can use the compression module to compress the content and then send the response to the browser. If the browser does not advertise that it supports compressed content, the response will always be delivered in an uncompressed format.

The Accept-Encoding header tells the web server whether the browser supports compressed content. This header can support a few different values, as follows:

```
Accept-Encoding: gzip
```

```
Accept-Encoding: compress
Accept-Encoding: gzip, compress
```

When more than one value is listed, the browser supports more than one compression format. Most modern browsers will announce multiple values.

If you can enable your web server to support compression, any browsers that also support compression should benefit, while those browsers that do not support compression will continue to work.

Configuring mod_gzip

The installation of mod_gzip is fairly straightforward and well documented. You simply need to place the module into the directory containing all your other Apache modules (usually in the libexec directory). It's also recommended that you use the separate configuration file (mod_gzip.conf) for all the mod_gzip-related configuration and include this new configuration file from your main Apache configuration file (httpd.conf), rather than placing the mod_gzip configuration directly in the main file.

▨ **Caution** `mod_gzip` is not officially supported by Oracle. So if you are the least bit wary of changing the configuration on your OHS, or you are worried that you may be left in an unsupported position, consider using Apache 2 to proxy requests to the OHS, and load the `mod_deflate` module on the Apache 2 server instead. Having said that, we have successfully run `mod_gzip` for a long time now without any ill effects. In any case, you are well advised to try this on a test system before using it on your production setup.

Here, you can see that the module is located in the `ORACLE_HOME/Apache/Apache/libexec/mod_gzip.so` directory.

```
[jes@pb OraHome]$ ls -al Apache/Apache/libexec/mod_gzip.so
-rwxr-xr-x  1 oracle oinstall 90998 Dec 9 2004 Apache/Apache/libexec/mod_gzip.so*
```

Remember that `ORACLE_HOME` refers to where the Apache server is installed, rather than the database's location.

We also copied the sample `mod_gzip.conf` to the Apache configuration file directory, as follows:

```
[jes@pb OraHome]$ ls -al Apache/Apache/conf/mod_gzip.conf
-rw-r--r--  1 oracle oinstall 14837 Jan 6 2006 Apache/Apache/conf/mod_gzip.conf
```

Although the sample `mod_gzip.conf` should work fine in most cases, we have made a few changes, one of which is adding the following line:

```
mod_gzip_item_include        handler    ^pls_handler$
```

The purpose of this line is to include compression on anything that is being handled by the `pls_handler`. The `mod_plsql` handler is responsible for handling requests for our DAD, which is how our APEX sessions are handled. We have added this because we've found in certain cases, where the MIME type is not detected properly, some items will not be compressed, even though they may be highly compressible items, such as CSS and JavaScript files. You may want to check whether this line is suitable for your own configuration (you can determine this through testing).

Next, we need to include the `mod_gzip` configuration by adding the following line to the main Apache configuration file (`httpd.conf`):

```
# Include the mod_gzip settings
include "/u1/app/oracle/OraHome/Apache/Apache/conf/mod_gzip.conf"
```

Make sure you use the correct path to the `mod_gzip.conf` file for your own installation.

Now restart Apache. You should have a working installation of `mod_gzip`.

▪ **Note** If you get a warning along the lines of "This module might crash under EAPI!" you don't need to worry. The module seems to work fine despite this warning. If you want to get rid of the error, you can try recompiling the module yourself.

Configuring mod_deflate

You can use mod_deflate on an Apache 2 server if you don't want to modify your existing OHS installation. You can then proxy requests from the Apache 2 server to the existing OHS server.

If you have downloaded the binary distribution of Apache, you should already have the precompiled mod_deflate module; otherwise, you can quite easily compile the module yourself, either into the main binary or as a separate loadable module. The instructions for compiling are included in the Apache distribution.

In the example, we have compiled mod_deflate so that it is part of the Apache binary. In Listing 14-15, we use the -l (lowercase letter *L*) parameter to list the modules that are compiled into Apache.

Listing 14-15. Listing the Modules Compiled into Apache

```
[jes@ap Apache] bin/httpd -l

Compiled in modules:
  core.c
  mod_access.c
  mod_auth.c
  util_ldap.c
  mod_auth_ldap.c
  mod_include.c
  mod_deflate.c
  mod_log_config.c
  mod_env.c
    ... extra output removed
```

This means that we do not need to explicitly load the module, since it is already compiled into Apache. If you have compiled it as a loadable module, you need to add the following line to your httpd.conf file:

```
LoadModule deflate_module libexec/mod_deflate.so
```

We add the following line to our main Apache configuration file:

```
AddOutputFilterByType DEFLATE text/html text/plain text/xml text/css
```

This line tells Apache that mod_deflate should be used for the content using the text/html, text/plain, text/xml, or text/css MIME types.

Once you restart the web server, you should have a working mod_deflate module.

For the rest of this section, we will discuss mod_gzip specifically; however, you should find that the results with mod_deflate are very similar in terms of the compression ratio and the benefits you receive.

Testing Compression

To test that the compression module is working correctly, we will use the GET tool to request the default page of our OHS installation (you can use any static page you like for this test), as shown in Listing 14-16.

Listing 14-16. Retrieving an Uncompressed Static Page

```
[jes@pb bench]$ GET -d -e http://localhost:7777

Connection: close
Date: Sun, 18 Feb 2007 23:47:07 GMT
Accept-Ranges: bytes
ETag: "46cbac-37a3-4159b828"
Server: Oracle-Application-Server-10g/9.0.4.0.0 Oracle-HTTP-Server
Content-Length: 14243
Content-Type: text/html
Content-Type: text/html; charset=windows-1252
Last-Modified: Tue, 28 Sep 2004 19:14:48 GMT
Client-Response-Num: 1
Link: </ohs_images/portals.css>; rel="stylesheet"
Title: Oracle Application Server - Welcome
```

You can see that the size of the returned HTML is 14,243 bytes, or around 14KB. By making the GET command use the Accept-Encoding header, we should be able to get the web server to compress the response content, as shown in Listing 14-17.

Listing 14-17. Retrieving a Compressed Static Page

```
[jes@pb bench]$ GET -d -e -H "Accept-Encoding: gzip,compress" http://localhost:7777

Connection: close
Date: Sun, 18 Feb 2007 23:50:50 GMT
Accept-Ranges: bytes
ETag: "46cbac-37a3-4159b828"
Server: Oracle-Application-Server-10g/9.0.4.0.0 Oracle-HTTP-Server
Content-Encoding: gzip
Content-Length: 2838
Content-Type: text/html
Last-Modified: Tue, 28 Sep 2004 19:14:48 GMT
Client-Response-Num: 1
```

This time, the content length is only 2,838 bytes, which is around a fifth of the size of the uncompressed version.

If you enabled logging in the mod_gzip.conf configuration file, you should be able to see an entry in the log file similar to the following:

```
pb - - [18/Feb/2007:23:55:01 +0000] "ws1 GET / HTTP/1.1" 200 3150
 mod_gzip: OK In:14243 -< Out:2838 = 81 pct.
```

The log entry tells you the original size of the document (14,243 bytes), what it was compressed to (2,838 bytes), and the resulting compression ratio (81%). This log can be extremely helpful in determining the benefit of using compression on particular files.

OK, so we know we can compress static HTML files. How about some of our APEX pages? If we try the URL of our report page, we should get results similar to those shown in Listings 14-18 and 14-19.

Listing 14-18. Retrieving an Uncompressed APEX Report Page

```
[jes@pb bench]$ GET -d -e "http://localhost/pls/apex/f?p=273:2:2807160253709943::NO"

Connection: close
Date: Sun, 18 Feb 2007 23:58:53 GMT
Server: Oracle-Application-Server-10g/9.0.4.0.0 Oracle-HTTP-Server
Content-Length: 8541
Content-Type: text/html; charset=UTF-8
Content-Type: text/html; charset=utf-8
Client-Response-Num: 1
Link: </i/css/core_V22.css>; /="/"; rel="stylesheet"; type="text/css"
Link: </i/themes/theme_15/theme_V2.css>; /="/"; rel="stylesheet"; type="text/css"
Title: Report
```

Listing 14-19. Retrieving a Compressed APEX Report Page

```
[jes@pb bench]$ GET -d -e -H "Accept-Encoding: gzip,compress"

"http://localhost/pls/apex/f?p=273:2:2807160253709943::NO"
Connection: close
Date: Sun, 18 Feb 2007 23:59:22 GMT
Server: Oracle-Application-Server-10g/9.0.4.0.0 Oracle-HTTP-Server
Content-Encoding: gzip
Content-Length: 2136
Content-Type: text/html; charset=UTF-8
Client-Response-Num: 1
```

Success! Once again the compression ratio is quite high, as we can see, as follows, from the log file:

```
pb - APEX_PUBLIC_USER [18/Feb/2007:00:08:40 +0000]

 "ws1 GET /pls/apex/f?p=273:2:2807160253709943::NO HTTP/1.1"
200 2365 mod_gzip: OK In:8541 -< Out:2136 = 75 pct.
```

The report page compresses to around a quarter of the uncompressed size.

Notice that the document contains the other linked items core_V22.css and theme_V2.css, which should also be compressible, shown as follows:

```
pb - - [18/Feb/2007:00:22:02 +0000] "ws1 GET /i/themes/theme_15/theme_V2.css

HTTP/1.1" 200 4626 mod_gzip: OK In:23836 -< Out:4315 = 82 pct.
pb - - [18/Feb/2007:00:22:02 +0000] "ws1 GET /i/css/core_V22.css HTTP/1.1" 200 2037
mod_gzip: OK In:6509 -< Out:1726 = 74 pct.
```

As you can see, we have achieved quite a significant compression ratio on these files, too.

Benchmarking Compression

So far, we have managed to compress the size of some of the files being downloaded to the users' browser, but what does that mean in terms of performance and resources?

We used the httperf tool to query the report both with the mod_gzip module enabled and disabled. We created a custom script that will perform a fetch of the main report page plus the linked CSS files and JavaScript files, so that the test is representative of a real user browsing the page.

▪ **Note** Many different tools can help you to benchmark the performance of your web server. We used httperf, a complex tool in itself, which allows you to script the URLs to retrieve. We encourage you to test compression results yourself on your own test systems. You can use httperf, ApacheBench, or another tool of your choice.

We performed three different tests to simulate the system being used by different volumes of end users. In the first test, we compare a single connection with no multithreading. In the without compression example, the page was requested first, then each resource in the page was requested in a sequential manner. Many modern browsers allow subrequests to be handled in parallel, although this is sometimes throttled to only one or two simultaneous subrequests at a time. Table 14-1 shows the results of the first test.

Table 14-1. Test 1: Single Connection, No Multithreading

	Mod_gzip Off	Mod_gzip On	Factor
Connection rate (conn/s)	8.6	12.1	~ 1.4 times faster
Connection rate (ms/conn)	116.8	82.8	~ 1.4 times faster
Session lifetime (sec)	0.4	0.2	~ 2 times faster
Total content size returned (KB)	38	8	~ 5 times smaller
Average session rate (sessions/sec)	0.47	4.03	~ 8.5 times faster

As you can see, using compression improves performance in all areas. The response content is downloaded in roughly half the time it takes without compression. Also, the average session rate when using compression is roughly 8.5 times higher. This is due to the compressed sessions being processed by the web server much quicker (since there is less data to transfer).

In the second test, we tried a more realistic case, where the browser is able to make multiple simultaneous subrequests for the resources (CSS, JavaScript, and so on). This test essentially simulates ten different users requesting the report page at more or less the same time. Table 14-2 shows the results of the second test.

Table 14-2. *Test 2: 10 Connections, 10 Parallel Subrequests*

	Mod_gzip Off	Mod_gzip On	Factor
Connection rate (conn/s)	8.7	23.1	~ 2.6 times faster
Connection rate (zms/conn)	115.2	43.4	~ 2.6 times faster
Session lifetime (sec)	1.1	0.5	~ 2.2 times faster
Total content size returned (KB)	380	80	~ 5 times smaller
Average session rate (sessions/sec)	2.89	7.69	~ 2.6 times faster

This time, the connection rate for the noncompressed version remained more or less uniform. Because the compressed response can be delivered to the browser quicker, it frees up the Apache processes to deal with other requests faster, so the connection rate increases. The average session rate factor drops a little however. This is probably mainly due to the initially bad session rate returned in the previous test.

In the third test, we are really starting to push the web server, approximating the effect of 200 users all accessing the report page simultaneously. Table 14-3 shows the results.

Table 14-3. *Test 3: 200 Connections, 10 Parallel Subrequests*

	Mod_gzip Off	Mod_gzip On	Factor
Connection rate (conn/s)	3.2	34.6	~ 11 times faster
Connection rate (ms/conn)	312.7	28.9	~ 11 times faster
Session lifetime (sec)	4.9	3.8	~ 1.2 times faster

	Mod_gzip Off	Mod_gzip On	Factor
Total content size returned (MB)	7.4	1.5	~ 5 times smaller
Average session rate (sessions/sec)	1.06	11.55	~ 11 times faster

As before, once we start really hitting the web server with a lot of simultaneous requests, the noncompressed test starts to show signs of stress. The compressed test shows that the web server is able to deal with an order of magnitude more requests per second. Also note that while the ratio of total content size returned is showing a similar ratio to the previous tests, we are now seeing measurable differences in terms of the actual quantity of bandwidth that would be saved with compression. In this simple example, we have saved 6MB of bandwidth. That might not sound like a lot, but remember that this is just a simple test system. Scale that number up to the figures you would achieve each day, then each week, then each month and each year. You could end up saving huge amounts of network bandwidth by taking advantage of compression.

Remember also that it is not just people who pay for their bandwidth that will benefit from these savings. Reduce one application's bandwidth to 20% of what it was formerly, and other applications will benefit from the newly available bandwidth. In fact, the savings on bandwidth might mean that you do not have to pay to upgrade the infrastructure as soon as you might otherwise. Tell your network manager that you can cut your usage by 80% today, and he's sure to be interested.

We've demonstrated the huge impact that configuring your web server to support compression can have. You may be wondering whether there is a risk that the processing overhead of compressing the response output will actually make using compression slower rather than faster. The only time this might be the case is when you're compressing extremely small files (say 2KB or less). Fortunately, the mod_gzip configuration file lets you specify a minimum file size, so that you don't try to compress files smaller than this size (see the mod_gzip_minimum_file_size parameter for more information).

Summary

The techniques we've discussed in this chapter can be of great benefit to many projects, even if you don't have to pay for your bandwidth, or you don't use that many images in your application so you don't think it would be worthwhile.

The good thing about these techniques is that their benefits also scale with your project. As the number of application users grows, so will the savings in terms of bandwidth and resource usage. Also, by using the image and region caching techniques, your application will be able to scale to support a larger number of users than if you didn't use them.

Please don't think you need a lot of users to implement these techniques. We advise using them from day one of your project. If you set up the mod_gzip module, then not only will the users of your application benefit, but so will you, as you use Application Builder during your project development (yes, you'll also benefit from compression of the web pages!).

It's very tempting to look at these examples and think, "Well, it's only a few kilobytes here and there. Who cares?" It may not look like a lot in terms of a single page view, but if you are saving 80% to 90% bandwidth on a weekly, monthly, or yearly basis, that could equate to considerable savings. Likewise, if you use image caching and manage to substantially cut down on the number of unnecessary requests that are made to your web server and database, that will equate to tangible savings in terms of investment, scalability, and performance.

CHAPTER 15

Production Issues

This chapter is a bit of a catch-all. It covers some of the common issues you might encounter when running your applications in a production environment. You'll find a number of techniques and features that can make managing your applications a bit easier.

Managing URLs

One very commonly recurring question regarding APEX is how you can provide a "nice" URL for your end users to access your application. In other words, rather than the user needing to type the following to access the home page (page 1) of application 101:

```
http://yourdomain.com:7777/pls/apex/f?p=101:1
```

you can give them a URL like this:

```
http://yourdomain.com/accounts.html
```

or perhaps the following:

```
http://accounts.yourdomain.com
```

As you should expect by now, there are actually a few different ways to achieve this goal:

- Use a location redirect
- Use frames
- With Apache mod_rewrite
- By proxying requests

The following sections discuss each of these techniques.

Using a Location Redirect

You can create an HTML file that contains a redirect to your APEX application. For example, suppose we create a file called buglist.html with the following content:

```
<META HTTP-EQUIV="Refresh" CONTENT="0; URL=/pls/htmldb/f?p=101:1">
```

This code causes the browser to redirect the specified URL (our APEX application) after the specified period, which in this case is 0 seconds, or immediately.

■ **Note** One thing to keep in mind when using the redirection method is that if the user presses the browser's Back button immediately after being redirected, he will return to the page containing the redirect. That page will send the user back to the APEX application. We will review some more elegant solutions to URL management shortly.

You need to place the buglist.html file somewhere that will be accessible by the web server. You can place it anywhere you like, but we're going to put it in the root location of the web server, which you can find by looking for the DocumentRoot directive in your Apache configuration (the httpd.conf file), as shown in Listing 15-1.

Listing 15-1. Searching for the DocumentRoot Directive

```
[jes@pb ~]$ cd $ORACLE_HOME

[jes@pb ohs]$ cd Apache/Apache/conf
[jes@pb conf]$ grep DocumentRoot httpd.conf
DocumentRoot "/Users/oracle/service/u01/app/oracle/product/OHS/Apache/Apache/htdocs"
```

Here, we changed the current working directory to the value of the ORACLE_HOME. Remember that this is the ORACLE_HOME assigned to your OHS or Internet Application Server (IAS) installation, not the ORACLE_HOME for your database. Then we changed to the configuration directory for the Apache installation and used the grep command to search for the DocumentRoot directive in the httpd.conf file. In our case, the document root is actually $ORACLE_HOME/Apache/Apache/htdocs; your installation might differ.

After you copy the buglist.html file in this directory, you can use the following URL to access the file from your browser:

```
http://127.0.0.1:7780/buglist.html
```

As soon as you do this, the URL in your browser will be changed to http://127.0.0.1:7780/pls/htmldb/f?p=108:1 as a result of the redirect.

Thus, we have provided the end user with a nicer shortcut to use for the URL to access the application; however, the typical APEX-style URL will still be displayed in the browser's address bar.

Using Frames

In HTML, a *frame* is an element that allows you to include content from another HTML document inside the main HTML document, effectively letting you break up the main document into separate areas (frames) that receive their source from different HTML documents.

So, how can you use frames to give the end users a nicer URL? Let's look at an example. Suppose you modified the buglist.html file with the code shown in Listing 15-2.

Listing 15-2. Contents of the buglist.html File

```
<html>

<head>
  <title>Buglist Application</title>
</head>
<frameset rows="100%,*" border="0">
  <frame src="http://192.168.56.101:8080/pls/apex/f?p=108:1" frameborder="0" />
  <frame frameborder="0" noresize />
</frameset>
</html>
```

You should now see the application as though you had used an APEX-style URL to access it, as shown in Figure 15-1.

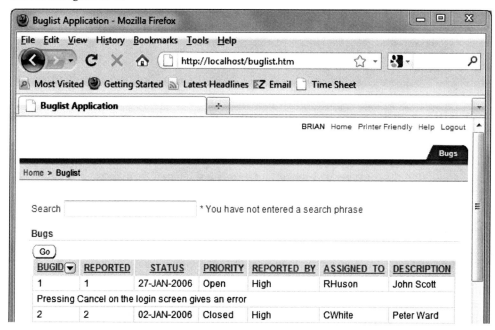

Figure 15-1. Accessing the application via the buglist.html URL

Notice how the address bar in Figure 15-1 no longer shows the APEX-style URL. Even if you navigate to different pages using the tabs and links, the URL shown in the browser will not change. Depending on your exact requirements, you might find this a slight disadvantage of using frames, since even if you follow a link in your application to another web site, the address bar will still display the same URL—there is no indication in the address bar that the user has moved away from that URL.

■ **Note** In this example, we have Apache 2.2.14 running on our local machine on port 80. Your browser will look at the web server's listen port and if it sees 80 or 443 (standard for HTTP and HTTPS respectively) it does not show the port number in the URL. The URL shown in our browser, `http://localhost/buglist.htm`, tells you that Apache is running on our local machine at port 80 and we're accessing a file called "`buglist.htm`." The Buglist application could be anywhere. When you use another port, like 7777, the browser will show the port number.

You can also make the URL a bit more traditional. Rather than have the `buglist.html` file in the document root, you can create a subdirectory called `buglist`, move the file into that subdirectory, and rename it to `index.html`, as shown in Listing 15-3.

Listing 15-3. Creating a Subdirectory in htdocs

```
[jes@pb htdocs]$ mkdir buglist
[jes@pb htdocs]$ mv buglist.html buglist/index.html
```

Now you can access the application by using the following URL:

```
http://127.0.0.1/buglist/
```

You can use this URL because the web server automatically uses the `index.html` file in that directory as the default file to serve if no file is specified. In other words, this URL is equivalent to the following:

```
http://127.0.0.1/buglist/index.html
```

However, you might find the previous URL looks a bit more pleasing to the eye than needing to specify the `index.html` file.

Using Apache mod_rewrite

Using Apache `mod_write` is definitely a bit more complex than the previous two methods, but it also gives you a lot more control and flexibility. This method relies on the `mod_rewrite` module for Apache to rewrite the incoming URL and modify it dynamically to point to your application.

To use this method, you must first ensure that the `mod_rewrite` module is included in your Apache configuration and is also enabled. Check that you have a line similar to the following in your main Apache configuration file (typically `$ORACLE_HOME/Apache/Apache/conf/httpd.conf`):

```
LoadModule rewrite_module       libexec/mod_rewrite.so
```

By default, the `mod_rewrite` module is shipped with the standard OHS distribution, so you should be able to simply add this line to your configuration. If you are using Oracle Database 11*g* or Oracle XE, and you're using the embedded PL/SQL gateway rather than an external HTTP server, you can still use this method by using an external HTTP server and proxying requests to the gateway (as discussed in the next section, "Proxying Requests").

You can enable the `mod_rewrite` module by including the following line in the same configuration file:

```
RewriteEngine On
```

Adding Rewrite Rules

Now you can add some extra directives to the configuration file to perform the actual rewrite logic, as in this example:

```
RewriteRule ^/buglist$
http://127.0.0.1:7780/pls/apex/f?p=108:1 [R=301]
```

This should all be on one line, but has been broken up to make it more readable. You will need to restart the web server before this rule will take effect. After you restart the web server, you will be able to use the following URL to access the application:

```
http://127.0.0.1:7780/buglist
```

Note that the rewrite rule will not work if you specify a trailing slash (as in http://127.0.0.1:7780/buglist/) because the rewrite rule uses a regular expression to match the requested URL: ^/buglist$. This means that the URL needs to begin with a forward slash followed by the exact text phrase buglist. If you wanted to make the trailing slash mandatory, you would modify the rewrite rule so that it reads as follows:

```
RewriteRule ^/buglist/$
http://127.0.0.1:7780/pls/apex/f?p=108:1 [R=301]
```

The rewrite rule has the following format:

```
RewriteRule url-pattern new-url [[flag, ...]]
```

The first parameter after the RewriteRule directive is a regular expression to match against incoming requested URLs. The second parameter is the new URL that should be used if the url-pattern parameter matches the requested URL. You can also pass a number of flags to the rule; in this example, we are using R=301. The purpose of the R=301 flag is to make the web server return the HTTP-301 response code to the browser, which is the code used for a permanent redirect, causing the browser to redirect to the new URL. Using this permanent redirect code should (in theory) enable robots and web spiders to learn that the new URL should be your APEX URL, rather than the shortened URL (however, our experience has been that this is not always as straightforward as it should be).

Rather than using a permanent redirect, you might choose to cause a temporary redirect using the HTTP-302 response code, by changing the [R=301] to [R=302]. You would do this if you were temporarily changing the page that the url-pattern should redirect to, rather than making a permanent change. This is a good way to temporarily take your applications offline for routine maintenance, for example.

Using Domains

An extension to this method is modifying the rewrite rule so that you can handle pointing a different domain name at your application. For example, rather than using http://127.0.0.1:7780, you might want to use http://buglist.yourdomain.com. In this case, you first must make sure that the Domain Name System (DNS) records for the domain (buglist.yourdomain.com) are correctly set up so that the domain points to the machine that is running your web server. In other words, when the user enters http://buglist.yourdomain.com into a browser, the user's machine will perform a DNS query to see to which web server (that is, which IP address) the request needs to be sent.

> ■ **Note** In most medium-sized companies, someone will have the responsibility of configuring the DNS settings for your domain. If you are using this technique for a domain that you have registered on the Internet, your name registrar will usually provide a web control panel where you can configure the DNS settings for the domain.

As an example, we have made some changes to our DNS configuration so that the buglist.localdomain address points to the IP address 192.168.1.7, which is on our local test network. We have used the Unix dig command to verify that the domain name is resolvable via DNS and also that it points to the correct IP address, as shown in Listing 15-4.

Listing 15-4. Using dig to Verify the DNS Configuration

```
[jes@pb ~]$ dig buglist.localdomain

; <<>> DiG 9.3.4 <<>> buglist.localdomain
;; global options:  printcmd
;; Got answer:
;; ->>HEADER<<- opcode: QUERY, status: NOERROR, id: 1122
;; flags: qr rd ra; QUERY: 1, ANSWER: 1, AUTHORITY: 0, ADDITIONAL: 0

;; QUESTION SECTION:
;buglist.localdomain.              IN      A

;; ANSWER SECTION:
buglist.localdomain.      86400   IN      A       192.168.1.7

;; Query time: 51 msec
;; SERVER: 192.168.1.1#53(192.168.1.1)
;; MSG SIZE  rcvd: 49
```

Next, we need to modify the httpd.conf file to enable a virtual host for that domain name. A *virtual host* is a way of serving multiple domain names (and corresponding web sites) from a single Apache configuration. There are different ways to configure virtual hosts, depending on whether you have a single IP address or multiple IP addresses available. For this example, we are using a single IP address and will have multiple virtual hosts listening on the same IP address. Listing 15-5 shows the VirtualHost entry in our Apache configuration for this domain.

Listing 15-5. Using a VirtualHost Entry

```
<VirtualHost *>

   ServerName buglist.localdomain
   ServerAlias buglist.localdomain
   RewriteEngine On
   RewriteRule ^/$ /pls/apex/f?p=108:1 [R=301]
</VirtualHost>
```

We have removed the previous `RewriteEngine On` directive from the main body of the `httpd.conf` file, since we just need to locally enable it within this new `VirtualHost` section. We also moved the `RewriteRule` directive so that it is now contained within the `VirtualHost` section.

If a request is now made to the web server where the requested domain name is `buglist.localdomain`, the directives within this `VirtualHost` section will be used. If the domain name does not match the settings in this `VirtualHost` section, they will not be used.

If we now enter `http://buglist.localdomain` into a browser's address bar, the request will be sent to the web server (since the DNS resolves this domain name to the IP address of the web server). The Apache web server will then recognize that the domain name matches this `VirtualHost` section and will apply the `RewriteRule` directive, which states that if the URL matches `^/$` (nothing other than the trailing slash on the end of the domain name), the web server should issue an HTTP-301 redirect to the browser to point to our APEX application.

One of the benefits of this method is that you can include many other directives in the `VirtualHost` section to process different domains separately. For example, if you want to place static files (images, CSS, and so on) on the web server file system, rather than storing them in the default location specified by the `DocumentRoot` directive you saw earlier, you can assign a new `DocumentRoot` for each `VirtualHost` section, like the following:

```
<VirtualHost *>

   ServerName buglist.localdomain
   ServerAlias buglist.localdomain
   DocumentRoot /www/buglist
   RewriteEngine On
   RewriteRule ^/$ /pls/apex/f?p=108:1 [R=301]
</VirtualHost>
```

Here, we have specified that the root directory for the `buglist.localdomain` virtual host is the `/www/buglist` directory on the web server file system (or possibly on networked storage). This means we could create a subdirectory in the `/www/buglist` directory called images and upload a file called `logo.gif`. We would then be able to refer to the `logo.gif` file via a relative URL within the application, as follows:

```
<img src="/images/logo.gif"></img>
```

Using this approach makes it easy to maintain static files and resources on a domain basis. For example, if you are in the process of testing a whole redesign of your web site with new images (and perhaps JavaScript and CSS), rather than having to copy all those new files over the old ones, you could create a new virtual host for your beta test, modifying the `DocumentRoot` directive to point to the directory containing all your new files, like the following:

```
<VirtualHost *>

   ServerName beta.buglist.localdomain
   ServerAlias beta.buglist.localdomain
   DocumentRoot /www/buglist/beta
   RewriteEngine On
   RewriteRule ^/$ /pls/apex/f?p=108:1 [R=301]
</VirtualHost>
```

This would enable you to easily test your application with the new files without needing to modify the old version of the application.

There are many more Apache directives that you might find useful to include in your `VirtualHost` sections. We encourage you to look through the Apache documentation.

Proxying Requests

In the previous section, we discussed how you can use the `mod_rewrite` module to rewrite the URL. However, you can do much more than just rewriting the URL. You can actually request the content from another web server, and then pass that content back to the user's browser as though it had come from the original web server. This could be useful in a number of scenarios, such as the following:

- Your end users cannot directly access your OHS/IAS for networking reasons.

- You are using the built-in embedded PL/SQL gateway in Oracle XE or Oracle Database 11*g*, but require more advanced features than Apache provides.

- You wish to make your application available on the Internet, but you do not want to move your OHS/IAS so that it is visible from the Internet.

- You are using the embedded PL/SQL gateway, but your security policy does not allow you to open a firewall route from the outside to the database.

In these cases, you can install a stand-alone Apache server and make it the one that resolves requests. This Apache server will then proxy requests to the OHS/IAS or embedded PL/SQL gateway by using some special Apache directives.

As an example, consider the scenario shown in Figure 15-2. Here, the end users are accessing the application over the Internet, but we wish to hide the database and OHS from direct access, so they are behind the firewall. We have situated the proxy Apache server outside the firewall, but have configured the firewall to allow the proxy Apache server to talk to OHS. (The details of how you would secure a configuration like this are up to your network administrator, DBA, and everyone else concerned.) We are going to allow requests to be made via the proxying server to the OHS and have the responses sent back again.

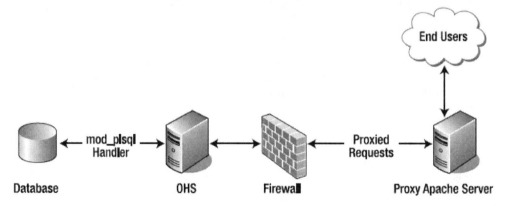

Figure 15-2. A typical proxying configuration

This technique relies on the `mod_proxy` module, so you will need to include that module in your Apache configuration, in the same way that you include the `mod_rewrite` module. You can either compile the module into your Apache binary file or include it as a module. In this example, we use the module method, so we add the following line to the `httpd.conf` file:

```
LoadModule proxy_module libexec/mod_proxy.so
```

Now we can create a `VirtualHost` section, as we did in the previous section, as shown in Listing 15-6.

Listing 15-6. *VirtualHost Entry with Proxying Directives*

```
<VirtualHost *>

ServerName buglist.foo.com
ServerAlias buglist.foo.com
DocumentRoot /www/buglist

RewriteEngine On
RewriteRule ^/$ /pls/apex/f?p=108:1 [R=301]
ProxyPass /pls/apex http://ohs:7777/pls/apex
ProxyPassReverse /pls/apex http://ohs:7777/pls/apex
ProxyPass /i http://ohs:7777/i
ProxyPassReverse /i http://ohs:7777/i
</VirtualHost>
```

First, we have the directives that define which domain name and URL the `VirtualHost` section applies to, and also the `DocumentRoot` for this virtual host.

```
ServerName buglist.foo.com
```

```
ServerAlias buglist.foo.com
DocumentRoot /www/buglist
```

Next, we have the main rewrite rules, as before.

```
RewriteEngine On
RewriteRule ^/$ /pls/apex/f?p=101:1 [R=301]
```

Any requests made to `http://buglist.foo.com` will be redirected to `http://buglist.foo.com/pls/apex/f?p=101:1`. This redirect will still be handled by the proxying web server. This is within the same domain, so the DNS will still resolve to the IP address for the proxying Apache server.

Finally, we have the proxying directives:

```
ProxyPass /pls/apex http://ohs:7777/pls/apex
```

```
ProxyPassReverse /pls/apex http://ohs:7777/pls/apex
ProxyPass /i http://ohs:7777/i
ProxyPassReverse /i http://ohs:7777/i
```

You can see that there are actually two different directives: `ProxyPass` and `ProxyPassReverse`. As the names suggest, these directives are responsible for the proxying in different directions.

The first directive checks to see if the URL contains the `/pls/apex` location. If it does, the request is passed to `http://ohs:7777/pls/apex`. This is actually a URL that corresponds to the OHS web server. In other words, if we make a request to `http://buglist.foo.com/pls/apex/f?p=108:1`, then the proxying server makes this same request to the OHS web server and uses the content returned from the OHS to pass back to the user's browser.

The second directive, `ProxyPassReverse`, is specified in a similar way. However, the purpose of this directive is to hide the fact that the proxy was used from the user's browser. If we did not perform this step, the content might contain references to URLs from the OHS rather than the proxying Apache server. For example, returned URLs cannot contain the OHS hostname, since that hostname is not resolvable from the user's machine (because it is on our internal network). Also the port number used for the OHS (port 7777) needs to be hidden; otherwise, the user's browser would try to connect to the proxying web server on port 7777. In other words, these directives allow the proxying server to act as a gateway or conduit between the user's browser and the OHS. However, you can also use directives such as `DocumentRoot` so you can store static files on the proxying web server rather than the OHS.

One thing you need to watch out for when you perform proxying like this is that as far as the OHS/IAS/embedded gateway is concerned, all of the web requests are coming from the proxying Apache server, rather than from the user's browser. So, if you need to know which hostname was used in the web request, rather than the value that was specified in the `ProxyPass` directive, you may need to add the following line to your configuration:

```
ProxyPreserveHost On
```

This will enable the OHS/IAS to evaluate the value used in the HTTP Host header correctly. In other words, it will be able to determine that the request was made for `buglist.foo.com`, rather than `ohs`, which was specified in the `ProxyPass` directive.

Although Oracle is moving toward using the embedded PL/SQL gateway as the method of accessing APEX, we certainly do not see the benefits of using an external proxying server decreasing—in fact, quite the opposite. Until the PL/SQL gateway supports all (or the majority) of the features that are present in Apache, such as HTTP compression, there will always be a reason to use a proxying web server in this way. This is also a good way to conceal the fact that your application is running in APEX.

Backing Up Applications

Another common issue is ensuring that applications are backed up, so they can be restored in case of disaster. We are talking specifically about the application here, not the schema objects or data that the application uses. For data and database backups, you should already have a well-defined business policy (if you don't, then you need to establish one!).

Of course, there are a number of different ways in which you can perform application backups, including as manual or automatic exports and through the database.

Manual Exports

You can export your application from the Application Builder interface. However, since exporting is a manual task, if you have a large number of applications, using this as a backup method is rapidly going to become laborious. Other drawbacks are that it is easy to forget to make a backup and that you need to come up with a manageable workflow to enable you to archive versions of application exports.

We do not advise that you rely on manual exports as your backup policy for your application. However, they can be extremely useful for making a backup just before you do something that you consider risky.

Easy Backups the Database Way

One of the best features of APEX is that it runs entirely inside the database. This has the obvious side effect that if you back up your database, you have also backed up your applications, since each application is stored as metadata within a schema in the database. As long as you have a recent backup of the database, your applications will also be contained within that backup (assuming that it is either a full database backup or you also backed up the tablespace/schemas associated with APEX).

If you are using RMAN to manage your database backups, it can be extremely easy to restore the tablespace/schema in which APEX is installed, thereby reverting all of the applications back to a prior state (although if you just wanted to restore a single application, this method would not be suitable).

The Oracle database also has another great feature known as Flashback, which enables you to go back to a prior point without needing to perform a full restore from backups. To demonstrate how you can use this feature to recover from a problem with your APEX application, imagine that a developer has gone into SQL Workshop and accidentally executed the following command:

```
delete from apex_application_files
```

This command deletes files from the underlying table (apex_application_files is a view) that are associated with the current workspace. The developer only meant to delete a single file but forgot to include a where clause restriction. Even worse, the SQL Workshop environment has automatically committed the transaction, so the developer cannot perform a rollback. So, what now?

If you had backups of those files, you could upload them back into the APEX environment. But if there were hundreds or thousands of those files, or you didn't have external backups of some of the files, you would be in trouble.

A solution is to take advantage of the Oracle Flashback technology to return the database to the state it was in before the files were deleted. You can use this technique for any situation where you need to get the database back to a prior point in time without reaching for the backups. For example, if you make the mistake of deleting the wrong application and do not have a recent backup of that application, you can use this Flashback method to take the database back to the point before you deleted the application.

As an example, we're going to simulate that disastrous delete command (in fact, we're not just going to simulate it, we're going to actually do it!). We'll use SQL*Plus for this example. First, we connect, via SQL*Plus, to the schema associated with our workspace, as follows:

```
apexdemo@DBTEST> select count(*) from apex_application_files;

COUNT(*)
--------
0
```

By default, we cannot see the files in that view, since we are not running the query inside the APEX environment (that is, our workspace is not defined in SQL*Plus). We can fix that as follows:

```
apexdemo@DBTEST> select

  2  wwv_flow_api.get_security_group_id
  3  from dual;
GET_SECURITY_GROUP_ID
---------------------
0

apexdemo@DBTEST> exec wwv_flow_api.set_security_group_id;
PL/SQL procedure successfully completed.
```

```
apexdemo@DBTEST> select
  2  wwv_flow_api.get_security_group_id
  3  from dual;
GET_SECURITY_GROUP_ID
--------------------
1.1830E+15
```

Note that you need to execute only wwv_flow_api.set_security_group_id. In this example, we used wwv_flow_api.get_security_group_id to show that before the wwv_flow_api.set_security_group_id call, the SGID was set to 0, and afterward it was set to the correct value.

Now we can re-query the apex_application_files view, as follows:

```
apexdemo@DBTEST> select count(*) from apex_application_files;

COUNT(*)
--------
8
```

We can see that eight files have been uploaded for this workspace. Now we can simulate what the user did by deleting the files. However, before we do that, let's check the current SCN in another SQL*Plus session, since we'll need that later.

```
SQL> select dbms_flashback.get_system_change_number from dual;

GET_SYSTEM_CHANGE_NUMBER
------------------------
3334372
```

This shows the current SCN is 3334372.
We can now delete the records, as follows:

```
apexdemo@DBTEST> delete from apex_application_files;

8 rows deleted.

apexdemo@DBTEST> commit;
Commit complete.

apexdemo@DBTEST> select count(*) from apex_application_files;
COUNT(*)
--------
0
```

They're gone—deleted. How do we get them back? We could restore from backups, of course, but there are a couple of ways that are much easier. First, since we only deleted records from one table we can execute a flashback query that will grab the records we just deleted from the flashback database. Using the SCN from above the flashback query would look like the following:

```
insert into apex_application_files
select * from apex_application_files
```

```
    as of  scn 3334372

/
```

This query actually re-populates the apex_application_files table using data from the flashback database. If we had done more damage to the database, we could flash the whole database back to a point in time before the damage was done. To flash the database back, we must first shut down the database and mount it, as follows:

```
SQL> shutdown immediate;

Database closed.
Database dismounted.
ORACLE instance shut down.

SQL> startup mount;
ORACLE instance started.
Total System Global Area 452984832 bytes
Fixed Size 779648 bytes
Variable Size 133175936 bytes
Database Buffers 318767104 bytes
Redo Buffers 262144 bytes
Database mounted.
```

Now we use Flashback to go back to the state we were in before we deleted the files (SCN 3334372).

```
SQL> flashback database to scn 3334372;
Flashback complete.
```

So now we can open the database, but we also need to remember to reset the logs, since we have used Flashback (the current logs are no longer needed/valid).

```
SQL> alter database open resetlogs;
Database altered.
```

Now we can re-query the apex_application_files view, as follows:

```
apexdemo@DBTEST> exec wwv_flow_api.set_security_group_id;

PL/SQL procedure successfully completed.

apexdemo@DBTEST> select count(*) from apex_application_files;
COUNT(*)
--------
8
```

And we see that the data is back!

You could be saying at this point, "So what? I could do that if I was using Java instead of APEX. All you've done is use Flashback technology to flash back the database."

To see what's so great about this, imagine for a moment that instead of performing a delete on apex_application_files, you are in the process of a massive, enterprisewide change management task. Suppose you have just run 394 SQL scripts to upgrade your production application from version 3.41 to

3.42, and then you update your APEX application. Now imagine that something terrible happens, and it doesn't work in production (every developer has this experience at least once in his life, right?). How easily can you regress your production environment back to the working environment you had before? With APEX, you can do this extremely easily by using the Flashback feature of the database. Not only will you go back to the working versions of your schema (the old versions of objects such as tables and their data), but because your APEX applications also live inside the database, you will automatically go back to the version of the application as it was at that point (that is, the working version).

Compare this with a traditional client/server solution or a middle-tier solution, where not only would you need to regress the database, but you would also need to regress the middle-tier applications back to the previous versions. You would also need to remember to revert back to the old versions of any configuration files that the applications might need. In our experience, the fewer things you need to do, the less chance there is of forgetting something.

Note that the usual caveats apply here. Don't test the sample code on your production system. The best advice we can give for critical tasks is this: read the documentation, read the documentation, read the documentation.

Also, note that we're not advocating that using the database Flashback feature should be your first course of action. You should consider using some of the other Flashback technologies, such as Flashback Table, where appropriate, since flashing back the entire database is desirable only in certain circumstances. However, if you need this feature, you've seen how easy it is to use.

Automated Backups

You may not be aware that tucked away in the APEX installation package that you downloaded are a couple of utilities (written in Java) that you can use to export your applications. In fact, the utilities can do much more than that. You can use them to export all the applications within a workspace or even all the applications within the instance.

If you have already deleted the APEX installation files after successfully installing APEX, you'll need to download APEX again, since the utility files are not available individually.

The files can be found in the utilities subdirectory of the root installation directory. We're using a Unix machine for the examples here; however, due to the portability of Java applications, they will also work quite happily on other operating systems—assuming that you followed the directions in the readme.txt file to set up your Java environment. If you already have Java installed, you should just need to set up your Java CLASSPATH environment variable, like the following:

```
[jes@pb ~]$ export CLASSPATH=.:${ORACLE_HOME}/jdbc/lib/ojdbc5.jar
```

But do read the readme.txt file in this directory. There have been some subtle changes in the use of APEXExport in that the JDBC drivers have changed. You now have the choice of either odjbc5.jar or ojdbc6.jar. The difference between these drivers is that ojdbc5 is for use with JDK 1.5 where odbcj6 is for use with JDK 1.6. The 11g database no longer supports JDK 1.4, so the ojdbc14.jar is not delivered with the database.

Many Linux distributions have Java 1.4 installed by default in the /usr/bin directory. The /usr/bin directory is also in the system path by default, so the 1.4 version of Java will be used when you run the java command. To determine which version of Java you have, use the following command:

```
[jes@pb ~]$ java -version
java version "1.6.0_25"
Java(TM) SE Runtime Environment (build 1.6.0_25-b06)
Java HotSpot(TM) Client VM (build 20.0-b11, mixed mode, sharing)
```

As you can see, we are running Java version 1.6.0_25. Since the JDBC drivers for 11g only support java version 1.5 and 1.6, APEXExport will work on our machine. If your machine is running Java version 1.4 or earlier, you will have to upgrade.

In Listing 15-7, we have set the current directory to the directory where we downloaded the APEX distribution, and then we perform a directory listing (using the ls -al command). We have highlighted the utilities directory in bold.

Listing 15-7. Contents of the APEX Distribution Directory

```
[jes@pb apex]$ pwd
/home/oracle/downloads/apex

[jes@pb  apex]$ ls -al
total 1076
drwxr-xr-x  8 oracle dba    4096 Mar  2 01:53 .
drwxr-xr-x  4 oracle dba    4096 Mar  2 01:17 ..
-rw-r--r--  1 oracle dba     857 Mar  2 01:53 afiedt.buf
-r--r--r--  1 oracle dba   16068 Apr 16  2010 apex_epg_config_core.sql
-r--r--r--  1 oracle dba     690 Sep 10  2008 apex_epg_config.sql
-r--r--r--  1 oracle dba    6831 Aug  4  2010 apexins.sql
-r--r--r--  1 oracle dba   14642 Apr  5  2010 apexvalidate.sql
-r--r--r--  1 oracle dba    1628 Apr  5  2010 apxchpwd.sql
-r--r--r--  1 oracle dba    2909 Apr  5  2010 apxconf.sql
-r--r--r--  1 oracle dba    7733 Nov  4 07:17 apxdbmig.sql
-r--r--r--  1 oracle dba   10582 Nov  4 07:17 apxdevrm.sql
-r--r--r--  1 oracle dba    3160 Apr  5  2010 apxdvins.sql
-r--r--r--  1 oracle dba    1028 Apr  5  2010 apxe101.sql
-r--r--r--  1 oracle dba     538 Mar  7  2008 apxe102.sql
-r--r--r--  1 oracle dba    2917 Apr  5  2010 apxe111.sql
-r--r--r--  1 oracle dba    8255 Apr 16  2010 apxldimg.sql
-r--r--r--  1 oracle dba    1478 Apr  5  2010 apxrelod.sql
-r--r--r--  1 oracle dba    4404 Apr  5  2010 apxremov.sql
-r--r--r--  1 oracle dba    4389 Aug  4  2010 apxrtins.sql
-r--r--r--  1 oracle dba      44 Apr 26  2007 apxsqler.sql
-r--r--r--  1 oracle dba    8939 Apr  5  2010 apxxemig.sql
-r--r--r--  1 oracle dba    1570 Apr  5  2010 apxxepwd.sql
drwxr-xr-x 11 oracle dba    4096 Nov 19 13:25 builder
-r--r--r--  1 oracle dba    4371 Apr  5  2010 catapx.sql
drwxr-xr-x  2 oracle dba   20480 Dec 17 09:41 core
-r--r--r--  1 oracle dba   93963 Nov  4 07:17 coreins.sql
-r--r--r--  1 oracle dba   12162 Nov  4 07:17 devins.sql
drwxr-xr-x 12 oracle dba    4096 Oct 22 11:01 doc
-r--r--r--  1 oracle dba    2400 Apr  5  2010 endins.sql
drwxr-xr-x 26 oracle dba   36864 Nov 10 17:07 images
-rw-r--r--  1 oracle dba  729625 Mar  2 01:42 install2011-03-02_01-23-27.log
-r--r--r--  1 oracle dba    1374 Apr  5  2010 load_trans.sql
drwxr-xr-x  2 oracle dba    4096 Nov 15 08:32 owa
drwxr-xr-x  4 oracle dba    4096 Nov 10 17:06 utilities
-rw-r--r--  1 oracle dba    4775 Jun  8  2010 welcome.html
```

Two Java utilities are available: APEXExport and APEXExportSplitter. Both reside in the oracle/apex subdirectory, as shown in Listing 15-8.

Listing 15-8. APEXExport and APEXExportSplitter Utilities

```
[jes@pb  utilities]$ ls -al
total 36
drwxr-xr-x 4 oracle dba 4096 Nov 10 17:06 .
drwxr-xr-x 8 oracle dba 4096 Mar  2 01:53 ..
-r--r--r-- 1 oracle dba 4197 Aug  4  2010 enable_sso.sql
drwxr-xr-x 2 oracle dba 4096 Nov 10 17:06 fop
drwxr-xr-x 3 oracle dba 4096 Nov 10 17:06 oracle
-r--r--r-- 1 oracle dba 4964 Nov  4 07:17 readme.txt
-r--r--r-- 1 oracle dba 2602 Apr  5  2010 reset_image_prefix.sql

[oracle@oim utilities]$ find . -print
.
./oracle
./oracle/apex
./oracle/apex/APEXExport.class
./oracle/apex/APEXExportSplitter.class
./enable_sso.sql
./fop
./fop/fop.war
./readme.txt
./reset_image_prefix.sql
```

Here, we used the find command to list the files contained in the oracle/apex subdirectory. Note that we did not change the working directory to the oracle/apex subdirectory, since we need to run the command from the utilities directory using the command shown in Listing 15-9.

Listing 15-9. APEXExport Usage Information

```
[jes@pb utilities]$ java oracle/apex/APEXExport
Usage APEXExport -db -user -password -applicationid -workspaceid -instance -expWorkspace -
skipExportDate -expPubReports -expSavedReports -expIRNotif -expTeamdevdata -expFeedback -
deploymentSystem -expFeedbackSince -debug
     -db:           Database connect url in JDBC format
     -user:         Database username
     -password :    Database password
     -applicationid : ID for application to be exported
     -workspaceid : Workspace ID for which all applications to be exported or the workspace
to be exported
     -instance :    Export all applications
     -expWorkspace :  Export workspace identified by -workspaceid or all workspaces if -
workspaceid not specified
     -skipExportDate : Exclude export date from application export files
     -expPubReports :  Export all user saved public interactive reports
     -expSavedReports: Export all user saved interactive reports
     -expIRNotif :   Export all interactive report notifications
     -expFeedback :   Export team development feedback for all workspaces or identified by -
workspaceid to development or deployment
     -expTeamdevdata : Export team development data for all workspaces or identified by -
workspaceid
```

```
-deploymentSystem : Deployment system for exported feedback
-expFeedbackSince :  Export team development feedback since date in the format YYYYMMDD

Application Example:
    APEXExport -db candy.us.oracle.com:1521:ORCL -user scott -password tiger -applicationid
31500
  Workspace  Example:
    APEXExport -db candy.us.oracle.com:1521:ORCL -user scott -password tiger -workspaceid
9999
  Instance Example:
    APEXExport -db candy.us.oracle.com:1521:ORCL -user system -password manager -instance
  Export All Workspaces Example:
    APEXExport -db candy.us.oracle.com:1521:ORCL -user system -password manager -
expWorkspace
  Export Feedback to development environment:
    APEXExport -db candy.us.oracle.com:1521:ORCL -user scott -password tiger -workspaceid
9999 -expFeedback
  Export Feedback to deployment environment EA2 since 20100308:
    APEXExport -db candy.us.oracle.com:1521:ORCL -user scott -password tiger -workspaceid
9999 -expFeedback -deploymentSystem EA2 -expFeedbackSince 20100308
```

Since we did not use any parameters, the command simply output some default usage help information. As you can see, the usage and parameters are pretty intuitive. For example, if you wanted to export application 101, all you would need to do is pass in the database, account, and application details, as shown in Listing 15-10.

Listing 15-10. Exporting an Application

```
[jes@pb utilities]$ java oracle/apex/APEXExport -db localhost:1521:dbtest

  -user apexdemo -password pass -applicationid 108
Exporting application 108
  Completed at Thu Jan 25 03:25:26 BST 2007

[jes@pb utilities]$ ls -al
  total 760
  drwxr-xr-x   5 jes  jes     170 Jan 25 03:25 .
  drwxr-xr-x  21 jes  jes     714 Jan 25 03:07 ..
  -rw-r--r--   1 jes  jes  382591 Jan 25 03:25 f108.sql
  drwxr-xr-x   3 jes  jes     102 Mar 14 17:45 oracle
  -r--r--r--   1 jes  jes    3747 Feb 27 14:35 readme.txt
```

Here, we pass in the database connection string in the format of hostname:port:sid (localhost:1521:dbtest) and also specify the username (or schema) that is associated with the workspace in which the application resides. Finally, we pass the ID of the application we wish to export (108 in this example). The command produces some output while it executes, showing which application is being exported.

After the command has executed, you will see that a file named f108.sql is created, which is exactly the same sort of application export file that you would get if you used the Application Builder interface to export the application. In other words, you could now use the Application Builder interface to import this application into another workspace (perhaps on another machine) if desired. You can also import the application by running the SQL script file while connected as your

APEX_040000 user if you prefer to perform the import at the command line (or perhaps as part of a batch import).

You can also export all of the applications for a particular workspace. Unfortunately, you need to do a little work here, because the APEXExport utility requires the workspace ID rather than the workspace name (yes, it would be a nice feature if we could just pass in the workspace name instead). You can get your workspace ID by running the following query in SQL Workshop:

```
select v('WORKSPACE_ID') from dual
```

Alternatively, you can execute the following commands in SQL*Plus:

```
apexdemo@DBTEST> select v('WORKSPACE_ID') from dual;

V('WORKSPACE_ID')
-----------------
0

apexdemo@DBTEST> exec wwv_flow_api.set_security_group_id;
PL/SQL procedure successfully completed.

apexdemo@DBTEST> select v('WORKSPACE_ID') from dual
V('WORKSPACE_ID')
-----------------
      1280317158978593
```

You can see that before the call to wwv_flow_api.set_security_group_id, the value of V('WORKSPACE_ID') is 0. After the call, you get the correct workspace ID, which you can now use with the APEXExport command, as follows:

```
[jes@pb utilities]$ java oracle/apex/APEXExport -db localhost:1521:orcl
-user apexdemo -password pass -workspaceid 1280317158978593
Exporting Application 100:'Sample Application'
  Completed at Fri Apr 08 15:01:20 CDT 2011
Exporting Application 101:'BUGLIST'
  Completed at Fri Apr 08 15:01:22 CDT 2011
Exporting Application 102:'Theme Master'
```

As you can see, it took around two seconds to export three applications from our workspace, which is certainly quicker than doing it via the Application Builder interface. In the following, also note that each application is exported into its own separate file, rather than a single file:

```
[jes@pb utilities]$ ls -al
total 2736
drwxr-xr-x 4 oracle dba     4096 Apr  8 15:04 .
drwxr-xr-x 8 oracle dba     4096 Mar  2 01:53 ..
-r--r--r-- 1 oracle dba     4197 Aug  4  2010 enable_sso.sql
-rw-r--r-- 1 oracle dba   564711 Apr  8 15:01 f100.sql
-rw-r--r-- 1 oracle dba  2064229 Apr  8 15:01 f101.sql
-rw-r--r-- 1 oracle dba   121448 Apr  8 15:01 f102.sql
drwxr-xr-x 2 oracle dba     4096 Nov 10 17:06 fop
drwxr-xr-x 3 oracle dba     4096 Nov 10 17:06 oracle
```

```
-r--r--r-- 1 oracle dba      4964 Nov  4 07:17 readme.txt
-r--r--r-- 1 oracle dba      2602 Apr  5  2010 reset_image_prefix.sql
```

You can also export all of the applications in the entire instance, as shown in Listing 15-11.

Listing 15-11. Exporting All Applications in the Workspace

```
[jes@pb utilities]$ java oracle/apex/APEXExport -db localhost:1521:orcl
-user system -password pass -instance
Exporting Application 100:'Sample Application'
  Completed at Fri Apr 08 15:06:40 CDT 2011
Exporting Application 101:'BUGLIST'
  Completed at Fri Apr 08 15:06:40 CDT 2011
Exporting Application 102:'Theme Master'
  Completed at Fri Apr 08 15:06:41 CDT 2011
Exporting Application 103:'Global App'
  Completed at Fri Apr 08 15:06:41 CDT 2011
Exporting Application 104:'BUGLIST_TABTEST'
  Completed at Fri Apr 08 15:06:41 CDT 2011
Exporting Application 105:'BUGLIST1'
  Completed at Fri Apr 08 15:06:41 CDT 2011
Exporting Application 106:'Theme Subscriber'
  Completed at Fri Apr 08 15:06:41 CDT 2011
```

So we now have export files for all of the applications in our test instance. Note that this has exported the applications, but you would still need to manually export the workspace itself, if required.

You might be wondering how you know which workspace these export files belong to. In a disaster recovery situation, which workspace would each application need to be installed into? The information for that is contained within the application export file itself. For example, if we look at the f101.sql file, we find the following:

```
prompt  Set Credentials...

begin

  -- Assumes you are running the script connected to SQL*Plus as the Oracle user APEX_040000
or as the owner (parsing schema) of the application.

wwv_flow_api.set_security_group_id(p_security_group_id=>nvl(wwv_flow_application_install.get_w
orkspace_id,1280317158978593));

end;
/
```

You can see that the file has a call to the same wwv_flow_api.set_security_group_id procedure that we used in our earlier SQL*Plus session, except in this case, the script is passing a value in the p_security_group_id parameter. This value (1280317158978593) is the same value that we obtained when we queried v('WORKSPACE_ID'). In other words, the script will install back into the same workspace if we execute it from SQL*Plus (assuming that workspace exists in the instance in which we install it).

We can now use a Unix cron entry (a way of scheduling commands) to run the APEXExport command at predefined intervals. First, we create a Unix shell script (called backup_apex.sh), which wraps the APEXExport command, as shown in Listing 15-12.

Listing 15-12. Contents of the backup_apex.sh Script

```
#!/usr/bin/bash

export CLASSPATH=.:/u1/jdbc/lib/classes12.zip:/opt/local/apexbkup
cd /opt/local/apexbkup/
/usr/local/bin/java oracle.apex.APEXExport
-db localhost:1521:dbtest -user apexdemo -password pass
-workspaceid 1280317158978593
```

This script sets the CLASSPATH environment variable so that the APEXExport command can find the required Java libraries (in the same way that we had to set CLASSPATH variable at the command line before).

```
[jes@pb apexbkup]$ ls -al

total 8
drwxr-xr-x   3 jes   jes      512 May 12 15:01 .
drwx--x--x  10 jes   jes      512 Jun  4 19:49 ..
-rwxr-xr-x   1 jes   jes      223 May 12 15:00 backup_apex.sh
drwxr-xr-x   3 jes   jes      512 May 12 14:46 oracle
```

So far, we have placed the backup_apex.sh script in /opt/local/apexbkup and have also copied the directory containing the APEXExport Java command to this directory. You could locate this in a different directory and modify the backup_apex.sh script so that it pointed to the correct directory, but we have done it this way to keep the example simple.

We can now run the backup_apex.sh script rather than having to type the full command line in full, as in the earlier example, as follows:

```
[jes@pb ~]$ /opt/local/apexbkup/backup-apex.sh

Exporting Application 100:'Sample Application v2.0'
  Completed at Thu Jan 25 10:43:55 BST 2007
Exporting Application 101:'Sample Application v2.0'
  Completed at Thu Jan 25 10:43:57 BST 2007
Exporting Application 102:'OJ API'
  Completed at Thu Jan 25 10:44:00 BST 2007
. . . extra output omitted
```

The exported files will be located in the /opt/local/apexbkup directory, due to the cd /opt/local/apexbkup command in our script. You could modify this if you wished, or perhaps change the script so that it copies the files to another directory (perhaps creating a new directory for each day's exports so that it is easier to locate previous exports).

The following code shows the contents of the crontab file that we have created in our Unix account:

```
jes@pb[10:44am]~> crontab -l
0 1 * * * /opt/local/apexbkup/backup-apex.sh
```

This `crontab` entry means "run the `/opt/local/apexbkup/backup-apex.sh` script at 1 a.m. every day." Now, this is quite a simplified example, and there are a few obvious flaws, as follows:

- The username and password credentials are stored in the `backup-apex.sh` script. You could tie down the permissions on that file so that no one else can read it (it would still be executable by the owner of the file and via the cron entry, of course).

- You cannot easily configure where the export scripts should be output to from the `APEXExport` command itself (it would be a nice addition if you could), so you would need to control this from the `backup-apex.sh` script itself. This means that you would need to develop this simple example further if you wanted to use it in a production environment.

- You cannot export the workspace definitions in the same way that you can export the applications. This means that you will also need to export the workspaces manually at regular intervals (where your own policy defines what "regular" means).

If you are familiar with Unix shell scripting, you can do some incredibly sophisticated things. We have set up one of our test environments with a similar automated export routine, but we have adapted the shell script, so that once the files are exported, the shell script automatically checks them into our source control system. Alternatively, you could e-mail those exported files to some offsite location, which you could then access in the event of a problem.

These examples demonstrated just how easy (and incredibly useful) automating your application backups can be. We encourage you to use the command-line tools to reduce the burden of performing the exports manually for backup purposes.

"As of" Backups

If you have used the Application Builder interface to export your application, you might not have noticed an incredibly useful setting that enables you to export your application as it existed at a previous point in time. This is the "As of" setting, as shown in Figure 15-3.

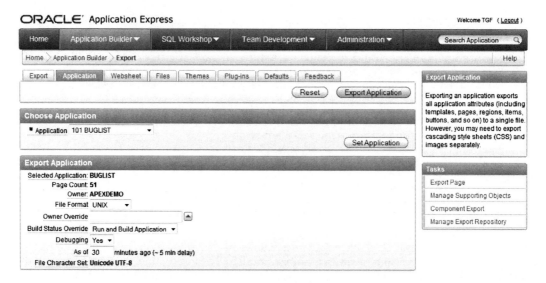

Figure 15-3. *Exporting a previous version of the application*

In Figure 15-3, a value of 30 is entered in the "As of" field before performing the export. This will have the effect of creating an export file for the application as it existed 30 minutes ago; in other words, without any of the changes made in the last 30 minutes.

Suppose you have spent all day making changes to your application, but you have also accidentally changed some code that you shouldn't have, which has now broken your application. In this situation, if you restored your application from the previous day's export (that, of course, you made with the automated backup method we have already covered), you would lose all the changes you made today. However, if you use the "As of" setting to export your application to a point in time before you made those fatal changes, you will be able to effectively keep the changes you spent all day making, but lose the more recent changes that broke your application.

This method is loosely analogous to recovering the database to a previous point in time, rather than restoring it to a previous backup. If the last backup you have is yesterday's, or last week's, you are going to lose all the changes made since that backup. The "As of" setting allows you to create another export of your application that will contain changes made up to that point.

You might not be surprised to know that this ability to export your application at a previous point in time uses the same Flashback technology that we covered earlier. Behind the scenes, the application export function uses the Flashback features to query the metadata about your application at that point in time.

However, there is a limit to how far back in time you can go. This is a configurable limit, but it is nonetheless a limit. The limit relies on the undo_retention parameter setting for your database, which in a default installation is set to 900 seconds or 15 minutes. You can query the current value on your database by connecting as a privileged user and running the following command:

```
sys@DBTEST> show parameter undo_retention
```

```
NAME                 TYPE         VALUE
-------------------- ------------ --------
undo_retention       integer      21600
```

On our test system, the retention is set to 21600, which is 21,600 seconds (or 6 hours). We highly recommend that you increase the default setting of 900 seconds (15 minutes) to enable you to go further back in time for your exports (this also enables you to use the other Flashback features, such as Flashback Table and Flashback Query, within this time window). But bear in mind that increasing the retention period will increase your disk space storage requirements (since your database will need to store that extra information). Yet, there would be nothing worse than one day finding out your undo retention was just that bit too small to help you. So, we feel that it's better to think in terms of hours (or days in some circumstances), rather than minutes, when it comes to the undo_retention parameter.

Migrating Between Environments

Another common need is to migrate your applications from one instance to another instance. For example, suppose you have made some changes to your application in your development environment. What is the best way to migrate those changes to your test environment and then later to your live environment? In this case, you want to upgrade your application. Another alternative is to clone your application.

Upgrading Applications

To help with change management, we advise that you do not give your end users (in the production environment) the direct URL to your application. In other words do not use the URLs like this:

```
http://yourserver:7777/pls/apex/f?p=108:1
```

Instead, use the techniques we covered earlier in the "Managing URLs" section to have URLs like the following:

```
http://yourserver/buglist/
```

Using these types of URLs means that you can manage upgrades to the production environment in the following way:

1. Export the application from the test environment.

2. Import the application into the production environment but give it a new application ID (say application 208).

3. Test the application in production to make sure it works correctly.

4. Switch the method you're using to manage the http://yourserver/buglist/ URL to point to application 208 once you're sure it works correctly.

This means that rather than replacing the application in the live environment, you are installing a new application, testing it, and then switching to point at the URL once you're satisfied with the upgrade. For example, if you are using the virtual host method to manage your URLs, you might have the entry shown in Listing 15-13 for your production application.

Listing 15-13. VirtualHost Entry for a Live Application

```
<VirtualHost *>

  ServerName buglist.live.localdomain
  ServerAlias buglist.live.localdomain
  RewriteEngine On
  RewriteRule ^/$ /pls/apex/f?p=108:1 [R=301]
</VirtualHost>
```

You can then install the new application as application 208. You can choose to either test this application by using the full URL (for example, http://buglist.localdomain/pls/apex/f?p=208:1) or set up another VirtualHost entry for testing the application in live, as shown in Listing 15-14.

Listing 15-14. VirtualHost for Testing a New Application in live

```
<VirtualHost *>

  ServerName buglisttest.live.localdomain
  ServerAlias buglisttest.live.localdomain
  RewriteEngine On
  RewriteRule ^/$ /pls/apex/f?p=208:1 [R=301]
</VirtualHost>
```

Once you install the new application in live, you can use the URL buglisttest.live.localdomain. When you're happy with the way it works, you can change the VirtualHost entry for the live application to point to 208 instead of 108, and then restart the web server (which should just take a few seconds).

This method offers some distinct advantages over replacing the currently live application, as follows:

- You can test the new application in parallel with the live application still running.

- You can easily regress to the old live application if you discover problems after making the switch.

- There is minimal downtime. The users don't need to wait while you replace the current version with the new version.

You can improve on this further by using application aliases, which removes the need to manually change the application ID. In that case, your VirtualHost entries would reference the application name rather than the numeric ID, as shown in Listing 15-15.

Listing 15-15. Using Application Names in the VirtualHost Entry

```
<VirtualHost *>

  ServerName buglist.live.localdomain
  ServerAlias buglist.live.localdomain
  RewriteEngine On
  RewriteRule ^/$ /pls/apex/f?p=BUGLIST:1 [R=301]
</VirtualHost>

<VirtualHost *>
  ServerName  buglisttest.live.localdomain
  ServerAlias buglisttest.live.localdomain
  RewriteEngine On
  RewriteRule ^/$ /pls/apex/f?p=BUGLISTTEST:1 [R=301]
</VirtualHost>
```

Notice how we now use BUGLIST and BUGLISTTEST as the application names. This means that we no longer need to worry about which numeric ID the applications use and can instead rely on a distinctive name to differentiate them.

If you use aliases, you will need to give your new application a different name before you export it from your development environment. However, this may be a more manageable solution than using the numeric ID in a production environment.

In this example, once we were happy with how the new application worked, we could go into the Application Builder interface and rename the live application (BUGLIST) to something like BUGLISTOLD, and then rename the new application from BUGLISTTEST to BUGLIST. We would not even need to restart the web server. Since we did not make any configuration changes to the VirtualHost section, the http://buglist.live.livedomain URL will now just resolve to the new application (since it now uses the BUGLIST application name).

This makes for a much simplified and controllable change-management process for migrating your applications across environments.

Cloning an Application

Sometimes you might want to test an application on another database instance. Or, perhaps you want to make some changes to the application and the underlying schema objects, and you want to do that in a completely separate environment (if, for example, you don't have the luxury of development, test, and live instances). If you're doing some major changes to an application, you may want to create a completely separate workspace on the application, associated with a completely separate schema, and then clone the application and underlying schema objects from the original workspace into the new environment.

There are many different ways to perform this sort of "environment cloning," depending on your exact requirements. For example if you require a complete clone of every workspace and every application in an instance to install on a new instance, you might find that cloning via RMAN or using database backups to make a clone of the database is the best way to do this. However, you might just need to clone your application and data within the same instance, perhaps on your laptop or to test some major changes in your development environment. In this case, you can perform the cloning in a different way, as we'll demonstrate in this section.

With APEX installed and working in your environment, you need to perform the following steps:

- Clone the workspace or create a new one.

- Clone the application.

- Clone all of the associated schema objects (tables, procedures, packages, and so on).

You don't need to perform the steps in this order. In fact, it makes sense to do them in a slightly different order because you need to have the new schema created before you create the workspace (since the workspace needs to have the schema assigned to it when the workspace is created).

In this example, we'll clone the Buglist application, which is in our APEXDEMO workspace (which is using the APEXDEMO schema).

Exporting the Workspace and Application

First, we export the APEX workspace using the Export Workspace function in the APEX administration section, as shown in Figures 15-4 and 15-5. You will need to be logged in to APEX as one of the instance administrators to access this functionality.

Figure 15-4. Choosing the workspace to export

Figure 15-5. Exporting the APEXDEMO workspace

This creates a file (called apexdemo.sql in this case), similar to the application export file, which contains all of the DML and DDL commands needed to create the workspace. One thing to be aware of is the file format that you use when you export the workspace, as shown in Figure 15-5. Your options are Unix and DOS. Make sure that when you import the workspace again, you use the correct file format. In other words, if you export it in the Unix file format, be sure to import it in the Unix format; otherwise, you may encounter problems due to the different way that line feeds and carriage returns are handled in the Unix and DOS formats.

So, we now have our workspace export. We can also export our application in one of the ways covered earlier in this chapter (either manually or by using the APEXExport command). The end result of this step is an application export file called f101.sql (for the Buglist application).

Cloning Schema Objects and Data

Now we get to the slightly trickier step. We need to be able to clone all of our schema objects and data. There are many different ways to do this, including the following:

- Use scripts that you have maintained to create all of your schema objects.

- Use a tool such as TOAD or SQL Developer to generate the scripts necessary to rebuild the schema objects.

- Use the SQL*Loader tool to load the data into the new schema (after extracting it from the original schema in some way).

- Use the external tables feature of the database to load data into the new tables.

- Use the exp tool to export a dump file of the original schema, and then use the imp tool to import the dump file into the new schema.

- Use Data Pump, which is particularly suitable for moving large amounts of data very quickly and efficiently. If the other methods prove too slow, Data Pump is your salvation (but Data Pump can take some work to configure).

All of these methods are viable options.

Using Scripts to Clone Schemas

The script method, which is commonly used, relies on you maintaining external scripts every time you make changes to your schema objects. For example, you might have a script (called create_foo.sql) with this command:

```
create table foo(
  id number,
  name varchar2(20)
)
/
```

If you wanted to add a new column, such as for e-mail addresses, to the foo table, you would need to modify the create_foo.sql script as follows:

```
create table foo(
  id number,
```

```
  name varchar2(20),
  email varchar2(30)
)
/
```

You would also need to maintain another script to handle the situation where the foo table already exists in the old format, without the email column. You might create a new script called upgrade_foo.sql.

```
alter table foo

  add (email varchar2(30))
/
```

You can see how maintaining scripts like these can quickly become hard work. And you need discipline to make sure that anyone who makes changes to your schema objects will make the necessary changes to the scripts. This is why using tools such as TOAD, SQL Developer, and others become an attractive option: they can be used to generate the scripts for you.

Some advanced tools let you maintain separate versions of your schema definition and will generate the scripts required for upgrading from one version of the schema to another version automatically (although you should always check these scripts by eye first before running them just to make absolutely sure you're happy with what they will do).

Using exp/imp to Clone Schemas

In our example, we just want to completely copy the original schema. We're not upgrading in any sense, because the new schema does not exist (we need to create it). This is where most people would opt to use the exp and imp tools, which are designed to do exactly this sort of schema-level copying. Let's see how to use these tools to perform the cloning and what problems you might encounter. It is worth noting that imp and exp are likely to be deprecated in future releases of the database in favor of DataPump Import and Export (which are covered later in this chapter).

exp and imp are command-line tools that enable you to export (exp) and import (imp) export files, called *dumpfiles*, containing schema objects. Using them, you can simply copy the contents of a schema into another schema.

First, we need to create a dumpfile of the original APEXDEMO schema, as shown in Listing 15-16.

Listing 15-16. Exporting the APEXDEMO Schema with exp

```
[jes@pb apexdemo]$ NLS_LANG=AMERICAN_AMERICA.AL32UTF8

[jes@pb apexdemo]$ export NLS_LANG
[jes@pb apexdemo]$ echo $NLS_LANG
AMERICAN_AMERICA.AL32UTF8

[jes@pb exports]$ exp

Username: apexdemo
Password:

Enter array fetch buffer size: 4096 >
```

```
Export file: expdat.dmp >

(2)U(sers), or (3)T(ables): (2)U >

Export grants (yes/no): yes >

Export table data (yes/no): yes >

Compress extents (yes/no): yes > no

Export done in AL32UTF8 character set and UTF8 NCHAR character set
. exporting pre-schema procedural objects and actions
. exporting foreign function library names for user APEXDEMO
. exporting PUBLIC type synonyms
. exporting private type synonyms
. exporting object type definitions for user APEXDEMO
About to export APEXDEMO's objects ...
. exporting database links
. exporting sequence numbers
. exporting cluster definitions
. about to export APEXDEMO's tables via Conventional Path ...
. . exporting table              APEX_ACCESS_CONTROL          2 rows exported
. . exporting table              APEX_ACCESS_SETUP            1 rows exported
. . exporting table              APEX_CUSTOM_LOG              0 rows exported
. . exporting table                        BIG_EMP           14 rows exported
. . exporting table                        BUGLIST           19 rows exported
. . exporting table              DEMO_CUSTOMERS               7 rows exported
. . exporting table                 DEMO_IMAGES              11 rows exported
. . exporting table                 DEMO_ORDERS              10 rows exported
. . exporting table            DEMO_ORDER_ITEMS              16 rows exported
. . exporting table          DEMO_PAGE_HIERARCHY             18 rows exported
. . exporting table           DEMO_PRODUCT_INFO              10 rows exported
. . exporting table                 DEMO_STATES              51 rows exported
. . exporting table                  DEMO_USERS               2 rows exported
. . exporting table                        DEPT              4 rows exported
. . exporting table                       DUMMY              0 rows exported
. . exporting table                         EMP             14 rows exported
. . exporting table              REPORT_HEADINGS              8 rows exported
. . exporting table              TREE_NAVIGATION              4 rows exported
. . exporting table              UPLOADED_FILES               1 rows exported
. . exporting table             USER_REPOSITORY             12 rows exported
. . exporting table               USER_SEARCHES             32 rows exported
. . exporting table            VERIFICATION_LINK              1 rows exported
. exporting synonyms
. exporting views
. exporting stored procedures
. exporting operators
. exporting referential integrity constraints
. exporting triggers
. exporting indextypes
. exporting bitmap, functional and extensible indexes
. exporting posttables actions
```

```
. exporting materialized views
. exporting snapshot logs
. exporting job queues
. exporting refresh groups and children
. exporting dimensions
. exporting post-schema procedural objects and actions
. exporting statistics
Export terminated successfully without warnings.
```

In this example, we executed the exp command without passing any parameters, so we were prompted for a username and password. We use APEXDEMO, which is the schema we want to export. It is also possible to connect as a DBA or privileged user, and then export any other user's schema.

We are then prompted for some parameters, such as whether to export grants (yes, in this example) and whether to compress extents (no, which is usually the answer you should give). After these prompts, the command begins to export each schema object. It also works out the relationships between the objects, so that the resulting export file will contain the creation of the objects in the correct order; for example, so that indexes can be created after the corresponding table has been created.

Before we ran the exp command, we set the NLS_LANG environment variable to AMERICAN_AMERICA.AL32UTF8 so that it matched the NLS parameters of our database. Before you export or import, you should make sure of the following:

- Your exp client character set matches your database character set when you export.

- The exp client and imp client character sets match.

- The imp client character set matches your database character set when you import.

If any of these character sets do not match, you may end up with your data being converted between the character sets, and potentially losing data due to the conversion process. You should be concerned if you ever see the message "Possible charset conversion" during either the import or export procedure.

We should now have a dumpfile containing all the schema objects and data within the APEXDEMO schema, as follows:

```
[jes@pb apexdemo]$ ls -al

total 336
drwxr-xr-x    3 jes  jes     102 Feb 26 15:12 .
drwxr-xr-x   19 jes  jes     646 Feb 26 14:58 ..
-rw-r--r--    1 jes  jes  169984 Feb 26 15:13 expdat.dmp
```

We'll import this schema into the same instance, but create another user to receive the schema objects. You would use the same procedure if you wanted to load the objects into another instance (where you could use the same username).

We connect to the database as a privileged user to create a new user, which we'll call APE-XCLONE, as shown in Listing 15-17.

Listing 15-17. *Creating the New APEXCLONE User*

```
dba@DBTEST> create user apexclone

2  identified by pass
```

```
3  default tablespace users;
User created.

dba@DBTEST> grant connect, resource to apexclone;
Grant succeeded.
dba@DBTEST> revoke unlimited tablespace from apexclone;
Revoke succeeded.

dba@DBTEST> alter user apexclone quota unlimited on users;
User altered.
```

We have created a user with a password of pass (not very imaginative) and assigned the user to the default USERS tablespace. We have also granted APEXCLONE the connect and resource roles so that the user can connect to the database and create schema objects (otherwise, we would not be able to perform the import).

We have used the connect and resource roles because this is a simple example. In your own production systems, you would probably want to grant explicit system privileges, such as create table and create trigger, rather than using these roles. This is because by using the roles, you might be granting your users more rights than they actually need. Make sure you carefully examine which rights any roles you use allow. One of the riskier privileges that goes along with the resource role is the unlimited tablespace privilege, which means the user will be able to create objects in any tablespace, regardless of any quotas that are in force. This is obviously usually extremely undesirable, so we have revoked the unlimited tablespace privilege from the APEXCLONE user (which is part of the resource role) and explicitly granted a quota on the USERS tablespace.

Now we can run the imp command and import the dumpfile that was just created, as shown in Listing 15-18. Note that we did not need to set the NLS_LANG environment variable again, since we are still within the same shell session (otherwise, we would need to execute the same commands we performed before the export).

Listing 15-18. *Importing the New Schema Objects*

```
[jes@pb exports]$ imp


Username: apexclone
Password:

Import file: expdat.dmp >

Enter insert buffer size (minimum is 8192) 30720>

Export file created by EXPORT:V10.02.00 via conventional path

Warning: the objects were exported by APEXDEMO, not by you

import done in AL32UTF8 character set and UTF8 NCHAR character set
List contents of import file only (yes/no): no >

Ignore create error due to object existence (yes/no): no >

Import grants (yes/no): yes >
```

```
Import table data (yes/no): yes >

Import entire export file (yes/no): no > yes

. importing APEXDEMO's objects into APEXCLONE
. . importing table        "APEX_ACCESS_CONTROL"        2 rows imported
. . importing table        "APEX_ACCESS_SETUP"          1 rows imported
. . importing table         "APEX_CUSTOM_LOG"           0 rows imported
<extra output omitted>
. . importing table        "VERIFICATION_LINK"          1 rows imported
About to enable constraints...
Import terminated successfully without warnings.
```

We have omitted some of the output in Listing 15-18 (it shows the same tables being imported that were exported).

We can check how the new schema and the original one compare by querying the user_objects view in both schemas, as follows:

```
apexdemo@DBTEST> select status, count(*) from user_objects

  2  group by status;

STATUS    COUNT(*)
-------  ----------
INVALID         3
VALID          87

apexclone@DBTEST> select status, count(*) from user_objects
  2  group by status;

STATUS    COUNT(*)
-------  ----------
INVALID         3
VALID          87
```

So we can see that all the objects have been copied, and the status (VALID or INVALID) is identical to the original schema. However, you may sometimes find that the status is different in the new schema, simply because objects that were invalid in the original schema might have been recompiled during the import, which has changed their status to VALID.

On the face of things, this looks like a great way to clone the schema and data (the data is also copied across, although you have the option to omit the data if you wish to re-create only the objects themselves). However, there are some potential issues with this method. Recall our previous example where we created the table foo:

```
create table foo(
  id number,
  name varchar2(20)
);
```

This is the way you would typically write DDL. However, sometimes you find that automated tools that generate the DDL for you might produce something like this for a table that contains a CLOB column. Let's take a look at the following:

```
CREATE TABLE "APEXDEMO"."FOO"

   ("ID" NUMBER,
    "NAME" VARCHAR2(20 BYTE),
    "DATA" CLOB
    )
  TABLESPACE "APEXDEMO"
  LOB ("DATA") STORE AS (TABLESPACE "APEXDEMO");
```

We actually used a GUI tool to create this table, and then used the tool to show the DDL that would be needed to re-create the table. The difference here is that the schema has been specified in the create statement. In other words, rather than saying "create the foo table in the default schema," we are saying "create the foo table in the APEXDEMO schema." This might seem like quite a subtle difference; however, if we repeat our exp/imp procedure, a couple of errors appear, as shown in Listing 15-19.

***Listing 15-19.** Import Fails with Errors*

```
[jes@pb apexdemo]$ imp


Username: apexclone
Password:

Import file: expdat.dmp >

Enter insert buffer size (minimum is 8192) 30720>

Export file created by EXPORT:V10.01.00 via conventional path

Warning: the objects were exported by APEXDEMO, not by you

import done in AL32UTF8 character set and UTF8 NCHAR character set
List contents of import file only (yes/no): no >

Ignore create error due to object existence (yes/no): no >

Import grants (yes/no): yes >

Import table data (yes/no): yes >

Import entire export file (yes/no): no > yes

. importing APEXDEMO's objects into APEXCLONE
. . importing table          "APEX_ACCESS_CONTROL"        2 rows imported
. . importing table            "APEX_ACCESS_SETUP"        1 rows imported
. . importing table             "APEX_CUSTOM_LOG"         0 rows imported
. . importing table                     "BIG_EMP"        14 rows imported
. . importing table                     "BUGLIST"        19 rows imported
```

```
. . importing table                     "DEMO_CUSTOMERS"        7 rows imported
. . importing table                        "DEMO_IMAGES"       11 rows imported
. . importing table                        "DEMO_ORDERS"       10 rows imported
. . importing table                   "DEMO_ORDER_ITEMS"       16 rows imported
. . importing table                "DEMO_PAGE_HIERARCHY"       18 rows imported
. . importing table                  "DEMO_PRODUCT_INFO"       10 rows imported
. . importing table                        "DEMO_STATES"       51 rows imported
. . importing table                         "DEMO_USERS"        2 rows imported
. . importing table                               "DEPT"        4 rows imported
. . importing table                              "DUMMY"        0 rows imported
. . importing table                                "EMP"       14 rows imported
IMP-00017: following statement failed with ORACLE error 1950:
 "CREATE TABLE "FOO" ("ID" NUMBER, "NAME" VARCHAR2(20), "DATA" CLOB)  PCTFREE"
 " 10 PCTUSED 40 INITRANS 1 MAXTRANS 255 STORAGE(INITIAL 65536 FREELISTS 1 FR"
 "EELIST GROUPS 1 BUFFER_POOL DEFAULT) TABLESPACE "APEXDEMO" LOGGING NOCOMPRE"
 "SS LOB ("DATA") STORE AS  (TABLESPACE "APEXDEMO" ENABLE STORAGE IN ROW CHUN"
 "K 8192 PCTVERSION 10 NOCACHE  STORAGE(INITIAL 65536 FREELISTS 1 FREELIST GR"
 "OUPS 1 BUFFER_POOL DEFAULT))"
IMP-00003: ORACLE error 1950 encountered
ORA-01950: no privileges on tablespace 'APEXDEMO'
. . importing table                     "REPORT_HEADINGS"       8 rows imported
. . importing table                      "TREE_NAVIGATION"       4 rows imported
. . importing table                      "USER_REPOSITORY"      12 rows imported
. . importing table                        "USER_SEARCHES"      32 rows imported
. . importing table                    "VERIFICATION_LINK"       1 rows imported
About to enable constraints...
Import terminated successfully with warnings.
```

This time, the import procedure was unable to create the foo table in the APEXCLONE schema. The following error message explains why it failed:

```
ORA-01950: no privileges on tablespace 'APEXDEMO'
```

Even though we are trying to import into the APEXCLONE schema, the import is trying to create an object in the APEXDEMO schema. This is why it was important to revoke the unlimited tablespace privilege after we created the APEXCLONE user; otherwise, the import would have succeeded because the APEXCLONE user would have been able to create objects in the APEXDEMO schema. The import process is trying to create the object in the wrong schema because, when the foo table was created, we fully qualified the schema in the DDL, as follows:

```
CREATE TABLE "APEXDEMO"."FOO"

   ("ID" NUMBER,
    "NAME" VARCHAR2(20 BYTE),
    "DATA" CLOB
   )
 TABLESPACE "APEXDEMO"
 LOB ("DATA") STORE AS (TABLESPACE "APEXDEMO");
```

The problem here is that when the imp process ran, it managed to rewrite the first tablespace definition it found from APEXDEMO to USERS (remember the new APEXCLONE uses the USERS tablespace); however, the imp process does not rewrite the second tablespace definition; that is, the part within the

STORE AS definition. If we had not specified a STORE AS in the DDL, the import would have worked, since the CLOB column would have been created using the default tablespace for the user (in this case, the USERS tablespace).

This is one of the major issues you will have using the exp/imp method to clone schemas if your objects contain fully qualified tablespace definitions: sometimes the imp command will be unable to rewrite the definitions to use the new schema and will try to create the objects in the original schema instead.

One solution is to run the imp command with the special parameter INDEXFILE=Y, which, instead of importing the data, will create a file containing all the DDL from the dumpfile, which you can then edit by hand to rewrite the tablespace definitions. You would then use this new file to pre-create all the schema objects (this time using the correct tablespaces), and then rerun the imp command, this time just to import the data (since the objects have already been created).

▓ **Note** The imp/exp method is well documented in the imp/exp documentation. It is also covered in the excellent *Expert One-On-One* book by Tom Kyte (Apress, 2003), as well as Tom's "Ask Tom" web site (http://asktom.oracle.com).

While this method works, it can be extremely cumbersome, particularly if you need to perform the cloning on a regular basis. Next, we'll look at another, much easier schema cloning method.

Using Data Pump to Clone Schemas

Data Pump, at first glance, looks quite similar to the exp/imp tools in that you can use it to export and import data. However, Data Pump is capable of things that are just not possible using exp/imp and also has the following advantages (based on the Data Pump documentation, so your own figures for performance may vary):

- Data Pump Export and Import utilities are typically much faster than the original export and import utilities. A single thread of Data Pump Export is about twice as fast as the original export tool, while Data Pump Import is 15–45 times faster than the original import tool.

- Data Pump jobs can be restarted without loss of data, whether the stoppage was voluntary or involuntary.

- Data Pump jobs support fine-grained object selection. Virtually any type of object can be included or excluded in a Data Pump job.

- Data Pump supports the ability to load one instance directly from another (network import) and unload a remote instance (network export).

One of the major differences between imp/exp and Data Pump is that with imp/exp, the export file will be created on the client side (you run then on the client machine, which might actually be the same machine as the database is on); but with Data Pump, the export and import files will reside on the server—in other words, the export file will be created on the same file system that the database resides on. So, setting up Data Pump does require a bit more work than using exp/imp.

Let's walk through an example. First, we need to connect to the database as a privileged user and create a directory object that specifies a directory path for the location of the files that Data Pump is going to use later, as follows:

```
dba@DBTEST> create directory datapump as '/home/oracle/datapump';
Directory created.
```

Note that this is just an example. You should check which directory structure is appropriate for your infrastructure. We are using the /home/oracle/datapump directory. We could have given the directory another name (such as apexdemo), but we used the name datapump just to clearly show its use within our directory structure. Also remember that the Oracle processes will attempt to read and write to this directory, so you must ensure that the permissions in that directory are correct, allowing the user or ID of the process that Oracle is running to access that directory.

We could perform the export and import of the schema as the users themselves (as we did with the exp/imp procedure). We would need to grant privileges so these users could access the directory we just created (using the grant read, write on directory datapump to <user> command). However, we want to use some advanced Data Pump parameters, which require elevated privileges that are not ordinarily available to normal users, such as the very dangerous sounding import full database privilege. Thus, we are going to perform the process as a privileged user.

Now, we can perform the actual export, as shown in Listing 15-20.

Listing 15-20. *Using Data Pump to Export the APEXDEMO Schema*

```
[jes@pb datapump]$ pwd

/home/oracle/datapump
[jes@pb datapump]$ expdp schemas=apexdemo directory=datapump
dumpfile=apexdemo.dmp logfile=export.log

Username: dba
Password:

FLASHBACK automatically enabled to preserve database integrity.
Starting "SYSTEM"."SYS_EXPORT_SCHEMA_01":  system/******** schemas=
apexdemo directory=datapump
dumpfile=apexdemo.dmp logfile=export.log
Estimate in progress using BLOCKS method...
Processing object type SCHEMA_EXPORT/TABLE/TABLE_DATA
Total estimation using BLOCKS method: 1.687 MB
Processing object type SCHEMA_EXPORT/USER
Processing object type SCHEMA_EXPORT/SYSTEM_GRANT
Processing object type SCHEMA_EXPORT/ROLE_GRANT
Processing object type SCHEMA_EXPORT/DEFAULT_ROLE
Processing object type SCHEMA_EXPORT/TABLESPACE_QUOTA
Processing object type SCHEMA_EXPORT/SE_PRE_SCHEMA_PROCOBJACT/PROCACT_SCHEMA
Processing object type SCHEMA_EXPORT/TYPE/TYPE_SPEC
Processing object type SCHEMA_EXPORT/SEQUENCE/SEQUENCE
Processing object type SCHEMA_EXPORT/TABLE/TABLE
Processing object type SCHEMA_EXPORT/TABLE/INDEX/INDEX
Processing object type SCHEMA_EXPORT/TABLE/CONSTRAINT/CONSTRAINT
Processing object type SCHEMA_EXPORT/TABLE/INDEX/STATISTICS/INDEX_STATISTICS
Processing object type SCHEMA_EXPORT/TABLE/STATISTICS/TABLE_STATISTICS
```

```
Processing object type SCHEMA_EXPORT/TABLE/COMMENT
Processing object type SCHEMA_EXPORT/PACKAGE/PACKAGE_SPEC
Processing object type SCHEMA_EXPORT/PACKAGE/GRANT/OBJECT_GRANT
Processing object type SCHEMA_EXPORT/FUNCTION/FUNCTION
Processing object type SCHEMA_EXPORT/PROCEDURE/PROCEDURE
Processing object type SCHEMA_EXPORT/PROCEDURE/GRANT/OBJECT_GRANT
Processing object type SCHEMA_EXPORT/PACKAGE/COMPILE_PACKAGE/PACKAGE_SPEC/ALTER_PACKAGE_SPEC
Processing object type SCHEMA_EXPORT/FUNCTION/ALTER_FUNCTION
Processing object type SCHEMA_EXPORT/PROCEDURE/ALTER_PROCEDURE
Processing object type SCHEMA_EXPORT/PACKAGE/PACKAGE_BODY
Processing object type SCHEMA_EXPORT/TABLE/CONSTRAINT/REF_CONSTRAINT
Processing object type SCHEMA_EXPORT/TABLE/TRIGGER
Processing object type SCHEMA_EXPORT/TABLE/INDEX/SE_TBL_FBM_INDEX_INDEX/INDEX
. . exported "APEXDEMO"."USER_REPOSITORY"          8.054 KB      12 rows
. . exported "APEXDEMO"."UPLOADED_FILES"          53.67 KB       1 rows
. . exported "APEXDEMO"."APEX_ACCESS_CONTROL"      7.156 KB       2 rows
. . exported "APEXDEMO"."APEX_ACCESS_SETUP"        5.562 KB       1 rows
. . exported "APEXDEMO"."BIG_EMP"                  7.820 KB      14 rows
. . exported "APEXDEMO"."BUGLIST"                  8.585 KB      19 rows
. . exported "APEXDEMO"."DEMO_CUSTOMERS"           8.984 KB       7 rows
. . exported "APEXDEMO"."DEMO_IMAGES"              5.906 KB      11 rows
. . exported "APEXDEMO"."DEMO_ORDERS"              6.429 KB      10 rows
. . exported "APEXDEMO"."DEMO_ORDER_ITEMS"         6.585 KB      16 rows
. . exported "APEXDEMO"."DEMO_PAGE_HIERARCHY"      5.984 KB      18 rows
. . exported "APEXDEMO"."DEMO_PRODUCT_INFO"        7.664 KB      10 rows
. . exported "APEXDEMO"."DEMO_STATES"              6.054 KB      51 rows
. . exported "APEXDEMO"."DEMO_USERS"               7.179 KB       2 rows
. . exported "APEXDEMO"."DEPT"                     5.648 KB       4 rows
. . exported "APEXDEMO"."EMP"                      7.812 KB      14 rows
. . exported "APEXDEMO"."REPORT_HEADINGS"          6.062 KB       8 rows
. . exported "APEXDEMO"."TREE_NAVIGATION"          6.312 KB       4 rows
. . exported "APEXDEMO"."USER_SEARCHES"            6.632 KB      32 rows
. . exported "APEXDEMO"."VERIFICATION_LINK"        5.593 KB       1 rows
. . exported "APEXDEMO"."APEX_CUSTOM_LOG"             0 KB        0 rows
. . exported "APEXDEMO"."DUMMY"                       0 KB        0 rows
. . exported "APEXDEMO"."FOO"                         0 KB        0 rows
Master table "SYSTEM"."SYS_EXPORT_SCHEMA_01" successfully loaded/unloaded
******************************************************************************
Dump file set for SYSTEM.SYS_EXPORT_SCHEMA_01 is:
  /home/oracle/datapump/apexdemo.dmp
Job "SYSTEM"."SYS_EXPORT_SCHEMA_01" successfully completed at 11:11
```

Note that we are actually performing the Data Pump export while connected to the same machine as the database, just so you can see the file that has been created. However, you could perform exactly the same command from a client machine, and the export file would still be created on the server (rather than the client machine). The following is the actual command used to perform the export:

```
expdp schemas=apexdemo directory=datapump
dumpfile=apexdemo.dmp logfile=export.log
```

Here, we specify the schema name (APEXDEMO) and pass the name of the directory we created earlier (datapump). We then see the output of the Data Pump Export command running through the various schema objects.

When the export has finished, we should be able to see the export file created in the directory (on the server), as follows:

```
[jes@pb datapump]$ ls -al

total 2240
drwxr-xr-x    4 oracle  oinstall      136 Jan 27 11:11 .
drwxr-xr-x   28 oracle  oinstall      952 Jan 24 23:59 ..
-rw-r-----    1 oracle  oinstall  1138688 Jan 27 11:11 apexdemo.dmp
-rw-r--r--    1 oracle  oinstall     4389 Jan 27 11:11 export.log
```

Now we drop the APEXCLONE user (since it is the quickest way to remove all the objects we imported earlier) and re-create the user as we did earlier, as shown in the following:

```
sys@DBTEST> drop user apexclone cascade;

User dropped.

sys@DBTEST> create user apexclone identified by pass
2  default tablespace users;
User created.

sys@DBTEST> grant connect, resource to apexclone;
Grant succeeded.

sys@DBTEST> revoke unlimited tablespace from apexclone;
Revoke succeeded.

sys@DBTEST> alter user apexclone quota unlimited on users;
User altered.
```

We can now perform the import using Data Pump, as shown in Listing 15-21.

Listing 15-21. Using Data Pump to Import into the APEXCLONE Schema

```
[jes@pb datapump]$ impdp remap_schema=APEXDEMO:APEXCLONE

 REMAP_TABLESPACE=APEXDEMO:USERS
DIRECTORY=datapump dumpfile=apexdemo.dmp logfile=import.log

Username: system
Password:

Master table "SYSTEM"."SYS_IMPORT_FULL_01" successfully loaded/unloaded
Starting "SYSTEM"."SYS_IMPORT_FULL_01":  system/********
remap_schema=APEXDEMO:APEXCLONE REMAP_TABLESPACE=APEXDEMO:USERS
DIRECTORY=datapump dumpfile=apexdemo.dmp logfile=import.log
Processing object type SCHEMA_EXPORT/USER
ORA-31684: Object type USER:"APEXCLONE" already exists
Processing object type SCHEMA_EXPORT/SYSTEM_GRANT
```

```
Processing object type SCHEMA_EXPORT/ROLE_GRANT
Processing object type SCHEMA_EXPORT/DEFAULT_ROLE
Processing object type SCHEMA_EXPORT/TABLESPACE_QUOTA
Processing object type SCHEMA_EXPORT/SE_PRE_SCHEMA_PROCOBJACT/PROCACT_SCHEMA
Processing object type SCHEMA_EXPORT/TYPE/TYPE_SPEC
Processing object type SCHEMA_EXPORT/SEQUENCE/SEQUENCE
Processing object type SCHEMA_EXPORT/TABLE/TABLE
Processing object type SCHEMA_EXPORT/TABLE/TABLE_DATA
. . imported "APEXCLONE"."USER_REPOSITORY"        8.054 KB      12 rows
. . imported "APEXCLONE"."UPLOADED_FILES"         53.67 KB       1 rows
. . imported "APEXCLONE"."APEX_ACCESS_CONTROL"    7.156 KB       2 rows
. . imported "APEXCLONE"."APEX_ACCESS_SETUP"      5.562 KB       1 rows
. . imported "APEXCLONE"."BIG_EMP"                7.820 KB      14 rows
. . imported "APEXCLONE"."BUGLIST"                8.585 KB      19 rows
. . imported "APEXCLONE"."DEMO_CUSTOMERS"         8.984 KB       7 rows
. . imported "APEXCLONE"."DEMO_IMAGES"            5.906 KB      11 rows
. . imported "APEXCLONE"."DEMO_ORDERS"            6.429 KB      10 rows
. . imported "APEXCLONE"."DEMO_ORDER_ITEMS"       6.585 KB      16 rows
. . imported "APEXCLONE"."DEMO_PAGE_HIERARCHY"    5.984 KB      18 rows
. . imported "APEXCLONE"."DEMO_PRODUCT_INFO"      7.664 KB      10 rows
. . imported "APEXCLONE"."DEMO_STATES"            6.054 KB      51 rows
. . imported "APEXCLONE"."DEMO_USERS"             7.179 KB       2 rows
. . imported "APEXCLONE"."DEPT"                   5.648 KB       4 rows
. . imported "APEXCLONE"."EMP"                    7.812 KB      14 rows
. . imported "APEXCLONE"."REPORT_HEADINGS"        6.062 KB       8 rows
. . imported "APEXCLONE"."TREE_NAVIGATION"        6.312 KB       4 rows
. . imported "APEXCLONE"."USER_SEARCHES"          6.632 KB      32 rows
. . imported "APEXCLONE"."VERIFICATION_LINK"      5.593 KB       1 rows
. . imported "APEXCLONE"."APEX_CUSTOM_LOG"           0 KB        0 rows
. . imported "APEXCLONE"."DUMMY"                     0 KB        0 rows
. . imported "APEXCLONE"."FOO"                       0 KB        0 rows
Processing object type SCHEMA_EXPORT/TABLE/INDEX/INDEX
Processing object type SCHEMA_EXPORT/TABLE/CONSTRAINT/CONSTRAINT
Processing object type SCHEMA_EXPORT/TABLE/INDEX/STATISTICS/INDEX_STATISTICS
Processing object type SCHEMA_EXPORT/TABLE/STATISTICS/TABLE_STATISTICS
Processing object type SCHEMA_EXPORT/TABLE/COMMENT
Processing object type SCHEMA_EXPORT/PACKAGE/PACKAGE_SPEC
Processing object type SCHEMA_EXPORT/PACKAGE/GRANT/OBJECT_GRANT
Processing object type SCHEMA_EXPORT/FUNCTION/FUNCTION
Processing object type SCHEMA_EXPORT/PROCEDURE/PROCEDURE
Processing object type SCHEMA_EXPORT/PROCEDURE/GRANT/OBJECT_GRANT
Processing object type SCHEMA_EXPORT/PACKAGE/COMPILE_PACKAGE/PACKAGE_SPEC/ALTER_PACKAGE_SPEC
Processing object type SCHEMA_EXPORT/FUNCTION/ALTER_FUNCTION
Processing object type SCHEMA_EXPORT/PROCEDURE/ALTER_PROCEDURE
Processing object type SCHEMA_EXPORT/PACKAGE/PACKAGE_BODY
Processing object type SCHEMA_EXPORT/TABLE/CONSTRAINT/REF_CONSTRAINT
Processing object type SCHEMA_EXPORT/TABLE/TRIGGER
Processing object type SCHEMA_EXPORT/TABLE/INDEX/SE_TBL_FBM_INDEX_INDEX/INDEX
Job "SYSTEM"."SYS_IMPORT_FULL_01" completed with 0 error(s) at 11:27
```

The following is the command we used to perform the import:

```
impdp remap_schema=APEXDEMO:APEXCLONE
  remap_tablespace=APEXDEMO:USERS
  DIRECTORY=datapump dumpfile=apexdemo.dmp logfile=import.log
```

The `remap_schema` parameter allows Data Pump to map from the original schema (APE-XDEMO) to the new schema (APEXCLONE). The `remap_tablespace` parameter allows Data Pump to map from the original tablespace (APEXDEMO) to the new tablespace (USERS).

As you can see, the output from Data Pump is different from that of the exp/imp method. Unlike using exp/imp, Data Pump Import successfully manages to import the foo table, even though the tablespace for the CLOB column was fully qualified against the APEXDEMO schema, since it was mapped to the new tablespace with the `remap_tablespace` parameter.

Clearly, using these parameters is a much easier way of mapping between schemas and tablespaces than trying to do it with the exp/imp tools, which cannot always successfully rewrite the schema references within the DDL, as you saw in the previous section.

Notice that the output from the Data Pump Import contains the following line:

```
ORA-31684: Object type USER:"APEXCLONE" already exists
```

We get this message (it's not an error; just a message) because we pre-created the APEXCLONE user. Let's see what happens if we delete the user and try the import again. First, drop the user as follows:

```
dba@DBTEST> drop user apexclone cascade;
User dropped.
```

Now run the import again. You'll get the same results as in Listing 15-21.

You might be surprised to see that even though we did not pre-create the user, the import was successful. This is because the export file contains all the necessary DDL to create the user for us. However, if we let Data Pump create the user for us, the password that we know for that user will not work. For example, we'll try to log in as follows:

```
[jes@pb datapump]$ sqlplus


Enter user-name: apexclone
Enter password:
ERROR:
ORA-01017: invalid username/password; logon denied
```

What happened here is that during the export, the hashed password for the APEXDEMO user was included in the dumpfile, so the APEXCLONE user was created using the same hash value, as shown :

```
dba@DBTEST> select username, password from dba_users
  2  where username in ('APEXDEMO', 'APEXCLONE');

USERNAME                        PASSWORD
------------------------------- -------------------------------
APEXCLONE                       E3OFB3C8B61086A3
APEXDEMO                        E3OFB3C8B61086A3
```

However, and this is where things get tricky, the login procedure uses *both* the username and password when generating the hash that should be compared against the value stored in the database.

Therefore, because the usernames are different, the same password would not hash to the same value. So, we need to set a new password for the APEXCLONE user, as follows, before we can log in:

```
dba@DBTEST> alter user apexclone identified by pass;
User altered.
```

We should now be able to log in as the APEXCLONE user and check that the objects were created properly, as follows:

```
[jes@pb datapump]$ sqlplus

Enter user-name: apexclone
Enter password:
apexdemo@dbtest> select count(*) from user_objects;

  COUNT(*)
----------
        90
```

Success! So, as you can see, although Data Pump requires a bit more configuration before you can use it, it is far more flexible and saves time compared with using the exp/imp method.

Closing the Loop: Setting Up the Workspace

Now that we have successfully cloned the schema, we can import the workspace file and application. Since we are re-creating the application on the same instance (and the workspace specified in the workspace export already exists), we won't import the workspace file, but will instead create a new one, as shown in Figures 15-6 and 15-7.

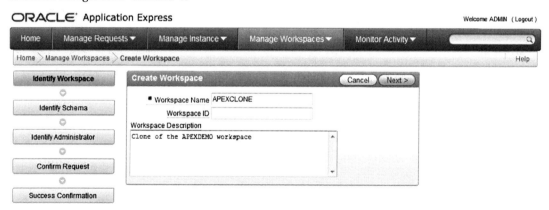

Figure 15-6. Creating the new APEXCLONE workspace

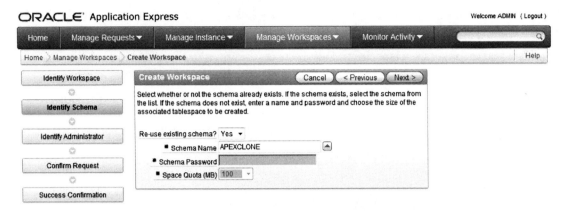

Figure 15-7. Reusing the APEXCLONE schema for the APEXCLONE workspace

Importing with Application Builder

After creating (or importing) the workspace, we can import the application. If we log in to the APEXCLONE workspace, we can use the Application Builder interface to import the application, as shown in Figure 15-8.

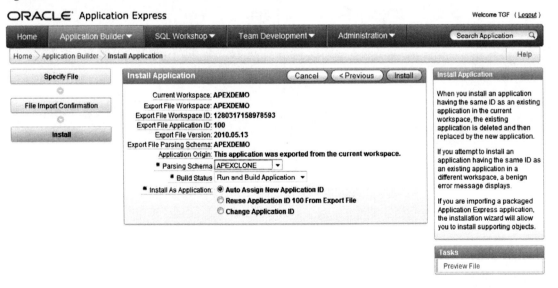

Figure 15-8. Importing the application with Application Builder

You can see that we are warned that the application was exported from another workspace, and that the original parse as schema in the export file is the APEXDEMO schema. We can assign APEXCLONE as the new parse as schema. Since we are importing into the same instance, we need to choose to auto-assign a new application ID; otherwise, it would conflict with the existing application.

We now have a fully working application, running within the APEXCLONE schema, which is an exact copy of the application we had in the APEXDEMO schema.

Importing with SQL*Plus

If we used SQL*Plus to import the application, instead of using Application Builder, we would get the following error:

```
apexclone@DBTEST> @f101.sql

APPLICATION 108 - Buglist Application
Set Credentials...
Illegal security group id value for this schema.
Check Compatibility...
API Last Extended:20070525
Your Current Version:20070525
This import is compatible with version: 20070108
COMPATIBLE (You should be able to run this import without issues.)
Set Application ID...
begin
*
ERROR at line 1:
ORA-20001: Package variable g_security_group_id must be set.
ORA-06512: at "FLOWS_030000.WWV_FLOW_API", line 46
ORA-06512: at "FLOWS_030000.WWV_FLOW_API", line 238
ORA-06512: at line 4
```

The problem here is that with this method, the script is trying to use the workspace ID of the workspace from which the application was exported. Therefore, we need to modify the script to use the ID of the new APEXCLONE workspace, as follows:

```
[jes@pb exports]$ sqlplus

Enter user-name: apexclone
Enter password:

apexclone@DBTEST> exec wwv_flow_api.set_security_group_id;

PL/SQL procedure successfully completed.

apexclone@DBTEST> select wwv_flow_api.get_security_group_id
  2   from dual;

GET_SECURITY_GROUP_ID
---------------------
    5379828196761673
```

So we now change the line in the f101.sql script from the following:

```
begin
  -- Assumes you are running the script connected to SQL*Plus as the
```

```
-- Oracle user FLOWS_030000 or as the owner (parsing schema) of
-- the application.
wwv_flow_api.set_security_group_id(
  p_security_group_id=>986113558690831);
```

```
end;
/
```

to this:

```
begin
```

```
-- Assumes you are running the script connected to SQL*Plus as the
-- Oracle user FLOWS_030000 or as the owner (parsing schema) of
-- the application.
wwv_flow_api.set_security_group_id(
  p_security_group_id=>5379828196761673);
```

```
end;
/
```

Note that if you used the original workspace export file to re-create the workspace on another instance, you would not need to perform this step, since the new workspace ID would match the original workspace ID. It is only because we are importing into a workspace with a different ID that we need to make this change.

If we now rerun the script, we will get the following error:

```
apexclone@DBTEST> @f108.sql

APPLICATION 108 - Buglist Application
Set Credentials...
Check Compatibility...
API Last Extended:20070525
Your Current Version:20070525
This import is compatible with version: 20070108
COMPATIBLE (You should be able to run this import without issues.)
Set Application ID...
begin
*
ERROR at line 1:
ORA-20001: Application 108 was not deleted. Import will not be attempted.
ORA-06512: at "FLOWS_030000.WWV_FLOW_API", line 261
ORA-06512: at line 4
```

The problem here is that the script is trying to use an application ID of 108 when we already have that application installed in this instance. We can resolve this by doing a search and replace through the file and replacing the application ID of 108 with another (unique) number (such as 1108). Also, it is important to change the following line in the export file:

```
begin

    -- SET APPLICATION ID
    wwv_flow.g_flow_id := 1108;
```

```
   wwv_flow_api.g_id_offset := 0;
null;
end;
```

Here, we have already changed the g_flow_id (which represents the application ID) from 108 to 1108. We also need to change the g_id_offset value if we are installing on an instance that already contains this application; otherwise, many of the internal IDs would conflict with the already installed application. So we have changed this line to the following:

```
wwv_flow_api.g_id_offset := 100000;
```

This is sufficiently large enough to ensure that it does not conflict with other applications in our instance (you should check which value makes sense in your own instance). Again, you would not need to do this if you were installing into a different instance (unless another application used the same ID, of course).

We can now rerun the script, and this time, it should execute successfully, as shown in Listing 15-22.

Listing 15-22. Executing the f108.sql Script

```
[jes@pb exports]$ sqlplus


Enter user-name: apexclone
Enter password:

apexclone@DBTEST> @f108.sql
APPLICATION 1108 - Buglist Application
Set Credentials...
Check Compatibility...
API Last Extended:20070525
Your Current Version:20070525
This import is compatible with version: 20070108
COMPATIBLE (You should be able to run this import without issues.)
Set Application ID...
...authorization schemes
...navigation bar entries
...application processes
...application items
...application level computations
...Application Tabs
...Application Parent Tabs
...Shared Lists of values
...Application Trees
...page groups
...comments: requires application express 2.2 or higher
...PAGE 0: 0
...PAGE 1: Report Page
...PAGE 2: Insert Form
...PAGE 3: Update Form
...PAGE 4: Success Page
...PAGE 5: Analysis
...PAGE 6: Analyze Reported
...PAGE 7: Analyze Reported
```

```
...PAGE 8: Analyze Status
...PAGE 9: Analyze Status
...PAGE 10: Analyze Reported By
...PAGE 11: Analyze Reported By
...PAGE 12: Analyze Assigned To
...PAGE 13: Analyze Assigned To
...PAGE 14: Empty Report Page
...PAGE 15: New User Registration
...PAGE 16: Help
...PAGE 17: Big Emp
...PAGE 19: Charts
...PAGE 24: Uploaded Files
...PAGE 101: Login
...lists
...breadcrumbs
...page templates for application: 1108
......Page template 1221013001094394
<extra output ommited>
...button templates
......Button Template 1223605281094424
......Button Template 1223820688094430
......Button Template 1224023773094431
......Button Template 1224205308094432
...region templates
......region template 1224405629094433
<extra output ommited>
...List Templates
......list template 1230704349094467
<extra output ommited>
...web services (9iR2 or better)
...shared queries
...report layouts
...authentication schemes
......scheme 1240217348094545
......scheme 1240527785094547
......scheme 1391009692011209
...done
```

We have omitted some of the output, but you can see that the script successfully completes this time.

In the Application Builder interface, we will see that the application is now available to edit and run in the APEXCLONE workspace, as shown in Figure 15-9 (note the workspace name at the bottom of the page).

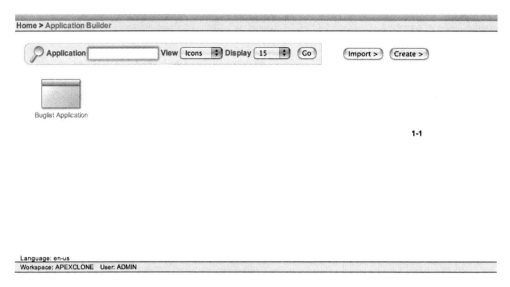

Figure 15-9. Application installed into the APEXCLONE workspace

If you are slightly nervous about editing the export file in this way, feel free to use the Application Builder interface, which will automatically create the new application ID for you. However, you might want to automate this process, which is obviously easier if you use SQL*Plus.

Summary

We've covered several diverse topics in this chapter, but they are all necessary to running an efficient production environment. You can help your users a lot by taking advantage of URL management to provide friendly URLs. And we all agree on the need to back up applications, because disaster will surely befall all of us sooner or later. And finally, being able to quickly clone an APEX environment is incredibly helpful when developing and testing new versions of an application. Cloning is also a useful troubleshooting tool, enabling you to take a snapshot of an application in order to diagnose and resolve a problem.

APEX Dictionary

The APEX dictionary (or *repository*, as it is also known) is arguably one of the most exciting features in APEX, and perhaps also one of the most underutilized.

During training sessions and presentations, we frequently like to ask the attendees, "Who is currently using the APEX Dictionary?" A varying number of hands are usually shown (at the time of writing, typically less than ten percent). It is a bit of a trick question, since everyone using APEX is using the APEX Dictionary, whether they know it or not.

The APEX Dictionary gives you access to a huge amount of information about your APEX environment, your applications, and the way that users are using your application. As you'll learn in this chapter, the APEX Dictionary is a great tool that you can use to make your applications even more feature-rich. After reading this chapter, we think you will be excited by the number of ways in which using the APEX Dictionary will not only make your life as a developer easier, but will also make your end users and managers happier.

Accessing the APEX Dictionary

Within the APEX environment, your applications are not stored as a single executable program (in contrast to the way that a Windows .exe file is stored, for example). Instead, the metadata for your application is stored in separate tables, in much the same way that the Oracle Data Dictionary itself stores information about objects in the database. These tables are located in the schema in which APEX was installed (in the APEX_ schema; for example, APEX_040000 for APEX version 4.0).

The APEX Dictionary allows you to query the metadata about your application, as well as retrieve many other useful bits of information. There are two different ways you can query that information: via the Application Builder interface (or rather reports accessible via the Application Builder) or by programmatically accessing a number views, which typically have an apex_ prefix. When you use the Application Builder interface, you are really accessing the same apex_ views, but in a graphical way.

Using the Application Builder Interface

The APEX Dictionary reports are available from the APEX Utilities menu, as shown in Figure 16-1. This figure shows the menu that appears when you click the drop-down arrow on the Utilities button. If you click the button itself, you will see the window shown in Figure 16-2. In the Utilities window, the button says APEX Views rather than APEX Dictionary; however, they will both take you to the same window, as shown in Figure 16-3.

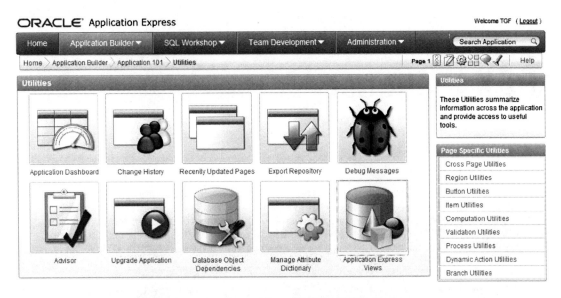

Figure 16-1. Accessing the Application Express Views from the Utilities menu

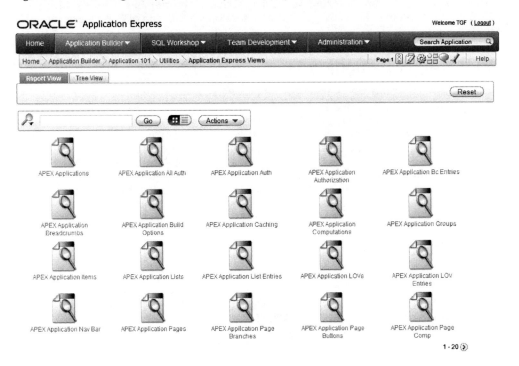

Figure 16-2. The Application Express Views window

The Application Express Views window shown in Figure 16-2 is your launchpad into the APEX Dictionary. From here, you can access all the different types of information. Each of the icons represents a different set of information that is available, including APEX workspaces, APEX applications, APEX application build options, and so on. It may not be immediately apparent, but all of these different views are defined in a view themselves, called apex_dictionary. You will see how that works later, but for now, it is enough to know that this graphical window is initially driven from entries in the apex_dictionary view.

In the Application Express Views window, you can change the View option to see the information in a different format. Figure 16-3 shows the information displayed in Report format.

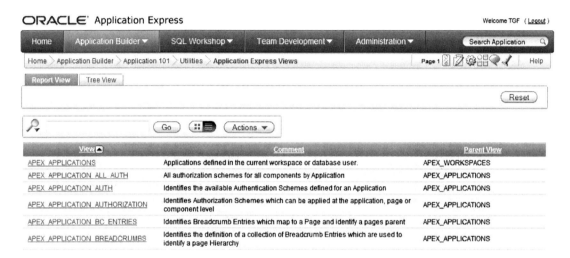

Figure 16-3. *The APEX Dictionary in Report Format*

In Report format, each view is listed with a Comment column and a Parent View column (remember that each entry in the report represents a distinct view that you can query). The Comment column gives information about the purpose of each view. If you are searching for a particular piece of information but are not quite sure which view provides it, you can look (or indeed search) through the Comment column to try to find a view that matches your search criteria. The Parent View column reflects a hierarchy for the views. For example, if you are interested in anything related to lists, you might search all the views that have apex_application_lists as the parent view (which would match, for example, the apex_application_list_entries view).

You can see this hierarchy in a more logical way by switching the Application Express Dictionary Views window to Tree view, as shown in Figure 16-4. In this figure, we have expanded the apex_workspace_activity_log entry. You can see that it has two child views related to it: apex_workspace_log_archive, apex_workspace_log_summary, and apex_workspace_log_summary_usr.

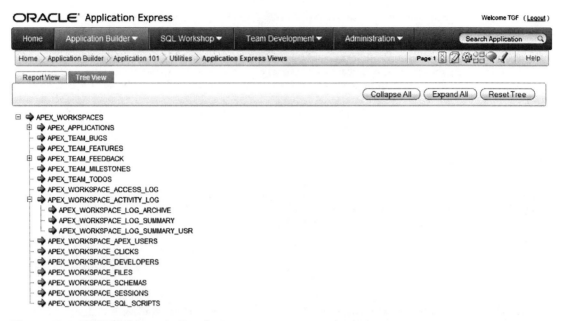

Figure 16-4. APEX Dictionary in Tree format

Let's see what we can do with this nice graphical interface using the APEX Dictionary. Let's say that we're interested in finding out information about our applications. We can search for the word "applications," as shown in Figure 16-5.

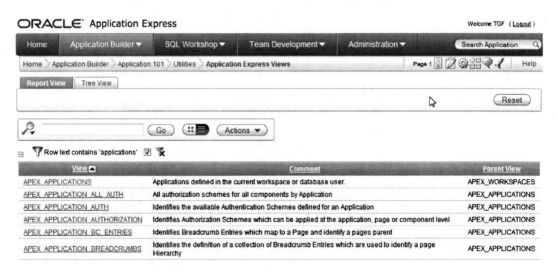

Figure 16-5. Searching the APEX Dictionary for "applications"

We see that three views might be useful. Let's click the link for the apex_applications view (since the name implies it might be directly related to what we want). Now we will see a window with a lot of information about the apex_applications view, including a description, query columns, query conditions, and so on. Figure 16-6 shows the table from which the APEX_APPLICATIONS view is constructed (the left-most column). The column on the right shows the columns that are included in the view. You can actually temporarily modify the contents of a view on this screen and produce the results by clicking on the Results button.

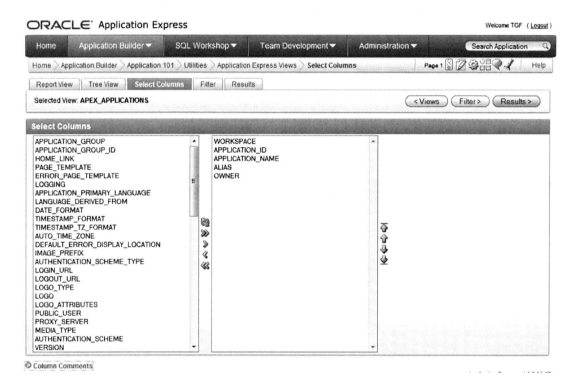

Figure 16-6. Description of the apex_applications view

Clicking on the Column Comments link, as shown in Figure 16-7, opens a window that displays the comments on the columns of the source table.

Column Name	Comments
WORKSPACE	A work area mapped to one or more database schemas
APPLICATION_ID	Application Primary Key, Unique over all workspaces
APPLICATION_NAME	Identifies the application
ALIAS	Assigns an alternate alphanumeric application identifier
OWNER	Identifies the database schema that this application will parse SQL and PL/SQL statements as
APPLICATION_GROUP	Identifies the name of the application group this application is associated with
APPLICATION_GROUP_ID	Identifies the ID of the application group this application is associated with
HOME_LINK	URL used to navigate to the home page of the application

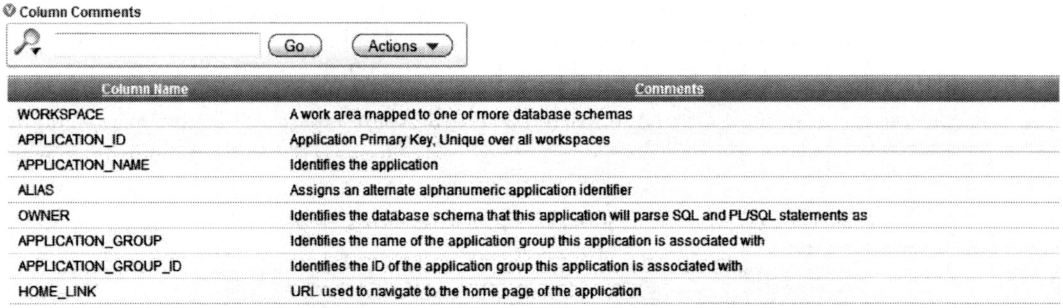

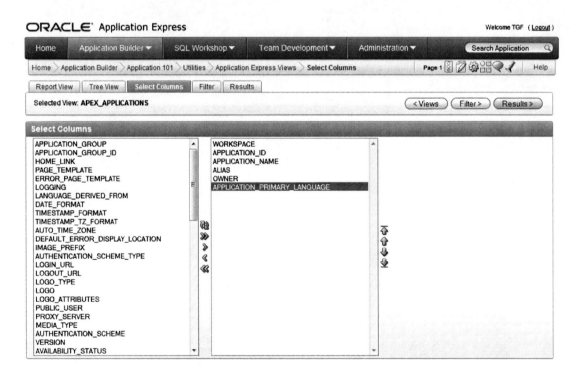

Figure 16-7. *Description of the apex_applications view*

We can select columns to be included and add query conditions. In Figure 16-8, we are including the `application_primary_language` column. This, in effect, modifies the previous query for this session. Click Results to see the output of the query.

Figure 16-8. *Modifying the apex_applications view*

Figure 16-9 shows the results of the modified query. You can also click on the Query link in the bottom left corner of the page to see the text of the query.

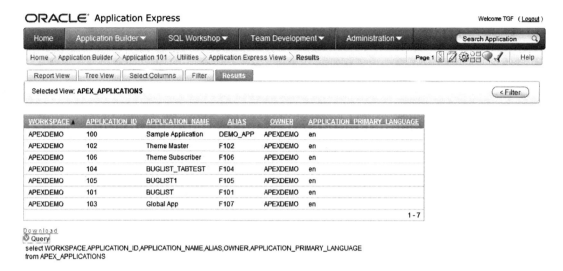

Figure 16-9. *Viewing the data from an APEX Dictionary view*

It is important to remember that when you query the APEX Dictionary in this way, you are seeing information that relates to applications within the current workspace. You won't see information about applications in other workspaces, unless those other workspaces also happen to use the same primary parsing schema as this one.

From Figure 16-9, you can see that the apex_applications view is a great way to quickly view different information about all of your workspace applications in a single report, without needing to go into each application individually.

By modifying the query conditions, you can be specific about the information you would like to see. For example, you could remove the Sample Application from the report, as shown in Figure 16-10. Note that we need to use single quotation marks around the string in the Value box in Figure 16-10. This changes the SQL query to be as follows:

```
select  WORKSPACE,
        APPLICATION_ID,
        APPLICATION_NAME,
        ALIAS,
        OWNER,
        APPLICATION_PRIMARY_LANGUAGE
from    APEX_APPLICATIONS
where   APPLICATION_NAME != 'Sample Application'
```

Figure 16-10. Adding a query condition

If we ran this query again, we would see every application installed in the workspace, with the exception of any applications with the application name set to Sample Application (that is, the Sample Application that is often installed by default when a new workspace is created). You can be very imaginative with the types of query conditions you construct to really drill down into the data you wish to see.

As you've seen, the Application Builder interface makes it easy to access the APEX Dictionary. In the next section, we'll concentrate on using the APEX Dictionary directly via the apex_ views in your own queries, rather than through the graphical interface, because that approach allows you to take control and to incorporate the APEX Dictionary into your own applications. But we do encourage you to use the graphical interface to see exactly how the information is stored and get an idea of the views and columns available.

Using the apex_dictionary View

The apex_dictionary view is the top-level interface into the dictionary for all the other views and information. The apex_dictionary view is a regular view on top of one of the internal tables used by APEX.

The apex_dictionary view was introduced in APEX version 2.2. (The underlying internal tables were there before that, and some view information was also available; however, the apex_dictionary view was first publicly made available and its use encouraged in version 2.2.) There are more than 2,700 entries in the apex_dictionary view (in version 4.0), presented in around 70 distinct views. This information represents both application metadata and monitoring information. Whenever there is a new release of APEX and the Oracle team makes a new view available, there will be a corresponding entry made into the apex_dictionary view (thus enabling us to find it and for it to appear in the graphical interface).

We mentioned in the previous section that the initial view of the APEX Dictionary graphical tool shows the information stored in the apex_dictionary view itself, and that this is your launchpad for working with the APEX Dictionary. By examining the apex_dictionary view itself, you can see how this relationship works, as shown in Listing 16-1.

Listing 16-1. Definition of the APEX_DICTIONARY View

```
jes@DBTEST> SQL> desc apex_dictionary
Name                                     Null?    Type
---------------------------------------- -------- ----------------------------
APEX_VIEW_NAME                                    VARCHAR2(30)
COLUMN_ID                                         NUMBER
COLUMN_NAME                                       VARCHAR2(30)
COMMENTS                                          VARCHAR2(4000)
COMMENT_TYPE                                      VARCHAR2(6)
PARENT_VIEW                                       VARCHAR2(34)
```

The columns contain the following information:

- apex_view_name: The name of another view that is available to be queried.

- column_id: The numeric value of the column for that particular view. If this value is zero, then it represents the description for the view itself.

- column_name: The name for each distinct column in the view. Note that there will always be $n + 1$ columns (since column 0 represents the view itself).

- comments: Comment for the individual column, or the comment for the view if column_id contains a zero.

- parent_view: String representing the name of another view that this view should be considered a child of.

You can query the apex_dictionary view in exactly the same way as the graphical interface, as shown in Listing 16-2 (which uses SUBSTR to show only the first 30 characters of the comments field for brevity).

Listing 16-2. Querying the apex_workspaces View

```
1  select
2      column_id as id,
3      column_name as name,
4      substr(comments, 1, 30) as comments
5  from
6      apex_dictionary
7  where
8*     apex_view_name = 'APEX_WORKSPACES'

        ID NAME                                COMMENTS
---------- ----------------------------------- ------------------------------
         0                                     Available Application Express
         1 WORKSPACE                           A work area mapped to one or m
         2 SOURCE_IDENTIFIER                   Identifies the workspace when
         3 SCHEMAS                             Number of database schemas cur
         4 LAST_PURGED_SESSION                 Creation date of the most rece
         5 ALLOW_APP_BUILDING_YN               Controls availability of ident
```

```
 6 ALLOW_SQL_WORKSHOP_YN              Controls availability of ident
 7 ALLOW_WEBSHEET_DEV_YN              Controls availability of ident
 8 ALLOW_TEAM_DEVELOPMENT_YN          Controls availability of ident
 9 ALLOW_TO_BE_PURGED_YN              Controls availability of ident
10 SESSIONS                           Number of non-purged APEX sess
11 APPLICATIONS                       Number of applications created
12 APPLICATION_PAGES                  Number of application pages cr
13 APEX_USERS                         Number of APEX users created i
14 APEX_DEVELOPERS                    Number of APEX users with deve
15 APEX_WORKSPACE_ADMINISTRATORS      Number of APEX users with work
16 FILES                              Number of APEX files associate
17 SQL_SCRIPTS                        Number of APEX SQL Scripts ass
18 TRANSLATION_MESSAGES               Number of translatable and tra
19 FILE_STORAGE                       Size in bytes of all files ass
20 LAST_LOGGED_PAGE_VIEW              Date of most recent page view
21 PAGE_VIEWS                         Count of page views recorded f
22 WORKSPACE_ID                       Primary key that identifies th
```

23 rows selected.

You can see that the column_id of 0 represents the view itself since there is no column_name value against it. The full value of the comments column is "Available Application Express (APEX) workspaces." So, this view is showing us the workspaces associated with the schema in which we executed the query. It is important to differentiate between querying the apex_dictionary view versus querying the apex_ view for information itself.

Now let's examine the apex_dictionary view in a bit more detail. Listing 16-3 shows the available views defined in the apex_dictionary view (note we have omitted some of the output).

Listing 16-3. *Querying the apex_dictionary View*

```
1  select
2     apex_view_name, count(*)
3  from
4     apex_dictionary
5  group by
6     apex_view_name
```

```
APEX_VIEW_NAME                      COUNT(*)
---------------------------------- ----------
APEX_APPLICATION_BC_ENTRIES              22
APEX_APPLICATION_LIST_ENTRIES            40
APEX_APPLICATION_PAGE_FLASH_CH           57
APEX_APPLICATION_PAGE_IR_CGRPS           13
APEX_APPLICATION_PAGE_IR_COMP            21
APEX_APPLICATION_PAGE_RPT_COLS           73
APEX_APPLICATION_TEMP_LABEL              19
APEX_APPLICATION_TREES                   35
APEX_APPLICATION_WEB_SERVICES            27
APEX_APPL_PLUGIN_ATTR_VALUES             14

...
```

Recall that the COUNT(*) is actually showing us the number of columns in that view plus one, since column 0 refers to the view itself. We can query information from a particular view by using a query similar to the one we used earlier, but substituting the name of the view we're interested in, as shown in Listing 16-4 (again truncating the output and the comments column for brevity).

Listing 16-4. *Querying the apex_dictionary View*

```
1  select
2     column_id as id,
3     column_name,
4     comments
5  from
6     apex_dictionary
7  where
8*    apex_view_name = 'APEX_APPLICATIONS'

       ID COLUMN_NAME       COMMENTS

---------- ----------------- -------------------------------------------------------------
        0                    Applications defined in the current workspace or database
        1 WORKSPACE          A work area mapped to one or more database schemas
        2 APPLICATION_ID     Application Primary Key, Unique over all workspaces
        3 APPLICATION_NAME   Identifies the application
        4 ALIAS              Assigns an alternate alphanumeric application identifier
        5 OWNER              Identifies the database schema that this application will
        6 APPLICATION_GROUP  Identifies the name of the application group this
...
```

Notice that this is the same information that we queried in the previous section using the graphical interface. There are actually around 70 columns available in the apex_applications view, giving you access to almost every piece of information about your application you could ever want.

So, to get a listing of all the applications installed in your workspace, you can run the query shown in Listing 16-5.

Listing 16-5. *Listing Applications in the Workspace*

```
apexdemo@DBTEST> select
2     workspace,
3     application_id as app_id,
4     application_name as app_name,
5     alias
6  from
7*    apex_applications
WORKSPACE       APP_ID APP_NAME              ALIAS
---------- ---------- --------------------- ----------
APEXDEMO          104 Sample Application    DEMO_APP
APEXDEMO          103 Buglist Application   F108
```

As mentioned earlier, it's important to remember that this is showing only applications in the workspace that has the parsing schema set as the schema connected to the database. If we ran this query while connected to a different schema, we would get different results:

```
jes@DBTEST>  select
   2     workspace,
   3     application_id as id,
   4     application_name as app_name,
   5     alias
   6  from
   7*  apex_applications

WORKSPACE            ID APP_NAME                           ALIAS
------------ ---------- ------------------------------ ------------
APEXDEMO            100 Sample Application             DEMO_APP
APEXDEMO            102 Theme Master                   F102
APEXDEMO            106 Theme Subscriber               F106
APEXDEMO            103 Global App                     F107
APEXDEMO            105 BUGLIST1                       F105
APEXDEMO            101 BUGLIST                        F101
APEXDEMO            104 BUGLIST_TABTEST                F104
```

If we connect as the schema associated with the APEX installation (the schema that was used when APEX was installed), we can see every application that is installed:

```
apex_040000DBTEST> select count(*) from apex_applications;

  COUNT(*)
----------
        20
```

So the information you see is related to which workspace the schema is associated with, with the exception of the APEX_ user, who can see everything.

Uses for the APEX Dictionary

So, why is the APEX Dictionary so useful? Well, it gives us the following features:

- We get a consistent view of an application's state at a particular point in time.

- We can view (and use) information about the application within the application itself.

- We can use it for quality assurance, tuning, and reporting purposes.

- We can use it to dynamically provide information about our applications, which could be used for a site maps, graphs, flowcharts, and so on.

You'll better understand the power and flexibility of the APEX Dictionary once you see a few examples of what you can do with it. In the following sections, we will show you some different ways to use the APEX Dictionary within your applications (and outside your applications). However, the number of possible ways of combining and using the information in the APEX Dictionary is huge. We encourage you to experiment and try to find new and ingeniously useful ways to use the APEX Dictionary in your own applications.

There are three main categories in which you can use the APEX Dictionary:

- Quality assurance (QA)

- Self-documentation

- Automated monitoring

This is by no means a definitive list; however, these are perhaps among the most widely used categories. The following sections show some sample uses of the APEX Dictionary in each of these categories, although some of the queries and reports certainly are cross-category; that is, you can use the results in whatever way you like.

For the examples, we use SQL*Plus, while connected to the Buglist application schema (the one used by the Buglist application for parsing). You could also use SQL Workshop to write these queries. Or you might find certain queries easier to do using APEX's graphical interface.

Quality Assurance

Often when you design an application, you need to abide by certain guidelines or criteria stipulated by your client, department, or company. However, as every developer knows, there is often a difference between the guidelines you are supposed to obey and the code that you actually write.

The APEX Dictionary offers the capability to query information about the metadata of your application (or indeed any application) to check whether it meets your QA guidelines (assuming that the guidelines can be interpreted in such a way that makes sense to query through the APEX Dictionary).

The following are examples of typical application requirements:

- Are all labels correctly aligned?

- Do all text fields have a maximum width assigned?

- Have all fields had help text assigned?

Let's take a look at how you can implement some of these simple QA checks.

Checking Label Alignment

Let's imagine that when we designed the Buglist application, we should have ensured that all of the labels were correctly aligned. In our case, correctly aligned means that the fields should be right-aligned. Listing 16-6 shows the query that we can use to determine the alignment of all the fields in an application.

Listing 16-6. Determining the Alignment of All the Fields in an Application

```
1  select
2     page_id as page,
3     item_name,
4     label_alignment as align,
5     item_element_width as width,
```

```
 6    item_element_max_length as max
 7  from
 8    apex_application_page_items
 9  where
10    application_name = 'BUGLIST'
11  and
12    display_as = 'Text Field'
13  order by
14    page_id,
15*   item_name
```

PAGE	ITEM_NAME	ALIGN	WIDTH	MAX
22	P22_SEARCH	Right	30	4000
23	P23_SEARCH	Right	30	4000
27	P27_ASSIGNED_TO	Right	32	30
27	P27_DESCRIPTION	Right	32	255
27	P27_PRIORITY	Right	32	30
27	P27_REPORTED_BY	Right	32	30
27	P27_STATUS	Right	32	30
28	P28_ASSIGNED_TO	Right	32	30
28	P28_DESCRIPTION	Right	32	255
28	P28_EMAIL	Right	30	4000

```
10 rows selected.
```

Notice in Listing 16-6 that we specify the application name in the query, as follows:

```
 9  where
10    application_name = 'BUGLIST'
```

We could have specified the numeric application ID instead. However, we cannot specify the application alias directly, since the view that we are querying (apex_application_page_items) does not include the alias as one of its columns. We could use a join against the apex_applications view to look up the application ID from the alias, if we wanted to avoid hard-coding the application ID (which could change if the application were deleted and re-imported).

The output from the query in Listing 16-6 shows that it returns a record for every item in our application. For example, page 15 contains a page item (a text field, since we are interested in only those items) named p15_email, which has the label right-aligned, a width of 30 characters, and allows a maximum of 2,000 characters to be entered.

PAGE	ITEM_NAME	ALIGN	WIDTH	MAX
28	P28_EMAIL	Right	30	4000

Now let's go into the Buglist application and modify the p28_email field so the label is left-aligned, as shown in Figure 16-11.

Figure 16-11. Modifying the alignment for p28_email

If we now run the query again, we should see the change in alignment immediately. In Listing 16-7, we have modified the query in Listing 16-6 to show only the records where the fields are not right-aligned.

Listing 16-7. Show Any Fields That Are Not Right-Aligned

```
 1  select
 2     page_id as page,
 3     item_name,
 4     label_alignment as align,
 5     item_element_width as width,
 6     item_element_max_length as max
 7  from
 8     apex_application_page_items
 9  where
10     application_name = 'Buglist Application'
11  and
12     label_alignment <> 'Right'
13  and
14     display_as = 'Text Field'
15  order by
16     page_id,
17*    item_name

PAGE ITEM_NAME     ALIGN        WIDTH       MAX
----- ------------  ----------  -------  ----------
   28 P28_EMAIL     Left             30        4000
```

As you can see, the query has immediately picked up the change to the alignment property of the p28_email page item. This is really amazing if you think about it. You have the ability to dynamically query the status of your applications at any point in time, seeing the changes that developers are making *as the developers make them.*

You might have noticed that in order to perform this query, we needed to know a few details about how APEX names and stores page item types. Here, we needed to know that the display_as column for a text field is stored as 'Text Field' and that the label_alignment column stores the values as 'Right', 'Left', and so on (as opposed to using a foreign key).

```
12     label_alignment <> 'Right'

13  and

14     display_as = 'Text Field'
```

Unfortunately, there is no document that lists all the different `display_as` values you can use. But you can effectively generate this yourself via the APEX Dictionary. For example, to get a list of all the page item types we are using in our Buglist application, we could run the query shown in Listing 16-8.

Listing 16-8. Querying the Different Page Item Types

```
apexdemo@DBTEST> select
  2    distinct(display_as)
  3  from
  4    apex_application_page_items
  5  where
  6    application_name = 'BUGLIST';

DISPLAY_AS
--------------------------------------------------------------------------------
Number Field
Star Rating
Hidden
Password
Text Field
Required In Color
Display Only
Date Picker
Select List

9 rows selected.
```

As you can see, the names correspond to what you would select via the Application Builder interface for the item type. Remember that this is not a full list of available page item types; it is just a list of the ones currently in use in the Buglist application. We could make this query arguably even more useful by showing where each of those page item types are used, as shown in Listing 16-9.

Listing 16-9. Querying the Different Page Item Types and Where They Are Used

```
  1  select
  2    count(*) as count,
  3    page_id as page,
  4    display_as
  5  from
  6    apex_application_page_items
  7  where
  8    application_name = 'Buglist Application'
  9  group by
 10    display_as,page_id
 11  order by
 12*   count desc, page

   COUNT        PAGE DISPLAY_AS
---------- ---------- ------------------------------
        6          28 Text Field
```

```
5        2 Text Field
5       27 Text Field
5       40 Text Field
4        3 Text Field
3        3 Hidden
3       27 Number Field
2       12 Text Field
2       19 Hidden
2       23 Display Only
2       27 Date Picker
2       28 Date Picker
2       29 Text Field
2       30 Text Field
2       45 Text Field
...
```

So we can now clearly see which item types we use most frequently and on which pages those types are.

Now, the original purpose of this example was to perform a QA check to determine whether the field alignment was correct for the application, and you can see just how easily that can be done. We could perhaps schedule a job that runs once a day (or at the end of every week) to ensure that all the applications in the workspace have correctly aligned labels. This would ensure that all newly created fields had correctly aligned labels and would also check to make sure someone had not changed the alignment of an existing label.

Checking Maximum Widths

In Listing 16-6 (shown earlier), we included in the query the maximum allowed width of the fields. Maximum widths are one of those things that we often forget to set when we create the page items. Then it looks somewhat sloppy when users type in a long string and get an error because there is a constraint on the database that allows them to enter only a maximum number of characters (32, for example). You can use a query like the one in Listing 16-6 to see which items still have default maximums defined and then correct them.

If you have a way to relate the page item to the underlying database column in which you will be storing the data, you might even be able to extend this example to show you where the maximum length of the on-screen page item differs from the maximum allowed to be stored in the database (we leave this as an exercise for the reader).

In general, we encourage you to define sensible maximum limits for your fields. You can use the User Interface Defaults section in the Application Builder to apply default values against tables that are used for the page items if you build a form or report against that table. This approach is definitely an improvement over needing to define defaults every time you create a form or report on a table. Obviously, this does not work for page items that you create manually (where there is no table from which to pick up the default).

Checking for Fields Without Help

APEX makes it incredibly easy to create applications. The drawback is that you may sometimes use the wizards and features to quickly create a prototype, and think "I'll come back to that bit later," but never get around to those fixes.

One area that often seems to suffer from this oversight is associated field help. When you create a new page item, depending on which theme you use, the default template type for that page item might be Optional Label with Help. You can change the default template that is used, but, in practice, people rarely do. This means that when you run your application, the label next to your page item will typically be a link that will create a pop-up window displaying (in theory) context-sensitive help for that particular field, as shown in Figure 16-12. As you can see, the pop-up window for the Search field simply says that no help exists. This behavior is obviously of limited usefulness and would get rather annoying for the end user.

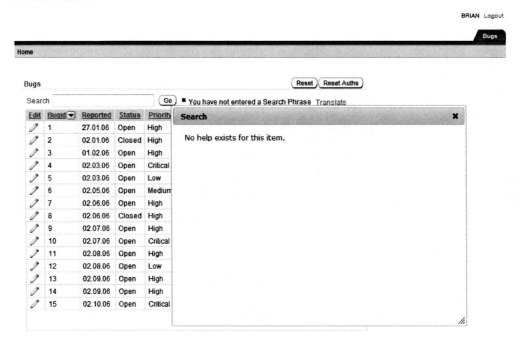

Figure 16-12. A typical label without pop-up help

Generally, you should either provide the help that the user expects or disable the links for the pop-up help. If you are providing help for only a few fields, the user will become frustrated by clicking links and never seeing any contextual help, and might never click the few fields that actually have help.

So, how can you find out for which fields the developer (even if that developer is you!) failed to enter any help text? As you might expect, that's easy to do using the APEX Dictionary. Listing 16-10 shows a query, again against the apex_application_page_items view, which searches for any fields that do not have help text and which are a visible page item type (we are obviously not concerned about hidden items having help text, since the user would never be able to access them anyway).

Listing 16-10. Reporting on Page Items Without Help

```
1  select
2     page_id as page,
3     item_name,
```

```
 4    display_as
 5  from
 6    apex_application_page_items
 7  where
 8    application_name = 'Buglist Application'
 9  and
10    display_as <> 'Hidden'
11  and
12    item_help_text is null
13  order by
14    application_name,
15    page_id,
16*   item_name
```

```
     PAGE ITEM_NAME           DISPLAY_AS
---------- -------------------- ------------------------------
        1 P1_REPORT_SEARCH     Text Field
        1 P1_SEARCH_MESSAGE    Display Only
        2 P2_ASSIGNED_TO       Text Field
        2 P2_BUGID             Number Field
        2 P2_DESCRIPTION       Text Field
        2 P2_EMAIL             Text Field
        2 P2_PRIORITY          Text Field
        2 P2_REPORTED          Date Picker
        2 P2_REPORTED_BY       Text Field
        2 P2_STATUS            Select List
        3 P3_ASSIGNED_TO       Select List
        3 P3_BUGID             Number Field
        3 P3_DESCRIPTION       Text Field
        3 P3_ID_COUNT          Display Only
        3 P3_PRIORITY          Text Field
        3 P3_REPORTED          Date Picker
        3 P3_REPORTED_BY       Text Field
        3 P3_REQUIRED          Required In Color
    ...
```

This output is very interesting, because not only does it show you that there are fields without help text associated with them, but it also gives you enough information to be able to locate those page items and either change the template they use or add some help. Once again, to demonstrate how dynamic this is, let's modify the p1_report_search field and add some contextual help, as shown in Figure 16-13.

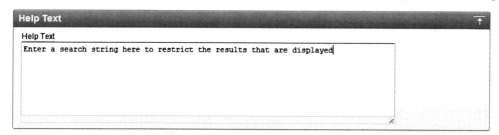

Figure 16-13. Adding contextual help to p1_report_search

We can now rerun the query, this time with an additional restriction to just show the items that are on page 1 (to minimize the output), as shown in Listing 16-11.

Listing 16-11. Viewing Page Items Without Help After Adding Help to p1_report_search

```
 1  select
 2     page_id as page,
 3     item_name,
 4     display_as
 5  from
 6     apex_application_page_items
 7  where
 8     application_name = 'Buglist Application'
 9  and
10     page_id = 1
11  and
12     display_as <> 'Hidden'
13  and
14     item_help_text is null
15  order by
16     application_name,
17     page_id,
18*    item_name
```

```
    PAGE ITEM_NAME               DISPLAY_AS
---------- -------------------- ------------------------------
       1 P1_SEARCH_MESSAGE     Display Only
```

You see that p1_report_search no longer appears in the output, since the item_help_text column is no longer null. If you now click the Search label in the application, you will see a pop-up window containing some (slightly) more useful contextual help, as shown in Figure 16-14.

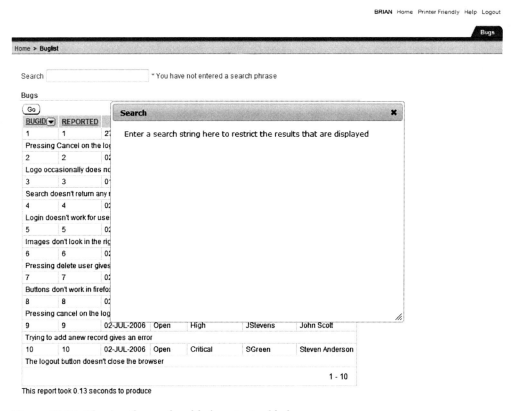

Figure 16-14. Viewing the newly added contextual help pop-up

Self-Documentation

Traditionally, you might develop an application and also maintain a separate Microsoft Word or Visio document that defines the structure of the application and how the different pages relate to each other. The primary problem with this sort of documentation is that it can quickly become out of sync with the application itself if you do not continue to update the document as changes are made to the application.

Self-documentation refers to the ability for the application to document itself. Here, we mean the ability for the developer to generate current, completely up-to-date information about the application via the information in the APEX Dictionary. This information will reflect any changes made to the document right up to the moment when you generate the report (run the query).

We are not suggesting that you replace your Word documents and Visio diagrams with SQL queries. However, some areas of the application documentation, such as the following, can be better addressed by using the APEX Dictionary:

- Report of all pages and comments on those pages

- A list of all page items and which pages they are on

- The flow of page branches and how pages relate to each other

As we mentioned earlier, some of those requirements are cross-category. For example, the list of all page items and pages on which they reside could certainly be filled by one of the queries presented in the "Quality Assurance Uses" section.

The following are some examples of using the APEX Dictionary for self-documentation. Once again, remember that this is not intended to be an exhaustive list; you are really limited only by your imagination.

Retrieving Page Comments

Many people are not even aware that you can store comments against the pages in the Application Builder. This facility can be very useful to retain a history of changes for the page, or perhaps just to add a temporary comment to detail why you are working on the page.

You can access the developer comments for the page by using the small icon that looks like a speech bubble in the top-right corner of the Application Builder when you are editing a page definition, as shown in Figure 16-15.

Figure 16-15. *Accessing developer comments*

Notice that below the icons there is a helpful piece of text that tells you there are currently zero comments for this page. When you click the speech bubble icon, as shown in Figure 16-16, you will have the opportunity to not only enter a comment, but also to create a Bug or a To Do entry in the Team Development system.

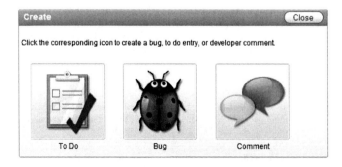

Figure 16-16. *The Developer Comments pop-up window*

In figure 16-17, you can see that we have added a couple of comments for the page to illustrate the process. We would recommend using the To Do or Bug Team Development features so the information is centrally available.

Figure 16-17. The Developer Comments pop-up window

If you don't know which APEX Dictionary view to use, you can always use the top-level apex_dictionary view to help you find a relevant view. So you could, for example, use a query like the one shown in Listing 16-12 (with some results omitted for brevity).

Listing 16-12. Finding Views with Information About Comments

```
1  select
2    distinct apex_view_name,
3    comments
4  from
5    apex_dictionary
6  where
7*   upper(comments) like '%COMMENT%'
```

```
APEX_VIEW_NAME                  COMMENTS
------------------------------  ---------------------------------------------------
APEX_APPLICATION_GROUPS         Identifies comments for a given application group
APEX_APPLICATION_PAGE_COMP      Developer comment
APEX_APPLICATION_PAGE_RPT_COLS  Comment on Report Column
APEX_APPLICATION_PROCESSES      Developer comment
APEX_APPLICATION_BUILD_OPTIONS  Developer Comment
APEX_APPLICATION_PAGES          Page comment
APEX_APPLICATION_PAGE_REGIONS   Developer comment
APEX_APPLICATION_SHORTCUTS      Developer comments
APEX_APPLICATION_TEMP_LABEL     Developer comment
APEX_APPLICATION_TEMP_PAGE      Developer comment
APEX_TEAM_FEEDBACK              Comment provided by application user
...
```

You could look through the returned list to find a view that seems relevant, and then perhaps drill down a bit and review the columns that are available in that view.

However, looking through the list of views in Listing 16-12, we find that none of them are immediately obvious candidates to use to obtain the developer comments for the pages. That is because, unfortunately, currently there is no APEX Dictionary view that exposes the developer comments. So, what was the point of all of this?

The point was to illustrate that the APEX Dictionary is a set of views that expose certain internal information to us. There may be some internal information that we still cannot get access to since no view exposes it, which is currently the case for developer comments. The comments themselves are stored in the `wwv_flow_app_comments` internal table, which we can query only if we connect via SQL*Plus as the APEX_ user (in our case, APEX_040000), or if you prefix the table with APEX_040000 as shown in Listing 16-13.

Listing 16-13. Querying the wwv_flow_app_comments Table Directly

```
flows_030000@DBTEST> select
  2     pages,
  3     created_by,
  4     app_comment
  5  from
  6     apex_040000.wwv_flow_app_comments
  7  where
  8*    flow_id = 103

PAGES    CREATED_BY    APP_COMMENT
-------- ------------- -----------------------------------------------------
1        TGF           Examined the help for page items
1        TGF           Updated the maximum widths for the fields
```

Be extremely careful if connected as your APEX_ user. In fact, you should almost never need to do anything as the APEX_ user. We're showing this example to illustrate that even though the underlying data is there, developers might not be able to access it until the Oracle APEX development team gives us access via the APEX Dictionary.

You could, in theory, create your own views to access any data from the underlying tables if there is no APEX Dictionary view that provides it. But bear in mind that you could be creating a maintenance nightmare for yourself, since you would need to remember to re-create these custom views should you need to upgrade or reinstall your APEX environment. In general, you should not resort to using such custom solutions unless they are absolutely required. It is far more preferable to submit a request to the Oracle team to create a view with the information you need (the OTN Application Express Forum is a great place to ask for this, as the Oracle development team members frequent the forums).

So, we cannot access the developer comments for the page using the APEX Dictionary. However, we can query comments from other areas of the application. For example, every page and every page item can have a comment assigned to it. Each region on a page can also have a comment assigned to it. To demonstrate how to query these comments, let's add a comment to page 1 of the Buglist application, as shown in Figure 16-18. We have also added a comment to the Report region on page 1. We can now query the comments for the application, as shown in Listing 16-14.

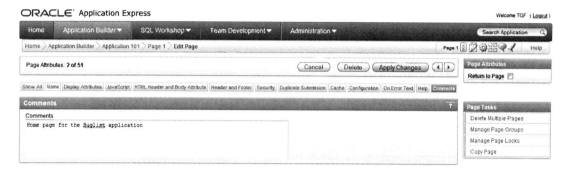

Figure 16-18. Assigning a page comment

Listing 16-14. Retrieving the Page Comments

```
apexdemo@DBTEST> select
  2     application_id as app_id,
  3     page_id as page,
  4     page_comment
  5   from
  6     apex_application_pages
  7   where
  8*    page_comment is not null

   APP_ID      PAGE PAGE_COMMENT
---------- ---------- --------------------------------------------------
      100       102 This page was generated by the feedback wizard
      101         1 Home page for the Buglist application
```

Notice that we have again connected as the schema user associated with our APEX workspace. Also notice that the apex_application_pages view contains only comments for the pages, which is logical. In order to retrieve the comments for the page regions, we use the apex_application_page_regions view instead, as shown in Listing 16-15.

Listing 16-15. Retrieving the Region Comments

```
  1  select
  2     application_id as app_id,
  3     region_name,
  4     page_id as page,
  5     component_comment
  6   from
  7     apex_application_page_regions
  8   where
  9*    component_comment is not null
```

```
    APP_ID REGION_NAME           PAGE COMPONENT_COMMENT
---------- -------------------- ---- --------------------------------------------------
       101 Bugs                    1 Report showing the bugs
```

The apex_application_page_regions view contains many different columns, allowing us to retrieve all sorts of useful information.

Retrieving Page Branches

In your application, users may be able to get from one page to another in multiple ways, such as directly by clicking a link, or by some page process in response to the user clicking a button or pressing Enter in a text field. It could be extremely useful to be able to see which pages link to which, how your pages relate to each other, and how the user navigates through them.

We can examine the page branches by using the apex_application_page_branches view, as shown in Listing 16-16.

Listing 16-16. Viewing Page Branches

```
1  select
2    page_id as id,
3    branch_action
4  from
5    APEX_APPLICATION_PAGE_BRANCHES
6  where
7*   application_id = 103

        ID BRANCH_ACTION
---------- -------------------------------------------------------------
         2 f?p=&APP_ID.:4:&SESSION.&success_msg=#SUCCESS_MSG#
         3 f?p=&APP_ID.:1:&SESSION.&success_msg=#SUCCESS_MSG#
         3 f?p=&FLOW_ID.:3:&SESSION.::&DEBUG.::P3_ID:&P3_ID_NEXT.
         3 f?p=&FLOW_ID.:3:&SESSION.::&DEBUG.::P3_ID:&P3_ID_PREV.
        12 f?p=&APP_ID.:12:&SESSION.&success_msg=#SUCCESS_MSG#
        19 f?p=&APP_ID.:19:&SESSION.
        23 f?p=&FLOW_ID.:23:&SESSION.
        27 f?p=&APP_ID.:26:&SESSION.&success_msg=#SUCCESS_MSG#
        28 f?p=&APP_ID.:23:&SESSION.&success_msg=#SUCCESS_MSG#
        29 f?p=&APP_ID.:29:&SESSION.&success_msg=#SUCCESS_MSG#
        30 f?p=&APP_ID.:30:&SESSION.&success_msg=#SUCCESS_MSG#
        34 f?p=&FLOW_ID.:34:&SESSION.
        40 f?p=&APP_ID.:39:&SESSION.&success_msg=#SUCCESS_MSG#
        42 f?p=&APP_ID.:42:&SESSION.&success_msg=#SUCCESS_MSG#
        45 f?p=&APP_ID.:45:&SESSION.&success_msg=#SUCCESS_MSG#
        46 f?p=&APP_ID.:46:&SESSION.&success_msg=#SUCCESS_MSG#
        47 f?p=&APP_ID.:47:&SESSION.&success_msg=#SUCCESS_MSG#
        54 f?p=&APP_ID.:54:&SESSION.&success_msg=#SUCCESS_MSG#
        55 f?p=&APP_ID.:55:&SESSION.&success_msg=#SUCCESS_MSG#

19 rows selected.
```

As you can see, the branch_action column contains an APEX URL, which means that if we want to get a nice branch mapping between pages, we need to do some work and parse the URL. One way to do that is to use regular expressions, as shown in Listing 16-17.

Listing 16-17. Querying the Flow Between Pages

```
1  select
2    page_id as page_from,
3    regexp_replace(branch_action,
4      '(.*)(\:)([[:digit:]]+)(\:)(.*)', '\3') as page_to
4  from
5    APEX_APPLICATION_PAGE_BRANCHES
6  where
7*   application_id = 103

PAGE_FROM PAGE_TO
---------- ----------
         2 4
         3 1
         3 3
         3 3
        12 12
        19 19
        23 23
        27 26
        28 23
        29 29
        30 30
        34 34
        40 39
        42 42
        45 45
        46 46
        47 47
        54 54
        55 55

19 rows selected.
```

This query allows you to produce a report that details how your pages link to each other, perhaps to help you find outdated or unwanted links between pages. For example in Listing 16-17, notice how page 3 has two branches to itself. Perhaps this is a potential issue that we need to look into (or it might be desired behavior, since the branches could be acting on very different criteria or performing different processing).

One nice extension of this sort of query is that you could use the advanced features of Oracle Business Intelligence Publisher (BI Publisher) to produce a nice report that you can export to a PDF file, a Microsoft Word document, or a Microsoft Excel spreadsheet to get a hard copy showing the state of your application at a particular point in time. The APEXLib, which is a free framework for APEX, also provides the facility to produce a nice graphical flowchart of how your application behaves.

We can also extend the example to find out exactly when the branching occurs, as shown in Listing 16-18.

Listing 16-18. Viewing the Branch Points Between Pages

```
1  select
2    page_id as page_from,
3    regexp_replace(branch_action,
4      '(.*)(\:)([[:digit:]]+)(\:)(.*)', '\3') as page_to,
5    branch_point
6  from
7    APEX_APPLICATION_PAGE_BRANCHES
8  where
9*   application_id = 103
```

```
PAGE_FROM PAGE_TO    BRANCH_POINT
---------- ---------- ------------------------------
        2 4          AFTER_PROCESSING
        3 1          AFTER_PROCESSING
        3 3          BEFORE_COMPUTATION
        3 3          BEFORE_COMPUTATION
       12 12         AFTER_PROCESSING
       19 19         AFTER_PROCESSING
       23 23         AFTER_PROCESSING
       27 26         AFTER_PROCESSING
       28 23         AFTER_PROCESSING
       29 29         AFTER_PROCESSING
       30 30         AFTER_PROCESSING
       34 34         AFTER_PROCESSING
       40 39         AFTER_PROCESSING
       42 42         AFTER_PROCESSING
       45 45         AFTER_PROCESSING
       46 46         AFTER_PROCESSING
       47 47         AFTER_PROCESSING
       54 54         AFTER_PROCESSING
       55 55         AFTER_PROCESSING

19 rows selected.
```

We can now see at exactly which point the branch would be fired.

Retrieving Modification Dates

Another common requirement is to be able to determine when things were last changed in
the application. Perhaps you want a list of anything changed in the last week, or perhaps you want to
know when each page was last modified. You can do this very easily using the APEX Dictionary. For
example, if we wanted to list the most recently updated pages in the Buglist application, we could use
the query in Listing 16-19.

Listing 16-19. Viewing the Most Recently Updated Pages

```
 1  select
 2    page_id,
 3    last_updated_by,
 4    to_char(last_updated_on,
 5      'DD/MM/YYYY HH24:MI:SS') as last_updated
 6  from
 7    apex_application_pages
 8  where
 9    application_id = 103
10  order by
11*   last_updated_on desc

  PAGE_ID LAST_UPDATED LAST_UPDATED
---------- ------------ --------------------------------------------------
        1 TGF          08/04/2011 21:10:58
       28 TGF          08/04/2011 20:18:23
        2 TGF          08/04/2011 20:05:26
       62 TGF          08/04/2011 04:49:11
       61 TGF          07/04/2011 22:18:33
       59 TGF          07/04/2011 21:06:25
       57 TGF          07/04/2011 04:14:16
       56 TGF          06/04/2011 21:52:33
       55 TGF          06/04/2011 21:07:42
       54 TGF          06/04/2011 21:06:00
...
```

This presents a very interesting usage, since we could include this information on the page itself in our application. For example, we can modify the Buglist application and add a hidden item on page 1 (the main report page) called p1_last_modified. We can then create an on-load before-header page process that retrieves the last modification date of the page, as shown in Figure 16-19. Notice how the query in Figure 16-18 uses the :APP_ID and :APP_PAGE_ID bind variable notation to use the current application and page IDs and retrieve the last_updated_on value into the p1_last_updated hidden page item.

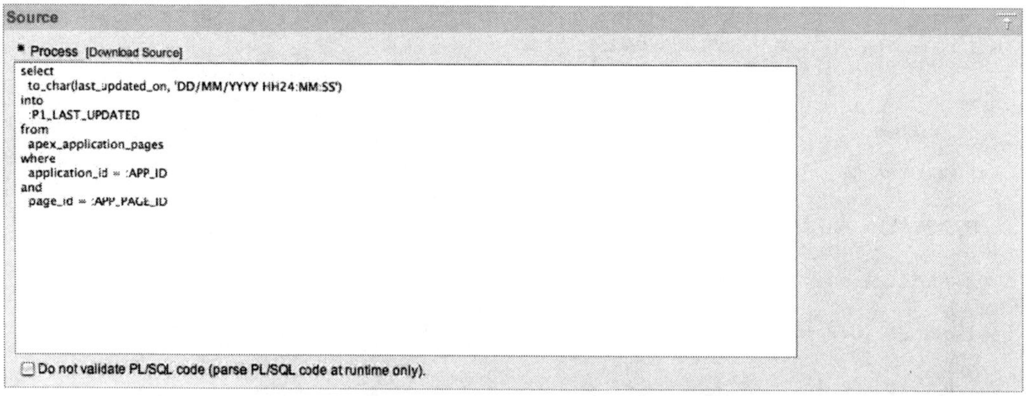

Figure 16-19. PL/SQL page process to retrieve modification date

We can now add some footer text to the page that references the p1_last_updated page item, as follows:

```
This page was last updated: &P1_LAST_UPDATED.
```

When you run the page, you should now see that the footer text shows the last modified date. We could extend this example to include the name (or rather login name) of the person who last modified the page, by adding another hidden page item and modifying the query to retrieve the last_updated_by column, as follows:

```
select
  to_char(last_updated_on, 'DD/MM/YYYY HH24:MM:SS'),
  last_updated_by
into
  :P1_LAST_UPDATED,
  :P1_LAST_UPDATED_BY
from
  apex_application_pages
where
  application_id = :APP_ID
and
  page_id = :APP_PAGE_ID
```

We could then modify the footer text to reference the new page item:

```
Last updated by &P1_LAST_UPDATED_BY. (&P1_LAST_UPDATED).
```

Automated Monitoring

The next major use for the APEX Dictionary is in the area of automated monitoring of your applications, such as for the following tasks:

- Check for application changes.

- Query user access to applications.

- Compare historical timing information.

By default, APEX records information every time a user accesses an application (this includes the Application Builder itself). Let's take a quick look at a query we can use to examine user access times for the Buglist application. The view that we need to query is apex_workspace_activity_log, whose definition is shown in Listing 16-20.

▓ **Note** You can disable the default logging (look in the Application Definition under the Logging setting). However, the benefits of leaving the logging enabled will usually far outweigh any performance benefits you might get from disabling it. Without this automated logging, you will find it extremely difficult to track down the performance problem areas in your application. Therefore, by disabling logging (in order to make the application run faster), you are actually making it more difficult for yourself to produce scalable, responsive applications.

Listing 16-20. Definition of apex_workspace_activity_log

```
apexdemo@DBTEST> desc APEX_WORKSPACE_ACTIVITY_LOG

Name                           Null?    Type
------------------------------ -------- --------------------
WORKSPACE                      NOT NULL VARCHAR2(255)
APEX_USER                               VARCHAR2(255)
APPLICATION_ID                          NUMBER
APPLICATION_NAME                        VARCHAR2(255)
APPLICATION_SCHEMA_OWNER                VARCHAR2(30)
PAGE_ID                                 NUMBER
PAGE_NAME                               VARCHAR2(255)
VIEW_DATE                               DATE
THINK_TIME                              NUMBER
SECONDS_AGO                             NUMBER
LOG_CONTEXT                             VARCHAR2(4000)
ELAPSED_TIME                            NUMBER
ROWS_QUERIED                            NUMBER
IP_ADDRESS                              VARCHAR2(4000)
AGENT                                   VARCHAR2(4000)
APEX_SESSION_ID                         NUMBER
ERROR_MESSAGE                           VARCHAR2(4000)
ERROR_ON_COMPONENT_TYPE                 VARCHAR2(255)
ERROR_ON_COMPONENT_NAME                 VARCHAR2(255)
PAGE_VIEW_MODE                          VARCHAR2(15)
APPLICATION_INFO                        VARCHAR2(4000)
INTERACTIVE_REPORT_ID                   NUMBER
IR_SAVED_REPORT_ID                      NUMBER
IR_SEARCH                               VARCHAR2(4000)
```

677

```
WS_APPLICATION_ID              NUMBER
WS_PAGE_ID                     NUMBER
WS_DATAGRID_ID                 NUMBER
CONTENT_LENGTH                 NUMBER
REGIONS_FROM_CACHE             NUMBER
WORKSPACE_ID                   NUMBER
```

The apex_workspace_activity_log has two underlying tables that store the user activity information periodically (currently every 14 days), which means that the apex_workspace_activity_log view will contain up to a maximum of 28 days' worth of history. If you wish to retain more than that, you will need to create your own process that periodically appends the new contents of the view to your own table.

Listing 16-21 shows a query that retrieves the average elapsed_time for page requests for the Buglist application.

Listing 16-21. Querying Average Elapsed Times for the Pages

```
1  select
2     page_id,
3     avg(elapsed_time) as average_time
4  from
5     apex_workspace_activity_log
6  where
7     application_id = 103
8  group by
9*    page_id
```

```
  PAGE_ID AVERAGE_TIME
---------- ------------
       51   .150756287
        1   .364408112
       54   .165111481
       57   .191758743
       30   .221034857
       43    .34228725
       42    .3667415
       22     .069138
```

This type of query can be invaluable for helping you to identify potentially slow or problematic pages in your application. You can see at a glance which pages are consuming the most time to process and generate.

Knowing the average time is extremely useful, but we can make it even more useful by showing how the average relates to the minimum and maximum times for those pages, as shown in Listing 16-22.

Listing 16-22. Querying Minimum, Maximum, and Average Elapsed Times

```
1  select
2     page_id,
3     min(elapsed_time) as min,
4     avg(elapsed_time) as avg,
5     max(elapsed_time) as max,
```

```
 6    count(*) as count
 7  from
 8    apex_workspace_activity_log
 9  where
10    application_id = 103
11  group by
12    page_id
13  order by
14*   page_id
```

```
   PAGE_ID       MIN         AVG         MAX       COUNT
---------- ---------- ---------- ---------- ----------
         1  .00026298 .364408112   2.300985         67
         2    .011347  .0377878    .076486          5
         3     .30938    .30938     .30938          1
        11    .207099   .207099    .207099          1
        17    .208001   .208001    .208001          1
```

This sort of information is even better for helping to diagnose performance issues, since you can see how the maximum times relate to the averages. For example, are the average times being skewed by a handful of slow requests, or do most user requests get responses in a reasonable amount of time?

As we've said, some of these queries have cross-purpose applications. For example, if your department has the QA guideline that all web applications must respond within 2 seconds, then the query in Listing 16-22 can be used to automatically monitor the applications and to send out an e-mail warning if any applications exceed this threshold. This sort of proactive monitoring can help you to act on problems as they occur, rather than waiting for users to call and complain that the application is running slowly.

As an example, Listing 16-23 shows a simple package that can be used to check for applications exceeding a time threshold for page requests.

Listing 16-23. Automatic Threshold Monitoring with PKG_MONITOR

```
1  create or replace package pkg_monitor as
2           procedure CheckElapsed(p_Elapsed in number,
3                                  p_ToEmail in varchar2);
4           procedure Run;
5  end pkg_monitor;
6* /

Package created.

1 create or replace package body pkg_monitor as
2   procedure CheckElapsed(p_Elapsed in number,
3                          p_ToEmail in varchar2) is
4     v_text CLOB;
5   begin
6     -- necessary to set up the APEX environment from SQLPlus
7     wwv_flow_api.set_security_group_id;
8     -- loop round the apex_workspace_activity_log view
9     for x in (select
10                application_id,
```

```
11                      page_id,
12                      elapsed_time
13                  from
14                      apex_workspace_activity_log
15                  where
16                      elapsed_time > p_Elapsed
17                  order by
18                      elapsed_time desc) loop
19          -- build up the email body
20          v_text := v_text || 'Application: ' || x.application_id;
21          v_text := v_text || ' Page Id: ' || x.page_id;
22          v_text := v_text || ' Elapsed Time: ' || x.elapsed_time;
23          v_text := v_text || utl_tcp.crlf;
24        end loop;
25        -- send the email
26        apex_mail.send(p_to   => p_ToEmail,
27                       p_from => 'alert@localhost',
28                       p_body => v_text,
29                       p_subj => 'Elapsed Time Metric Warning');
30          -- push the mail out to the mail server
31          apex_mail.push_queue('localhost', 25);
32      end CheckElapsed;

33      /* Simple test harness */
34      procedure Run is
35      begin
36        CheckElapsed(3, 'jes@dbvm.localdomain');
37      end run;
38*   end pkg_monitor;
39    /
```

Package body created.

The code is Listing 16-23 is fairly straightforward. It contains two procedures:

- procedure CheckElapsed(p_Elapsed in number, p_ToEmail in varchar2)

- procedure Run

The CheckElapsed procedure is the main procedure. The Run procedure is just a simplified test harness procedure that allows us to call the CheckElapsed procedure with some hard-coded parameters.

We are using the apex_mail package to send e-mail messages via our mail server. We have hard-coded the values that we need to work with our mail server, such as the push_queue method:

```
apex_mail.push_queue('localhost', 25);
```

You will need to modify the hard-coded values or parameterize the procedures to work with your own environment.

Now we can call our test harness procedure to check whether any pages in the application have taken more than 3 seconds to generate. Note that in the Run procedure, the value of 3 is hard-coded again; if you want to specify another threshold, call the CheckElapsed procedure directly.

The following is the output of calling the pkg_monitor.run procedure.

```
apexdemoDBTEST> exec pkg_monitor.run;

Pushing email: 3371913588187709
Pushed email: 3371913588187709

PL/SQL procedure successfully completed.
```

The output is the result of the call to apex_mail.push_queue, which pushes out the e-mail to our local mail server. If we check our e-mail, we should see a message with a body similar to the one shown in Figure 16-20.

```
Application: 4000 Page Id: 580 Elapsed Time: 54.038137
Application: 4000 Page Id: 580 Elapsed Time: 54.038137
Application: 101 Page Id: 46 Elapsed Time:44.606271
Application: 4000 Page Id: 580 Elapsed Time: 54.038137
Application: 101 Page Id: 46 Elapsed Time:44.606271
Application: 4000 Page Id: 580 Elapsed Time: 35.047103
Application: 4000 Page Id: 580 Elapsed Time: 54.038137
Application: 101 Page Id: 46 Elapsed Time:44.606271
Application: 4000 Page Id: 580 Elapsed Time: 35.047103
Application: 4000 Page Id: 560 Elapsed Time: 25.305091
Application: 4000 Page Id: 580 Elapsed Time: 54.038137
Application: 101 Page Id: 46 Elapsed Time:44.606271
Application: 4000 Page Id: 580 Elapsed Time: 35.047103
Application: 4000 Page Id: 560 Elapsed Time: 25.305091
Application: 101 Page Id: 38 Elapsed Time: 23.489265
Application: 4000 Page Id: 580 Elapsed Time: 54.038137
Application: 101 Page Id: 46 Elapsed Time:44.606271
Application: 4000 Page Id: 580 Elapsed Time: 35.047103
Application: 4000 Page Id: 560 Elapsed Time: 25.305091
Application: 101 Page Id: 38 Elapsed Time: 23.489265
Application: 4000 PageId: 580 Elapsed Time: 22.604886
Application: 4000 Page Id: 580 Elapsed Time: 54.038137
Application: 101 Page Id: 46 Elapsed Time: 44.606271
Application: 4000 Page Id: 580 Elapsed Time: 35.047103
Application: 4000 Page Id: 560 Elapsed Time: 25.305091
Application: 101 Page Id: 38 Elapsed Time: 23.489265
Application: 4000 Page Id: 580 Elapsed Time: 22.604886
```

Figure 16-20. *Threshold notification e-mail body*

Notice that the message shows every page, including the Application Builder pages that took more than 3 seconds to generate. The message also lists the pages in descending elapsed_time order, which means that at a glance, we can determine which pages might need attention (or perhaps we might need to look at our infrastructure for some of those times!).

Many of the techniques we have demonstrated are very powerful, and when you begin to combine techniques, you can achieve fantastic results. For example, rather than sending a plain-text e-mail message, you could produce a PDF report containing graphs showing how your applications are behaving and regularly (via a scheduled job) e-mail that PDF report to key people. Alternatively, you could integrate the ability to send out an alert via Short Message Service (SMS) or a pager by using one of the commercial or free web services that provide this ability.

Using the API

This section is not strictly related to the APEX Dictionary. Rather, it deals with using API functions to manually create and manipulate items in APEX without using the Application Builder.

The material in this section is contentious, because there is certainly the argument that you should be doing this work via the Application Builder interface, not from the API directly, to protect yourself from mistakes or from potentially corrupting your application (or even worse). However, the techniques we describe here can lead to some really labor-saving results.

So, the material in this section can be considered "unsupported." If you are going to try these techniques, do that in a sandbox or on a test machine first. Take backups before doing anything from the API (and test those backups!). Also, bear in mind that because, in many cases, the API routines are considered unsupported and/or undocumented, they can change from version to version, so you should not rely on the functionality being the same between versions or indeed even included.

Now given all the warnings, why would you want to use the API at all? Sometimes you will want to perform a task that will take too long using the Application Builder. Or, you may want to automate the building of an application. This really is possible—you can build APEX applications that create other APEX applications for you.

▓ **Tip** The APEX export facility uses the API. Reading an application export file is a great way to learn about the internals of APEX.

Adding Items to Your Pages

Imagine that we have an application with a large number of pages (think in terms of hundreds of pages). For some reason, our business requirements decree that we add a hidden page item on each of those pages (perhaps to be used in some footer text). How would we do that?

We can do it by using the wwv_flow_api.create_page_item procedure. The APEX application export files use this exact procedure to create page items when you import an application (and, indeed, when you create a page item using the Application Builder).

Listing 16-24 shows the code to add a new hidden page item to page 1 of the Buglist application.

Listing 16-24. Using wwv_flow_api.create_page_item

```
1   declare
2       vId number;
3       vPageId number := 1;
4   begin
5       -- set up the APEX environment
6       wwv_flow_api.set_security_group_id;
7
8       wwv_flow_api.set_version(
9           wwv_flow_api.g_compatable_from_version);
10
11      -- set the application id
12      wwv_flow.g_flow_id := 101;
```

```
13
14      -- get a unique id for the item
15      vId := wwv_flow_id.next_val;
16      wwv_flow_api.create_page_item(
17                  p_id => vId,
18                  p_flow_id => wwv_flow.g_flow_id,
19                  p_flow_step_id => vPageId,
20                  p_display_as => 'HIDDEN',
21                  p_name => 'P' || vPageId || '_HIDDEN_ITEM');
22* end;
```

```
API Last Extended:20070525
Your Current Version:20070525
This import is compatible with version: 20070525
COMPATIBLE (You should be able to run this import without issues.)
```

```
PL/SQL procedure successfully completed.
```

Notice that we get some output telling us that the API we are calling is valid for the version of APEX we are using. This is the same type of output you get when you import an APEX file from the command line.

Because we are running Listing 16-24 via SQL*Plus, we need to set up the environment as though we were running it through the APEX environment. We do this with a call to `wwv_flow_api.set_version`. We pass in the current version that we have installed by referencing the `wwv_flow_api.g_compatable_from_version` packaged variable.

Next we need to provide the ID of the application that we want to manipulate:

```
wwv_flow.g_flow_id := 101;
```

Every item in APEX needs a unique ID, and the safest way to obtain one is to use the sequence that APEX itself uses:

```
vId := wwv_flow_id.next_val;
```

The final step is to make the call to the `create_page_item` procedure:

```
wwv_flow_api.create_page_item(
            p_id => vId,
            p_flow_id => wwv_flow.g_flow_id,
            p_flow_step_id => vPageId,
            p_display_as => 'HIDDEN',
            p_name => 'P' || vPageId || '_HIDDEN_ITEM');
```

Notice that we are dynamically generating the item name using the value of vPageId (for example, for page 1 the item would be called `p1_hidden_item`). Also note that the page ID parameter is called `p_flow_step_id`.

We should now be able to go back into the Application Builder and see the newly created application item, as shown in Figure 16-21.

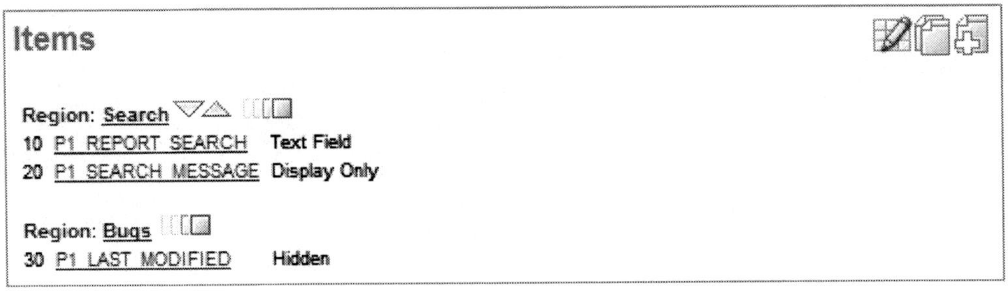

Figure 16-20. After running the create_page_item code

However, as you can see, the p1_hidden_item item is not listed. This is because we did not commit our session in SQL*Plus. Once we do commit our session, the item appears, as shown in Figure 16-22.

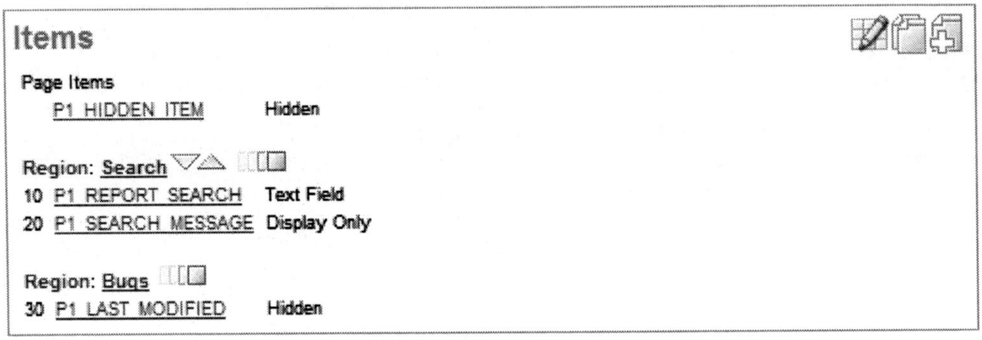

Figure 16-21. The create_page_item code has been committed

As we said, you really need to exercise caution when using the API, since you are not afforded much of the protection that you get when you use the Application Builder interface. However, what you lose in protection you definitely gain in control.

You saw how easy it is to programmatically create a page item. Now imagine that we had to add a page item (or perhaps a region) to 10, 20, or 100 different pages in the application (we could use page zero for the region; however, we might require a distinct item on the page for some reason, too). Imagine how much time that would take to do manually via the Application Builder versus programmatically looping around one of the APEX Dictionary views (for example, apex_application_pages) to extract the page number and then calling the create_page_item procedure. You will have turned something that would take minutes (or potentially hours) into something that completes in mere seconds.

■ **Note** Bear in mind that APEX was actually developed using the very API that we are showing you. In effect, APEX was developed using APEX.

Creating Text Fields Programmatically

If we want to create a text field rather than a hidden page item, we can take our code from Listing 16-24 and amend it as shown in Listing 16-25.

Listing 16-25. Creating a Text Field

```
 1  declare
 2    vId number;
 3    vPageId number := 1;
 4    vAppId  number := 103;
 5  begin
 6    -- set up the APEX environment
 7    wwv_flow_api.set_security_group_id;
 8    wwv_flow_api.set_version(
 9      wwv_flow_api.g_compatable_from_version);

10    -- set the application id
11    wwv_flow.g_flow_id := vAppId;
12    -- get a unique id for the item
13    vId := wwv_flow_id.next_val;
14    wwv_flow_api.create_page_item(
15      p_id => vId,
16      p_flow_id => wwv_flow.g_flow_id,
17      p_flow_step_id => vPageId,
18      p_display_as => 'TEXT',
19      p_prompt => 'Surname',
20      p_name => 'P' || vPageId || '_TEXT_ITEM');
21* end;
```

```
API Last Extended:20070525
Your Current Version:20070525
This import is compatible with version: 20070525
COMPATIBLE (You should be able to run this import without issues.)

PL/SQL procedure successfully completed.

apexdemoDBTEST> commit;

Commit complete.
```

Notice that the only modification needed was to change the p_display_as parameter to use TEXT rather than HIDDEN.

Now suppose you had to create a number of pages in an application that would be used to fill out information in the form of a matrix. For a matrix of modest size (such as 4 × 4), it definitely would be more productive to create those pages via the Application Builder. However, suppose you needed to create an 8 × 8 matrix of fields. You might decide to save a bit of time (since you could reuse the code later) by adding the fields programmatically. An example of code that does this is shown in Listing 16-26.

Listing 16-26. Creating a Matrix of Fields Programmatically

```
 1  declare
 2     vId number;
 3     vPageId number := &PAGE_NUMBER.;
 4     v_NewLine varchar2(20);
 5  begin
 6     -- set up the APEX environment
 7     wwv_flow_api.set_security_group_id;
 8     wwv_flow_api.set_version(
 9        wwv_flow_api.g_compatable_from_version);
10     -- set the application id
11     wwv_flow.g_flow_id := &APPLICATION_NUMBER.;
12     for v_y in 1..5 loop
13       for v_x in 1..5 loop
14         -- get a unique id for the item
15         vId := wwv_flow_id.next_val;
16         if (v_y = 1) then
17           v_NewLine := 'YES';
18         else
19           v_NewLine := 'NO';
20         end if;
21         wwv_flow_api.create_page_item(
22           p_id => vId,
23           p_flow_id => wwv_flow.g_flow_id,
24           p_flow_step_id => vPageId,
25           p_display_as => 'TEXT',
26           p_prompt => 'Y' || v_x || 'X' || v_y,
27           p_begin_on_new_line => v_NewLine,
28           p_begin_on_new_field=> 'YES',
29           p_name => 'P' || vPageId || '_X' || v_x || 'Y' || v_y);
30       end loop; -- x
31     end loop; -- y
32* end;
```

```
Enter value for page_number: 18
old    3:    vPageId number := &PAGE_NUMBER.;
new    3:    vPageId number := 18;
Enter value for application_number: 101
old   12:    wwv_flow.g_flow_id := &APPLICATION_NUMBER.;
new   12:    wwv_flow.g_flow_id := 101;
API Last Extended:20070525
Your Current Version:20070525
This import is compatible with version: 20070525
COMPATIBLE (You should be able to run this import without issues.)

PL/SQL procedure successfully completed.

apexdemoDBTEST> commit;
```

The code in Listing 16-26 is really not much more complicated than the code you have previously seen, other than it uses an inner loop and an outer loop, allowing correct positioning of the text fields using the p_begin_on_new_line and p_begin_on_new_field parameters. Also notice that the &PAGE_NUMBER. and &APPLICATION_NUMBER. variables in this script allow you to specify the application and page numbers dynamically (these are not the same as APEX substitution variables).

▓ **Note** There are a huge number of potentially useful routines that you can use programmatically. We encourage you (if the situation warrants it!) to look through an application export file to see which routines it contains and how they can be used. The routines you've been reading about in this chapter are the same ones APEX uses to import new applications. That's why reading an export file is such a good way to learn the use of those routines.

Generating Applications

You can see just how powerful the techniques illustrated in this section can be in automating your application development. We have seen these techniques used to pre-create skeleton applications based on the answers to a series of wizards that were in fact part of another APEX application—in other words, an APEX application that is used to create another APEX application.

As a final example, Listing 16-27 shows a helpful piece of PL/SQL that we have used to dynamically create an application that used different definitions for shortcuts.

Listing 16-27. Creating Shortcuts Dynamically

```
Declare
    c1 varchar2(32767) := null;
    l_clob clob;
    l_length number := 1;
begin
    c1 := c1 || 'Are you sure you want to delete?';
    wwv_flow_api.create_shortcut(
      p_flow_id => wwv_flow.g_flow_id,
      p_shortcut_name => 'DELETE_CONFIRM_MSG',
      p_shortcut_type => 'TEXT_ESCAPE_JS',
      p_shortcut => c1);
end;
```

This technique lets us create an application that we can use to generate other applications, which can be a great time-saver in certain situations.

A Final Warning!

In this section on using the API, we showed you that some of the API routines can be very useful in certain circumstances. You might go your whole life as an APEX developer without having to ever use them programmatically yourself (although they're used under the hood of the Application Builder), but we just wanted to make you aware that they are there if you need them.

We are definitely not saying that you should be using these API routines. We would go so far as to say that if you ever think you need to use them, then think again and see if you can use the Application Builder instead. You need to really understand the consequences of using the API directly.

There is a difference between using the API and updating the internal tables yourself. These API routines do not afford as much protection as the Application Builder; however, they do perform a certain amount of "sanity checking" of the parameters you pass in and the way you try to use them. If you try to manipulate the underlying internal tables yourself however, you are definitely running the very real risk of destroying your APEX environment, losing data, and corrupting your applications. So, in short, don't do it!

Summary

Together, the APEX Dictionary and the API allow you to work "under the hood" of the APEX interface. Rather than use the GUI to view, say, field definitions one at a time, you can query the dictionary and review dozens of field definitions at a glance. Similarly, using the API allows you to bypass the GUI and create fields, pages, and even whole applications programmatically. You can write applications that modify themselves to accommodate user preferences. You can write applications to generate completely new applications. In fact, APEX itself is essentially an application allowing you to generate other applications. The sky is the limit. Be as a creative as you like, and put the power of APEX to work for you.

Index

▚ Q

■ T

U

■ W

CPSIA information can be obtained at www.ICGtesting.com
Printed in the USA
LVOW122147280911

248365LV00005B/1/P